WHAT DOES THE BIBLE SAY ABOUT...

The Ultimate A TO Z RESOURCE

FULLY ILLUSTRATED

THOMAS NELSON
Since 1798

NASHVILLE   DALLAS   MEXICO CITY   RIO DE JANEIRO   BEIJING

Published in Nashville, Tennessee, by Thomas Nelson, Inc.

Most of the material in this book originally was published in another form in *The Word in
Life*™ *Study Bible,* copyright © 1993, 1996 by Thomas Nelson, Inc.

Unless otherwise indicated, Scripture quotations are from the *New King James Version* of the
Bible, copyright © 1979, 1980, 1982, 1990 by Thomas Nelson, Inc.

Illustrations by Jonny Hawkins.

Library of Congress Cataloging-in-Publication data is available from the Library of Congress.

What does the Bible say about . . .

ISBN 978-0-7852-4270-3

Printed in the United States of America

13 14 15 16 RRD 10 09 08

MORE THAN ANOTHER BIBLE FACT BOOK

It seems there is no end to books written *about* the Bible. We can learn about its organization, its historical sources, and its human writers. We can enter into the ongoing debate about when and where certain portions were written. We can even delve into the ancient languages in which it first was inscribed on parchment.

If we believe, however, that the Bible is God's message to humanity, we must turn our attention to what the Bible *says* about the matters and issues of our daily lives. This book was conceived and produced to shed specific light on that question. Hundreds of brief articles, almost all of them tied to one or more Scripture references, have been collected under topics that clearly relate to modern life. Each article seeks to help the reader find a biblical solution to questions arising from contemporary living experiences—often with some rather pointed questions.

You may read this book "from cover to cover," gathering a wide variety of insights along the way. Or you may check the Contents for a topic of interest and find the article(s) related to that. A listing in the back of the book includes all the topics and every article by title under each topic. The alphabetic sequence of both lists makes it easy to find the topic you want.

An extra bonus can be found at the very back of the book in the Scripture Index. Here you can look up a particular passage and be directed to specific articles that deal with the issues it raises. Not every passage is addressed (we had less than 500 pages to work with), but we trust that every reader will find a number of articles of interest—and challenging for daily living.

CONTENTS

ABANDONED

(see Forgotten)

ABORTION

Abortion and the Bible

The contemporary debate over abortion usually pits pro-life advocates against those who hold to the pro-choice position. To pro-lifers, life in the womb begins at the moment of conception. This life, like all human life, should be respected as a gift from God. They speak of the fetus as an "unborn child," and they see abortion as the killing of that child.

Pro-choicers, on the other hand, do not recognize the fetus as a person until it becomes viable (able to live on its own) or until the moment of birth. Thus the fetus has no rights apart from the woman. Only the woman who carries the fetus has the right to decide whether it will be born or not. If carrying the fetus to full term will have a negative effect on her physical or emotional health, abortion may be medically warranted.

There are other considerations in the abortion issue that need to be taken into account along with the "when-does-life-begin" question. Many people of faith cite biblical principles that they believe speak directly to this controversial subject.

1. *Human beings are made in the image of God.* Genesis 1:27 declares, "So God created man in His own image." We are more than a batch of random cells thrown together in haphazard fashion. As human beings, we reflect the eternal God, who called us into being with design and purpose. Each person, even the unborn, has the right to achieve the potential for which he was created.

2. *Children are a blessing from God.* The psalmist declared, "Behold, children are a heritage from the Lord, the fruit of the womb is His reward" (Ps. 127:3). Parents cooperate with God in bringing human life into the world. We have the right to participate in the creative process but not to take the life of the innocent unborn.

3. *Life is sacred to God.* Because life is sacred to God, we are commanded not to murder (Ex. 20:13). No life is to be taken without a justifiable reason. God is the Creator and

giver of life. Only He has the sovereign right to take life away.

The Creator's Craftsmanship

Psalm 139 speaks of God's intimate knowledge of each individual. He has that knowledge because He has created each person from the womb (Ps. 139:13).

The Hebrew word translated "formed" (or "created" in some translations) is not *bara*, which conveys the idea of creation from nothing (compare Gen. 1:1), but *qanah*, which has to do with ownership. God knows us intimately because He owns us. He is like the inventor who carefully designs and builds a device and then becomes the owner of its patent.

Paired with *qanah* is a word translated "covered" (or "knit together"). This language communicates the idea of a person's body and soul being intricately molded and crocheted together in the mother's womb. It is a process that involves time, skill, and craftsmanship.

People are not thrown together haphazardly, even less do they come together through random processes. Rather, God intentionally and masterfully creates human life in the womb. He works everything together into a whole, according to His will.

The same God whose mind and power fashioned the stars, the seas, the animals, and all other human beings has carefully, intentionally, and individually crafted you. That means you are unique. No one else has been given exactly the same makeup as God has given you.

ABSOLUTES

(see Standards; Truth)

ABSTINENCE

Saying No with a Purpose

Abstinence is the voluntary, self-imposed, and deliberate denial of certain pleasures, such as food, drink, and sex. The noun "abstinence" is found only once in the KJV (Acts 27:21), where the apostle Paul is described as having experienced "long abstinence." The verb "abstain" is found six times in the KJV (Acts 15:20, 29; 1 Thess. 4:3; 5:22; 1 Tim. 4:3; 1 Pet. 1:11).

Abstinence is basically of two kinds: (1) a total abstinence involving an absolute renunciation of a forbidden thing, such as in a

Nazirite vow; and (2) a temporary abstinence as, for example, the mutual consent of husband and wife to give up sexual relations for a time, in order to give themselves "to fasting and prayer" (1 Cor. 7:5).

The Israelites were commanded to abstain from eating meat that contained blood (Gen. 9:4). They were to refrain from eating certain animals (Leviticus 11). Priests could not drink wine while exercising their holy ministries (Lev. 10:9). Others abstained from drinking wine (Jer. 35:6).

The apostle Paul taught that Christians live by the laws of love and freedom—and that they should voluntarily abstain from food sacrificed to idols if it caused a weaker brother or sister in Christ to stumble (Rom. 14:1–23; 1 Cor. 8:1–13). The believer's body, said Paul, is the "temple of the Holy Spirit" (1 Cor. 6:19) and should not be polluted by unclean things.

Paul also exhorted the church of the Thessalonians to "abstain from sexual immorality" (1 Thess. 4:3); indeed, they were to "abstain from every form of evil" (1 Thess. 5:22).

ABUNDANCE

The Christian is called to live a life of unselfish and sacrificial love. Abstinence should always seek to glorify God and to build up fellow believers in the faith.

ABUNDANCE

Celebrating Abundance

When was the last time you celebrated a pay raise, bonus, new position, promotion, or even just a steady job by praising the Lord publicly for His bounty? That's partly what the Old Testament concept of the tithe was about (Deut. 14:22).

A *tithe* meant "a tenth part." God commanded the Israelites to part periodically with one-tenth of their produce or income for three reasons: to celebrate the abundance that He had provided (14:22–26); to provide for the Levites, who owned no land because they were responsible for the tabernacle and worship (14:27; Num. 18:20–24); and to provide for the poor (Deut. 14:28–29).

Believers today are not bound by the law of the tithe. However, the principles still apply—to celebrate God's blessing, to support those in vocational Christian work, and to provide for the poor. Do you observe these disciplines out of your financial resources?

God wants us to feast and be joyful in light of His provision and goodness. How might you show joy and gratitude with what He has given you?

The God Who Gives Wealth

There are two extremes today about the connection between God and wealth. One is that wealth and money are inherently evil and therefore God is opposed to them. The other is that God is just waiting to shower wealth on those who satisfy certain expectations that He has.

Moses' word to the Israelites that "God . . . gives you power to get wealth" (Deut. 8:18) helps to clear up both misunderstandings. On the one hand, it shows that ultimately wealth is a gift of God; therefore, it cannot be evil as such, or else God would not provide it (compare James 1:17). Numerous other Scripture passages reinforce the fact that whatever one possesses, one has God to thank for it (for example, 1 Sam. 3:7; Hos. 2:8).

On the other hand, Moses' statement shows that God is not a celestial Santa Claus dispensing toys to good children. In the first place, no one today can claim this passage as a direct promise from God. These words were spoken to Israel because, as the text plainly states, the nation was involved in a covenant relationship with God. The terms of that covenant called for blessing on the nation (but not necessarily on individuals within the nation) if it kept the Law (compare Lev. 26:3–5). Moses was concerned that, in the face of abundance, the people would forget the source of their wealth.

For people today, who live outside that special covenant that God had with ancient Israel, Moses' words imply only the general truth that all that we have ultimately comes from God.

God's words also show the importance of human responsibility in obtaining wealth. God did not give His people wealth directly so much as He gave them the ability to work their fields and develop their resources so that they prospered. Thus, we ought never to expect God to simply drop a check in the mail so that we effortlessly enjoy financial gain. Rather, we can turn to Him for strength and wisdom as we do our work to provide for our needs.

ACCOUNTABILITY

The Believer's Accountability

The discipline of a Corinthian believer (2 Cor. 2:6) points to one of the important functions of the body of Christ—to hold its members accountable for how they conduct their lives. In the case mentioned here, the censure of the church caused the offender to repent and change his ways, restoring his spiritual life and bringing joy to the church.

Accountability is easy to talk about but difficult to practice. No one likes to be judged by others. In modern society it's especially easy to feel that one's personal life is no one else's business. But a study of Scripture reveals a number of important principles about accountability:

1. *As believers, we are accountable not only for our actions, but also for our attitudes.* In the performance-oriented work world, evaluations tend to measure results alone—higher sales, greater cost control, more clients served. Everything is quantitative. But God is

interested in our innermost heart. He looks at the quality of our character. As God told Samuel, "The LORD does not see as man sees; for man looks at the outward appearance, but the LORD looks at the heart" (1 Sam. 16:7).

2. *Accountability depends on trust.* To hold ourselves accountable to others is to trust their judgment and to believe that they are committed to the same truths and values that we are. It also helps if we can sense that they have our best interests at heart. That's why Paul pleaded with the Corinthians to forsake their divisions and "be perfectly joined together in the same mind and in the same judgment" (1 Cor. 1:10). Without that unity, they would never submit to each other.

3. *Accountability is directly related to the principle of submission.* Every person must struggle with the natural tendency toward rebellion against God. Accountability involves allowing others to enter into that struggle with us. But that means that sometimes we must defer to the judgment or counsel of others, especially when they challenge us with clear-cut scriptural truth or the wisdom of personal experience. Paul told the Ephesians that part of living in the will of the Lord involves "submitting to one another in the fear of God" (Eph. 5:21).

It's not surprising that participation in the body of Christ would involve accountability, because all of us experience accountability in many other areas of life. For example, the government holds us accountable for obeying the law and paying taxes. Likewise, government officials are accountable to the public for their decisions. Employees are accountable to the boss for their work. Likewise, corporate officers are accountable to stockholders for quarterly financial results. In short, accountability touches us at home, at work, at church, and even at play.

But our attitudes toward accountability in general ultimately reflect our attitude toward accountability to God. If we are rebellious toward the One who created us and loves us most, how able will we be to submit to others?

Accountability of a Leader

Jehoash's dealings with the priests concerning temple repairs is a useful lesson in accountability:

- Jehoash delegated specific responsibilities to the priests with clear instructions concerning the collection and use of money (2 Kings 12:4–5).
- He personally confronted the priests, including their leader, Jehoiada, for their non-performance (12:7).
- He suggested a course of remedial action (12:7–8) and then saw to it that an alternative solution to the problem would be carried out (12:9–12).

Accountability involves far more than simply telling someone what to do and then coming back later to see if instructions have been carried out. It means that a leader commits to overseeing the workers' performance and making sure that the project is completed.

Accountability of the "Gods"

Psalm 82 presents modern readers with a puzzling reference to "gods" (Ps. 82:1, 6). We know that the ancient Israelites believed in one God. So what are we to make of this enigmatic allusion to other "gods" (Hebrew, *elohim*, "mighty ones")?

Two main suggestions have been proposed in answer to this riddle. One is that the "gods" mentioned here are demons, fallen angels who not only oppose God but harass human beings. The Book of Job tells of two occasions when "sons of God" met with the Lord, and Satan sought permission to oppress Job (Job 1:6–12; 2:1–7).

The second suggestion is that the "gods" are actually corrupt human judges who were either honored with or took upon themselves the title of "mighty ones." Some believe that they issued their rulings in the names of certain pagan gods in order to claim more authority for themselves.

Neither suggestion is without problems, but both seem to fit the description in Psalm 82. The evil judges oppress the poor and helpless (82:2–4), and the demons do their work in spiritual darkness, creating instability wherever they go (82:5).

Whatever the identity of these "gods," the point of Psalm 82 is that ultimately all authorities are accountable to God. He is their final Ruler and Judge, as He is of the whole earth. He measures the integrity of those to whom He has delegated power according to their treatment of the poor, the fatherless, the afflicted, and the needy.

Public Accountability

The idea that public officials need to be publicly accountable was a fundamental principle for David. Thus he charged the leaders of the kingdom "in the sight of all Israel" to follow the ways of the Lord (1 Chr. 28:8).

Visibility is an essential part of accountability. By setting themselves under the scrutiny of others, leaders help to ensure that their actions and decisions will be aboveboard—or at least that others will be able to pass judgment on what is done.

David's charge to Israel's leadership suggests three ways to handle accountability and maintain integrity:

1. *Allow others to review plans and performance.* David had developed plans for the temple with the Lord's help (28:11–19). But as he passed them on to Solomon, he pointed out that many professionals and craftsmen were available to refine the plans and carry out the work (28:21).

2. *Act within a community of others.* Leaders need others for advice and perspective. David called on the entire community of Israel to work together with his son to accomplish the construction of the temple (29:1–9).

3. *Acknowledge God's presence in everything.* This was the most important objective of all. Solomon and his leaders needed to seek out the Lord's commandments and fear Him in everything they would do (28:8–9). He was the One to whom they were ultimately accountable.

Do you place yourself under this kind of accountability? Are you involved with others in a way that protects and promotes your integrity and development?

ACHIEVEMENT

A Kingdom Perspective on Significance

Jesus wants His followers to evaluate turbulent times of change (Mark 13:33) not just from the perspective of history, but even more from the perspective of His kingdom. As believers, we are citizens of eternity. Therefore, our confidence needs to be rooted in something far more important than our positions and achievements here and now. It's not that the here and now has no importance. But as we live our lives, God wants us to be loyal workers for His kingdom, serving the people He sends our way.

Is your significance tied too closely to achievements—building buildings, reaching business goals, acquiring material possessions, climbing career ladders? There's nothing inherently wrong with these. But if you lost them, would your confidence completely crumble? If your sense of worth depends on them, what happens when you reach the top of the ladder, only to discover that the ladder is leaning against the wrong wall?

The problem is that our world has a system of values that is upside down from the way God determines value. It lacks any sense of what Scripture describes as "calling," or what Christians later termed "vocation"—a perspective that God has called and equipped people to serve Him through their work in the world. Instead, our culture encourages us to climb a work/identity ladder that is ultimately self-serving, and often self-destructive.

Climbing that ladder can be very misleading. The higher one goes, the more one's identity, value, and security tend to depend on the nature of one's work. But what happens if we lose our position, titles, or high-level compensation? Perhaps this explains why severe emotional problems—drug and alcohol abuse, abuse of spouse and children, divorce, even suicide—often accompany job loss. If our significance relies on our job, then it dies with our job.

God calls us to a far more stable basis for significance. He wants us to establish our identity in the fact that we are His children, created by Him to carry out good works as responsible people in His kingdom (Eph. 2:10). This is our calling or vocation from God. According to Scripture, our calling:

- is irrevocable (Rom. 11:29).
- is from God; He wants to let us share in Christ's glory (2 Thess. 2:14).
- is a function of how God has designed us (Eph. 2:10).
- is an assurance that God will give us everything we need to serve Him, including the strength to remain faithful to Him (1 Cor. 1:7–9).

- is what we should be proclaiming as our true identity (1 Pet. 2:5, 9).
- carries us through suffering (1 Pet. 2:19–21).
- is rooted in peace, no matter what the circumstances in which we find ourselves (1 Cor. 7:15–24).
- is focused on eternal achievements, not merely temporal ones (Phil. 3:13–4:1).

Above all else, believers are called to character development, service to others, and loyalty to God. These can be accomplished wherever we live or work, whatever our occupational status or position in society. If we pursue these, we can enjoy great satisfaction and significance. No matter what happens on the job, we can join Paul in saying, "We know that all things work together for good to those who love God, to those who are called according to His purpose" (Rom. 8:28).

Success

To what extent should Christ's followers today pursue success? The declaration of John the Baptist that "He [Jesus] must increase, but I must decrease" (John 3:30) seems to repudiate the idea of personal achievement, recognition, or material gain—common measures of success in our society. Indeed, John himself showed none of the outward trappings of a successful ministry.

So should believers avoid success as the world defines it? Can people be successful in their careers as well as in their spiritual lives, or are the two mutually exclusive? Some Christians say that success on the job creates credibility for them to talk about Christ with coworkers. Others, however, claim that they have no interest in being successful. But is that a genuine conviction, or are they merely avoiding the rough-and-tumble of a competitive marketplace?

Questions like these barely scratch the surface of the complex, emotional issue of success. The people of Jesus' day were no less interested in prospering than we are, even if they defined success in slightly different terms. So it's not surprising that Scripture speaks to human ambition and achievement. It seems to affirm at least three important principles, as illustrated by John the Baptist:

1. *Success is always measured by a set of standards established by some person or group.* Many people of John's day felt that they were assured of the blessing of God simply because they were descendants of Abraham. Their religious leaders aggressively promoted and reinforced that idea (Matt. 3:7–9; Luke 3:8; John 8:39). John challenged them to reconsider that way of thinking. What mattered, he said, was faith in Jesus. That was the ultimate criterion by which God would measure people's lives. Thus, unbelief would result in the ultimate failure—eternal death (3:36).

2. *Why and how we pursue success is just as important as whether or not we achieve it.* John's listeners were ordinary people caught up in the everyday scramble to get ahead. But in their pursuit of gain they tended to ignore the needs of others and to take ethical shortcuts. John challenged them to make internal changes (that is, to repent) and to demonstrate those changes in their day-to-day responsibilities through charity, honesty, and justice (Luke 3:8, 10–14).

3. *Obtaining success always carries a cost.* John warned the people of God's judgment using a simple, well-known image: "Even now the ax is laid to the root of the trees. Therefore, every tree which does not bear fruit is cut down and thrown into the fire" (Luke 3:9). Just as a lumberjack would lay his ax at the foot of a tree while he decided which trees in a forest to cut, so God had sent John and Jesus as His final messengers before letting His judgment fall.

The people could choose what they wanted to do. But either way, there would be a cost involved. For John, the cost of faithfully proclaiming his message was imprisonment and, eventually, execution (Matt. 14:1–12). Yet he gained a treasure all out of proportion to the price of martyrdom—the praise of Christ (11:7–11).

So should believers pursue success? Judging from the experience of John the Baptist and the people who followed him, the issue seems to be not so much *whether* we should pursue it, but *how.* In light of John's message, it's worth considering three crucial questions:

- Who sets the standards by which I measure success?

A

- What are my motives and behavior in pursuing success?
- What price am I willing to pay to achieve success?

ADDICTION
The Respectable Idol

It's easy to ridicule the ancients for worshiping idols of wood and stone (Jer. 18:15). "How could they be so foolish?" we might wonder. "How could they worship man-made objects as gods?" Thus we might assume that we are in agreement with the Lord, who strongly condemned idolatry (18:17).

But are we really that different? Just as the Israelites worshiped the work of their hands (10:3–4, 8–9), don't many of us today worship the work of our hands? Haven't the process and product of our careers become virtual gods for some of us? In fact, hasn't work become an addiction for many, the controlling center and defining identity of their lives?

Moreover, work is an especially respectable idol in our society. A person can sacrifice everything else—family, friends, even personal health—on the altar of work, and actually be praised for it, actually be rewarded for showing commitment, determination, and the "right stuff."

That is a profound tragedy. Work was intended by God to be a wonderful means of serving Him. He Himself is a worker, and He has created us in His image to be His coworkers. But work was never meant to become an end in itself, and certainly not an idol. Likewise, our work may express who we are, but it was never meant to become who we are.

Perhaps to keep us from turning work into an idol, the Lord modeled an important principle when He ceased from His own work on the seventh day of creation. He was showing us that work is not what life is all about. Work has its place, but there is something far more important than our labors—the Lord Himself. The point of the Sabbath, and later the Lord's Day, which Christians began observing in New Testament times, is to show our ultimate trust in and devotion to the Lord.

Isn't it interesting that the people of Jeremiah's day were abusing the Sabbath at the same time as they were practicing idolatry (Jer. 17:21–27)? Apparently sins of work and sins of worship can often go hand in hand. Is that the case for you?

ADULTERY
David in Sin

For many people in today's world, the importance of sin as a concept is gradually eroding. Some dismiss any belief in sin as a quaint notion left over from a bygone era. Others accept the reality of sin, but deny or ignore their own sins. Still others use sin as an opportunity for entertainment, delighting in the exposure of others caught in sin, or even parading their own moral failures before a prying public.

For King David, there was ultimately only one way to deal with sin: face it, confess it, and be forgiven. Psalm 51 shows him doing precisely that. In total contrast to the pretense of confession practiced by so many today, David's prayer expresses utter brokenness.

What exactly was the sin to which David was admitting? The Bible tells us plainly that he committed adultery with Bathsheba, the wife of Uriah the Hittite, and that when she became pregnant David tried in vain to cover his sin, eventually engineering Uriah's death (2 Sam. 11). Yet Psalm 51 does not mention the adultery, and it only touches upon the murder (51:14). Instead, the main transgression confessed is, "Against You, You only have I sinned, and done this evil in Your sight" (51:4).

David was not evading responsibility for the sexual immorality and murder, but he recognized that ultimately sin is an offense against a holy, righteous God. Even when other people are hurt by our sins, it is God whose standards have been violated. Thus, while sinners owe apologies and restitution to people, they owe contrite confession to God. He alone is able to forgive sins (Mark 2:7).

The Bible is extraordinarily realistic. Its account is not filled with "super saints" whose perfection we must admire from a distance. Instead, it presents the lives of real people and makes a full disclosure of their failings. It does this for our instruction and growth—we who also struggle with sin, imperfection, and doubt.

God helped David. He desires to help you, too. What sins do you need to confess to Him right now, in order to find His forgiveness and restoration?

The Ordeal of Jealousy

What does a spouse do when the marriage partner breaks faith in the relationship? What can other believers do to address the wrong which has been done and see that justice is accomplished?

In the case of an Israelite's wife suspected of adultery, the Law acknowledged the pain of the offended spouse (Num. 5:14). It recognized the destructive potential of jealousy. So it instructed an offended husband to bring his wife before the priest, who in turn would "set her before the LORD" (5:15–16), who was the only One to be trusted to properly detect the sin.

It's interesting to note the sensitivity involved in the ritual for determining guilt or innocence. Rather than placing the woman before a crowded, noisy room of hostile examiners or curious spectators, she was brought quietly before the Lord. There the priest placed her under oath and gave her a drink of "bitter water" by which the Lord would assess and judge her guilt or innocence.

The implication is clear: people are not likely to exhibit much justice when they are hurt, angry, or jealous. Those feelings are understandable, especially if a spouse has been unfaithful. But wounded love usually tempts a person to vengeance rather than justice. Ultimately, revenge belongs only to a holy, righteous God. Only He can be trusted to mete

ADVICE

out an absolutely fair punishment (Deut. 32:35–39; Rom. 12:19).

Like the Law, Jesus counseled a wise, sensitive approach in dealing with sin among believers. He cautioned His followers to privately confront an alleged offender rather than creating a public spectacle. Great care should be taken to assess guilt or innocence. And always the driving spirit behind any inquiry needs to be the restoration of the sinner and reconciliation in the relationship between offender and offended (see Matt. 18:15–22).

*For more on this topic, see **POLITICAL SCANDAL,** "Scandal and Cover-Up," page 304; **RAPE,** "Unbridled Sexual Passion," page 331.*

ADVERSITY
(*see* Opposition)

ADVICE
Bad Advice
By consulting a medium (1 Sam. 28:7), Saul not only made a poor choice, he got bad advice—"bad" in the sense of evil. His use of witchcraft was a violation of the Law and ultimately led to his death (1 Chr. 10:13–14). Scripture is clear that God's people are to have nothing to do with mediums, oracles, soothsayers, or other elements of witchcraft.

God has spoken clearly against seeking spirituality and guidance apart from Him. We need not resort to witchcraft or other occult practices, as He has given us His Word to guide us and the Spirit to help us. He also gives us the counsel of wise friends in the faith (Prov. 20:18; 24:6).

Be Careful of Counsel
As you make decisions and strategize plans, you'll do well to gain counsel from wise, trusted confidants. In fact, Proverbs says that utilizing input from many counselors offers safety (Prov. 11:14). Their variety of opinions tends to ensure success (15:22; 20:18; 24:6).

The people of Isaiah's day could have benefited by heeding wise counsel, but they had a hard time distinguishing good counsel from bad. So Isaiah contrasted the two. Reliable counsel . . .

- listens carefully to God (Is. 8:11);
- is not quick to identify "conspiracies" (8:12);

- avoids acting solely out of fear (8:12); and
- praises and respects the Lord (8:13).

Unreliable counsel . . .

- ignores God's law and testimony (8:19–20);
- allows anger to distort things (8:21); and
- leads to trouble and anguish (8:22).

Can you identify the sources of good and bad counsel in your life? Would anyone be able to mention you as a source of wise counsel and advice?

*For more on this topic, see **EXPERIENCE,** "Listening to the Voice of Experience," page 139.*

ADVISORS
David's Folly
The head of a large company resists the advice of his trusted advisors and bulls ahead with ambitious plans. Is that brave leadership or arrogant folly? In the case of King David, his insistence on numbering Israel seemed innocent enough at first, but ultimately proved perilous to the nation (1 Chr. 21:2–8). The tragic incident of David's census provides some important lessons for those in authority:

1. *Follow the will of God.* No one knows exactly why David decided to conduct a census, but it was not because God told him to. Perhaps he wished to assess his military strength. Or maybe he was preparing to raise a labor force to construct the temple that he so desperately wanted to build for the Lord (1 Chr. 17:1–6; 22:1–5). In any event, the census was not God's will (1 Chr. 21:7). If you're a leader, you'll want to carefully consider whether your plans go with or against God's will, particularly as it is revealed in Scripture.

2. *Listen when your advisors oppose you.* David ignored the advice of his closest counselors (21:4). Joab, the general of his army, recognized that David was going contrary to God's will. He and his captains warned the king that a census was unnecessary. In fact, Joab was so incensed when David persisted that he refused to count the Levites and Benjaminites (21:6).

Proverbs 11:14 says that when counsel is lacking, people fall. But people also fall when counsel is present but ignored. As a leader, you'll want to pay special attention when you receive opposition from those whose advice normally seems sound. It could be a sign that you are headed for serious trouble.

3. *Recognize that your choices affect others.* David committed the sin, but it was his people who came under God's judgment (1 Chr. 21:14). The king's stubborn choice resulted in the deaths of seventy thousand of his subjects. In the same way, choices made by leaders today often affect many innocent people under them. For that reason, if you are a leader you'll want to carefully consider the consequences that your decisions may have for others. What happens if you are wrong is at least as important as what happens if you are right.

The Wisdom of Taking Counsel

Leaders are often praised for their decision-making abilities. But wise decision making is rarely a solo performance. Effective leaders invariably surround themselves with people who can provide accurate and timely information, give insight as to the meaning of that information, and offer suggestions and advice about the best course of action to take. In the end, the leader has to make the call, but getting to that point is usually a team effort.

The Book of Proverbs reflects the need for counsel, not only for leaders, but for every person who wants to honor God in life. In fact, the book offers its own principles for making use of wise counsel:

- Sound advice is a part of wisdom (1:5; 8:14).
- Fools despise counsel and refuse to listen to it. They are so convinced that they are right that they don't pay attention to anyone else (1:25, 30; 12:15).
- Many counselors offer safety (11:14). Their variety of opinions tends to ensure success (15:22; 20:18; 24:6).
- Heeding good advice often avoids conflict (13:10).
- Listening to advice has long-term benefits. Wisdom compounds itself over time (19:20).
- It is worth the effort to tap the reservoirs of wise people (20:5).
- Pick your advisors carefully (12:26; 13:20).
- Beware of rumor and gossip—especially when they concern a close, trusted friend (16:28).
- Look for people who can honor confidences (17:9).
- Integrity and courtesy are admirable qualities in an advisor (22:11; 27:9).
- Avoid the opinions of angry people (22:24).
- Allow people who know your situation to help you (27:10).
- No matter what plans and strategies you devise, the will of God will ultimately prevail (19:21; 21:30).
- True friends will tell you the truth (27:6).

Understanding the Times

People of faith are called to be people of wisdom and discernment. That requires an understanding not only of Scripture, but also of the world in which Scripture must be applied. In ancient Israel, David was blessed to have a group of counselors "who had understanding of the times" and thus could advise him on what the nation should do (1 Chr. 12:32).

The tribe of Issachar was especially known for such wise men. In fact, tradition holds that representatives from Issachar tended to be the wisest members of Israel's Sanhedrin, the nation's highest ruling body in the days of Jesus.

No one knows exactly how David's counselors went about "understanding the times." But it seems reasonable to infer that that their job was to perceive trends, discuss major issues, evaluate information, and consider strategy. Thanks in part to them, David was able to unify the kingdom and a establish a growing empire (1 Chr. 14:2, 17).

Today, God's people still need those who can "understand the times." Our world now faces changes of such magnitude that some have described the situation as nothing short of chaos. For that reason we need people who can buttress their faith with discernment more than ever. God has not called us to shut down our critical faculties in order to follow every wind of doctrine and promise. Instead, Jesus exhorted His followers to "be wise as serpents and harmless as doves" (Matt. 10:16). That means knowing God *and* knowing the times.

AEROBICS

(*see* Physical Fitness)

AFFLUENCE

A Chicken in Every Pot

Peace and prosperity are the goals of many countries today. When a nation enjoys such blessings, it has much for which to be thankful. But with affluence and power comes a temptation to forget that God is the source of every good thing. We see this in Israel's history.

Under Solomon, Israel briefly emerged as a powerhouse of wealth and military might. Its influence extended from the Euphrates to Egypt (1 Kin. 4:21) and its affluence to a majority of its citizens, whose prosperity is summarized as "eating and drinking and rejoicing" (4:20). As Solomon's reign put a temporary stop to threats from without and strife from within, everyone lived in safety, "each man under his vine and his fig tree" (4:25). In twentieth-century terms, David's successor put "a chicken in every pot."

Yet storm clouds were brewing. The cost of maintaining Solomon's court was enormous

AFFLUENCE

(4:22–23). His many building projects, including his gilded temple and his even more lavishly appointed palace, required increased taxes that created unrest and ultimately led to a tax revolt (10:14–15; 12:4, 18).

The system also created a two-class society of privileged citizens and menial workers, an underclass made up mostly of foreigners (9:15, 20–23). And while trade was lively (9:26–28; 10:22–23), it contributed to the depletion of natural resources.

However, these problems remain in the background of 1 Kings 4–10, which describes the general peace and prosperity that Israel enjoyed after so many years of turmoil. Glowing reports of the empire's power and prestige cascade from the text until the beginning of chapter 11, where the good news suddenly comes to a halt with the transition, "But King Solomon loved many foreign wives" (11:1).

Things head downhill from there as Solomon turns away from the Lord to idols (11:4–8), God pronounces judgment on him (11:9–13) and raises up adversaries against him (11:14–25), Jeroboam rebels (11:26–28), and the kingdom divides after Solomon's death (12:1–19).

What happened? Why did Solomon's brilliant reign end on such a tragic note? How could the wisest king who ever ruled (3:12; 10:3, 6–7, 24) violate the Law so foolishly and blatantly by accumulating wives who would lead him into idolatry?

One answer is that times of prosperity can easily dull the spiritual sensitivity of even the most devoted of God's people. It's not that prosperity is evil in and of itself. But Jesus described the "deceitfulness" of riches which can choke the spiritual life out of a person (or a nation; Matt. 13:22). Likewise, the New Testament warns believers to stay alert and spiritually vigilant, lest they fall into temptation (1 Cor. 10:12–13; 1 Pet. 1:13; 5:8).

What happened to Solomon and Israel can happen to any of us. We who live in relative affluence are especially vulnerable to losing touch with God, even as our possessions and power multiply. Perhaps Israel and its king should have paid more attention to the warning signs that it was headed for spiritual disaster. Can you detect warning signs in your own life and country?

National Prosperity

What is it that causes a nation to prosper? For Israel, national prosperity was directly linked to its moral and spiritual health, as measured by adherence to the Law (Deut. 11:13–17). If the people obeyed the Lord and followed His ways, the Lord promised to bless their lands with abundance. If they forsook Him and turned to other gods, He threatened to cause drought and economic ruin.

Does the same relationship between obedience and prosperity hold true for nations today?

Our reading of this promise and others like it is informed by the fact that Deuteronomy defines a special covenant between God and a people of His choosing. The Lord has never entered into a similar agreement with any other nation. The promises were made to Israel and fulfilled just as they were given. They cannot be transferred to other nations.

Even so, there are tremendous benefits to a nation that fears God. All nation-states are ultimately accountable to Him. Therefore, He pays attention to what governments and their citizens do. He will not allow evil to go unchecked; neither will He reward faith and obedience with unmitigated disaster. There is a general correspondence between honoring God and prospering as a people.

The Dangers of Success

Doing well has its dangers. Success can bring changes for the worse in one's values and behavior. Isaiah tried to alert the wealthy people of ancient Israel to what was happening to them as a result of their financial success (5:8–10). They were accumulating houses and lands, but losing their ethical integrity. The same kind of thing can happen to us, too:

- We can start resorting to unethical practices to increase our gains (1:23; 5:20, 23).
- We can turn away from caring about the poor, such as orphans and widows (1:23; 3:14–15).
- We can heap up material things far beyond what we really need (2:7; 3:18–24; 5:8).
- We can begin to worship our own accomplishments (2:8; 5:21).
- We can start abusing people (3:15).

We may not even recognize these patterns as we get caught up in hard work and success. Nevertheless, we can experience the impact of these attitudes and behaviors in powerful ways:

- Our children can become spoiled and insolent (3:5).
- We can experience a breakdown in leadership (3:6–7).
- Wars can break out (3:25–26; 5:26–30).
- We can experience the loneliness of the wealthy (5:8).
- Self-indulgence can replace work and lead to failure (5:11–13, 22).

Does this describe your life? If you are prospering materially, you are at risk for the temptations and dangers of affluence. Maybe you need to pause and take stock, lest your blessings turn out to be snares.

For more on this topic, see PLEASURE, "Self-Indulgent? Who, Me?" page 302; SELF-ISHNESS, "The Delusions of Affluence," page 361.

AGING

From Success to Significance

"What am I going to do with the rest of my life?" This is a question that countless retirees struggle with as they make the transition out of their careers. The prospect of twenty or more years with time on one's hands can be a scary thing. Likewise, many people who have reached middle age start to wonder what they will accomplish during the second half of life, especially if they have met or exceeded their career goals. For many, there is a longing to move beyond success to significance: "What am I going to do that *matters?*"

David's words in Psalm 71 should inspire and direct anyone who is contemplating how to have a meaningful, satisfying life in the later years. David was determined to declare the Lord not only to his own generation, but to later ones as well (Ps. 71:18). To that end, he asked God for continued strength. We can well imagine that the mere fact that David had such a clearly defined purpose was itself a source of vitality and strength.

To what purpose will you give your life in your final years? Is it big enough to energize you and keep you motivated? The elderly tend

to have control over valuable resources, such as money, property, time, wisdom, experience, friendships, and memories. Can you find ways to make these available to others, in order to accomplish something significant for God?

Declining Years

Young people commonly think and act as if they were going to live forever. For that reason, Ecclesiastes 12 paints a picture of old age and introduces it to young people with the warning, "Remember your Creator in the days of your youth."

As presented in Eccl. 12:1–5, old age is not a pretty picture:

- It is a period of "difficult days" in which one takes "no pleasure."
- It is a time of disorientation.
- The hands ("keepers of the house") shake and tremble.
- The legs and back ("strong men") now bend and stoop.
- The teeth ("grinders") begin to fall out and chewing becomes difficult.
- The eyes ("windows") grow dim.
- The hearing ("doors") grows weak.
- One loses one's appetite ("grinding").
- Insomnia (waking up "at the sound of a bird") sets in.
- The voice ("daughters of music") grows feeble and faint.
- One is terrified of falling.
- The hair turns white, like almond tree blossoms.
- Getting around is much harder, like an old grasshopper dragging itself along.
- The will to hang onto life begins to fail, and death awaits.

Certainly there are many elderly who defy this portrait. Yet in the main, the conditions mentioned are typical. Ecclesiastes warns the young to remember God before earthly life ends. Several images convey the coming of death and mourning: a silver cord is loosened, a bowl is broken, a pitcher is shattered, a wheel ceases to turn (12:6), the "dust" of the body returns to earth (12:7; cf. Gen. 3:19; Job 34:15), and the spirit goes to God, presumably for judgment (Eccl. 12:7, 14).

This is the fate of every human being. No matter how young or old we are, every day each of us is a bit closer to death. Given that reality, Ecclesiastes challenges young people to live unto God, for life is empty and meaningless without Him.

Growing Old Gracefully

Do you fear the weariness of growing old? Are you resisting the aging process?

David discovered that a loss of vitality—one of the signs of old age—is sometimes related to unconfessed sin. The only way to deal with that was confession and repentance (Ps. 32:3–5).

David also learned that life is a choice between obeying God voluntarily or stubbornly resisting His ways, like a horse or a mule which has no understanding and must be harnessed to be brought under control (32:8–9).

In his later years, David brought together what he had learned about the connection between physical vitality and spiritual obedience when he wrote, "I have been young, and now am old; yet I have not seen the righteous forsaken, nor his descendants begging bread" (Ps. 37:25).

You might see in David's words a challenge to ask what pattern you are choosing—voluntary cooperation with God, which tends to lead to a long life of vitality, or stubborn resistance against His will, which will drain and ultimately break you. Are there sins in your life that have gone unconfessed, perhaps for years? Why not settle the account with the Lord right now by praying a prayer of repentance from sin, and openly admitting your need for God's forgiveness and cleansing?

Flourishing or Fading in Old Age?

Consider your feelings about growing old. Who are the elderly people you know? Perhaps you already are among them, but if not, how does it feel to know that before long, you will be joining the ranks of senior citizens?

The Book of Psalms speaks in several places about the kind of life the aged live. One possibility is to still be "bearing fruit" in old age, like a magnificent old fruit tree that is still flourishing (Ps. 92:14). But another psalm expresses fear of being cast aside and ignored when age causes the psalmist's strength to falter (71:9). What accounts for this contrast?

The difference between flourishing or fading in old age seems to be the issue of righteousness (92:12). Those who have lived for God during their lives tend to keep bearing fruit even in their senior years. In fact, many of the seeds they have planted, either in their own lives or in the lives of others, sprout up and mature into a harvest of goodness (compare Gal. 6:7–10). But those who have squandered their lives in self-centered pursuits that ignore God's ways usually have little to show as they come to the end of their days.

This psalm challenges us to consider whether we are preparing for our final years by living with righteousness today. What seeds are we sowing, and what harvest are we planning for?

AGREEMENT

A Done Deal

There are many ways to signal that an agreement has been reached—with a handshake, a formal signing, an exchange of gifts, or perhaps a ceremony. The Israelites ratified their covenant with God by assembling at Mount Gerizim and Mount Ebal in central Canaan (Josh. 8:30–35).

Half the people stood in front of one hill and half in front of the other, while Joshua and the Levites reviewed the conditions of the Law. The people voiced their commitment to the terms by shouting, "Amen!" It must have been a spectacular sight—and an unforgettable experience.

AIDS

What Does Leprosy Have to Do with AIDS?

In Jesus' day, leprosy was a slowly progressing, chronic, highly infectious, incurable skin disease with serious social implications. Today, leprosy is rare thanks to sulfone drugs and better hygiene. Now known as Hansen's Disease, the once-dreaded malady has been virtually eliminated.

Now the world struggles with acquired immune deficiency syndrome (AIDS), a scourge that bears some remarkable similarities to leprosy. Biologically the diseases are quite different. But like the lepers of the ancient world, many AIDS sufferers are socially ostracized out of fear that they will contaminate others.

The situation is complicated by the fact that many AIDS cases have resulted from sex outside of monogamous, heterosexual marriage or from intravenous drug abuse—behaviors that oppose biblical precepts and principles. That introduces a moral dimension to the problem. But if there are moral issues involved in the spread of AIDS, there is also a moral issue involved in determining a Christlike response to AIDS.

In biblical times, leprosy was thought to be very contagious and hereditary. It was also believed to be a divine punishment for sin, even though the actual instances of that, such as Miriam (Num. 12:9–10) and Uzziah (2 Chr. 26:16–23), were exceptional. The Law was very specific about the diagnosis and treatment of leprosy (see Lev. 13). If a priest detected suspicious symptoms—pimples, scabs, sores, nodules, or white spots on the skin "like snow"—he ordered a quarantine of the infected person for seven days to protect the rest of the society. If the symptoms did not fade away within a week, another week of quarantine was prescribed.

Weeks could drag into months and months into years. Quarantined persons became social outcasts, living outside the Israelite camp. They fended for themselves as best they could. Some perhaps received occasional supplies from relatives, but most were reduced to begging. Those who actually had the dreaded disease slowly wasted away. As the disease took away sensation, they easily injured themselves without feeling pain, leading to deformity and "half-eaten flesh" (Num. 12:12) and, eventually, death.

Quarantines never cured a leper. Only divine intervention could. So when Jesus healed lepers, it demonstrated His divine nature and caused people to turn to Him. Surely His compassionate treatment of lepers is instructive for those of us living in a day of AIDS. We continue to seek for a cure, just as leprosy was eventually cured through modern medicine.

In the meantime, believers need to consider what a Christlike response would be to people with AIDS. Jesus reached out to lepers with love and healing. What compassionate, redemptive responses can we show toward our own, modern-day "lepers"?

ALCOHOLISM

Merry—and Sad—with Wine

The misuse of fermented beverages has caused untold grief throughout human history. Absolom's strategy of getting Ammon drunk and then murdering him (2 Sam. 13:28) was yet another sad tale involving wine. The Bible often reports on the sad effects of alcohol abuse.

- Amnon (2 Sam. 13:28–29), David's oldest son, was murdered by his half brother Absalom while drunk.
- Ahasuerus (Esth. 1:10), the Persian king, commanded Queen Vashti to display herself while he was drunk at a royal feast. When she refused, he had her removed.
- Elah (1 Kin. 16:9), the fourth king of Israel, was murdered while drunk.
- Lot (Gen. 19:32–33), having survived the fire of brimstone that fell on Sodom, was seduced by his daughters to commit incest while drunk.
- Nadab and Abihu (Lev. 10:1, 9) may have been intoxicated when they offered "profane fire" to the Lord; afterward, the Lord prohibited the priests from drinking on duty.

The misuse of anything in God's creation is sin, and the misuse of alcohol causes especially serious problems socially, morally, and spiritually.

The Dangers of Alcohol

The Book of Proverbs reminds us of the tremendous human suffering than can result from the abuse of alcoholic beverages and warns us about the dangers of losing control to alcohol (Prov. 23:29–35). In a day of widespread alcoholism, and with alcohol consumption a factor in countless crimes, including accidents caused by drunk drivers and workers, the warnings of Scripture need to be taken more seriously than ever.

Proverbs paints a picture of the person whose life has come under the control of alcohol:

- He is marked by woe, sorrow, contentions, complaints, wounds, and red eyes (23:29).

- He wastes most of his time either looking for a drink or lingering over it when he finds it (23:30).
- He lives in a fantasy by glorifying the properties of drink (23:31).
- He comes off his time of drinking with the feeling that he has been snakebitten (23:32).
- He hallucinates and says things he doesn't mean (23:33).
- He becomes numb and foolish (23:34–35).

Anyone who has ever lived with a person like that knows all too well how destructive alcohol can be, not only to the person, but also to everyone else in his world. That is why the Bible shows us tragic examples and gives careful instructions and strong warnings about alcohol:

- In ancient Israel, vows of abstinence were sometimes taken when a person assumed a significant responsibility. For example, the priests were not allowed to drink on duty (Lev. 10:9). Abstinence was part of the Nazirite vow (Num. 6:3).
- Rulers are admonished to not drink lest they pervert justice and forget God's ways (Prov. 31:4–5).
- Isaiah included drinking parties as a contributing factor in the Israelites' downfall (Is. 5:11–12). In fact, many priests and prophets were so frequently inebriated that they could not fulfill their God-given responsibilities (28:7–8).
- Paul listed revelry and drunkenness with sins such as lewdness, lust, strife, sexual immorality, coveting, idolatry, slander, extortion, and envy. He warned believers not to associate with professing Christians who persisted in such behaviors (Rom. 13:12–13; 1 Cor. 5:11). He also warned that drinking alcoholic beverages can contribute to the downfall of younger and weaker believers (Rom. 14:19–21).
- Peter included drunkenness with the kinds of sins listed by Paul, pointing out that heavy drinking is part of a lifestyle of unbelief, which dissipates people's health and character (1 Pet. 4:3–4).

The Bible does not demean people in trouble. In fact, it encourages us to find ways to assist people in the grip of alcohol, and not just condemn or reject them.

ALLIANCES
The Perils of Misplaced Allegiances

In about 701 B.C., the Assyrian king Sennacherib sent forces to quell numerous uprisings among the kingdoms in the western empire. First they attacked the Phoenicians, deposing the king of Tyre. Then they moved south along the coast to the Philistine city-states of Ashkelon and Ekron, which had openly rebelled after the death of Sargon II (705 B.C.).

As Sennacherib's armies bore down on Jerusalem, King Hezekiah considered how he would defend his capital. He had made extensive preparations (2 Chr. 32:3–6, 30). But were they adequate to withstand the full force of Assyrian might?

One option open to Hezekiah was to appeal for help from the Egyptians. For years they had supplied Judah, Israel, the Philistines, and other neighbors to the north with military forces and arms. The Egyptians routinely used these smaller nations as a buffer between themselves and the Assyrians. Now that Jerusalem itself faced attack, Hezekiah was certain to get help if he wanted it.

But Isaiah's counsel was to reject such an alliance (Is. 30:1–5). To pursue it would show a lack of faith in the Lord to deliver His people. In fact, the Law prohibited the Israelites from allying themselves with the Egyptians or even importing armaments from them (Deut. 17:16).

Apparently Hezekiah heeded Isaiah's word. When Sennacherib's general taunted him and demanded a surrender, he asked the prophet to pray and ask God for help. Isaiah did so, and the Lord responded by delivering the city (2 Kin. 18:13–19:37; 2 Chr. 32:1–21).

This contrasted sharply with the actions of Hoshea, the last of Israel's kings. Faced with a situation similar to Hezekiah's, Hoshea had appealed for help from So, king of Egypt. Before long, the Assyrians had overrun Israel, destroyed its capital of Samaria, and deported its inhabitants (2 Kin. 17:1–18).

AMBITION
(*see also* Pride)

Image-Consciousness

When other people look at you, what do they see? What image do you project to co-workers, customers, friends, and neighbors? As Paul traveled through the cities of the Roman Empire, he always gave thought to how he would be perceived, but his biggest concern was whether observers would see Jesus in him.

To illustrate this principle, Paul recalled a phenomenon that occurred during the period in which Moses received the Law (2 Cor. 3:7, 13). As Israel wandered through the wilderness, God revealed Himself to the people through what looked like a consuming fire (Ex. 24:17). But to Moses He spoke face to face (33:11). This encounter with the Living God had such an effect on Moses that his face would shine with an afterglow whenever he returned to the people. To dispel their fear, he put a veil over his face to hide the glory that resulted from his proximity to God.

Paul argues that we as believers have an even closer proximity to God than Moses did,

for God Himself lives inside us (2 Cor. 3:8). Thus, when we meet others, they ought to see the glory of God shining out of us (3:9–11, 18). In other words, they ought to see Jesus.

Is that who people see when they look at us? Do they see Jesus' love, integrity, and power? Or do we "veil" the Light of the World (Matt. 5:14–16) under a mask of selfish ambition and worldly concerns?

Pride Goes Before a Fall

Arrogance is an occupational hazard for those in authority. Sitting in positions of power, prestige, and privilege can easily seduce people into thinking that they got there solely by their own abilities and assets. Furthermore, they can begin to assume that rules that apply to others don't apply to them.

King Uzziah of Judah fell into that pitfall of pride (2 Chr. 26:16). He was young when he came to the throne, but he succeeded because he honored God and listened to the wise advice of the prophet Zechariah (26:1–5). But in his later years, after he had achieved many military victories, he made the mistake of presuming to perform temple rites reserved only for the priests, which led to his downfall (26:16–21).

Scripture offers many examples of people whose pride and ambition blinded and eventually destroyed them:

- Pharaoh, the ruler of Egypt, resisted the Lord's command to let the Israelites go. This brought down plagues on his people and eventually led to the destruction of the firstborn of his nation as well as his military forces (Ex. 6:1; 8:15; 15:1–18).
- Solomon, David's successor, allowed his idolatrous wives to turn his heart away from the Lord. God promised to divide his kingdom and raised up adversaries against him (1 Kin. 11; compare Eccl. 2).
- Lucifer, God's chief angel, was cast out of heaven and committed to eternal destruction after he made it his ambition to exalt himself above the Lord (Is. 14:12–17).

Modern-day Bible readers do well to consider their outcomes and take them as a warning against thinking more of ourselves than we ought to think (Rom. 12:3; 1 Cor. 10:6, 11–13).

ANCESTRAL ROOTS

Genealogies—Records of God's Grace

The genealogies of Abraham's sons, Ishmael and Isaac, are far more than just a collection of names or an extended family tree. They tell the story of God's work and purposes from generation to generation.

As such, these genealogies have much to teach us today about how we look at our heritage. They remind us to . . .

1. *Look back with gratitude.* Genealogies show us our roots. As the Israelites looked back on their past, they had much for which to praise God. He had chosen them as His people, brought them out of slavery in Egypt, given them a land, and established a kingdom. Through it all, He had remained faithful to His promises to such leaders as Abraham, Moses, and David.

2. *Look around at our connections.* First Chronicles reminds the reader of the kinship between Edomites and Israelites—a fact that has important implications to this day. In a world where ethnicity so often seems to divide, Scripture encourages us to look also at what we have in common.

3. *Look ahead with faith.* The past is often an indication of the future. Because Israel's past showed God's faithfulness to the people's forebears, it gave a basis for trusting God to fulfill His Word among their descendants. Likewise, we today can count on God to honor what He has told us.

Following God is more than just an immediate, momentary experience. Certainly it involves what we do in the here and now. But our spirituality is also part of the tapestry of history—a history that God oversees and in which He participates. In 1 Chronicles 1–8 we see His work in the history of one family. How has God been involved in the people from whom you are descended?

Jesus' Roots

Matthew opens with a family tree of Jesus' ancestors (Matt. 1–16). Don't skip this genealogy and begin at verse 18! Matthew includes it for at least three important reasons:

1. To show that God's Son was also a real, flesh-and-blood human. This was a crucial concept for Matthew's first-century audience.

2. To show that Jesus was the long-awaited Messiah of Israel. Notice the prominence of David and Abraham.

3. To show that Jesus is also the international Christ, the Savior of the whole world. His genealogy reaches beyond Jews to include several ethnic groups that populated the Middle East during Israel's Old Testament history. Jesus came to "make disciples of all the nations" (Matt. 28:19).

The Gift of an Ethnic Heritage

Culture provides people with a common set of experiences and values that bind them together over time. As Paul concludes his letter to the Colossians, he mentions three men who shared his Jewish heritage: Aristarchus, Mark the cousin of Barnabas, and Jesus who was called Justus (Col. 4:10–11). He says that they were the only Jews still working with him.

Even though Paul was "the apostle to the Gentiles," he still cherished his Jewish roots. No Gentile could fully appreciate what it meant to grow up and live with the traditions of Judaism. But Aristarchus, Mark, and Justus could. No wonder Paul calls them "a comfort" to him.

God never asks us to reject our roots. We can affirm our ethnic heritage as a rich gift from Him, no matter how our surrounding culture regards it. To be sure, ethnicity ought not to create barriers with other people (Gal. 3:28; Col. 3:11). But we need not hide the cultural background from which God has called us. We need never deny who God has created us to be.

The Three Sisters

Family resemblances account for a great deal, not only among families, but among cities and nations as well. Ezekiel's prophecy showed that as he warned the exiles from Judah about Jerusalem's imminent collapse under God's judgment.

The primary reason for that judgment was idolatry, and in order to illustrate the extent of that sin, the prophet likened Jerusalem to a woman born into a family of idolators (Ezek. 16:44–47). Just as we have the saying, "Like father, like son," so the people of Ezekiel's day were apparently fond of saying, "Like mother, like daughter" (16:44). Applying that proverb to Jerusalem, Ezekiel said that its parents were members of two Canaanite tribes, the Hittites and the Amorites.

Ezekiel was not saying that the Israelites were actually descended from a Canaanite couple; the Hebrews came from Abraham and Sarah, who were of Aramean stock (Deut. 26:5, where "Syrian" means Aramean). Instead, Ezekiel was saying that because of their extensive idolatry, the Israelites might as well have come from the Canaanites, who were notorious idolators.

But in addition to the Canaanites, Ezekiel linked Jerusalem to two other symbols of idolatry and wickedness, the cities of Sodom and Samaria. These were "sisters" to Jerusalem in that both tolerated so many evils that God eventually destroyed them in judgment. Sodom (see Gen. 18:20) and her four "daughter" cities were consumed by brimstone and fire for numerous sins, including injustice to the poor in the midst of incredible wealth (Ezek. 16:49) and sexual immorality (Jude 7).

Likewise, Samaria (see 1 Kin. 16:24), the capital city of the northern kingdom of Israel, and her "daughter" cities had been captured by the Assyrians in 722 B.C. as a punishment for their entrenched idolatry (2 Kin. 17).

Apparently the Judeans thought that God was willing to overlook their own idols, but they were wrong. Devastating wrath was coming because Jerusalem had outdone her "sisters" in turning to other gods (Ezek. 16:48–52).

In drawing application for today from Ezekiel's ancient prophecy, it seems clear that we need to take our spiritual "roots" seriously, both as individuals and societies. Biologically we may not be related to people and cultures who disobey and dishonor God, or who perhaps do not even believe in God. But that matters little if we import their spiritual beliefs and attitudes, and adopt their godless practices. We might as well be members of the same family. If we bear that family resemblance, we will join them in facing God's judgment.

ANGELS

Angels—Servants of God

The four angels that John saw standing at the four corners of the earth (Rev. 7:1) are among the countless ministering spirits that serve God and His people (Heb. 1:7, 14). Angels figure prominently in the Book of Revelation (for example, Rev. 1:20; 5:2, 11; 7:2, 11; 8:2, 6; 12:7; 14:6; 15:1; 18:21; 20:1; 22:8). But they also played a part in many other events of the New Testament.

- Calmed Joseph's doubts about Mary's faithfulness (Matt. 1:20–25).
- Warned Joseph to flee from Herod's plan to kill Jesus (Matt. 2:13).
- Encouraged Joseph to return to Israel with his family (Matt. 2:19–20).
- Ministered to Jesus after His temptation in the wilderness (Matt. 4:11).
- Told the women at the empty tomb that Jesus was alive (Matt. 28:2–6).
- Foretold to Zacharias the birth of John the Baptist (Luke 1:11–20).
- Told Mary that she would bear the Christ (Luke 1:26–38).
- Announced Jesus' birth to shepherds near Bethlehem (Luke 2:8–15).
- Appeared to Jesus in the Garden of Gethsemane to give Him strength (Luke 22:43).
- Promised the crowd observing Jesus' ascension that He would return in like manner (Acts 1:10–11).
- Brought Peter and John out of prison (Acts 5:17–20).
- Told Philip to go into the desert where he met the Ethiopian treasurer (Acts 8:26).
- Told the centurion Cornelius to send for Peter (Acts 10:3–8).
- Released Peter from prison (Acts 12:7).
- Struck down Herod for not giving glory to God (Acts 12:23).
- Stood by Paul during a storm at sea to assure him that he would stand before Caesar (Acts 27:23–24).

God's Line of Defense

One of the most popular topics of speculation in recent years has been the subject of angels. Many books have been published that claim to offer first-hand accounts of experiences with angels. But as always, the Bible must remain our authority on the supernatural.

Daniel 10 is an important passage pertaining to angels. Daniel records a vision in which the archangel Michael, described as "one of the chief princes," is said to defend Israel from the "princes" (probably evil angels) of Persia and Greece (Dan. 10:10–21). Later during the end times, Michael will help to deliver Israel from all her enemies (12:1).

The Bible presents angels as real beings and provides limited information about them, but for the most part it leaves them veiled in mystery. Apparently God wants us to know reality extends beyond our normal perceptions, yet He does not want us to know too much about it. However, He sometimes lifts the veil and allows humans to catch a glimpse of the spiritual activity and warfare taking place around us. Daniel saw some of that reality and found it overwhelming and troubling (7:15; 8:27; 10:15–16). On the other hand, Elisha experienced it and found it reassuring (2 Kin. 6:16–17).

As you develop your understanding and beliefs about angelic forces, good and evil, cosmic battles in the heavens, and other topics of the supernatural, be sure that they accord with Scripture. Sensational stories and wild speculations may make for interesting reading, but ultimately truth is at stake. God's revelation in Scripture can help you sort it all out.

Spiritual Realities Beyond You

Jesus often encountered demons like those that possessed the men at Gadara (Matt. 8:28–34). The mention of demons affirms the reality of powerful spiritual forces in the universe. Scripture has much to say about angels and demons.

Angels are members of an order of heavenly beings who are superior to humans in power and intelligence (Heb. 2:7; 2 Pet. 2:11). However, unlike God they are not all-powerful or all-knowing (Ps. 103:20; 2 Thess. 1:7). God often sends them to announce good news, such as the birth of Jesus (Luke 1:30–31), or to warn of coming dangers, such as the destruction of Sodom (Gen. 18:16–19:29).

Angels played a particularly active role in the events surrounding Jesus' birth, resurrection, and ascension. Since Pentecost, the frequency of angelic activity in human affairs appears to have diminished, perhaps because of the larger role played by the Holy Spirit in the lives of believers.

Demons are fallen angels that have been cast out of heaven. They seek to undermine the cause of righteousness in the world (1 Pet. 3:19–20; 2 Pet. 2:4; Jude 6). Scripture describes them with various names: "unclean spirits" (Mark 6:7), "wicked or evil spirits" (Luke 7:21; Acts 19:12–13), "spirit of divination" (Acts 16:16), "deceiving spirits" (1 Tim. 4:1), and "spirit of error" (1 John 4:6).

The Reality of Angels

The Book of Zechariah contains more references to angels—all the way from Satan to the Angel of the Lord—than almost any other book of the Old Testament. Because of the apocalyptic nature of these writings, some might be tempted to see these angels as figurative or mythological. But the Bible shows that angels are real spiritual beings who serve God and His people.

Satan is a fallen angel who leads a vast army of other fallen angels in open rebellion against God. The Angel of the Lord is frequently mentioned by Zechariah (Zech. 1:11–13; 3:1–6; 12:8). Some believe the appearances of this angel in Old Testament times were actually appearances of the preincarnate Christ. Other angels in Zechariah served as special messengers or agents of revelation (1:9, 14, 19; 2:3; 4:1, 4–5; 5:5, 10; 6:4–5).

It is interesting that whereas the prophets who preached before the Babylonian exile rarely mentioned angels, the prophets after the exile, especially Daniel and Zechariah, frequently alluded to them. This may be because the exile was a particularly dark time spiritually. The temple at Jerusalem had been destroyed, and the glory of the Lord had departed from Israel. Angels may have been a way for God to reassure His people.

ANGER

Compassion and Anger in One Person?

It isn't easy to show both compassion and anger in appropriate ways. With most people it seems like it's one or the other, often in extremes—sugar-coated sentimentality or vicious, destructive rage, neither of which helps anyone.

In Luke 19:41–46, we see that Jesus acted out of both compassion and anger. As He drew near Jerusalem and saw the plight of its people, He was moved to grief, and His eyes filled with tears (19:41). But before long He saw one source of the city's problem— the unjust moneychangers in the temple. With stern but controlled anger, He drove them out, taking care to put a name on their offense: "robbery" (19:45–46).

As you consider Jesus' responses in these two situations, it's worth asking: What moves you to tears? What injustices make you indignant? What productive or corrective action do you take in light of how you feel? Do you even allow yourself to react emotionally to the pain around you, or do you choose detached, dispassionate analysis or just plain apathy?

The Use and Abuse of Anger

How you handle anger says a lot about what sort of person you are. Jacob's sons Simeon and Levi apparently were so controlled by anger that their father cursed them for it (Gen. 49:7).

Anger is like fire. When handled appropriately, it can bring about great good. But out of control it can destroy people's lives.

In the New Testament, Jesus became angry when the religious leaders tried to prevent Him from helping a disabled person because of their religious traditions (Mark 3:5). Later, Paul cited Ps. 4:4 in exhorting us to "be angry and do not sin" (Eph. 4:26). And Hebrews says that the Holy Spirit was angry at the deadening effects of sin on the Hebrew patriarchs (Heb. 3:7–19).

So then, anger can be used for good. But what makes for "good anger"? Here are some characteristics to consider:

1. Good anger often is a response to an injustice or something destructive. For example, Jesus reponded with anger over the misuse of the temple and the abuse of God's people (John 2:13–17; compare Is. 10:1–2). His anger was not self-serving or vindictive; actually it served a purpose of mercy. A similar example of good anger Can be seen in God's expression of wrath against sin. His judgment fell on Christ, who bore our judgment (John 3:16–17).

2. Good anger is slow to develop but increases as it encounters more and more wrong (Is. 4:4; Nah. 1:1–11; James 1:19).

3. Once anger is recognized, one should act on it instead of harboring it and allowing it to fester and become destructive (Mic. 7:18; Eph. 4:26–27).

4. Good anger acts and then forgives; it doesn't keep a scorecard of past wrongs (Ps. 103:9; 1 Cor. 13:5).

5. Good anger is rooted in a sustained and thoughtful understanding of justice and mercy (Zech. 1:1–15). By contrast, impulsive anger is dangerous and should be avoided (Prov. 22:24; 29:22; 1 Cor. 13:5).

6. Whether good or bad, anger is powerful (Ps. 18:7, Prov. 27:4; Jer. 10:10), so it needs to be harnessed and used with a calculated intent for good (Eph. 4:26), so that everyone benefits.

Why Did Moses Hit the Rock?

Some people live with lifelong consequences for choices made in a moment of passion or foolishness. Moses was such a person. In a sudden and rare display of anger, he lashed out at a rock—a seemingly insignificant and harmless act. Yet it cost him entrance into the Promised Land (Num. 20:10–12).

What caused Moses to strike the rock, rather than speak to it as God had commanded? This question is worth pondering, because Moses' life turned on this incident. And if Moses, who was described as the most humble man on the earth (12:3) and the greatest prophet of Israel (Deut. 34:10), could fall so far and so quickly, what about the rest of us? Aren't we also at risk for making sudden choices that we may regret the rest of our lives? How can we avoid that peril?

In the end, only Moses can answer for why he struck the rock. Yet it seems clear that he was acting out of anger, which was out of character for him. For years, Moses patiently put up with the Israelites' grumbling. Instead of lashing out at them, he interceded with God time and again, pleading for the Lord to have mercy on His people. What, then, was the source of the anger that boiled over at the waters of Meribah?

A reasonable possibility is that Moses carried deep wounds from his early life. Consider the fact that he was born in a minority culture of slaves, with a death sentence on his head; yet he was raised in the palace of the king by a woman who was not his mother (Ex. 2:1–10). Who can say what permanent scars and tensions this conflicted background may have left on Moses? Perhaps we see an early result in Moses' murder of an Egyptian who was mistreating a Hebrew (2:11–12). If so, we have a record of two incidents in which an ordinarily mild-mannered and unusually self-controlled man strikes out in anger, doing long-term harm to his future, in response to a flawed past.

Is there a lesson here for the rest of us? It would seem that deep, unresolved anger and other emotions can leave us vulnerable to impetuous choices. Ordinarily we may be able to keep things under control. But under certain circumstances, we are liable to act on impulse and do things that we deeply regret later on. The problem is not just our past, but our failure to bring the past to the Lord for perspective and healing.

The Lord judged Moses because, for whatever reason, he failed to believe God and honor Him before the people (Num. 20:12). What is it that has the potential to keep you from obeying and fearing the Lord? Whatever it is—whether it is from your past or your present—it needs to be dealt with so you can love and serve the Lord with all that you are and have (Deut. 6:5).

ANIMALS

Animals Do Have Rights!

One of the most complex issues of modern society is the impact that meeting the needs of people has on animals and their environment. Does the Bible have anything to say about this often divisive topic?

One principle that Scripture seems to affirm is that animals do, in fact, have certain God-given rights. For example, the Lord regards a person's care and concern for the life of an animal as righteousness, while cruelty to an animal is an act of wickedness (Prov. 12:10). The point is that animals have a right to be treated with wisdom and kindness, not cruelty. God pays attention to how we treat animals.

However, it is also true that God has given human beings dominion, or authority, over the other creatures (Gen. 1:26). Animals are a resource to be managed and used as humans see fit. Yet people are accountable to God for exercising this dominion. Wisdom, or the "fear of the Lord" (Prov. 1:7), suggests that we treat animals as God their Creator would treat them. For example, we know that God has an interest in the preservation of species (Gen. 7:1–5, 23–24; 8:1, 17; Luke 12:6). Likewise, He is concerned that farm and work animals be cared for properly (Ex. 23:12; Deut. 22:4). Shouldn't these concerns influence the way we treat animals today?

Learning from Creation

One of the primary ways by which God has revealed Himself is through the world that He has created. As Job discussed his troubles with his critical friends, he challenged them to learn about God through the creatures that God has made (Job 12:7–8). There are other places where Scripture invites us to discover wisdom and find wonder through some of the creatures of God's world:

- Dogs serve as guards against danger for flocks of sheep and other livestock; generally disparaged in Scripture (1 Sam. 17:43; 2 Kin. 8:13; Job 30:1; Phil. 3:2).

- Ostriches are not particularly good parents, but they can outrun swift horses (Job 39:13–18).

- Eagles are known for their sharp eyes that can spot their prey from hundreds of feet in the air (Job 39:27–30).

- Ants can carry loads many times their own weight, and they show unusual discipline, organization, and industry (Prov. 6:6–8).

- Camels have a capacity to travel for days without water and can move quickly, but they can also be wild and stubborn (Jer. 2:23).

- Sparrows are small and seemingly inconsequential, but they are fed by God and are of great concern to Him (Matt. 6:26; 10:29–31).

In looking at creation, wisdom recognizes that "the Lord has done this" (Job 12:9). Are you a wise observer of the incredible wonders of the animal kingdom? The Bible

CREATURES AS TEACHERS

ANIMALS

encourages us to look and learn from nature's testimony (Rom. 1:20).

Learning from Little Creatures

The earth is full of small, virtually unnoticed creatures. Yet Agur, the writer of Proverbs 30, studied four inconspicuous species and found in them attractive traits that display wisdom:

- The tiny ants plan in advance for the long winter months by storing up food in the summer (Prov. 30:25).
- Rock badgers build secure nests in the strongholds of rocks (30:26).
- Locusts stick together and move in unison even without an obvious leader (30:27).
- Spiders do their skillful work in king's palaces (30:28).

Foresight and planning, safe building, teamwork, and excellence are valuable traits. If tiny creatures such as these exhibit such qualities, how much more should human beings, who have been created in God's image? Reflecting on these creatures, we do well to ask: In what ways do we need to improve our work?

ANXIETY

From Despair to Praise

How do you respond when everything in life seems to be going badly? Can you find any hope for good? In Ps. 22:1–18, David cried out to God with anxiety and despair. He felt:

- abandoned and helpless;
- ignored;
- despised and rejected;
- ridiculed for his faith;
- taunted by vicious enemies;
- drained and on the verge of death; and
- surrounded by a murderous mob.

However, like Job at the end of his sufferings, David was able to affirm that God was still near and capable of delivering him (22:19–20; compare Job 42:1–6). As a result, despite the injuries and insults he had suffered, he came back from the brink of despair. He was able to praise God before his family, his countrymen, and ultimately the entire world (22:22–28).

To whom do you turn when things go badly? As with David, the God who created you wants to join with you in your worst times. He is willing to walk with you all the way through the "valley of the shadow of death" (23:4).

APOSTLES

Who Were the Apostles?

Paul was counted among a group of early church leaders known as "apostles" (2 Cor. 11:5). Each apostle was chosen by Jesus and given authority to carry out certain tasks, especially the task of making disciples of "all the nations" (Matt. 28:19).

The word *apostle* means "messenger." The term was first used of the twelve disciples whom Jesus sent out, two by two, into Galilee to expand His ministry of preaching and healing (Mark 3:14; 6:30). These same disciples, with the exception of Judas Iscariot, were recommissioned as apostles after Jesus' resurrection to be His witnesses throughout the world (Acts 1:8). After Jesus' ascension, the group brought their number to twelve again by choosing Matthias (1:23–26).

However, the term *apostle* came to apply to others besides the Twelve. It included people like Paul who had seen the risen Christ and were specially commissioned by Him (1 Cor. 15:10). James, the Lord's brother, was counted as an apostle (Gal. 1:19). And when Paul wrote that Jesus was seen not only by James but also by "all the apostles" (1 Cor. 15:7), he seemed to be describing a wider group than the Twelve to whom Jesus appeared earlier (15:5).

The authority committed to the apostles by Christ was unique and foundational (12:28; Eph. 4:11). The apostles could install elders or other leaders and teachers in the churches, and they could authorize believers to assume special responsibilities.

ARBITRATION

The Scandal of Litigating Christians

Scripture is explicit: for a Christian to take another Christian to court is "an utter failure" (1 Cor. 6:7). What, then, should we as believers do when we have disputes that normally call for litigation? Paul recommends that we take the matter before wise believers who can make a judgment (6:4–5). But suppose we can't arrange that? Then Paul says it would be better to "accept wrong" than to go before unbelievers for judgment.

Does that categorically rule out lawsuits between Christians today? Not necessarily. Modern Christians disagree over how to apply this passage. Our society is very different from the first-century Roman Empire. But we know that early churches took Paul's instructions literally. They forbade their members to resort to the pagan courts of the day. Instead, they appointed their own elders to judge civil disputes between members.

Those courts gained such a reputation for justice that they even attracted non-Christians, who found them preferable to the notoriously corrupt imperial courts. Eventually, church courts replaced secular courts and for some six centuries were the most important, if not the only, courts in Europe.

Some Christians today are trying to restore this judicial function of the church. In the United States, Christian attorneys are working with church leaders to arbitrate church members' disputes. The decisions can even be legally binding if the disputants agree to that in advance.

How do you settle legal problems when other believers are involved? Are you willing to try everything short of litigation first, before even considering going to court?

Third-Party Mediation

When a relationship has broken down, what can be done? When broken promises separate friends, how can the two people be reunited? It helps if a third party can be found to mediate a settlement. That was a function of the priests in ancient Israel. By favoring Aaron's rod over those of others, God made it clear who should stand between Him and the people (Num. 17:10–11).

God's relationship with Israel repeatedly broke down as a result of violated commandments and rebellious complaints on the part of the Israelites. Sometimes the offenses were so substantial that God immediately punished the offenders (14:40–45; 15:32–36; 16:31–35). Yet even when His character was violated and the people deserved judgment, God listened

to Moses and Aaron as they intervened on the people's behalf (16:22, 46–48).

After Korah was taken away, the situation continued to deteriorate (16:41). Apparently the people had already forgotten whom God had made priests. So the Lord devised a plan to again make it clear that one group—the sons of Aaron—were to serve as intermediaries or priests between Him and the rebellious nation (17:1–11).

The Lord Jesus Christ is the intermediary between God and sinful people. All who depend on Christ's atoning work on their behalf have direct access to God (Heb. 10:19–25). Christ has become our High Priest (8:1–6; 9:11–15), a permanent third-party Advocate who is fully worthy to intercede for our sin.

Have you allowed Christ to act as your Advocate? Do you regularly enter into God's presence through the finished work of Christ on your behalf?

If so, how might you follow Christ's pattern and intervene between opposing parties? Are there situations in your family, community, or workplace where a reasoned and compassionate third party could help the adversaries hear each other and perhaps reconcile them? Would you consider acting as that go-between?

ARROGANCE

(see Ambition; Pride)

ART

God Is Not Against Art

Down through history, some have thought that because God commanded His people not to make carved images (Ex. 20:4–6), He is opposed to art in general. But such is not the case. The point of the second commandment is to avoid substituting anything for God. This is clear from the command, "You shall not bow down to them nor serve them," meaning idols (20:5). In Egypt, where the Israelites had been living for four hundred years, carvings of animals and other idolatrous images were worshiped. Scripture denounces such foolish practices (Ps. 115:4–8).

But Scripture does not denounce art. In fact, the Hebrews were called by God to use art to help them worship Him:

- They were told to use costly materials to make beautiful furnishings for the tabernacle and vestments for the priests (Ex. 25–28).
- They were led by the skilled artisans Bezalel and Aholiab, to whom the Spirit gave ability to create a work of art (Ex. 28:3; 35:30–36:5).
- Years later they were told to construct the temple at Jerusalem, a magnificent architectural achievement that dazzled those who came to worship.
- They created masterful hymns and psalms that not only helped them worship the Lord, but became a source of inspiration for Christians to worship Him as well.

All of these artistic achievements were used in vastly different ways than the golden calf which the Israelites fashioned in the wilderness (Ex. 32:1–6). On that occasion, having been called and equipped by God to create a beautiful center of worship, they instead resorted to idolatry. They broke the second commandment shortly after it had been given. But the problem was their own rebelliousness, not art.

ASTROLOGY

(see Occult)

ASTRONOMY

The Failure of the Stars

The prophet Isaiah predicted that the heavenly bodies would fail to give light when the day of the Lord came against Babylon (Is. 13:10). This suggested the catastrophic destruction that God would bring on this evil empire. Darkness would descend on a nation that exalted itself above all others (14:12–15).

Isaiah's prophecy may also have been mocking the Babylonians' reliance on astrology and astronomy to make plans and interpret history. Calendars surviving from the Assyrians and Babylonians show that they linked important events such as battles, floods, famines, and the death of kings to the movement of the stars and planets. (These artifacts have helped modern-day researchers carefully estimate the dates of these events and construct a fairly accurate timetable of ancient history.)

Thus, if the stars were to fail, the Babylonian worldview would fail as well, leaving the nation in utter confusion.

ATTITUDE

"It Serves Them Right!"

Paul's willingness to speak up is remarkable in that he was on his way to prison and had no need to warn anybody of anything (Acts 27:10). Nor did he have any control over the situation. Of course, he knew that God could preserve him from any and all dangers. Yet he reached out beyond his own interests and safety and spoke up for the safety of others.

Is that your perspective, especially when things don't go your way? Or do you keep your mouth shut with the attitude . . .

- "It serves them right!"
- "They won't pay attention anyway."
- "Let them stew in their own juices."
- "Why should I say anything? My boss doesn't listen anyway. It won't make any difference."
- "If they want to play that sort of game, I can, too."
- "I'll be out of here in a few weeks anyway."
- "She doesn't care about me. Why should I care about what happens to her?"
- "He made his bed, now let him lie in it."

AUTHORITY

A Challenge to Authority

Sooner or later, almost all leaders have their authority questioned. Sometimes they are challenged directly, but more often indirectly by rumor and innuendo.

Jesus faced a direct challenge to His authority from the chief priests and elders, the top leadership in Israel (Matt. 21:23–27). In this instance He didn't argue with them, but simply tossed the ball back into their court. He showed that one very effective way of responding to threatening questions is to ask questions in return.

But observe two aspects of the interaction between Jesus and the Jewish leaders:

1. *The motives of the challengers.* The scribes and Pharisees had no interest in an honest understanding of the nature or source of Jesus' authority. They were only concerned

with protecting their own interests and power. In light of their behavior, you might ask yourself whether you ever question or resist people in authority over you because you are afraid or jealous of them.

2. *The security of Jesus.* Jesus was neither upset nor caught off guard by His attackers. For one thing, He had endured their criticism before, and no doubt expected it to increase. But He also knew with absolute certainty about the very thing that His challengers were attacking: He knew who He was and whose authority He wielded (28:18). His response is a reminder that intimidation is something we allow to occur. People may threaten and confront us, but only we allow ourselves to feel fear. The real question is, Are we certain who we are as followers of the King?

A Symbol of Authority— and Responsibility

Those in authority should hold that authority as a trust on behalf of others. That's what the stones on Aaron's breastplate symbolized (Ex. 39:14). The gems were a reminder that the priests were representatives of the tribes of Israel. Whatever Aaron and his descendants did, whatever choices they made, whenever they wore the breastplate they were to keep the people in mind.

In a similar way, if you hold authority, you should weigh carefully and frequently your responsibility to those who depend on you. Authority is as much a privilege as a right. You may enjoy its "perks," but you also need to fulfill the obligations and honor the trust that others have placed in you.

Empower, Not Overpower

One of the most important things authority figures can do is to make it possible for those under them to act responsibly, wisely, and independently. Moses did that by giving the Hebrews God's laws (Deut. 4:5). As a result, the Hebrews had the potential to become a great ation of "wise and understanding people" (4:6).

This is a useful lesson for anyone in authority today. If we view authority as merely telling others what to do, then we'll slowly train subordinates to become passively dependent, waiting for their next orders. But if instead we view authority as an obligation and opportunity to invest in others and help

them develop their expertise, then we can empower them to exercise their own judgment and skills.

Lessons on Authority

Sooner or later every authority figure will probably face a challenge of authority. Moses faced one from two major Israelite leaders, who happened to be his sister and brother. How he handled the situation, including his plea for God to deliver his sister, Miriam, from leprosy (Num. 12:13), proves instructive. There are several lessons to be gained about the nature of godly authority and the challenges people in authority face:

1. *Subordinates often find authority difficult to accept.* Even outwardly submissive people and close associates may harbor jealousy and suspicions about an authority figure. These issues may be unspoken, but nonetheless they can create a low-level current of dissatisfaction.

2. *Rebellion against authority is not necessarily related to any particular failure on the part of an authority figure.* Resistance to authority is not always a well-considered response to a lapse of leadership. Sometimes it can break out almost spontaneously as a result of imagined grievances.

3. *Rejection of authority can be infectious and contagious.* It's interesting that the challenge by Miriam and Aaron immediately preceded the people's refusal to enter Canaan (Num. 13–14) and Korah's rebellion (Num. 16). Rebellion can spread through gossip, half-truths, and emotional appeals. Because of the sin nature, people have a tendency to join with others in rejecting authority. In fact, rebels often become folk heroes.

4. *Authority needs to be tempered by humility.* The text points out that Moses was a leader with humility (12:3). That's a good model to follow. Especially when faced with "rebellion," authority figures need to respond with prayer, humility, and dependence on God's wisdom and strength, whatever else they may do. The primary goal is not simply to reassert one's power or overcome opponents— though those may be necessary—but to act in a way that honors God's purposes and name.

5. *Christians are always called to mercy, even as they administer authority and justice.*

When Christ was attacked by angry people, He responded mercifully, even if He also used strong words. In the same way, He calls His followers to show mercy and love toward opponents. Often when people challenge authority, it creates an opportunity for correction and clarification. Thus conflict can result in stronger and better relationships through the mercy, love, and power of Christ.

Positive Authority

Authority can be used in ways that bring liberty to people, not just limitation.

Sometimes people think of authority as nothing more than telling others what they cannot do and keeping people in line. But in God's instruction to Moses (Ex. 6:13), we are reminded that authority can bring freedom to others when it is applied wisely and under the Lord's direction.

For example, a judge can use authority to release an innocent person from jail. A high school principal can use authority to obtain resources so that teachers are able to teach effectively. A manager can use authority to reward a worker's performance and encourage creativity and excellence.

So in its best use, authority can be affirming and supportive rather than controlling and punitive. How are you inclined to use authority?

Spiritual Authority

If you exercise leadership among other believers, you'll want to carefully study Paul's comment about his authority (2 Cor. 13:10). Like many of us, Paul liked to be in charge, and he felt frustrated when people failed to follow his lead, as the Corinthians had. As an apostle, he had spiritual authority over them, which at times led him to deal severely with them (1 Cor. 4:21; 5:5; compare Titus 1:13).

But it's important to notice how Paul exercised his authority, especially as he grew older in the faith. He didn't lord it over others or try to use his authority to personal advantage. Nor did he abuse his power by using it to work out his own anger. Instead, he recognized that spiritual authority is given "for edification and not for destruction" (2 Cor. 10:8; 13:10), for building others up, not for tearing them down.

Is that how you use your position and authority? Do you exercise leadership in order to accomplish the best interests of those who follow you? As they carry out your directives, are they built up in Christ, or torn down?

The Transfer of Authority

The transfer of authority is always a delicate task. Changing leaders can be a time of great stress for an organization, as old alliances and political forces vie with new ones to determine who will shape the future.

The death of Aaron (Num. 20:22–29) was a major event in the life of Israel. He was not only high priest for the nation but the nation's first high priest. Furthermore, he had been Moses' primary spokesman (Ex. 4:16; 7:1). He was also Moses' brother.

Aaron's successor, Eleazar, was his third son. Nadab and Abihu, Aaron's two older sons, had been consumed in the Lord's anger after offering "profane fire" before the Lord (Lev. 10:1–3). Thus Eleazar was, in a sense, the "third choice" for the position of high priest.

Despite these and other factors, the transition from Aaron to Eleazar went smoothly. Perhaps it was because God Himself oversaw the transfer of power. Scripture tells of several other transitions, not all of which went as smoothly.

Under Authority

The centurion pointed out that, like Jesus, he was also "a man under authority" (Matt. 8:9). The encounter between the two suggests several lessons of authority and leadership:

1. *Effective leaders willingly admit when they need help (8:5).* The centurion faced a problem that went beyond his own considerable power. But he was willing to go outside his resources to enlist Jesus to deal with the situation.

2. *Effective leaders respond to matters of the heart and spirit (8:6, 8).* The centurion was moved by compassion for his suffering servant, and perceived that Jesus had insight and power that went beyond a physician's skill.

3. *Effective leaders are able to approach others on their terms (8:5, 8).* The centurion came in faith, pleading with Jesus to help his servant. As a Roman officer, he could have ordered Jesus, or offered Him money. But instead, he approached the Lord in a manner consistent with His nature.

4. *Effective leaders understand and accept*

the nature of authority (8:9). The centurion understood what submission is all about. When he issued a command, his soldiers simply obeyed. He recognized that Jesus had the same authority over illness.

5. *Effective leaders invest trust in those under their authority (8:9–10).* Great leaders display great faith in their people. The centurion trusted that Jesus could do what He said He would do.

6. *Effective leaders know whom to trust (8:10).* Trust is only as useful as the trustworthiness of the one in whom it is placed. The centurion's faith was marvelous because it was invested in the right person—Jesus. Leadership based on blind faith, either in others or in a system, is foolhardy.

In light of these observations:

- Do you rely too much on your own competence, or do you honestly assess both your strengths and your weaknesses?
- Do you respond to people only in terms of "the facts," or are you sensitive to the feelings and unexpressed needs of others (as well as your own)?
- Are you willing to meet and work with people on their terms, in their arena? Or must everyone come to you and play by your rules?
- Are you willing to be in charge, but unwilling to submit?
- In whom and in what do you place your faith?

For more on this topic, see **SUPERVISION,** *"The Godly Use of Power," page 390.*

B

BANKING
Banking

When Jesus incorporated a bank into His parable of the talents (Luke 19:23), He was referring to a relatively recent development in Jewish society. Institutional banking was not known in ancient Israel until the time of the Babylonian Captivity (587 B.C.). Lending money at interest (a traditional function of banks) was forbidden in the Law (Ex. 22:25; Deut. 23:19–20). People protected their valuables by burying them or depositing them in temples or palaces.

During the Captivity the Israelites became familiar with Babylonian banking practices. Some Jews joined the industry and became prominent bank officers. By New Testament times banking had become an established institution.

Although Jesus' parable shows that bankers received money for safekeeping and also paid interest, the most common New Testament reference to banking is to moneychanging (Matt. 21:12).

Banking in the Old Testament

The "creditor" mentioned in the Law (Deut. 15:2) was not what we today think of as a banker or credit institution, but merely a neighbor who had loaned something to someone. Institutional banking was not known in ancient Israel until the time of the Babylonian Captivity (586 B.C.).

The absence of banks was in part the result of laws against lending money at interest (at least to fellow Israelites), a traditional function of banks (Ex. 22:25; Deut. 23:19–20). As for protection of valuables, people tended to hide them (Josh. 7:21; Matt. 13:44; Luke 19:20), leave them with a neighbor (Ex. 22:7), or, in Solomon's time, deposit them at the Temple or palace, where the national wealth was stored (1 Kin. 14:26).

However, during the Captivity, the Israelites were exposed to Babylonian banking institutions. Some of these practices were later incorporated into Jewish society. By the first century banking was well established.

Charitable Loans to the Poor

Does the Bible prohibit charging interest on loans? Some Christians today believe that it does, citing texts such as Exodus 22:25–27. Yet in applying biblical principles to modern financial transactions, it's important to remember that the Old Testament Law helped to define a *theocracy,* a society that was to be wholly dedicated to the Lord. That is very different from today's world, where societies and their economies usually operate on more secular and pluralistic terms.

Nevertheless, God's people can still pursue the spirit of the Law. God prohibited charging interest on loans to the poor because it meant oppressing them. The assumption was that the "poor" were those who had no choice but to seek a loan to survive. In fact, they were so destitute that they had nothing else to offer as collateral but the clothes off their back (Ex. 22:26). To profit from such a person's plight would be oppressive. It would mean economic gain by causing a poor person to be cold at night.

But if one lends at no interest, wouldn't that mean some actual loss of value to the lender? Yes, because money's present value is greater than its future value. Money loaned out cannot, while it is out of a lender's hands, be used by the lender to buy more goods or services. Thus lending money at no interest to a poor person means that the lender inevitably experiences some loss. Yet God views the lost interest as an outright gift to the poor borrower. In fact, He promised to bless His people if they would operate with open hands toward the poor and needy (Deut. 15:11).

Does this law apply to interest charged on commercial loans? Generally the opinion is that it does not. The command against charging interest applied specifically to the "poor" and essentially involved charity. Interest on

BANKING

RENT A
SAFETY
DEPOSIT
HOLE
TODAY!
* FREE SHOVEL
WHILE SUPPLIES
LAST

noncharity loans, such as commercial loans, would not be inherently oppressive because it would not take advantage of someone's crisis for food, clothing, or shelter.

BANKRUPTCY
Foreclosure!

If you've ever had to file for bankruptcy protection or lost your home through foreclosure, perhaps you can appreciate Amos' warning to the affluent property owners of Israel. He predicted that God's judgment would effectively repossess and demolish their expensive houses (Amos 3:15).

The fact that wealthy Israelites often had two homes reflects the climatic realities of Palestine. It can be quite cold in the highlands during the winter, with snow in the upper elevations. Meanwhile, it can be fairly warm down by the Dead Sea or along the Mediterranean coast. These extremes caused the affluent to build two homes—a summer house and a winter house—much like many people today, who have a home in the city and a second home in the country.

These Israelites were living in a time of renewed prosperity as Israel extended its borders. They poured their wealth into their homes, lavishly decorating them with expensive paneling and ivory carvings (3:15; 6:4). However, their opulence was too often paid for by defrauding the poor (2:6; 5:11–12; 8:4–6). For that reason, the Lord promised to foreclose on the proud Israelites' expensive real estate.

There is a lesson here for rich Christians today. There may be nothing inherently wrong with owning two homes or furnishing them attractively. But God always pays attention to our treatment of others, especially the poor (James 5:1–6). It is a dangerous thing to lavish luxury on ourselves, particularly if we are doing so at the expense of others. We may find God not only "foreclosing" on our material lifestyle, but bringing us into a time of spiritual crisis as well.

The Year of Jubilee

Israel's Jubilee year (Lev. 25:9) occurred every fiftieth year. It was like a sabbath year (25:3–7) except that it had the additional purpose of returning property and lands to their owners and servants to their families (25:10). This meant that twice each century, the economy of Israel was somewhat leveled, though by no means redistributed. The point was that no family's lands should be permanently lost to creditors, and no one's freedom should be permanently lost to servitude.

BARRENNESS
(*see* Infertility)

BARRIERS
Breaking Down Ethnic Walls

A major breakthrough in race relations is described in Acts 10. For years a virtual wall between Jews and Gentiles had hampered the apostles in sharing Jesus with the Gentile world. But when Peter met Cornelius—an officer of Rome's occupation troops in Palestine—two conversions took place: Cornelius, his family, and his friends came to faith; and Peter came to realize that God wants Gentiles in the church.

God easily could have used Philip the evangelist (see Acts 8:5) to bring the gospel to Cornelius. After all, he lived in Caesarea and had already shown his willingness to share the gospel across ethnic lines. But no, God called Peter to bring His message to the Roman centurion. Apparently He wanted to break down barriers against Gentiles in Peter's heart.

Here is how Peter saw Cornelius:

- Living in Caesarea, Roman military capital of Palestine (Acts 10:1).
- A centurion, commander of one hundred occupying Roman troops (10:1).
- Of the Italian Regiment, all men from Italy (10:1).
- Gentile (10:1).
- Unclean, like the unclean animals of the Old Testament dietary laws (10:11–16).
- Unlawful for a Jew to visit, as he was from another nation (10:28).
- Uncircumcised, therefore not right to eat with (11:3).

In Peter's mind, these factors disqualified Cornelius from serving him dinner, let alone coming to faith. But Peter was following a "Jewish gospel."

God's intention had been that Hebrews would treat their Gentile neighbors cordially (Num. 35:15; Deut. 10:19; Ezek. 47:2). Of course, He also charged His people to exclude heathen practices, particularly idolatry (Lev. 18:24–19:4; Deut. 12:29–31). Intermarriage was condemned, though sometimes allowed (compare Ex. 34:16; Deut. 7:3; Ezra 9:12; 10:2–44; Neh. 10:30). But the main concern was moral purity.

Through rabbinic tradition strict separation became the rule. By Peter's day, four hundred years of Greek and Roman oppression had only hardened Jewish resolve to avoid as much contact as possible with foreigners.

Peter and the other Jewish believers brought these attitudes with them into the church, which made it almost impossible for them to reach out to Gentiles.

Here is how God saw Cornelius:

- Devout (Acts 10:2).
- A God-fearer, along with his household (10:2).
- Generous to the poor (10:2).
- A man of prayer whose prayers and alms were received by God (10:2, 4).
- Obedient to God's angel (10:7–8).
- Cleansed by God, so not unclean (10:15).
- Crucial for Peter to visit (10:5, 19–20).

God's view of Cornelius was a contrast to Peter's. Because of Christ, God was ready to throw the doors of faith wide open to Gentiles: "What God has cleansed you must not call common," He sternly declared to Peter (10:9–16). Because of Christ, the centurion could be "cleansed" from sin and be acceptable to God. God broke down the wall in Peter's heart by pouring out the Holy Spirit on these Gentile believers (10:44–45).

Attitudes of prejudice and legalism trouble the church today just as they did the early church. But true believers must seek out *all* people, look at them from God's perspective, love them for the gospel's sake, and rejoice over those who respond in faith.

*For more on this topic, see **OBSTACLES**, "Overcoming Obstacles—with the Lord's Help," page 281.*

BEAUTY
Beauty in Creation

One has only to consider the awesome effects of natural phenomena such as the eruption of a volcano or the passing of a powerful hurricane to imagine the massive destruction that must have occurred as a result of the Flood. Yet after the waters subsided, Noah led his family in worship and thanksgiving (Gen. 8:20). In doing so, he reaffirmed for the next generation the value of life and the need for people to follow God's ways.

In response, the Lord resolved never again to curse the ground or destroy every living thing. He also promised to renew the cycle of the seasons (8:21–22). Then God created a memorial or sign of His promise—a beautiful rainbow as a permanent reminder of His covenant with every living creature (9:12–17).

This episode highlights an important fact that we do well to consider: that even though people today continue to rebel against God, and even though the curse of Genesis 3:14–19 has not been lifted, creation is still to be valued and managed wisely (Lev. 25:2; Ps. 24:1–2).

BEREAVEMENT

(*see* Grief)

BETRAYAL
Judas Iscariot, the Betrayer

The New Testament never mentions Judas Iscariot without reminding the reader that he was the man who betrayed Jesus (for example, Matt. 10:4; Mark 3:19; John 12:4). Consequently, to this day the name Judas is a symbol of betrayal.

Why did he do it? His portrayal in the Gospels suggests that he had a keen interest in money. But the amount that the priests paid him—thirty pieces of silver—was relatively small. Besides, he had access to the disciples' money box and apparently was known for helping himself to its contents (John 12:6).

Some have suggested that Judas thought that his betrayal would force Jesus into asserting His true power and overthrowing the Romans. Others have suggested that Judas became convinced that Jesus was a false Messiah and that the true Messiah was yet to come.

Or perhaps he was upset over Jesus' seemingly casual attitude toward the Law in regard to associating with sinners and violating the Sabbath.

In the end, no one knows what Judas' exact motives were for turning against Jesus. He remains a shadowy figure in the Gospel accounts, unknown by his companions, unfaithful to his Lord, and unmourned in his death.

BIBLE

God Has Spoken—to You!

Imagine hearing God's voice! Moses did (Num. 1:1). Scripture gives little indication of what that experience was like, but it does say that the Lord spoke to Moses "face to face, as a man speaks to his friend" (Ex. 33:11). Perhaps you wish that God would speak to you that directly. But actually, He has—through the Bible.

The Bible claims to be from God. Though its words were written down by people, they are words that God has spoken. Throughout the first five books of the Bible, Moses states again and again that he is presenting what God said to him (for example, Ex. 24:4).

Likewise, Moses declares that the Law was revealed to him by God (Ex. 25:1; Lev. 1:1; Num. 1:1; Deut. 1:6). In fact, the phrase "the Lord spoke to Moses" is repeated thirty-three times in Leviticus alone. Later, the New Testament would affirm Moses' insistence that his commandments came from God:

- Jesus used the words "God spoke" in citing the incident of the burning bush (Mark 12:26).
- Both Jesus and the Pharisees acknowledged the authority of the Law as coming from God (Matt. 19:4–7; John 9:29).
- Stephen cited Moses' writings as God's words (Acts 7:6).
- Peter indicated that Moses and the other prophets "spoke as they were moved by the Holy Spirit" (2 Pet. 1:21; compare Heb. 1:1).

God spoke clearly to Moses. He has likewise spoken clearly to us, through His written Word, the Bible. Countless Jews and Christians down through history have preserved His message since it was given. Many have spent their careers and even their lives to make it available to us today. The Bible has been banned, burned, and, to some, supposedly "debunked," yet still its truth stands. It remains the test of orthodoxy for all who claim to be of God or speak of God's ways.

Yet the question remains: Do we read and obey what God has said?

A Word to Live By

For many people today, the Bible remains a closed book. One reason is that some people have the mistaken idea that the Bible is a mysterious collection of encoded teachings that only a few wise or holy people can interpret. But God's Word is not a mystery. It never has been. From the beginning of time, God has spoken clearly, in terms that humans can understand (Heb. 1:1–2).

Moses reminded the Israelites of this fact as they prepared to enter the Promised Land. God had given them His Law at Sinai (Deut. 5:4–5, 22), so there was no need to go searching to find out what He wanted (30:11–14). He had already made plain what His will was. He even wrote down His Law on stone tablets so that the people would have a permanent record of it.

Believers today also have a permanent, written record of God's Word—the Bible. And though a few parts of Scripture may be hard to understand (2 Pet. 3:15–16), it is generally not a mystery. We need not resort to subjective revelations or any other strange practices to interpret its meaning. The Bible's message becomes evident when we read it according to normal principles of reading.

However, the most important thing about Scripture is not just that we read it or study it, but that we *live* it, that we obey the Lord (James 1:22). God did not give us His Word merely to inform us, but to change our lives.

A Completed Story

Peter wants us to feel confident that the Scriptures are as valid and trustworthy today as they were when they were first written (2 Pet. 1:21). He also gives some information on the process God used to get His Word written down in a permanent form.

The "older testament," which exists today in thirty-nine books, was written mostly in Hebrew over a thousand-year period, hundreds of years before Christ. The twenty-seven books of the "newer testament" were written in Greek during the first century after Christ's birth. As the various writings came into existence over the centuries, the people of God corporately studied and recognized them as being the Word of God.

The two testaments together tell a completed story. *Testament* means "covenant" or "agreement" between God and humanity. The Old Testament is "old" in the sense that it reveals a covenant made at Mount Sinai (Ex. 19:3–6; 24:3–8). The New Testament or covenant was accomplished by Christ through His death on the cross (Luke 22:20; 1 Cor. 11:25)

The Bible: Getting the Big Picture

As Paul indicates to Timothy (2 Tim. 3:16–17) and many other passages affirm, the Bible is the ultimate authority for Christian faith and practice. It is crucial to interpret Scripture in light of its overall context.

The Bible as it has come down to us is laid out in two parts: the Old Testament, covering the period before Christ, and the New Testament, the period after Christ. The biblical record is a three-part story:

Part I: God's Original Creation (Gen. 1–2). The eternal God created a perfect, beautiful world and put it under the management of Adam and Eve and their successors (Gen. 1–2). No one knows how long this part of the story lasted, but Scripture devotes only the first two of its 1,189 chapters to telling it.

Part II: The Human Dilemma and God's Response (Gen. 3—Rev. 20). The second part of the story takes up all but the last two chapters of the Bible. Two story lines weave throughout the record. One reveals how the balance and beauty of creation is terribly damaged by sin and rebellion. The other unfolds God's response to rescue His creatures and the creation from this dilemma. His redemptive work is promised through Israel (as recorded in the Old Testament), provided through Christ (as recorded in the Gospels), and then applied in and through the church (as told in Acts and the letters). The Book of Revelation's first twenty chapters display events related to Christ's return to earth.

Part III: The Achievement of God's Original Design (Rev. 21–22). The last two chapters of the Bible tell the final third of the story. They offer great hope to the reader by promising a new heaven and earth. God's original intentions for the creation will finally and fully be achieved. This parallels and fulfills Genesis 1–2 and also reflects the values of Christ, who is the focus of the whole Bible.

The Bible: Trustworthy and True

Is the Bible a trustworthy document? Are the Scriptures true as written? Or are they full of myths that may have symbolic value but little if any basis in fact? People have been questioning the biblical record almost from its beginnings. Peter, for instance, encountered skepticism as he presented the gospel in the first century. His claims about Jesus were nothing but cleverly devised fables, some said—a charge he vehemently denied (2 Pet. 1:16).

Today the Bible's credibility and authority are still attacked. Yet how many of its critics have carefully studied its teaching? How many have even looked at the story of how it came to be written?

A careful reader will recognize that the Bible is not so much a single book as a library of sixty-six books. It contains a variety of literary genres: history, poetry, narrative, exposition, parable, and "apocalyptic" (see Rev. 10:1–10). Its many authors wrote during a period of some two thousand years using three languages—Hebrew, Greek, and Aramaic. Probably all but one were Jews.

Remarkably, the writers tell one unified story:

- They offer the same understanding of God throughout. He is one God, Creator, Savior, and Judge. He is all-powerful, all-knowing, and eternal. His character is holy, good, loving, and just.
- They offer the same understanding of human nature. People are made in God's image and are capable of great good. Yet they are also sinful and capable of great wickedness. The great need of humanity is to be reconciled to God and to each other.
- They offer a common understanding of Jesus Christ. He is both God and man.

He became a real human being in order to show the world the God it could not otherwise perceive. Something deeply significant happened as a result of His death on the cross, making it possible for God and humanity to be reconciled.

- They offer the same hope. God will accomplish His purposes for His creation.

Aside from the internal evidence that Scripture is what it claims to be—the very words of God—is a growing body of external evidence that supports its reliability as a document. For example, scholars have found many contemporary sources that parallel the Scriptural record. For instance, Jesus is mentioned by two Roman writers of the first century, Tacitus (*Annals* 15.44) and Pliny the Younger (*Letters* 19.96), as well as by some Jewish writings of that period, including Josephus (*Antiquities* 18.3.3) and the *Mishnah*, a collection of traditions under compilation in Jesus' day.

Another body of research that proves invaluable for biblical studies is archaeology. Countless discoveries have helped to verify the text of Scripture, most notably the Dead Sea Scrolls. Likewise, digs throughout the Mediterranean have supported biblical references to various places and people and the events of which they were a part thousands of years ago.

The more one examines the evidence, the more one becomes convinced that the Bible is more than a cleverly devised tale. It has the ring of authenticity. But in that case, readers ought to pay attention to its message. That is the ultimate issue. As Mark Twain aptly put it, it is not the things in the Bible that people can't understand that prove troublesome, but the things they can understand. Even if people are convinced that the Bible is true from cover to cover, will they heed its message?

The Power of God's Word

This publication that you are reading is based on the belief that Scripture really is the living and powerful Word of God (Heb. 4:12). As this verse shows, the Word speaks to heart matters—intentions and motives. Ultimately, people make choices and act on the basis of their underlying values and notions about what is true and right. God's Word is the authoritative standard by which all thoughts and actions are to be measured.

BIGOTRY

(*see* Prejudice)

BIRTH CONTROL

Children—A Blessing, Not a Burden

The modern world tends to send mixed messages about the value of children, but the Bible is unequivocal in its affirmation that children are a blessing from the Lord, and a source of happiness for parents (Ps. 127:3–5). This biblical view stands in contrast to modern thinking, which slowly but surely has come to regard children as a burden on families and communities, rather than a blessing.

Scripture is not blind to the realities of raising children. In fact, it faithfully records many of the difficulties inherent in bringing children into the world. Nevertheless, the Bible insists that children are ultimately a heritage and a reward from God.

As believers today consider this truth, it should create a level of tension about easily accepting modern attitudes. For example, it seems to question the often unquestioned use of artificial birth control. Does preventing pregnancy mean turning down a gift from God, from whom every good and perfect gift comes (James 1:17)? Likewise, Psalm 127 seems to challenge current popular opinion, which holds that two or three children make a big family, and more children tend to indicate a couple's ignorance, carelessness, or indifference toward the environment. How does this square with the psalmist's assurance that "the fruit of the womb is a reward"?

Problems such as "unwanted" pregnancies and overpopulation deserve careful thought and genuine discussion. But those thoughts and discussions, as well as the decisions that flow out of them, need to be informed by biblical truth and values. Psalm 127 challenges us to consider whether we still value children as much as God does.

BITTERNESS

(*see* Hatred)

BLASPHEMY

Dishonoring God's Name

God takes His name very seriously, as the incident with Shelomith's son reveals (Lev. 24:10–23). When the young man "went out among the children of Israel," perhaps he was taunted by racial insults because of his Egyptian roots. That would help to explain his fight with one of the Israelites (24:10). It might also explain why he ended up reviling the name of Israel's God. Perhaps he felt that one insult deserved another. But in dishonoring God, he was committing the sin of blasphemy.

God had warned His people in the Ten Commandments that He would "not hold him guiltless who takes [My] name in vain" (Ex. 20:7). In this landmark case involving Shelomith's son, God followed through on His Word. First He told Moses to remind the

BIRTH CONTROL

IF KIDS ARE THE "FRUIT OF THE WOMB", THESE MUST BE CLING PEACHES.

people that there would be a death penalty for blasphemy (Lev. 24:15–16). Then the horrible sentence—execution by stoning—was carried out (24:23).

In light of this sobering incident, it's worth considering ways that we today may dishonor God's name. Here are three possibilities:

1. *Blaming God for evil.* It is common to call floods, tornadoes, and other natural disasters "acts of God." There may be nothing wrong in such a euphemism. But if we impute to God responsibility for things that are actually the result of sin and evil, that amounts to blasphemy.

God cannot be the author of evil (James 1:13, 17). He gives only good gifts. Therefore, we are out of line whenever we assign to Him acts that are unworthy of Him.

2. *Dishonoring another person.* Some people who would never curse God somehow think it's all right to curse another human being. Again, James 3:9–10 strongly warns us against that practice, for every person is created in the image of God. Therefore, to dishonor another human being is to dishonor the Creator—a sin amounting to blasphemy.

3. *Willful, persistent rebellion and unbelief.* It is bad enough if we demean the character of God by what we say. But the ultimate insult to God is to turn our backs on His clearly revealed will—especially in regard to Christ's work on our behalf and the spiritual growth that ought to result from faith in Him.

Jesus was accused of blasphemy by the religious leaders of His day, but He warned them that it was they who were blaspheming, because they were resisting the Holy Spirit. In a similar way, the New Testament strongly cautions believers against "falling away" from a vital relationship with God into unbelief and disobedience.

BLOOD
Images of Life and Death

The red fluid circulating in our body takes nourishment to the body parts and carries away waste. The word "blood" is often used literally in Scripture. Sometimes the word refers to the blood of animals (Gen. 37:31); at other times it refers to human blood (1 Kin. 22:35). The word is also used figuratively in the Bible. It may mean "blood red" (Joel 2:31)

or murder (Matt. 27:24). The phrase "flesh and blood" means humanity (Heb. 2:14).

But the most important biblical concept in regard to blood is the spiritual significance of the blood of sacrificial animals. Although some scholars believe the blood primarily means the animal's *life,* most agree that blood refers to the animal's *death.* Most of the Old Testament passages that discuss sacrifices mention the death of the animal, not its life (Lev. 4:4–5). The Bible makes it clear that the satisfaction or payment for human sins was made by the death of a specified animal substitute: "For the life of the flesh is in the blood, and I have given it to you upon the altar to make atonement for your souls; for it is the blood that makes atonement for the soul" (Lev. 17:11).

In the New Testament, this Old Testament idea of sacrifice is applied to Christ's blood. References to the "blood of Christ" always mean the sacrificial death of Jesus on the cross. References to the blood of Christ were made by Paul (Rom. 3:25); Peter (1 Pet. 1:19); John (Rev. 1:5) and the author of Hebrews (Heb. 9:14). Although all have sinned, "we have redemption through His blood, the forgiveness of sins" (Eph. 1:7).

BLOOD MONEY
Tainted Money

The chief priests knew that the coins tossed back at them by Judas were unacceptable to God (Matt. 27:6). It was blood money, money they had paid to apprehend their enemy, Jesus (26:14–16). Yet they turned around and used it to buy a cemetery for the poor—a good deed, yet hypocritical all the same.

Do you ever present "tainted" money to the Lord—money not necessarily obtained through outright crime, but perhaps through deception, shady deal-making, or dirty politics? When we donate money to churches, missions, schools, ministries to the poor, and the like, we hide nothing from God. He knows all of our motives. He knows whether our gifts are from the first and best of what we've accumulated, or whether we're giving "leftovers." He knows whether our gifts cost us little or nothing (2 Sam. 24:21–24). And He certainly knows—and hates—whatever we have come by unjustly (Mal. 1:6–14). We deceive no one but ourselves if we pretend to honor God while giving Him the fruit of unrighteousness.

BODY

The Shape of Who We Are

Our body defines our existence. Some religions consider the body evil or inferior to the soul, but the Bible teaches that the body is God's good gift to us (Gen. 1:31). It is a necessary ingredient for a fully human existence (Gen. 2:7). In the Old Testament the word "body" sometimes means "corpse" (Num. 6:6). Occasionally the reference is to the body as that part of a person that is involved in reproduction (Deut. 28:4).

In the New Testament these Old Testament meanings are carried forward, but new insights appear. Paul teaches that the body is often the instrument of sin (1 Cor. 6:18); that the body must die as a penalty for sin (Rom. 7:24); and that sin dishonors a person's body (Rom. 1:24). On the other hand, believers in Christ may "put to death the deeds of the body" (Rom. 8:13) and present their bodies as holy sacrifices that please God (Rom. 12:1).

Since human life requires a body, sometimes the term "body" symbolizes the whole person. Both Jesus and Paul used the word in this way (Matt. 6:22–23; Phil 1:20). The Bible reveals little about existence after the death of the body. But complete salvation and full humanity begin not at death but at the return of Christ. Then believers will receive their eternal resurrection bodies (1 Cor. 15:35–49).

BONDAGE

(*see* Debt; Slavery)

BOTTOM LINE

The Bottom Line

Busy people often demand that others come to the point by asking, "What's the bottom line?" In other words, what matters? What's important? What's worth paying attention to?

Many people want to know what the "bottom line" in Scripture is. There's a lot of information in the Bible and a lot of stories. But when you boil it all down, what's the point? What does God want? What's expected of an individual?

Moses gave us the "bottom line": *fear God* (Deut. 10:12). That is, respect God, keep His commandments, love Him, and serve Him with all that we are and have. Nothing else is more important.

The Real Bottom Line

Businesspeople commonly talk about the "bottom line," usually meaning the *financial* bottom line. In Luke 9:25 Christ challenges us to look at another bottom line—the final accounting each of us will give to God for how we have spent our lives.

Clearly one can be very successful from a human point of view and yet be finally lost. Moreover, a careless Christian's works will be judged adversely. That can happen both actively and passively. Actively, we can sell out to the world's values by lying to a customer, cheating on a deal, or running over others to advance our position. Passively, we can drift away from God by leaving Him out of our work and lives, or perhaps by sacrificing our families in order to pursue wealth and status. Either way, the "bottom line" is clear: we will bring ourselves to ultimate loss.

BREAD

The Bread of Life

When Jesus called Himself the "bread of life" (John 6:35; also 6:32–33, 41, 48), He was using as an image more than a staple of the diet, He was drawing on a rich symbol of Jewish life.

Bread played an important role in Israel's worship. During the celebration of Pentecost, two loaves of leavened bread were offered as sacrifices (Lev. 23:17). In the tabernacle, and later in the temple, the Levites placed twelve loaves of unleavened bread, or bread without yeast, before the Lord each week to symbolize God's presence with the twelve tribes (Ex. 25:30).

Throughout the Exodus, God miraculously sustained His people by sending manna from heaven each morning (Ex. 16). The bread-like manna was a "small round substance as fine as frost" (16:14). It looked "like white coriander seed" and tasted like "wafers made with honey" (16:31) or "pastry prepared with oil" (Num. 11:8).

It was this manna that Jesus was recalling when He called Himself "the true bread from heaven" (John 6:32), "the bread which came down from heaven" (6:41), and the "bread of life" (6:48–51, 58). Symbolically, Jesus is the heavenly manna, the spiritual or supernatural food given by the Father to those who ask, seek, and knock (6:45; Matt. 7:7–8).

However, it's also interesting that Jesus' "bread of life discourse" (as John 6:26–58 is called) was given during Passover, also known as the Feast of Unleavened Bread (6:4, 22). Passover celebrated the deliverance of Israel from slavery in Egypt. On the night before leaving Egypt, the Israelites made unleavened bread, as they had no time to let their bread rise before taking flight (Ex. 12:8; 13:6–7).

In this context, Jesus had just fed at least five thousand people (John 6:1–14), an event that led directly to the bread of life discourse (6:22–27). Clearly, He was indicating that He was God's provision for the people's deepest spiritual needs. Just as God had provided for His people as they came out of Egypt, so Jesus had provided physical food for the five thousand and was ready to provide spiritual nourishment and life to all of them as well.

Tragically, the people balked at His teaching (6:30–31, 41–42, 52, 60). Their hearts were hardened in unbelief. Soon, many began to turn away (6:66). But to those who believed, like Peter who declared, "You are the Christ, the Son of the living God" (6:69), Jesus gave abundant and eternal life.

BREVITY OF LIFE
(see Death)

BURIAL AND FUNERAL CUSTOMS
Burial Practices
Paul's doctrine of the resurrection (1 Cor. 15:42) flew in the face of prevailing ideas about the afterlife. To the Greek mind, death released a person's spirit from the prison of the body. The last thing a Greek would want was to be reunited with a corruptible body (15:35).

Burial practices in Corinth and the other cities of the Roman Empire were largely a function of one's status in life. If the deceased was a member of the upper classes, the job of preparing the body was delegated to professional undertakers. They usually dressed the body in a toga adorned with badges and other tokens of the person's accomplishments and offices. Professional mourners and musicians then led a funeral procession to the burial site. Sometimes actors were recruited to follow the cortege, wearing masks that depicted the family's ancestors.

In Greek and Roman cultures, bodies were as likely to be cremated as buried. Either way, the rich tended to bury their dead in elaborate tombs. Some even formed cooperatives in which hundreds of urns were placed.

The poor, by contrast, laid their dead to rest in common, often unmarked graves. Or, if they lived in or near Rome, they might use the catacombs, a maze of underground tunnels outside the city. In the later years of the first century, Christians were not permitted to use regular cemeteries, so they resorted to the catacombs for their funerals. As persecution increased, some eventually fled there for survival.

Among the Hebrews, bodies were laid either in a shallow grave covered with stones or in a cave or tomb hewn out of stone and secured by a circular stone rolled and sealed over the entrance. Graves were often marked with a large, upright stone.

Due to the hot climate of Palestine, dead bodies decayed rapidly, so burial usually took place within a few hours after death. If someone died late in the day, burial took place the next day, but always within twenty-four hours after death.

The Hebrews did not follow the Greek custom of cremation, except in emergencies, nor did they generally use coffins. And even though they had historical ties to Egypt, they did not embalm their dead as the Egyptians did.

Mummification was invented by the Egyptians more than three thousand years ago. They believed that the preservation of the body insured the continuation of the soul after death.

According to the Greek historian Herodotus, there were three different methods of embalming. The least expensive method involved emptying the intestines by flushing them with a cleaning liquid, after which the body was soaked in natron. A second method called for placing the body in natron after the stomach and intestines had been dissolved by an injection of cedar oil.

The most elaborate method of embalming required the removal of the brain and all internal organs except the heart. The inner cavity of the body was then washed and filled with spices. The corpse was soaked in natron, then washed and wrapped in bandages of linen soaked with gum. Finally, the embalmed body was placed in a wooden coffin. These processes proved remarkably effective in preserving bodies from decay.

Funeral Preparations

Jesus told the dinner crowd that Mary was preparing Him for His burial (John 12:7). It's difficult for us today to appreciate the significance that burial rituals had for ancient peoples. Nearly every ancient religion gave explicit and sometimes elaborate instructions for preparing and burying the dead.

For Hebrews at the time of Christ, women and men participated in the mourning ritual, but women likely prepared the corpse for interment. First they washed the body, then scented it with fragrant oil, an act of devotion that might be repeated at the tomb.

The oil that Mary used on Jesus (12:3) was probably nard, a perfume used by women. Imported from India, it was extremely costly and was known for its strong fragrance. It was the same perfume used by the woman that Solomon praised in his Song of Solomon (1:12; 4:13).

Washed and scented, the body was dressed in the person's own clothes or else wrapped in specially prepared sheets. Then, as soon as possible, it was carried upon a bier to the tomb. Relatives, friends, and professional mourners (see Matt. 9:23) formed a procession, and anyone meeting it was obliged to show honor to the deceased and the relatives by joining. A eulogy was often delivered at the grave site.

The body was placed on a shelf in the tomb, which was then sealed by a heavy, tight-fitting slab. Jews were expected to visit the tomb often, partly as a precaution against burying someone who only seemed dead.

The Mourners

In the ancient world, paid professional mourners (Matt. 9:23), most often women, aided families in their public expression of grief upon the death of a loved one. They composed poems or dirges praising the deceased, which they chanted to the accompaniment of a flute or other musical instrument in an attempt to stir the audience emotionally. They usually wore sackcloth and scattered dust in the air and on their heads. Weeping, wailing, and beating their breasts, they created an unmistakable tone of grief. It was also common for mourners to sit on the ground, perhaps to represent the low estate to which the family of the deceased and the wider community were brought by the death of the person (compare Is. 47:1, Ezek. 26:16). There was no denial of death or distancing themselves from loss.

Perhaps Jesus was making use of the image of professional mourners when He spoke of those who mourn in the Sermon on the Mount (5:2).

Whitewashed Tombs

Jesus drew upon a grim, arresting image in His denunciation of the self-righteous Pharisees (Matt. 23:27–28). At the end of a Jewish funeral procession, which everyone was obliged to join, the body was placed on a rock shelf in a tomb. Once the flesh had decomposed, the bones would be collected and removed, allowing the shelf to be reused. Since Jews were made ritually unclean by touching graves (Num. 19:16), rocks used to seal tombs were whitewashed as a warning to stay away. The glaze gave the tombs a clean image on the outside—even though there were decomposing corpses on the inside.

BURNOUT

Jethro Performs an Intervention

Moses was a classic case of a workaholic heading toward burnout. Fortunately, he had in Jethro an astute father-in-law who could see what Moses could not—that eventually his failure to delegate authority would wear himself and his people out (Ex. 18:18). Jethro had the courage to speak up and warn his son-in-law about the looming danger, not unlike caring relatives and friends of people today who are addicted to various substances or habits. Often their "intervention" can literally make the difference between life and death.

Such drastic action is often necessary with workaholics because they are often the last to see the damage their compulsive work habits are doing to themselves and to others around them. When things are not working out, their tendency is to work harder, making the problem even worse.

Might you be a Jethro in someone's life by taking the person aside and explaining the damage that excessive work is causing? Can you offer some strategies for change, or perhaps suggest some resources for getting help?

On the other hand, perhaps you're the one who tends toward overwork. Is there already a Jethro in your life who is asking you to slow down? Maybe your Jethro is a spouse whom you haven't spoken to at length for days or weeks. Maybe it's a son or daughter who long ago gave up expecting you to take time just to play. Maybe it's a friend you've been avoiding, who always seems to nag you about working too hard.

Moses responded right away to Jethro's suggestions (18:24). How long will it take you?

BUSINESS

The Four Way Test

In many ways, the issue Micah raises in Micah 6:6–8 is, How can you develop an ethical yardstick for life and work? How do you know when your practices, products, and relationships are acceptable to the Lord?

This question was heavy on the heart of Herbert J. Taylor as he labored to rescue a troubled manufacturing company in Chicago in 1932, during the Great Depression. One morning, Mr. Taylor was praying and reflecting on Jesus' Sermon on the Mount (Matt. 5–7), a passage that expands Micah's three-part summary of the Law—justice, mercy, and humility (Mic. 6:8). Mr. Taylor rendered the same truth in what has come to be known worldwide as the Four Way Test:

1. Is it the truth?

2. Is it fair to all concerned?

3. Will it build goodwill and better friendships?

4. Will it be beneficial to all concerned?

Despite the disaster that struck the national economy, Mr. Taylor's company not only survived but thrived as its management embraced these biblical standards. Later, the Four Way Test was adopted by a major international service club, and Mr. Taylor became its president. By now, the organization has spread these principles to more than one hundred countries, through clubs, programs, schools, and service projects.

As you look at situations in your workplace, family, and community, consider the three-way test of Micah and the Four Way Test that Mr. Taylor devised. How would your actions change if you applied this test to every situation in your life?

A Public Transaction

Abraham's purchase of the field of Ephron was a public transaction, as is evident from the phrase, "before all who went in at the gate of his city" (Gen. 23:18). In the ancient Middle East, a city's gates were where much of its civic business was conducted. Those who "went in at the gate" were primarily adult males who owned property. A similar reference occurs in Genesis 34:24 to indicate the adult males of Shechem.

C

CALLING

All Believers Are "Ministers"

A simple way to define "ministry" is that it is the work of God by the people of God (Eph. 4:12). It is the work of serving others, using the gifts, resources, and power that God gives us.

This is important for the church today to understand, because many Christians assume that "ministry" belongs only to professional ministers, or clergy. But ministry belongs to everyone in the body of Christ. All believers are "ministers." All have been gifted to carry out the work of God (Rom. 12:4–8; 1 Cor. 12).

What, then, is the role of the clergy? To equip, or prepare, the "ministers" to do their work of ministry (Eph. 4:11–12). This involves teaching the truth of God's Word, helping believers overcome the problems that hinder them, giving them a vision for reaching out

to others with the love of Christ, and helping them develop and utilize the practical skills required to carry out their God-given tasks.

Ministry is the calling, privilege, and responsibility of every member of the body of Christ. Some congregations help to remind their people of this truth by listing professional workers under the title of "staff" or "pastors" in their bulletins and newsletters, and reserving the term "ministers" for all members.

It has been said that when believers are baptized, they are ordained into the ministry. Perhaps it would help to recover this perspective. It might free pastors and other church leaders to focus on their crucial role of equipping the saints for the work of ministry. It might also help to redistribute the load, which is often crushing for clergy and their families. Broadly shared ministry would mobilize and affirm the whole church and enrich every part of the world where the "ministers" live and work.

Different Experiences of Calling

The circumstances of Ezekiel's call to be a prophet were rare and dramatic, yet the same God who called Ezekiel also calls believers today to carry out His assignments. Each person experiences calling in a somewhat different way. The main thing is that God has called all believers to serve Him with all of their lives.

For some, like Ezekiel, calling has also occurred through an incident in which God has spoken to the person with a commission to be a prophet or leader (Ezek. 2:1–5). For most, however, God's call has been much less dramatic, but no less significant. It affects everything about a person's life—career, family, identity, faith, relationships, and even one's outlook for the future.

One of the most evident aspects of God's call is the way He creates people with unique skills and abilities that fit them for specific purposes. Here are some of the people in the Bible who were called by God, and what happened when they responded to His call.

- Abraham left his homeland and relocated to Canaan by way of Haran (Gen. 11:31–12:4; Acts 7:2–5).
- Moses became the liberator and leader of the Israelites (Ex. 3:1–12; 5:1).

LOCAL CALLS OUT OF STATE CALLS CALLS INTO THE MINISTRY

CALLING

- Nehemiah negotiated with the king to lead a group of Jews back to Jerusalem to rebuild the city, particularly its walls (Neh. 1:1–2:10).
- Esther intervened to save the lives of her people, the Jews, from a genocidal plot (Esth. 4:1–6:10).
- Daniel became an advisor to kings, and a prophet (Dan. 1:19; 7:1)
- Jonah, after initially running from the Lord, went to Nineveh and warned of God's judgment, resulting in citywide repentance (Jon. 1:1–3; 3:1–10).
- Barnabas served as a friend and mentor to young believers, including Saul (Acts 9:26–27; 11:25–26) and John Mark (15:36–39).
- Saul became God's principal spokesman during the later part of the first century A.D. (Acts 9:15).

Who Is "Called"?

Are only certain people "called" by God to do important work for Him? Many people assume that occupations such as the pastorate or missionary work are true "callings" that have significance before God, while other jobs are just jobs.

Even though work is an important part of life, by itself it falls far short of describing the significance of an individual. There are many other aspects to being a person—personal growth and development, family, citizenship, friendships, and faith. So to define oneself by one's occupation is inadequate. It tends to place more value on the self than on God; more on activity than on character; and more on success than on relationships. In short, it tends to equate employment with human worth.

From the Bible's point of view, "calling" describes *all* of the responsibility of all believers to serve God with all of their lives:

Every believer is called to belong to God. Paul indicated to the Christians at Rome that both he and they had the same calling (Rom. 1:1, 6). Likewise, he wrote to the believers in Ephesus that just as there is one Spirit and one body (that is, the church), "you were called in one hope of your calling" (Eph. 4:4).

Every believer is called a child of God. In His love, God brings us into His family (1 John 3:1), through faith in Christ Jesus.

Every believer is called to accept the work of Christ on our behalf. Though we are sinners deserving of judgment, Christ's death on the cross has "justified" us, made us able to stand before a holy God and receive His salvation and grace (Rom. 8:28–30; 2 Tim. 1:9). For this we have every reason to live lives of gratitude (1 Thess. 2:13).

Every believer is called to become like Christ. Living the life God calls us to involves change in which we take on the character of Christ. That means resisting the temptation to turn away from Him, even though others may encourage us to do so (Gal. 1:6–9). It involves fleeing evil and pursuing good, fighting to maintain our faithfulness (1 Tim. 6:11–12). Just as Christ is holy, so we are to develop holiness in everything we do (1 Pet. 1:15; 3:9). As we pursue Christlikeness, we can do so with the certainty that the Lord is helping us, equipping us for every good work (Phil. 2:12–13; 2 Pet. 1:3–10).

Every believer is called to serve God and other people. Christ has called us to Himself to live out our faith in a manner that is worthy of Him (Eph. 4:1–4). We have the privilege of declaring God's work through everything we do and say (1 Pet. 2:9–10, 21).

Every believer is called to become a citizen of the new heaven and new earth. The Christian life leads ultimately to the end of being "glorified," raised up to stand with Christ in eternal glory, pure and holy at last (1 Pet. 5:10; 2 Pet. 3:10–11). In that day, we will celebrate the final coming together of Christ and all His faithful ones (Rev. 19:9–10). Our obedience to the Lord right now confirms this ultimate calling (Matt. 5:19).

If you are a believer in Christ, you have the same, significant calling as any other believer in Christ, no matter what your workday occupation may be. Calling is not just a matter of what job one has. It means living as a child of God. Is that the calling that you are pursuing?

*For more on this topic, see **VOCATION**, "'Called' to a New Purpose," page 414.*

CAPITAL PUNISHMENT

A Grim Means of Execution

Would-be assassins Bigthan and Teresh were "hanged on a gallows" (Esth. 2:23), but the punishment was probably not hanging as we know it today but impalement. As far as we know, rope hangings were not used in Persia during the biblical period, and the word translated "gallows" refers not to a scaffold but to a pole or stake.

Execution by impalement was a common practice of the Assyrians, who killed war captives by forcing their living bodies down onto pointed stakes. The Persians continued this grim means of execution. Thus references to "hanging" in Esther (5:14; 6:4; 9:14) probably refer to impalement, or possibly crucifixion.

Stoning

The intensity of the Jews' hostility against Jesus can be seen in their readiness to stone Him (John 10:31; 8:59). Stoning was an ancient method of capital punishment reserved for the most serious crimes against the Mosaic Law, including:

- child sacrifice (Lev. 20:2);
- consultation with mediums and occultists (20:27);
- blasphemy (24:16);
- Sabbath-breaking (Num. 15:32–36);
- the worship of false gods (Deut. 13:10);
- rebellion against parents (21:21);
- adultery (Ezek. 16:40); and
- certain cases of direct disobedience against God's express command (Josh. 7:25).

Stoning was usually carried out by the men of the community (Deut. 21:21) upon the testimony of at least two witnesses, who were to cast the first stones (17:5–7). The execution usually took place outside the camp or city (Lev. 24:14, 23; 1 Kin. 21:10, 13).

Jesus must have known He was headed for trouble when His enemies "surrounded" Him (literally, "closed in on Him,") as He walked in Solomon's porch (John 10:23–24). In the same way, a victim of stoning would be surrounded as the executioners cut all means of escape from their fury.

CAREERS

A Dramatic Career Change

Most people go through a number of job changes in their lives, and sometimes even several different careers. Each transition tends to be filled with tension, uncertainty, and sometimes doubt. In fact, many Christians facing a career change hope that God will somehow give them an indication of what He wants, effectively making the decision for them.

That happened to Isaiah. He was given a vision of the throne room of heaven when God called him to become His prophet (Is. 6:1–9). Thus there was no doubt as to what the Lord wanted. This same kind of dramatic encounter with God, leading to a major career decision, was experienced by a number of other people in the Bible:

- Moses came upon a burning bush while tending his father-in-law's herds in Midian. The Lord directed him to return to Egypt and lead His people out of slavery into the Promised Land (Ex. 3:1–10).
- Gideon met the Angel of the Lord, who was sitting under a terebinth tree, while threshing wheat in a secluded location. The Lord appointed him to save the Israelites from the oppressive Midianites (Judg. 6:11–14).
- David was tending sheep when the Lord directed Samuel to anoint him with oil as the next king of Israel (1 Sam. 16:1–13).
- Saul encountered a blinding light and the voice of Jesus on the road to Damascus, and was told that he was to become the Lord's spokesman (Acts 9:1–22).

The primary example is Jesus Himself, who left carpentry for public ministry after hearing His Father's voice at the Jordan River (Matt. 3:17). Each of these encounters was initiated by God, and each one led to a career change involving a special task or purpose. Yet despite the drama of these encounters, they appear to be the exception rather than the rule. Most people are not given a sign from heaven as to what God wants them to do in life. Instead, they must make decisions about how best to use their God-given skills and abilities

C

in whatever opportunities the Lord brings their way.

In the meantime, are you being faithful in the tasks and responsibilities that God has currently given you, in your family, work, and community? Those are the places of God's assignment for you right now.

Bloom Where You Are Planted

Modern workers place a high value on mobility and freedom of choice. So how should Christians in our culture deal with Paul's admonition to remain in the situation where God has called us (1 Cor. 7:17–24)? That sounds terribly antiquated in a society where the average person changes careers at least four times in life. In the ancient world, people normally worked for a lifetime at the same job.

Paul wrote that becoming a believer doesn't necessarily mean a career change. Wherever God has assigned us, that is our calling and we should pursue it to God's glory. On the other hand, there is nothing in the faith that locks a person into a work situation, any more than an unmarried woman must remain single all her life (7:8–9).

Paul's teaching about vocation parallels what he wrote about pre-conversion marriage (7:10–16). A believer is not compelled to leave his or her unbelieving spouse. On the other hand, the marriage may be dissolved if necessary to maintain peace. In the same way, believers should not use conversion as an excuse to leave their jobs.

This is an important point because Christianity introduces new values into our lives that may make us anxious to escape our work environment. The atmosphere of language and jokes, competition and politics, quotas and numbers may begin to feel uncomfortable. Wouldn't it be easier to quit one's job and go to work for a Christian employer—or better yet, pursue a career in a church or ministry? But Paul didn't encourage that choice as the normal path. A job change may be a possibility, as Jesus' disciples found out. But it is not necessarily virtuous to leave our "nets," especially if our only reason is to escape the realities of the work world.

Career Tracks

In today's workplace, change occurs so rapidly and radically that many experts describe the situation as nothing short of chaos. As a result, many workers will likely change careers—not just jobs but careers—as many as four to seven times or more in the course of their lives.

As believers deal with such a world, it helps to study the life of Moses. Even though he lived thousands of years ago in a vastly different society, his life nevertheless offers a couple of important lessons on how one travels the career path.

One way to look at Moses' career history is to notice that he worked in at least three different careers:

1. *Member of the royal family.* Raised in Pharaoh's court (Ex. 2:10), Moses became a master of Egyptian culture and politics (Acts 7:22). He probably did not have the level of responsibility that Joseph had before him (Gen. 41:41). But he enjoyed a privileged position that gave him access to the "treasures of Egypt" (Heb. 11:26). Perhaps he thought he could use that position to assume leadership of his people the Hebrews. But Moses was not yet ready for that, and this phase of his life, which lasted about forty years, ended abruptly with Moses' murder of an Egyptian and flight to Midian (Ex. 2:11–15).

2. *Shepherd.* The second forty years of Moses' life were spent tending sheep for his father-in-law Jethro (Ex. 3:1). This had to have been a complete contrast to Moses' previous career: from royal splendor to rustic simplicity, from urban sophistication to rural isolation, from ruling an empire to chasing dumb sheep.

3. *Leader of the Exodus.* During his last forty years, Moses led Israel out of Egypt (Ex. 4:27–12:36) and through the wilderness to the Promised Land (12:37–40:38; Lev.; Num.; Deut.). In many ways, this career utilized strengths and experiences from his two previous careers. The leader from Egypt and the shepherd from Midian combined to make Moses the "servant of the Lord" (Deut. 34:5).

These three careers were very different. Yet for that reason they offer encouragement to modern-day workers who may end up in several different assignments during the course of a life. God can use the same person to accomplish vastly different tasks. The question is, are we willing to accept new challenges and assignments and make the most of them for the Lord?

Getting Ready for the Future

During his first eighty years, Moses was learning important truths about himself, his world, and his God. This accumulated wisdom became invaluable during the Exodus, particularly after the unfortunate incident at Kadesh Barnea (Num. 13–14) and the nation's subsequent wanderings in the wilderness. It's easy to imagine that Moses could never have carried out that leadership assignment without an eighty-year curriculum to prepare him.

One advantage of looking at Moses this way is the hope and value it affords retirees in our own culture. The elderly are one of the fastest-growing population groups in developed nations today. Many have left behind years in the workforce and now wonder how they can spend the rest of their lives productively and meaningfully.

The life of Moses shows the way. God can take the accumulated experience and knowledge of older, mature adults and put it to powerful use, especially in tasks that require insight, wisdom, and experience. These need not necessarily be paid positions. The point is that nothing in one's life has to be wasted. If we see our lives as having a purpose under God's direction, then we can look back at our history and consider: what has God prepared us to accomplish before He takes us home?

For more on this topic, see LIFE PLANNING, "Building a Life by the Blueprints," page 244.

CELEBRATION

A Celebration for Everybody

Sometimes God's people are prone to celebrate their faith for their own benefit. David, however, tried to reach out to those who tended to be left out or left behind. He recognized that praising the Lord was a way to include everybody.

Notice some of the groups mentioned in Psalm 68 who had cause to celebrate God's greatness (Ps. 68:5–6, 10, 12, 31):

- orphans (the fatherless)
- widows
- the lonely
- prisoners
- the poor

- victims of war
- people of other races.

How can you recognize others in your worship and celebration of the Lord today? Who do you know that is left out or left behind? Why not provide a way for that person or group to "join the party"?

Leaders Celebrate Often

Effective leaders appreciate the value of celebrating the great things that God has done in and through their organization. When the task is completed, when results have been achieved, when people have been served, then it is appropriate to take time to celebrate.

That is what Nehemiah did when the people completed the rebuilding of the wall (Neh. 8:1, 10). First he had Ezra read from the Law—the motivation for Nehemiah's mission in the first place. The words kindled a godly sorrow (9:1–3), but also genuine joy (8:10–12). Thus with heartfelt praise, choice food, and even an "amen" chorus (8:6), the community rejoiced in the Lord for the work it had accomplished.

One interesting sidelight to the celebration was Nehemiah's instruction to "send portions to those for whom nothing is prepared" (8:10). In other words, bring the poor to the party! Share the wealth. No one should be deprived of joy just because he cannot afford even a small feast.

If you are in a leadership position, do you know how to celebrate your group's milestones? In the end, celebration can be a way of worshiping the Lord, because He is the source of all good gifts. We can praise Him for giving us a task and the means to accomplish it.

Let's Celebrate!

Does Christianity have to be morbid or cheerless? Should nonbelievers have all the fun? Does God disapprove of merrymaking? Is the only way to celebrate with wild wingdings and horrid hangovers?

No! Christians have ample reason to enjoy life, as James hints when he urges us to sing songs of praise with those who are happy (James 5:13). Likewise, Paul says (twice) to "rejoice in the Lord" (Phil. 3:1; 4:4). Even Jesus challenges a too-somber attitude. To be sure,

He was "a Man of sorrows and acquainted with grief" (Is. 53:3). Yet His enemies called Him a "winebibber" (Matt. 11:19). He enlivened a wedding with a gift of fine wine (John 2:1–12) and attended a "great feast" with a converted tax collector and his friends (Luke 5:27–39).

We might also note that the Bible opens in celebration. God creates the world and then sets aside an entire day to commemorate what He has done (Gen. 2:1–3). In fact, He tells His people to follow that pattern weekly and annually (Ex. 20:8–11; Lev. 23:1–44). At the other end of Scripture, we find a wedding-like celebration in heaven as God removes all pain and suffering (Rev. 19:1–10). Hallelujah!

How, then, can we cultivate celebration and joy on earth, here and now? Scripture encourages us to be the joyous people of God who have hope:

Weddings. Weddings are a cause for celebration because the "one flesh" union of a man and a woman reflects God's image on earth. The Song of Solomon is an entire love poem that celebrates this theme.

Concerts and Artfests. Major events or accomplishments call for celebration in song, dance, poetry, and other arts. Scripture memorializes the victory or work of God among His people in numerous songs, such as those of Deborah (Judg. 5), Moses and Miriam (Ex. 15:1–21), Hannah (1 Sam. 2:1–10), David (Ps. 18), and Mary (Luke 1:46–55). We do not have the words to the songs of Jephthah's daughter (Judg. 11:34), David's followers (1 Sam. 18:6–7), or Paul and Silas (Acts 16:25–26), but their songs of deliverance set a joyous pattern for us to follow.

Harvest Celebrations. Israel's agricultural economy revolved around harvest time, which it celebrated by honoring God in songs of joy and parading samples of produce (Ps. 126:5–6; Is. 9:3). Other festivals included the week-long feasts of unleavened bread, weeks, and tabernacles (Ex. 23:16; Lev. 23; Num. 28–29; Deut. 16:9–17). The Sabbath year festival, held every seven years (Lev. 25:1–7), and the jubilee celebrations, held every fiftieth year (25:8–55), linked the nation's worship and celebration with social legislation.

Sabbath. Having finished His work, God established one day each week to remind His people that all of creation belongs to Him, that work is not endless, and that His people must depend on Him (Gen. 2:1–3; Ex. 20:8–311). Early Christians moved their weekly observance to the first day of the week to commemorate "Resurrection Day" or the "Lord's Day" (see Rev. 1:10), the day on which Jesus proved that He was "Lord of the Sabbath" (Matt. 12:1–14) by rising from the dead.

As was the Sabbath, the Lord's Day is a time for worship, celebration, rest, and renewal. Unfortunately, both in Jesus' day and our own, the joy of the day has too often been lost under layers of legalistic rules and restrictions, making it more of a burden than a delight. But Jesus declared that "the Sabbath was made for man, and not man for the Sabbath" (Mark 2:27).

Special Occasions. Scripture records a variety of occasions that called for special, spontaneous celebrations, such as escape from captivity (Ps. 126:1–3), conversion from sin (Acts 2:40–47; 16:25–34), and miraculous deliverance (Ex. 14:30–15:21). On occasions like these we need to pause to enjoy God's good gift, and to give thanks for what He has done in our lives.

CENSUS
A Temptation to Trust in Numbers

David's census of Israel (2 Sam. 24:1) was one of seven major censuses mentioned in Scripture.

Scripture's record of this census raises several questions. Second Samuel attributes it to "the anger of the Lord," whereas the parallel account in 1 Chronicles attributes it to Satan (1 Chr. 21:1). One solution to this apparent discrepancy is to consider that in the Old Testament, Satan is presented as a fallen angel of God who exercises only as much power as the Lord allows him (for example, Job 1–2; Zech. 3:1–5). God apparently allowed Satan to incite David to number the people. In that way both accounts are accurate, but provide different perspectives.

David's purpose in counting his population was probably to assess his military strength, much like the second census taken under Moses (Num. 1:2–3). David found eight hundred thousand men eligible for military service in Israel and five hundred thousand men in Judah (2 Sam. 24:9), more than double the previous head count.

Yet this census displeased the Lord. The Bible does not explain why, but it may be that David was falling into the temptation of trusting in the size of his army rather than in the Lord. God punished David and reduced his forces somewhat by bringing a plague that killed seventy thousand men (24:15; 1 Chr. 21:14).

Atonement Money

Modern-day citizens are familiar with national censuses that are taken periodically. The counts are used in a multitude of ways, from planning to budgeting to representation. In a similar way, Moses was instructed to count the children of Israel as they prepared to cross the wilderness (Ex. 30:12–16). This census was used to raise funds for the tabernacle.

This first nationwide census of Israel counted all those twenty years or older (30:14; probably all the men of that age, who were heads of families). The count was used to levy a tax of half a shekel upon each person numbered, whether rich or poor. That amount— perhaps about eighty cents in today's silver market—was small enough that every family could pay it.

The money collected was to furnish the tabernacle (30:16), but it also had an important symbolic value: it was a "ransom . . . to the Lord" (30:12), and "atonement money" (30:16). It represented the atonement for sin, made by Christ and foreshadowed in the blood of the sin offering of atonement (30:10). Perhaps the small size of the tax was intended to remind everyone that no amount of money can possibly satisfy God or purchase one's soul.

New Reasons for Taking a Census

Census data has been used by governments throughout history for a variety of purposes: for example, to draft soldiers for military service, to collect tax revenue, and to conscript laborers for public works projects. However, when a census was taken of the Jews who returned to Palestine from Babylon (Ezra 2:1), the results were put to several new and interesting purposes:

1. *To return properties to their rightful owners.* Generations earlier, Moses had taken a census of the Israelites as they prepared to

enter Canaan, to obtain data to be used to divide the land among the tribes of Israel (Num. 26). Later, when the people took possession of the land, they settled in their allotted territories (Josh. 13–19).

From that time forward, each family's land was intended to stay in the family. In fact, an intricate set of laws was established to ensure that no family lost its land permanently.

Thus when the exiles returned, it was important that they be able to trace their lineage in order to verify their claims to family lands or, in the case of priests and Levites, to Levitical cities (Ezra 2:3–58). Certain priests who could not prove their heritage were made to wait until a priest could consult God as to their status (2:59–63; Neh. 7:61–65).

2. *To collect resources for rebuilding the temple.* Indirectly, the census became an occasion for the returnees to give a freewill offering that was used toward the building of a new temple (Ezra 2:68–69).

3. *To redevelop and repopulate Jerusalem.* Several years after this census was taken, Nehemiah reviewed it when he realized how empty Jerusalem was (Neh. 7:4–5). Then the people cast lots in such a way that one-tenth of the population of Judah was relocated to the capital city in order to reclaim its public life (11:1–2).

This latter use of Ezra's census makes for intriguing thoughts about using census data today. Many inner cities have buildings and even entire neighborhoods that are abandoned and lifeless. What might happen if one-tenth of God's people from nearby suburbs moved into these areas to rebuild, revitalize, and reclaim them for good? Not only could these "enterprise zones" become valuable centers of economic and cultural life, but they could have a positive impact on entire cities as they touch people with the light and life of the gospel.

A Time to Be Counted

Just as the United States numbers its population every ten years, so governments in biblical times kept track of their citizens. Several major censuses are mentioned in Scripture, including the one in Luke 2:1–3, when Quirinius was imperial legate in the Roman province of Syria.

Censuses were important for taxation, administration, military planning and conscription, recruitment of (sometimes forced) labor for public works projects, and for tithes and offerings to maintain religious institutions. Caesar Augustus used censuses to inventory the resources and needs of his empire, to raise money, and to determine where to allocate his troops. The Romans are believed to have held an empire-wide census every fourteen years, and Luke could have been referring to one of those.

In biblical times, as today, censuses had major political implications. They certainly aided the strategic delivery of services. But registration was experienced by many as a tool of exploitation and oppression, especially where government was maintained without the choice of the governed and with little concern for their welfare. Such was the case in Israel under the Romans.

Nevertheless, God used a census to bring Joseph and Mary to Bethlehem, where Jesus was born, in fulfillment of His plan.

CHANGE

Does Change Threaten You?

A stubborn allegiance to old habits and traditions can sometimes seriously hinder maturing faith. Every believer should pay attention to that, because new life in Christ inevitably leads to innovation and timely change. Fear of change is understandable, but too much fear may be a sign of sinful resistance or of clinging to the past only because it feels safe and familiar.

Jesus understood our human tendency toward predictability and the natural resistance to new things. He also knew that not all changes are good, and He never advocated change for the sake of change. But He warned against making tradition, particularly religious tradition, the standard by which all things should be tested (Luke 6:36–39). His parable of the wineskins pleads for at least the openness to consider something new. It affirms timely change in matters of growth and new life.

Are you resistant to the dynamics of change in your life, work, family, or church? If so, could you be resisting the very work of God or the ongoing dynamic of life itself? Pay attention to Jesus' image of the wineskins!

Old-timers' View of Change

Have you ever longed for the "good old days"? Do you find yourself shaking your head over seemingly shoddy products and declaring, "They just don't make 'em like they used to"? That might have been part of the sentiment expressed by some of the "old-timers" when they saw the foundation for the temple (Ezra 3:12). Comparing it to Solomon's temple, which they could remember from their youth, they seem to have had mixed emotions.

On the one hand, they probably realized that the second temple was not going to be nearly as nice as the first one. So they wept out loud (compare Hag. 2:3). Yet on the other hand, they might also had been crying for joy to see at least some of Israel's past glory restored.

Memories die hard, and believers today may also feel mixed emotions, living in times of rapid and far-reaching change. On the one hand, the older we become, the more we realize that newer is not necessarily better. For that reason we may find it easy to dismiss all change as needless inconvenience and seek for security in the past.

Yet God calls us to meet the needs of today, not yesterday. Moreover, it would be a contradiction for people of faith to encourage growth and then resist the very idea of change. At least some change and newness are inescapable if we intend to remain relevant to those among whom God has placed us. We can remember and respect the past, but we can also greet the challenges of today and tomorrow with joy. After all, God does not change; His faithfulness endures forever.

Token Gestures or Genuine Change?

Perhaps the hardest sins to root out are those which are socially acceptable and part of a society's institutions. King Zedekiah of Judah discovered this when he tried to put a stop to a form of slavery in Jerusalem (34:8–9).

The Old Testament Law allowed people who could not satisfy their debts to become slaves of their creditors. But the length of servitude was a maximum of six years. In the seventh or Sabbath year, slaves were to be released, and not only were their debts to be forgiven, but their former owners were to help them get back on their feet by loading them down with material provisions (Deut. 15:12–18).

This was the ideal. But as the economy of Judah faltered in its later years, the wealthy devised ways to keep their Hebrew neighbors in permanent bondage (compare Is. 3:14–15). Faced with the Lord's imminent judgment, Zedekiah arranged for the people to renew the covenant and release their slaves (Jer. 34:10). But once they perceived the threat of punishment to be past, the slaveowners broke their commitments and returned their debtors to slavery (34:11).

Thus the renewal of the covenant appears to have been a token gesture. It was like so many pledges that people make, even today, that are symbolic rather than substantive. These vows may look good for publicity purposes, but they are hypocritical. Institutionalized evil demands genuine, fundamental change from the top to the bottom of society. Judah never made that kind of change, and so eventually it was judged by the Lord (34:17–22; 52:4–27).

For more on this topic, see **RENEWAL,** *"Starting Over," page 336.*

CHARACTER

(*see* Ethics; Integrity)

CHASTITY

(*see* Sexual Intercourse)

CHILD ABUSE

City Kids Die over Adult Matters

In the tragic account in Matthew 2:16–18, we read of an entire village of baby boys being slaughtered due to the insane rage of a jealous king. The story reminds us that growing numbers of children today die needlessly for the sins of adults.

Like Rachel (2:18), mothers all over the world, particularly in urban ghettos and developing nations, weep over their dead children. Rachel had lots of experience with tears. Her father tricked her fiancé into marrying her sister, and she remained childless for years (Gen. 29:1–30:24). Later, Jeremiah the prophet described her as wailing over the exiled tribes (Jer. 31:15, the passage quoted by Matthew).

The weeping and wailing in Bethlehem must have gone on for days. It could not have been quickly silenced, nor could Rachel's wailing be comforted. The babies of Bethlehem and the people in exile had a common bond: in both cases, innocent people suffered as a result of the proud, ungodly acts of powerful leaders.

Jesus can offer particular comfort to those who grieve the loss of a child. In effect, the babies of Bethlehem died for Him. He must have carried the pain of that throughout His life and onto the cross. It doubtless shaped His special concern for children (compare Matt. 18:6–7). And His concerned activity toward them beckons us to find ways to serve children today.

Matthew's retelling of this slaughter is a very significant part of the Christmas story. In a powerful way, it reminds city kids today that they need not die in vain: Jesus lived and died for them, too.

CHILD WELFARE

Children and Childcare

When Jesus welcomed the little children (Matt. 19:14), He was making a major statement to everyone standing by about the value and significance of children.

Perhaps the disciples, who rebuked the mothers who brought their babies to Jesus (Matt. 19:13), had adopted the prevailing Graeco-Roman view of childhood as an insignificant phase of life. To be sure, children were necessary for a family's survival, but they were not valued for their own sake.

Indeed, unwanted infants in pagan cultures were routinely abandoned on roadsides and at garbage dumps. Tragically, gender and economics often determined an infant's fate: more girls than boys were exposed since girls represented a future financial burden while boys could eventually contribute to the family's income.

Most exposed infants died, but a few were rescued and raised to become slaves, gladiators, or prostitutes.

Children were held in such low esteem in Jesus' time that some professional beggars collected exposed children, mutilated them, and then used their misery to gain sympathy and thus increase profits from their begging.

However, among the Jews children were traditionally considered a blessing from God, and childlessness a curse. In fact, children were so desired that barrenness was grounds for divorce.

Jewish fathers had ultimate authority over all aspects of their children's lives, but both fathers and mothers were instructed by the Law to nurture and care for their children. Fathers were particularly obligated to teach their children God's commands and to raise them as members of God's chosen people (Deut. 6:6–8). In return, children were obliged to honor both mother and father (Deut. 5:16).

Mothers usually took care of infants who typically nursed until the age of two or three. In some wealthy Greek and Roman homes, women employed wet nurses and, as the children grew, slaves who were assigned to their total care. Poor women, however, worked while their babies hung from slings on their backs. But as soon as the children were old enough, they were taught to help.

First-century women did not have to confront the childcare dilemma faced by many women today. Their work and their homes were tightly linked, so they did not have to surmount the challenges of specialization and separation.

For more on this topic, see CHILD ABUSE, "City Kids Die over Adult Matters," page 51.

CHILDBIRTH
A Woman in Labor

An alternative translation to sorrow (John 16:21) is "pain." There were few options available to first-century women for pain relief during labor. Since births took place at home, all of the disciples had probably heard a woman scream out in pain while giving birth.

As in most undeveloped countries today, childbearing in biblical times was often fatal for the child, the mother, or both. Many pagan women sought help from their gods, along with special charms, to protect them during pregnancy and delivery.

So Jesus was using a graphic metaphor by comparing the coming "sorrow" of His followers with that of a woman in labor. He was indicating that their pain could not be avoided. But He did give them a hope: He promised that they would see Him again, and when they

did their joy would be as great as a woman whose baby has finally been delivered safely.

Do you live with the hope of seeing Jesus, even as you confront the pain of this world?

CHILDLESSNESS
(*see* Infertility)

CHILDREN
Protecting Your Heritage

Psalm 127 links the welfare of the family to the welfare of the city, and also connects both of them to God. God is the ultimate source of strength to home builders and city planners alike (Ps. 127:1–2). Those who build their house according to God's power and wisdom will have the heritage of children who can "speak with their enemies in the gate," or public arena (127:3–5).

One implication of this psalm is that God's people belong in the public sector. In fact, the objective of raising godly children is to produce godly people who will be involved in public discourse.

However, there is a vast difference between ancient Israel in Solomon's day and the pluralistic society of today. Modern-day believers face tensions unknown to the ancient Israelites, particularly when it comes to raising their children. For example, should they educate their young people in the public sector, which has become increasingly secular and at times unruly, or should they seek alternative schooling?

There are no hard and fast answers to this question. In the end, parents must do what they believe is best for their children and right before the Lord. There are reasons why a godly family might withdraw its children from public schooling. One of the most important is that children are a valued heritage from the Lord. Yet that could also be a reason to remain involved in the public system: children are a heritage—not just one's own children, but all children.

God's people have a civic duty to be a part of the public debate about schooling, however they decide the question for their own children. There is no place for believers to withdraw from the world. Scripture calls us to engage our "enemies (and presumably our friends) in the gate."

C

Rearing Children with Discipline

A popular belief today is that people are basically good. An extension of this belief is that children come into the world as morally pure and pristine creatures who are then "socialized" into harmful, hurtful patterns by parents and society.

The Book of Proverbs, along with the rest of the Bible, presents a very different picture of children and child-rearing. Although children are seen as a blessing, they tend toward evil if left to their own nature (Prov. 22:15). For that reason, parents are urged to discipline their youngsters. Neglecting to do so amounts to condemning a child to death (19:18).

Opinions vary as to the best way to discipline children. But disagreements about means must never lose sight of what Proverbs says are the ends involved—to bring a child into adulthood with strong character and the ability to make wise choices (29:15). Whatever the term "rod" means to you as a parent, Proverbs encourages you to use discipline in raising your children (23:13).

Several principles of discipline are found in Proverbs:

- A child needs far more than discipline. In fact, discipline is only one part of a much broader home environment required to set a child on the path toward wisdom, self-appreciation, understanding, and humility (2:1–22; 4:3–9; 15:31–33).
- Punishment for wrongdoing is not only corrective but preventive in that it can steer a young person away from more powerful forms of evil and ultimate destruction (5:12–14; 23:14).
- Correction demonstrates love, whereas lack of it is a form of hate (13:24).
- Discipline is intended to purge children of the inherent "foolishness" that the Bible says they have (22:15).

Discipline is indispensable to healthy child-rearing. But Proverbs also observes that there are no guarantees as to how a child will turn out. Many people see a promise in the proverb, "Train up a child in the way he should go, and when he is old he will not depart from it" (Prov. 22:6). But like much of the rest of Proverbs, this is not a promise so much as an observation about child-rearing. Children may receive excellent discipline, yet still refuse the path shown them by their parents:

- A child may grow up to be lazy, abusive, or immoral, and thus a cause of shame to his parents (10:5; 19:26; 29:3).
- A child may turn out to be a scoffer who rejects instruction and rebuke, no matter how well intended or administered (13:1).
- A child may grow up to despise his parents (15:20).
- A child might rob his parents and not even see it as wrong (28:24).
- A child may grow up to curse, mock, and scorn his parents (30:11, 17).

Given this sobering reality, God calls us as parents to demonstrate lives of wisdom, truth, and service to our children, knowing that they may or may not choose to follow in that path. Ultimately, no parent can force a child to honor either them or God; that is a choice that each of us makes on our own. We as parents are simply called to do our best and leave the results to God.

Set Apart to the Lord

The Lord vowed to kill the firstborn of the Egyptians, but He commanded the Hebrews to set apart their firstborn children to Him when they came into the Promised Land (Ex. 13:11–16). It's hard to say exactly what "setting a child apart to the LORD" meant, but it likely involved a spiritual and psychological release of the child to fulfill whatever God's plans for the individual might be. Thus it was a sign of trust in and obedience toward a good God.

This release of the child to the Lord was symbolized by a ritual of redemption, in which the newborn was "exchanged" for an offering brought by the parents (compare Ex. 13:13). Scripture highlights a few cases in which firstborn children were dedicated to the Lord. A few of the more significant include Samson (Judg. 13:5, 24–25), Samuel (1 Sam. 1:11, 24–28), John the Baptist (Luke 1:66, 80), and Jesus (2:7, 22–24).

Pass On the Story

The older we get, the more important it is that we tell what we have learned about God and about life to our children, to our grandchildren, and even to generations yet unborn. The elderly are one of the most valuable links there are to the past.

Joel urged the elders of Judah to tell their descendants the story of what God had done among them (Joel 1:3). It is hard to say exactly what events the prophet had in mind, but apparently the elders would know: things more profound than anything that had happened in their days and the days of their fathers (1:2), important things that needed to be remembered.

Today, we as God's people still need to pass on the story of what God has done in our lives and our societies. That requires that we first discern His work, then that we communicate it memorably to future generations. We must tell both the good and the bad, the pleasant and the unpleasant. Doing so will help to equip younger generations not only to walk wisely with God, but also to be ready when it is their turn to "prophesy" and see "dream dreams" (2:28).

The Faith of Our Children

Faith is always just one generation away from extinction. No matter how much people may love and serve God, they cannot believe for their children. Young people must develop their own walk with God.

Yet parents can help them take their first steps of faith. That's why Moses urged the Israelites to teach the words of the Law to their children (Deut. 6:7–9, 20–21; see also 4:9–10; 11:19). He offered a number of suggestions for teaching these statutes to young people. The following principles are just as useful to believers today:

1. *Know what you are talking about.* Know the Word of God for yourself first before trying to pass it on. Moses wanted his people to be known as a "wise and understanding [or discerning] people" (Deut. 4:6).

2. *Cultivate your own faith.* Moses exhorted the people to develop personal contact with God (Deut. 6:1–9). He told them to fear the Lord all the days of their lives, to love the Lord with all their being—heart, soul, and strength; and to establish habits and strategies for recalling and rehearsing the story of God's dealings in their own lives and in the lives of their ancestors.

Parents cannot give to their children a faith that they do not have. It's one thing to talk about religion; it's another thing to speak to the issues of life out of a vibrant relationship with the living God.

3. *Teach by example.* Moses urged the Israelites to practice the Law so that their children see it in action, not just hear it recited (Deut. 10:12–13; 11:1–2, 7–8). He reminded them to live with the perspective that God owns everything, to maintain a commitment to integrity by refusing bribes, by ensuring justice for orphans and widows, to worship the Lord regularly, and to keep a singular focus on the Lord and avoid any other loyalties, especially to idols.

Children quickly see through empty religion. They know instinctively what their parents truly believe and where their loyalties lie. Thus parents today have the same need to model Christlikeness before their children if they want to see their children take any interest in the things of the Lord.

4. *Be creative.* Moses wrote a song to declare God's ways to Israel (Deut. 32:1–47). It was a good lesson in the use of the arts to celebrate the Lord and encourage children to learn about the faith (Deut. 31:9–13, 19, 22, 30). Likewise, Moses urged the people to rehearse the law for the entire community, including children and aliens, every seventh year during the festival of booths, to develop music that would bring honor to the Lord and tell of His mighty works, and to teach the children music that praised God (Deut. 32:46–47).

With so many creative, affordable resources now available, parents have an unprecedented opportunity to impact their youngsters for the Lord in a positive way.

The Friend of Children

In Jesus' day it was common for mothers to ask famous rabbis to bless their children. With Jesus, however, they sought more than a blessing; they wanted the touch of this Rabbi (Mark 10:13). No doubt the power of His touch had become well known.

Mark did not explain why the disciples tried to keep the children away. Perhaps they viewed the little ones as ritually unclean, or, like most of society, unworthy of an important man's attention.

But Jesus rebuked the disciples and invited the children into His arms (Mark 10:16). The way that He spoke to them and embraced them must have shocked those who stood by. Such tenderness and respect were rarely given children in that society.

The Problem of a Difficult Child

Perhaps no heartache is greater than that of a parent whose child grows up to be stubborn, rebellious, and wayward. In dealing with that kind of painful sorrow, a parent may react with hostility and rejection, as if the prodigal child were no longer deserving of love, or with self-recrimination, as if the parent were entirely to blame for the way the youngster turned out.

But Scripture offers a model for the parent of a difficult child—God Himself. His "dear son" Ephraim, that is, the northern kingdom of Israel (Jer. 31:20), had completely departed from the Lord's ways and turned to pagan practices (2 Kin. 17:7–18). For that reason, the

Lord had allowed Assyria to take the Israelites into exile in 722 B.C.

Nevertheless, the Lord never forgot His people, as Jeremiah pointed out. Like the loving father in Jesus' parable of the prodigal son (Luke 15:22–32), the Lord never lost His affection for Israel. He was ready to welcome the people back whenever they wished to forsake their rebellious ways. In fact, Jesus Himself was the ultimate evidence of God's undying loyalty to His faithless children: "He came to His own, and His own did not receive Him" (John 1:11).

If you are the parent of a prodigal, you can take some comfort from the fact that even the ultimate Parent had wayward children. Unfortunately, because each of us is sinful and human, you may find it difficult to love your children with the kind of love that God has. Nevertheless, as you consider how best to deal with your children, you can ask God to empower you to love them with wisdom and grace.

For more on this topic, see **BIRTH CONTROL,** *"Children—A Blessing, Not a Burden," page 35.*

CHOICES

A Reckless Choice

Someone has well said that there are good decisions and there are quick decisions, but there are few good quick decisions. Herod made a very bad decision on the spur of the moment when he rewarded his stepdaughter with a blank check (Mark 6:23).

It's easy to condemn Herod for his foolishness. Yet how often we act in a similar manner, making decisions that have the most far-reaching consequences in haste, in a flush of wild excitement. Carried away by our passions, we choose impulsively, to our misfortune.

Herod's mistake is easily understood. He was drunk, he was distracted, and he was impulsive by nature. Believers ought never to make their decisions in such a manner. As Paul challenges us, we need to live as wise people, not as fools (Eph. 5:14–17).

Convenience Makes for Odd Choices

Faced with difficulty, most of us tend to choose convenience and expediency over sacrifice and integrity, particularly when the personal costs are likely to be high. Our desire to avoid negative outcomes can stir up odd reactions in us.

Jesus triggered some odd choices of convenience and expediency in the political system of Jerusalem. For example:

- Two leaders who had been longtime enemies suddenly became allies and friends (Luke 23:12).
- Pilate chose to free Barabbas, an insurrectionist and murderer (Luke 23:19), and allow the execution of Jesus, the innocent man (Luke 23:22), in order to maintain order and appease an angry mob (Luke 23:23–25).
- The rulers chose popularity with the people, and the people chose fawning subservience to the rulers, over justice for the accused (Luke 23:23–24; Matt. 27:20, 25; John 19:15).

These kinds of sinful tendencies are part of the reason Christ came to die. He wants to save us from opportunistic, self-serving ways of life, because ultimately they lead to death. Evil alliances, political manipulation, rigged votes, and injustice are a stench in the nostrils of God (Is. 2:5–3:26).

As believers, we may have to make odd choices, too. But ours should be rooted in Christlike values of love, truth, and humility, rather than expedience, popularity, and selfishness.

Gray Areas

In first-century Corinth, meat sacrificed to idols (1 Cor. 8:1) proved to be an issue on which believers vehemently disagreed. It was a "gray" area of life, a matter for which there seemed to be no clear-cut instruction. How should Christians settle such disputes? Through a predetermined set of dos and don'ts? No, Paul offered a different perspective, one that appeals to conscience.

Paul argued that food and drink do not determine our relationship to God (1 Cor. 8:8). Meat offered to idols is inconsequential because, ultimately, there is no such thing as an idol (1 Cor. 8:4–6). An idol is not God, so the mere fact that a priest blesses meat and offers it to an idol means nothing. From that point of view, Christians should be able to enjoy whatever food they want.

However, questionable practices may affect one's relationships with fellow believers or unbelievers (1 Cor. 8:9). As members of Christ's family we are obligated not to be a "stumbling block," but a loving neighbor. Our faith is not merely private, but has a corporate ethic and public responsibility as well.

So we live in a tension: God's grace frees us to choose as we please, but God's love requires us to ask questions of conscience about our choices. From what we eat, to whom we live and work with, to where we live, to what we do with our money and time—almost everything we do affects our neighbors (1 Cor. 8:10–13). So we need to ask, Are we treating them with love?

We need not allow others to manipulate us through legalistic criticism. But we do need discretion as to how our choices affect those around us. It's not enough to follow Christ just in our hearts; we also need to follow Him in our consciences.

Which Is Better?

They say that sometimes good is the enemy of the best, yet making the best choice is not always easy. Still, our choices in life can have profound implications, so Scripture exhorts us to weigh them carefully. The Book of Proverbs helps us by frequently setting two alternatives before us and then using the word "better" to describe which one is the best—or wisest—choice:

- Wisdom is better than much wealth; it is more profitable (Prov. 3:13–14; 8:11).
- Fearing the Lord is to be preferred over great treasure associated with trouble (Prov. 15:16).
- A simple meal with love is better than a feast with hatred (Prov. 15:17).
- Associating with the humble is better than getting wealthy with the proud (Prov. 16:19).
- Self-control is better than getting to rule your own city (Prov. 16:32).
- It is better to be poor and honest than rich and crooked (Prov. 19:1, 22; 22:1; 28:6).
- An open rebuke is to be preferred over love that is never expressed (Prov. 27:5).

Proverbs challenges us to use every resource at our disposal—information, intuition, a knowledge of right and wrong, love, and truth—to make wise choices rather than just coasting through life letting come what may. Our choices have implications. Let's put our God-given abilities to work in order to choose the *best!*

For more on this topic, see **ANGER,** *"Why Did Moses Hit the Rock?" page 22.*

CHURCH
Are We Still a Light to the World?

The Servant songs of Isaiah offer a powerful hope for Israel and the other nations of the world. The prophet promised a great Servant of God who would come to "raise up the tribes of Jacob" and be a "light to the Gentiles," and His salvation would reach "to the ends of the earth" (Is. 49:6–7).

Later history would show that Jesus Christ is this Servant, this light of the world (Matt. 12:17–21; John 1:4–13; 8:12). However, Jesus has also commissioned His followers to be lights as well, spreading His light to every corner of the earth. As believers, we are servants of the Servant, bearing His light. Are we still a light to the world? If not, there could be at least five reasons for a breakdown:

Lack of doctrinal clarity or authority. The light of Christ was intended to illumine the truth about God (John 7:16–18; 8:31–32). But if we ourselves are still in the dark about what we believe, then we have nothing to persuade others to believe.

Moral or ethical compromise. It is impossible to sustain a credible message about a pure and holy light if we ourselves are living in moral darkness (1 John 1:5–6). God wants us to live a lifestyle that is morally attractive to unbelievers (Matt. 5:14–16; Titus 2:9–10).

Disunity or a lack of love for other believers. Perhaps nothing undercuts the mission of the church more than internal conflict. Why should the world believe in Christ's message of love if His followers are at war with one another? Jesus was fully aware of this when He prayed for the unity of His people (John 17:22–23).

Ethnic and racial prejudice. The gospel penetrated beyond the borders of ancient Judea because Jesus broke down traditional walls of separation between Jew and Gentile (Eph. 2:14–22), and because a few brave believers acted on that truth. Are believers still willing to break through cultural barriers today?

A lost passion for evangelism and mission. No one will spread the light of Christ if no one believes that His light still needs to be spread. Someone brought Christ into the midst of your own spiritual darkness. Is there any credible reason why you should not introduce someone else to His grace? Or were you the last unsaved person on earth?

Churches—Keys to the Cities

Christianity eventually prevailed as the dominant worldview and social force in the Roman world. One reason: it planted churches in dozens of the empire's major cities by the end of the first century. Christians spread the gospel "to the end of the earth" (Acts 1:8) by establishing strategic, visible communities in urban areas such as Antioch (Acts. 11:22, 26; see Acts 13:1). These groups of believers stood apart from the culture in their beliefs and values, yet engaged the culture in their daily lives and work.

The New Testament word for "church," *ekklesia,* means assembly or congregation. In the Greek world, the *ekklesia* was a public assembly called together by a herald to discuss legal issues and make community decisions. For example, Paul faced such a gathering at Ephesus, a town meeting that turned into a riot (Acts 19:32–41). But *ekklesia* always referred to people—originally to the citizens of a city, and later to a gathering of believers. There is no evidence that it meant a church building until the fourth century A.D.

Interestingly, eight times out of ten the New Testament uses the word *ekklesia* to refer to all of the believers in a specific city, such as "the church that was at Antioch" (Acts. 13:1) or "the church of God which is at Corinth" (1 Cor. 1:2). Elsewhere it implies all Christian believers, regardless of geographic location or time in history—what is often called the universal (or catholic) church (Eph. 1:22; 3:10, 21; 5:23–32).

In forming churches, the early Christians did not drop out of society, nor did they form congregations that competed with each other

for members (though sometimes members competed with each other, 1 Cor. 1:10–12). Instead, they lived and worked as members of the larger community. Meanwhile, they related to the other believers in their cities as members of a common family in Christ. This proved to be a radical concept—so powerful, in fact, that by the end of the second century, one author was able to write:

"Christians are not distinguished from the rest of mankind by either country, speech, customs; the fact is, they nowhere settle in cities of their own; they use no peculiar language; they cultivate no eccentric mode of life. Yet while they dwell in both Greek and non-Greek cities, as each one's lot was cast, and conform to the customs of the country in dress, food, and mode of life in general, the whole tenor of their way of living stamps it as worthy of admiration and admittedly extraordinary."

This remarkable reputation of the early Christians compels modern believers to ask: What will the church today be remembered for?

The Church as a Family of Faith

Paul had once been a dangerous enemy to the followers of Christ. But his dramatic encounter with the Savior and subsequent change of heart brought him into the family of God (Acts 9:1–30). Courageous Christians such as Ananias (see Acts 9:10) and Barnabas (see Acts 4:36–37) began to nurture and aid the new believer. He had become a brother.

In the same way, Christ makes believers today into a new family. Having experienced the same gift from God—forgiveness and hope—we are now brothers and sisters in Christ.

Paul acknowledged several of his family of faith as he closed 1 Corinthians:

- Young Timothy, who needed acceptance and affirmation (1 Cor. 16:10–11).
- Gifted Apollos, one of the Corinthians' former leaders who was unable to go to them at that time (1 Cor. 1:12; 16:12).
- Stephanas, baptized by Paul in the early days of the Corinthian church; the Corinthians needed to respect him (1 Cor. 16:15–16).
- Fortunatus and Achaicus, encouragers of Paul who may have delivered to him the

letter from the Corinthians that he was answering with 1 Corinthians; like Stephanas, they too needed recognition (1 Cor. 16:17–18).

- Priscilla and Aquila, cofounders of the Corinthian work and business partners with Paul (Acts 18:1–4); they now were leading a similar work at Ephesus and sent warm greetings to their brothers and sisters (1 Cor. 16:19).

Once an enemy, Paul became a true friend, partner, and advocate of other believers. Just as others had once cared for him and his needs, he wrote to the Corinthians of the needs and concerns of his brothers and sisters in Christ.

Who are some of your friends in the faith? Who among them needs support or advocacy right now? To whom can you appeal on their behalf?

Isaiah's Vision, the Church's Mission

Isaiah refers to Tarshish (Is. 66:19) more than any other Old Testament writer does. Tarshish may have been a city or region in southern Spain, though no one knows for sure (see Jon. 1:3). But in the vision that climaxes Isaiah's prophecy, Tarshish and the other cities listed represent the ends of the earth. These distant lands have not heard of God or seen what He has done, but He will send messengers to them who will recruit representatives to come to Him at the "holy mountain Jerusalem" (Is. 66:20).

Isaiah's vision is interesting to read from the perspective of the New Testament. Jesus sent His followers out from Jerusalem to "all Judea and Samaria, and to the end of the earth" (Acts 1:8). He sent them to these places to "make disciples of all the nations" (Matt. 28:19)—a mission that sounds very much like a fulfillment of Isaiah's prophecy.

In obedience to the Lord, the early church sent gospel workers throughout the Roman world. In fact, Paul, the church's most widely traveled ambassador, wrote to believers in Rome that it was his intention to make a trip to Spain (Rom. 15:28). Could it be that he had Isaiah 66 in mind? It is a distinct possibility, though no one can say for sure.

What is certain is that Isaiah's vision and the church's mission have not changed. Christ still wants His people to take His message to the ends of the earth. He is still building a people for Himself from "all nations and tongues." To the extent that we participate in that effort, we help to bring about the completion of God's plan.

The Business of the Church

There are many reasons why people seek positions of authority in a church. Some do it because they have authority at their normal job and therefore feel they should have authority at church. Some do it for just the opposite reason: authority is denied them at work, so they seek it in the church.

Peter reminds overseers (1 Pet. 5:2–4) that the presence or absence of authority or success on the job is more or less irrelevant to positions of authority at church. That may shock church members and leaders who have uncritically adopted models of church management from the business world. It's not that churches can't benefit from many of the practices found in business. Certainly in administration and finances, churches have much to learn from the efficient and effective policies of the marketplace. But the church is not a business, and philosophies and practices from that sphere need to be carefully evaluated and sifted in light of Scripture before they are put into effect.

Why Attend Church?

David declared that he was glad to "go into the house of the LORD" for worship (Ps. 122:1). Today, many Christians are glad to go into their church buildings to worship Christ, but a growing number are not. In fact, unprecedented numbers have become dropouts from church attendance.

Their reasons for quitting vary. But in light of David's joy in coming before the Lord, it might help to consider reasons for maintaining church attendance:

- Because believers need help to reflect on the past week and see it as just a small part of the journey of life.
- Because they will benefit from being taught and led in worship by others, rather than feeding on a constant diet of their own choosing.

- Because they need regular reminders of their standing in Christ, help in acknowledging and confessing their sins, and teaching about God's truths.
- Because they need to hear how believers in the past struggled, grew, and lived out their faith.
- Because they need to experience artistic and creative expressions of the faith, such as music, ritual, prayers, architecture, or creeds.
- Because they will benefit from silence before the Lord once in a while.
- Because they need help to face the issues of life and faith as presented through the teaching.
- Because they need to hear about the experience of other contemporary believers.
- Because they need an alternative to the constant messages of a culture that ignores God.
- Because they need a conscious break from work and self-interests in order to concentrate on the Lord.
- Because they need to hear reminders of God's love.
- Because they need help in praying.
- Because they need to belong to a community of faith that includes others who are trying to live out the gospel.

CHURCH AND STATE

Family, State, and Church: Three Inseparable Institutions

As the Book of Genesis is the "book of beginnings," it is not surprising that it presents the beginnings of three fundamental institutions of society: the family, the state, and the community of faith.

The family is the primary institution established by God (Gen. 2:23). Before there were any nations, cities, or other human communities, there was a family. Logically and chronologically, family comes first.

But when the world's first family began to break down because of sin, God established the state. After Cain killed Abel (Gen. 4:8), his judgment and punishment came from God (Gen. 4:9–15). There was no court of law or other governmental authority to deal with the case. But when God placed a mark on Cain as a peace-bond, He gave a law to prevent

other members of the family from killing Cain (Gen. 4:15). This rule of law was the beginning of the state. As in the case of the family, however, it was not long before sinful people began to corrupt the state as well (Gen. 4:23–24).

But a third institution can also trace its beginnings to the early days of the world. After righteous Abel was buried, Adam and Eve had another son named Seth. This man and his son Enosh were linked with an increasing tendency of people to "call on the name of the Lord" (Gen. 4:26). This kind of commitment to righteousness was preserved in Noah (Gen. 6:8), and continued later with Abraham, through whom God promised to bless "all the families of the earth" (Gen. 12:1–3).

The promise to Abraham was fulfilled in Jesus Christ. He has brought the blessing of salvation from sin. But He has also brought the blessing of a community based on a common faith, known as the church (Eph. 2:14–22).

Ideally, these three institutions—the family, based on biological unity; the state, based on geographical unity; and the church, based on spiritual unity—are intended to reinforce each other and be mutually dependent. Each one needs the other two to function in an effective, godly way. Otherwise, all three suffer. Yet when one institution is struggling or breaking down, the other two need to offer support and assistance, though they cannot replace it.

Hannah's Song: Praising the True King

Many people today debate the potential as well as the limits of big government. The books of 1 and 2 Samuel make interesting reading in light of that discussion, for they offer an account of Israel's transition from rule by judges to a Jerusalem-based monarchy.

Under the judges, the nation went through periods of political and spiritual health. But for the most part, the people turned away from God (Judg. 21:25). Would they do better under the kings?

Hannah's song (1 Sam. 2:1–10) answers that question from the outset of the book: No matter who "rules" Israel, whether judge or king, the Lord is Israel's true King (1 Sam. 2:3, 10), salvation is from Him (1 Sam. 2:1), and God's concern is often for the outsiders, the poor—people on the "bottom of the heap" (1 Sam. 2:4–9).

The rest of 1 and 2 Samuel, as well as 1 and 2 Kings, bear out these truths:

- When the people demanded a king (1 Sam. 8:4–5), the Lord said that it was because they had rejected Him as their King (1 Sam. 8:7).
- When the nation faced crises, it was not their king who delivered them, but the Lord (for example, 1 Sam. 11:13; 17:46; 2 Sam. 5:22–25).
- It was not Saul, the people's favorite, who firmly established the monarchy, but David, the eighth and youngest son of Jesse, a shepherd of Bethlehem (1 Sam. 16:7, 9–13; 18:23; 2 Sam. 7:12–16).

Thus Hannah's song is a helpful corrective to overconfidence in government of any kind. All government is ultimately established by God (Rom. 13:1–7). Ideally, governments should seek justice for all. But in the end, one's faith must not rest in the power of centralized control, but in the power of God's justice, mercy, and salvation.

State-Established Religion?

In many countries of the world today, Christians are in the minority and struggle with how to live under unsympathetic or oppressive governments. By contrast, the Jews of Ezra's day, who were a minority in the Persian empire, enjoyed enough freedom to return to their homeland and rebuild their temple (Ezra 6:3, 6–7). In fact, the Persian state officially sanctioned their religion and contributed resources toward the temple project (Ezra 6:4, 8–10).

Is state-supported religion a goal that Christians today should pursue? There are different opinions worldwide on that issue. But whether or not governments support Christians, Scripture exhorts Christians everywhere to pray for the governments under which they live (1 Tim. 2:1–2).

*For more on this topic, see **REVOLUTION**, "A Tax Revolt," page 346.*

CHURCH BUILDINGS

(*see* Worship Centers)

CIRCUMSTANCES

Seeking the Peace of the City

Christians live with a future hope in the return of Christ and eternity with Him. In the meantime, we are visitors or "sojourners" on earth (1 Pet. 2:11). What should be our attitude toward this less-than-perfect world? We can gain some insight into our situation from the Lord's instructions to the captives of Judah living in Babylon (Jer. 29:4–7).

The Babylonians came against Judah in 605 B.C., and again in 599–597 B.C. In both cases they carried off the best and the brightest of the nation's leaders (2 Kin. 24:14–16; Jer. 27:20; 29:2; Dan. 1:1–6). Jeremiah sent a letter to the exiles in Babylon to tell them to expect seventy years of Babylonian captivity (29:1, 10). But the message opened with a remarkable statement: God had caused the exiles to be carried away to Babylon (29:4). Ultimately their plight was not merely the result of Nebuchadnezzar's policies, but of God's purposes. They were people sent to fulfill a mission.

Jeremiah told the refugees to put down roots—to build houses, plant gardens, marry, and have children (Jer. 29:5–6). They were not going anywhere for at least a couple of generations, so they might as well make the best of it. Furthermore, the Lord intended for His people to survive the Captivity in order to bring a remnant of them back to the land.

Another part of the exiles' mission was to "seek the peace of the city" of Babylon and to pray for it (29:7). This must have been unthinkable to them—to pray for their enemies who had taken them from their homeland, and to work for peace in Babylon! Yet Jeremiah affirmed that their own well-being was tied to the well-being of the Babylonians (29:7).

This perspective has implications for the way we as believers today look at the circumstances in which God has placed us. Like the exiles of Judah, we may live in cities and countries that depart from godly values and even promote ungodliness. Nevertheless, we too are to seek the peace of the places where we live and work, and to pray for leaders (1 Tim. 2:1–2).

Who Knows?

Suppose you lived in a time and place where you did not have the Bible as a moral or theological compass. How would you know what God was up to as you tried to interpret the events of life? Mordecai faced that problem as he lived in Persia sometime during the reign of Ahasuerus (486–465 B.C.).

One would never know from the Book of Esther that Mordecai's people, the Jews, had been chosen to be the Lord's people, or that the Lord had given them His Law, had spoken to them through His prophets, and was using the exile to chasten them for their disobedience against Him. In fact, the book does not even mention God—a fact that caused some to question whether Esther belonged in Scripture.

Thus it might seem that Mordecai and the Jews had little to guide them as they faced the prospect of annihilation (Esth. 3:13). Mordecai reacted with mourning (Esth. 4:1), but did so in a way that caught the attention of his cousin Esther (Esth. 4:2–9). Apparently he challenged her to speak to the king on her people's behalf (Esth. 4:10–12).

Then Mordecai made a reflective statement that suggests he was aware that God was working out His purposes: "Who knows whether you have come to the kingdom for such a time as this?" he asked his cousin. Who knows? Mordecai could not be certain, but he was proposing the idea that the remarkable turn of events in Esther's life—becoming the queen of Persia—had not come about by accident. She was placed in a strategic position at a timely moment to carry out a purpose. Whose purpose? Mordecai does not say, but the fact that he and Esther were Jews makes it plain that the Lord's hand was behind it all.

Like Mordecai and Esther, you may face circumstances about which you have little if any insight. Whether or not Scripture is silent on the issue, you may wonder what God is up to. What does it all mean? In moments like these, you can engage in the kind of reflection that Mordecai practiced—comparing the events of life with what you know about God to suggest what His purposes might be. The same God who worked through Esther is at work in your life today. Who knows what

circumstances He might bring you into "for such a time as this"?

*For more on this topic, see **NOSTALGIA**, "The Good Old Days," page 280.*

CITIES

At Home in the City

The Lord's words to Paul (Acts 18:9–10) offer hope for believers who live and work in cities. While there are many evils in the city—as well as in the country—the city itself is not an evil. Nor does evil prefer urban over rural settings. In his nighttime vision, Paul derived comfort from the affirmation that God was at work in the city. It was not a strange place for him, nor a place of alienation and fear. He felt at home there.

Today, cities continue to be strategic for the work of the church in an increasingly urbanized world. Believers might as well get used to living and working in them as God's people. After all, they will spend eternity in a heavenly city (Rev. 21:1–27)!

Cities Can Change Their Names

Every city has a history, a profile, and a personality. This identity is not static, but can change over time. The city of Beth Aven (Hos. 10:5) is a case in point.

After the death of Solomon, Jeroboam I founded the northern kingdom of Israel. Fearing that his people might return to Judah if they made religious pilgrimages to Jerusalem, he set up rival worship centers at Bethel in the south and Dan in the north (1 Kin. 12:28–33). In time, Bethel, which means "house of God," became so infamous as a shrine of idolatry that it was renamed Beth Aven, "house of harlotry."

The transformation of Bethel to Beth Aven, from holiness to harlotry, represented a tragic reversal in the city's legacy. The early Hebrews often built an altar to mark a sacred place, or bethel, where God had intervened in human history and fulfilled His promises. Thus Abraham and Jacob had erected pillars at or near ancient Bethel to mark their covenant with God and His promises of blessing (Gen. 12:8; 28:22; 31:13). Under Jeroboam, this sacred space had been defiled.

Yet the downward spiral of a city can be reversed. Cities can be restored, as Bethel

C

was by King Josiah of Judah. As part of his campaign of sweeping reform, he tore down Jeroboam's idols and high places (2 Kin. 23:15). He showed that with God's help a city can be changed for the better, and not just for the worse.

What is the legacy in your city's name? Is that legacy on the rise or on the decline? If your city were to be given a new name reflecting its current identity, what might it be called? What changes need to be made, and how could you promote that process of change?

In Search of One to Save the City

The prophets frequently compared Jerusalem to the ancient city of Sodom. God destroyed Sodom for its persistent wickedness and rebellion against Him. However, the Lord would have spared the city if Abraham could have found even ten righteous people living there. Apparently he could not (Gen. 18:32–33; 19:24–25).

How many righteous people would have spared Jerusalem from similar judgment? Only one, according to Jeremiah (Jer. 5:1). But the prophet searched in vain for that one.

First he went to the poor, but quickly discovered that they were ignorant of justice and truth (Jer. 5:4). Then he went to the "great men," the leaders, because they at least could read the Law, which had been rediscovered by Josiah (2 Kin. 22:8–23:3). Yet he found every single one of them to be guilty of departing from God's ways (Jer. 5:5).

So Jerusalem was bound for judgment. It had become so degenerate that God would have settled for even one righteous person rather than ten.

By this standard, how would you evaluate the cities of today? Are they morally better or worse than Sodom? How do they compare with Jerusalem? If Jeremiah were to search in your city for the "one righteous person," would he find one? Would that person be you? If not, what changes do you need to make in your life? What changes do the people of your city need to make?

Urban Redevelopment

Cheers and celebration usually greet the news of urban redevelopment when it benefits those living in the redevelopment zone.

Citizens look forward to new streets, housing, schools, businesses, or other improvements to their community's infrastructure. Sometimes a special ceremony is held to announce funding for the project.

In an even grander way, the prophet Isaiah envisioned a celebration for the good news of Jerusalem's redevelopment. The city had been laid waste by the Babylonians (587 B.C.; 2 Kin. 25:8–9). But the day would come when a messenger would arrive with "glad tidings of good things" (Is. 52:7). In effect, he would announce to the handful of inhabitants left in Jerusalem (Zion) that the Lord was reviving the city by bringing back its inhabitants from exile.

This news would so brighten the city that even its "waste places," or ruins, would "break forth into joy" and song, praising God for the great things He was about to do (Is. 52:9). Likewise, a choir of the city's watchmen would begin singing when they saw the exiles approaching their hometown at last (Is. 52:8).

As we walk through the "waste places" of modern-day cities—the deserted tenements, boarded-up storefronts, shuttered factories, and skid row alleys—and meet the battered, broken people who inhabit them, is anything more needed than Isaiah's "glad tidings" that God reigns (Is. 52:7) and can comfort and redeem a city (Is. 51:3; 52:9)? Can anything else quite rekindle the same hope, where only hopeless ruins stand?

God is still in the business of reclaiming and reviving cities and their people. What the cities of Judah had to sing about—redemption and return from Babylon—prefigured the good news of redemption and freedom from the curse of sin in Christ. Therefore, as we bring that good news to our communities, we become the "beautiful feet" that Isaiah celebrated (Is. 52:7; compare Rom. 10:15). So let's start walking and talking for God!

Was the Birth of the City Good or Bad?

Many of us are familiar with Cain, the world's first murderer. But how many are aware that Cain was also the first known builder of a city, and that, ironically, from this violent man's lineage came the first signs of civilization?

Cain's motivation to found a settled town may have sprung from the punishment he received for killing his brother, Abel. God placed a curse on Cain and forced him to wander the earth (Gen. 4:10–12). But he feared for his life, so God marked him to protect him from enemies (Gen. 4:13–15). Still, he wandered east of Eden ("delight") to the land of Nod ("wandering")—a stark contrast!

Perhaps to end his fugitive status, offset the effects of God's judgment, and maybe even recapture something of the original Eden, Cain founded Enoch. It's interesting that he names the settlement after his firstborn son.

But was the birth of the city good or bad? Some would say bad, pointing out that the idea of the city came from a man who "went out from the presence of the LORD" (Gen. 4:15). They would ask, how could a man who was alienated from God create anything positive?

Yet Cain's descendants brought much good into the world, though none of them totally escaped the effect of either Adam's fall or the curse placed on Cain. Cain's progeny included Irad (meaning uncertain), Mehujael ("smitten of God"), Methushael ("man of God"), and Lamech (meaning unknown) (Gen. 4:18).

The sons born to Lamech included another nomad or wanderer, Jabal ("nomadic"), but also a musician, Jubal ("playing"), and a skilled craftsman, especially in metals, Tubal-Cain ("smith" or "striker," Gen. 4:21–22). Thus from Cain came both pastoral and urban descendants, with the artist perhaps moving between both worlds. Their sister was named Naamah ("lovely" or "graceful"), reinforcing the idea that these were relatively cultured people.

Yet before long another tragedy struck the Cain family. Lamech came to his two wives one day and admitted to murder. But Lamech pled self-defense as his reason for killing a man (Gen. 4:23–24). He insisted that he be avenged ten times as much as his ancestor, Cain, who committed premeditated murder. In this way Lamech took the law into his own hands, perpetuating the violence and the "curse of Cain."

So in the end, Cain left a legacy of good as well as evil. We see that dual heritage in the city to this day. For instance, certain cities in Europe gave rise to the Reformation, yet also to the Holocaust; they produced both an Ein-stein and a Hitler. Such a history reminds us of the sobering truth of God's words to Cain, "If you do not do well, sin lies at the door. And its desire is for you" (Gen. 4:7).

For more on this topic, see **RAPE,** *"Supposed Safety in the City," page 331;* **URBAN MINISTRY,** *"Paul's Urban Strategy," page 409; "The City Is the Lord's!" page 411.*

CITIZENSHIP

Governmental Authority

Scripture challenges us as believers to subject ourselves to whatever governments we live under (Rom. 13:1–7). Submission to authority is never easy. Human nature tends toward resistance and even rebellion, especially if government is imposed, incompetent, and/or corrupt. But as we struggle with how to respond to the systems in which we live, this passage offers some helpful perspectives:

1. *God is the ultimate authority (Rom. 13:1).* Government as an institution has been established by God to serve His purposes. God raises up and does away with leaders.

2. *Both followers and leaders are ultimately accountable to God (Rom. 13:2).* Submission to human authorities reflects our submission to God's authority.

3. *God uses governments to carry out His good purposes on earth (Rom. 13:3).* Without question, some governments sometimes persecute those who do good. Paul had firsthand experience with that. But mainly, it's the lawbreaker, not the law-abiding citizen, who has something to fear from government.

4. *Obedience is a matter of inner conviction as well as external law (Rom. 13:5).* Our motivation to obey must go beyond fear of punishment. As believers, we serve the highest of all authorities, God Himself.

Pledging Allegiance

David spared Saul's life twice—once in the cave at En Gedi (1 Sam. 24:1–7), and again in the Wilderness of Ziph (1 Sam. 26:2, 7–12). Even though Saul was demented, unfit for office, and bent on destroying David, David refused to take his life, because Saul was the Lord's anointed (1 Sam. 24:6).

In fact, David was troubled for having violated even the *garment* that Saul was wearing (1 Sam. 24:5). It's similar to the way Americans "pledge allegiance to the flag of the United States . . . and to the republic for which it stands." To David, the robe of Saul represented the king.

David's respect for Saul's position serves as model for the high respect that God's people today should have for government and its officials. Like David, we may not care for the people in office or their actions, but we can at least respect the position, since government is ordained by God.

In fact, all officeholders—whether or not they are Christians or even God-fearing people—deserve our respect and prayers (1 Tim. 2:1-2). A governmental position invested by the prayers of God's people, anointed by God's representative, and confirmed with an oath of office invoking God's help—such an office is undeniably God-ordained.

In a day when disrespect for government is in vogue, Christians have a challenge to adopt a different attitude. David respected even a morally degraded, insanely driven Saul. How much more ought believers today to honor duly elected public officials.

Paul indicated that even "secular" governments, such as the autocratic Roman Empire, are God-ordained (see Rom. 13:1-7). Likewise, secular governments carry out God's sovereign purposes. For example, He called Cyrus, the pagan king of Persia, His shepherd and His anointed (see Is. 44:28–45:1).

As we think about governments, particularly those that seem to oppose God's ways, it helps to remember that God will always be glorified. Despite a Pharaoh, a Nebuchadnezzar, or a Herod who seeks to thwart God's purposes, God will accomplish His will. For a profile of a person committed to God while working for a foreign, pagan government, see the Book of Daniel.

For more on this topic, see **CHILDREN,** *"Protecting Your Heritage," page 52.*

CIVIL DISOBEDIENCE

A Case of Civil Disobedience

Is it ever right for God's people to participate in acts of civil disobedience? The behavior of the Hebrew midwives (Ex. 1:15) suggests that there can be times when it is.

It's interesting that the Book of Exodus, a story of deliverance from oppression, begins with a case of political resistance as two women refuse to do Pharaoh's bidding. Because his command was the law of the land, they were consciously and deliberately breaking the law.

This may seem to contradict biblical teaching elsewhere that believers should obey the law and respect the governing authorities (for example, Rom. 13:1-2). But it's important to realize that there are limits to human authority. Sometimes God's people must resist human officials in order to obey God (Acts 5:29). That was the type of situation here. Pharaoh was commanding nothing less than infanticide.

The text states plainly why he would do that: he was afraid of the Israelites (Ex. 1:8-10, 12). That fear translated into public policy designed to discriminate against and subjugate the Hebrews.

But whereas Pharaoh feared the Israelites, their midwives did not fear him; they feared God (Ex. 1:17, 21). That is, they held to the Lord's command to respect and preserve human life (Gen. 9:3-7; compare Ex. 20:13). Perhaps they also knew that God's promise to make a great nation from Abraham and to give them the land of Canaan literally rested in their hands (Gen. 12:1-2; 13:14-17). So when it came to a conflict between Pharaoh's command and God's command, the midwives determined to obey God.

In our own time, thousands of children die every day as a direct or indirect result of political, economic, social, or religious policies. Some of these policies are as cold and calculated as was the command of Pharaoh, others are not. But either way, the outcome is the same: infanticide. Children are still being killed by the harsh decisions of people who do not fear God.

As Christians, we have a model to follow in the example of the Hebrew midwives. When asked to do something that goes against God's ways, we can resist and even disobey. We may not be as fortunate as the midwives to escape retribution. But we can rest in our conscience, knowing that we have feared God who is our ultimate authority.

In a way, Pharaoh's command to kill the Hebrew boys foreshadowed the last of the ten plagues, in which God sent an angel of death to kill the Egyptian firstborn.

The edict also foreshadowed King Herod's order to execute all the baby boys around Bethlehem in an insane attempt to destroy the baby Jesus. Like the Exodus account, that story, too, has social implications: it reminds city kids today that they need not die in vain.

(Almost) All the People

It is unrealistic to think that any of us will go through life without having to choose between submission to a human authority and obedience to God. Sooner or later, we will likely be told by someone in authority to do something opposed to God. When that happens, what should be our response?

There is a great tension here for believers. The Bible tells us to obey those in authority (Rom. 13:1–7), yet it also gives us examples of godly people who resisted human authorities when their commands violated the commands of God (Acts 4:13–22). There is no simple formula to relieve this tension. In fact, it is this very tension that requires us to rely on God rather than some list of dos and don'ts.

Furthermore, if we feel no tension between the authority of God and human authority, we have to wonder where our commitments lie. Apparently next to no one in ancient Babylon felt any tension or anxiety about bowing down to Nebuchadnezzar's golden image, or if they did, they feared the fiery furnace (Dan. 3:6) more than they feared God.

But Shadrach, Meshach, and Abed-Nego did not submit. They refused to violate the first and second commandments, which forbid idolatry (Ex. 20:3–5). Furnace or no furnace, they were determined to honor the Lord (Dan. 3:17–18).

Is this how Christians today should respond to laws and directives with which they disagree? Again, there are no simple answers. Situations vary. Perhaps the following questions will be useful as you wrestle with yours:

- Is this truly a matter of biblical principle, or just one of preference, taste, or style?
- Why exactly do I have problems with what I am being asked to do? Is it really an issue of conscience and morality, or is it something else—perhaps a personality conflict, or just feelings of discomfort?
- Have I made an effort to listen and understand exactly what the authority is asking me to do? Have I checked out my perceptions by telling the authority what I think I heard?
- Do I really understand how what I am being asked to do conflicts with godly values? Have I studied God's Word diligently, prayed for His insight, and thought things through?
- Is this really an either/or situation, or are there alternatives that might satisfy everyone involved? Daniel dealt with an issue of conscience by coming up with a creative alternative to his superior's command (Dan. 1:8–16). Can I think of a way to meet the authority's needs while preserving my own integrity?

Convicts with Conviction

In an unjust society, it is often the righteous who are imprisoned. A number of leaders in the Bible, such as Hanani the seer (2 Chr. 16:10), spent time behind bars. Their loyalty to God's calling, to biblical convictions, and to genuine faith sometimes made them vulnerable to persecution or required them to resist laws or rulers—which landed them in jail.

The Bible shows us many cases where imprisonment has been used to persecute the innocent. Christ Himself, who was without sin, became a prisoner and was executed for our sakes.

But even in cases where wrongs have been committed, the fact remains that Christ's good news is for captives and prisoners too. Forgiveness, restoration, and reconciliation are at the heart of the message of the cross (Luke 4:18; Heb. 13:3).

"We Ought to Obey God Rather Than Men"

What should Christians do when faced with a conflict between human authority and God's authority? Notice what Peter and the other apostles did (Acts 5:22–32):

- Their aim was to serve and glorify God. They were not motivated by ego or out to protect their own power.
- Their point of disobedience was specific and particular. They did not resist the authority of the Jewish council in total.

- They approached the situation with a spirit of submissiveness toward both the council and God. They did not harbor rebellious anger toward authority in general.
- They delivered a positive, factual message about God's plan and power in loving truth. They did not slander or show disrespect to their superiors.
- They accepted the cost of being loyal to the truth without rancor or bitterness.

CIVIL RIGHTS

Faith and Rights

"Human rights" is not a new concept. Nearly every social structure has at least some rules to protect its members.

As a Roman commander arrested Paul and ordered that he be beaten, Paul used his Roman citizenship to protect his rights (Acts 22:25–29). He had done the same thing at Philippi after being illegally jailed (Acts 16:36–40). In Jerusalem, he insisted on due process rather than endure unjust mob retaliation. He set the record straight so that the authorities could intervene appropriately.

Rumor, anger, or distortion regarding the faith need to be met forthrightly, as Paul's example shows. There's no need to allow discrimination to hinder one's practice of Christianity in society, particularly in one's workplace. As believers we need a clear understanding of the laws and rules and their application, and we need to ensure that they are applied fairly on behalf of everyone—including ourselves.

Playing Favorites

Countless laws and legal battles have been and continue to be fought over civil rights and the effort to end discrimination. James calls on the ultimate law, the "royal law" (James 2:8), to speak out against discrimination in the one place it ought least to exist—the church. He specifically condemns favoritism toward the rich and discrimination against the poor. When believers discriminate on the basis of socioeconomic status, they violate the core of God's law.

Yet it happens all the time, doesn't it? How about where you work, or in your church or community? Are only the wealthy considered likely candidates for church leadership? How do you respond to customers at work, visitors at church, or shoppers at a grocery store who look "down-and-out"?

On the other hand, does James's stern warning against favoring the rich and dishonoring the poor imply that we should favor the poor and dishonor the rich? Do you ever practice "reverse discrimination"? Does your church condemn wealthy people for their wealth? Do you assume that someone who has riches gained them by dishonesty or oppression, rather than by honest work and service?

James says that favoritism is as much a transgression of the law as adultery or murder (James 2:10–11). Apparently God takes economic discrimination seriously!

COALITION

A Remarkable Coalition

We live in a world where groups of people tend to exclude others rather than include them. Seldom do people from vastly different backgrounds band together, unless it's to fight a common enemy. Distinctions such as race, money, position, language, and gender often keep people from cooperating with each other.

But for those who followed Jesus, divisive walls began to break down. As a result of His influence, people who were far apart socially began to come together for the benefit of others.

Such was the case at Jesus' burial. His death brought about a surprising coalition: two men who were prominent Jewish leaders, and two women, one who had been delivered from demon possession and the other an obscure mother (Luke 23:50–56). Who were these people?

Joseph of Arimathea was a wealthy community leader and a member of the Jewish council. He had access to Pilate and gained permission to take away Jesus' body. He helped prepare the body for burial and deliver it to his own tomb (23:50–53; compare Matt. 27:57–60; Mark 15:42–46).

Nicodemus was also a member of the council (John 3:1–2). He challenged some of the accusations against Jesus (7:50–51). After the Lord's death, he brought nearly one hundred pounds of embalming supplies (19:39–42).

Mary Magdalene came from Galilee. She had been demon-possessed before following Jesus (Luke 8:2). Along with other women she observed the tragic ordeal of the Crucifixion (23:49). After Joseph retrieved the body, she helped with the embalming (23:56). Later, after Jesus' resurrection, she helped spread the amazing news that He was alive (24:10).

Mary of Galilee was the mother of James and Joses (Mark 15:40). Little else is known about her, but she played enough of a part in the burial coalition to have her participation recorded in Scripture.

Does your faith connect you with people different from yourself? Believers often have more in common with other believers than they do with family, friends, or coworkers. That fact can sometimes be just the bit of evidence needed to make the faith attractive to its worst critics.

An International Work Group

The rapidly growing Christian movement recruited members from a wide variety of places. That created significant cultural diversity, as the traveling team mentioned in Acts 20:4 shows. Note the rich differences of background:

- Sopater of Berea (perhaps the same as Sosipater in Rom. 16:21);
- Aristarchus (Acts 27:2) and Secundus of Thessalonica;
- Gaius of Derbe;
- Timothy of Lystra, the product of a mixed marriage (Acts 16:1);
- Tychicus, possibly from Ephesus (Eph. 6:21–22; Col. 4:7–8);
- Trophimus of Ephesus (Acts 21:29);
- Luke the physician from Antioch in Syria, who possibly was writing the Acts account while on the trip;
- Paul of Tarsus, Jerusalem, and Antioch in Syria (see Acts 13:1)

This varied coalition shows how the people of God have a foundation for unity beyond all other causes. The common faith can bridge differences that circumstances like a depression, war, or natural disaster cannot. It fulfills Jesus' prayer for His followers that they would demonstrate a oneness that demands the world's attention (John 17:20–23).

COMMERCE
A Valuable Trading Partner

Hiram of Tyre was probably the most valuable ally that David and Solomon had, for he supplied them not only with raw materials for their many building projects, but expert craftsmen as well. He also helped launch Israel's shipping industry by providing experienced sailors and ships (1 Kin. 9:26–28; 10:11, 22).

During the twenty-year period in which Solomon built the temple and his own palace complex, Israel incurred a trade imbalance with Phoenicia, for which twenty cities along the Galilean-Phoenician border were given to Hiram. However, the cities were later returned when Hiram determined them to be cabul, "good for nothing" (5:1–18; 9:10–14; 2 Chr. 8:1–2).

The Cedar Trade

The parched and war-torn landscape of modern-day Lebanon makes it difficult to imagine, but three thousand years ago the area was flourishing with massive cedar trees. The timber was so plentiful that Solomon sent thousands of laborers to cut and transport cedar wood to Jerusalem, where he built numerous structures with it, including his impressive residence, appropriately called the House of the Forest of Lebanon (1 Kin. 7:2).

Cedar was also used for the construction of the temple (1 Kin. 5:6–10; 6:9–10, 15–18). It was used again many years later in the construction of the second temple, after the Babylonian exile (Ezra 3:7).

Solomon was by no means the only ruler to import the fragrant, durable, and attractive cedar, as well as cypress and fir. Lebanon is known to have traded these woods with Syria, Egypt, and the nations of Mesopotamia.

Yet something happened to this lively economy between the time of Solomon and the time of Christ. In fact, a massive change occurred in the overall ecology of the Palestine area. Scripture suggests that it was part of God's judgment of Israel for turning away from Him.

The forests of Lebanon were decimated by overcutting. Solomon contributed to that, yet even his demand for cedar was apparently exceeded by that of the Babylonian ruler Nebuchadnezzar, according to extrabiblical sources and possibly the biblical prophets as well (for example, Hab. 2:17). As a result, the ancient cedar forests vanished within a matter of generations, never to be replaced, despite attempts to reforest the land.

The Trade in Purple

Lydia's hometown, Thyatira, was a thriving manufacturing and commercial center. Its trade in purple was renowned in the Roman world. The most expensive of dyes and a mark of wealth or royalty, purple came from the murex, a shellfish found only along the northeastern section of the Mediterranean coast. Purple cloth was ranked in value with gold and was important not only for adorning emperors and temples but for tribute and international trade.

We don't know when or why Lydia relocated to Philippi, but it was a smart business move. A Latin inscription found there mentions the dyeing trade and its economic importance to the city. Philippi was the leading Roman colony of the region, located on the major east-west highway connecting Europe to the Middle East. Its people were known for trying to outdo Rome in dress and manners.

Lydia probably belonged to a local dyer's guild, a professional association. Guilds sometimes involved such pagan customs and practices as worship of the trade's patron god, feasts using food sacrificed to idols, and loose sexual morality.

Lydia's conversion didn't change her occupation, but it dramatically changed her loyalty. Her business contacts likely introduced Paul to the "movers and shakers" of the Macedonian area.

Trade in Ancient Israel

While the strip of land that Israel inhabited had little in the way of proven natural resources, its location geographically made it a strategic corridor through which much of the military and economic traffic between Europe, Asia, and Africa had to pass. As a result, Israel became a major factor in international trade and commerce and a much-prized possession of ancient empires.

Grain, especially wheat and barley, grew abundantly in the shallow valleys along the foothills of Judea and Samaria and became major export crops. Figs, grapes, and olives were plentiful in the hill country of Judea.

Hebron produced magnificent grapes that it turned into large quantities of raisins and wine for domestic consumption and export. Olives were used as food or crushed for cooking oil. Olive oil was also used in lamps or as a body rub, making it a major product of the region.

Palestine also boasted large herds of sheep and goats from which wool and cloth were produced. Fish were taken along the Mediterranean coast and especially at the Sea of Galilee. Along the northern section of the Mediterranean coast could be found the murex shell, used to make a very valuable dye called purple. Extensive textile industries, using both wool and the linen made from flax grown on the coastal plain, produced the distinctive Tyrian purple cloth that was in great demand throughout the Mediterranean world.

The southern end of the Jordan valley was the source of a large and profitable salt-mining industry. Asphalt or bitumen was easily obtained from the tar pits in the Dead Sea area. This substance was used as caulk in boats and rafts, as mortar in building, and for making monuments and jewelry. Israel exported few metals except during the reign of Solomon when copper mines in Sinai and the iron mines in Syria were worked commercially. However, timber from the Lebanon mountains was a major trade item.

Little pottery was exported, except for simple containers for wine and oil. This may have been because Israelite pottery was more practical and less artistic than Philistine and Greek pottery. However, a major industry was the manufacture of millstones from the high-quality basalt stone found in the volcanic hills of northern Gilead. These were shipped as far away as Spain, Italy, and North Africa.

In Ezekiel 27:1–24 we read of numerous products that were traded through the city of Tyre: fir, cedar, oak, ivory, ebony, fine embroidered linen, blue and purple cloth and clothes, white wool, finished garments and multicolored apparel, saddlecloths for riding, caulk, silver, gold, iron, tin, lead, vessels of bronze, emeralds, corals, rubies, precious stones, wheat, millet, honey, the herb cassia, spices, cane, oil, balm, horses, mules, lambs, rams, goats, wine, luxury goods, and slaves.

COMMITMENT

Do You Fear God for Nothing?

We live in a world of "you scratch my back and I'll scratch yours." For many, this principle of give-and-take extends to their faith. Ask them why they believe in God and they'll reply that it's because of all the wonderful things He has done for them. In effect, their walk with God operates on the basis of reciprocity: He gives to them, and in exchange they follow Him.

Satan accused God of having that kind of relationship with Job. He charged Him with "buying" Job's loyalty by rewarding Job with wealth and security (Job 1:9–10). As Satan accurately pointed out, purchased devotion is suspect because it is liable to vanish the moment the rewards cease (Job. 1:11).

However, Satan misjudged Job's character. Stripped of his possessions and struck with the tragic loss of his family, Job nevertheless blessed the name of the Lord and refused to blame God for his troubles (Job. 1:21–22). Later, when Satan touched Job's body, he still refused to turn away from God. Should one accept only good from God, and not adversity, he asked (Job 2:9–10)?

Job's integrity was a powerful response to Satan's question, "Does Job fear God for nothing?" (Job 1:9). The answer was yes, Job feared God for nothing in return. His devotion was not bought; it was a gift.

Could the same be said of you? Do you follow God because of the "rewards" you believe He has given you? Suppose they were all taken away. Would you still honor Him? Is your commitment to the Lord out of a simple, genuine faith—the kind of steadfast faith that declares, "Though He slay me, yet will I trust Him" (Job 13:15)?

God's Family Album

The names that Peter calls believers (1 Pet. 2:9–10) are important because they reveal our identity. We know *who* we are because we know *whose* we are: we belong to God. We have received His call, mercy, and claim on our lives. As a result, we can commit our-

selves to others and work with them to achieve common goals.

Peter draws on the Exodus account for his language here: "I . . . brought you [out of Egypt] to Myself. . . . You shall be to Me a kingdom of priests" (Ex. 19:4–6). God first identified with and redeemed the people of Israel, then He made covenant agreements with them. Likewise for us, first God's grace secures our identity, then our commitment to His service.

Our modern culture tears at that sense of identity and security. If we want to effect change and serve others, we need to know whose we are and why. Do you? Can you find yourself in God's family portrait framed in this passage?

Just Do It

There's an old saying that "talk is cheap." It's easy to express sentiments such as loyalty, love, or respect. But the real question is, What happens when our commitments cost us something?

Leviticus, along with the rest of the Law, spelled out practical ways in which Israel could demonstrate its loyalty and love for God, as well as ways for the people to demonstrate their commitment to each other as a covenant community. One of the most important of these practical steps was the sacrificial system (Lev. 7:37–38).

The sacrifices were inconvenient and costly. But by carrying them out, the people showed in a very evident way that they were God's people. The sacrifices turned words into actions.

In the same way, believers today need to translate their words and thoughts into actions, even if it costs them something. "My little children, let us not love in word or in tongue, but in deed and in truth. And by this we know that we are of the truth, and shall assure our hearts before Him" (1 John 3:18–19).

The message is clear: Just do it!

Singleness of Heart

Many believers today pray for revival, but one of the conditions of revival is unity among believers. If God's people are divided in what they believe or contradictory in what they say, it can be very difficult for unbelievers to take the gospel message seriously.

During Hezekiah's reign in Judah, spiritual revival came about largely because the Lord gave the people "singleness of heart" to obey His commandments, as given through the leaders (2 Chr. 30:12). This newfound unity to obey God and honor the covenant contrasted sharply with the disunity that had marked the Israelites since the days of Rehoboam (2 Chr. 10:1–19). Hezekiah invited the survivors of the northern kingdom to rejoin their brothers and sisters in the south (2 Chr. 30:6–9). Most of the northerners resisted this call, but a few responded (2 Chr. 30:10–11).

One reason why the people were again able to follow God wholeheartedly was that Hezekiah was doing so. Scripture attests that in everything he did, Hezekiah honored the Lord "with all his heart" (2 Chr. 31:21). In this he was honoring what Jesus later declared to be the first and foremost commandment: to love the Lord with all one's heart (Deut. 6:5; Matt. 22:37–38).

Jesus also prayed that His followers would be one in order that the world would know that He was the Christ (John 17:20–21). Do you want revival? Perhaps the place to begin is with an examination of your own heart. See whether you are like Hezekiah and the people of his day—committed to the Lord and to His people with *singleness of heart.* In what ways can you unite with believers from Christian traditions other than your own?

The Covenant-keeping God

Perhaps you've heard someone in business sarcastically say, "Contracts were meant to be broken." Tragically, that is all too often true. People today make and break commitments with seeming abandon. On paper they may agree to certain terms. But when the terms are no longer convenient, they renege on their commitments. Or they will end the relationship at the first sign of failure on the other person's part.

But when God says He'll do something, He does it. His covenant with David (Ps. 89:3–4) is an unconditional commitment that God will honor no matter what. It is much like a parent's commitment to a child. Indeed, God tells His people, "Can a woman forget her nursing child, and not have compassion on the son of her womb? Surely they may forget, yet I will not forget you" (Is. 49:15).

God has made a covenant with believers today that is just as firm as His covenant with David. He does not back out of the relationship just because we may disappoint Him. God will still be true to His word:

- His commitment is incomparable because He is without equal (Ps. 89:6).
- He is overwhelmingly faithful (89:8, 24, 33).
- The covenant with Him lasts forever (89:28–29, 36).
- His commitment is unbreakable and unalterable (89:34).

When God agrees to do something—whether it is to send the Messiah or to save a believer—His commitment is built on a love that far exceeds human love, sticking with the object of its affection sometimes in the face of outright rebellion or abject failure. As Paul described it to his spiritual son Timothy, "If we are faithless, He remains faithful; for He cannot deny Himself" (2 Tim. 2:13).

Are you looking for a love that will not fail? If so, your deepest longings can be met in a relationship with the covenant-keeping God.

The Nazirite Vow

Have you ever felt a desire to dedicate yourself to the Lord in some special way for a period of time? The Nazirite vow (Num. 6:2) was a way for the ancient Hebrews to do that. Just as they were encouraged to pay vows of their possessions, they could also make a vow of their own lives.

The term *Nazirite* meant "one separated or consecrated." Thus, a person taking a Nazirite vow devoted himself to God. As a sign of his commitment, the Nazirite abstained from all products of the vine—grapes, raisins, wine, and vinegar—from the use of a razor, and from touching a dead body, even that of a family member (Num. 6:3–7).

The text does not explain why a person would make such a vow. But many believe that it was an act of devotion, or possibly of penitence after atonement for a sin. It is also possible that one became a Nazirite as a way of expressing single-minded commitment to some important task.

Along these lines, parents were known to make a Nazirite vow on behalf of their unborn children. For example, Hannah pledged that she would dedicate to the Lord any child that He might give her. The nature of her vow suggests that her son, Samuel, was probably a Nazirite throughout his life (1 Sam. 1:11, 27–28). In a similar case, the Angel of the Lord told Manoah that his wife would bear a son who would be a Nazirite. Thus the judge Samson was born (Judg. 13:3–5).

These lifetime vows appear to be exceptional. Numbers implies that the Nazirite vow normally lasted for a fixed period of time (Num. 6:13). If so, that would have made it accessible to the average person. One could show special devotion to God for several days, weeks, months, or perhaps even years. But there was no need to drop out of society or practice extreme forms of abstinence.

Like so many forms of religious devotion, however, the Nazirite vow became corrupted over time by those who saw it as a means of gaining favor with God. Abuses included setting a minimum number of days on the duration of the vow, getting wealthy people to finance the offerings involved, and even betting on how long one could keep the vow.

There is no New Testament equivalent to the Nazirite vow. Even so, Christians can vol-

COMMUNITY

LOVE ONE ANOTHER!

OUT OF MY WAY, BUDDY, PEOPLE NEED TO SEE THIS!

untarily devote themselves to God in special ways. For example, some Christian traditions call for abstinence and intensified devotional activity during the Lenten season. More generally, the disciplines of prayer and fasting are ways of focusing oneself on God whenever one might choose.

But one thing needs to remain clear: Nothing that we do ever puts God in our debt. Rather, we are forever obligated to Him. Vows are simply a way of reminding ourselves of that fact.

For more on this topic, see **PERSECUTION,** *"The Cost of Commitment," page 296.*

COMMUNICATION
Show Them Who's in Charge!

It's not enough to be called a leader; one must *act* as a leader to expect any results. That's the challenge that Moses and Aaron faced as they prepared to meet with Pharaoh (Ex. 7:1–2).

God had already given them authority to speak on His behalf. We might call that *positional authority,* the sort of status that a title or rank might confer. But actions speak louder than words. So now their task was to *communicate* to Pharaoh the authority they had been given, and to do so clearly and with power.

Poor communication can seriously undercut a leader's authority. If one fails to make one's goals and purposes clear, or to communicate in terms that those listening can easily understand, or to repeat the message as many times as it takes to get the point across, then it doesn't matter what title or position one holds. No one is going to pay much attention.

Showing as Well as Telling

They say that a picture is worth a thousand words. Jeremiah painted many pictures for the people of Judah, such as the broken flask (Jer. 19:1–15). His purpose in using these visual aids was to help his listeners grasp the significance of what God was saying to them.

This is an important lesson in communication. To say what we need to say clearly, it helps to use more than words—especially in today's society, which has become more visu-

ally oriented than ever. We will tend to say more if we show as well as tell. Telling tends to confront listeners with information; showing tends to involve listeners in the communication process.

Of course, it could be argued that Jeremiah's visual demonstrations were of little value, since most of the people did not turn from their wicked ways after watching and listening to him. But communicators have little control over how people respond to what they say. Their primary responsibility is to make sure that they communicate as clearly and effectively as they can, which is what Jeremiah did.

Are people of faith today as skillful in speaking to our society as Jeremiah was to his? It will certainly help if we have something for people to see, as well as hear. We might also improve communication in our families, workplaces, and communities by employing creative, memorable "visuals." And as always, our most powerful means of communicating the gospel will be not just what we say, but how we live.

COMMUNITY
Corporate Solidarity

The battle between David and Goliath illustrates a time-honored principle called "corporate solidarity," in which the one stands for the many. Thus when Goliath came out to challenge the Israelites, he called for a champion from their ranks to fight with him, one on one (1 Sam. 17:8–10). Goliath would represent the Philistines, and the Israelites' man would represent Israel.

This was a not uncommon way of settling disputes in the ancient world (for example, 2 Sam. 2:12–17; 1 Chr. 11:22–23). And the principle of corporate solidarity extended beyond warfare. For example, Adam's sin included the whole world in sin (Rom. 5:12–19). Achan's sin brought judgment on his entire community—family, clan, and nation (Josh. 7:11, 20, 24).

Conversely, if one person turned to God, especially if that person were the head of a family, such an act could preserve the entire family in certain cases. Thus Rahab's decision to protect the Hebrew spies delivered her and her family from the destruction of Jericho (2:12–13; 6:17).

A unique representative is Jesus, who was able to be a substitute for all humanity and carry the sins of the world onto the Cross (Rom. 5:15–19; compare Is. 53:11).

In our own day, we still see the application of "one equals many." For example, the United States government is a representative system in which one elected official's vote stands for the vote of an entire district of the country. Likewise, sports teams represent cities, and Olympic athletes lift up the collective spirit of entire nations. In business, a salesperson represents an entire company. In fact, corporations are legally liable for the actions of their employees.

Corporate solidarity is a key to understanding many of the incidents recorded in Scripture, such as David's encounter with Goliath. It also has many implications for people's participation in families, organizations, communities, and societies. We are not as independent as we might like to believe. The lives that we live impact others, just as others' lives impact our own.

From Me to My Community to the World

One of the worst things about going through tough times is that the stress and strain of testing tend to concentrate all of our focus on ourselves. It's hard to be concerned about the needs of others when our own needs demand attention.

Self-care is vitally important, and in fact, if we neglect our own needs, we will probably be less effective in helping others. We'll also tend to burn out. Yet while taking care of our personal concerns, it's also important to pass along whatever grace and strength God sends our way. At least, that was the pattern for the writer of Psalm 102.

The psalmist cried out to the Lord from the depths of profound, personal distress (Ps. 102:1–11). His prayer honestly expressed his heart: he felt that God had abandoned him to his enemies. His only hope was in the Lord's eternal nature and undying love for His people (102:12–14).

In the midst of his prayer, the psalmist envisioned God looking down from heaven to view the earth (Ps. 102:19). This was a worth-while exercise; it helped the psalmist look at things from God's perspective. The first thing the writer realized was that God could see him, and people like him—the prisoners, and especially those condemned to die (Ps. 102:20). The Lord could hear their groaning, and would eventually release them.

But the point of freeing them was that they would talk about the Lord in Zion, the center of Israel's religious life (see 2 Sam. 5:7). In other words, the grace of God was given to the individual so that it would be shared with the community. In turn, the people at Jerusalem had a mission to live for God in a way that attracted other nations to worship and serve the Lord (Ps. 102:22).

God Is a Community

Something profoundly important is revealed about the nature of God in the statement, "Let *Us* make man in *Our* image, according to *Our* likeness" (Gen. 1:26, emphasis added). God is not speaking as a solitary figure, but as a *plurality*, as a Being of more than one Person. Christians trace the doctrine of the Trinity beginning at this passage.

The picture that emerges from a number of texts is that God exists in three Persons; not three Gods, but one God in three Persons. The text uses the Hebrew word *Elohim*, the plural form of *Eloah* ("God"), for this communal, supreme Creator-God. Later we discover the three Persons included in "Us": the Father (James 1:17–18), the Son, Jesus Christ (John 1:3; Col. 1:16), and the Holy Spirit (Gen. 1:2; Ps. 104:30).

In a very real way, God is a community and exists in relationship to Himself. This is important for Genesis 1–2, because it implies that God had no need to create anyone else. He was not lonely, nor was He somehow deficient and in need of help. He was and is completely self-sufficient, and would be so even if He had never created any creature. But He chose to create the world and its people as a gift given out of His abundant love. In Genesis 1:26, God is saying, in effect, "Let us create Adam and Eve and their descendants as creatures who can share the love and community we already have among Ourselves."

Thinking of God in the plural, as a community, may seem odd, but it has very practical implications. It is the basis for understanding marriage and the family. It says that relationships matter, and that as people created in God's image, we need each other. It also encourages us as God's people to build communities, not to run from them.

COMMUNITY DEVELOPMENT
Christ Cares About Cities

The account of Nehemiah rebuilding the city of Jerusalem (Neh. 2:20) may seem like a footnote of history, but it illustrates a fundamental principle that has implications for every Christian living today: *Christ cares about cities.*

A key passage for understanding this concept is Paul's New Testament letter to the Colossians. There we learn that Christ is the Lord of all of life, whether public or private. He not only transforms us personally, but uses us in the global arena to transform societies and systems as well.

Therefore, Christ wants His followers to participate in public institutions for the benefit of all. As believers, we can use the systems of the city—education, health care, transportation, housing, community development—as instruments for good. By doing so, we can help create healthy cities that promote healthy neighborhoods that encourage healthy families and lead to healthy individuals—and vice versa.

This was the sort of work in which Nehemiah was ultimately involved. He was concerned about far more than a wall. He wanted to see his people restored and revitalized. He wanted his nation to return to the covenant with God outlined in the Law. The rebuilding of the city of Jerusalem was the first step in that process.

Are you committed to the city in the way that Christ is? How might you use your resources—job, money, relationships, influence—to accomplish tangible benefits for people in your community?

Community Development Begins with Worship

Effective community developers and project managers looks for ways to help people come together and work to better their circumstances. When Jeshua and Zerubbabel and their brothers surveyed the situation at Jerusalem (Ezra 3:1), they began their community redevelopment efforts by calling the people together for worship (Ezra 3:2–11).

In many ways this event was to be expected. All of these leaders were priests, and to a priest, the first priority in a plan to revitalize community life was to reestablish worship services and rebuild a worship center. Thus, even before the city walls were rebuilt, an altar was set up and temple construction was started.

Apparently the Israelite priests realized that worship celebrations help to mobilize a community while also giving glory to God. Their example encourages us today to place a priority on seeking the Lord and worshiping Him as we launch projects aimed at community development.

The Ten Percent Solution

How do you revitalize dead or dying urban neighborhoods that have many abandoned homes and buildings, few if any businesses, and an infrastructure that lies in ruins? Nehemiah came up with a novel solution for that problem in Jerusalem: let the outlying suburbs donate one-tenth of their people to move into the city (Neh. 11:1–2). In effect, the districts surrounding Jerusalem tithed people for the purpose of community redevelopment.

Could a similar "ten percent solution" be applied to run-down neighborhoods today? It is intriguing to imagine what might happen if ten percent of all the believers in the suburbs surrounding any of today's largest cities relocated into the most blighted sections of their cities; if they put their children in neighborhood schools; if they rebuilt abandoned or neglected houses; if they shopped at neighborhood stores and restaurants; if they established or worked at businesses in the community; if they participated in local political and civic affairs; if they built up churches in the inner city.

Nehemiah's recruitment for the repopulation program involved casting lots to determine who would relocate (Neh. 11:1; see Josh. 18:8–10). Those who were selected were "blessed" or ordained (Hebrew, *barak*, Neh. 11:2) to the task by their fellow citizens. This suggests a formal commissioning of these families to carry out the redevelopment of Jerusalem.

In a similar way, people who move back into the city today to help revitalize urban life need not come with a spirit of know-it-all condescension or quick-fix triumphalism, but rather with a sense of mission. Just as urban blight happens over many years, so urban renewal takes years to accomplish.

But it must start somewhere. Nehemiah began with ten percent of God's people living nearby. Where will God's people today begin?

Why Start with the Wall?

The city of Jerusalem to which Nehemiah returned was in gross disrepair. Its temple had been restored by Ezra, but little else was functioning effectively. The wall was broken down, the gates were burned, the roads were cluttered with debris, and most of the homes and buildings stood vacant. It must have been a depressing place to visit, let alone live.

If you were Nehemiah, where would you have started to rebuild the Holy City? After a private nighttime site inspection (Neh. 2:11–15), Nehemiah chose to start with the rebuilding of the wall. Why?

The text does not give us the details of Nehemiah's reasoning, but several points seem clear:

1. *The project was achievable.* Restoring the city's many systems of commerce and public life required complex, long-term processes. By contrast, the wall could be rebuilt in a mere fifty-two days (Neh. 6:15). Thus Nehemiah provided a means of success to a people who had experienced nothing but defeat for decades.

2. *The task was something in which everyone could participate.* The physical labor of rebuilding the wall did not require highly technical or intellectual skills. A few carpenters and masons were needed, but most of the work required nothing more complicated than lifting stones and clearing a path. Thus everyone could get involved. As a result, the task brought together the entire community.

3. *Rebuilding the walls had both practical and symbolic value of restoring security to the city.* For too long, Jerusalem had been wide open to the domination of strongmen such as Sanballat, Tobiah, and their cronies (Neh. 4:1, 7; 6:1). By closing up the walls, Nehemiah was improving the safety of the citizens. He also was serving notice that the Israelites were back, putting thugs and thieves out of business.

Nehemiah's wisdom serves as a model for those involved in community development today. Often the place to begin revitalization of a neighborhood is with simple tasks that are doable and achieve tangible yet significant results.

For more on this topic, see **CITIES**, *"Urban Redevelopment," page 63.*

COMMUNITY SERVICE
Faith Impacts the World

Jesus sent His followers into "all the world" (Mark 16:15). Clearly He had global impact in mind. But spreading Christ's message involves more than just broadcasting a statement or set of facts. How does faith *impact* the world?

One way is through followers of Christ who live out the gospel and proclaim it to the world. That's why the lifestyles and relationships of believers are so important. People are watching to see how we as Christians handle our responsibilities and resources. Is there any evidence that Christ really makes a difference in our lives?

Another way is through Christian institutions, such as local churches, parachurch organizations, and the Christian media. If you work or volunteer for one of these kinds of organizations, you have an important opportunity to touch the needs of the world with Christ's love and power.

A third sphere of influence is through lobbying and advocacy. Here Christians attempt to influence the institutions and people that control society. This might mean something as simple as voting, or something as complex as running for office or working to enact a particular piece of legislation. In our culture, Christians have the right to participate actively in public policy decisions, and we should use that right in ways that we believe honor the Lord.

As we attempt to take Christ's message to "all the world," it helps to understand how our world operates.

The Public Side of Our Faith

Much of the Christianity that has come down to us today dwells on private spirituality—prayers, private devotions and Bible reading, self-examination and confession, personal holiness, individual acts of charity, and so on. This is all to the good, inasmuch as Christ is a Person who seeks a relationship with individuals.

But what about the public side of our faith? For example:

- How do we as believers live as Christians in the public arenas—work, community, relationships, civic responsibilities, and so on?
- What about our communities of faith, such as our churches? How vibrant and strategic is our collective witness as God's people to a watching world?
- In what ways do we as believers influence our society as a whole—its institutions, its needs, and its values?

These are broad, complex questions that have no easy answers. But we cannot afford to ignore them—not when we consider the public side of Jesus' ministry. Unlike others of His day who withdrew from society to practice and perfect their own private spirituality (such as the Essenes, see Matt. 16:1), Jesus actively engaged His culture. He participated in its rituals. He focused His work on its cities. He interacted with its leaders. He welcomed its crowds (as seen in Matt. 14:13–14). He particularly reached out to its poor—not only the financially poor but the "poor in spirit," those left behind, those left without hope.

In short, Jesus not only affects our private lives, but our public lives as well. We need to recover that dimension of the gospel today. As believers we are no longer simply individuals, but have been made part of a "royal priesthood" and a "holy nation." Out of those who were once "no people," we are now "the people of God" (1 Pet. 2:9–10). We need to discover how to live out our faith in visible, public ways, as the collective people of God, in order to powerfully impact our world.

COMPANIONSHIP

The Value of Companionship

People these days often celebrate the myth of rugged independence, praising the self-made, self-reliant individual. Yet whatever feats people may accomplish on their own, far greater achievements are won by dedicated, united teams working together toward common goals.

The writer of Ecclesiastes recognized this. He placed a high value on companionship for four reasons:

Greater productivity. No matter how hard a single person works, he can rarely do as much as two people working together (Eccl. 4:9). A team has to expend far less effort to achieve the same results, and a team can maximize results through increased efficiency.

Access to immediate assistance. Sooner or later everyone fails. It is only human to do so. But if someone is alone in failure, the results can be devastating—not just to the product, but to the person. However, by working in partnership with others, people have a buffer against failure. It is less likely to occur, and when it occurs, companions are standing by to offer consolation, and to help their friend get back on track (Eccl. 4:10).

Human comfort. The world can be a cold place. It can tear people apart without a second thought. That's why it helps to have companions. They can offer comfort when life is harsh, not necessarily by anything they say, but just by being there (Eccl. 4:11).

Security. The world can be indifferent, but it can also be dangerous. One need not even go looking for trouble; trouble can come stalking on its own. But wolves tend to attack the solitary sheep, not the entire flock. That's why it makes sense to travel through life in the company of others (Eccl. 4:12). There is safety in numbers.

Have you made the effort to establish a solid, lasting friendship with one or two other people? If not, you are missing out on some valuable benefits that God intended for you. It is not wrong to be alone, or to be independent by nature. But all human beings need someone with whom to share themselves. That is how God has made us.

COMPASSION

A Prophet's Anguish

The prophets of the Bible have sometimes been stereotyped as angry people whose lives were devoted to scolding others. Jeremiah does not fit that profile. As he reflected on the tragic destruction that was coming on Jerusalem, he was not gloating with a sense of "I can't wait," but rather was full of tears and tender sympathy (Jer. 9:1). His heart was broken over the slaughter that he knew was coming.

Nor did the prophet forsake his fellow citizens as they faced their peril. He may have wished to flee to a wilderness retreat (Jer. 9:2), but instead he stood by the doomed people of Jerusalem.

Jeremiah, the weeping prophet, well illustrates the true messengers of the Lord who agonize over the pain and suffering they can foresee. They are not driven by rage, but by compassion for people. They may have to deliver unpleasant news, but their aim is to heal people, not hurt them.

Abandoned

Disease and suffering can bring families together, but they can also tear families apart. This is often the case for those whose problems are largely the result of their own choices, especially choices that have gone against what the family would have wanted.

David saw his family torn apart by choices he had made (Ps. 38:11–12), even as his body was ravaged by sickness, possibly an acute skin disease (Ps. 38:3, 5, 7). Yet however serious his physical problems may have been, they were overshadowed by the pain of his troubled heart (Ps. 38:8, 10). Worst of all, he was unable to communicate his true thoughts and feelings (Ps. 38:13–14).

Have sin and its consequences created distance between the members of your family? Has someone been abandoned to suffering because of anger or disapproval by the others? Psalm 38 offers several insights for redeeming the situation.

First, the psalmist who cries out is willing to confess his own sin and foolishness (Ps. 38:3–5, 18). This is crucial in cases where someone's sickness or suffering is the result of sin. That sin needs to be acknowledged, confessed, and repented of (compare James 5:13–16).

But the psalm offers hope in the certainty that God sees and hears, even if family members cannot or will not (Ps. 38:15). This hope in the Lord is available not only to the sufferer, but to innocent bystanders as well, such as parents, spouses, or children. By trusting in God's goodness, they can see themselves no longer as victims, but as victors.

Finally, Psalm 38 challenges all of us not to abandon anyone to silent suffering in sin and sickness. The psalm may express David's predicament, but it also reminds us of the plight of everyone who has ever been brought low by their own foolishness. Rather than stand aloof from someone with the attitude, "You made your bed; now lie in it," we can draw near with understanding and compassion. Psalm 38 can help us respond to the plea of a lonely sinner, "Remember me."

Competition vs. Compassion

Do you compete to prove your significance? Do you crave greatness? Do you measure your self-worth not only by whether you win, but by how much?

Jesus saw that His followers were in the grip of this common way of thinking (Luke 9:46). So He placed a child in front of them and affirmed that childlikeness is more desirable to God than competition. He went so far as to state that welcoming the child in His name would be like welcoming Him. While the disciples aspired to positions of power and prestige, their Lord exalted the humble act of serving a child as more important.

Jesus calls us to follow a very different value system than our world's. Position, success, and beating the competition fade in comparison to caring for those around us who are weak and forgotten. He beckons us as His followers to replace competition with compassion.

Who near you needs affirmation and help?

Remembering Our Frailty

Perhaps you have attended a graveside service in which the minister committed the dead person's body to the grave with the words, "Ashes to ashes, and dust to dust."

This saying recognizes the reality of human mortality and the frailty of human life.

David was keenly aware of the human condition, and of the way God keeps it in mind in His dealings with His people (Ps. 103:14). The psalmist could trust God to do that because he knew that God is a God of mercy (Ps. 103:11). The Hebrew word for mercy means that the Lord remains loyal to those with whom He makes a covenant. He does not take advantage of their weakness as human beings.

In a similar way, we as God's people are challenged to extend mercy to others. We do that by living up to our promises, and by doing good for others (Is. 1:17; Matt. 5:44; Gal. 6:10). We also do it by mercifully recognizing the frailty and fallibility of every person with whom we ever enter into an agreement. Just as God "knows our frame" and "remembers that we are dust," so we need to remember that everyone who makes a promise to us is also "dust"—weak and prone to failure. Therefore, we should mercifully pardon them when they fall short of fulfilling their intended commitments, thereby covering a multitude of sins (1 Pet. 4:8).

Support the Weak

Paul begins the concluding words of his letter with four sharp exhortations (1 Thess. 5:14). The "unruly"—the lazy, the undisciplined, those looking for a free ride—need a bit of a jolt. (Paul later gave them one in 2 Thess. 3:6–12.) Those who are losing heart need encouragement. And everyone needs patience.

But Paul's third directive, "uphold the weak," has to do with one's responsibilities toward the poor. Wherever Scripture raises this issue, it challenges us to share at least some of our material wealth with people in desperate need. It is the only Christlike response there is.

Indeed, Christ serves as the ultimate model of compassion. He even staked His credibility on His work among the downtrodden and destitute when John the Baptist inquired as to whether He was the Christ.

Paul hardly needed to challenge the Thessalonian believers to be generous. He knew by experience that even though they lived in deep poverty, they were willing to give "beyond their ability" (2 Cor. 8:3) to help others in need.

If the Thessalonians, poor as they were, could give "beyond their ability," what should affluent believers today be giving?

*For more on this topic, see **ANGER**, "Compassion and Anger in One Person?" page 21.*

COMPETITION

Daniel Spares His Competitors

In politics and government today it is frequently expected that one must do whatever it takes to neutralize and, if possible, eliminate the opposition. "Don't get mad—get even!" seems to be the motto of the day. As a result, officeholders, candidates, lobbyists, and special interest groups often wage "total war" in which the only objective seems to be to win at any cost—even if it means smearing an opponent's character or hobbling the person through dirty tricks.

However, as rough-and-tumble as politics might be today, things were far worse in ancient kingdoms such as Babylon. In those days, the price of losing a political battle was not merely a loss of power or electability; often it was the loss of one's life (Dan. 6:24; compare Esth. 7:10).

This is the world in which Daniel lived and served, and he was keenly aware of the stakes involved. It is interesting, then, to consider his reaction to the news of Nebuchadnezzar's decree to execute all the wise men of Babylon (Dan. 2:12–13). Daniel could have allowed the king's edict to eliminate many of his opponents, whose occult-based advice (2:2) competed with his own godly counsel (Dan. 2:17–18). Instead, he pleaded with Arioch to stop the killing and allow him to speak with the king (Dan. 2:24). Thus he saved the lives of pagan sorcerers who were in fact his enemies (compare Dan. 3:8).

Would you have done the same? Consider how you regard and treat your opponents and competitors. Are you committed to their destruction? Or can you look beyond ideologies and political jockeying and see the people involved? Daniel shows the way to fulfilling the admonition of Scripture: "If your enemy is hungry, feed him; if he is thirsty, give him a drink" (Rom. 12:20; compare Matt. 5:43–48).

Who Gets the Credit?

Paul pointed out that the work of planting the church at Corinth was a joint venture between himself, Apollos, and the Lord (1 Cor. 3:5–8). Actually, many others were involved as well. But the point was that cooperation, not competition, is what God desires.

Paul was speaking about the start-up of a church, but the principles apply in the workplace as well. An attitude of competition worries about who gets the credit for success, which is really a selfish concern. By contrast, cooperative efforts over time generally result in achievements far greater than what any individual could do in isolation. That's because the skill, insight, and energy in an organization's work force have enormous potential. But that potential will never be realized if everyone's chief objective is to take credit for results.

Who gets the credit where you work? Do you promote cooperation toward mutual goals rather than competition between individual agendas?

COMPROMISE

Aiming to Please

Success is pleasing, and we often obtain success by pleasing others—our bosses, customers, shareholders, and so forth. But who do you most seek to please? Yourself? Other people? Or God? Conflict is not always inevitable. Sometimes you can, with integrity, please all of these. But sometimes there is a dilemma because it's not always possible to please everybody. Preferences and standards may contradict each other. So when you have to make the tough decision about whom to please and therefore whom to displease, perhaps a better question is, how much does pleasing God really matter to you?

"All Will Be Yours"

Satan promised to give Jesus authority over all the kingdoms of the world. "The father of lies" spoke the truth when he boldly declared, "This has been delivered to me, and I give it to whomever I wish" (Luke 4:6). He neglected, of course, to mention who had delivered the world powers to him—God the Son Himself, who possessed authority over the entire created universe (Col. 1:15–17)!

No wonder Jesus turned him down, one might say. But notice: Jesus did not respond by laying claim to His rightful authority. No, rather than focusing on the substance of the offer, He responded to its cost. To accept it would have required idolatry—a violation of His Father's unique position as the Lord God who alone deserves worship.

Jesus' response compels us to ask: When we receive an enticing offer that, in effect, promises "all will be yours" (Luke 4:7), what do we focus on—the benefits or the costs? The benefits may be extremely attractive. But what are the costs? Does it involve "selling out" our Lord by compromising His commands, His values, or His honor? If so, then the cost is simply too high, and we need to respond as He did: "Get behind me, Satan!"

"Everybody's Doing It"

People sometimes excuse or justify their immoral behavior with the attitude that "everybody's doing it." But that notion is false. Not everyone is doing it. Not everyone is giving way to popular opinion. Some people maintain their moral convictions—even those that are not based on specific biblical teachings.

Jeremiah shows us an example. The wicked people of Judah were faithless when it came to keeping the covenant, so God gave them a case study in loyalty. He told Jeremiah to offer wine to a group of people called the Rechabites (Jer. 35:2), a family descended from Jonadab the son of Rechab (Jer. 35:6). The Rechabites refused Jeremiah's offer (as God knew they would), based on a centuries-old tradition established by their ancestor.

In the days following King Ahab's evil rule in Israel, God raised up Jehu (see 2 Kin. 9:2) to completely destroy Ahab's descendants. In carrying out this task—which Jehu did with zeal—he recruited Jonadab to join with him (2 Kin. 10:15–117). Perhaps to display his loyalty to the Lord, Jonadab commanded his descendants to refrain from drinking any alcohol, and to live in tents as nomads (Jer. 35:6–7), just as the Israelites had lived in former times. The Lord did not command Jonadab or his family to live this way. Jonadab established these rules, and his descendants followed them of their own free will.

Thus the Rechabites showed that it is possible to remain faithful and obedient to God, no matter what other people may be doing. After all, if this family could remain loyal to convictions that were not even prescribed by God, then surely the rest of the people could hold fast to beliefs and standards that God had commanded (Jer. 35:12–16).

The same principle applies today. Here and there in modern society, we find groups of people who steadfastly maintain traditions or lifestyles that they have inherited from their ancestors. They go about their business seemingly undeterred by the fads and fashions of the surrounding culture. But if these groups are able to hold onto their convictions, is there any reason why those of us who claim to follow Christ should not maintain the moral standards and doctrinal truths that the Lord has established in Scripture?

In Whom Do You Trust?

The encounter between the emissaries of Assyria and those of Judah was a high-level, high-stakes meeting involving the fate of nations (2 Kin. 18:17–18). A dramatic struggle was taking place between the seen and the unseen, between confidence in military might and faith in God.

The Assyrian chief of staff asked the Jewish leaders to relay an important question to King Hezekiah: "In whom do you trust?" (2 Kin. 18:19). It was a question worth pondering. Hezekiah's reign, like most of those before his, was marked by spiritual inconsistency. Periods of great trust in God alternated with times of compromise and collusion with the enemies of God.

The same had been true of the northern kingdom of Israel, which had relied on Egypt (rather than the Lord) for protection from the Assyrians (2 Kin. 17:1–4). The result was the capture of Israel's capital and the deportation of the people into captivity (2 Kin. 17:5–6).

The question, In whom do you trust? is still worth pondering today. God's people have many things vying for their allegiance and confidence: education, money, career status, political power, military might, and technology, to name but a few. Each of these

has its place. But ultimately, in what do we place our trust? What is our confidence? If we give up on God's provision and power, we make the same mistake as the ancient Israelites.

CONFESSION

Confessions That Bring Healing

What does it mean to tell God, "I'm sorry," and admit that we have sinned? Samuel's confrontation of Saul about sins that Saul had committed and responsibilities that he had betrayed (1 Sam. 15:17–31) makes an interesting study in confession.

Saul acknowledged his error and described its source: fear of his people rather than of God's commands (1 Sam. 15:24, 30). Samuel informed Saul that he would lose his kingship because of what he had done (1 Sam. 15:22–31). Here we see an example of sin's long-lasting consequence regardless of confession and forgiveness.

What things do you need to confess before God? What areas of your life do you need to examine as to whether you are following God's ways? Remember, the Lord delights in forgiving repentant sinners (1 John 1:9). Therefore, give Him the gift of your own brokenness and receive the refreshment of His forgiveness and acceptance. Read Psalm 51 for more on what it means to be cleansed by God from sin.

Corporate Confession

In thinking about the sins of one's ancestors, a common tendency is to resist the sense of personal responsibility. "I'm not to blame for what happened back then. I wasn't even born yet! My forebears may have committed various evils, but they have to bear responsibility for those, not me."

While that argument is not totally without merit, the Bible teaches that there is such a thing as corporate sin—an entire group of people being held accountable for the sins of some of their members. And if there is corporate sin, then there is a need for corporate confession.

Lamentations offers an example of corporate confession. Jeremiah speaks in terms of personal sin and sorrow: "I rebelled. . . . Behold my sorrow" (Lam. 1:18). Likewise, "I have been very rebellious" (1:20). But clearly Jeremiah was identifying with his people. His first-person statements reflect a sense of collective guilt for what the nation of Judah as a whole has done.

God's people today also bear corporate responsibility. We may not have contributed directly to wrongs committed in the past, but just as we inherit benefits from our predecessors, so we must accept legacies of sin. Like Jeremiah, we can humbly make confession and seek healing for what "we-as-a-people" have done, and recognize the consequences that may still be with us as a result of past sins.

In addition, we do well to think carefully about how we conduct our own lives, knowing that today's choices may affect our children's children.

Out of the Depths

How should we tell God we are sorry for something we have done (or not done), or that we need His help? Is there a right way or a wrong way to come before Him? Does God even want to hear about our weaknesses, failures, and sin?

The psalms record a number of prayers offered "out of the depths" of human pain and moral misery (Ps. 130:1). They not only demonstrate that God lends an ear to honest prayers of brokenness and failure, but they also provide a model for how we might express ourselves to Him.

- Psalm 6: A plea for help in the midst of illness.
- Psalm 10: An expression of perplexity over the success of the wicked and a prayer for blessing.
- Psalm 35: A prayer for help when under attack or in conflict.
- Psalm 51: A confession of sin and plea for cleansing.
- Psalm 102: A prayer in the midst of depression.
- Psalm 130: A cry to God out of deep guilt.
- Psalm 143: A prayer about inadequacy and failure.

God delights to hear His people call upon Him. He is not embarrassed by our troubles or failures. In fact, He invites us to make a sincere confession of sin (1 John 1:5–10). We have nothing to gain by denying or hiding our spiritual needs or by delaying to come before God. So what prayer do you need to pray to Him right now?

CONFIDENCE

Gain Confidence from Perspective

Our troubles can easily cause us to lose the larger picture about life. Daily routines and pressures can create doubts about our significance. And because we are bound in a world of time, it's easy to assume that difficulties such as sickness, conflict, loneliness, insecurity, or fear will become a permanent state of affairs.

The Ephesian believers lived with a lot of pressure. Their faith was born in a crucible of riots, courtroom conflict, and economic change (Acts 19:23–40). Later, when Paul wrote this letter to the Ephesians, he encouraged them to develop and maintain God's perspective on their lives and faith:

- Looking back, he rehearsed what God had done for them before they were even born (Eph. 1:3–8).
- Looking forward, he listed the future benefits that their faith would bring (Eph. 1:9–14).
- In the meantime he prayed that they would be aware of and comprehend these realities, and experience God's power (Eph. 1:15–23). He also prayed that their identity would be rooted in eternal truths and in God's present power in them (Eph. 3:14–21).

What doubts and stresses have caused you to lose perspective? Ephesians suggests that you relax—and join Paul in prayer. Take a look at the big picture of God's work on your behalf. It began long before you arrived and long before your first steps in Christ. It will continue long after you pass from this life. Seeing things in this way can lend perspective to the harsh realities that may dominate your life right now.

Crises of Confidence

If you struggle with a lack of self-confidence, you'll do well to look carefully at Moses' conversation with God when the Lord gave him the task of liberating the Israelites from Egypt (Ex. 3:11–4:17). Moses seriously questioned his ability to carry out the Lord's assignment. He gave God five excuses, each of which indicates a crisis of confidence in a certain area.

The Crisis of Identity. When Moses asked, "Who am I?" (Ex. 3:11), he appears to have had an answer already firm in his mind: "I'm a nobody!" Moses was an Egyptian by upbringing, but he had left behind a reputation for murder and perhaps rebellion. He no longer had influence among Egyptian royalty. Perhaps Moses was like many people today who struggle to integrate their ethnic or cultural heritage into a larger society. Often they go through a crisis of identity and self-doubt.

But God reassured Moses by giving him two strong promises: the promise of His presence and the promise to bring Moses back to the very spot where he was standing (Ex. 3:12). God gives His people today the same strong word of encouragement.

The Crisis of Authority. Moses' second concern was that he wouldn't know what to tell his fellow Hebrews. He especially wondered how he ought to explain who had sent him: "What is [God's] name?" (Ex. 3:13). This was an issue of authority. Why should the people believe an old man coming out of the wilderness claiming to be from God? To meet that concern, God reaffirmed His special role as the Lord God of the Hebrews (Ex. 3:14–18). God is in control. He is the Lord. He rules over all the earth and its people.

The Crisis of Faith. Moses' third concern was that his people would neither believe him (Ex. 4:1). In response, God gave Moses three "signs," or miracles, to perform (Ex. 4:2–9). These supernatural acts would demonstrate God's presence and power.

The Crisis of Communication. Moses' fourth concern had to do with a perceived lack of ability as a spokesperson: "I am not eloquent" (Ex. 4:10). God indicated to Moses that He is the Lord of communication. He promised to be with Moses' mouth in a way that Moses' words would be understood (Ex. 4:11–12). This is an encouragement for all of us who are called to represent the Lord to our associates (1 Pet. 3:15).

The Crisis of Obedience. Moses' final excuse was a clear case of unwillingness to carry out the Lord's command. In effect, he was asking, "Isn't there someone else You could send?" (Ex. 4:13).

Moses' question may seem incredible after all the promises and signs that God had given. Apparently God felt put off, because His anger was kindled as a result of Moses' statement (Ex. 4:14). We can imagine how God must feel when we as believers today resist His clearly revealed will or refuse to carry out His purposes for our lives.

But God had anticipated Moses' reluctance. He had already started Aaron on the way to meet his brother Moses (Ex. 4:14). Perhaps God had intended to surprise Moses with that joyous and encouraging news. Instead, He related the coming of Aaron out of exasperation with Moses' refusal to trust Him.

This conclusion to Moses' conversation with God points to an important truth: Doing God's will is ultimately a matter of obedience. We may have legitimate concerns and needs as we consider God's directives. But after all our issues have been addressed, the question remains: Are we going to obey Him? Thankfully, Moses did obey God (Ex. 7:6), with the result that the Israelites were liberated. What good things, great or small, might God want to accomplish through us if we would but follow His Word and obey His commands?

Peace within the Chaos

We live in a turbulent world. Change is rapid and frequently dramatic. Jesus said that He alone can provide the help and peace we need to live and work with integrity and wholeness (John 14:25–28). Certainly our work cannot be depended on for that. No job is engaging enough, no position powerful enough, and no material rewards substantial enough to give us the kind of inner peace and confidence we long for. Only Christ will never leave us nor forsake us.

Are You Confident of Your Character?

Sooner or later, most of us will run into someone who challenges our integrity and may even question our motives. That can be very unsettling, especially if we know that our character is not above reproach.

Job's friend Eliphaz questioned whether Job was as upright and blameless as he liked to think he was (Job 4:6). He argued that Job wouldn't be suffering if his ways were right before God (Job 4:7–11). But Job was confident that his character was aboveboard. He felt certain that whatever the cause of his troubles, it was not that he was in sin.

As you think about your own reputation and character, where is your confidence? "Reverence" and "integrity" (Job 4:6) go hand in hand. Reverence relates to our respect for God and our passion to honor Him with our lives. Integrity relates to our behavior before other people, whether or not they are watching. By approaching every aspect of our lives with this concern for what God thinks and a commitment to live with purity, we can develop confidence in our character.

CONFLICT

From Conflict to Cohesion

After escaping from Egypt, the children of Israel struggled with numerous problems in the desert that threatened the cohesiveness of their community:

- They complained over a lack of good food (Ex. 16:2–3).
- They quarreled with Moses over water (Ex. 17:2–3).
- Their many needs for arbitration brought Moses to the point of exhaustion (Ex. 18:13–27).
- Impatient over their leader's absence during his stay on Mount Sinai, they fell into idolatry, resulting in judgment from God (Ex. 32:1–35).

So when Moses finally "broke ground" on the monumental task of building the tabernacle and its furnishings, it gave the people a unifying cause to rally around, and also unleashed a tide of generosity (Ex. 36:2–7). As a result, the entire community came together in some encouraging ways. Suddenly the people showed willing hearts (Ex. 35:21, 26), diligence in the work, and generosity that exceeded the needs of the project. In fact, their leaders had to restrain the people from bringing more resources.

Are the people at your workplace consumed with conflict and complaining? What project or cause might draw everyone together and result in care and generous service toward others?

*For more on this topic, see **ARBITRATION**, "Third-Party Mediation," page 25; **DISAPPOINTMENT**, "My Way or No Way!" page 108.*

CONFLICT RESOLUTION

Conflict Resolution

It seems that no matter what one does, conflicts are bound to happen. Peter's report of his visit to Cornelius aroused hostility and opposition among some of the believers at Jerusalem (Acts 11:2–3). His behavior in Joppa, socializing with the hated and feared Gentiles, was unacceptable—even scandalous.

But Peter responded with a clear, honest description of what happened (Acts 11:4–17). He filled in the gaps in their understanding and gently interpreted his activities. As a result, he not only achieved understanding, but created acceptance and approval for the new converts (Acts 11:18).

Is there a need for advocacy, interpretation, or gentle persuasion in your world? Can you be a source of grace and truth between adversaries?

Sedition or Solidarity?

In giving Israel the tabernacle and establishing the sacrificial system, God clearly warned His people that all burnt offerings had to be presented at the door of the tabernacle (Lev. 17:8–9). Thus the altar that the tribes of Gad and Reuben and the half tribe of Manasseh set up east of the Jordan River appeared to be a blatant violation of a divine absolute. The rest of the tribes prepared for civil war (Josh. 22:10–12).

However, the "great, impressive altar" turned out to be nothing more than a monument (Josh. 22:26–27). Rather than forsake the commandments of the Lord, the three tribes had built it so that they and their children would *not* forsake them. They even named the monument Witness as a sign of their commitment (Josh. 22:34).

This incident is interesting in light of conflicts today over when, where, and how Christians should worship and serve the Lord. One group's practice will offend another group, who sometimes appeal to biblical statements to denounce the practice. But a question worth considering is whether the practice leads people toward or away from the Lord.

Perhaps the most important lesson of this incident is the value of talking things over. A young nation was on the verge of civil war, but after both sides had a chance to air their perspectives, hostilities were averted. The same thing could happen today. Christians of different persuasions would do well to ask questions and listen to each other rather than jumping into conflicts that create needless disunity.

For more on this topic, see COUNSEL, "Wise Believers Seek Counsel," page 92.

CONFRONTATION
You Are the Man!

Just as David was a man after God's own heart (1 Sam. 13:14), so Nathan was God's gift to the man after His own heart. Scripture introduces him suddenly when David sought to build a temple to the Lord (2 Sam. 7:1–2). Nathan revealed that God promised to establish David's dynasty, but that He wanted the construction of a temple to be left for Solomon (2 Sam. 7:3–17).

Nathan's next appearance followed David's sin with Bathsheba. He pinpointed David's guilt with the stinging accusation, "You are the man!" Nathan's prophecy concerning David's house (2 Sam. 12:10–12) came to pass with Amnon's rape of Tamar (2 Sam. 13:1–20), Absalom's murder of Amnon (2 Sam. 13:21–29), and Absalom's rebellion against his father and the violation of David's concubines (2 Sam. 15:1–18; 16:20–23).

Nathan helped to prevent another of David's sons, Adonijah, from seizing the throne by reminding the king of his promise to make Solomon his successor (1 Kin. 1:11–27). He then assisted in the crowning of Solomon (1 Kin. 1:32–40) before disappearing from the account.

For more on this topic, see EVASION, "Is Evasion Ethical?" page 133.

CONSCIENCE
Knowing Right from Wrong

The conscience provides our inner awareness of conforming to the will of God or departing from it, resulting in either a sense of approval or condemnation.

The term does not appear in the Old Testament but the concept does. David, for example, was smitten in his heart because of his lack of trust in the power of God (2 Sam. 24:10). But his guilt turned to joy when he sought the Lord's forgiveness (Psalm 32).

In the New Testament the term "conscience" is found most frequently in the writings of the apostle Paul. Some people argue erroneously that conscience takes the place of the external law in the Old Testament. However, the conscience is not the ultimate standard of moral goodness (1 Cor. 4:4). Under both the old covenant and the new covenant the conscience must be formed by the will of God. The law given to Israel was inscribed on the hearts of believers (Heb. 8:10; 10:16), so the sensitized conscience is able to discern God's judgment against sin (Rom. 2:14–15).

The conscience of the believer has been cleansed by the work of Jesus Christ; it no longer accuses and condemns (Heb. 9:14; 10:22). Believers are to work to maintain pure consciences. They also must be careful not to encourage others to act against their consciences. To act contrary to the urging of one's conscience is wrong, for actions that go against the conscience cannot arise out of faith (1 Cor. 8:7–13; 10:23–30).

A Nation Loses Its Conscience

Amos' description of Israel is sobering, if not downright frightening: "They do not know to do right" (Amos 3:10). Wickedness overflows the nation like a mighty river. As a result, the people are drowning in sin. They can no longer tell right from wrong. There is no longer any national conscience.

A nation is on the verge of collapse when good and evil look the same. If questions of right and wrong no longer even enter the people's minds, then that nation is in desperate trouble. In Israel's case, enemies were waiting just around the corner (Amos 3:11–12).

Has your nation lost its conscience? Do people call good bad and bad good? Or can they even tell right from wrong? Or worse, do questions of morality not even concern them? If so, consider how you could act as an agent of conscience. Perhaps you could challenge people to consider their ways, and apprise them of their responsibility to fear God. You may not be received well, but God will honor you for standing up for righteousness.

Matters of Conscience

One noticeable difference between Christianity and most other religions is that Christians are not bound by ritualistic rules. Paul discusses two examples in Romans 14: special days of religious observance (Rom. 14:5–13) and food (Rom. 14:2–4, 14–23). However, the principles he sets forth apply to all matters of conscience, the "gray" areas of life for which Scripture prescribes no specific behavior one way or another.

Special observances and food were apparently trouble spots for the Roman believers. No doubt those from Jewish backgrounds brought their heritage of strict Sabbath-keeping and were shocked to find Gentile believers to whom Sabbath days were inconsequential. Likewise, some from pagan backgrounds may have encouraged the church to form its own counterparts to the festival days they had practiced in their former religions.

The pagan religions of the day offered meat as sacrifices to their idols. The meat was then sold to the general public. But many believers objected to eating such meat, or meat of any kind, lest they give tacit approval to the practice of idolatry. Others, however, saw no problem (Rom. 14:2). Again, Christians lined up on both sides of the issue. Predictably, people began to question each other's spirituality and dispute over whose position was "right" (Rom. 14:1).

Do these situations sound familiar? Perhaps meat sacrificed to idols is not an issue for believers today. But plenty of issues have managed to divide modern believers. Paul offers some principles for settling such disputes:

1. No Christian should judge another regarding disputable things (Rom. 14:3–4, 13). We may have opinions about what is right and wrong. But Christ is the Judge, for us and for others.

2. Each person needs to come to his or her own convictions regarding matters of conscience (Rom. 14:5, 22–23). God has given us a mind and the responsibility to think things through and decide what is best for ourselves in cases where the Scriptures are not clear.

3. We are not totally free to do as we please; we must answer to the Lord for our behavior (Rom. 14:7–8, 12).

4. We should avoid offending others by flaunting our liberty (Rom. 14:13). It is easy to offend believers who lack the knowledge and confidence of their liberty in Christ (Rom. 14:2; 1 Cor. 8:9–12). Even actions that are not inherently sinful can produce sin if they cause others to stumble.

5. We should practice love, pursuing peace in the body and that which builds others up in the faith (Rom. 14:15, 19). Christianity is just as concerned with community and healthy relationships as it is with morality. To be sure, there are matters that are worth fighting for. But where God is either silent or has left room for personal choice, believers need to practice tolerance and consider what is best for all.

For more on this topic, see CHOICES, "Gray Areas," page 56.

CONSEQUENCES

The Consequences of Sin

God never delights in sin, but He does delight in forgiving sin (John 3:16–18; 1 John 1:9). He has promised to remove the believer's guilt "as far as the east is from the west" (Ps. 103:12). Yet even though God deals with the wages of sin (Rom. 6:23), He often leaves us to face the tragic consequences of sin.

Moses and Aaron committed acts that cost them participation in the "land of milk and honey" (Deut. 32:48–52). Even though they doubtless confessed their sins and offered the required sacrifices to atone for them, they still had to face the consequences of their disobedience.

This is sobering lesson for us all. Like Moses and Aaron, we can find forgiveness of sin from God. But we are not immune to the practical effects of our sin. For example, to recover from some sins we may have to live under strong disciplines to avoid repeating the mistakes of the past. Some sins produce indelible physical or emotional marks. Or, like Zacchaeus, we may need to make costly restitution to those we have wronged (Luke 19:1–11). In some cases, we may have to let go of certain relationships that are permanently broken, at least in this world, as a result of what we have done (Rev. 21:4).

Sin does have a price. Christ paid the ultimate penalty for sin on the cross. But when it comes to the practical consequences of our actions, we can often expect to pay for those ourselves.

The Peril of Ignoring Consequences

From time to time newspapers carry tragic stories of people who have fallen into serious trouble by failing to consider the consequences of their actions. Often they admit to the error of their ways with a statement such as, "I didn't think anyone would get hurt"; "I didn't know it was loaded"; "Things just got out of hand"; "I guess we didn't think it through."

The people of Judah failed to think through the consequences of their choices (Lam. 1:9). For generations they ignored the Law's warnings against idolatry, oppressing the poor, cheating in business, relying on foreign governments (especially Egypt) for security, and other sins of public life. They maintained a pretense of worshiping the Lord by keeping up temple rituals, but the reality was that they had turned their backs on God.

The Lord sent numerous prophets to warn His people of impending disaster, but the Judeans routinely ignored them (2 Chr. 36:15–16). As a result, they were shocked when the Babylonians finally came and destroyed their way of life.

As you consider your own life, what consequences are you perhaps ignoring? Is there a relationship that needs healing, a problem that needs to be solved, a habit that needs to be broken or established, or a decision that needs to be made? Procrastination will only invite sudden disaster and ruin. Why not get started today on making changes—before it's too late?

CONSERVATION

A Rest for the Land

One of the most unusual laws that God imposed on Israel was a requirement to let the Promised Land lie fallow every seventh year (Lev. 25:2–8). This was not unlike the requirement for the people to rest every seventh day, or Sabbath (Lev. 23:3), and therefore was called the sabbath year or "sabbatical."

The sabbath year seemed to enforce two concepts. First, the land belonged to God (Lev. 25:23). He created it and put it under humanity's management to "tend and keep" it (Gen. 2:15). Even after people first sinned, God charged them with the responsibility of restoring the earth, so far as that is possible, from the effects of the curse, such as natural infertility, weeds, pests, germs, pollution, and the like. Letting the land lie fallow would help in this regard by restoring the ground's nutrients.

A second reason for the sabbath year had to do with dependence on God. To go without a harvest every seventh year would be a powerful reminder that one is ultimately dependent on God. That's why God promised to send three years' worth of harvest in the sixth year—food enough for the remainder of the sixth year, for the unplanted seventh year, and for the first year of the next cycle (Lev. 25:20).

From the standpoint of our highly technological society today, the concept of a sabbath year seems thoroughly out of date. Yet the two truths behind the sabbath year have not changed. Ultimately, God still owns the means of production; we are simply workers using His resources. Likewise, we are still ultimately dependent on Him.

*For more on this topic, see **CREATION**, "Creation: 'Very Good,' but Not Sacred!" page 93.*

CONSPIRACY

Plots and Coups

Access to power—whether in the workplace, family, or community—invariably seems to give rise to schemes and strategies to gain control. The royal court of the northern kingdom of Israel, like other centers of power in the ancient Middle East, was constantly thrown into chaos by intrigue and plots against the kings. The overthrow of Pekah (2 Kin. 15:30) was just one in a long line of coups and coup attempts during the time of the divided kingdom.

- Rehoboam imposed even higher taxes than those levied by his father before him. Ten tribes rejected his leadership and stoned his chief tax collector (1 Kin. 12:12–20).
- When Ben-Hadad, king of Syria, lay sick, he sent his representative Hazael to ask the prophet Elisha about his recovery. Hazael returned with encouraging words, but then murdered his master and gained the throne for himself (2 Kin. 8:7–15).
- After being informed by Elisha that he would become king of Israel, Jehu plotted to overthrow King Joram by killing him at a supposed peace conference (2 Kin. 9:1–29).
- Jehu also purged Israel of Baal worship by inviting prophets of Baal from throughout the land to convene at the temple. After declaring to them his loyalty to Baal, he had his soldiers execute them.
- Pekah came to power by assassinating his predecessor. But during Pekah's rule, Assyria plundered more than half of his land, stripping it of its inhabitants. A conspiracy then rose up and Pekah was assassinated (2 Kin. 15:25–30).

CONTENTMENT

A Lifestyle of Contentment

Paul sounds so positive in Philippians 4:10–13, so confident! It would be easy to assume that life was rosy when he wrote these words. But where was he? According to 1:12–14, in prison—quite possibly in Rome, facing a death sentence!

Given that sobering context, this passage speaks powerfully to the issue of contentment, not only with material possessions, but with circumstances as well.

Paul makes no idle boast here. He knew firsthand the wealth and privileges of prominence in the Jewish community and of Roman citizenship (Phil. 3:4–6; Acts 22:3–5, 25–29; 26:4–5). On the other hand, he had suffered extraordinary hardships in his work—

jailings, beatings, stonings, forcible ejection from several towns, shipwrecks—to say nothing of emotional and spiritual disappointments and setbacks (2 Cor. 11:23–33).

Either extreme would test a person's character. What was Paul's secret? "Christ who strengthens me." Rather than looking to the possessions he had or didn't have, or to his circumstances, good or bad, he looked to Christ to satisfy his needs. The result, he says, was contentment.

This passage poses a strong challenge to Christians living and working in today's society. Some of us live at the upper levels of material prosperity—"abounding," as Paul puts it. The temptation is to forget God (Luke 12:16–21). Likewise, much in our culture urges us to feel discontent with our lot—to long for more, for bigger, for better. Jesus warns against that attitude. On the other hand, failures and disappointments can also draw us away from trusting in the God who cares (see Luke 12:22–34).

"Give Us This Day . . ."

Wisdom tells us that both extremes of wealth and poverty are laden with dangers. Riches can seduce one into disowning God, whereas poverty can reduce one to stealing (Prov. 30:8–9). To avoid either temptation, Agur offered a simple prayer for daily bread with contentment.

Christians today are invited to do the same by thanking God for their daily bread in the tradition of the Lord's Prayer (Matt. 6:11).

CONTRACTS

The New Covenant

Even a casual reader of the Bible soon discovers that it is divided into two major sections, the Old Testament and the New Testament. But how many readers realize that "testament" is just another word for "covenant"? Thus the New Testament describes the new covenant (1 Cor. 11:25), or agreement, that God has made with humanity, based on the death and resurrection of Jesus Christ.

In the Bible, a covenant involves much more than a contract or simple agreement. A contract has an end date, but a covenant is a permanent arrangement. Furthermore, a contract generally involves only one aspect of a person, such as a skill, while a covenant covers a person's total being.

God entered into numerous covenants with people in the Old Testament. For example: with Adam and Eve (Gen. 3:15); with Noah (8:21–22; 2 Pet. 3:7, 15); with Abraham (Gen. 12:1–3); with Israel (Deut. 29:1–30:20); and with David (2 Sam. 7:12–16; 22:51).

The agreement with Israel was especially significant, because it established a special relationship between God and the Hebrews. They were made His "chosen people" through whom He would bring blessing and hope to the rest of the world. However, because the recipients of God's Law could not keep it perfectly, further provision was necessary for them as well as for the rest of humanity.

That's why God promised a new covenant through the prophet Jeremiah. Under the new covenant, God would write His Law on human hearts. This suggested a new level of obedience and a new knowledge of the Lord.

The work of Jesus Christ brought the promised new covenant into being. When Jesus ate His final Passover meal with the Twelve, He spoke of the cup as "the new covenant in My blood" (Luke 22:20), the words that Paul quoted to the Corinthians to remind them of the need for purity and propriety in their worship (1 Cor. 11:25–34).

The new covenant in Jesus' blood rests directly on the sacrificial work of Christ on the Cross (which was prefigured by Israel's system of sacrifices) and accomplishes the removal of sin and the cleansing of the conscience by faith in Him (Heb. 10:2, 22). So every time Christians celebrate the Lord's Supper, they remind themselves that God has fulfilled His promise: "I will be their God, and they shall be My people . . . I will be merciful to their unrighteousness, and their sins and their lawless deeds I will remember no more" (Heb. 8:10, 12; compare Jer. 31:33–34).

For more on this topic, see **COMMITMENT,** *"The Covenant-keeping God," page 71;* **EXPECTATIONS,** *"The Need for Clear Contracts," page 138.*

CONVERSION
Christians and Social Conditioning

Paul's statement that he persecuted the church prior to his conversion (1 Cor. 15:9–10) is a strong piece of evidence against the commonly held notion that religious preference is mainly a result of upbringing.

Without question, cultural circumstances play a part in people's religious beliefs. But can social conditioning alone explain why people believe and behave as they do? After all, a Christian upbringing is no guarantee that a person won't someday abandon the faith. On the other hand, countless people who have had no exposure to Christianity in their youth nevertheless convert as adults.

Christian conversion is much misunderstood. It is often regarded as sudden, irrational, selective, and even illusory. But what are its essential elements? Paul's experience is instructive. While certain aspects of his conversion were unique, four elements stand out that are present in every authentic conversion:

- *His conversion touched his conscience.* Paul recognized that he had been fighting God and that his vicious treatment of Christians was wrong (Acts 26:9–11; 1 Tim. 1:13).
- *His conversion touched his understanding.* He discovered that the Jesus he was persecuting was no less than the risen Messiah, the Son of God (Acts 9:22).
- *His conversion touched his will.* He gave in to Jesus and began following Him (26:19–20).
- *His conversion produced noticeable change in his life.* His ambitions, his character, his relationships, his outlook—everything changed as a result of his encounter with Christ (Phil. 3:7–11).

But suppose, as some have, that it all amounts to nothing but an illusion? Three tests can be applied to determine whether religious experience in general and Christianity in particular is illusory.

First, there is the test of history. Christianity makes historical claims. There is nothing illusory about Jesus or His impact on the world. His death and resurrection are well attested. Nor is there any doubt about the reality of the church.

A second test is the test of character. When drunkards become sober and crooks become honest, when self-centered people become generous and unbelievers become giants of faith, it is very difficult to explain this away as illusion.

Finally there is the test of power. Delusions and neuroses tend to destroy people's character. They produce unbalanced behavior and keep people from achieving their goals. Christianity has precisely the opposite effect. It makes people whole. It even enables people to face death with confidence and courage.

History, character, power: these cannot be attributed to social conditioning. Rather they strongly suggest that something far deeper lies behind Christianity, something good, powerful, and alive.

The Responsibility for Conversion

Do you stagger under a heavy load of expectation that you alone (or that you primarily) are responsible for bringing your friends and coworkers to faith? Do you feel guilty because you can't get them converted? If so, you may be surprised to discover that not even Jesus felt that kind of load for the lost!

While explaining how people enter the kingdom, Jesus clearly declared that it is God the Father who draws them (John 6:44). That means that people's response to the gospel does not depend primarily on you or on Jesus. Elsewhere, Jesus taught that:

- "All that the Father gives Me will come to Me" (6:37).
- "No one can come to Me unless it has been granted to him by My Father" (6:65).

Clearly, the responsibility for conversion ultimately belongs to the Father. Then is there anything we can do as Christ's followers to motivate others toward the Savior? Yes, we can give evidence of how God works in our lives as we grow. We can offer clear, truthful information about the gospel as we have opportunity. And we can invite and even urge others to believe.

But the ultimate responsibility for salvation is God's, not ours. So relax! Live the faith, talk about it, and offer it to others. But let the dynamic of conversion be from God alone.

CONVICTION
Values in the Workplace

Perhaps in no other area do we as Christians today have as great an opportunity to influence people around us as in our ethics and morality in the workplace. How we behave on the job tells others everything they need to know about our values and commitments. The question is, are we standing for what is right?

Daniel and his three companions made up their minds to stand for godly values right from the start of their careers (Dan. 1:8). As ambassadors-in-training in Babylon, they declined to eat the specially prepared food provided by the government. Scripture does not tell us why. It may be that the food had been offered to idols or blessed by the pagan priests. That would have made it ritually unclean according to the Jewish Law, and to eat it would have been a compromise of their faith. Another possibility is that accepting the provisions would have been a sign of loyalty to King Nebuchadnezzar, and a means by which the foursome would have been obligated to his service.

The exact reasons why they found the food objectionable matter little. The important point is that once they realized that eating it would result in "defilement," they took a stand. They refused to just "go along to get along."

Therein lies the real challenge of workplace ethics today. Occasionally we may struggle to discern the right from the wrong, which is a matter of the intellect. But most of the time our need is to summon the conviction and the courage to do what we know is right, which is a matter of the will. Ultimately, ethics and morality have less to do with the head than with the heart. Daniel and his friends settled in their hearts what they needed to do and not do, based on biblical principles. As a result, they were able to carry out a plan with tough-minded resolve. In other words, they showed some moral backbone.

You can do that! As you face ethical choices where you work, you can choose to stand for what is right. It may cost you, but God will give you the strength to deal with whatever consequences come your way. Furthermore, the cost of losing your integrity is infinitely greater than whatever it costs you to keep it.

For more on this topic, see DEATH, "Death Threats," page 98.

COOPERATION

(see also Teamwork)

Leaders Build Community

In many Western countries of the twentieth century, the labor force often has been sharply divided between management and labor. One problem of this rigid distinction is that it tends to create a mentality of "us" versus "them." History shows that most of the greatest achievements of humanity have been accomplished by teams and communities of people working together toward common ends.

Nehemiah understood the power of community as he undertook the task of rebuilding Jerusalem's walls. After surveying the situation, he gathered the people and gave a speech in which he mobilized the community around the rebuilding project. First he raised their awareness that something *should* be done, then he instilled confidence in them that something *could* be done—by them (Neh. 2:17–18).

It is interesting to notice that Nehemiah spoke in terms of "we" and "us," even though in his written account he used "they" and "them." Clearly he saw himself as a participant in the dire circumstances, even though he had just arrived from the royal palace. In fact, he bridged the class division between himself and his people by sharing the discussion he had had with the king, thereby showing that the people had a friend in the royal court.

If you are in a leadership position, have you learned how to break down walls that divide, and instead build community? Like Nehemiah, do you know how to overcome communication barriers? Do you address individuals and families by name, involve people right where they live, respect their limitations, and take a personal interest in their circumstances?

United for the Work

Working without phones, faxes, cars, or planes, a dedicated, diverse team of first-century believers spread the good news about Jesus throughout the Roman world. Paul mentioned several of these coworkers to Titus—Artemas, Tychicus, Zenas the lawyer, and Apollos (Titus 3:12–13)—but there were many others; for example, Barnabas (see Acts 4:36–37), Priscilla and Aquila (see Rom. 16:3–5), Silas (see Acts 15:34), and Junia (see Rom. 16:7).

The task of proclaiming the gospel in the face of sometimes fierce opposition knit these early believers together. They planned their travel not only around the tasks of ministry, but also around their relationships with each other. For example, Paul encouraged Titus to come to him at Nicopolis during a seasonal break (Titus 3:12). They also took care to provide necessities for each other (Titus 3:13).

The principle emerges from this pattern that the cause of Christ goes forward even in the face of opposition when the workers are united for the work.

For more on this topic, see COALITION, "A Remarkable Coalition," page 67; COMMITMENT, "Singleness of Heart," page 70; COMPETITION, "Who Gets the Credit?" page 80.

CORRUPTION

A Nation Sells Its Soul

What would you say about a country where justice is for sale, truth depends on what you can afford, and spirituality is determined by your ability to pay? You might say that such a land had sold its soul. When even the moral values of a culture are defined in terms of money, then the society is in deep trouble.

Judah was a deeply troubled society in Micah's day. Three categories of leaders—the judges, the priests, and the prophets—had put their services up for sale (Mic. 3:11). The issue was not that they were being paid; obviously they needed to earn a living. But they had corrupted their *offices* by allowing money to distort their leadership. Rather than saying what was true, right, and just, they said whatever they were paid to say. They grew wealthy from their positions, but their integrity went bankrupt.

The amazing thing was that these so-called leaders somehow believed that the Lord would continue to underwrite their hypocritical ways. They brushed off the warnings of an impending invasion by a foreign army that Micah and other prophets were giving. "Is not the LORD among us?" they replied. "No harm can come upon us."

But they were sorely mistaken. The Lord had written them off in their impenitence. He was not about to allow them to go on violating His Law and still enjoy peace and affluence.

Do you see any parallels between ancient Judah and our own society today? If you are in a position of leadership, especially where you are rendering moral and ethical decisions or giving advice, consider whether you ever allow money to taint your official responsibilities. If so, remember that the Lord has been known to deal with corrupt leaders.

A Nation in Decline

Those who speak of a moral and spiritual decline in society today might want to borrow a page from the Book of Hosea. The prophet denounced ancient Israel by heaping up metaphors that sound a lot like what is being said about modern culture. He described Ephraim (Israel) as:

- *Corrupted* (Hos. 7:8). Israel "mixed" itself with surrounding nations by allowing their pagan religions to corrupt its religious and spiritual life. In doing so, God's people violated the first and second commandments (Ex. 20:3–4). They also formed political alliances to prop up their defenses rather than relying on the Lord (for example, 2 Kin. 16:5–6).
- *Half-baked* (Hos. 7:8). An unturned cake was like a pancake that is burned on one side and gooey on the other. Israel was half-baked in that its prosperity under Jeroboam II was purely material and not at all spiritual. Its vapid, self-absorbed culture had nothing significant to offer.
- *Weakened and feeble* (Hos. 7:9). The "aliens" (Hebrew, zarim) mentioned by Hosea were foreign "allies" such as Assyria and Egypt who seemed to be friends but were actually enemies (2 Kin. 15:17–20; 17:3–4). These nations "devoured" Israel's strength by requiring heavy pay-

ments and tribute. Yet this "aging process" occurred imperceptibly over a period of about forty years, so that the Israelites hardly even noticed their loss of power.
- *Arrogant* (Hos. 7:10). Despite the many reversals that took place between the prosperous reign of Jeroboam II (c. 793–753 B.C.) and the foolish reign of Hoshea, Israel's last king (c. 732–722 B.C.), the nation lived with an illusion of strength and virility. The people arrogantly resisted the Lord right up to the end of their kingdom (2 Kin. 17:13–18).

No nation can survive for very long when it actively turns away from God. The experience of Israel shows that material prosperity is not enough to sustain a culture. Without godliness at the core, a society has to keep propping itself up with expensive yet unreliable crutches. Sooner or later, though, moral weakness will bring it down—proud and foolish to the end.

CO-SIGNING FOR LOANS

(*see* Loans)

COUNSEL

Wise Believers Seek Counsel

If you've ever tried to resolve a deep-seated controversy, you may have found how easy it is to "agree to disagree" over a highly controversial issue, but how difficult it is to actually carry that out. It takes concerted effort. In his exchange with the apostles at Jerusalem (Gal. 2:1), Paul demonstrated how believers should honor one another by seeking each other's counsel, especially when strong convictions and difficult issues are at stake.

In this situation, Jewish followers of Christ were finding that their faith was influenced by deeply rooted ethnic and cultural bias against Gentiles. Paul had once been a champion of Judaism (Gal. 1:13–14), but then became "the apostle to the Gentiles" (Gal. 1:15; see Acts 13:2–3). Paul came to Jerusalem to meet with the leaders of the Jewish believers and discuss his activities.

Note several elements in the encounter between the two different positions:

- Paul voluntarily went to the leaders of the other side (Gal. 2:1–2).
- He met privately to discuss a potentially volatile situation (Gal. 2:2).
- He sought the input of recognized leaders (Gal. 2:2–9).
- He evaluated his position and behavior in light of God's truth, in order to avoid working "in vain" (Gal. 2:2).
- He brought along an actual test case, uncircumcised Titus, which caused some to demand that Titus conform to the Jewish rite of circumcision (Gal. 2:3–5).
- Clarity was achieved, but in this case it did not require uniformity of practice (Gal. 2:9).
- The leaders reached agreement on another matter, serving the poor among both Jews and Gentiles (Gal. 2:10).

Commitment to Christ calls for believers to pay each other honor and respect. Even if they decide to "agree to disagree," they still need each other.

*For more on this topic, see **ADVISORS**, "The Wisdom of Taking Counsel," page 10.*

COURAGE

"Give Me This Mountain!"

Caleb is a case study in unflinching faithfulness and seasoned courage. When the entire nation wanted to quit its journey at Kadesh Barnea and return to Egypt, he and Joshua (see Josh. 1:1) stood against them, convinced that God would deliver on His promise to give them the land (Num. 13:30; 14:6–9). As the older man, Caleb was probably the spokesperson, even though Joshua became the successor to Moses.

As a result of his courageous stand for God, Caleb not only entered Canaan but helped Moses divide the land (Num. 34:16, 19) and led his people, Judah, in the possession of their territory. God seemed to prolong Caleb's life as a reminder to a younger generation that He fulfills His word.

Convinced of that truth, 85-year-old Caleb could be heard to cry, "Give me this mountain!" as he looked upon Hebron (see Gen. 23:19). Once granted his request, he boldly drove out the Anakim who lived there—a direct response to the timidity shown by his peers forty years earlier at Kadesh, who wailed about "giants" in the land (Num. 13:31–33; Josh. 14:12; 15:13–14). In the end, Caleb's persevering faith won out over both the size of his enemies and the fear of his friends.

*For more on this topic, see **CONVICTION**, "Values in the Workplace" page 90.*

COVENANT

(*see also* Contracts)

The Freedom of the New Covenant

Have you ever noticed how terms like "binding," "enforceable," and "limits" tend to make their way into negotiations of contracts and agreements? Words like that suggest that contracts rarely free people, but rather hedge them in with terms and commitments.

The Bible presents two contracts, called *covenants*, between God and people: the old covenant (Heb. 9:1) described in the Old Testament ("testament" means covenant), which was based on God's Law, and the new covenant described in the New Testament, which is based on God's grace.

Actually, God's new covenant differs from a contract in that it is one-sided in initiative, not unlike a conqueror declaring the terms of victory. However, God's covenant is vastly different from a victor's terms in that God's driving motivation is love, grace, and the desire to restore people into His family.

Based on His new covenant, God offers the forgiveness of sins and eternal life to all who respond and place faith in Jesus. Have you responded? Is there someone you need to tell about God's offer?

*For more on this topic, see **AGREEMENT**, "A Done Deal," page 14; **CONTRACTS**, "The New Covenant," page 88.*

CRAFTSMANSHIP

(*see* Excellence)

CREATION

Creation: "Very Good," but Not Sacred!

When God made the world, He declared it to be "very good" (Gen. 1:31). But is the universe itself divine? Is Mother Nature sacred? No, because God made the world and its natural systems out of nothing (Heb. 11:3). Nor is the creation self-sustaining; it depends on God for its continued existence (Col. 1:17; Heb. 1:3).

This means that:

1. People can work only within the framework of preexisting physical realities. Humans are not God, and cannot call things into existence from what was nonexistent.

2. The universe is not God. Some philosophies and religions teach that the material universe and all it contains are a form of God, and/or that every human, animal, plant, and object contains a piece of God. But God is distinct from His creation.

3. The earth is not sacred. Some conservationists ascribe a false value to creation by treating the earth and its flora and fauna as sacred. God wants humanity to manage the earth carefully, but not because the earth is sacred.

4. The earth is a resource that God has given humans to manage. God has called His creation "very good" and has placed it under our rule for His glory and our benefit (Gen. 1:26–30). We are to tend it, cultivate it, conserve it, reshape it, mine it, and consume it with the certainty that each of us will give a full accounting to God for what we do with and to His world (Rom. 14:11–12; 1 Cor. 4:5).

CREEDS

*For more on this topic, see **ANIMALS,** "Learning from Creation," page 23.*

CREEDS
Creeds and Confessions

King Asa and the people of his day renewed their covenant with the Lord by taking an oath that declared their revitalized commitment (2 Chr. 15:13–15). This formal oath was apparently spoken or shouted in unison, punctuated by blasts from trumpets and rams' horns.

The intent of Asa's oath was similar to that of other creeds and confessions that believers have used down through the ages to formally state their beliefs and publicly declare their spiritual commitments. In fact, God's instruction to the Israelites to *diligently* teach His ways to their children (Deut. 6:6–9) has encouraged many to formulate creedal summaries.

Scripture itself contains numerous assertions of faith:

- The Ten Commandments: These commandments summarize God's moral code.
- Psalm 78: This instructional song about God's faithfulness and the Israelites' unfaithfulness may have been sung or read as a teaching device in ancient Israel.
- 1 Corinthians 15:3–7: Paul labeled his summary of Christ's death, burial, and resurrection as "the gospel" (1 Cor. 15:1), suggesting that these doctrines comprise the core truths of the good news of salvation.
- Ephesians 4:4–6: This affirmation of the nature of the church is a list of seven elements comprising the unity of the body, organized around the three Persons of the Trinity.
- 2 Timothy 2:11–13: This "faithful saying" may have been used by the early church in baptizing new believers.

CRIME
A Law for Criminals and Their Victims

Jailing criminals may protect society and punish offenders, but what does it do for the victims of crime? Wandering Israel had no jails, so it punished criminals in other ways. However, a major part of serving justice was for the offender to make restitution to the wronged person (Num. 5:7).

Restitution involved restoring or repaying losses in a way that made amends for the crime. In that way, the Law took into account both criminal and victim. Ultimately it regarded crimes against property and persons to be "unfaithfulness against the Lord." Note some of the formulae given for restitution under different situations:

- Loss or theft of a beast of burden (for example, an ox killed): Restitution of five times the value.
- Animal grazes in another's field or vineyard: Restitution made from one's own field or vineyard (Ex. 22:5).
- Causing a crop-destroying fire on a neighbor's land: Full restitution of the loss (Ex. 22:6).
- Borrowed animal dies or is injured while in use (in the owner's absence): Payment of full value to the owner (Ex. 22:14–15).
- General crimes against persons: Full restitution plus twenty percent, payable to the victim, next of kin, or the priest (Num. 5:7–9).

Modern-day laws handle crimes and restitution much differently. But quite apart from the criminal justice system, are there situations in your past or present in which paying back someone you have wronged would be appropriate, no matter how difficult?

Making the Punishment Fit the Crime

One of the hardest things for any legal system to do is to devise just penalties. But the laws concerning the theft of animals (Ex. 22:1–4) provides a good case study in making the punishment fit the crime.

The penalty for stealing and then slaughtering or selling an animal was more than double the penalty for stealing an animal and then getting caught. Why would this be? Probably because slaughtering or selling the stolen goods increased the costs of apprehension, trial, and conviction of the thief. It also demonstrated the criminal's determination to avoid repayment. So a heavier punishment was appropriate.

Here we have a solid biblical basis for graduated penalties based on a criminal's attempt to evade capture and conviction.

CRITICISM
Dried-up Friends

Water was the lifeblood of ancient caravans. That made the oasis of Tema (Job 6:19) a popular and indispensable rest stop for Sabean traders traversing the major north-south highway across the Arabian Desert. Their camels could travel up to a week without water, but sooner or later they had to have refreshment. If a caravan came to the watering hole and for some reason found it dry, disaster loomed.

Job was probably quite familiar with the caravans of Sheba. As the wealthiest man in the Middle East (Job 1:3), he probably had traded with them on numerous occasions. Perhaps he had even arranged caravans himself. Likewise, he may have visited Tema; the site was only about three hundred miles to the southeast from Edom, where some believe he lived.

In any case, Job described his disappointment over the lack of kindness shown by his friends (Job 6:14) as like a caravan arriving at a dried-up oasis. Not only expecting but desperately needing water, the weary travelers find only dust. Their hopes dashed and their situation perilous, they face the terrifying prospect of dying of thirst (Job 6:21).

In a similar way, Job turned to his friends in his hour of need, expecting to find much-needed comfort. To his shock, they responded with rebuke and criticism.

CRUELTY
Bloody Assyria

In pronouncing woe on the "bloody city" of Nineveh (Nah. 3:1), Nahum was denouncing the entire culture of the Assyrians for their numerous sins against God and crimes against humanity. These included horrible acts of violence and cruelty designed to terrify and humiliate victims.

Evidence for these atrocities comes from the testimony of Assyria's own kings. For example, Ashurnasirpal II (883–859 B.C.) boasted of dyeing the peaks of mountains red with the blood of his slaughtered enemies. He was known to flay his captives (possibly while they were still alive), and spread their skins on the walls of conquered cities.

Another atrocity cited by Ashurnasirpal, as well as by his successor, Shalmaneser II (859–824 B.C.), was to have the heads of slain enemy warriors cut off and stacked into a pillar in front of a defeated city. Then the conquerors threw boys and girls from the city into bonfires.

Sennacherib (705–681 B.C.), who sent a force against Judah and Jerusalem in the time of Hezekiah (2 Kin. 18:13–19:36), described cutting the throats of his enemies like lambs, and cutting off their lives as one cuts a string. Apparently he took grim pleasure in eviscerating his captives.

Assyrian descriptions of these cruelties might have been exaggerated. Nevertheless, the claims are generally corroborated by murals and other artwork surviving from that era. For example, a frieze depicting the capture and ruination of a city shows the bodies of the enemy impaled and hanging from long stakes. It is believed that this was a precursor to the Roman practice of crucifixion.

D

DANCING
Dancing Before the Lord

Among the Israelites, dancing generally occurred among women, either singly or in groups. It was a way of celebrating joyous occasions. Indeed, dancing became a symbol of joy, the opposite of mourning (Ps. 30:11; Eccl. 3:4; Luke 15:25).

The Bible gives several examples of dancing. Groups of women danced at celebrations of military victories (1 Sam. 18:16). The dancing of the virgins at Shiloh was probably part of a religious celebration (Judg. 21:19–23). Occasionally, children imitated the dance in their play (Job 21:11; Matt. 11:17).

The Bible also gives a well-known example of a man dancing. Wearing a linen ephod (the outer garment worn by priests), David "danced before the LORD with all his might" (2 Sam. 6:14) when the ark of the covenant was brought up to Jerusalem from the house of Obed-Edom.

Dancing by the Israelites was usually accompanied by the rhythmic beating of timbrels—or tambourines (Judg. 11:34). On great national occasions, Israel also praised the Lord with stringed instruments, flutes, and cymbals (Ps. 150:4). Men and women never danced together. Even on those occasions where both sexes participated in the sacred professional dances, they always danced separately (Ps. 68:25; Jer. 31:13). Dancing for sensual entertainment was unheard of in Israel.

Salome's infamous dance, which won her John the Baptist's head on a platter, was in the tradition of Greek dancing, a sensual art form rather than an act of worship (Matt. 14:6).

DEATH

Beyond Death

How should the believer view death? Daniel looked into the future and saw hope in the midst of death. He described the state of the dead in terms of "those who sleep" (Dan. 12:2), which is a metaphor. The "sleep" of death means that the dead will someday "wake up" from their temporary condition and go on to an eternal state—"some to everlasting life, some to shame and everlasting contempt" (Dan. 12:2).

Other Old Testament writers reflect this same view that death is not the end of existence. Some describe it euphemistically as a reunion with one's ancestors (Gen. 15:15; 35:29; 1 Kin. 2:10). Others refer to it in a way that shows they expected to meet God when they died (Ps. 17:15; 73:23–24). Likewise, in the New Testament, Paul used language similar to Daniel's in describing the sleep of death (Eph. 5:14; 1 Thess. 4:13–14).

God does not let death have the final say over us. He invites us into eternal life with Him through the provision of Christ, who died and came back to life in order to deal with our sin and enable us to escape condemnation and death.

Death Loses Its Power

Are you afraid of death? Many people are. Death seems to be the ultimate enemy, taking away our most cherished possession—life it-self. Some people, faced with the inevitability of dying, try to deny what is coming, as if ignoring it would make it go away.

But the Bible faces death head-on. Its pages are filled with accounts of death and dying, of both the good and the bad, the powerful and the weak, kings and paupers, faithful and sinners. Even God confronted the painful reality of death in the crucifixion of His Son, Jesus.

However, the Bible offers hope in the face of death by challenging death's ultimate victory. For example, Hosea promised that God would ransom His faithful people from the power of the grave: "I will redeem them from death," the Lord vowed (Hos. 13:14). The prophet's declaration is actually a taunt song that ridicules death's power.

A number of other biblical writers affirm God's power over death:

- In recording Adam and Eve's sin in the Garden of Eden, which allowed death to enter the world, Moses also recorded God's curse, which included a word of hope: the tempter who brought sin and death into the world would eventually be conquered (Gen. 3:14–15). The implication is that death will not have the final word in this life. God will, through Jesus.
- Isaiah promised that God will "swallow up death forever, and the Lord GOD will wipe away tears from all faces" (Is. 25:8).
- Even as Jeremiah lamented the tragic death of the holy city Jerusalem, he sounded a bright note of hope by reminding his listeners of God's mercies, which are "new every morning." One can "hope in Him," because salvation is from the Lord. (Lam. 3:22–27).
- Paul echoed Hosea's words when he rhetorically asked, "O Death, where is your sting? O Hades, where is your victory?" Then he added, "Thanks be to God, who gives us the victory through our Lord Jesus Christ" (1 Cor. 15:55–57).
- John foresaw the end of death in his vision of a new heaven and new earth (Rev. 21:1, 4).

Because Christ offers everlasting life in His presence to those who believe in Him (John 11:25–26), Christians can sing songs of hope and praise at the funerals of fellow believers. Even as the mourners lament the loss of their loved ones in this life, they can rest in the confidence and hope of being reunited with them in heaven.

Is death the ultimate defeat for you? Or do you have hope in Christ of experiencing the ultimate victory?

Life Is Short

Young people often act like they think they think they are immortal. Likewise, people whose lives are basically going well can be lured into the trap of thinking that the good times will never end. But when sudden difficulties or death confront us, they can shake us into the awareness that life is very short.

Job came to that realization (Job 16:22). The sudden loss of his family, wealth, and health helped him gain perspective on life— and death. For example, he came to see his life as passing more swiftly than a skilled weaver's shuttle as it runs through the loom (Job 7:6). Likewise, he compared his life to the existence of a flower or a passing shadow (Job 14:1–2).

These thoughts may sound morbid, but facing the fact of life's brevity can help us do a better job of living the time that is allotted to us. We don't have to go through the kinds of sufferings that Job did to gain that perspective.

Life is on loan from God. Therefore we do well to understand as much as we can of its length and breadth, its strength and weakness, and its place in human history. By doing so, we can honor the truth of the psalmist who wrote, "My times are in Your hand" (Ps. 31:15).

Death Threats

Sometimes faith in God can be very unpopular. It can even trigger death threats by those who are hostile to the Lord. This kind of violent opposition to the faith still takes place in various countries of the world today, when followers of Christ choose loyalty to their Lord over compromising their convictions.

Jeremiah was threatened with death in reaction to his message of God's impending judgment of Jerusalem and its people (Jer. 26:11). Fortunately, the prophet's influential friends prevented any harm from coming to

him (Jer. 26:16, 24). But many others in Scripture (and throughout history) proved their commitment to God with their blood, as the accompanying table shows. Their sacrifice challenges believers today, especially those who live where they are not openly persecuted, to examine their hearts carefully. Would we be as brave and loyal to the Lord if the penalty for following Him were death?

DEBT

Debt-Free Living

Paul's admonition to owe nothing but love (Rom. 13:8) is a powerful reminder of God's distaste for all forms of unpaid debt.

Usually we think of debt in terms of monetary loans. But in light of the context of this passage (Rom. 13:1–7, 9–10), Paul seems to have a broader view of debt in mind (Rom. 13:7). He speaks to us of:

- Taxes, levies placed on us by governing authorities, such as income and social security taxes
- Customs, tolls and tariffs arising from trade and business, such as highway tolls, airport landing fees, and import fees
- Fear, the respect we owe to those who enforce the law, such as police officers and military personnel
- Honor, the praise we owe to those in high authority, such as judges and elected officials.

All of us are debtors to God's grace. As He has shown us love, we need to extend love to those around us with whom we live and work—even those who tax and govern us.

Freely You Have Received, Freely Give

Modern-day investors and financiers pay close attention to interest rates, as vast sums of money stand to be gained or lost by even the slightest movement. In fact, charging interest on loans has become a way of life in today's society. But in ancient Israel, the Law prohibited charging interest on at least one category of loans—those made to the poor (Lev. 25:35–38).

This law had many social, financial, and spiritual implications, but two are especially worth mentioning. First, the law genuinely helped the poor by not making their situation worse. It was bad enough to have fallen into poverty, and it could be humiliating to have to seek assistance. But if in addition to repaying the loan a poor person had to make crushing interest payments, the obligation would be more hurtful than helpful.

Secondly, the law taught an important spiritual lesson. For a lender to forego interest on a loan to a poor person would be an act of mercy. He would be losing the use of that money while it was loaned out. Yet that would be a tangible way of expressing gratitude to God for His mercy in not charging His people "interest" for the grace He had extended to them. Just as God had mercifully brought the Israelites out of Egypt when they were nothing but penniless slaves, and had given them a land of their own (Lev. 25:38), so He expected them to do a similar kindness to their own poor citizens.

Christians are in a parallel situation. The life, death, and resurrection of Jesus has paid our sin debt to God. Now, as we have opportunity, we can help others in need, particularly fellow believers, with loans that do not escalate their troubles. Jesus even gave a parable along these lines about two creditors and their attitude toward forgiveness (Matt. 18:23–35). He also instructed His followers: "Freely you have received, freely give" (10:8).

For more on this topic, see FINANCIAL ASSISTANCE, "The Redeeming Relative," page 156.

DECEIT

Playing Games with God

The dramatic account of Ananias and Sapphira (Acts 5:1–11) immediately after the mention of Barnabas (Acts 4:36–37) draws a stark contrast between two kinds of people. On the one hand, Barnabas serves as a positive model of sincere faith, as evidenced by his open-handed generosity. On the other hand, Ananias and Sapphira serve as negative models.

Externally, they appeared the same. Like Barnabas, they sold land and brought money to the church, where they "laid it at the apostles' feet" (Acts 4:37; 5:2). But internally, they had a radically different commitment.

The sins that Peter named—lying to the Holy Spirit (Acts 5:3) and testing the Spirit (Acts 5:9)—indicate that they were playing games with God. Peter noted that the source of their deception was Satan. As the ultimate liar (John 8:44), Satan had filled their hearts with lies, in contrast to the Holy Spirit, who fills the heart with truth (John 14:16–17; Eph. 5:6–21). And like Israel, they were testing the Spirit (1 Cor. 10:1–13), testing the limits of what He would permit, trying to see how much they could get away with.

God dealt severely with this couple by making an example of them. As a result, fear came upon the church (Acts 5:5, 11)—not a cringing fear of dread, but a heightened respect for God's holiness, His moral purity. The incident still stands as a bold warning to believers today about relating to God. No one is perfect, and God forgives. But when given a chance to confess the truth, it's important to confess the truth, not lie as they did.

Trick Questions

Have you ever seen someone try to manipulate someone else by asking for one thing in order to get another? Perhaps you've tried to outwit or embarrass someone with a less-than-direct approach.

The Sadducees did precisely that when they tried to trap Jesus in front of a crowd (Matt. 22:23–33). Using the subject of serial marriage relationships, they attempted to paint Him into a corner on His teaching about the resurrection, a belief that they rejected (Matt. 22:23).

Jesus confronted them on their thinly veiled pretext and at the same time affirmed the resurrection. He even used the very Scriptures they loved to quote: Matthew 22:32 is from Exodus 3:6. Jesus refused to let them get away with using subtle inferences to twist things to their own advantage. He cut to the heart of the matter.

There's nothing wrong with being discreet, using inference, or stating things subtly and diplomatically. Some situations call for planting seed ideas in someone else's thinking, then allowing time for the idea to take shape. Here, however, Jesus was challenging selfish manipulation and trickery which had no benefit for others.

Are you known as a speaker of truth among your peers? Are there ways you could be more forthright and helpful in your communications?

DECISION-MAKING

Casting Lots

Imagine being in Joshua's shoes, with the responsibility of helping the tribes of Israel divide the land of Canaan among themselves. At your direction, seven tribes who have not yet received their inheritance send out surveyors to inspect their allotted territories. After the surveyors report back, your job is to use the information they have gathered to divide their lands proportionately. How would you go about making your final decisions?

Joshua elected to cast lots (Josh. 18:8–10). No one knows the exact method he used, but apparently an element of chance was involved. Doesn't it seem odd that in making such an important decision, Joshua would leave the outcome up to chance? Shouldn't he have used a decision-making process that involved more direct communication from God?

Actually, the text says that Joshua cast the lots "before the LORD in Shiloh" (Josh. 18:8, 10), that is, at the tabernacle there (Josh. 18:1). Perhaps God was superintending the outcome of the lots, so that there was no chance involved. Some believe that the items known as the Urim and Thummim were used in that manner (see Ex. 28:30).

But it is equally possible that Joshua cast lots "before the LORD" simply to demonstrate that the division of the land was proceeding according to the Lord's command, as well as to show that the process was being carried out with the utmost integrity, with no manipulation on anyone's part.

Does Joshua's action imply that believers today are free to use games of chance such as drawing straws, flipping a coin, or rolling dice in making important decisions? Not everyone will feel comfortable using such an approach, but Joshua's example at least offers it as a possibility. However, several principles are worth keeping in mind:

1. No approach to making decisions should avoid the role of human responsibility. God expects us to make choices and accept the consequences. Joshua sent surveyors to evaluate the land. In the same way, we need to gather information and the counsel of others in order to make wise, informed decisions.

2. No approach to making decisions should be a substitute for God's clearly revealed will. The Bible plainly tells us the main things we need to know to follow God. We need to concentrate on those pursuits. When we make choices, we must never violate the express teaching of Scripture, no matter what the outcome of our decision-making process.

3. The point of casting lots and similar methods is to ensure fairness, integrity, and objectivity. So one must make sure that the method is indeed fair, with no manipulation of the results. Doing so will help avoid and even end conflicts (Prov. 18:18). However, such an approach is perhaps best used when one cannot decide among essentially equal alternatives.

Effective Planning, Together

Plans created in isolation tend to be less effective than they could be. That is why wise planning encourages participation and input from a variety of people (Prov. 15:22).

Oftentimes, however, in the rush to get something done, decision-makers make the mistake of bypassing or ignoring advice. That invariably leads to problems—sometimes catastrophic—because hasty planning is rarely effective. Too many details fall through the cracks. By seeking the counsel of others, leaders can decrease the possibility of overlooking crucial factors in their decisions.

Another reason for including rather than excluding others in the decision-making process is that sooner or later others must carry out the plans that are laid. To the extent that they are involved in formulating those plans, the implementers will tend to support the decisions that are made.

Determining God's Will

Christians believe that they should carefully obey God's will. But how can we know what His will is? How should we go about making decisions that honor the Lord?

The example of Gideon is frequently cited as a model for godly decision-making. Before acting, Gideon carefully considered whether the Lord wanted him to rally an army and attack the Midianites. Twice he set out a fleece (a clump of wool) to make sure of God's intentions (Judg. 6:36–40). On this basis, some have argued that before Christians make major decisions with long-range consequences, they should "put out a fleece before the Lord," seeking some tangible sign that indicates His will with certainty.

Is that an appropriate way to know God's will? In considering the question, it is important to note that this is the only occasion in the Bible when God revealed His will through a fleece. It is also worth noting Gideon's extreme hesitation, doubt, and fear. The Lord had already told him what to do through the Angel of the Lord (Judg. 6:11–16). In fact, the Angel had already given Gideon a confirming sign (Judg. 6:17–22).

In light of these facts, Gideon's use of the fleece would appear to demonstrate a lack of faith more than any zeal to be certain of God's will. Fortunately, God was very patient with him and granted his request for a confirming sign. But it seems that using a fleece to determine God's will was the exception rather than the rule, and thus does not serve as the best pattern for how we can depend on God for guidance.

Is there a more reliable way? Yes, God has clearly and objectively told us what He wants throughout the Bible. For example, the Ten Commandments give straightforward instructions to guide our behavior in numerous areas of life. Likewise, one of the New Testament letters to the Thessalonians says plainly, "This is the will of God" (1 Thess. 4:3). The passage then goes on to outline some of God's will in regard to sexuality.

Thus when it comes to making choices in life, God calls us to clear thinking—thinking that is based on our relationship with Him and our allegiance to His values, which are clearly spelled out in Scripture. God has made us to be thinking, discerning, analytical persons who assume responsibility for working our way through life in accordance with His general plans and purposes. He challenges us to learn all that we can about any situation, relationship, responsibility, or opportunity that we have, weigh it in light of His precepts and principles, and then act. As we

act, we can take comfort from the fact that He is at work within us, "both to will and to do for His good pleasure" (Phil. 2:13).

DEFENSE

Prayer—*Before* the Crisis

Some people think of prayer primarily as a last resort, an act of desperation to try when all else fails and one is faced with overwhelming odds. But the example of Asa shows that while prayer ultimately is the best defense, it also is the best offense, a discipline that should be practiced long before trouble strikes.

Faced with an army more than three times the size of his own three-hundred-thousand-man force, Asa cried out to God for help. He humbly acknowledged that the Lord, not military might, was his ultimate defense (2 Chr. 14:11). The Lord responded by defeating the Ethiopians (2 Chr. 14:12–15).

This incident showed that what matters in battle is not the size of the armies, but trust in the Lord. As always, what counts with God is faith.

Yet Asa's trust in God was not just a "foxhole faith," motivated by fear. He was able to pray as he did because he had been praying, worshiping, and honoring the Lord for years (2 Chr. 14:3–7). In fact, his reign had reversed many of the sins initiated by his great-grandfather Solomon.

Less than two decades earlier, Solomon's successor Rehoboam had been defeated by Egyptian forces, which included Ethiopians. The invaders from the south overran Judah and captured Jerusalem with far fewer military resources (2 Chr. 12:1–12) than the army which Asa saw crushed. This emphasizes the point that when the people of God made worship and prayer their first priorities, God was faithful to take care of them. But when they turned away from the Lord and made other things such as wealth and prestige their top priorities, then God allowed them to fail.

So it is with spiritual warfare today. God wants to see whether we respond in faith when circumstances overwhelm us. But He also is interested in the quality of our faith before tragedy strikes, when things are going well. Either way—in calm or in crisis—we need to pray to the Lord in faith (1 John 5:4).

D

DELEGATION

Delegation and Affirmation

Is delegation hard for you? When faced with a choice between letting others do a task or doing it yourself, do you tend to sigh, "It's easier to do it myself"? Do you give others, such as coworkers, relatives, or friends, not only the responsibility but the needed authority to get the job done—even if it means seeing it done their way instead of yours?

Certainly Jesus had more reason than any of us to avoid delegating His work to others. When it came to proclaiming His kingdom, He had every right to lack confidence in His band of followers. He had experienced their failings firsthand (Luke 9:10–50). Yet He sent out seventy workers with full appointment to preach and heal on His behalf (Luke 10:1, 16).

In doing so, Jesus affirmed the often heard but less often practiced concept of people and their development as the most important task of a manager. Certainly He gave the seventy workers detailed instructions before sending them off (10:2–12). But a study of His discipleship methods shows that he was just as concerned with their growth as he was that the task be accomplished or done in a certain way.

Jesus accomplished the work He came to do. He hardly needed seventy neophytes to help Him! But He was clear that people matter, and that His disciples would grow only if they held real responsibility and authority. No wonder the seventy returned "with joy," excited by their experiences (Luke 10:17). They would never be the same again.

To whom do you need to give more responsibility and affirm with greater encouragement?

Moses' Swan Song

When an executive retires, it is common for the person to meet with the various lieutenants and others that have been of support to offer final words and instructions. As Moses came to the end of his life, he gathered the elders of Israel to him to hear some parting words (Deut. 31:28–29).

Apparently Moses had real doubts as to whether the people would remain faithful to God after he was gone. His concern raises the question of how leaders can have confidence that the values and vision they have tried to honor will be maintained by the organization after their departure.

Solomon puzzled over that issue and felt even greater doubts than Moses (Eccl. 2:18–21). As he pointed out, ultimately there is no way to guarantee that one's successors will act wisely or pass along worthy convictions to future generations. Still, there are some things that leaders can do to help prolong their impact:

1. *Articulate values and dreams frequently.* Moses spelled out the Law twice—once in Exodus and again in Deuteronomy. He also caused it to be written on a memorial for all to see. Likewise, wise leaders know how easy it is for their followers to become lost in the tasks at hand, so that they forget the fundamental purposes and perspectives behind the work.

2. *Mentor people.* Moses mentored Joshua so that he left behind a highly trained, qualified leader. Mentoring involves working transparently before others in a way that allows them to see not only what one does and how, but also why—the underlying motivations and passions that sustain the leader's energy.

3. *Delegate to others.* Delegation doesn't mean just passing off work to someone else. Rather, it involves assigning them tasks for which they are qualified, providing the resources necessary to accomplish those tasks (including authority), monitoring progress, and providing feedback and evaluation both during and after the assignment. Thus delegation is an investment, not an assignment. Moses would have worn himself out had he not delegated authority to qualified leaders among the people.

DEMONS

Demons as Real Beings

Popular culture tends to dismiss demons as nothing but an imaginative fantasy similar to the "daemons" of Greek mythology, supposedly supernatural beings that mediated between the gods and humans. But Scripture presents demons not as mythological creatures, but as real beings involved in historical events. Jesus, for example, frequently encountered demons during His ministry, as in the case of the demon-possessed mute (Luke 11:14).

Demons are fallen angels who joined with Satan in rebellion against God. The Bible does not explicitly discuss their origin, but the New Testament does speak of the fall and later imprisonment of a group of angels (2 Pet. 2:4; Jude 6). Their rebellion apparently occurred before God's creation of the world. Afterward, Satan and his followers roamed the new creation, eventually contaminating the human race with wickedness (Gen. 3; Matt. 25:41; Rev. 12:9). To this day they continue to oppose God's purposes and undermine the cause of righteousness.

Whatever Became of "Demon Possession"?

For all the good they've contributed to the healing professions and pastoral care, some theories of psychology have done a great disservice by casting doubt on the objective reality of evil and the devil. That presents a problem for those who read the Bible's accounts of demon possession (for example, Luke 9:38–42) and believe that demonic powers can play a hand in physical illnesses.

Some schools of psychology reduce religious experience to nothing but unconscious drives projected onto the external world. Satan, they say, is no more than a personification of one's deepest, darkest emotions. Likewise, God is reduced to the embodiment of a fully authenticated self, parental ideals, social mores, or universal symbols of goodness.

Without question, a genuine encounter with God or with Satan may involve intense emotional and psychological experiences. But that does not make either one any less real. The existence of Satan and demons is affirmed in scores of scriptural texts. (A demon is a fallen angel or spirit that has joined with Satan in his futile rebellion against God.) At war with Jesus and His followers, these evil powers have played a major role in such events as the Fall, the Flood, and Jesus' crucifixion, and will figure in the tribulations that will someday wrack the earth and in the final judgment.

The Gospels record several dozen encounters between Jesus and the powers of evil. In many of those instances, demon possession had produced any number of physical maladies and manifestations, such as:

- deafness (Mark 9:25);
- muteness (Matt. 12:22; Mark 9:17–25);
- bodily deformity (Luke 13:10–17);
- blindness (Matt. 12:22); and
- epileptic seizure (Luke 9:39).

Ailments like these did not automatically imply demon possession. In fact, distinctions were made between possession and physical illness unrelated to evil spirits (Matt. 4:24; 10:8; Mark 1:32; Luke 6:17–18).

By casting out demons and restoring people both physically and spiritually, Jesus showed that the kingdom of God was as real as, and more powerful than, the forces of Satan (Matt. 10:7–8; 12:28). Today, that same work has been delegated to the church (Luke 10:17; Acts 16:18). Psychology is often helpful in the task, but it is no match for the kingdom of darkness. Only the "whole armor of God" can help believers prevail (Eph. 6:10–18).

For more on this topic, see ANGELS, "Spiritual Realities Beyond You," page 20.

DESPAIR

(*see* Anxiety)

DIETING

The Value of Fasting

Responding to modern society's obsession with image and appearance, some weight-loss programs have started to prescribe fasting as a means of losing weight. But in ancient Israel, fasting was observed for more purposes than that. For example, the gallant men of Gilead fasted for seven days to express their grief over King Saul's death (1 Chr. 10:12). Rather than hide their sadness and feelings of loss, they openly expressed it by using fasting as a cleansing discipline.

Other purposes for fasting among the Israelites included:

- commemorating special occasions of God's deliverance (Zech. 8:19);
- repenting of and grieving for disobedience and sin against the Lord (Judg. 20:26; 1 Sam. 7:6);

- expressing humility before God (Lev. 16:29; Ps. 69:10); and
- seeking guidance from the Lord by clearing out the senses and focusing on Him (Ex. 34:28; 2 Chr. 20:3–4).

Today one hears much about "focus," "concentration," and "working the program" in areas such as sports, the workplace, and psychotherapy. Fasting is a means toward spiritual focus by concentrating on God rather than on food and other personal needs. In what ways might you benefit from the discipline of fasting? Are you facing major challenges or decisions? Perhaps fasting would be a fitting way to honor God in the situation and ask for His help. You may be surprised at how depriving yourself of a day's food in order to concentrate on the Lord can build spiritual muscle and moral fiber.

Here are some examples of fasting from

the Bible that might encourage you in this discipline:

- David fasted to show his repentance after learning that he would lose the child conceived by adultery with Bathsheba (2 Sam. 12:15–16). The child died anyway according to the judgment of the Lord.
- Ahab fasted to show his repentance after Elijah warned him of judgment because of the murder of Naboth (1 Kin. 21:27). The Lord decided to delay punishment until his son assumed the throne (1 Kin. 21:29).
- Ezra fasted before journeying from Babylon to Jerusalem in order to ask God's blessing, guidance, and safety (Ezra 8:21–23). The trip was without incident (8:31–32).
- Daniel fasted and repented on behalf of the Jews in order to entreat God to restore them from exile in Babylon (Dan. 9:3–4). God allowed His people to return to their land.
- Jesus fasted for forty days in the wilderness after being baptized by John at the start of His ministry (Matt. 4:2). Satan came to tempt Him into sin, but He withstood the test.
- Paul and Barnabas were fasting and praying when God called them for a journey to take the gospel to Asia Minor (Acts 13:1–5). Several new churches were planted as many people came to faith.

DIFFICULTIES

(see Problems; Troubles)

DILIGENCE

Faithfulness

All of us must deal with authority and responsibility. The parables Jesus told (Luke 12:35–48) talk about the believer's faithfulness to God. But they also remind us of faithful conduct on the job.

To be sure, our work relationships are more complicated—and civilized—than those between slaves and masters. But in light of the principles raised in this passage, we might ask: Are we as productive when our supervisors are gone as when they are looking over us? Do we try to anticipate their needs and desires, or do we wait until told what to do? Do we pray for our bosses and the work we do under them?

Jesus has a high regard for faithfulness. In this passage He challenges us to carry out our spiritual responsibilities in a faithful, diligent way. But clearly we need to fulfill our everyday work responsibilities with the same reliable, faithful spirit.

Laziness—The Path to Ruin

No one schedules a burglary. Thieves break in when *they* feel the time is right. But as security experts point out, there are many things that property owners can do to keep the time from ever being right for stealing their property. In the same way, there are many things that people can do to ward off poverty and financial need—but not if they are lazy (Prov. 24:33–34).

Proverbs is not suggesting that all poverty is the result of laziness, but that laziness invites sudden disaster and ruin. Notice that the lazy man's vineyard, which requires careful and diligent care, shows every sign of neglect. It is overgrown with thorns and nettles, and its protective stone wall is broken down (Prov. 24:31). As a result, it is both unproductive and vulnerable to attack from foxes and other pests. There can be only one outcome for the owner: no grapes.

Is this a picture of your life? Think about some of the areas in which diligence and responsibility are crucial: your job, your family, your finances, your health, your relationship with God. What thorns and thistles have you allowed to grow in these areas, so that they are not as productive as they could be? What breaches in the walls have you allowed, making you vulnerable to setbacks and even disasters? Consider carefully and take instruction from what happens to the lazy man (24:32).

DISABILITIES

(see Handicaps)

DISADVANTAGED PERSONS

(see also Poverty)

A New Slant on Poverty

Pain is a great leveler. Whether one is high and mighty or lowly and unknown, physical and emotional suffering attack without discrimination, treating the one the same as another. Job discovered that truth, and in the process found a whole new set of friends—the poor (Job 31:13–23).

Before his troubles, Job had been a champion of the poor (see Job 29:12–17). But his enormous wealth and position of importance in his community had probably distanced him from their pain. Not unlike many government officials and well-to-do citizens today, he was aware of their plight, but had never experienced it for himself.

Then a series of disasters struck, and overnight Job was reduced to poverty. As a result, the poor were no longer just a class of people that needed help, but fellow sufferers with whom Job was in the same boat. With a new set of eyes, he began to identify with slaves who feared unjust treatment from their masters (Job 31:13). He now understood what widows and orphans felt when they were forced to go without food, clothing, and shelter while watching others live in luxury (Job 31:16–21; compare Job 24:2–12).

In the end, Job discovered a new sense of equality as a result of his downfall: "Did not He who made me in the womb make them?" he asked rhetorically (Job 31:15). He realized that people are basically the same. Possessions and position have nothing to do with their fundamental humanity.

Perhaps one reason that Job was able to come to that perspective had to do with the Near Eastern culture in which he lived. Modern Westerners tend to interpret Job's situation as a case study in personal suffering. To them, the key issue to resolve would be, "Why is this happening to me?" But in Job's society, people were more likely to make sense of a person's troubles from the standpoint of collective suffering. The idea was that one person's pain had significance for the entire community.

Thus Job went beyond the question of, "Why am I, of all people, facing these trials?" His condition enabled him to embrace others who were slighted and slandered by society. Job's experience challenges Bible readers today to consider what it would take for us to befriend the friendless and seek justice for the powerless.

Always the Poor

Unfortunately, some people use Jesus' statement in Mark 14:7 as an escape hatch to avoid caring for the poor. "Jesus Himself said there will always be poor people," the logic goes, "so what good does it do to offer aid? The problem won't go away." But Jesus had nothing of the sort in mind. On the contrary, He was mandating that we should always care for those who have need.

An Inventory of Evil

One of the best ways to assess the integrity of someone's heart is to look at that person's treatment of the poor and disadvantaged. Job recognized that principle. He knew that God takes a special interest in the downcast. In fact, Job was distressed because he knew of evils against the poor that were going unpunished.

Job mentioned what some of those evils were. His list provides a useful inventory by which anyone can self-evaluate character:

- Do you cheat in business or steal other people's possessions (Job 24:2)?
- Do you take away the resources of the powerless and drive them into needless debt (Job 24:3)?
- Do you abuse the poor and force them out of your way (Job 24:4)?
- Do you cause the poor to lose work, so that they must fend for themselves as best they can to find food, clothing, and shelter (Job 24:5–8)?
- Do you lock powerless people into situations and systems that bleed them but benefit you (Job 24:9–10)?
- Do you live lavishly, even as people nearby are dying for lack of basic resources (Job 24:11–12)?

Job had been an extremely wealthy man (Job 1:3), so he probably knew many people who practiced these evils. What would Job say if he were a formerly wealthy citizen living in our culture today?

Compassion is a mark of real faith toward God (James 1:27). As we read Job's six-point inventory of evil, how do we score?

Gleaning and the Poor

If you've ever walked through a field or orchard after harvest and picked up a discarded ear of corn or a spare apple left behind, you're familiar with the activity of gleaning (Lev. 19:9–10; 23:22). Gleaning was the process of going back over a field, orchard, or vineyard after the main harvest to gather every last growing thing, reaping thoroughly into every corner and stripping bare every stalk or branch of its produce.

By instituting a law related to gleaning, God showed his concern for the poor. The law prohibited landowners from gleaning their lands after harvest. Instead, they were to leave the corners and whatever the harvesters missed for poor people to glean. To emphasize this statute, God punctuated it with the reminder, "I am the Lord your God" (Lev. 19:10).

It was a reminder of who stood behind the commandment. But it also was a reminder of who owned the land. The poor obviously did not own it. Yet neither did the "landowners," at least not directly. The land belonged to God. He graciously provided it for people to grow their food, along with the strength for plowing, sowing, cultivating, irrigating, and harvesting. Therefore, what grew on the land actually belonged to God. He graciously gave it to His people to provide for their needs.

But this gift was given with some conditions attached. One of them was that the poor be allowed to eke out a living by picking up the leftovers. If the people followed God's ways, there would be more than enough food for everyone (Lev. 26:4–5).

Heaven Rules! Feed the Poor!

There is a direct correlation between the spiritual health of societies and their treatment of the poor. Those that honor God show mercy to the weak and disadvantaged. Those that depart from godly ways abuse and manipulate the poor. An example of this principle can be seen in ancient Babylon.

The Babylonian King Nebuchadnezzar had much of which to be proud. He won almost every military battle that he ever fought. His empire spanned the Middle East. He extensively rebuilt his capital city of Babylon. He had unimaginable wealth and power. For these reasons, his heart was lifted up in pride—so much so that he apparently forgot a basic truth: "Heaven rules" (Dan. 4:26).

God warned Nebuchadnezzar through his dreams that judgment was coming (Dan. 4:1–26), and his advisor Daniel took the risk of challenging his boss to change his ways before it was too late. It is interesting to observe Daniel's advice: "Break off your sins by being righteous, and your iniquities by showing mercy to the poor" (Dan. 4:27). The parallelism of Daniel's statement suggests that righteousness for Nebuchadnezzar equated with showing mercy to the poor.

The king apparently disregarded Daniel's advice. He persisted in his pride and arrogance, ignoring God. As a result, the Lord took away his position and power (Dan. 4:33) until he turned to the Lord and admitted that heaven rules (Dan. 4:34–35). He then instituted a reign based on truth, justice, and humility (Dan. 4:36–37).

Nebuchadnezzar's experience challenges us to ask: What values drive you? What rules your life? An easy way to answer these questions is to reflect on your attitude toward the poor. Are you committed to seeing that they benefit from truth and justice? How might you demonstrate that commitment in your job and community?

Respect the Poor!

People sometimes dismiss the poor by misapplying Jesus' remark that "you have the poor with you always" (Mark 14:7). This can be a smug way of disavowing responsibility to help or even care about the plight of poor people. The rationalization is, "They'll always be around, and there's nothing I can do about it, so why even try?"

But the Book of Proverbs declares that God so identifies with the poor that to mock the poor is to insult God (Prov. 17:5). Consider a few ways in which we may be "mocking" the poor: by laughing at their condition; by jumping to conclusions about why they are poor; by taunting them with words; by training our eyes to look past them, as if they were invisible; or even by adopting the pious attitude, "There but for the grace of God go I."

Jesus' words about the inevitability of there being poor people can also be read as a call to His followers to serve the poor after He was gone. His other statements would certainly support that. By serving the poor, we are continually serving Jesus. But if we close our eyes and ears to their plight, then God warns that we will not be noticed when we fall on hard times (Prov. 21:13).

The Underclass

Nearly every society and every city in biblical times had a large *underclass*—people scraping by on the margins of society. Tending to congregate in the cities, the underclass included the poor, the sick, the disabled, the lepers, the blind, the insane, the demon-possessed, widows, orphans, runaways, castaways, and refugees. Lacking resources to provide for even their basic needs, many turned to begging, stealing, menial labor, slavery, and prostitution. Few cultures made provision for these desperate, destitute wanderers, and so they remained largely powerless to change their condition.

Yet it was to the underclass that Jesus intentionally directed much of His life and ministry. They were among the "blessed" in His opening remarks in the Sermon on the Mount (Matt. 5:3–10). And He declared that He had come to bring them good news in His inaugural sermon at Nazareth (Luke 4:17–18). So it was no surprise that when John's questioning disciples came to ask whether He was indeed the Messiah, they found Him ministering among the underclass (Luke 7:20–21).

Nor was it any surprise that the early church continued this outreach. They used their resources to meet material needs among their own members (Acts 2:44–45; 4:32, 34–35). They attracted the sick and afflicted (Acts 5:12–16). They appointed leaders to manage social programs for widows (Acts 6:1–6). They sent famine relief (Acts 11:27–30). They urged new leaders to remember the poor (Gal. 2:10). They even evaluated their success in part by how much they collected in charitable contributions (Rom. 15:26–27).

To what extent will Christians today follow in the footsteps of Jesus and the first believers? Our cities, like theirs, are filling up with an underclass. How can we offer "good news" to them? Can we touch their bodies as well as their souls? Do we take them as seriously as our Savior did?

For more on this topic, see SOCIAL SERVICES, "God's Safety Net," page 376.

DISAPPOINTMENT
My Way or No Way!

When things don't go your way, do you pout and dig in your heels? Do you take a stubborn attitude that resists authority and insists on your own way? That's the response that Dathan and Abiram had to Moses' invitation to a meeting (Num. 16:12). Moses wanted to settle differences raised by Korah (Num. 16:1–3). But Dathan and Abiram refused to show up. Their attitude seemed to be the all-too-common one of "My way or the highway!"

That's a perilous mind-set to have in any organization or group setting. It puts a chill on communication, stifles constructive dialogue, and poisons everyone's outlook. It can only lead to more conflict and confrontation, as the dramatic ending of Korah, Dathan, Abiram, and the rest of their band of rebels illustrated (Num. 16:31–33, 35).

The tragic outcome of Korah's rebellion is a lesson in conflict resolution. Stubbornness can be a valuable asset in overcoming obstacles. But when the "obstacle" standing in one's way is a divinely appointed authority, as Moses was, then resistance is not the right course. How different the outcome might have been if Korah and the others had brought their concerns to Moses and the Lord and discussed them in an open, honest way.

How do you go about resolving conflict and dealing with disappointment? Have you worn out your shoes—and your relationships—by digging in your heels too many times? Why not try a different approach?

For more on this topic, see CRITICISM, "Dried-up Friends," page 96.

DISCERNMENT
Tough-Minded Believers

Christianity has rightly been characterized as a religion of love, but it's important not to take that emphasis to an unhealthy extreme. If, in the name of love, we uncritically accept every idea or value of others, we open ourselves up to error. God never asks us to put our brains in neutral when it comes to matters of faith.

John repeatedly appeals for love (1 John 2:10; 3:3, 10–24; 4:7–12, 16–21), but he also places a premium on truth—not the wishy-washy opinions that pass for "truth" in our society, but the absolute, eternal truths of God's Word. For example, John challenges us to "test the spirits" (1 John 4:1) and learn to discern between truth and error (1 John 4:6). He calls for us to avoid sin, which requires that we discern what is sinful (1 John 2:1; 3:4–10). He tells us to distinguish between the things of the world and the will of God (1 John 2:15–17), and he appeals for us to identify deceivers and avoid them (1 John 2:18–29; 3:7).

Paul echoes this appeal to be tough-minded when it comes to our faith. To be spiritual, he writes, means to be able to "judge" (discern or test) all things (1 Cor. 2:15). Likewise, we are to have the mind of Christ: tough in discernment, loving toward all, and fearless in the face of judgment (Phil. 2:5–11, 17–18).

Are you discerning on issues of faith and spirituality? If not, consider starting your own study of the Scriptures to understand what they say and mean, or perhaps enroll in a Bible class where you can learn more about God's truth in a systematic way.

*For more on this topic, see **ADVISORS**, "Understanding the Times," page 10; **HOSPITALITY**, "When and How to Disagree," page 204; **SPIRITUAL DISCERNMENT**, "Judge All Things?" page 377.*

DISCIPLESHIP

Discipleship—or Mentoring?

In the Great Commission (as it is frequently labeled; Matt. 28:19), Jesus commanded His disciples to "Go . . . and make disciples." The objective was not that they attract their own disciples, but that they win new followers of Jesus. Acts tells the story of how the Spirit-filled apostles obeyed that command.

But closely related to the making of disciples is the *mentoring* of leaders. "Mentoring" has become a buzzword among Western business and professional people. But the concept is as old as Homer's *Odyssey* (c. 900–810 B.C.), in which Odysseus entrusts to his friend, Mentor, the education of Telemachus, his son. A mentor, then, is a trusted counselor or guide—typically an older, more experienced person who imparts valuable wisdom to someone younger. Countless figures throughout history have recalled the powerful influence of mentors on their development.

The Old Testament is filled with mentoring relationships: Jethro, a wealthy livestock owner, helped his overworked son-in-law, Moses, learn to delegate authority (Ex. 18:1–27); Deborah, judge over Israel, summoned Barak to military leadership and helped him triumph over Jabin, a Canaanite king, bringing forty years of peace to the land (Judg. 4:4–24); Eli, a priest of the Lord (but a failure as a father), raised young Samuel to succeed him (1 Sam. 1:1–3:21); the prophet Elijah, who oversaw the evil end of Ahab and Jezebel, passed his office on to young Elisha, who received a double portion of his spirit (2 Kin. 2:1–15).

Barnabas, a wealthy landowner in the early church, became an advocate and guide for Saul, the former enemy and persecutor of the movement (Acts 9:26–30). Over time, with Barnabas's coaching and encouragement, Saul (later called Paul) became the central figure in the early spread of the gospel.

Close observation reveals four key functions of a kingdom-style mentor:

1. *Mentors care about those who follow them.* Their primary interest is not what they can gain from the relationship, but with what they can give to it. They also realize how much they have to learn from their protégés. Ultimately, they fulfill Paul's admonition to look out not only for their own interests, but also for the interests of others (Phil. 2:4).

2. *Mentors convey wisdom and skill.* Through modeling and coaching, and eventually by turning over responsibility to their followers, kingdom-style mentors seek to make their disciples more capable than the mentors have been (Matt. 10:25).

3. *Mentors correct their followers when they are wrong.* An excellent example is Barnabas's challenge to Paul over taking John Mark along on the second missionary journey (Acts 15:36–39). Later Paul changed his perspective and asked Timothy to bring John Mark to him (2 Tim. 4:11). Kingdom-style mentors do not avoid confrontation.

4. *Mentors connect their followers to significant others.* As Acts 9 shows, Saul's entrée into

the early church was Barnabas. Kingdom-style mentors introduce their protégés to relationships and resources that will further their development and increase their opportunities.

Passing on the Mantle

The New Testament offers models of "making disciples" and mentoring. However, neither discipleship nor mentoring were invented by the early church. The principles involved had been around for centuries.

Take the relationship between Elijah and Elisha as an example. When Elisha literally took up the mantle of Elijah (2 Kin. 2:13), he was taking over Elijah's role as the main prophet of Israel, a role for which Elijah had helped to groom him (1 Kin. 19:16).

A number of similar mentoring relationships can be found in the Old Testament:

- Jethro and Moses. Jethro drew alongside his overworked son-in-law and helped him organize leaders over the people of Israel (Ex. 18).
- Moses and Joshua. Moses helped Joshua prepare to assume the leadership of Israel when the people were ready to enter Canaan (Deut. 31:1–8, 34:9).
- Samuel and David. Samuel anointed David into leadership and stood by him when Saul was trying to hunt David down (1 Sam. 16; 19:18–24).
- Mordecai and Esther. A Jew living in Persia, Mordecai mentored his cousin when she found herself in a surprising role as queen, with the opportunity to rescue her people from their enemy, Haman (Esth. 1–10).

Mentoring involves a voluntary investment in others for their growth, development, and success. It is rooted in faith in the value of the other person. The goal is the gain of the one being mentored, whether or not the mentor benefits. Thus mentoring often requires loving sacrifice.

Is there someone you could serve—especially someone younger—by giving them your friendship, experience, and knowledge? As you reflect on your own development, can you identify those who have given themselves to you? In what ways have you thanked them?

The Price of Discipleship

As John points out in John 12:42–43, the Pharisees held a powerful grip on Jewish society in Jesus' day, stifling dissent through fear. Apparently Jesus had some support even at the highest levels of society. But it did Him no good, as fear of rejection overcame the impulse for justice and truth.

Have you ever been embarrassed or afraid to identify publicly with Christ because of possible rejection by others, especially superiors? Scripture is clear that one price of authentic discipleship will almost certainly be some rejection and persecution (John 15:18–25; 2 Tim. 3:12). To believe that you can avoid any tough choices between acceptance by the world and loyalty to God is both naive and dangerous. If God does not hold your highest allegiance, how real can He be to you in any meaningful way?

DISCIPLINE

God's Model of Discipline

How do you handle the disobedience of people over whom you have authority, such as subordinates, students, or children? Hopefully, you look for ways to discipline that benefit the offender rather than just exploding in anger. If so, you're following in the footsteps of God, whose discipline of Israel offers insight into dealing with disobedience.

Israel repeatedly broke God's commandments. For example, within a generation or two of entering the Promised Land, the people were worshiping idols (Judg. 2:10–13). Throughout their history, they failed to keep the Sabbatical and Jubilee years (Jer. 34:12–16). And they repeatedly dishonored the Lord's sanctuary and its implements (1 Sam. 4:3–4, 11; 13:7–13). These were direct violations of the covenant (Lev. 26:1–2). And Israel broke almost every other law as well.

In every case, God responded with firm correction, just as He had warned (Lev. 26:14–39; compare Judg. 2:14–15; Jer. 34:17–22; 1 Sam. 7:2; 13:14). Finally He allowed foreigners to take His people into exile (2 Chr. 36:17–21).

Nevertheless, God's relationship with his recalcitrant and rebellious people always included a place for forgiveness if they repented:

- He would remember His covenant with Israel's ancestors, Jacob and Abraham (Lev. 26:42, 45).
- He would remember the Promised Land (26:42).
- He would not cast His people away completely, or "abhor" them (26:44).
- He would not utterly destroy them or break His covenant with them (26:44).
- He would remain their God (26:44–45).

God shows that a leader must practice loyalty toward disobedient followers even when correcting them. Following His example, can you exercise discipline in a way that helps people rather than destroys them? Can you "bend" under the pressure of disobedience, but not totally break?

Tightening the Screws—Carefully

Even with someone as stubborn as Pharaoh, God showed incredible patience. God could have brought the final plague—the death of the firstborn (Ex. 11:1)—immediately after Pharaoh's first refusal to free the Hebrews.

Instead, God began a systematic plan of attrition, as if to wear down the ruler's resistance. Yet Pharaoh remained steadfast. He was not easily influenced to change his mind. As Moses and Aaron negotiated with him, he became increasingly difficult to deal with (Ex. 7:13, 23; 8:15, 19, 28, 32; 9:7, 12, 34; 10:27–28).

Finally, after the last plague, an agreement was reached. But what a long, intense, and hard process it took to get to that point! Even then, Pharaoh's true colors resurfaced as he and his armies pursued the fleeing Hebrews (Ex. 14:5–9).

Sooner or later, most of us will confront someone who seems as stubborn as the king of Egypt. It may be a coworker, a boss, the government, or even one of our own children. When that moment comes for you, will you handle it with patience? God's treatment of Pharaoh shows the value of "tightening the screws" slowly rather than suddenly.

So as you deal with resistance, can you devise a carefully graduated sequence of consequences that might help the other person understand what is happening and perhaps have a change of heart? Discipline and correction need to help the recipient discover a problem and provide a chance to make changes. There's no point in jumping immediately to the harshest outcomes.

*For more on this topic, see **CHILDREN**, "Rearing Children with Discipline," page 53; **SUPERVISION**, "Stick to Your Word," page 389.*

DISCRIMINATION

Discrimination Based on Wealth

The soldiers seemed to enjoy mocking Christ (John 19:2–3). But they were also mocking wealth and authority, perhaps having lived and worked too long under Rome's iron fist. The crown of thorns was a grisly caricature of the ultimate symbol of royalty. But the purple robe was the genuine item: the purple dye used to make it was very costly, and only the very rich could afford it.

This incident reminds us that wealth and its symbols can be used to send many kinds of messages. Frequently wealth is the starting point for deciding who should be respected, accepted, included, and honored, and who should not. Scripture explicitly states that sin lies at the root of such judgments (James 2:1–9).

Do you judge people, in your heart of hearts, by their possessions and financial achievements? Do you work hard at getting close to people of position and wealth? Do your friends come from many different levels on the social and economic ladder?

Ushers on Trial

To discriminate is to sin. In James 2, a congregation—particularly the ushers—is on trial for discrimination. Their behavior is an example of how "faith without works" operates: without cause it excludes people on the basis of social standing rather than welcoming them into the household of God. Paul made a similar case when he affirmed that, in Christ, "we are all one" (Gal. 3:28).

When Money Talks, Do You Listen?

Are you more likely to listen to the counsel of the rich person than that of the poor? Does your church tend to choose only wealthy businesspeople to serve as leaders, perhaps assuming that their financial success shows that they must be wiser than others? Ecclesiastes recognizes the diminishing of the poor person's perspective as a common fact of life (Eccl. 9:16).

But is it wise to turn a deaf ear to the poor person's counsel? Probably not, since the issue when it comes to counsel is not the size of one's portfolio but the wisdom of one's words (Eccl. 9:17). Furthermore, a variety of perspectives is always helpful. The poor and the working class have insights into problems and issues that the rich cannot have because of their very wealth.

Besides all of this, Scripture warns believers not to shut out the poor from the church and its decision-making process. To do so amounts to discrimination (James 2:1–9).

For more on this topic, see **CIVIL RIGHTS,** *"Playing Favorites," page 67.*

DISEASE

(*see* Sickness)

DISOBEDIENCE

Disobedience Has a Price

Breaking the rules has far-reaching implications. All societies have rules, along with penalties for violating those rules. This pattern of morality is rooted deep in God's design of humanity at the creation. At the end of Leviticus, we find that the intricate relationships between creation and its Creator cannot be violated without costly consequences to His people:

- God will be known as a "terror" rather than as a Friend and Companion, as was His original intention (Lev. 26:16, 23, 24).
- Life will become painful and passing (Lev. 26:16).
- The people's efforts at production will feel vain, as others profit from their labors (Lev. 26:16, 20).
- Enemies will create both true and false fears to dominate them (Lev. 26:17, 25, 36–38).
- Their reputation will suffer (Lev. 26:19).
- Violence will become their lot (Lev. 26:22).
- Their children will die before them (Lev. 26:22).
- Their food will be limited and unsatisfying, such that in extreme circumstances they become cannibalistic (Lev. 26:26–29).

- Their dwellings and cities will become abhorrent to them, smelling foul and lying devastated (Lev. 26:30–34).
- They will become refugees (Lev. 26:34, 39).

But the passage ends on a bright note: God repeats His offer to forgive and receive His people back. He wants them to enter into life as He planned it, with all the blessings that were intended for a holy and obedient people (Lev. 26:40–46). In the end, forgiveness and holy living can bring stable, gratifying life to God's people.

The Pattern of Bochim

God told the Israelites to dispossess the Canaanites by taking over their cities, destroying their idols and altars, and refusing to enter into agreements with them (Judg. 2:2). Apparently the citizens of Bochim failed to carry out those instructions. No one knows the exact circumstances, but the offenses were serious enough for the Angel of the Lord to come up from Gilgal to this village near Bethel and cry against it (Judg. 2:1).

The timing of the sermon was important. The days of Israel's conquest of Canaan were drawing to a close, yet many cities remained in the hands of, or at least were still influenced by, the Canaanites (Judg. 1:27–35). Joshua's life was over (Judg. 2:8), and a new generation was coming into power (Judg. 2:10).

So Bochim's spiritual failures were a serious matter. They set a dangerous precedent of idolatry that persisted from that day forward (Judg. 2:3), as the Book of Judges shows. Apparently the people of Bochim tearfully repented of their wrongs and, in the presence of Joshua, offered a sacrifice to atone for their sins (Judg. 2:5–6). But the pattern of spiritual adultery was established.

Unbelievers today are free to worship whatever "gods" they will. But God's people cannot adapt to their ways. Like Israel, believers may need to limit their neighborliness if necessary to preserve their own faith and godliness. They must allow nothing to distract them from unswerving allegiance to the Lord. Otherwise they invite a host of thorny issues and a legacy of tears.

DIVERSITY

From Babel to Pentecost:
Scattering and Gathering

American literature often celebrates the pioneer spirit and a love for open spaces. But that spirit seems to have been lacking among the world's inhabitants in the years after the flood (Gen. 11:4). Only a profound change in language patterns caused the people to quit Babel and migrate to the ends of the earth (Gen. 11:8–9).

The confusion of languages at Babel was an explosive moment in history. It introduced geographic and linguistic barriers that survive to this day. However, in breaking up the unified community at Babel, God was working out His purposes. He knew that the people were united around a sinful desire to thwart His will, not to honor it (Gen. 11:6). Therefore, He miraculously disrupted their communication as an act of grace. He was preventing humanity from committing itself en masse to rebellion and eventual self-destruction.

Many centuries later, the same God who scattered the peoples at Babel began to gather them together again. At Pentecost, His Spirit began to create a new community unified around Jesus Christ. The Lord even breached linguistic barriers on that day—a miracle to match the miracle of creating different languages at Babel.

Since the beginning of history, God has been at work to save people from sin. He still uses the principles of scattering and gathering to do that. Only now, after Pentecost, the people that He "scatters" are equipped with the message of His grace and the power of His Spirit. He is helping them overcome every barrier that stands in the way of people knowing Him.

Issues of Truth and Love

As the gospel expanded "to the end of the earth" (Acts 1:8), the first Christians encountered new cultures that challenged accepted beliefs and practices. Then as now, the frontiers of mission required the church to meet as an international body to sort out issues of faith and culture (Acts 15:6).

Some controversies involve "truth issues," others "love issues," and others both truth and love issues. Truth issues call for clarity of doctrine and understanding of Scripture. Love issues call for open-mindedness and toleration. The situation in Acts 15 required the early church to deal with both.

What issues in today's church are truth-related? What issues are love issues demanding tolerance for legitimate differences of opinion and practice? What issues demand the perspective of both truth and love?

Many Nations Under God

The peoples and nations listed in Genesis 10, if traced forward in time and named with modern names, might read like a directory of the United Nations today. The listing presents the world as it was in ancient times. But it also reminds us that just as the flood spread the judgment of God throughout the earth, so the blessings of God on Noah have spread through his descendants, through these nations, to the ends of the earth. God made "from one blood every nation" of the world (Acts 17:26), the outcome of His charge to Noah (Gen. 9:1).

The Pledge of Allegiance says the United States is "one nation under God." Given the perspective of Genesis 10, one could almost say that there are "many nations under God." Not that any nation has always served God or brought itself "under" His sovereignty. Far from it. Some have violently opposed God's ways. Nevertheless, this passage implies that God is concerned about the *whole* world; He loves *all* peoples (compare John 3:16–17). Likewise, as we survey the many nations of the world today, we need to keep in mind that ultimately we are all part of the same family, descended from the same righteous man, Noah (Gen. 10:32).

DIVINATION

(*see* Occult)

DIVORCE

Do We Divorce God?

The more a nation's divorce rate increases, the more God regards the situation as a national scandal. That seems to be the import of Malachi's words concerning divorce (Mal. 2:14–16). Apparently a substantial number of husbands in postexilic Judah were "dealing treacherously" by divorcing their wives. This treachery involved a retraction of their marriage vows, but it also represented treachery against the Lord.

What provoked this skyrocketing divorce rate? The books of Ezra and Nehemiah tell of those two leaders challenging the men of the land to "put away" the wives that they had married from among the Canaanites and other peoples of the land (Ezra 9–10; Neh. 13:23–27). These divorces were regarded as a means of national cleansing and a return to the covenant.

But is it possible that this policy of dissolving mixed marriages helped to create a jaded attitude about divorce? Could it have contributed to a climate in which divorce became an easy alternative even when both partners were Jewish, evidence of which we continue to see in Jesus' day (Matt. 19:3–9)?

Malachi, a contemporary of Ezra and Nehemiah, spoke clearly about God's attitude: "I hate divorce" (Mal. 2:16). The prophet warned the people to "take heed to your spirit." A casual attitude toward divorce was a symptom of a problem with one's heart attitude toward the Lord. Loyalty to Him was what counted.

The Bible and Divorce

Divorce is nothing new. It was common throughout the ancient world, usually favoring the man. Thus the Law did not establish divorce, but brought justice to an existing practice. Moses spoke of a "certificate of divorce" (Deut. 24:1). Apparently the husband was to initiate the preparation of this official document dissolving the marriage. He could have it written if he found any "uncleanness" in his wife. No one knows exactly what "uncleanness" (literally "a thing of nakedness") meant, but it was sufficient grounds for divorce.

How should believers today regard divorce? Is it prohibited by the Bible? This is a very complex issue, and various traditions hold different points of view. But several biblical principles suggest that questions about divorce should start with a proper understanding of marriage:

1. *Marriage is a holy institution established by God.* When God created the world, He made male and female and established that they be united in marriage (Gen. 1:27; 2:24).

The marital union should be characterized by singular faithfulness; indeed, God considers the marriage bond sacred.

2. *Marriage is based on trust and faithfulness.* God considers marriage a sacred bond, and He expects the partners to honor that union with exclusive, lasting commitment (Matt. 19:6).

3. *God hates unfaithfulness.* The primary reason for divorce is unfaithfulness—not only sexual infidelity, but emotional unfaithfulness, allowing one's affections and commitments to wander away from one's mate so that trust, commitment, and communication break down. God hates unfaithfulness. He judged Israel severely because His people proved unfaithful to their covenant with the Lord. Because He hates unfaithfulness, He also hates divorce (Mal. 2:16).

4. *Divorce is a concession by God.* As Jesus explained, God hates divorce, but He permits it as a concession to the fallen nature of humanity (Matt. 19:8). Easy divorces were the standard of the day in the cultures surrounding ancient Israel. The Law established guidelines to limit the Hebrews from abusing each other through divorce.

5. *Grounds for divorce are few.* Today, a marriage can be dissolved easily. But if one considers the Bible, there are few reasons why divorce is permissible. (It was never mandated, except when Ezra commanded certain Jews returning from the exile to dissolve their marriages to pagans, Ezra 9–10.) The New Testament appears to allow two reasons for divorce: adultery (Matt. 5:32; 19:9) and the desertion of a Christian by an unbelieving spouse (1 Cor. 7:12–16). There could possibly be other valid circumstances not addressed in Scripture, such as persistent physical or emotional abuse.

6. *There is a place for compassion for the divorced.* As much as God hates unfaithfulness and divorce, He shows compassion for divorced people, and is ready to forgive and to restore any who have come short of His expectations when they seek His pardon. Divorce, whatever the grounds, is not the unforgivable sin. Yet neither is it something to take lightly. Marriage is a solemn commitment that should be entered into carefully and with a view toward permanence.

Divorce is an acknowledgment that sin wreaks havoc on God's design. Yet it need not be the only response to a troubled relationship. Marriage is important enough for partners to try all available means to preserve it when they face obstacles. Help may come from friends, church, or professional counsel. But most of all, help is available from God Himself, who wants to see marriages succeed.

DOUBLE STANDARD

A New Standard for Judgment

The woman presented to Jesus (John 8:3) must have been utterly humiliated at being dragged into the temple by self-righteous men who were only using her to try to trick the Teacher they hated. According to the Law, adultery required capital punishment of *both* parties (Lev. 20:10). Did the accusers forget to bring the man? Or had they allowed a double standard to creep in?

If so, Jesus refrained from challenging their hypocrisy, but He did set a new standard for judgment: Let someone perfect decide the case (John 8:7; compare Matt. 5:48). Ironically, He was the only one who fit that qualification, and He did decide the case—declining to condemn the woman, but admonishing her to "go and sin no more."

Are there double standards in your moral judgments? Are you eager to point out the speck in someone else's eye, while ignoring the plank in your own (Matt. 7:4–5)? Or, perhaps, like the woman, you've experienced the forgiveness of God for grave offenses against His holiness. If so, live in His grace—and sin no more.

DOUBT

Skeptics Welcome

Have you ever struggled with doubts or troubling questions about Christ, the Christian faith, or the church? Do you sometimes feel that tough questions are not welcome or acceptable among believers?

Thomas (John 20:24) was a classic skeptic. Even though he had traveled with Jesus and learned from His teaching for at least three years, he needed time, evidence, and personal convincing before he would accept the resurrection (John 20:25–26). But Jesus responded to his doubt by inviting him to check

it all out. He presented Himself for Thomas' inspection (John 15:26–27) and did not chide him for wanting to be certain.

Jesus seeks to honor the mind and heart of every seeker or doubter. He knows that easily developed loyalties often lack staying power. By contrast, many tenacious people who probe the corners of their doubts and fears finally reach the truth—and faith in the truth is what Christ desires. He even promised that the Spirit would aid those who seek it (John 16:12–16).

The encounter with Thomas should encourage every skeptic to bring his or her doubts to God. He delights in hearing our arguments and questions.

DREAM

A Glimpse of the Future?

Dreams are the images, thoughts, and impressions that pass through our mind when we are asleep. Dreams have had a prominent place in the religious literature of ancient peoples. In ancient times, dreams—especially those of kings and priests—were thought to convey messages from God (Num. 12:6; Gen. 31:10–13). In the Bible these were sometimes prophetic in nature. Elihu stated clearly his belief that God speaks through dreams (Job 33:14–15).

In a dream God warned Abimelech, the king of Gerar, not to touch Sarah, because she was Abraham's wife. The Lord spoke to Jacob in a dream in which He renewed the covenant and assured Jacob of His protection and presence.

Two special cycles of dreams in which expert interpretation was involved occur in the Old Testament. The first cycle related to Joseph (Gen. 37:5–10). The second cycle involved Daniel (Dan. 2:14–45), with the dreams coming to Nebuchadnezzar of Babylon. The dreams in each case pertained to events of the future. God granted the ability to interpret these dreams to Joseph (Gen. 40:8; 41:12) and Daniel (Dan. 2:20–45).

In the Old Testament dreams were frequently associated with the prophets of Israel (Deut. 13:1–5; Jer. 23:25–32). But dreams, with their proposed prophecies, were not accepted uncritically. False prophets and their prophecies had to be recognized and rejected. Jeremiah, especially, denounced the prophets who spoke with lies.

In the New Testament, God appeared to Joseph in a dream after His announcement of the forthcoming birth of Jesus (Matt. 1:20). God also spoke through these dreams to protect the infant Jesus (Matt. 2:13–14).

DROUGHT

Days of Powder and Dust

If ever there were a testimony to the fact that God keeps His word, it is the droughts that came on Judah in the days of Jeremiah (Jer. 14:1). Hundreds of years earlier, God had promised that if His people followed Him, He would bless their land with abundance. But if they turned away from Him, disobeying His laws and worshiping other gods, He would turn the annual rains to "powder and dust" (Lev. 26:18–19; Deut. 28:1–24).

Judah surpassed Israel in its idolatry and wickedness, so the Lord kept His promise by sending a series of droughts. Jeremiah pleaded for mercy, but God told him that it was too

late; He had given His people over to judgment (Jer. 14:11–12).

There was a certain irony in using drought to punish the Israelites. The people were following the gods of the Canaanites who supposedly had power over nature (see Deut. 32:39). Yet now God had shown the futility of these idols by holding back the rains (Jer. 14:22).

DRUG ABUSE

(*see also* Alcoholism)

Smashed!

The Bible characterizes drunkenness as a drugged or deranged condition that results from drinking intoxicating beverages (1 Cor. 5:11; 6:10; Eph. 5:18). Drunkenness regularly appears in lists of vices in the New Testament (Luke 21:34; Rom. 13:13; Gal. 5:21).

Noah, who planted a vineyard and drank its wine after the Flood, is the first intoxicated man mentioned in the Bible (Gen. 9:20–21). While intoxicated, Lot fathered sons by his daughters (Gen. 19:32–38). People thought the apostles were drunk on the Day of Pentecost (Acts 2:15), and drunkenness was apparently a problem in the Corinthian church (1 Cor. 11:21).

Common symptoms associated with drunkenness and mentioned in the Bible include the drunkard and his songs (Ps. 69:12), his reeling and staggering (Job 12:25; Jer. 23:9), his vomiting (Is. 28:8; Jer. 25:27; 48:26), and his drugged condition (Joel 1:5).

Drunkenness is also spoken of figuratively in the Bible to describe a helpless people whose ways have brought them punishment from the Lord (Is. 29:9; Jer. 13:13; Ezek. 23:33). Symbolically, one may also be drunk from the Lord's fury (Is. 63:6; Jer. 25:27; Lam. 4:21) and the "wine" of fornication (Rev. 17:2).

DUTY

Doing Your Duty

Jesus' words in Luke 17:6–10 raise many puzzling questions. Did He intend that we should never thank people for doing what is expected of them? Should workers never expect praise for doing their jobs? Why are the workers "unprofitable" if in fact they did what was their duty? Should we always do

more than expected? Was this a sermon on initiative and creativity? Who was Jesus addressing, bosses or employees?

Actually, He was responding to the disciples' request for more faith (Luke 17:5). That's a key to understanding this passage. Jesus had just challenged His followers to forgive others freely and repeatedly (Luke 17:1–4). But they replied, "Give us more faith," as if it took great faith to forgive.

But it does not. Forgiveness is not some supernatural ability that only God can give. It is not the product of great faith, but rather of simple obedience. That's what the servant in the parable must do—obey his master. It doesn't take great trust on the part of the servant to get a meal prepared; it just takes doing it. In the same way, forgiveness is expected of us as Christ's followers, since Christ has forgiven us. We are *obligated* to forgive others, so there's no reward attached to it.

The disciples expected a payoff for following Jesus (Luke 9:46–48; Matt. 20:20–28). But Jesus wanted them to see that following Him was a reward in itself!

DYSFUNCTIONAL FAMILIES

Our Sins Can Affect Our Grandchildren

How often we assume that our "private" sins hurt no one but ourselves. For instance, how could the sin of envy affect anyone else? Isn't coveting strictly a matter between us and the Lord?

But sins of character have a way of touching everyone with whom we have contact—especially those we love the most, our family. That is what happened in three generations of Isaac's family. His wife Rebekah determined to gain Isaac's blessing for her favorite son Jacob, even if it meant deceiving her husband (Gen. 25:28; 27:5–29). Thus she helped her son Jacob grow up to be a deceiver (Gen. 27:35–36).

Years later, Jacob's second wife Rachel became frustrated as her sister and rival Leah bore four sons for Jacob. Rachel's anguish developed into such strong envy that it created tension and anger in her husband, even though he loved Rachel dearly (Gen. 29:34–30:2).

A bitter harvest of Rebekah and Jacob's deception and Rachel's envy was reaped in the third generation when Joseph's brothers began to envy him (Gen. 37:11). They sold him into slavery and then deceived their father about it (Gen. 37:23–35). Where had they learned to treat their sibling with jealousy and their father with such cruel deception? Clearly, they were following in their elders' footsteps!

Sin can pass from generation to generation, not just by what is said, but by what is lived. Attitudes are not so much taught as caught. In light of this reality, consider the relationships in your own extended family. In what ways may you be harming others by harboring envy, covetousness, lust, pride, or other "private" sins? Is there a need for repentance and a change of attitude, as well as behavior? Would you change your ways for the sake of your children and grandchildren?

Like a Spider's Web

Esau had been cheated by the schemes of his mother and brother (Gen. 27:1–39). When he realized what had been done to him, he was outraged—some would say justifiably (Gen. 27:34–36). Yet how did he deal with his anger and hurt? He nursed it into a grudge and determined to retaliate by killing his brother after his father was dead (Gen. 30:41; compare Heb. 12:16–17).

However, he failed to take into account the complicity of his mother. When she learned of Esau's plan, she helped Jacob escape. And rather than confront the deception that she and Jacob had committed, and apologize to Esau, she merely suggested that time would heal all wounds (Gen. 27:42–45). Perhaps she

was more concerned for her own situation than for either of her sons.

What a web of evil!

The patterns of trickery and manipulation continued into the next generation. Jacob's sons committed such evils as destroying an entire city out of revenge (Gen. 34:1–31), and selling one of their brothers into slavery and then lying to their father about what had happened (Gen. 37:23–28, 31–35). Apparently they had learned from their father and grandmother that the way to deal with sin was not to acknowledge it, but to hide it.

Such is the nature of sin and evil. It binds people the way a spider wraps a fly in more and more threads until no escape is possible—no escape, that is, apart from divine intervention. God's response to sin was to offer Jesus Christ as a sacrifice for us. He took on Himself the penalty for sin that we deserve. Therefore, He is able to break the bonds of sin that ensnare us (Rom. 5:6–9).

Have you taken God up on His offer to deliver you from sin? Are there continuing patterns of evil and destruction from which you need to be set free? Are there things for which you need God's forgiveness? Apart from Him you can be sure—things won't get any better with time.

The conflict between Esau and Jacob (Gen. 27:41) was eventually patched up (Gen. 33:4, 10–11). Nevertheless, the two brothers set a precedent for their descendants that grew into a centuries-long feud between the Edomites and Israelites.

For more on this topic, see **MURDER,** *"Family Chaos," page 274.*

E

ECOLOGY

An Ecological Disaster

The infestation of frogs (Ex. 8:8–15) and the other nine plagues that God visited on Egypt created an ecological nightmare. The Nile and its related waterways, the air over Egypt, the flora and fauna of the region, and many other natural systems were degraded by the upset of the region's ecological balance.

However, let there be no mistake: the re-

sponsibility for these natural disasters was Pharaoh's, not God's. The ruler's refusal to obey God, or even to treat his Hebrew laborers with simple compassion, brought about the ten judgments. It was only after God allowed the natural systems of Egypt to fail, one after the other, that Pharaoh relented.

As the Creator, God knew exactly how to upset the intricate and delicate balance of Egypt's environment in a way that would bring proud Pharaoh to his knees. The plagues were awesome and undeniable demonstrations of His power, and the fact that the Israelites were spared showed that God was in control of nature's forces.

Bless the Lord by Blessing the Earth

Psalm 104 begins and ends with a blessing: "Bless the LORD, O my soul!" (Ps. 104:1, 35). This is easy to say; but how might we actively bless the Lord, given that His blessings to us are so practical (Ps. 104:14–15)? One way would be to take care of the earth that the Lord has created.

The Bible gives us a great deal of insight into why stewardship of the earth is a legitimate concern for God's people, and how we can fulfill that responsibility:

1. God created the earth (Gen. 1:1), and everything about the creation reflects His handiwork and glory (Ps. 19:1–6; 33:5–7; Is. 6:3).

2. God assessed His creation as "very good" (Gen. 1:10, 12, 18, 21, 25, 31).

3. God gave human beings dominion, or authority, over the earth and its creatures (Gen. 1:28), a responsibility that in a sense makes people coworkers with God. One of

E

ECOLOGY

the first tasks given to the first human beings was to manage and develop the Garden of Eden (2:15).

4. The earth belongs to God (Ex. 9:29; Ps. 24:1–2). It is essentially "on loan" to humanity, and we will give an account to Him for how we have used it.

5. Creation is an intricate system in which the various parts affect each other (Ps. 65:5–13; 104:10–23).

6. Nature is a reminder of God's enduring mercy. It should cause us to praise and worship Him (Ps. 136:1–9).

7. God's creation of the earth and His gift of life is tied to His command to care for the world's poorest and most deprived people—the bruised, the blind, the imprisoned, and the oppressed (Is. 42:5–9).

8. The world currently "groans" with birth pangs, waiting to be set free from the curse. Meanwhile, believers are called to demonstrate the love of God, even in the midst of the tribulations, distresses, persecutions, famines, nakedness, peril, and wars of the world (Rom. 8:18–39).

9. The simple act of eating is a privilege and a benefit of God's wonderful gift of creation. Scripture encourages us to eat "to the glory of God," not just for the satisfaction of our pleasures (1 Cor. 10:23–33).

Are you concerned about God's good earth? Do you live with any limits on consumption, the use of natural resources, or the creation and disposal of waste? Does the industry you work in demonstrate any stewardship of the earth? If not, what changes could you help to bring about?

Faith and the Environment

Global warming. Overpopulation. Acid rain. The destruction of rain forests. Is the Bible concerned with the earth's ecology? Or does it teach that the earth's resources exist purely for people's pleasure, to be used as they will, with little thought for long-term consequences?

"The earth is the Lord's, and all its fullness," declared the psalmist (Ps. 24:1). Again, "The earth is full of [God's] possessions" (Ps. 104:24). These and many other passages indicate that creation is not ours to plunder, but rather a resource which God has entrusted

to our management, to be used in service to each other. We will ultimately answer to God for its use.

In John's description of the end times, there is much destruction and violence. But not all is to be consumed. Nor does the earth exist only for people's pleasure and consumption. The command not to harm "the grass of the earth, or any green thing, or any tree" (Rev. 9:4) is a curious echo of Genesis 1:29–30: "every herb that yields seed which is on the face of all the earth, and every tree whose fruit yields seed . . . every beast of the earth, to every bird of the air, and to everything that creeps on the earth."

The same concern for earth's resources occurs when God sends one of His angels to cry with a loud voice to the four angels "to whom it was granted to harm the earth and the sea . . . 'Do not harm the earth, the sea, or the trees'" (Rev. 7:2–3). Likewise, the new heaven and earth include a "pure river of water of life, clear as crystal . . . the tree of life, which bore twelve fruits, each tree yielding its fruit every month. The leaves of the tree were for the healing of the nations" (Rev. 22:1–2).

When God created the world's resources, He declared them to be "very good" (Gen. 1:31). He assigned people to care for them, develop them, and use them for good (Gen. 1:26–31). This management role is part of our calling to live according to the image and likeness of God. He has made us to be more than mere consumers who gratify their own desires. He wants us to serve Him as we manage His creation. Our work is a gift from God to develop and deliver the benefits of that resource to other people.

Do you treat the world with respect as a resource for which God has given you responsibility? Does your work please God and serve other people? Can you think of ways to do a better job of managing the environment in a way that God would approve?

God and the Environment

Not only has God created the world, He sustains it with loving attention. His concern extends even to the needs of birds and animals, for which He provides food and drink (Ps. 104:10–23). Scripture shows clearly that the Lord watches over every aspect of the creation, including its conservation. For example:

- In the beginning, God commanded Adam and Eve to cultivate and keep the garden. That kind of stewardship ruled out wanton destruction (Gen. 2:15).
- Later, God was sorry that He had created humans because of their total wickedness (Gen. 6:5–6). So He determined to destroy everyone through a flood. However, He saved not only Noah and his family, but animals as well (Gen. 6:13–14, 19–22).
- After the flood, God made a covenant that "all flesh shall never again be cut off by the water of the flood" (Gen. 9:8–11).
- Later, God instructed the Hebrews to allow their cropland to be rested (left fallow) every seventh year in order to rejuvenate it and preserve it (Ex. 23:10–11; Lev. 25:2–7; 26:34–35).
- The Law also prohibited the unnecessary destruction of fruit and nut trees and the killing of mother birds, even for food (Deut. 20:19–20; 22:6–7).

God cares about what He has created, and He has charged us as people to wisely manage those resources (Gen. 1:26), to use them for our good and for His glory. As we face increasingly complex environmental issues, we need to view the earth as a sacred trust from God's hands, for which He will hold us accountable. If He cares about every single creature on the planet, shouldn't we?

Lord of the Land

The numerous wars of this century have shown the terrible devastation that war brings on the environment. By recalling these catastrophes, modern-day Bible readers can imagine some of the awesome destruction caused by the "day of the Lord" described in Joel 2. For example, before-and-after photos of Hiroshima, where the first atomic bomb was dropped, give some indication of what the prophet had in mind when he described a Garden of Eden turned into a wilderness (Joel 2:3).

Yet after the devastation, the Lord will clean up the damage. Joel tells the land not to fear, but to rejoice, because God will restore health to the environment, bring about new life, and cause the revived vegetation to yield abundant produce (Joel 2:19–27). Thus there is a close connection between the redemptive work of God and the creative work of God.

This has important implications for believers today. If God is concerned with all of life—the natural as well as the spiritual—God's people should be, too. We have good cause to preserve and wisely manage the natural world and the urban environment. Indeed, we act as God's agents on the earth, "to tend and keep it" (Gen. 2:15). We will give an account to our Lord, who is concerned with land as well as people.

The Ruin of the Land

The desolation that the Lord promised to bring upon the "forest" of Assyria (Is. 10:19) was a judgment of that nation's arrogance, inhumanity, and idolatry. Isaiah's vision hinted at ecological disaster. A similar judgment was to fall on other parts of the Middle East, including Canaan. In fact, the prophets frequently spoke in terms of environmental catastrophe.

Isaiah saw the earth being "defiled under its inhabitants," and warned that the "curse has devoured the earth" (Is. 24:5–6). As a result, the vineyards would fail and death would come to the cities (Is. 24:7–13). Ezekiel likened Assyria to a cedar in Lebanon, and prophesied that its glory would be cut down (Ezek. 31:1–14). Joel warned of devouring locusts that would strip the produce from Judah's fields and vineyards (Joel 1:2–4). Joel's vision probably referred to an invasion by a foreign army, but his description accurately reflected the ruination of an agricultural economy (Joel 1:10–12, 17–18).

Whether or not the prophets were speaking of literal disasters in the ecology of the Middle East, the fact is that between the eighth and first centuries B.C., the Mediterranean coastal regions experienced an extreme change in their environments. The forests of Lebanon and Ephraim disappeared. The firs on Mount Hermon ("Senir") became unavailable (Ezek. 27:5). The lions that lived in the Jordan River valley were no longer to be found. To a large extent, the land became "desolate," just as the prophets had warned (Mic. 7:13).

No one can say exactly what brought about this massive destruction of the natural environment. But the impact of human activity certainly played a part, especially:

1. *Overcutting of forests, especially in Lebanon.* The Bible describes how Solomon imported as much cedar as he wanted from the Phoenicians (1 Kin. 5:10). In fact, one project used so much cedar that the building was called the House of the Forest of Lebanon (1 Kin. 7:2). Prolonged and indiscriminate cutting of Lebanon's ancient forests eventually wiped them out.

2. *Frequent battles and military campaigns.* When an ancient army besieged a city, it plundered nearby fields and forests to feed itself, and then burned the countryside in order to cut off any potential food supplies for the defenders. Siege ramps and towers were constructed from whatever timber could be found. As a result, a military campaign usually ravaged the environment of the invaded territory.

A temporary reversal in this situation occurred during the time of the Roman Empire. Roman engineers implemented a carefully coordinated program of water conservation and land use, and built an impressive infrastructure of canals, aqueducts, and reservoirs. They even attempted to replant trees in Lebanon. But with the passing of the Romans, many areas reverted to desert, and much of the land that was said to flow with milk and honey (Num. 13:27) once again became unproductive.

The Voice of the Lord in Creation

David could hear the "voice of the LORD" in the phenomena of nature (Ps. 29:3). Can we? In a day of increasing concern over the world's environment, psalms such as this one deserve regular review in our thinking, worship, and prayers.

Psalm 29 ascribes to the Lord all power and authority over nature. The Canaanites worshiped natural forces such as wind and fire as their gods (called "mighty ones," Ps. 29:1). But Israel worshiped the God of creation, not the creation itself. Thunderstorms, lightning, and floods were but means by which the Lord might express Himself; they were not themselves divine.

Yet today, some people view the earth as sacred or divine, and for that reason champion the environment. By contrast, people who believe the Bible see the earth as a resource from God for which human beings are responsible. Armed with this belief, God's people have tremendous motivation to manage the environment wisely, to protect and preserve it equitably, and to worship with humility the God who created it.

For more on this topic, see CONSERVATION, "A Rest for the Land," page 87.

EDUCATION
Jesus the Student

What kind of student was Jesus? Did He come into the world already knowing everything He needed to know? Was He able to acquire knowledge without even studying? The snapshot of Jesus in the temple (Luke 2:46–47) suggests otherwise. Though He apparently held His seniors spellbound with questions and responses, He nevertheless went through a lifelong process of education, learning and growing through "on-the-job training" from expert teachers.

Luke paints a picture of Jesus as a model student. The rabbis He encountered at Jerusalem were the preeminent experts in Judaism who researched, developed, and applied the body of Old Testament Law and rabbinical tradition to issues of the day. Some were members of the council, the governing tribunal of Judea. These teachers were fond of waxing eloquent on religious and legal questions in the temple courtyard for the benefit of any who would listen (Matt. 6:5; 7:28–29; 23:1–7).

Nevertheless, Jesus made strategic use of these authorities during His visit to the big city for Passover. Now age 12, He was considered a man. So He went to the temple to learn all He could about the Law of God. He proved to be an avid student, listening carefully and asking questions about His "Father's business" (Luke 2:49). Rather than embarrass His parents and offend His teachers by spouting off what He knew, He humbly subjected Himself to the discipline of education (Luke 2:51). His turn to teach would come later. For now, He accepted the role of a learner.

It's a good example for all of us who must go through school and learn on the job. Like

Jesus, we need to learn all we can from the best teachers we can find, showing ourselves to be teachable, with an attitude of humility.

The Value of Learning

"It doesn't matter whether you have an education," some people say, "God can use you anyway." True, God can use anyone, with or without formal education. But Moses' learning "in all the wisdom of the Egyptians" (Acts 7:22) proved to be a valuable asset when the Lord called him to lead Israel out of captivity.

Moses spent the first third of his life—forty years—in Egypt. Raised among royalty, he was exposed to the impressive culture of the pharaohs. The curriculum likely included political science, public administration, religion, history, literature, geometry, and perhaps even engineering and hydraulics.

But that was not the end of Moses' education. He spent another forty years in "graduate school" in the desert, studying animal husbandry while interning as a shepherd. He also learned about public health and primitive communities. Altogether, the first two-thirds of Moses' life prepared him for his most challenging job—leading Israel through the wilderness.

Intelligence and education alone don't make someone fit to serve God. Indeed, an educated person can hide behind his or her learning in order to avoid dealing with God. Young Saul fell into that trap (Acts 22:3–5), as did his fellow Pharisees. So did the philosophers at Athens (Acts 17:16–34). But as Stephen pointed out, the problem is not with the intellect but with the will; the danger comes not from embracing knowledge but from resisting God (Acts 7:51).

EMBALMING

Grave Procedures

Embalming is a method of preparing the dead for burial and preserving the body from decay. The practice of treating a corpse to preserve it dates back more than three thousand five hundred years. Mummification was invented by the Egyptians, who believed that the preservation of the body insured the continuation of the person after death.

According to the Greek historian Herodotus, there were three different methods of embalming. The least expensive method involved emptying the intestines by flushing them with a cleaning liquid, after which the body was soaked in natron. The second method called for placing the body in natron after the stomach and intestines had been dissolved by an injection of cedar oil.

The most elaborate method of embalming required the removal of the brain and all internal organs except the heart. The inner cavity of the body was then washed and filled with spices. The corpse was soaked in natron, then washed and wrapped in bandages of linen soaked with gum. Finally, the embalmed body was placed in a wooden coffin.

The Bible mentions embalming only once, in reference to Joseph and his father Jacob (Gen. 50:2–3, 26). Even this single reference is surprising, since the ancient Israelites did not generally embalm their dead because of laws concerning the touching of dead bodies (Num. 5:1–4; 19:11–22). But both Joseph and Jacob died in Egypt. They were apparently embalmed so their bodies could be taken back to Israel for burial.

Preparation for burial of the dead among the Jews usually consisted of washing the body (Acts 9:37) and then anointing it with aromatic ointments. Burial was normally on the day of death or the following day. The body was wrapped in cloth strips, with a separate cloth tied around the head. Spices were applied when the body was wrapped (Mark 16:1). Expensive spices were used to prepare Jesus' body for burial (John 19:39–42).

EMPATHY

A Kinder, Gentler Counselor

Elihu sat on the sidelines while Eliphaz, Bildad, and Zophar exhausted their pleas to Job (Job 32:4–5). Apparently Elihu assumed that these three counselors would be more knowledgeable than he because of their age. Yet when it became evident that they lacked convincing arguments, he offered a new perspective through four back-to-back addresses (Job 32:5–33:33; 34:1–37; 35:1–16; 36:1–37:24).

Elihu turned out to be far more empathetic in his treatment of Job. For example, he allowed for the possibility that neither Job's circumstances nor his rebuttals to his three friends' remarks necessarily implied sin or guilt. Instead, he suggested—probably correctly—that Job was being disciplined and refined by fire for his greater good, or to teach greater truth.

Perhaps because of the merit of Elihu's arguments, God did not reproach him the way he did Job's three other friends (Job 42:7–9). Apparently God did not take issue with what the young counselor had said. But Elihu's explanation for Job's condition did not go far enough. There is no higher principle of justice than God's to which humanity can appeal. God Himself is the ultimate standard of justice. We need appeal to God alone for mercy or vindication. We may also appeal for greater ability to understand our experience, but we have no guarantee of receiving that— at least not on this side of heaven.

Elihu and counselors like him are to be commended for first trying to put themselves in another person's place. By observing and listening before speaking, they are better equipped to apply abstract theological concepts to real, live human beings in sensitive, compassionate ways.

EMPOWERMENT

Empowering Leadership

Jesus' promise in John 14:12–13 shows that noble leadership seeks to empower others to achieve results even greater than the leader has achieved. The true leader seeks to achieve great goals more than great personal gain. Rather than being intimidated by his followers' potential, he rejoices in their growth, development, and achievements.

ENCOURAGEMENT

Barnabas—"Joe Encouragement"

The apostles chose the perfect Christian name for Joses of Cyprus when they called him Barnabas—Son of Encouragement. Every appearance of Barnabas in Scripture finds him encouraging others in the faith. In fact, he serves as the supreme model for how to mentor young believers. Numerous churches can trace their beginnings back to the efforts of "Joe Encouragement."

An interesting sidelight: Though Levites traditionally lived off the temple system, Barnabas had real estate. But on coming into the faith, he sold it and donated the proceeds for the care of the poor (Acts 4:36–37). Later, he joined with Paul in refusing to make a living from the gospel (1 Cor. 9:6).

Encouraging the Boss

Separation from close friends can bring feelings of loneliness and loss, especially when one is facing disappointment or failure. Paul felt that way in Athens. Despite his strident efforts to present and defend the gospel, he met with only lackluster response from the Athenians (Acts 17:16–34). Not surprisingly, his thoughts turned toward the Thessalonians with whom he felt an unusually deep bond (1 Thess. 2:8; 2:17–3:1).

Anxious for news, Paul sent his valuable associate Timothy north for a visit (1 Thess. 3:2). The young man's report buoyed Paul. Even as one city was resisting Christ, another was responding to Him in powerful and encouraging ways (1 Thess. 3:6–10).

Paul's emotional honesty here is refreshing and instructive. Rather than deny or spiritualize his pain, he acknowledged it and took action. He needed the warm affection of the Thessalonians and especially the capable companionship of Timothy. Rather than live as a "Lone Ranger Christian," Paul stayed connected to other believers and relied on them for insight, encouragement, and support. In this way he honored a basic principle of Christian community (Heb. 10:24–25).

Does your supervisor need encouragement, affirmation, or help in keeping the big picture? Often when people are under great stress or feeling a sense of failure, the only thing they hear is what's wrong. Can you encourage your boss with a word about what is right?

For more on this topic, see **RECOGNITION,** *"The Lord Knows," page 332.*

END-TIMES PROPHECIES

A Promise of Victory

Ezekiel describes a dramatic battle in which the Lord promises to defeat a powerful army of allied forces that will come against Israel (Ezek. 38–39). The emphasis of the prophecy seems to be that God will fight for His people. He will not allow their enemies to destroy them. On the contrary, He will so completely destroy Israel's enemies that it will take seven months to bury their bodies (38:12), and their arms will provide seven years' worth of firewood (Ezek. 38:9).

One difficulty in understanding these chapters is that they are to some extent related to a style of literature known as *apocalyptic* (see Rev. 10:1–10). This means that their message is given in somewhat veiled terms through the use of vivid imagery. So readers must beware of drawing quick conclusions based on a too-literal a reading of the text. On the other hand, one need not dismiss Ezekiel's vision as allegorical, or assume that it was a coded message that could only be understood and applied by his original hearers.

The identities of Gog, Magog, and the other names mentioned (Ezek. 38:2–3) are perhaps impossible to establish with certainty. The name Gog appears in the Bible only in Ezekiel and in Revelation 20:8, which suggests prophetic significance. Around 660 B.C., the kingdom of Lydia in western Asia Minor (modern Turkey) was ruled by a King Gyges, who some have suggested was the Gog referred to in Scripture. Others identify Gog with an ancient god, Gaga, others with Alexander the Great or some other historical figure.

Whatever the identity of Gog, he includes in his army soldiers from Persia, Ethiopia, Libya, Gomer, and Togarmah (Ezek. 38:5). In Ezekiel's day, the first three of these referred to lands which were probably at the extremes of the world as the Jews knew it. Some see this international conspiracy of nations against Israel as a literal confederacy that will attack Israel in the end times, precipitating Armageddon. Others see it as a symbol of all of the evil forces that are gathered against the people of God.

It is possible that Ezekiel himself did not know the exact identity of this enemy alliance that would come against Israel. In his day, the Lord was dispersing the Jews throughout the world and tearing the land from their control. Promises of restoration had been given (Ezek. 36–37; compare Jer. 31), but even a restored Israel would have its enemies.

God promises to protect His people. His victory is cataclysmic, overwhelming, and total (Ezek. 39:1–16). He accomplishes it by Himself (Ezek. 38:17–23) in what sounds like the great and terrible "day of the LORD" foreseen by other prophets (Joel 2:28–32; Amos 5:18–20; Zeph. 1:14–18).

New Work for a New World

Did you know that in the world to come you will have work to do, and that your work will be gratifying, fulfilling, and enduring? According to the glimpse of the future that Isaiah was given, people will build houses and cultivate vineyards (Is. 65:21–22), an indication that God's new earth will be filled with meaningful activity.

This should come as a comfort to you if your present occupation seems insignificant, boring, or dissatisfying. In the world to come, you will "long enjoy the work of [your] hands" (Is. 65:22). That is, you will see the results of what you accomplish and enjoy the benefits of your efforts. You will not "labor in vain" (Is. 65:23) the way so many workers do now.

Isaiah's vision has reference to this world as it was originally created. It was "very good" in God's estimation (Gen. 1:31), and the work of the world was "very good" as well. In His new world, God will restore work to its original purpose.

In the meantime, we can serve God as His coworkers, using the abilities and resources that He has given us to wisely manage this earth and meet the needs of people. We can also anticipate our future with God by walking with Him through life and learning what He has in store for us. And we can share our future hope with others, encouraging them place their lives and future in the loving hands of Christ.

Issues for Doomsday

As you look at events in the world today, you may feel anxious about how history is going to turn out. Perhaps you're confused and troubled about end times. The buildup of weapons, the warnings of religious prophets of doom, shaky economies, and the turmoil of nations may feel very unsettling.

Jesus' words in Mark 13 (and Matt. 24:1–51 and Luke 21:5–36) speak to these issues. They left an indelible impression on His followers. What touched off the discussion was the disciples' comments on the solidity and significance of a downtown building (Mark 13:1). Jesus replied by noting how temporary such structures actually are (Mark 13:2). Later,

E

in a quiet setting (Mark 13:3), He went into far more detail about the end of history as we know it and the stresses believers would undergo (Mark 13:4–37). Rather than avoid the topic, He spoke of:

- deception, wars, earthquakes, and famines as the beginning of sorrows (Mark 13:5–8);
- how His followers would experience testing as His witnesses before councils, governors, and kings (Mark 13:9–11);
- how family members would turn against each other (Mark 13:12–13);
- how distress and deception would eventually reign, but such times would be limited by God (13:14–25);
- His eventual return for His own (Mark 13:15–31);
- the fact that no one knows precisely when He will return—and thus the need for His followers to be watchful and dutiful in serving God (Mark 13:32–37).

Jesus contrasted the strength and beauty of a downtown building with the faithful loyalty and service of His followers (Mark 13:2, 9, 13, 33–37). Human structures will inevitably crumble and fall, but the righteous works of God will last forever. Therefore, believers ought to stand firm, serving God faithfully—not just building monuments to their own accomplishments, and certainly not falling prey to the seductive dangers of the times.

Don't Panic

Are you anxious about the future of the world? Do dire predictions about coming disasters trouble you? Or do dramatic solutions to the world's many problems hold your curiosity?

Like many people today, the believers in Thessalonica were vulnerable to urgent warnings and announcements related to the future (2 Thess. 2:1–2). In fact, certain false teachers of the day pandered to people's interest in such things, playing to their greatest hopes and worst fears about the return of Christ (2 Thess. 2:3; 1 Thess. 5:2–5). In response, Paul appealed for reason and critical thinking based on the clear instructions he had given (2 Thess. 2:3–12, 15).

As we read 2 Thessalonians today, we, like the letter's original readers, need to "stand fast and hold the traditions which [we] were taught," the truths of God's Word. We should avoid fanciful, fearful guesswork about events related to the Lord's return and instead be busy about our responsibilities at hand (2 Thess. 3:6–13).

ENEMIES

Love My Enemies?

The Law commanded Hebrews to love their neighbors (Lev. 19:18), but Jesus challenged His followers to love even their enemies (Luke 6:27). Later He would be asked, "Who is my neighbor?" (Luke 10:29). Here we might ask, "Who are our enemies?"

Many believers today might think of our enemies as those we find unpleasant, people we just don't like. But that's not strong enough. By "enemies" Jesus meant those we actually hate, and those who hate us, for whatever reason.

Jesus' listeners didn't need to look far to understand who it was He was talking about. Luke 6:17 notes that a huge crowd had gathered around Him, including Gentiles from the seacoast cities of Tyre and Sidon. These centers of Baal worship had troubled the Hebrews for generations by introducing pagan ideas and practices. Elsewhere, Roman occupation troops held sway over the region, exploiting the Jews through oppressive taxation and political manipulation.

So it was immediately clear to the crowd who their enemies were—who was likely to curse and shame them (Luke 6:28), who was likely to strike and rob them (Luke 6:29), and who was likely to exploit them (Luke 6:30). "Love your enemies," Jesus told them. Love those you hate, and who hate you.

Those of us who follow Jesus in today's world also have "enemies." Basically we are no different from those first believers. If we look carefully, we will recognize people we *hate*, and who *hate us*. The bitterness may spring from racial, ethnic, political, economic, moral, gender, religious, or ideological conflicts. But they go beyond mere likes and dislikes. So Jesus' challenge to us is the same: "Love your enemies. Love those you hate, and who hate you."

Upside-Down Values

Enmity and hostility have a way of turning otherwise kind and compassionate people into vicious and vindictive people. That is one reason why Scripture cautions us against allowing bitterness and hatred to remain in our hearts. These attitudes can seriously distort our values, turning them upside down so that we care more about things such as our own honor, our material well-being, or our national or ethnic pride, than we do about people.

Jonah fell into this trap. God called him to preach repentance to the people of Nineveh, but Jonah resisted because they were bitter enemies of his people, the Israelites. Only after a near-death experience did the unwilling prophet finally comply (Jon. 1:17–3:3).

However, his values were still upside-down. When he complained about the repentance of the Ninevites (Jon. 4:1–3), God taught him a lesson using a shade plant. The Lord exposed the prophet's distorted attitudes by showing that he cared more for the loss of the plant than for the plight of an entire people whom God was determined to save (Jon. 4:10–11).

What do your attitudes toward others—especially your enemies—reveal about your values? Have you allowed yourself to become "upside-down" in your concern for people? If so, why not step back and take a long, hard look at what matters to God. Then take steps to reorient your life so that it honors what the Lord values.

For more on this topic, see COMPETITION, "Daniel Spares His Competitors," page 79.

ENGAGEMENT

(*see* Marriage)

ENVIRONMENT

(*see* Ecology)

EQUALITY

Finally, Full Equality

Will there ever be an end to discrimination, racism, elitism, and injustice? Will people ever regard each other as equals? John's vision of "every tribe and tongue and people and nation" standing before God and singing His praise (Rev. 5:9) gives us assurance that in the end, we will all experience full equality.

Scripture begins with a creation that was "very good" (Gen. 1:31). Adam and Eve were given authority over creation and responsibility to tend the garden as full partners. However, the horrible entrance of sin ruins this original design. Is there any reason to hope that God's original intention will be recovered?

Yes, Revelation 5 offers images of the original reality one day coming true again:

- One who is worthy to provide a renewed future arrives (Rev. 5:1–5).
- The Spirits of God pervade the creation (Rev. 5:6).
- Believers from every tribe and nation are among the leadership (Rev. 5:9).
- All of them are empowered to be "kings and priests to our God" who will reign on the earth (Rev. 5:10).
- Unhindered praise and worship breaks forth, uniting representatives of all peoples before God (Rev. 5:11–14).

God's original design will ultimately become a reality. Meanwhile, believers today are called to be signposts of Christ's coming kingdom so that others may choose to welcome Him into their lives.

Is there evidence in your life, family, and work that this kingdom is beginning in you?

What Is Headship?

What exactly did Paul mean when he used the word "head" (1 Cor. 11:3)? Some believe that the term by definition implies subordination of one person to another. Others disagree. For example, John Chrysostom, an early church leader, declared that only a heretic would understand "head" as chief or authority over. Rather, he understood the word as meaning absolute oneness, cause, or primal source.

Either way, it's important to note that while "the head of Christ is God" (1 Cor. 11:3), Christ is elsewhere shown to be equal with God (for example, John 1:1–3; 10:30; Col. 1:15). So the term "head" need not exclude the idea of equality. At the same time, even though Christ is the equal of God, He became obedient to the point of death (Phil. 2:5–8), demonstrating that equality need not rule out submission.

ESCAPISM
Schemes to Avoid Painful Realities

Many people in modern society act as if they should be able to live without pain, suffering, or disappointment. For many, self-indulgence, pleasure, and happiness appear as inalienable rights to which they are entitled. They not only feel that no limits should hinder them in achieving personal satisfaction, but that life somehow owes it to them.

But it takes some interesting mental tricks or "schemes" (Eccl. 7:29) to hold this view of life. Here are some of the schemes often used to deny the more painful realities of life:

1. *Escape.* We may seek to escape from unpleasantness by involving ourselves in a myriad of distractions. As a result, we become too busy to think, reflect, or even hear about things we can't handle, enjoy, or control. We may even set up elaborate ways to avoid negative information, such as skipping the hard news sections of the papers. There is nothing inherently wrong with busyness, but God offers a life that is busy with joy (Eccl. 5:20).

2. *Denial.* We may deny that life has problems by constantly telling each other, "Everything's fine." Our conversation may be filled with propaganda that we want to believe. In this way we can become like the false scribes that Jeremiah described, whose cry was "peace, peace" when there was no peace (Jer. 8:11). God is the God of peace, but He also uses adversity to build our character (Eccl. 7:14).

3. *Indifference.* We may become callous to people's pain—aware of their suffering, but unmoved by it. In reality, there may be very little we can do, yet God would have us show compassion for those who are oppressed (4:1).

4. *Hedonism.* We may deal with pain by engaging in an extreme pursuit of happiness, becoming "party animals" and living from one thrill to the next. There is a place in life for leisure and pleasure, but God shows how empty the worship of ourselves and our pleasure systems can become (Eccl. 2:1–11).

5. *Withdrawal.* We may also avoid the world's dark realities by turning inward, closing off as many contacts as possible with the outside world. We may protect our space behind privacy fences, answering machines, or security systems, always in control of the people and information that reach us. We may forsake the claims of others and instead insist that our values, interests, and rights are the ones that really matter. However, God reminds us that turning inward can lead to an empty existence (Eccl. 4:8).

Are you using one or more of these strategies to avoid some of the more painful realities of life? If so, you'll want to consider that only by facing reality with God's strength can you find real meaning and purpose.

ETERNAL LIFE

(*see* Immortality)

ETHICS
Be Holy, For I Am Holy

Both the reason and the goal of all God's ethical requirements is His own holy character (Lev. 11:44–45). As His followers, we should be holy because we should reflect His character. He is our Father. He has created us. He has chosen us as His own. Therefore, we should be like Him.

Also, we should be holy because He has determined to make us like Himself (Rom. 8:29–30). That is His goal in saving us: that we should be "holy and without blame" before Him (Eph. 1:4).

What areas of your character and conduct reflect something of God's holiness? Where do you need to grow?

Good Enough for God?

Psalm 15 presents a summary of what God expects of His people. The question under discussion is, who is good enough to meet with God? (Ps. 15:1).

The answer is interesting in that rather than giving a list of dos and don'ts, this psalm describes godliness in terms of *character.* The qualities extend to personal issues of integrity and honesty, our relationships with others, and the way we handle our money.

This passage shows that we should approach worship not only in terms of our inward, personal needs, but also in light of our outward, public responsibilities. It also shows that religion is a matter of character as well as conduct.

The Quality of Being

We live in a day of the "fast track," the "sound bite," and the "hurried child." But what is so attractive about the rush to achieve quick results? Is that the way life was intended to be?

A study of James 1 shows that God wants people to *be someone* more than to *get somewhere*. Rather than measuring our worth through achievements and acquisitions, He evaluates our character, looking for such virtues as peace, truth, serenity, and strength of character. He values us for who we are and who we are becoming. He wants us to be:

- people who can endure testing and trial (James 1:4).
- people who trust God to provide for their needs and feel free to ask for His help (James 1:5–9).
- people who can discern between good and bad choices and make wise decisions (James 1:12–16).
- people who give generously to others, just as God has given generously to us (James 1:17–18).
- people who listen well and respond thoughtfully (James 1:19–21).
- people who act instead of just talking and whose actions benefit others (James 1:22–25).
- people who value and show compassion toward others who are in need, especially those forgotten by society (James 1:26–27).

It takes time to develop character like that. But God is interested in long-term growth, not just a quick fix. We may need to slow down and take a long, hard look at the direction of our lives. If we're driven to gain as much as we can as fast as we can, we're headed down a road toward destruction.

Standing for God

While it's always easy to find people who want to be "in charge," it's far more difficult to find people of character and ability who will step into roles of leadership. Israel faced a chronic crisis of leadership during the days of the judges, when "everyone did what was right in his own eyes" (Judg. 21:25). Few could be found who were willing and able to offer moral and spiritual direction.

Perhaps that's why Deborah, in her song of praise composed after Israel's victory over Jabin and Sisera, celebrated *willing* leaders followed by willing people (Judg. 5:2, 9). Apparently the people were willing to follow if they could find *leaders who would lead* rather than despots who would dominate, such as Abimelech (Judg. 9).

Deborah and Balak were good models of leaders willing to lead. Their stand for God and integrity before the people were profoundly inspiring—so much so that even common people such as the woman Jael were emboldened to grab whatever was at hand, be it but a tent peg and a hammer, and strike down their enemies (Judg. 4:17–22; 5:24–27).

Will you be a willing leader for God today? Whatever your sphere of influence—at your job, in your home, at church, in the community—will you accept the challenge to stand for God's ways and encourage others to do the same?

ETHNIC CLEANSING

A Legacy of Genocide

David made a name for himself in the Valley of Salt (2 Sam. 8:13–14), probably the wasteland plain southwest of the Dead Sea. But while his exploits greatly increased his reputation among his own people, they were sowing lasting bitterness elsewhere that would come back to haunt his successor, Solomon.

The "name" that David earned came at the expense of the lives of eighteen thousand Syrians, who probably were people of Edom. God explicitly commanded his people not to "abhor" the Edomites, since they were descended from the same ancestor, Jacob (Deut. 23:7–8). Yet David's general, Joab, carried out a six-month campaign of genocide "until he had cut down every male in Edom" (1 Kin. 11:15–16). This delighted the Israelites, who had long hated the Edomites.

However, an Edomite boy named Hadad watched the slaughter before his father's servants escaped with him to Egypt. He never forgot what he had seen. Years later, after David had died and his son Solomon had turned away from the Lord, God allowed Hadad to come back to Palestine, where he become a perennial thorn in Solomon's side (1 Kin. 11:14, 19–22).

E

Thus the life of Solomon was affected by the brutal ethnic policies of David and Joab. The tragic fruit of this legacy raises the question: How will you be remembered by other people, especially your enemies? If you have made or are making a "name" for yourself, what is the basis of that name? Is it being made at someone else's expense?

ETHNIC CONFLICT

(*see* Prejudice; Racism)

ETHNIC DIVERSITY

To All Peoples

Jesus sent His followers to make disciples of all the nations or peoples of the world. As John takes us into the throne room of heaven, we see the fulfillment of Jesus' mandate. There, standing before the Lamb (Christ) is a crowd so large that it cannot be counted, made up of "all nations, tribes, peoples, and tongues" (Rev. 7:9).

Actually, two groups are present—representatives from God's people, the Jews (Rev. 7:3–8), and countless Gentile believers (Rev. 7:9–10). Just as Jesus said it would, the gospel has spread out from Jerusalem to reach people from "the end of the earth" (Acts 1:8). Now Jews and Gentiles have come together to receive the salvation that God has promised. Now God dwells among His people. Jesus is their Shepherd, supplying all their needs (Rev. 7:14–17).

In response to this spectacular, worldwide, multiethnic salvation, the creatures of heaven and earth fall down before God in worship and song (Rev. 7:11–12). What a breathtaking picture this is!

But of course this vision lies in the future. For now, we live in a world wracked by ethnic divisions and racial prejudice. Yet knowing that God intends to populate heaven with people from every ethnic background has important implications for those of us who claim to follow Christ. If God's heart reaches out to the whole world, then our hearts need to as well.

The Antioch Model

Even though first-century Christians made regular pilgrimages to Jerusalem and met annually in the upper room, the city of Antioch—not Jerusalem—was the center of early Christianity. In fact, modern churches might consider Antioch as a model for what God's people ought to be and do.

Like most cities today, Antioch was racially diverse and culturally pluralistic. As a result, when the scattered believers arrived there (Acts 11:19–20), they had to wrestle with how to make the gospel meaningful for a diversity of groups. Four factors help to account for their success.

1. *They saw ethnic division as a barrier to overcome rather than a status quo to be maintained.* Antioch walled off the four dominant ethnic groups of its population, Greek, Syrian, African, and Jewish. But the gospel breaks down walls of separation and hostility (Eph. 2:14–22) and brings diverse peoples together in Christ. We know that the Antioch believers broke through the ethnic barriers because . . .

2. *They soon had multiethnic leadership.* The church employed and deployed pastors, teachers, and evangelists who reflected the composition of the community

3. *They sent out ministry teams.* Just as the church at Antioch had been established by believers fleeing from Jerusalem, it, too, sent out ministry teams to tell the story of Jesus. Paul used Antioch as his base of operation for three successive tours (Acts 13:1–3; 15:36–41; and 18:22–23). Moreover, Antioch served as a crossroads for travelers from the Tigris and Euphrates River valleys to the east, Asia Minor to the north, and Egypt to the south. So the church was able to maintain an international outreach in its own hometown.

4. *They joined together to accomplish projects of compassion.* A famine in Judea became an opportunity for the multiethnic Christians at Antioch to serve their predominantly Jewish brothers in Judea (Acts 11:27–30). Paul recognized how powerful the "politics of compassion" could be at uniting otherwise disconnected churches. "Remember the poor" became his rallying cry to bring together believers in Ephesus, Corinth, Thessalonica, Galatia, and Rome with those at Jerusalem (Acts 20:17–18, 35; 2 Cor. 8:1–9:15; Gal. 2:10).

Overall, Antioch became the model for how the church ought to function when surrounded by diversity and cultural pluralism.

Out of Many, One

The city of Colosse included people from a wide variety of ethnic and cultural backgrounds (Col. 3:11):

- Greeks, whose cultural heritage dominated the Roman world;
- Jews, who prided themselves as "God's chosen people";
- Barbarians, who spoke no Greek and therefore lacked social standing;
- Scythians, a crude, cruel warlike people from the north; and
- slaves, menial workers at the bottom of the society.

Members from all these groups came to faith and joined the community of believers at Colosse. But their ethnic prejudices created problems, which Paul listed (Col. 3:8–9). He pulled no punches, calling them by their ugly names: anger, wrath, malice, blasphemy, filthy language, and lying. Paul challenged his culturally mixed group of readers to shed such behaviors like an old set of clothes and put on Christ instead, who "is all and in all." He was possibly reminding them of a first-century baptismal creed that reminded new converts that they were joining a new family in Christ.

God's family has no place for prejudice. Radically new ways of relating to others are called for (Col. 3:12–17). If believers today lived out these ideals, we would see God change our churches and begin to transform our culture.

ETHNIC DIVERSITY

God's Rainbow

Societies and their systems tend to encourage people to divide along racial, ethnic, and cultural lines, or else to abandon their distinctives by assimilating into the dominant power group. Paul called for a different approach. He didn't ask Jews to give up their Jewish heritage and become Gentiles, nor did he ask Gentiles to become Jews. Instead, he affirmed the rich ethnic backgrounds of both groups while challenging them to live together in unity (Rom. 15:7).

That kind of unity is costly, and the attempt to practice it is always under attack. Yet that is the church that God calls us to—a diverse body of people who are unified around Christ. Our backgrounds—whether Japanese, Anglo-Saxon, African, Middle Eastern, Puerto Rican, Chinese, Italian, or whatever—are God's gifts to each of us and to the church. He has placed us in our families as He has seen fit. We can rejoice in the background He has given us and be enriched by the background He has given others.

Jews, Gentiles, and Jesus

At the time Jesus was born, Hebrews saw the world divided into two types of people—Jews and everyone else. Jews regarded foreigners (known as *Gentiles,* or "nations") as morally unclean and spiritually lost. Jews were God's people; Gentiles were not. The attitude was well expressed by Peter upon meeting Cornelius, a Roman centurion: "You know how unlawful it is for a Jewish man to keep company with or go to one of another nation" (Acts 10:28).

The roots of this separation stretched deep into Israel's history. One important development occurred in about 450 B.C. when a remnant of Jews returned from captivity in Babylon to rebuild Jerusalem. Their leader, Ezra the priest, called for purification from all pagan influences, such as foreign-born wives (Ezra 10:2–4).

Later, after centuries of domination by the Greeks and Romans, Jews developed a hatred for all Gentiles and tried to avoid contact with foreigners. According to Tacitus, a Roman historian, "they regard the rest of mankind with all the hatred of enemies" (*Histories,* 5.5).

In Matthew's Gospel we see a recognition of the tension between the two groups. He presents Jesus as the long-awaited Christ of the Jews (Matt 15:24). Jesus fulfilled numerous Old Testament messianic prophecies (for example, 1:23; 2:6, 14, 18, 23). But Matthew also shows Jesus breaking through the Jew/Gentile wall of hatred and separation. Jesus dealt with Jews and Gentiles alike, shattering the caste system of His day—and shocking His Jewish brothers.

What ethnic or racial walls would Jesus tear down in the modern era? Perhaps He would have joined black slaves in the United States and lived among them as an equal. Perhaps He would have violated the customs of segregation and eaten with blacks in white restaurants earlier in this century. Perhaps He would open His door to Haitians in Miami, Chinese in Vancouver, or Vietnamese in Houston. Perhaps He would make friends with Palestinians in Israel, or reach out to Moslems in Iraq and Iran. Perhaps He would heal both Roman Catholics and Protestants in Northern Ireland.

Racism and ethnic hatred have never been God's desire. They come from the sin of men and women. Jesus repudiated such sin wherever He found it. As Matthew shows, His heart is for all the nations.

The City as a Melting Pot

Many cities today are called "melting pots" because of their large number of immigrants and the tendency of ethnic groups to assimilate into the larger culture over time. Jerusalem was, and always has been, a melting pot of cultures. But around 588 B.C., the city became a melting pot of a different kind.

The Babylonians began a siege then that lasted for about two years, with one brief respite, and culminated in the fall of the city. Hundreds of miles away in Babylon, the Lord told Ezekiel to utter a parable about a pot of stew (Ezek. 24:3–5). Jerusalem was portrayed as a stew pot full of water, choice meats, and spices, with "fuel bones" (logs) blazing underneath.

Some believe that Ezekiel's parable was based on a folk song commonly sung by women as they prepared their food. The Lord may have turned a well-known ditty into a powerful spiritual lesson.

The illustration provided a recipe for cooking up a yummy stew. But the parable introduced a problem in the preparations. Scum (or rust) in the pot was spoiling the stew so that no one would want to eat it (Ezek. 24:6). By analogy, the sins of God's people in Jerusalem had made them odious and distasteful. The Lord's remedy was to "turn up the heat" (24:9), so much so that the water would eventually evaporate, the meat would burn up, the pot would turn red hot, and the scum would burn off (Ezek. 24:10–11). Thus God would cleanse the city of its impurities. That was essentially what the Babylonian siege accomplished.

In thinking about cities today, the image of the boiling pot is still appropriate. If a city is relatively healthy, it can stand a certain amount of "heat" and even profit from it. To some extent, heat and pressure are necessary to fully cook the diverse ingredients and meld them together into an enjoyable, nutritious meal. On the other hand, when a city ignores its problems and allows spiritual and moral decline to go unchecked, an increase in heat can be explosive. In the worst case, it can lead to meltdown.

That is what happened to Jerusalem when Babylon conquered it. What steps are you and your community taking to ensure that you avoid a similarly bad outcome?

For more on this topic, see **BARRIERS,** *"Breaking Down Ethnic Walls," page 30.*

EVASION

Is Evasion Ethical?

As you deal with people at work and in your family, you no doubt encounter situations where it might seem better not to reveal the whole truth. What should you do? Is anything less than the actual, complete truth ever ethical or biblical? Can believers practice cunning when Scripture calls us to be honest (for example, Eph. 4:15, 25, 29)?

Christ faced this dilemma when certain leaders challenged His authority (Matt. 21:23). He replied by asking them a question that was almost impossible for them to answer (Matt. 21:24–27). Was He being fair?

Observe the context. Jesus' inquisitors were powerful religious leaders who felt threatened by His assault on their hypocrisies and His impact on the people. He had just challenged one of their sources of revenue by throwing the money changers out of the temple (Matt. 21:12–17). Now they were launching a counterassault by challenging His authority.

Rather than being unethically evasive, Jesus was merely diverting an evil plot in a discrete manner by posing a difficult question. A simple yes or no answer would have played right into their hands. It probably would have touched off a confrontation prematurely. Jesus was more interested in accomplishing His long-range purposes than in exposing these hateful leaders on the spot.

Have you developed the ability to discern the gray areas of conflict and competition? Do you take a long-term view when you face confrontation?

EVIL

God and the Problem of Evil

Few stories offer a more dramatic or thrilling climax than the closing chapters of Revelation. The scene of God ultimately destroying Satan and his hosts (Rev. 20:1–10) brings a joyful conclusion not only to the Revelation of John, but to the entire Bible. Once and for all, evil will be banished, never again to trouble God's creation.

Yet while Christians look forward to that day with hope, many other people reject God and the gospel precisely because of evil in the world. Their reasoning goes something like this:

- A God who is good and loving would not allow evil and suffering in His world.
- Yet evil exists in the world.
- If God is all-powerful, He could remove evil if He wanted to.
- Yet evil remains. In fact, at times it seems to grow worse.
- Therefore, a good and powerful God must not exist.

This is a powerful argument, and there can be no question that evil and pain are a big problem to both belief and behavior. Christianity offers no knock-down solution, but the

Bible does give us ground to stand on as we try to live in a world where suffering is real.

1. The Bible teaches that God did not create evil. The world He made was utterly good (Gen. 1:31). But people themselves turned against God, using His gift of free will to rebel against Him. With that moral rebellion, the perfection of God's world came tumbling down and people began to suffer.

The Bible also claims that behind human wickedness lies a great outside influence, Satan. This fallen angel hates God and everything to do with Him. He is out to destroy both humanity and the environment and does everything He can to attack God and His purposes. He promotes much of the evil and suffering that we see.

2. Even though God did not create evil, nor does He will it, He nevertheless uses it to accomplish His purposes. For instance, God sometimes uses pain to draw people to Himself, especially when they otherwise would not respond to Him. Likewise, the struggle against evil has led many people to strive for good, producing such admirable traits as courage, endurance, self-sacrifice, and compassion.

3. Why then, if God is all-powerful, does He not remove evil from the world? This question assumes that He has done nothing. But in fact, He has. First, God Himself came into this world, with all its sorrow and pain, and lived as a man. Jesus knew poverty, thirst, hunger, injustice, physical abuse, heartbreak, and betrayal. He ended his life in excruciating pain. So God certainly understands our condition. He has personally experienced it.

In the process, God dealt with the problem of evil at its root. On the cross, Jesus took on Himself the wickedness of every person who has ever lived in order to do away with it. Christ broke the grip of evil that holds the world captive. Already we can see among God's people a glimpse of the new life that He has brought about (Rom. 8:4, 11).

This brings us to God's final solution to evil, which John describes in Revelation 20. In the end, God will triumph by doing away with evil and those who promote it. He will restore His creation and His creatures to their original purpose, to the original relationship they enjoyed with Him. Suffering will be but a memory. Goodness, justice, and peace will characterize the moral climate of God's new heaven and earth.

Blaming Satan?

A common view today is that Satan (Job 1:6) is not a real person, but just a mythological way ancient peoples had of explaining evil and suffering. However, the Book of Job does not support that view, nor does the rest of the Bible.

Notice particularly how Satan figures in this book. He appears in the first two chapters, but then completely drops out of the narrative. Most of the rest of the book contains a discussion between Job and four of his friends as they try to make sense of Job's trials. But nothing is heard directly from or about Satan again. The speakers propose numerous suggestions and insights concerning suffering, but they never resort to blaming Satan, or even to mentioning him.

This has important implications for believers today, especially given that we live in a society with an increasingly secular worldview. On the one hand, the Book of Job shows us that Satan does exist and does influence what happens to individuals. In other words, we live in a universe where the supernatural affects day-to-day life. We cannot dismiss the Bible's teaching about angels and demons as nothing but myths from the past.

Yet on the other hand, the Book of Job cautions us against just blaming Satan for the troubles we face. Job and his friends disagree on the exact cause of Job's sufferings, but they all agree that people are morally responsible for the choices they make. Their focus is not so much on Satan as their adversary as it is on God as their Judge (Job 5:8, 17; 8:3–6; 9:1–3; 11:5–6).

God Limits Evil

The first couple gained a terrible new knowledge by breaking the rules. After eating the fruit, Adam and Eve, who had previously known only good, now came to know evil (Gen. 3:22)!

One of the first results of their newfound "knowledge" was that they were no longer unashamed of who they were as creatures made in God's image. Instead, they felt shame in their naked condition and immediately covered themselves (Gen. 3:7; compare 2:25).

What a sad gain—self-hatred! And that was but the beginning of humanity's troubles for acting on the serpent's deception. Soon the loss of respect for God's ways and for human dignity led to evil running rampant in God's good creation (Gen. 6:5–6).

God's response to the intrusion of sin into His world and into the lives of His human coworkers was to put limits on the evil. He refused to let it go unchecked. Notice several restraints that God appears to have imposed:

1. He provided clothing, perhaps to limit lust and sexual abuses (Gen. 3:21).

2. He drove Adam and Eve out of the garden, depriving them of access to the tree of life and thereby preventing them from living forever in a fallen condition (Gen. 3:22–24).

3. He prevented Cain, the first murderer, from continuing to farm the earth and benefit from its systems as before, possibly to keep him from using the world's resources to wreak further havoc (4:11–12).

4. He sent a flood to check the wickedness of Noah's generation, but preserved Noah and his family in order to repopulate the earth from an obedient people (Gen. 6:1–22).

5. After the flood He kept limits on what Noah and his descendants could eat and established a penalty for murder, and perhaps by extension for other abuses of people against people (Gen. 9:1–7).

6. When evil again gained momentum and the people of Babel tried to establish their supremacy, God frustrated their plans by confusing their languages and limiting their ability to build a tower (Gen. 11:1–9).

Many more biblical examples could be cited of God imposing limitations on evil. He is a kind and benevolent Sovereign who intervenes to protect His creation and prevent people from destroying themselves. God's ways may sometimes seem harsh. But He knows better than we do (Is. 55:8–9). He will not allow evil to undo what He loves and wishes to redeem.

God Restrains Evil

The presence of pain, suffering, and evil in the world causes some people to wonder whether a good God exists, and if He does, why He doesn't put an end to it if He can. John's vision of a beast rising up out of the sea (Rev. 13:1) and causing great havoc in the world does not explain why there is evil, but it does sound an important note of encouragement: the evils of the world happen only by "permission" and those that do occur have precise limits imposed on them by God. Notice that the beast "was given authority to continue for *forty-two months*" (Rev. 13:5, emphasis added).

Clearly, God has placed restraints on evil. We have not and will not experience the full onslaught of pain and suffering that could be delivered. This restraining work of God can be seen in several incidents in the Old Testament:

Adam and Eve (Gen. 3:22–24). After Adam and Eve sinned, God sent them out of the garden and sealed it off. According to Genesis, this was not a matter of retaliation by God but a protection from the possibility of eating from the tree of life and being separated from Him forever.

The Flood (Gen. 6:5–8). When evil had corrupted the entire world, God acted with "severe mercy" by sending the flood. This restricted evil and made possible a second start for the earth.

The Tower of Babel (Gen. 11:1–9). Again, widespread evil threatened to consume the creation. God intervened by confusing the languages of the peoples to limit their collusion in wickedness. This was a case of God preserving sinful humanity from itself.

Job (Job 1:6–2:10). Satan wanted to prove to God that Job's faithfulness was merely the result of God blessing him. So God granted Satan limited permission to inflict suffering.

John was writing to believers to help them maintain a realistic view of good and evil in the midst of intense persecution. Today, as we watch televised reports of death and disaster around the world, and as we experience pain and suffering in our own families and among our neighbors and associates, we too need to maintain a godly perspective. God has placed limits on evil. The very fact that we have a distaste for it reflects that we do indeed bear God's image as His creatures.

EXAMPLE   136   EXAMPLE

EXAMPLE

Faith at Home

Is your faith a part of your conversation at home with your children when you sit down at mealtimes, drive with them in the car, do household chores together, or travel on vacations? Or do your youngsters hear about the Bible and spiritual things only from other people outside the home?

Moses frequently told the Israelites to teach the Law to their children (Deut. 11:19). Whether or not their little ones ever knew God depended on the parents. The new generation of children had not seen the works of God during the Exodus from Egypt or during the wilderness journey. They had no firsthand experience of the Lord's provision of food, water, protection, and rescue, or of His appearance at Mount Sinai.

Like the Hebrew parents of old, parents today must find ways to convey spiritual truth about the goodness and greatness of God to the next generation. If you have children, you might consider:

- telling them stories from your own past about how you came to know God and how He has worked in your life;
- telling them how you have grown in the faith, especially through some of the tough times;
- praying with them at meals, bedtime, or when significant events are taking place; and
- inviting them to share in the joys, sorrows, successes, and failures of your life, so that they see you as a real person with real faith.

God's Name on the Line

How does God make Himself known to the nations and people of the world? Aside from the witness of Scripture and the life and work of Jesus Christ, His primary means is through men and women who are dedicated to Him and live as He wants them to live. They are the light of the world, whose good works light the way to the Lord (Matt. 5:14–16).

That means that God's reputation is at stake when it comes to how His people conduct their lives. That was certainly true for ancient Israel. He made a covenant with them to be

His people (Ezek. 20:5–6). Yet three times before they even got to the Promised Land, they reneged on their commitment and turned back to the idols that they had learned to serve in Egypt. Each time the Lord threatened to pour out His fury on them (Ezek. 20:8, 13, 21), but each time He spared them for one reason: He wanted the rest of the world's nations to know who He is (Ezek. 20:9, 14, 22).

If Israel were destroyed, the pagan nations would have lost an important witness to the living God. In fact, Moses pointed this out at Mount Sinai, when the Lord wanted to destroy the idolatrous Israelites and start a new nation from him. Moses argued that then the Egyptians and other nations would misinterpret God's purpose for bringing the people out of Egypt (Ex. 32:9–14).

In light of this history, believers today need to think about the reputation of our lives, and whether it is worthy of the Lord. Would people be attracted to God or repelled by our conduct? Are we winsome? Is God honored by unbelievers because of the things we do and say?

Leading by Example

As Paul recognized (Phil. 3:17), leaders always lead by personal example, whether they are aware of it or not. And their example extends far beyond the nature of the task at hand. People pattern their motives and values after executives, supervisors, and other leaders.

Paul encouraged others to follow his example. What sort of example do you set for others? Are you aware of how you influence them? Are you close enough to the people around you, and in touch enough with your own tendencies, to have confidence in how others might follow you?

Models of Faith

God's people often find themselves in the minority. For example, many believers run into values and practices in the workplace that go against godly principles. Likewise, many students encounter beliefs and ideas that run counter to the Bible's teaching. How should people of faith respond when the surrounding culture seems hostile to faith?

There is no one "right" answer. In the Old Testament, God called the Israelites to develop their own society. He established laws designed to keep out pagan practices and influences. By contrast, New Testament believers were sent into the world to have an impact for God on the prevailing cultures.

Christians today must reflect carefully on their relationship to modern society, which has become increasingly secular and at times even hostile to the things of Christ. It might help to consider several examples in the Old Testament of people who were taken out of their "safe" environments and placed in rather hostile circumstances, yet still honored God.

- Shadrach, Meshach, and Abed-Nego were taken to Babylon as captives of war and trained for service in a pagan government. They are models of integrity and commitment to the Lord while carrying out duties for unbelievers (Dan. 1–6).
- Nehemiah was a strategically placed official in the Persian court who was allowed to return to Jerusalem and rebuild the wall. He is a model of leveraging one's position to accomplish God's purposes while overcoming hostile opposition (Neh. 1–6).
- Esther and Mordecai were two members of an ethnic minority who found themselves in a position to influence a godless king. They are models of taking courage and acting wisely in order to withstand evil (Esth. 1–10).

There are many other models of faith in the Old Testament, but these have several things in common:

They were all laypeople. They were not among the priests or Levites, and so had no "professional" reasons to exercise faith in their day-to-day work. Yet they carried out God's purposes more faithfully than some of the professionals would have.

They were all believers living in foreign lands. The environments were spiritually hostile and therefore a temptation to abandon God. Yet these believers did a better job of following the Lord in antagonistic societies than many of their contemporaries did back in the Holy Land, in a society that was supposedly conducive to spiritual life.

They all remained committed to God, His people, and His Word. The pressures of the surrounding cultures seemed to harden their commitments, not destroy them. They seemed aware of a larger picture and purpose beyond their immediate circumstances, by means of which they evaluated the situation and made wise choices. While others around them caved in, they held on to fundamental convictions that governed their actions. As a result, Scripture presents them as models of faith worth emulating today.

*For more on this topic, see **ROLE MODEL**, "Always an Example," page 351.*

EXCELLENCE

Excellence in the Workplace

In recent years, numerous books have been written extolling the value of quality and excellence in the workplace. By and large, these studies have been based on the premise that quality work doesn't just lead to higher profits—it is a condition of staying in business today.

The emphasis on excellence has had major repercussions in the corporate world, where many managers and employees have embraced it as a new way of doing business. Yet the theme of excellence in work is as old as the Bible (Prov. 22:29). In fact, quality is one of the keys to a biblical view of work:

- God does His work with excellence. When He created the world, the end result was "very good" (Gen. 1:31).
- God equips people with specific skills and abilities that fit them for certain kinds of work. He wants us to use our skills for their intended purposes, thereby serving Him with all our mind and might (Matt. 22:37–38).
- Christians are to do their work as if Christ Himself were evaluating the effort—because He is (Eph. 6:5–8).
- Christians are commanded to be "well pleasing in all things" in their work, because doing so makes the gospel of Christ attractive to coworkers and customers.

In light of these principles, ask yourself what kind of quality and craftsmanship you put into your work. Would God be pleased with how you do your job? Would He be pleased with the end product or service? Are you proud of the way you do your job? If not, how could you make improvements?

The Pursuit of Excellence

Many of us will do our best as long as circumstances reward our efforts. But what happens if we work for a less than ideal boss, or if our company seems satisfied with mediocrity, or if we are treated unjustly? Are we as willing to pursue excellence when things aren't going our way?

Joseph is an encouragement to anyone who lives and labors in a less than perfect world. Unjustly jailed because he spurned the advances of his boss's wife (Gen. 39:6–18), he soon became a warden's assistant in the prison to which he was sent (Gen. 39:21–23). His proven ability was so strong that his keepers did not even bother to check his work. They trusted him implicitly.

Joseph maintained such a pursuit of excellence by applying himself to the task at hand rather than focusing on how he had been framed. As a slave he probably had no means of appeal anyway. So he turned the hardships of his life into opportunities for diligence and focus.

God honored this attitude with achievements that would be considered amazing under any circumstances. Ultimately, Joseph the minority slave rose to power and status as the nation's second-in-command (Gen. 41:41–45).

So if you honor God in your work and pursue an attitude of excellence, will God reward you with power and prestige? There is no guarantee of that. However, Scripture does make a promise: "Whatever you do, do it heartily, as to the Lord and not to men, knowing that from the Lord you will receive the *reward of the inheritance*" (Col. 3:23–24, emphasis added). God will reward you according to how you do your work. He challenges you to excellence!

Joseph's example of patience in the midst of suffering does not take anything away from the fact that believers should not ignore injustice, especially as it manifests itself in the workplace. Two books, Esther in the Old Testament and Philemon in the New, offer stories of God's people challenging the unjust systems of which they were a part.

Modeling Excellence

Moses set an excellent example for his workforce by doing his own job "according to all that the Lord had commanded him" (Ex. 40:16). That kind of precision set the pace for everyone else and reaped invaluable rewards.

For example, the management team for the construction of the tabernacle emulated Moses' example by performing their tasks with "wisdom and understanding, in knowledge and all manner of workmanship," so that they completed the project "according to all that the Lord had commanded" (Ex. 35:30–31, 35; 36:1). Likewise, all of the workers under them carried out their tasks "as the Lord had commanded" (Ex. 39:1, 5, 7, 21, 26, 29, 31–32, 43).

Excellence in Israel began with Moses. It spread to the group of managers helping to supervise and coordinate the project. Then the workers followed suit. Do you model excellence and quality for others at your job?

EXCUSES

Aaron's Excuses

Aaron was actually quite a competent leader. But in the incident with the golden calf, he abdicated his leadership role and allowed the people to corrupt themselves in Moses' absence. Nor did his lame excuses enable him to avoid responsibility (Ex. 32:22–24). What excuses have you used when your behavior was less than admirable?

EXECUTION

(*see* Capital Punishment)

EXPECTATIONS

The Need for Clear Contracts

Too often when people make commitments, they fail to clearly spell out the terms of the agreement. In God's covenant with Israel, he clearly stated what would happen to the nation if it obeyed or disobeyed His law. If the people obeyed, He would bless them with prosperity; if they disobeyed, He would bring judgment upon them (Deut. 7:9–11; compare Lev. 26).

If only people today could be as clear and straightforward in their contracts, especially their informal agreements! As a result of unwritten terms and unstated expectations, people are often shocked when others don't live up to what was thought to be their end of the bargain. Feelings are hurt, expectations are disappointed, and relationships suffer. It happens not only in business transactions but friendships and family relationships as well.

Can you think of situations in which you have failed to make clear your expectations and the rewards or penalties for performance or nonperformance? What have been the results? What could you do to restore any of your relationships that have been hurt in this way? What steps can you take to ensure that you make your terms clear in the future?

EXPERIENCE

(*see also* Advice; Counsel)

Listening to the Voice of Experience

Advice that too readily agrees with our own perspective or that promises personal gain at the expense of others should always be viewed with suspicion. Rehoboam ignored the counsel of older, more experienced advisors in favor of the opinions of his youthful companions (2 Chr. 10:6–8). As a result, the northern tribes rebelled, and the kingdom was permanently divided (10:19).

How do you respond to the experience and opinions of older people, for example, older workers in your workplace? Do you automatically dismiss them as uninformed or out-of-date? Age and wisdom do not always accompany each other, but frequently they do. The example of Rehoboam shows that there is merit in consulting and listening to people who have been around for a while. They can be a valuable, even irreplaceable resource.

F

F

FAILURE

A Wasted Opportunity

The Lord took Solomon's fall into idolatry so seriously that He offered to give most of Israel to Jeroboam (1 Kin. 11:9–13, 31–39). The offer was unexpected—and unimaginable! It was an invitation to a virtually unknown minor official to become the father of a dynasty ruling God's people.

Yet despite this incredible gift from the Lord, Jeroboam squandered the opportunity right from the start of his reign. Apparently he forgot or disbelieved the Lord's promise to establish his kingdom, for he began to fear the return of his people to Rehoboam (1 Kin. 12:26–27). Rather than turn to God to reassure him, he took matters into his own hands by setting up his own system of idolatrous worship (1 Kin. 12:28–33).

Thus, Jeroboam ended up promoting the very evil that he was raised up to surmount. Not only did God judge him by quickly snuffing out his line (1 Kin. 14:17–18; 15:29–30), he became the model of idolatry against which all who succeeded him were compared (for example, 1 Kin. 16:26; 22:52; 2 Kin. 3:3). So

while Jeroboam could have enjoyed lasting acclaim, instead he left a legacy of infamy.

Go Ahead and Try It

Have you rejected business and career opportunities because, like the person who "observes the wind [and] will not sow," or who "regards the clouds [and] will not reap" (Eccl. 11:4), you have been unwilling to take risks?

One of the secrets of successful businesspeople is failure. They know that for every major enterprise that is successful, scores of others have failed. Yet they are willing to risk failure, over and over if necessary, in order to find the winning combination. This is in complete contrast to people who will try nothing unless it seems to be a sure thing.

The inventor Thomas Edison spent more than forty thousand dollars in nearly a thousand fruitless experiments before, on October 21, 1879, he finally crafted an incandescent lamp that could burn for more than forty hours. His ultimate success was preceded by an incredible string of failures. But from every failure he learned something, new knowledge that eventually taught him not only what not to do, but also what to do to achieve his goal.

Ecclesiastes' reminder to the person unwilling to take risks is that "you do not know the works of God who makes everything" (Eccl. 11:5). In a universe governed by a personal, sovereign God, there is no "sure thing" except that the Lord's own plans and promises will take place. Therefore, those who wait for certainty before they act may wait forever. Better to sow and reap when you can, trusting God for the results.

The Wrong Stuff?

Jesus was close to the end of His earthly ministry. His life was about to come to an agonizing end at the hands of bitter opponents. Shortly thereafter, those He had trained would be assuming the reins of His new movement.

That transition period would prove to be rather awkward. It didn't help that it was forced on the group by hostile outsiders. But the most troubling aspect was what happened to Jesus' associates, the ones who would have to carry His banner into the future. During those final days and hours, they began to fall apart:

- Bravado caused them to overstate their commitment (Matt. 26:35). When the moment of truth came, they deserted the Lord (Matt. 26:56).
- Even though the Lord asked them to keep watch with Him during His final hours of freedom, they fell asleep twice (Matt. 26:40, 43).

FAITH

- At the very moment when Jesus was standing trial and enduring mockery and beatings, Peter, who had led the others in declaring their loyalty (26:35), denied any association with Him (Matt. 26:69–75).

In short, the disciples hardly seem to have had the "right stuff" for continuing the important work that Jesus began. Yet, even after all that He went through, Jesus returned to that very group of followers after His resurrection and declared that they were still His chosen representatives, the ones appointed to continue His work. He even affirmed His commitment to stick with them to the end (Matt. 28:19–20).

Jesus' treatment of the disciples shows that failure is not the unforgivable act. In fact, it seems to be the crucible out of which character is formed. It is certainly not a sifting-out process to eliminate weak or useless people. Christ does not look for perfect people, but rather faithful people who can experience His forgiveness and grow.

Do you stick with people even though they stumble? Do you allow the shortcomings of your spouse, children, boss, coworkers, and neighbors to open up bright futures? Do you give yourself freedom to fail?

FAIRNESS

(see Justice)

FAITH

A Perilous Journey of Faith

It is one thing to boldly proclaim what God *can* do. It is quite another to actually trust that God *will* do what He has promised. Ezra had been telling King Artaxerxes about the divine protection that God's people could expect (Ezra 8:22). But then he was allowed to lead a group of exiles back to Palestine. At that point, Ezra determined that he needed to demonstrate his faith by declining an armed escort.

The Persians must have thought the choice ludicrous. The route from Babylon to Jerusalem that Ezra selected followed the northern border of the Arabian Desert. At nine hundred miles, it was shorter than the northern route through Aleppo and Hamath, but it was also more dangerous. Bandits and warring clans frequented the highway and its watering holes, waiting to ambush travelers and caravans. To travel without soldiers virtually invited disaster, especially given the precious cargo that the group was carrying (Ezra 8:24–30).

Yet God rewarded the people's faith with an uneventful journey (Ezra 8:31). The trip took about four months to complete, averaging seven or eight miles per day. Such a relatively slow pace was perhaps due to the many children and elderly who made the journey.

Ezra's courage is a challenge to God's people today to follow through on their statements of faith, especially when unbelievers are watching the outcome. What good does it do to talk about trusting solely or primarily in God, only to abandon that position as soon as things get tough? We need to act in a way that is consistent with the faith we proclaim.

Danger Ahead

Yeast, or leaven, is a powerful fungus that can cause a lump of dough to rise into bread, ferment liquids into alcohol, or cause painful infections. When Jesus spoke of yeast in His comments about the Pharisees and Herod (Mark 8:15), His disciples were quite confused. What could He mean? What was the leaven of the Pharisees and Herod?

Jesus reminded His followers of His miracles of feeding the five thousand and the four thousand (Mark 8:19–21; 6:35–44; 8:1–9). What was the response of the Pharisees? They disputed with Him and tried to test Him by appealing for a miracle (Mark 8:11). In short, they refused to believe—despite the miraculous provision of meals for more than nine thousand people! Furthermore, they were already in league with Herod and his supporters to destroy Jesus (Mark 3:6; 12:13), just as Herod had done away with John the Baptist (Mark 6:14–29).

Clearly, Jesus was warning His followers against the insidious infection of unbelief. Like yeast in dough, a lack of faith can permeate one's life until it breaks out in open rebellion against God. No wonder the Lord was so displeased with the disciples' lack of perception (Mark 8:17–18). Perhaps the yeast of unbelief was already at work among them.

After all, they had apparently failed to understand the significance of a feeding miracle the first time around (Mark 6:52); now they were missing it a second time!

Jesus had grave concern about the condition of His followers' faith. He knew that there was danger ahead. Powerful enemies would lay hold of Him, and the disciples would be sorely tested. No wonder He took measures to keep a low profile (Mark 8:26, 30). He wanted to avoid exposing these men to the full force of His opponents before their faith was ready to handle such a trial.

None of us knows what dangers lie ahead for our faith. We may be headed for trials and challenges that we never imagined. Is our faith ready to meet whatever challenges come our way? Or have we let the yeast of unbelief gain a foothold, breaking down our trust in God and spreading resistance to Him throughout our lives?

Despair vs. Confident Faith

Whether you react to troubling news with a sense of desperation and despair or a quiet, confident faith will largely depend on the status of your relationship with God. For example, King Ahaz of Judah had turned away completely from the Lord, not only practicing idolatry, but even sacrificing his own children as burnt offerings to pagan gods. When he heard that Syria and Israel had formed an alliance and were preparing an attack, he had no faith to fall back on. Instead, he became so frightened that his heart began shaking like a tree in the wind (Is. 7:1–2).

In His mercy, God told Isaiah to help Ahaz gain some perspective by taking a long-term view of the forces aligning themselves against him and his people. The prophet pointed out trends that would mean the demise of Ahaz's enemies within sixty-five years (Is. 7:8). Instead of anxious desperation, Ahaz was invited to exercise quiet faith in the Lord.

In a similar way, believers today are called to take a different view of time and the events of history. The Bible helps us gain perspective by taking a long-term view of history's outcomes, not just the short-lived gains or losses from year to year. As God's people, we are part of a process spanning generations, in which we are building on the legacy of our predecessors and contributing to the future of our successors.

From that perspective, today's terrors can become tomorrow's joys (Is. 7:18–25).

Grow in Groups

The incidents at Troas (Acts 20:7–12) reflect a habit that believers do well to cultivate— gathering frequently in informal, small clusters to reflect on Scripture, pray, and support one another.

The working people of that key Roman seaport gathered around the visitors to spend an evening together and learn more about the faith. They were following a pattern established at the beginning of the movement, of coming together around the apostles' teaching, fellowship, the breaking of bread, and prayer (Acts 2:42). In fact, their appetite for the experience was insatiable: even the shock of Eutychus's fall could not deter them (Acts 20:9–11)!

Home- or work-based groups of believers have frequently been the foundation of significant Christian movements throughout history. It's worth asking: Do you meet regularly with peers at work, home, or church to sort out your faith and its application to your world?

Spectator Faith

Pollsters repeatedly report that as many as one-third of the population of North America professes to believe in Christ. Yet numerous surveys show a steady decline in public morality, not just among the unchurched, but among the churched as well. What accounts for this apparent contradiction between faith and practice? Perhaps we can gain a clue from what God told Ezekiel about the people of his day who seemed to follow a similar pattern.

Ezekiel must have had quite a following, because when it appeared that the Lord was about to reveal something through him, news of the event raced through the community (Ezek. 33:30). His prophecies were like a performance, with his listeners hanging on every word (Ezek. 33:32).

But when the show was over, so was the people's interest. They generally ignored the content of what the prophet had to say; only his presentation seemed to matter. To be sure, they talked as if their lives were going to exhibit genuine concern for others, but from day to day they lived only for their own self-interest (Ezek. 33:31). On the whole, their curiosity about Ezekiel's sermons amounted to little if any life change.

The problem in Ezekiel's day was not unlike a problem in our own day, in which "faith" is more entertainment than it is heart commitment. People become spectators rather than players. Their concern is more with *What is the latest word from the Lord?* rather than *What am I going to do with what God has said?* As James put it, one becomes merely a hearer of the word rather than a doer—deceiving oneself in the process (James 1:22).

That is the worst thing about faith as entertainment—self-deception. True conversion means a changed will, not just an expanded knowledge about spiritual things or good feelings toward God. As Jesus pointed out, true love for God means living according to His will (John 14:15, 21, 23–24).

Foggy Faith

Early morning fog can be a beautiful sight as it creeps over the mirrored surface of a lake or huddles over a silent meadow. Many a photographer has waited until just the right moment to capture a subject enshrouded in mists before the sunlight burns them away.

Yet while fog may be impressive in the natural world, it can be utterly perilous in the spiritual, as Hosea pointed out. He used the image of fog as a metaphor of Israel's faithlessness (Hos. 6:4). The nation's commitment to the Lord was as empty and fleeting as a cloud. As soon as the people felt the "heat" of moral and spiritual conflicts, their loyalty to God evaporated.

This same "foggy faith" characterizes many people today. In an emotional moment they may pay impressive lip service to loving and serving God, but as soon as their feelings of devotion fade, their "faith" is effectively vaporized.

Clearly, as the Lord evaluates faith, what seems to matter is not whether it is beautiful, but how long it will last.

Staying Focused

The world is a complex place. Many things vie for our attention. As a result, no matter how much we may want to honor God, it's easy to become distracted and even confused. It's easy to forget what really matters.

Moses made it clear to the Israelites what really mattered and therefore what they needed to stay focused on. After briefly reviewing how God had delivered them from Egypt and kept them alive during their desert journeys, he challenged the people to keep their attention focused on the "statutes and judgments" of the Lord (Deut. 5:1). He urged them:

- to "hear" the statutes and judgments— to listen to them clearly and repeatedly;
- to "learn" them—to go beyond beyond simple memorization to personal ownership; and
- to "be careful to observe" them—that is, to actually do them, to make them a way of life.

Moses reviewed the Ten Commandments (Deut. 5:6–21), the spine of the Law. Then he repeated his call for a three-part response to the Law at the end of the presentation (Deut. 5:32–33):

- "Be careful to do them"—a response of obedience.
- "You shall not turn aside from them"— a response of focus.
- "You shall walk in all the ways"—a response of integrating the Law into everyday life.

This emphasis on keeping one's focus on what God says is repeated throughout Deuteronomy (for example, "Hear, O Israel," Deut. 6:4–5; 9:1; 20:3; 27:9). In fact, it is repeated throughout Scripture (for example, Ps. 19:7–11; 119:9, 11; Matt. 4:4, 7, 10; Rom. 12:2). Thus, like the people of Israel, believers today need to remember what is central. We may have many pursuits, but we need to maintain a single-minded focus on the Lord and what He has said.

Tips for the Timid

For some followers of Christ, faith is not merely a private matter but a timid one as well. It's as if faith is such a delicate thing that unless one carefully protects it, the world will surely destroy it.

The Book of Hebrews challenges believers to a different way of living. Faith that is alive and growing need not be treated like a pet bunny rabbit that is periodically brought out of its cage to be adored and fed on special occasions, but then quickly returned to its haven of safety. To be sure, we live in a world of roaring lions (1 Pet. 5:8) and therefore must be on guard. Yet the safest way to live in a world of spiritual dangers is to build up our strength, not to hide our faith in secrecy. Hebrews offers some suggestions:

- We can take confidence by freely entering into God's presence through Christ (Heb. 10:19, 22).
- Our faith can rest in full assurance that because of Christ's work on our behalf, our sins have been forgiven (Heb. 10:21–22).
- We can keep a firm grip on the basics of our faith, which rest on the integrity of Christ (Heb. 10:23).
- As believers we can stir each other up to loving, active faith (Heb. 10:24).
- We can meet with other believers regularly for encouragement, accountability, worship, and prayer (Heb. 10:25).
- We can leave judgment and repayment up to God, who is the ultimate Judge of people (Heb. 10:29–31).
- We can keep a loose grip on privilege, comfort, and possessions and instead show compassion toward those in need, such as prisoners (Heb. 10:32–33).
- We can condition ourselves for the long haul so as to finish well (Heb. 10:35–39).

Spiritual strength and health means integrating our faith with every area of life. Faith is not just one more thing on a list of a hundred things, but rather the foundation of who we are. If our walk with Christ is real, it should become evident to others (James 2:14, 26; 3:13). Faith that is alive and growing is faith unleashed!

FAITH AT WORK
Bad Business
How should God's people do their work or run their businesses? Does faith make any significant difference in how believers approach the issues of the workplace? The prophet Isaiah believed that it should. He called the Israelites to very clear, godly standards against which they could measure their work. However, the people of his day were not measuring up (Is. 59:1–15):

- They had blood on their hands from injustice and wickedness.
- Their words and commitments were not to be trusted.
- Justice and truth did not characterize their transactions. Instead, they used manipulative, evil schemes for personal gain.
- They poisoned the economic system with their evil ways.
- They used intrigue and violence to take advantage of others.
- Wherever they went and whatever they did, they caused people to be destroyed.
- They ignored the possibility of doing business by peaceful, just means.
- Instead of bringing the light of justice and righteousness into their work, they brought darkness and a feeling of blindness.

How would Isaiah assess your work and the way you do it? Does your faith make any difference in the way you do your job? Consider whether your coworkers, customers, and others would see you as a source of long-term benefit and economic justice, or as a source of trouble and net loss to the business enterprise. If you're unsure how to evaluate the impact of your faith at work, who could you ask for an honest appraisal?

Less Talk, More Action
What evidence can new believers offer to validate their new faith? How can their commitment to Christ be seen as more than just one more spiritual path among many? They need to put their best foot forward among nonbelievers, spiritually speaking, but how?

Believers on the island of Crete faced such a challenge, and it was enormous. The Cretan culture had many gods. Its people filled their time with much idle chatter, empty promises, and lies (Titus 1:10–13). So how could the Christians' loyalty to yet one more God be taken seriously, let alone make any difference in the society?

Paul acknowledged the dilemma that these early believers faced by opening his letter to Titus with the affirmation that God never lies (Titus 1:2). In the same way, God's people must be people of truth and unimpeachable integrity. How can that happen? Through fewer words and more deeds. That was the way to build consistent evidence of a new and credible lifestyle with lasting impact.

The apostle called for that strategy among several sub-groups of the new believers: older men (Titus 2:2), older women (Titus 2:3), younger women (Titus 2:4–5), younger men (Titus 2:6), Titus himself (Titus 2:7–8), and slaves (Titus 2:9–10). Each of these groups was to carry out the deeds of faith listed in 3:1–8. In fact, Paul insisted that they all "be careful to maintain good works" (Titus 2:8). They were to avoid extended arguments as unprofitable and useless in their witness.

Do your coworkers see the Christlike deeds of believers where you work? Or has their main exposure to the faith been little more than Christians filling the air with statements and ideas? Has your own walk with Christ produced any visible fruit in front of your associates, such as patience, staying power, compassion, loyalty, better management, hard work, or faithful service? That's the kind of evidence that shows whether faith in Christ has any power and impact.

Reconnecting Sunday and Monday

Does the faith you celebrate on Sunday sometimes feel disconnected from the "real world" you face on Monday? The newly formed group of believers (Acts 2:46–47) closed that gap by practicing a rhythm of two kinds of experiences—*gathering* for growth and worship balanced by *scattering* into the world for work and to communicate the gospel to non-Christian friends and coworkers.

This pattern continues throughout Acts as the narrative moves back and forth between internal meetings of the church and external encounters with the surrounding culture. The account includes more than twenty refinement narratives and more than fifty engagement narratives. We clearly see a connection between the development of faith and its delivery.

Believers today could help to reconnect Sundays and Mondays by moving through this same cycle. The gathering process might include worship services, praise gatherings, prayer meetings, fellowship over meals, and teaching for growth. Such encounters prepare us for Monday's world of work and responsibility, filled as it often is with pressures, conflicts, and opportunities to engage unbelievers as they inspect or perhaps even oppose our faith.

Rather than being disconnected, these two worlds need to be vitally connected. The refinement of our faith as we gather for growth supplies much-needed strength as we engage the world Monday through Saturday. On the other hand, the realities of life outside the fellowship can alert us to areas where we need to grow in faith.

Are you reconnecting Sunday and Monday by practicing this rhythm? Is there a link between the resources of your faith community and the demands of your world? Are there ways to improve the connections?

The Divine Partnership

Christ was fully involved in the work of creation (John 1:3). In fact, all three persons of the Trinity worked together to bring the world into existence—Father (Gen. 1:1; John 5:17), Son (John 1:10; Col. 1:16), and Holy Spirit (Gen. 1:2; Job 33:4).

Many people tend to think of God's divine partnership only in terms of the work of salvation. But the three members of the Godhead are just as involved in the ongoing work of providing and caring for all creatures and maintaining the created order. In fact, their creative work continues even now in the heavens, as God prepares eternal dwelling places for believers (John 14:2–3; Rev. 21:1–2, 5).

Remarkably, this working, triune God invites people to work with Him as junior members in the partnership, to accomplish His work in the world. In our day-to-day jobs, God asks us to do only what He has been doing from the beginning.

*For more on this topic, see **COMMITMENT**, "Just Do It," page 70.*

FAITHFULNESS
Finishing Well

What would be an appropriate epitaph on your tombstone? What statement would describe your life overall rather than whatever current circumstances you are temporarily facing right now?

When Paul wrote to the believers in Thessalonica, they were in the midst of intense suffering (2 Thess. 1:4–5). But Paul encouraged them to look beyond their immediate troubles to the return of Christ and the affirmation they would receive from Him at that time (2 Thess. 1:6–7). Their enemies, who were really enemies of the Lord, would be judged and dealt with (2 Thess. 1:8–9). By contrast, they would join with their Savior in joy and praise (2 Thess. 1:10). Paul went on in the next chapter to expand on this theme and its impact on the Thessalonians' current difficulties (2 Thess. 2:1–12).

God calls us as His people to finish our lives well by holding on to the truths that last (2 Thess. 2:15). He challenges us to maintain lifelong faithfulness and not to be entirely caught up in the here and now, whether good or bad.

As you consider the long-term direction of your life, what memories are you creating in others about your values and reputation? What will people choose to remember about you?

The Hall of Faithfulness

Hebrews 11 takes us through a museum of Hebrew heroes—what we might call the Hall of Faithfulness, since faith is the operative value here (Heb. 11:1–2). This is a remarkable collection of social winners and losers, all of whom are now with God because of their faith.

We look back on the lives of these "greats," but they in turn fill a stadium to watch us run the race of life (Heb. 11:39–12:1). However, that race is not a solo event or one lonely individual against the world. It's more like a relay race, in which we have received a handoff from those who have preceded us. Now it's our turn to run, in full public view.

God's Measure of Success

The story of the talents (Matt. 25:14–30) is about the kingdom of heaven (Matt. 25:14), but it offers an important lesson about success. God measures our success not by what we have, but by what we do with what we have—for all that we have is a gift from Him. We are really only managers to whom He has entrusted resources and responsibilities.

The key thing He looks for is *faithfulness* (Matt. 25:21, 23), doing what we can to obey and honor Him with whatever He has given us. We may or may not be "successful" as our culture measures success, in terms of wealth, prestige, power, or fame. In the long run that hardly matters. What counts is whether we have faithfully served God with what He has entrusted to us. By all means we must avoid wasting our lives, the way the third servant wasted his talents, by failing to carry out our Master's business.

For more on this topic, see **WORKMANSHIP,** *"Faithful Workmanship," page 433.*

FALSE PROPHETS
Jezebel

The name Jezebel (Rev. 2:20; see 1 Kin. 19:1) instantly signified evil for John's readers. King Ahab's wife, Jezebel, left a bad taste in Israel (1 Kin. 16:31; 21:25; 2 Kin. 9:7–10, 22). After her passing, Jews avoided naming their daughters Jezebel.

In Revelation 2, a Jezebel is teaching people to worship false gods and encouraging immorality. The pagan religions of the day, including the emperor-worship of the Romans, usually involved idol worship and sometimes included sexual activity.

This Jezebel was no follower of Christ, but a false prophet leading people astray. Yet the believers at Thyatira stood by, watching and tolerating her teaching and promotion of sexual promiscuity in the name of religion.

FALSEHOOD
(*see* Lying)

FAME
A New Style of Fame

If you've ever encountered a famous person, you may have felt somewhat intimidated, especially if that person seemed arrogant. People of status and image can easily make us feel inferior, as if we have nothing to offer by comparison. No wonder we long for the traits of compassion and humility in society's leaders.

Jesus became famous among His own people. But as He entered Jerusalem, the capital of Palestine, He modeled a new style for handling acclaim from the crowd. The city was wild with excitement during its peak season of tourists and celebration. What a moment for Jesus to bring His campaign to a climax! He even had the prophecies of Zechariah (9:9) and Isaiah (62:11) to bolster His confidence.

But instead of a parade of chariots and trumpets and a well-orchestrated ceremony, Jesus chose to ride into town on a donkey, a common beast of burden; no prancing warhorse for Him! And instead of walking arm-in-arm with powerful city officials and other celebrities, He was accompanied only by a small band of common fishermen, rural Galileans, and even a former tax collector. For once, the common folks had a parade (Matt. 21:8, 10).

Once arrived at the end of the parade route, Jesus did not go to the halls of the powerful. Instead He marched into the place of worship, a national center for the Jews. There He overthrew the tables of unjust businesses that manipulated the poor and made the temple a place of moneymaking (Matt. 21:12–13). He focused on the blind, the lame, and children (Matt. 21:14–16). And when He completed the day's tasks, He spent the night not in the fashionable home of a city leader but in a humble house in a nearby suburb, Bethany (Matt. 21:17).

Jesus' final activities before His death focused on those most ready to hear of His love, forgiveness, and hope—the little people in (or even outside) the system of privilege and power (Luke 4:18).

Do you know people who need to be invited to join the humble King's procession? Are there coworkers, neighbors, or family members who need to receive good news through you? How are you dealing with the temptation to rub shoulders only with the powerful and elite?

FAMILY

Family Loyalty

Ancient society placed great emphasis on faithfulness to blood relatives. So Jesus' words in Matthew 12:48–50 must have sounded quite foreign to the crowd. He seemed to be breaking with tradition and disowning His family. But notice:

Jesus didn't deny that the woman and the men at the door were His family. He merely pushed beyond the normal understanding of family to a larger reality—the claims of spiritual kinship. This new "family" included anyone who does the will of the Father in heaven.

In no way was Jesus denying the value or benefits of solid family relationships.

For or Against Family?

Conflict seems inevitable within families. Family members can always find something to disagree about—personal values, current events, politics, possessions, sex, money, feelings. Why do some of the most bitter fights occur between people who married for love? How can people who are so familiar with each other sometimes find themselves so far apart?

One reason is that families are unions of sinners, and sinners will be themselves no matter how intense their love and commitment for each other (1 John 1:8, 10). This has been so from the beginning: the first eight families in Scripture displayed many kinds of dysfunction, revealing their condition as sinful human beings. Perhaps God recorded their stories to let us know that even though He instituted the family unit, families are made up of sinners who will inevitably hurt each other.

Was Jesus "too good" to associate with His family of origin? His words in Mark 3:33–35 might seem to imply that. But He was merely distinguishing between human expectations about how families should relate and what the values of the kingdom had to say about family relations. He was not against His own parents and siblings; He just wanted to stress obedience to God.

"His own people" had already shown that they understood very little about Jesus or the values of His kingdom (Mark 3:20–21). They were limited by their own sinfulness, and needed God's help like everyone else.

Learning at Home

As modern-day society is quickly discovering, there is no substitute for a solid, stable home life. Where parents are absent, negligent, or abusive, children will probably not learn to cope with the world in a healthy way. For that reason, Proverbs stresses that parents are given to children to impart wisdom (Prov. 4:3–4). Out of their own seasoning, struggles, and suffering, parents can offer experience and insight that will help the next generation get started on the right course.

God's intention is that both parents are to be involved in their family's learning process. Fathers are to take the lead as sources of guidance and direction, and mothers are to offer governing principles based on God's Word (Prov. 1:8; 4:1; 6:20). In addition, Proverbs 4:3–4 implies that grandparents play a role, largely through the parenting they have done with the parents of their grandchildren.

In this way, a family is to "train up a child in the way he should go" (Prov. 22:6). That is the gift that the home gives. The child might not appreciate that gift until he is older, but parents are urged to give it nonetheless. Indeed, they cannot afford not to.

What can you be thankful for as you consider the gifts your parents offered you? In turn, what gifts are you offering your children?

Learning Faith Through Songs

One of the most effective ways to teach spiritual truth is through song. Likewise, memories are often passed on most effectively through music. Aware of this, the ancient Hebrews composed Psalms 113–118 to be sung around the supper table during Passover.

The first two of the group were sung before the meal and the other four afterwards. Each of the psalms commemorated some aspect of the escape of the Israelites from their bondage to Pharaoh and the Egyptians (Ex. 12–15), and for that reason they are sometimes referred to as the Egyptian Hallel (*Hallel* means "praise"; compare Ps. 113:1). Jesus and His disciples probably sang these psalms at their last meal together in the upper room (Matt. 26:30; Mark 14:26).

The themes of these six Passover psalms are:

- Psalm 113: Praising God for releasing the downtrodden.
- Psalm 114: Escaping from Egypt.
- Psalm 115: Praising God together as a people.
- Psalm 116: Thanking God personally and giving oneself to Him.
- Psalm 117: Calling non-Jews to praise God.
- Psalm 118: Recalling God's steadfast, enduring love.

This pattern of worshiping the Lord through songs sung around the family table encourages us as believers today to ask: Does our family have songs that it can sing to encourage each member to give thanks to God, remember His acts, and learn important truths about Him? Do we occasionally pause to express our joy together in music? Who in our family might lead the rest in singing our praises to God?

Praying for Your Family

Our families can be a source of both joy and sorrow in our lives. Job saw his children as a great blessing, and was overwhelmed with grief when they were suddenly and tragically taken away. In the midst of his despair, he cried out to God, wishing that he had never been born (Job 10:18–22).

Do you pray for your family? Do you let God hear your deepest feelings and hopes for them? He longs for you to express yourself to Him. The Bible gives us numerous examples of people who prayed about their families. Their prayers tend to be honest expressions about belonging to a community where love and sin coexist. By considering their prayers, you can gain insight into how to pray constructively about your family situation.

- Abraham's servant prayed for help in finding a wife for Isaac (Gen. 24:12–14).
- Isaac prayed about Rebekah's barrenness (Gen. 25:21).
- Jacob prayed in preparation for meeting his estranged brother Esau, whom he had not seen in many years (Gen. 32:9–12).
- Hannah prayed for a son and promised to give him back to God if He would end her barrenness (1 Sam. 1:9–20).

- David prayed that God would spare the life of his infant son born to Bathsheba (2 Sam. 12:15–16).

Phases of Family Life

Family life is a decades-long process to which God calls His people. That's why Paul devoted so much space in Ephesians to the issues of married couples (Eph. 5:22–33), children (Eph. 6:1–3), and fathers (Eph. 6:4).

If a couple marry in their mid-twenties and live into their mid-seventies still married, they will spend fifty or more years together. There are roughly six phases of marriage. Each phase requires husband and wife to work together as a team, combining their unique temperaments and strengths. They must pull in the same direction if they expect to complete all six phases with their marriage intact.

The Honeymoon Years. During this first period of marriage, two people from different family experiences and value systems begin to discover one another. Differences and similarities surface in areas such as finances, sexuality, faith, use of time, and personal habits. Each difference affords an opportunity for conflict as well as growth. Patterns that the couple establishes during this phase will affect what happens during the next five phases.

The Childbearing Years. The birth or adoption of the first child brings a rapid transition. New babies can feel like an "invasion," an abrupt intrusion into what had been a relatively cozy twosome. Often the father particularly feels displaced as mother and infant bond through birth, nursing, and nurturing. The childbearing years can be extraordinarily draining. Young parents need to "deposit" lots of emotional support into each other's "reserve bank accounts" if they hope to maintain a positive balance during the demanding child-focused years.

The Child-Rearing Years. As a couple's children pass through elementary and high school, new authority figures emerge, such as teachers, coaches, youth pastors, and peers. Before, parents had the final word with their children. Now others impose new values, decisions, and schedules.

This is a great time for parents to help children think about themselves and the world. Discussion, prayer, and support can create an atmosphere of unity that is essential if youth are to face the many factors that compete with the family. If the parents are secure in their "bond of perfection," they can help their children tackle the tough issues.

The Child-Launching Years. With the onset of puberty, children begin to notice the opposite sex and discover "love" outside the home. This is the beginning of the "leaving" process, as children become adults in their own right and take steps toward independence. In this phase, young adults tend to experience numerous "trial runs" of freedom. It helps for parents to remain available when their children have lost their way. If young people never experience the freedom to fail, they may never learn to leave the nest and fly on their own.

The Empty-Nest Years. By this point many couples have developed a child- or career-centered marriage rather than a strong relationship between themselves. This is tragic, since the empty-nest phase typically outlasts the first four phases combined. No wonder so many marriages come apart as soon as the children grow up and leave. The couples have built their lives around their kids, and now they have nothing left in common.

But empty-nest couples who have built a strong relationship can experience a joyous recovery of full attention to their marriage. They have more time to spend with each other, and often more money to spend. They may also have the bright privilege of welcoming grandchildren into the world.

The Alone Years. The death of either spouse brings the survivor into the final phase of family life. The sudden experience of being alone again exposes the level of individual growth experienced during marriage. Some couples never establish patterns that make for strong individuality. They become so intertwined and dependent on each other that the loss of the partner causes the surviving mate to wither. But if the person has cultivated other relationships among friends and family and developed personal interests and hobbies, life can still be joyful and fulfilling.

Where is your family among these six phases of family life? God calls couples to a lifetime of work. Are you practicing "biblical family planning" with a view toward the long haul?

Hope for the Family

The fact that John's vision ends in a marriage between Christ (the Lamb) and His bride the church (Rev. 19:6–10) offers great hope to families. In this world, almost every family experiences some pain and suffering in its relationships. After all, families are made up of people who struggle under the burden of sin.

Of course, things were not intended to be that way. In the beginning, God instituted the family when He created Adam and Eve and joined them together as "one flesh" (Gen. 2:24). However, their sin and rebellion against God brought havoc into their relationship and into all subsequent families. In their own family they soon experienced violence as Cain murdered his brother Abel, causing an ongoing cycle of trouble (Gen. 4:1–16).

Even in a fallen world, however, God desires His best for the family structure. Scripture holds out great hope for the restoration of marriage. For example:

- It encourages parents to raise children in an environment of truth and integrity (Deut. 6:2–9).
- It offers a touching illustration of aid to a family devastated by death and the prospect of poverty (Ruth 1–4).
- It shows a family destroyed by senseless evil but restored twofold by a faithful God (Job 1:13–21; 2:9; 42:10–17).
- It affirms the beauty of sexual love within marriage in terms of passion, fidelity, and integrity (Song of Solomon).
- It encourages the restoration of broken relationships, just as God will do with His people (Hos. 1:2–2:23).
- It offers guidelines for marriage in terms of mutual submission, loyalty, love, and discipline for children that does not alienate them—a way of relating that is similar to Christ's relationship to His bride the church (Eph. 5:21–6:4).

God's original design for the family will not be destroyed. Right now you may be experiencing the struggle of human relationships or even the pain of a broken family. But you can take hope from the knowledge that God's healing and love will ultimately win out, and He will "wipe away every tear . . . there shall be no more death, nor sorrow, nor crying" (Rev. 21:4).

Family and Work

Do you ever experience tension between your work and your family life? Most people do. Yet ironically, work and family are two of God's primary callings for us. And often we find them side by side in Scripture (for example, Ps. 128:2–4).

Since the beginning of history, work and family have been the two realms in which people have tended to find both the greatest meaning and fulfillment and the deepest pain and frustration. The Bible reflects this paradox by opening with the painfully realistic account of Adam and Eve (Gen. 2–3). On the one hand, their work in the garden and their life with each other brought them great joy and significance. But after they sinned, work became "sweat" (Gen. 3:19) and family life produced pain, sorrow, and estrangement (Gen. 3:16; 4:8, 16).

The biblical account goes on to record more stress between work and family in the life of Abraham. Abraham used his wife Sarah as a bargaining chip as he negotiated for food with the Egyptians (Gen. 12:10–20). Later, he and his nephew Lot achieved so much wealth that they had to part ways in order to maintain a peaceful relationship (Gen. 13:1–18)!

Another prime example of frustration in work and family is Solomon. His success as a king was spectacular (1 Kin. 10:23), but his family life was not, affected as it was by the many political marriages he made (1 Kin. 11:1–3). In the end, he found both his work and family to be very unsatisfying (Eccl. 1:1–2:26), even though he believed that both were gifts from God to be treasured (Eccl. 3:12–13; 5:18–20).

Psalms 127 and 128 hold out hope for these areas as well. By centering our work in the Lord, we can find a measure of fulfillment and reward. Likewise, family life can be satisfying and secure when we build our homes on a godly foundation.

As you think about the connections between your family and work, how much do the members of your family know about your work? How much do you know about theirs?

In what ways could your church help to bridge the gap between work and family life?

*For more on this topic, see **CHURCH AND STATE**, "Family, State, and Church: Three Inseparable Institutions," page 60.*

FAMINE

A Spiritual Cause to a Natural Event

The three-year famine in the days of David was the result of Saul's violation of the standing peace treaty that Israel had with the Gibeonites (2 Sam. 21:1; see Josh. 9:15, 19–21). This suggests two things:

1. Political commitments, such as peace treaties, have spiritual implications. God takes people's words—including the words of governments—seriously and expects people to honor their commitments. To break a covenant is to sin against the very character of God, who always remains faithful to His promises.

2. Natural events sometimes have spiritual causes. Famines, floods, diseases, pestilence, and other destructive phenomena of nature can be shown to have natural causes. Nevertheless, Scripture offers many illustrations of the fact that God may sovereignly allow and ordain such events for spiritual reasons.

FARMING

Subsistence Farming

Although the word "farm" occurs only in Matthew 22:5, farming was an important occupation in Bible times. Practically every family owned a piece of land in Israel, and many families farmed a small area of their own.

Outside the cities, most Israelites lived in villages rather than on farms. Cultivated land usually was outside the village, situated near the water supply or on western or northern slopes where rainfall was greatest. Crops grown included wheat, barley, grapes, olives, and figs.

Farm animals lived in the houses with the families. All but the poorest owned at least one ox or donkey as a work animal. Cattle, sheep, and goats were common, providing milk products as well as skins for clothes. Richer families and royal estates employed farm managers and workers (1 Chr. 27:25–31) and hired laborers for special tasks, particularly at harvest time (Matt. 20:1–16).

Frequent difficulties, such as hilly ground, stony soil, and unpredictable rainfall, did not make farming easy. But there were certain rewards, such as the joys of shearing animals and gathering the crops at harvest time (1 Sam. 25:2–8; Is. 9:3).

FASTING

Fasting for the Upwardly Mobile

You may think of fasting as something done only by people who have taken vows of poverty, or perhaps by the highly devout. But Zechariah discussed fasting for people who were prospering materially (Zech. 7:5). Largely because their community was in the middle of a building boom, they were moving up the ladder economically. In today's terms they might be called upwardly mobile.

It is interesting that Zechariah challenged these people with fasting in the context of community development and social justice (Zech. 7:6–10). This leads to at least three reasons why fasting can be a valuable practice for people who are recovering economically and moving up in the world:

1. Fasting can help us remember what it was like to be hungry and to do without.

2. Fasting can help us remember the spiritual resources of God that sustained us when we didn't have much, and it can also enable us to focus on the Lord.

3. Fasting can help us remember and identify with those around us who are poor and hungry.

Scripture suggests a number of other purposes for fasting and offers numerous models of people who practiced it.

*For more on this topic, see **DIETING**, "The Value of Fasting," page 103.*

FATHERHOOD

Strained Relationships

David and his son Absolom had a troubled relationship that lingered in estrangement (2 Sam. 14:24), exploded into open rebellion (2 Sam. 15:1–12), and ended in a tragic death (2 Sam. 18:9–15, 33). Scripture records a number of other fathers and sons who experienced unusual conflict:

- Noah and Ham. When Noah's drunkenness was seen and exposed by his son

Ham, Noah cursed Ham's son Canaan and his descendants, even as he blessed Shem and Japheth (Gen. 9:20–27).

- Isaac and Jacob. Jacob manipulated his father into giving him what rightly belonged to his brother Esau (Gen. 25:28; 27:1–40).
- Eli and Hophni and Phinehas. When Eli reprimanded his sons for abusing the priesthood, they paid him no attention; later God's judgment fell on the family (1 Sam. 2:22–36).
- Samuel and Joel and Abijah. Samuel placed his unworthy sons at Beersheba (perhaps where they could do the least amount of harm); nevertheless, their wickedness caused the Israelites to demand a king, which led to the anointing of Saul (1 Sam. 8:1–6).
- An unnamed father and his two sons, one loyal and one prodigal. Having squandered his inheritance, the repentant prodigal of this parable returned home, where his overjoyed father threw a big party; but the celebration estranged the loyal son (Luke 15:11–32).

Eli, the Failed Father

Eli served as a priest and judge of Israel for forty years (1 Sam. 4:18). It was not an easy time in which to exercise leadership. Israel had no centralized government, and "everyone did what was right in his own eyes" (Judg. 21:25)—including Eli's own sons, Hophni and Phinehas. They abused the sacrificial system and committed immorality with the women at the tabernacle (1 Sam. 2:12–17, 22).

Eli was in a position to put a stop to these abuses, but he was not equal to the task. Eli was unable either to restrain his sons or to remove them from the priesthood, and he and his descendants fell under the scathing judgment of God (2:27–36).

Yet one bright spot of hope emerged from Eli's household—the boy Samuel, who, in contrast to Eli's wicked sons, followed the Lord and grew up to be one of Israel's greatest judges (2:17–18; 3:1, 19–20).

The Challenge of Wayward Children

Scripture urges parents to raise up their children in the ways of the Lord (for example, Prov. 22:6; Eph. 6:4), but it makes no guarantees as to how they will turn out. Sometimes parents of the utmost integrity see their children utterly reject God. Such was the case for Samuel (1 Sam. 8:2–3).

Scripture presents Samuel as a man who seemingly followed the Lord right from the womb (1 Sam. 1:11, 22; 2:18; 3:19). By contrast, his sons, like Eli's sons before them (1 Sam. 2:22–25), turned out to be quite immoral (1 Sam. 8:3).

Could Samuel have done anything differently? Who can say? But the fact that he installed the young men as judges in Beersheba (1 Sam. 8:2) raises the question of whether he was turning his back on his son's problems rather than facing them squarely.

Beersheba was located at the extreme southern end of Israel's territory (see Gen. 21:31). It may be that in sending his sons there, Samuel was placing them where they could do the least amount of harm. But in the end, their misdeeds caused great harm, as they created an excuse for the elders of Israel to demand a king (1 Sam. 8:4–5). The subsequent selection of Saul was a choice for which God Himself felt sorrow (15:11).

No one knows how differently things might have turned out had Samuel confronted his sons and, as a last resort, taken them before the elders. But the legacy of his family is a sober challenge to any parent of a wayward young person to face trouble head-on.

Fatherly Advice

Many of the Proverbs were originally addressed to young men as wisdom from fathers to their sons (Prov. 1:8; 2:1; 3:1, 11, 21; 4:1). This reflects the nature of ancient Hebrew culture, in which sons were expected to inherit leadership of the family and nation.

These youths are warned about many of the traps that commonly ensnare young men:

- sexual temptation (Prov. 5:15–20; 7:1–27);
- foolishness (Prov. 12:15–16);
- ill-gotten gain (Prov. 10:2: 13:11);
- verbal abuse (Prov. 13:2–3; 15:1);
- strong drink (Prov. 31:4); and
- pride or selfish ambition (Prov. 16:1–9).

However, the fact that the book has a masculine tone should not lead us to think that women are excluded from either the giving or the receiving of Proverbs' teaching. The book repeatedly urges youth to pay attention to the instruction of their mothers (Prov. 1:8; 6:20; 10:1; 30:17). Likewise, the principles and warnings of the book apply just as much to young women as they do to young men— particularly in our own culture, where both sexes engage in many of the same activities.

FAVORITISM

(*see* Discrimination)

FAVORS

Payback Time

Paul tells Philemon that "if" Onesimus has stolen anything, he should send Paul a bill for it (Philem. 18–19). But at this point he is writing somewhat tongue-in-cheek.

Paul knew that Onesimus really had "wronged" Philemon. Not only had he run away, apparently he had stolen property and owed Philemon restitution. Paul never questioned Philemon's right to have his slave returned or receive reimbursement for the theft. Conversion to Christ does not relieve anyone of obligations to others.

Nonetheless, Paul wanted Philemon to forgive Onesimus and receive him back as a brother (Philem. 16). But just in case the theft created a sticking point in the reconciliation, Paul volunteered to pay for the loss if Philemon was unwilling simply to forgive it. (Notice how Paul was imitating Christ in this regard.)

Of course, Paul anticipated that Philemon would be more than happy to bear the loss. After all, he owed Paul a large, intangible debt

of gratitude for all that Paul had done for him (Philem. 19). So in effect, he would be returning Paul a favor by accepting Onesimus back unconditionally.

Is there a lesson here about favors and paybacks? Consider: often when we impose on others, asking them to do favors for us or for our friends, our main concern is for our own interests. But Paul's main concern was for Philemon—not for his financial loss, which was trifling, but for his spiritual gain, which was considerable.

FEAR

Fear in the Workplace

One of the most widespread motivations in the workplaces of the world today is also one of the most destructive—fear. Workers fear losing their jobs. Managers fear a loss of productivity and profits. Investors and owners fear a loss of capital.

Yet fear as a dominating force in the work world is nothing new, as the conflict between Pharaoh and the children of Israel illustrates. The situation was fraught with tension and anxiety on both sides. A crushing demand for increased output (Ex. 5:6–9) was but one of the tragic ingredients.

Notice how fear influenced the three main parties involved:

1. Pharaoh was a harsh taskmaster, but his power and anger were ultimately the result of fear. The Egyptians had watched as the Hebrews multiplied rapidly, and the account says they were literally "in dread of" what might happen in the event of war (Ex. 1:10, 12). So when Moses, the Hebrew spokesman, asked for a long weekend holiday for the laborers, the Egyptians' fears conditioned Pharaoh's response (Ex. 5:4–5). The brickmakers were given an increased workload with no increase in the supply of basic resources or extension of deadlines. Clearly, the last thing Pharaoh wanted to do was "empower" his workers. Instead, he wanted to dominate them because he was driven by fear.

2. The Israelites, especially their supervisors, reacted to Pharaoh's new production policy by verbally attacking their own leader, Moses (Ex. 5:15–21. They knew the people could not meet Pharaoh's impossible demand, and they feared what would happen as a result (Ex. 5:19).

3. Moses responded to the Hebrew supervisors' rebuke by turning on God, challenging His Word and His purposes and complaining that he was the wrong man for the job (Ex. 5:22–23). While the text doesn't say so explicitly, it's easy to see that Moses deeply feared the rejection of the people and the prospect that his mission might be ending in failure.

Fear distorted reality for all three parties in the Exodus account—manager, workers, and spokesman. Ultimately God's plan prevailed. But how differently things might have gone had any one of the three handled their fears in a different way—for example, by being more reflective, flexible, negotiable, and trusting toward God.

What causes fear in your workplace? How do you respond?

Redefining Fear

Every culture seems to be afraid of someone or something. The Hebrews feared and hated the Romans because of the ruthless might of their occupation troops. Eventually those fears were realized as Rome viciously destroyed Jerusalem in A.D. 70. In recent years, the West feared destruction from Soviet nuclear missiles. Today there is growing alarm and outrage over drug- and gang-related violence in cities.

But in Luke 12:4–7 we see that Jesus redefines fear by rearranging our view so we look at things from God's perspective. He draws upon the Old Testament concept of the "fear of the Lord" (Prov. 1:7). This is not a fawning, cringing dread that keeps us wallowing in anxiety, but a respect for who God is—the One who holds ultimate power. When we have a balanced view of God, it puts our thinking in a proper framework. We view everybody and everything in relation to God's holiness, righteousness, and love. We can't ignore physical threats and violence, but we dare not ignore the One who holds sway over our eternal destiny.

FEAR OF GOD

Fearful Silence

Habakkuk 2:20 is sometimes used as a call to worship. It urges reverent silence before the Lord as He dwells in His holy temple.

However, the context shows that the silence which all the earth is to keep is a silence in light of God's judgment, not merely the respectful silence of a worship service. The Lord has just pronounced five "woes" on Babylon (Hab. 2:6–19), indictments for which He will bring the nation down.

The only appropriate response to this warning is fearful silence (compare Hab. 3:2). Mighty Babylon is going to be judged. There is nothing for the rest of the world to say. A holy God is having the last word.

A High View of God

Recent years have seen an increase in teaching that emphasizes God's love, forgiveness, and intimate presence with His people. These truths are important to hear in modern society, where many people feel lonely, isolated, guilty, and insignificant. But has the pendulum swung too far? Have some Christians perhaps become overly familiar in their view of the Lord, thinking of Him not just as the friend of sinners, but as their personal buddy? Has there been a loss of respect for God's authority and holiness?

The ancient Israelites repeatedly treated God with disrespect during their wilderness journey to the Promised Land (Ps. 78:40–41). They forgot that just as His power was able to punish the pagan Egyptians for oppressing them, so it was ready to punish their own disobedience and rebellion (Ps. 78:42, 59–61).

By contrast, the Psalms call us to maintain a high view of God:

- The Lord executes justice, which includes deposing those who exalt themselves (Ps. 75:2–10).
- He is awesome and deserves to be feared (Ps. 76:4–12).
- He is worthy of our reflection as we consider His many acts throughout the history of the Israelites (Ps. 77:11–20).
- He will judge those who do not serve Him (Ps. 78:32–55).
- He is like none other. We are to learn about Him in order to fear His name (Ps. 86:8–11).

Reflect for a moment on your own perceptions of God. Have you become overly familiar toward Him? If so, consider how you might become more realistic in your understanding—perhaps by meditating on the psalms cited above. As the writer to the Hebrews reminds us, we need to serve God with reverence and holy fear (Heb. 12:28–29).

Fear of God?

The Hebrew midwives had a healthy fear of God (Ex. 1:21), a fear that enabled them to risk Pharaoh's wrath. They are a good example of what Christ told His disciples years later about not being afraid of those who kill the body, but rather to fear "Him who, after He has killed, has power to cast into hell" (Luke 12:4–5). That fear of the Lord gave them courage, direction, and motivation to make tough choices and live with godly behavior.

Today, when there is so much emphasis on God's love, grace, and mercy, is it possible that we have forgotten that God is to be feared? He takes our sin very seriously; therefore we need to take His holiness very seriously. We need not cringe in horror, as though God were a tyrant who delights in punishing us. But neither should we wink at sin as though He were a kindly grandfather who laughs at a little mischief. As both the Egyptians and the children of Israel found out, "our God is a consuming fire" (Deut. 4:24).

God Remains Forever

The Book of Lamentations ends with a powerful bit of wisdom by affirming that the Lord remains forever (Lam. 5:19). This truth stands in dramatic contrast to the stark, sobering scene of Mount Zion (Jerusalem), silent and deserted except for a few wild animals that wander through its ruins (Lam. 5:18). The city is no more. But God remains.

So it is throughout Scripture. God always has the final word. For example, the flood carries away a wicked generation, but God remains (Gen. 7:21–23). Job despairs of life, but ultimately sees that God remains (Job 42:5–6). An entire generation of rebellious Israelites dies off in the wilderness, but God remains (Ps. 90:2). Successive empires rise and fall—Assyrian, Babylonian, Persian, Alexandrian, Roman—but God remains (Dan. 4:34–35; 7:13–14). Even the world itself is destroyed and remade, but God remains (Rev. 21:5–6; 22:13).

This is a fundamental truth that lends perspective to the events of our lives and of history. Families, businesses, cities, nations—everything in this world comes and goes. But God remains forever. Therefore, as Solomon concluded, "Fear God and keep His commandments, for this is man's all" (Eccl. 12:13).

Wisdom and the Unbeliever

In its purest sense, "wisdom" means knowing God and respecting His Law (Ps. 111:10; Prov. 1:7). But that doesn't mean that unbelievers can never acquire or demonstrate real wisdom. If even the simplest animals (Prov. 30:25–28) can display wisdom, then surely any human, even one who does not know God, can have wisdom of a sort, and benefit from it. In fact, many aspects of wisdom are as available to the unbeliever as they are to the believer.

For example, anyone can have the prudence to plan ahead, as the ants do by storing food in the summer (Prov. 30:25; compare Prov. 6:6–8; 10:5; 24:27). Anyone can defend himself from danger, as the rock badgers do by living in rocky crags (Prov. 30:26; compare Prov. 22:3). Any group of people can decide to work together to achieve their goals, the way the locusts do (Prov. 30:27; compare Prov. 13:20). And anyone can work hard and skillfully, as the spider does in weaving its web (Prov. 30:28; compare Prov. 22:29).

So wisdom is available to all. However, there is a danger associated with wisdom in the hands of unbelievers. It is possible for the immediate rewards of living according to wisdom to crowd out thoughts about God. As a result, people may reject Christ's call, the way the rich young ruler did, because they love the benefits of wisdom, such as riches, more than God (Luke 18:18–23). Then, like the man who multiplied his barns but had no fear of the Lord, unbelievers may one day hear God say to them, "Fool! This night your soul will be required of you" (Luke 12:16–21).

Wisdom has practical benefits for everyone, but it is not enough to just enjoy the end of wisdom. The beginning of wisdom—the fear of the Lord (Prov. 1:7)—matters even more.

For more on this topic, see FEAR, "Redefining Fear," page 154.

FEMALE-MALE RELATIONSHIPS

(see Male-Female Relationships)

FINANCIAL ASSISTANCE

The Redeeming Relative

To whom would you turn if you fell on hard times financially? Many people resort to family and close relatives. But more and more people today have no one to turn to if they need help.

In ancient Israel, by contrast, people generally could count on some family member to step forward with financial support if poverty forced them into slavery or caused them to lose their land. This relative was called a "redeeming relative" (Lev. 25:25) or "kinsman-redeemer."

The redeeming relative was usually a male relation—a brother, an uncle, a cousin (Lev. 25:48–49)—provided to protect the clan. The Hebrew word used for this kinsman meant "one who has the right to redeem." An Israelite could sell himself, his family, or his land (Lev. 25:39–43) in case of poverty. But the redeeming relative had the first option by law to buy back any land or person being sold, thus allowing ownership to be kept within the clan (Lev. 25:23–28; Jer. 32:6–10).

Thus the redeeming relative was an important figure in Israelite culture. In fact, God Himself is often represented in the Old Testament as a redeemer (Deut. 7:8; 2 Sam. 7:23). Likewise, in the New Testament, Jesus is described as our brother who redeems us from the power of sin (Heb. 2:11–12, 17).

FINANCIAL SECURITY

Peace with God

Ecclesiastes challenges us with a proverb that points out the relative value of little with contentment and great wealth with trouble (Eccl. 4:6). The comparison encourages us to ask: how important are material wealth and financial security in your life? What do you sacrifice to achieve them?

While the Bible sometimes depicts material wealth as a blessing from God (Deut. 7:1–14; 11:13–15; 28:1–14), it also warns against elevating riches above other things that are more valuable. These include:

- a right relationship with God (Prov. 15:16; Luke 12:13–21);
- love of family (Prov. 15:17);
- righteousness and justice (16:8);

- humility (16:19);
- peace in the home (17:1); and
- personal integrity (28:6).

As you evaluate your own life, consider ways in which you have perhaps chosen material prosperity over these things. What have been the results—for you and for others?

FIRST THINGS FIRST
(*see* Priorities)

FISHING
The World of the Fishermen
Fishing on the Sea of Galilee was big business. This now-famous body of water, eight miles wide and thirteen miles long, lay beside a fertile plain renowned for its agriculture. In Jesus' day, nine cities crowded its shorelines, each with no less than fifteen thousand citizens, possibly making the region's total population greater than Jerusalem's.

The names of the Galilean towns reflect the importance of fishing to the life and economy of the area. For example, at Tarichaea, "the place of salt fish," workers packed fish for shipment to Jerusalem and export to Rome. Bethsaida—from which at least four fishermen left their nets to follow Jesus (Matt. 4:18–22; John 1:44)—means "fish town"; most of the town was employed in the fishing industry.

Shoals just offshore were a fisherman's paradise. In Jesus' day, hundreds of fishing boats trawled the lake. Galileans ate little meat besides fish. It came highly salted, as there was no other way of preserving the "catch of the day."

Two kinds of nets were used—the *sagene* and the *amphiblestron*. The *sagene* (Matt. 13:47) was larger. Fitted with both weighted and buoyant material, it was used for trawling. In water, it stood almost upright and bagged fish as it was dragged behind a boat. The smaller *amphiblestron* was shaped like an umbrella and was used for casting off the side of a boat (see Mark 1:16).

The fisherman's day did not end with a return to shore. Mending and washing nets, preserving fish, maintaining boats and supplies, training and supervising crews, and negotiating with merchants and others in the shipping industry made for long, tiring hours.

FLEXIBILITY
A Foolish Order
Some situations call for tough-minded leadership that makes great demands on people. War is such a situation. In Saul's war with the Philistines, he ordered his troops to forego food until they had vanquished the enemy (1 Sam. 14:24).

Apparently Saul intended the command to be a noble challenge to his men. After all, why should they relax and enjoy a good meal when their longtime enemies, the Philistines, remained unbeaten?

Yet the order was actually a foolish one as it deprived the men of needed energy to fight the battle. The command came across as arbitrary and capricious and seemed to be based more on Saul's bravado than wise leadership. Thus it probably lowered morale more than it boosted it. Nor did it help when Saul insisted on enforcing his rash oath, even when the one who violated it was his own son, Jonathan (1 Sam. 14:43–44).

Silly directives by leaders, especially when followed by demands for rigid conformity, help to create a climate of fear and repression. But there are ways to avoid that kind of destructive leadership:

1. *Consult with others before issuing orders.* Saul had a strong tendency to act on his own. Things might have gone differently at Michmash if he had invited others to evaluate and even challenge his reasoning and the potential impact of his plans.

2. *Seek God's guidance.* The most important Person with whom any leader should consult is God. Yet Saul often ignored the Lord as he led his troops into battle—a habit that ultimately cost him his kingdom (1 Sam. 15:10–11) and even his life (1 Sam. 28:4–8, 16–19; 31:6).

3. *Realistically appraise the impact of orders.* Saul's desire for victory over the Philistines was admirable, but his policy of no food until after the battle was poorly thought through. The fact that his son, Jonathan, knowingly violated the directive (1 Sam. 14:28–30) was a clue that the order should have been rescinded.

4. *Be willing to consider exceptions to the rule.* Strictly enforced rules and policies help

F

to maintain order, but wisdom suggests that there may be a time to make an exception. Saul insisted on enforcing his policy by calling for the death of Jonathan (1 Sam. 14:44), but it only put distance between Saul and his army (1 Sam. 14:45). Apparently Saul forgot that rules should be a support for people, not a straitjacket.

5. *Admit it when the policy is wrong.* Apparently Saul's pride prevented him from backing away from his foolish decree. He emerged victorious from the battle (1 Sam. 14:46–47), but at what cost? He was at odds with his own son and the people (1 Sam. 14:44–45).

FOOD

Food in the New Testament World

Meat sold in the Corinthian meat market (1 Cor. 10:25) was meat that had been offered to the Greek gods. Thus Paul had to address the moral question of whether a believer in Christ should buy and eat such food. His conclusion: don't worry about it; the earth and all its products belong to God (1 Cor. 10:25–26).

Actually, beef was something of a luxury in ancient Greece and seldom eaten on a regular basis. A far more common source of meat was fish. Other items in a typical meal might be cheese, leeks, olives, wine, oil, and vinegar. Greece raised some wheat, but most of its bread was made from imported grain from Egypt or Asia Minor.

In Palestine, the land of "milk and honey" (Ex. 13:5), Hebrew farmers raised a variety of cereal grains such as wheat and related products, spelt, barley, and millet. They also cultivated cucumbers, squash, beans, lentils, leeks, onions, and garlic. Fruits and nuts included melons, grapes, raisins, figs, apricots, oranges, almonds, and pistachios.

Honey was gathered from bees or made from dates. Regional spices included mint, anise, dill, and cummin. As in the rest of the Mediterranean, olives were plentiful. They were eaten green or ripe, or they might be pressed into oil, which was used for cooking, seasoning, and as fuel for lamps.

Beef and mutton were a common part of the daily fare in Palestine, along with milk, butter, and cheese. A noon meal for a workman might consist of two small loaves of barley bread—one filled with cheese, the other with olives.

Animals were divided into two classes by the Hebrews, clean and unclean (Lev. 11:1–47; Acts 10:9–15). Only clean animals—those that chewed the cud and had divided hooves—could be used for food (Lev. 11:3), except the fat (Lev. 3:16–17). Pigs and camels were ceremonially unclean and therefore unfit for food. Camel's milk and cheese, however, were not forbidden.

Many kinds of fish could be eaten (Lev. 11:9–12), but not oysters or shrimp. Some twenty different species of birds, mostly scavengers, were rejected (Lev. 11:13–19). Insects that had legs and leaped, such as the grasshopper, were fit for consumption. All reptiles were considered unclean.

The major preservative for these foods was salt. An abundant supply was available from the Sea of Salt, or Dead Sea, in the south.

FOOLISHNESS

On Fools

Proverbs is very straightforward about the fact that some people pursue life in very foolish ways. By calling them "fools," Scripture places the full burden of responsibility for their condition on their own backs. Proverbs 26:1–12 gives us a series of truths concerning fools:

- They are not deserving of honor (Prov. 26:1, 8). Indeed, it seems out of place to honor them.
- They go through life suffering harsh treatment, punishment, and loss of freedom, like a beast of burden (Prov. 26:3).
- They cannot listen to reason (Prov. 26:4).
- They are convinced they are right, and have to be shown the error of their ways (Prov. 26:5).
- They are unreliable and irresponsible (Prov. 26:6).
- They are morally and spiritually impotent and even dangerous (Prov. 26:7, 9).
- God cares for them despite themselves (Prov. 26:10).
- They persist in their folly (Prov. 26:11).
- They are hopeless (Prov. 26:12).

The Foolishness of Fools

Perhaps at one time or another you have made a foolish commitment for which you now feel rather sheepish. The opportunity may have looked promising at the outset, but you ended up losing in the long run. As you look back, you may be able to see why the choice was poor to begin with, and why it ultimately failed to give you what you anticipated.

Proverbs describes one kind of "fool" as a person who makes poor choices about how and where to "invest" his life (Prov. 14:24). From beginning to end, he trades away the most valuable things that he has for the most

worthless. That is why Proverbs describes him as committing foolishness that yields nothing but folly. While the wise person wears a crown of riches, the fool can be said to wear a dunce cap of folly.

But this is not the only kind of fool we find in Proverbs. This book describes four distinct types of foolish people:

- *The simple.* This person can't tell the difference between truth and falsehood. Because he lacks direction, he is headed for a fall (Prov. 7:7; 9:4; 14:15).
- *The scoffer.* This person laughs at wisdom and toys with wickedness. Warned of the consequences of pursuing evil, he

FOOT-WASHING

says, "It won't happen to me" (Prov. 1:22; 13:1; 15:12).

- *The arrogant.* This person willfully ignores wisdom and lives unto himself. He has no interest in whether something is good or bad. All that matters, is "What's in it or me?" (Prov. 10:23; 12:23; 13:16).
- *The rebel.* This person actually hates wisdom. He so totally rejects it that he could be said to be an aggressive unbeliever (Prov. 1:7; 14:9; 16:22).

Carefully look over the characteristics of the four types of fools. Do any of them apply to you? What steps are you prepared to take to change from a life devoted to folly to one devoted to wisdom?

For more on this topic, see **CHOICES,** *"A Reckless Choice," page 56;* **FLEXIBILITY,** *"A Foolish Order," page 157;* **SINCERITY,** *"Being Sincere Is Not Enough," page 369.*

FOOT-WASHING
The Order of the Towel

Leadership is a fascinating topic. Business books offer models of leadership as diverse as Attila the Hun, Oriental warlords, and Abraham Lincoln. But Jesus painted a different picture of leadership.

As He wrapped up His work, Jesus held a dinner for his closest associates. Instead of delivering a state-of-the-union address or naming a successor, He chose to leave His seat at the head of the table and pick up some household servant's equipment—a basin of water and a towel. He then washed the feet of every person at the table—even Judas, His betrayer (John 13:1–20). Foot-washing was usually performed by household servants as an act of hospitality to weary, dusty guests (compare Luke 7:44). Leaders and hosts did not stoop to such a menial task. But Jesus did.

Seated once again at the table, the Lord asked whether His followers understood what He had done (John 13:12). He then exhorted them to adopt the same posture of serving others, thereby following His example. He assured them that they would be blessed if they did (John 13:15–17).

Jesus still calls believers today to become members of the "Order of the Towel." As Christ's followers, we need to lead others by serving them.

FORCED LABOR
(*see* Minorities; Oppression)

FORGIVENESS
Forgiveness Follows Repentance

Someone has well said that the grace of God is free, but it is not cheap; it costs. The grace of God cost Jesus the agony of death on a cross, and it costs those who wish to receive God's forgiveness the price of repentance, or turning from sin.

The Lord reminded His people of this relationship between forgiveness and repentance by stating His promise to heal their land in terms of a condition: "if . . . then" (2 Chr. 7:14). To God, forgiveness follows repentance. And repentance is not merely saying, "I am sorry." Neither is it accomplished by tears and a sad countenance. True repentance means turning *away* from wicked ways—from thoughts and acts that displease God—and turning *toward* a life that reflects godly ways.

God cannot bless evil, and He will not reward those who practice evil. To do so would violate His very nature. So if we want His blessing, we must honor His character by pursuing His ways. "Be holy," He urges us, "for I am holy" (Lev. 11:44; 1 Pet. 1:15–16).

No Forgiveness!

People speak of committing the "unpardonable sin," but in His severe comments to the Pharisees (Matt. 12:31–32), Jesus indicated that it is more than just a figure of speech—it is a matter with eternal consequences!

Can people ever sin so badly that God cannot forgive them? The answer is yes and no. It's important to realize that the blood of Jesus Christ on the cross paid for all of the sin of the world (John 1:29; Rom. 5:12–21; 8:3). There is no sin that God has not overcome through Christ. That means that no one ever has to fear going beyond the scope of God's grace or power. Sometimes people despair because they have committed certain sins that to them seem unforgivable. But no matter what their failure has been, God can and will forgive their sin if they come to Him in repentance (Acts 2:38; 1 John 1:9).

At the same time, it is possible to willfully place oneself beyond the grace of God—to persist in rebellion and sin and resist His call to repentance. This, essentially, is what the Pharisees and other Jewish leaders did (compare Acts 7:51–52). Jesus had healed a demon-possessed man by the power of the Holy Spirit (Matt. 12:28). His enemies claimed that He cast them out by the power of Satan ("Beelzebub," 12:24). The accusation was evidence that they had rejected Him.

It also slandered the Holy Spirit, revealing their spiritual blindness, a warping and perversion of their moral nature that put them beyond hope of repentance and faith—and therefore beyond forgiveness.

Is there an "unpardonable sin"? Not for those who cry out like the tax collector in a parable of Jesus, "God, be merciful to me a sinner!" (Luke 18:13). But those who, like the Pharisee in the same parable (as well as the Pharisees in this incident), trust to their own self-righteousness, reject Christ, and slander His Holy Spirit reveal a spiritual cancer so advanced that they are beyond any hope of healing and forgiveness.

Extreme Forgiveness

If Peter gasped when Jesus told him to forgive his brother up to seventy times seven times (Matt. 18:22), he must have gagged when he heard the parable that followed.

The first servant owed ten thousand talents to the king (18:24). The second servant owed one hundred denarii to the first servant (Matt. 18:28). This was an extraordinary difference in indebtedness. A talent was a lot of money, perhaps one thousand dollars in today's currency. But in that culture, it probably represented far more. A talent equalled six thousand denarii, and one denarius was what a common laborer could earn in one day.

So the first servant owed at least ten million dollars, but from the standpoint of common wages, he would have had to work sixty million days to pay off his debt! By contrast, the second servant owed sixteen to eighteen dollars, which he could earn in one hundred days. In other words, the first servant owed the king more than the second servant owed

the first servant by a ratio of at least six hundred thousand to one!

Somehow, after Jesus finished that parable, seventy times seven probably didn't look so bad to Peter!

Two Sides of the Coin

"Think positive" is the message preached from many pulpits today. And for good reason: the message of salvation in Christ is good, positive news in a world that sometimes seems more and more depressing by the day.

However, before we can fully embrace the good news about God's Son, we must first accept the bad news about our own sin. Psalm 106 is the flip side of Psalm 105. Both recall Israel's history. But whereas Psalm 105 is an enthusiastic celebration of the Lord's faithfulness, Psalm 106 focuses on the continuing unfaithfulness of His people. Still, the piece is not without hope: the Lord remains committed to mercy, forgiveness, and doing the mighty wonders necessary to sustain His wayward children (Ps. 106:44–46). No wonder the psalm concludes with a blessing for the Lord "from everlasting to everlasting" (Ps. 106:48).

If Psalm 105 stood alone, the forgetful student of history might assume that God swept His people into the Promised Land with no setbacks or opposition. But Psalm 106 puts things in perspective. As we look at that same history, it confronts us with the ugly face of sin and shows why people (and nations) so badly need forgiveness. Thus Psalms 105 and 106 show the two realities involved in salvation: sin and grace. Focusing on either one without the other will lead to distortion.

The Power of Forgiveness

The crowd that watched Jesus heal the paralytic responded enthusiastically to His dramatic display of power (Matt. 9:8). But they overlooked His more significant ability to forgive sins—a power that deeply troubled the scribes (Matt. 9:2–3).

The power of forgiveness is immeasurable. Jesus challenged us as His followers to forgive others who have wronged or hurt us (Matt. 6:14–15; 18:21–35). That may seem like a simple act, but anyone who has struggled with pain and anger knows that it takes enormous power to authentically forgive—to lay aside one's hurt and reach out to an offender with the embrace of a pardon. On the other side, forgiveness can release the wrongdoer from paralyzing guilt and even turn around the course of that person's life (James 5:19–20).

Forgiveness is as powerful and liberating as the healing of a paralytic. And it's a power that Jesus has delegated to His followers (John 20:23).

FORGOTTEN
Forsaken?

It is one thing to feel alone. It is another to feel abandoned. David felt abandoned by the one Person whose support he could least afford to lose—God (Ps. 22:1–2). This extreme sense of being forsaken and forgotten was the terror that Job experienced in the midst of his sufferings (Job 16:11; 30:20) and that Jesus felt in the agony of the Cross (Matt. 27:46).

Yet Psalm 22 offers hope. It assures us that God is acquainted with our suffering, no matter how horrible. He is with us even when we feel most forsaken. Why? Because He is the God who has known us from the womb (Ps. 22:9–10).

This is the unique power of the Christian message—that God knows us personally and intimately. Other religions may affirm God as the Creator and ultimate Ruler of the world. But the God of the Bible is intensely personal. He knows us better than we know ourselves. Even though we may feel abandoned, He never forgets us. He has our sorrows and grief in the center of His heart.

FORSAKEN
(see Forgotten)

FORTUNE-TELLING
(see Occult)

FRAUD
What's Wrong with Dross?

Isaiah listed a number of symptoms that indicated Judah had turned away from God: murder, silver turned to dross, wine mixed with water, rebellious princes, thievery, rampant bribery, and failure to defend the weak and vulnerable (Is. 1:22–23). Murder, rebellion, thievery, bribery, selfishness, and neglect

of the poor are clearly against God's ways. But what is the significance of silver turning to dross, or of wine being mixed with water?

Both were evidences of a corrupt economy. In the ancient world, deceptive merchants mixed wine with water in order to have more product to sell at less cost to themselves. A buyer might taste a sample from one or two wineskins filled with undiluted wine but be unaware that other skins held diluted wine. So, just as some meat packers used to mix sawdust into hamburger meat, these wine sellers mixed water with wine in order to defraud their customers.

Another means of fraud was to adulterate silver with dross, trace elements normally burned out of the precious metal during the refining process. Silver was a common medium of exchange in that day, but its value was affected by its weight and purity. Dishonest merchants could cheat their customers by representing their silver as being of a higher purity than it really was.

Whether the commodity is wine, hamburger, silver, or any other item of exchange, debasing it by mixing in impurities is fraudulent and unjust. God was determined to restore justice and righteousness to His people by ridding Jerusalem of its wicked rulers and merchants and replacing them with just ones (Is. 1:24–26). One sign of Jerusalem's restoration would be renewed integrity, as illustrated by a purified money supply: "I will . . . thoroughly purge away your dross, and take away all your alloy" (Is. 1:25).

How pure are the goods and services you exchange for money? Isaiah warns us that God takes our financial transactions very seriously. His standards of honesty and justice have not changed since Isaiah's day. Therefore, we do well to keep our trade pure and above reproach.

FREE WILL
Did Pharaoh Have a Chance?

If God "hardened" Pharaoh's heart (Ex. 9:12), did the ruler really have a fair chance to heed God's command to "let My people go"? Or was he a hapless pawn in God's plan to emancipate His chosen people?

Pharaoh had as fair a chance as any other person to hear and obey the Lord, but he used his encounter with the living God as a singular opportunity to "prove" his determination and might. This becomes plain when we understand that "hardening" means the "strengthening" of his heart or will.

God did not intervene in Pharaoh's decisions in a way that took control of Pharaoh's will. Pharaoh kept complete control—and responsibility—over his choices. Apparently God had made him to be what we would call a strong-willed individual. So it's not surprising that he was determined to resist God's plan. When the text says that God "hardened" or "strengthened" his heart, it is a way of saying that Pharaoh became even more determined; he was acting even more like the strong-willed person that God had made him to be.

It's interesting that not every Egyptian had the same response to the plagues as Pharaoh did. A number of them joined the Hebrews and left in the Exodus (Ex. 12:38). Furthermore, even some of Pharaoh's own magicians confessed that the miracles of Moses and Aaron were "the finger of God" (Ex. 8:19).

FREEDOM

Christianity and Personal Freedom

Freedom is the prevailing cry of the world today, the overwhelming preoccupation of individuals and nations. Yet even though Scripture speaks of a liberty that Christ offers (Gal. 5:1–12), some people resist Christianity as itself an obstacle to freedom. Is this view of the faith justified?

On the face of it, it seems strange to identify Christianity as an enemy of freedom. After all, Christians have historically stood up for the poor, the oppressed, the captive, and the underprivileged. Likewise, liberation from ignorance, disease, and political oppression have invariably resulted wherever Christian faith and principles have been adopted. Why, then, would some view the faith as repressive?

Perhaps part of the answer lies in the problem of legalism. Whenever Christianity is made into a list of dos and don'ts, it becomes intolerant and restrictive. Instead of enjoying an intimate relationship with a loving God, the legalist is obsessed with rules and regulations, as if God were a celestial Policeman just waiting to catch us out of line.

To be sure, Christ does make demands on us that sometimes limit our autonomy. But true Christianity sees this as part of a relationship based on love and grace, not unlike a healthy marriage in which both partners sometimes sacrifice their own desires in order to serve the other.

But even if there were no legalists, many people would still resist Christianity because they resist any absolute standards that would place claims on them. To them, freedom means pure autonomy—the right to do whatever they want, with no accountability to anyone else.

But surely that leads to irresponsibility and license rather than freedom. Nor do people really live that way. Sooner or later they choose one course of action over another, based on some set of values. In other words, they surrender their will to standards, whether good or bad, and act accordingly. So it is not just the values of Christianity that "stifle" personal freedom, but values in general.

The real question, of course, is what kind of people do we choose to be? What is our character? Christians try to mold their character after the pattern of Jesus. He was the most liberated person who ever lived. His ultimate standard of behavior was, what does My Father want Me to do (John 8:29)? Did that code stifle His freedom? Hardly: He was utterly free of covetousness, hypocrisy, fear of others, and every other vice. At the same time He was free to be Himself, free to tell the truth, free to love people with warmth and purity, and free to surrender His life for others.

True Christian freedom is Christlike freedom. It accepts absolute moral standards that are well known and well proven, and it takes its inspiration from the liberated life and teachings of Jesus of Nazareth.

Real Freedom

One of the greatest motivating factors for people throughout the world today is the quest for freedom, for self-determination. Armies fight for it. Nations vote for it. Individuals work for it.

But in Romans 6, Scripture teaches that, ultimately, no one is ever totally "free." In the end, everyone serves either God or sin. In fact, Paul uses the word "slaves" to describe the relationship (Rom. 6:16–20). We are either slaves of righteousness or slaves of sin.

What does that imply for our understanding of the nature of freedom? Is complete autonomy possible? Is there such a thing as self-rule or political self-determination? Yes, in a limited sense. But here as elsewhere, Scripture describes real freedom as a change of masters: being set free from slavery to sin in order to become slaves to righteousness instead.

All of us are enslaved to sin from the moment of conception. Our only hope is Christ, who is able to emancipate us from that bondage (Rom. 7:24–25). Then, having saved us, He enables us through His Holy Spirit to do what we could not do in and of ourselves—live in obedience to God's Law (Rom. 8:3–4). Therein lies true freedom.

For more on this topic, see COVENANT, "The Freedom of the New Covenant" page 93; LIMITATIONS, "Hemmed In," page 244.

FRIENDSHIP

Helping Someone in Need

The news was out: help was available for the sick! But a certain paralytic had no way to get to it. Physically disabled people like him were not only immobile, but usually poor. Useless to society and lacking help from the government, they invariably lived as social outcasts.

But some men knew of this man's dilemma and came to his need. They helped him get to a house where Jesus was teaching. Yet enormous crowds made access impossible. Fortunately, the men were determined and resourceful: they literally tore the roof off in order to connect their friend with the Helper (Luke 5:19).

Jesus noticed "*their*" faith" (Luke 5:20, emphasis added) and healed the paralyzed man.

Is there someone near you who is cut off from needed services—health care, transportation, access to community resources, financial assistance, or advocacy in the workplace? Can you band together with others to provide what is needed in the tradition of the unnamed but faithful helpers described in Luke 5?

Kindred Spirits

The friendship between Jonathan and David went far beyond personal affinity and camaraderie. Scripture records that "the soul of Jonathan was knit to the soul of David" (1 Sam. 18:1), indicating an unusually close bond between the two men. This commitment was formalized with a covenant in which David agreed to show "kindness" (Hebrew, *chesed;* 1 Sam. 20:11–17) to Jonathan's descendants. When he became king, David followed through on this promise by honoring Jonathan's son, Mephibosheth.

For his part, Jonathan showed amazing devotion to David by thwarting the evil intentions of his father, Saul, on several occasions (1 Sam. 19:1–7; 20:18–42). This loyalty was all the more remarkable given the fact that David was to become king, even though Jonathan would have inherited the throne if God had not decided otherwise (1 Sam. 15:27–28).

Prayer Partners

In a dangerous and trying time, Daniel made use of two valuable resources: a trio of close friends who shared his faith, and prayer (Dan. 2:17–18). Together this group of prayer partners fought a spiritual battle against despair and defeat. They enlisted divine help to understand the king's dream or otherwise deliver them from certain death.

When you face tough times, to whom do you turn for support, encouragement, and wisdom? A natural tendency is to seek out those whom we think will have the means to help us—position, influence, power, money. But these people may not necessarily be our most valuable allies, in that resorting to them may keep us from trusting God. By contrast, a trustworthy friend or two who can offer godly wisdom and prayer support may be worth more than a dozen acquaintances with the "right" connections.

For that reason, it is important in the best of times to be cultivating the kinds of friendships that will sustain us in the worst of times. Each day we make an investment in the quality of our relationships.

A Friend of God

Imagine speaking to God the way Moses did, as though He were your friend (Ex. 33:11)! Yet the fact is that Christians are God's friends, thanks to Jesus Christ: "No longer do I call you servants," He told His followers, "for a servant does not know what his master is doing; but I have called you *friends*" (John 15:15, emphasis added).

As believers, then, we need never think that we're alone when facing problems or crises. God is right there with us. Indeed, He is the Friend "who sticks closer than a brother" (Prov. 18:24).

Characteristics of Friendship

Can you think of anyone who would describe you as a good friend? What would they say about you if asked to talk about their relationship with you?

Scripture says that good friendships are a great treasure. While some people play at friendships, a true friend "sticks closer than a brother" (Prov. 18:24). Elsewhere, the Book of Proverbs describes other characteristics of good friends and neighbors:

- A good friend is one who makes honest commitments, and acknowledges quickly when those promises cannot be fulfilled (Prov. 3:28–29; 6:1–.5).
- A good neighbor refuses to despise poor neighbors, but instead shows kindness toward them (Prov. 19:7; 22:9).
- A good and true friend forgives, and then lets the matter rest. He does not keep bringing up past mistakes and failures (Prov. 17:9, 14).
- A good neighbor or friend is willing to share in one's adversity (Prov. 17:17; 18:24; 27:10).
- Good neighbors do not wear out their welcome by paying too many visits (Prov. 25:17).
- A good friend will sing one's praises to others (Prov. 27:1–2).
- Friends can sharpen one's thinking with good counsel (Prov. 27:17; 28:23).

Use this list of friendship characteristics to measure your own value as a friend. Do you follow the kind of guidelines for friendships laid down by Proverbs? Also think about the people you value as friends. Do they know how much you appreciate them?

FRUSTRATION

Bitter Prayers

For a book of worship, the Psalms contain some rather harsh expressions of hatred and vengeance. For example, Psalm 137 seems to delight in the image of Babylonian babies being dashed against rocks (Ps. 137:8–9). Likewise, David prays down curses on his enemy, asking that no one would extend kindness to him, nor to his orphaned children after him (Ps. 109:12). Similar expressions can be found in Psalms 35, 55, 58, 59, 69, 83, and 140.

What are we to make of these prayers? What are they doing in a collection of songs for worship? Opinions differ on the answer to that question. But one point of view is that worship means expressing to God our honest feelings, no matter how "ugly" they may seem. God is not intimidated by our pain nor unaware of the poison that lurks in our innermost being. He invites us to bare all before Him.

In fact, the Bible presents a number of accounts of people who brought their anger, disappointment, or pain to God. Their raw emotion is clearly expressed, providing encouragement to us to approach God when we are in personal agony. Some of these figures include:

- Job, whose cries of pain and loss were welcomed, heard, and responded to by God.
- Solomon, whose "diary" of reflections on life, at times bordering on depression and despair, can be found in the Book of Ecclesiastes.
- Habakkuk, whose despair over Israel's plight and complaint to God were heard (Hab. 1:1–17).
- Jeremiah, whose lament over the destruction of Jerusalem, including vivid and ugly descriptions of agony and pain, is included in Scripture in the Book of Lamentations.
- Paul, whose internal conflicts over sinful patterns speak eloquently for many of us (Rom. 7:14–25).

True worship involves speaking the truth. That includes the truth about how we feel, no matter how dark our emotions may be. God will hear us. However, He also expects us to hear Him, as each of those mentioned above did.

Do you bring your innermost hatreds, hostilities, fears, and frustrations to God? Where better to take them? If buried, they will only fester, sooner or later to emerge and cause great harm to us and those in our path.

FUND-RAISING

Anonymous Giving

Jesus' words in Matthew 6:1–4 challenge a lot of what goes on today in fund-raising and charitable causes. As any fund-raiser knows, one of the biggest motivations for people who give large gifts is the prestige that results.

Jesus questioned that spirit of giving, however. He detested people who made a great show of presenting their gifts in the temple and elsewhere (Mark 12:41–44) as if they were generous and upright, but behind the scenes practiced the worst sorts of greed and immorality (Matt. 23:23–24). He was not attacking giving but hypocrisy.

How can we be sure that we are giving with the right motives? One way is to give anonymously (Matt. 6:3–4). That way, our gifts will affect no one's opinion of us one way or the other. The matter will stay between us and God—and He can evaluate our motives.

FUNERAL CUSTOMS

(see Burial and Funeral Customs)

G

GANGS

Gang Behavior

One of the most troubling developments of life today is the rapid growth of gang activity, particularly among young people. Proverbs speaks to this issue by warning against associating with people committed to crime and violence (Prov. 1:10–19).

Somehow, joining a group can release a person from the usual restraints on behavior. Encouraged by others, one may commit an amount of evil that far exceeds anything he or she would do alone. The craving for significance and peer approval, combined with bitterness against society, can yield an appetite for destruction that overrides any sense of conscience.

However, gang-related behavior is not limited to wandering groups of youth on the streets. Even many "respectable" adults with good jobs can be found ganging up on others. For example, cliques may form in an office, alliances may come together in a university, or rival groups may square off on a construction site. By ganging up on individuals, the perpetrators may do little if any outward violence, yet their assaults can be remarkably vicious.

Do you find these tendencies where you work, or perhaps in your neighborhood or even within your own family? Does someone about whom you care deeply exhibit these behaviors? Proverbs challenges us to forsake these ways with a sobering warning: gang-ing up on others is a certain path to self-destruction (Prov. 1:18–19).

GARDEN

From Planting to Paradise

We usually think of a garden as a plot of ground where flowers, vegetables, or ornamental shrubs are grown. But the word "garden" as used in the Bible also includes parks, plantations, and orchards. Gardens that belonged to kings (2 Kin. 25:4; Neh. 3:15) were actually royal parks. The garden of the Persian King Xerxes, for example, was large enough to hold a week-long feast for thousands (Esth. 1:5).

Mesopotamian kings kept and hunted wild animals in their gardens. They also used these plots of ground for cultivating a wide variety of plants. The author of Ecclesiastes apparently regarded the planting of gardens and orchards as a royal task, demonstrating the king's prosperity (Eccl. 2:4). Occasionally, however, parts of royal gardens might be used for other purposes, such as vegetable gardens (1 Kin. 21:2) or even burial grounds (2 Kin. 21:18, 26).

Ordinary people also owned gardens. These gardens were not generally attached to individual houses, but were in a separate area, often outside city walls and near a good water supply. Their main function was to produce food (Num. 24:6; Jer. 29:5).

Gardens are also spoken of symbolically as

portraits of happiness and fruitfulness. For example, the lovers in the Song of Solomon compared one another to a garden of delights (Song 4:12; 5:1; 8:13). The Lord's blessings for His people are also described as a garden of delights (Is. 51:3; Ezek. 36:35; Amos 9:14).

The Garden of Eden represented God's ideal environment for man. Special characteristics of Eden were its wide variety of trees (Gen. 2:9; Ezek. 31:8–9), its precious stones and metals (Gen. 2:11–12; Ezek. 28:13–14), and its rivers (Gen. 2:10–14; Rev. 22:1–2), all of them portraying its richness and fertility. Eden is also sometimes referred to in the Bible as the garden of the Lord (Gen. 13:10; Is. 51:3) or the garden of God (Ezek. 28:13; 31:8–9). Some of this garden's features, especially its rivers and the Tree of Life, are also used to portray God's final blessings for His people (Ezek. 47:12; Rev. 22:1–2, 14).

GENERATION GAP

(*see* Parent-Youth Relationships)

GENEROSITY

Giving of Ourselves

Paul wanted the Corinthians to give generously toward a fund-raising project to help needy Christians. He linked generosity with spiritual benefits: the more one gives, the more one benefits (2 Cor. 9:6–11).

This principle goes beyond financial giving. At work, for example, you may donate toward the local United Way. But when a coworker asks for some of your time to talk about a problem, what is your response? Do you give your attention generously or grudgingly? When your boss gives you a special assignment, do you give the project just enough attention to get it over with, or do you jump in wholeheartedly with energy and creativity?

What about your time and emotional energy after hours? When your spouse or children need you, do you make yourself available generously or grudgingly? Do you give a fair contribution of yourself to assignments that you've volunteered for, or just a token effort?

We are constant recipients of God's generous grace. He promises that if we will give of ourselves, He'll enable us to have an abun-

dance of resources for the work to which He has called us (2 Cor. 9:8).

GIVING

A Parting Gift

What the disciples saw as waste (Mark 14:4–9) the Lord saw as worship. The woman's gift of costly oil was worth about one year's average wages, yet she poured it out, apparently sensing that her days with Jesus were drawing to a close.

This incident raises the issue of how one's material wealth enters into worship. While Jesus was still physically present and available to her, the woman did "what she could" (Mark 14:8). She took one of her most valuable possessions and gave it to Jesus in an unusual act of devotion. A waste? Not to the One she honored by it.

Today Jesus is not physically among us. Yet while we are alive, we control a certain measure of the world's resources. So we might ask: What act of worship might we give while we have opportunity? How might we honor the Lord materially?

There are no easy answers. But did Jesus give us a clue when He told His disciples that just as the woman had done Him "a good work," so they could do good to the poor at any time (Mark 14:6)?

Amount vs. Attitude

Jesus called the widow in Luke 21:1–4 "poor." The word He used referred to a person so destitute that she was literally in danger of death.

It is hard to reckon what the two mites that she threw into the treasury would be worth in today's currency. But even in her day they were not much. Each mite was worth about one-thirty-second of a denarius, the daily wage of a soldier, which would be less than fifty cents today.

The important thing to note is that the two coins were "all the livelihood that she had" (Luke 21:4). She was truly destitute—the sort of widow who would later be eligible for support from the church (1 Tim. 5:5). Nevertheless, she gave generously to the temple. Jesus praised her for her faithfulness, even though it meant sacrifice.

In doing so, the Lord showed that God's

accounting differs from ours. He pays attention to our attitudes in giving more than the absolute dollar amount of our gifts.

Saying Thank You

How do you say "thank you" to someone who has been extremely helpful? With a card? A small gift? An all-expenses-paid vacation? The size of the gift depends a lot on the nature of the person's help and the level of your gratitude. But whatever you give, your expression of thanks is not unlike the Old Testament idea of vows.

Vows were offerings that the Israelites gave, or at least pledged, to God as a way of thanking Him for His blessing or help. Vows were strictly voluntary. But once people made vows, they were obligated to pay them.

There were several common ways that Israelites paid their vows. One was by "consecrating" or setting apart a person from the household (Lev. 27:2). (These "donated" individuals may have been servants, though the text does not say.) Other vows were paid with animals, houses, or land.

"What shall I render to the LORD for all His benefits toward me?" the psalmist asked (Ps. 116:12). It's a question that every follower of God does well to ponder. God never demands that we pay Him vows. But doesn't it seem reasonable that if we give gifts to friends and associates as tokens of appreciation, we ought to consider tangible ways to say thanks to God, in light of "all His benefits"?

Giving with Compassion and Integrity

Money is powerful. It can bring out the best or the worst in a person. In our drive to gain lots of it or use it for personal comfort and convenience, we can become very cold and manipulative (1 Tim. 6:10). But that ought not to be the way for God's followers.

In 1 Corinthians 16, we see that Paul was coordinating a fund-raising drive to help some needy believers. He could have focused on the plight of the recipients. They were Christians in Jerusalem, perhaps suffering from persecution or famine. But instead he concentrated on how the Corinthians should initiate a regular pattern of giving to meet the need (1 Cor. 16:2). Their participation would be an act of loving worship as they met together on the first day of the week.

Paul also pointed out that the transfer of the funds would be carried out by responsible people chosen by the Corinthians themselves (1 Cor. 16:3). That guaranteed accountability and integrity. Apparently Paul was quite realistic about the human tendency toward manipulation and greed.

How are you using your money to alleviate suffering and meet the needs of others?

*For more on this topic, see **FUND-RAISING**, "Anonymous Giving," page 166.*

GOALS

Our Goals and God's

At first glance, Ecclesiastes 3:14 seems to suggest that nothing people do really matters. Ultimately, God's will is going to be done. But if nothing can be added or taken away from His work, then why should we attempt to do anything? Why not just wait for God to do everything?

But that perspective forgets that God has *chosen* to do things through us as human beings. We are agents of God's power and purposes—not puppets who mindlessly jump at His commands, nor parasites who mindlessly sup at His provisions. God calls us to an intimate partnership with Him (2 Cor. 1:5–7; 12:15; Phil. 3:10; Col. 1:24).

Given this reality, we can read Ecclesiastes 3:14 as an invitation for us to link our goals, our dreams, and our skills to God's great designs.

*For more on this topic, see **RESULTS**, "A Craving for Results," page 344.*

GOD'S GLORY

Considering God's Glory

As he began his letter to the Christians at Rome, Paul wrote that God's invisible attributes are clearly seen through the creation, so that everyone is without excuse if they refuse to believe in or give glory to God (Rom. 1:20–21). Centuries earlier, Isaiah was told essentially the same truth in his vision of God's throne room: "The whole earth is full of His glory!" (Is. 6:3).

God has revealed Himself to the whole world through what He has made (Ps. 19:1–4). The creation shows not only that He exists, but that He is just, righteous, and holy.

When Isaiah saw this holy God sitting on His throne, "high and lifted up" (Is. 6:1), and heard the praises of the seraphim (or angels), he cried out in humility before Lord, confessing himself to be an unclean sinner who had no right to stand in the presence of the living God (Is. 6:5), and he threw himself on God's mercy. The joy of the account is that God cleansed Isaiah from sin (Is. 6:6–7).

God has not allowed everyone to see Him through the kind of vision that Isaiah was given, but He has adequately revealed Himself through what He has made. He calls each and every person to come before Him. When we do, may we respond in the same way that Isaiah did—with sincere repentance that leads to hope and healing.

God Among Us

Psalm 48 celebrates Mount Zion, or Jerusalem, as the dwelling place of God, the city of God (Ps. 48:1–2). But the real focus of the psalm is not on an earthly city, but on the glory and wonder of God Himself. His presence makes the city significant and brings it joy. Therefore He deserves the praise of the city's inhabitants.

Notice some of the ways in which the psalmist reminds us that "this is God" (Ps. 48:14):

- God is great and deserving of great praise.
- He dwells with His people and is a refuge for them.
- He is the great King who is feared throughout the earth.
- He is a God of lovingkindness.
- His praise resounds to the ends of the earth.
- He is righteous and the source of righteousness.
- He is the God of justice.
- He is God forever and ever.
- He is the guide of His people.

Psalm 48 anticipates John's vision of a new heaven and new earth, which includes a new Jerusalem (Rev. 21–22). There God will dwell forever with people from every nation who have come to Him for salvation. What a wonderful picture and a magnificent hope: God personally living among His people, forever and ever!

GOD'S GUIDANCE
Reflecting on God's Guidance

Modern-day believers are able to examine the Scriptures to understand a host of everyday concerns—work, ethics, the church, marriage and family, decision making, and many others. But what do we do when we face a situation that the Bible doesn't address directly? How can we understand God's ways?

Joseph's remarks upon revealing himself to his brothers (Gen. 45:5–8) show the value of looking backward from time to time at how God has worked in our lives. Joseph had to wrestle with some tough life questions: Why was his life disrupted by his jealous brothers? Why was he wrenched from his family and sent to Egypt? Why should he suddenly find himself elevated to a position of unparalleled power and prominence over one of the world's great empires? Where was God in all of these experiences? And now, as he faced his brothers, why should he show them any mercy? Why should he not avenge himself for the wrongs they had caused him to suffer?

Joseph had no biblical passages to turn to for help with these matters. Nor did he have any wise, godly counselors that we know of. He was on his own to sort it all out. So he took what he knew of God and used it to interpret his experience of people and the world. His conclusion? "You meant evil against me; but God meant it for good" (Gen. 50:20).

To some that might sound like a pat answer or a simplistic attempt to "make lemons into lemonade." But it was not. Joseph never denied reality. He knew better than anyone that his enslavement and imprisonment had been brought about by wicked schemes. "You sold me here," he reminded his brothers (Gen. 45:5).

But Joseph also had to cope with his sufferings somehow, and he did so by discerning God's purposes in them: "God sent me before you to preserve life . . . to preserve a posterity for you in the earth, and to save your lives" (Gen. 45:5, 7). In effect, Joseph incorporated his pain into God's divine plan.

Such after-the-fact recognition of God's will does not absolve wrongdoers of the sins they have committed, nor does it remove pain from one's memory. But it does do justice to the events that have occurred and validates one's life experience. Reflecting on God's work in your life can be an especially valuable exercise if you live and work in a "secular" environment. You need to think carefully and critically about what God may be up to in your life, just as Joseph did in Egypt.

Marking Your Trail

Many of us are so busy that we never take time to consider where we are going—or why. Yet we humans are the only creatures that God created with the capacity for self-reflection. We can think about ourselves, evaluate our lives, and make changes in light of what we see.

Proverbs encourages us to stay on the path of wisdom, to be careful not to stray "to the right or the left" (Prov. 4:25–27). Is that the case for you? Use the questions below to "mark your trail" along the journey of faith. Take a look at your attitudes and behaviors using these "path" questions:

- Influence on others. Whose life have you genuinely touched and changed for the better in recent years?
- Direction and purpose. If you continue to work for the next ten years as you are now working, what will you have gained? Describe what your life will look like in ten years.
- Honoring God. Can you cite three things that you have done in the last year that you believe have clearly brought glory to God? Name ways in which you have honored Him at work, in your home, and in your community.
- Avoiding evil. What one thing have you said "no" to in the past year in order to "remove your foot from evil" (Prov. 4:27)? What did it cost you? What did you gain?
- Your testimony. What one characteristic would you say clearly distinguishes you from non-Christians in your workplace or neighborhood?
- Looking back. Think about where your life was ten years ago. Name three specific ways in which you have grown or changed for the better in that time. Or have you taken a step or two backward? If so, what practical changes do you need to make to turn your life around?

Pondering God's Plan

"I wonder why God allowed that to happen." Countless people have uttered statements like that, either to themselves or out loud. In a world of many mysteries and uncertainties, they wonder why?

Is it worthwhile to ponder the reasons behind events or to question the ways of God? Some people think not. "God has His own reasons," they say. "Ours is not to know why. We ought not to question the purposes of God. Besides, there are some things we'll never know until we get to heaven, so why bother our heads with them now?"

But judging by Paul's words in Philemon 15–16, thinking about what God may be up to in the events that come our way, what we might call "theological reflection," is both useful and encouraged. Paul had no scriptural text to turn to that would fully explain why Onesimus, of all people, had come to faith and was prepared to return to Philemon. So he offered Philemon his own reading of events.

Like Paul, we can and should reflect on the circumstances of our lives. We should think carefully about what God may be trying to show us or teach us. We should pay attention to the unusual or the unexpected, and even to the undesirable events that come our way. Such habits help us bring God and His Word into our understanding of life.

GOD'S KINDNESS

A Case Study in God's Kindness

Psalm 117 is the shortest of all psalms and the shortest of all chapters in the Bible. Its message is simple and straightforward: Israel is a case study for all the nations, about one nation that was shown God's "merciful kindness" (Ps. 117:1).

Some believe that this psalm was not composed until after the Assyrian and Babylonian captivities, when the Jews became scattered among the nations. Under those circumstances, they may have come to appreciate a truth that was rooted deep in their heritage—that God's salvation is not for Israel alone, but for all the nations of the world.

This universal offer of salvation goes back to Abraham, through whom God promised to bless "all the families of the earth" (Gen. 12:3).

Centuries later, the prophets would echo the same theme. For example:

- Isaiah foresaw the nations streaming to Jerusalem to worship the Lord (Is. 2:2–4; 66:18–24).
- Jeremiah predicted that someday the Gentiles would renounce their godless past and turn to the Lord (Jer. 16:19–21).
- Amos spoke of the Gentiles who are called by God's name (Amos 9:11–12).
- Micah, like Isaiah, envisioned the day when many peoples and nations would come to serve the Lord at Jerusalem (Mic. 4:1–5).
- Zephaniah said that God would form an "assembly of kingdoms," which He would purge until they spoke a "pure language" and followed the Lord "with one accord" (Zeph. 3:8–9).
- Haggai prophesied that all nations would eventually come to the Lord, "the Desire of All Nations" (Hag. 2:7).
- Zechariah foresaw the time when many nations and peoples would eagerly come to the Lord as His people (Zech. 2:10–11; 8:20–23).
- Malachi asserted the God was determined to make His name great among the nations (Mal. 1:11).

What assurance do we have that these promises will be fulfilled? In answer, Psalm 117 points to Israel. Israel is a case in point that when God commits Himself to people, He follows through. That is the nature of His "merciful kindness" (Hebrew *chesed*; Ps. 117:1). What He says "endures forever."

So when God pledges Himself to the Gentiles, His promises are as binding as they were in the case of Israel. As Paul pointed out in his letter to the Romans, citing Psalm 117, the salvation of the Gentiles is not God's "Plan B" (Rom. 15:7–13). All along He has been working to fulfill His word to Abraham that all the families of the earth will be blessed. Psalm 117 celebrates that promise. Therefore, "praise the LORD, all you Gentiles!"

GOD'S LOVE

Christ Became Poor

Almost anyone can "love" people in the abstract. But when it comes time to express that love—by lending a helping hand or writing a check—one can quickly determine the sincerity of a person's love for others. That was Paul's point in 2 Corinthians 8:8–9. To illustrate it, he used the ultimate model of tangible love—Jesus Christ.

Christ became poor in order to make us rich. Consider what He gave up when He left heaven and took on a human body:

1. He left His Father, whose immediate presence He would not enjoy again for more than thirty years. How long would you be willing to be away from your closest companion and friend in order to help a group of people—especially if you knew that most of them would reject and despise you, and might even kill you?

2. We can imagine that He left a joyful crowd that included Abraham, Isaac, Jacob, the angelic hosts, and all the redeemed saints who were worshiping Him, glorifying Him, and having fellowship with Him prior to His incarnation. He left those who loved Him to come and be misunderstood, rejected, scorned, hated, and scourged by most of those He came to help. Would you leave a position of honor and adoration to go help people who would by and large reject you?

3. He left a heavenly home that far exceeded in splendor, majesty, and comfort the physical environment of His earthly life. Would you give up the best accommodations this earth has to offer in order to help needy people in a bad neighborhood?

4. He left His pre-incarnate existence in the form of God, without limitations, to take on a physical body subject to fatigue, aches, and pains. Would you accept hunger, thirst, fatigue, pain, and limited physical abilities to help people who didn't even care whether you came or not?

The statement that Christ became poor puts into perspective Jesus' command to the rich young ruler to sell what he had and give the proceeds to the poor (Mark 10:21), and His instruction to the disciples to sell what they had and give alms, providing themselves treasure in heaven (Luke 12:33). What Jesus asked them to do, He had already done—to such a degree, in fact, that their obedience could never equal His selflessness.

He Did It for You!

To what extent have you ever sacrificed for someone else? Sacrifice can mean *giving up* something you really want in order for someone else to have it. But an even greater sacrifice involves *taking on* something that you really do not want so that someone else will not have to bear it.

That is what Jesus did when He was "wounded for our transgressions" and "bruised for our iniquities" (Is. 53:5). He took on Himself the "chastisement," or punishment, that we deserved for our sins so that we would not have to bear it. He did not want to suffer, but He submitted to suffering because of His great love.

Hundreds of years before Jesus came, Isaiah described in remarkable detail how the Messiah would suffer on behalf of others.

- He would be exalted (Is. 52:13; Phil. 2:9).
- He would be disfigured by suffering (Is. 52:14; 53:2; Mark 15:17, 19).
- He would make a blood atonement (Is. 52:15; 1 Pet. 1:2).
- He would be widely rejected (Is. 53:1, 3; John 12:37–38).

- He would bear our sins and sorrows (Is. 53:4–5; Rom. 4:25; 1 Pet. 2:24–25).
- He would be our substitute (Is. 56:6, 8; 2 Cor. 5:21).
- He would voluntarily accept our guilt and punishment (Is. 53:7–8; John 10:11; 19:30).
- He would die on behalf of transgressors (Is. 53:12; Mark 15:27–28; Luke 22:37).
- He would be buried in a rich man's tomb (Is. 53:9; John 19:38–42).
- He would save those who believed in Him (Is. 53:10–11; John 3:16; Acts 16:31).

In what ways can you follow Jesus' example of servanthood—even if it involves suffering (1 Pet. 2:18–25)?

Justice to the Gentiles

Imagine if you were suffering unjustly at the hands of ruthless, godless people. They have stolen your property, slaughtered your relatives, and threatened your own life. You have cried out to God for help, and now the Lord's reply comes: He promises to bring justice into the situation. However, to your shock, His justice will be not only for you, *but for your oppressors as well!*

This was the surprising message that Isaiah delivered to the people of Judah in his prophecy concerning the Servant of the Lord (Is. 42:1–9). The prophet said that God's Elect One was coming "to bring justice to the Gentiles" (Is. 42:1). This must have been a rude awakening for the Israelites! Yet throughout Isaiah's prophecies, the Lord said again and again that they were not the only people whom He cared about, and who fit into His plans. He was seeking the salvation of the Gentiles, too—even though many of the Gentile nations abused and oppressed His people.

The New Testament reveals that the Servant of the Lord predicted by Isaiah is Jesus Christ (Matt. 12:17–21). He came to establish justice for the whole world. He would open blind eyes and free prisoners (Is. 42:7; 61:1–3; compare Luke 4:16–30). In carrying out this mission, He encountered hostility from His own people as well as Gentiles.

From the beginning of creation, God has had the whole world in view as the object of His love, mercy, and salvation. What a wonderful hope this is for all people of all nations! Is this a truth that affects the way you deal with people who do not know God, especially if they are from cultures and backgrounds different from your own?

Describing God's Love

John has been called the apostle of love, and 1 John certainly offers plenty of evidence to show why. For example, he writes that one way to know that we are born of God is that we love Him and keep His commandments (1 John 5:2).

But what does John mean by love? People say they "love" all kinds of things today. One minute they "love" peanut butter and in the next they "love" their spouse. Likewise, they "love" pets, food, sports, vacations, cars, children—whatever!

Thankfully, Scripture defines love for us by describing God's love, using both nouns and verbs. As we examine various passages, we find that God's love is:

- Lasting (Ps. 136; Rom. 8:28–39; 1 Cor. 13:8).
- Sacrificial (John 15:12–13; Rom. 5:8; 2 Cor. 5:14–15; Gal. 2:20; 1 John 3:16–17).
- Reconciling and healing (Matt. 5:38–48; Luke 6:27–31; 2 Cor. 5:17–19).
- Mutual between Father, Son, and Holy Spirit (Matt. 11:27–30; John 14:31).
- Effective; it involves not just emotions or words, but deeds that benefit people (1 John 3:18–19; 4:21; 5:1–3).
- Fearless (Rom. 1:16; 1 John 4:18).
- Discerning (1 Tim. 1:3–7; 1 John 2:15–17; 4:1–7).
- Accepting, not condemning (Luke 15:11–32; 18:10–17; John 3:16–17; Rom. 8:1).
- Generous (Luke 10:25–37; Rom. 5:8, 15–17; 6:23; 1 Cor. 2:9; 1 Pet. 3:8–9).

Perhaps the best summary of true, godly love is 1 Corinthians 13, "the love chapter," in which Paul describes the love of God as it needs to be among the believers at Corinth. Likewise, the ultimate expression of God's love is Christ, who offered Himself up for the sins of the world (John 3:16).

In what ways does your love need to develop? Have you grasped the dimensions of God's love for you? How can you cultivate Christlike love and make it more tangible in your life, work, and relationships?

G

Prodigal Wife, Prodigal People

Perhaps you are familiar with Jesus' story of the Prodigal Son (Luke 15:11–32). Hosea describes the real-life stories of Gomer, his prodigal wife, and of Israel, the Lord's prodigal people.

Hosea's marriage was extraordinary in that he was called to marry "a wife of harlotry" (Hos. 1:2). Gomer's exact background is unknown, but it may be that she had been unfaithful to a previous husband, or she may have been a known prostitute. It may also be that she was one of the temple prostitutes believed to have been part of the idolatrous rites then being practiced in Israel.

Whatever Gomer's background, she was a powerful symbol of Israel's spiritual adultery against the Lord (Hos. 2:2). The nation had departed almost entirely from worship as prescribed in the Law. Instead, the people had adopted the religions of the cultures around them, particularly the Canaanites, Phoenicians, and Moabites. Canaanite religion was essentially a fertility cult in which ritual sexual intercourse with prostitutes is believed to have played a major role.

God utterly rejected these Canaanite practices, calling them what they were—"harlotries." The Lord, not the Canaanite god Baal, was Ruler over the land and Israel's faithful Lover and forgotten Provider of bounty (Hos. 2:8).

Like Israel, Gomer left her loving husband and returned to her life of harlotry. Apparently she ended up in the slave market, where Hosea redeemed her for fifteen shekels and some barley (Hos. 3:2). This was a fairly minor cost in terms of value, merely the common price of a slave (compare Ex. 21:32). But it was a great sacrifice of love on Hosea's part. The prophet was mirroring the love of God for His prodigal people, and symbolizing the reconciliation that would someday take place (Hos. 3:4–5).

Spiritual adultery is still a danger for God's people today. The New Testament likens the relationship between believers and Christ to marriage (Eph. 5:25–33). When Christians turn away from Christ and adopt beliefs, values, practices, and rituals that are unworthy of Him, they commit the same sort of "harlot-ries" as ancient Israel committed against the Lord (2 Cor. 11:2–4).

The Two Arms of God

The two arms of God—a strong right arm (Is. 40:10) and a tender left one (Is. 40:11)—together embrace His people with the "tough love" of power and comfort.

God's strong right arm rules with sovereign might. It can act like a powerful army to protect, defend, or (as in the case of Judah in Babylon) deliver hostages from captivity. In a similar way, it can protect, defend, or deliver people from the power and bondage of sin.

On the other hand, God exhibits tender sensitivity. He is the Good Shepherd who faithfully feeds His flock and makes sure that the little lambs are nursed. He watches over the vulnerable, the weak, and the innocent.

He is the God of power and comfort. How greatly we need Him today, as anyone who works with children can appreciate. Mothers, fathers, school bus drivers, day care workers, teachers, street crossing guards, child welfare workers—anyone whose job it is to nurture, protect, and advocate for children can look to the Lord described in Isaiah 40 for the personal and spiritual resources to carry out the task.

For more on this topic, see ADULTERY, "David in Sin," page 7; FORGIVENESS, "Two Sides of the Coin," page 161; SECOND CHANCE, "Forgiveness Unlimited," page 358.

GOD'S MERCY

God's Unfailing Mercy

What has been the deepest, darkest experience in your life, the time when you felt the worst emotions, perhaps to the point of utter despair? For Jeremiah and his contemporaries in Judah, it was the destruction of Jerusalem.

The death of the city was absolutely crushing. The Israelites' magnificent temple was reduced to ashes, the city walls were pulled down, the main part of the populace had been either killed or deported, and only starving elders, women, and children remained (Lam. 2:10–12).

Only one thing kept hope alive—knowledge of the mercies of the Lord (Lam. 3:22–24). God's mercy (Hebrew, *chesed;* see Deut.

7:9) involved His undying love and loyalty toward His people. Having committed Himself to Israel through His covenant with them, the Lord could be expected to follow through on that commitment. He might discipline His wayward people, allow them to be ravaged by their enemies, and even let their temple and the Law be destroyed (Lam. 2:9), but He would never ultimately forsake His people.

Neither will God forsake His children today. His mercy and grace have been extended to those who are in Christ Jesus (Rom. 8:1), and nothing can separate us from His love (Rom. 8:31–39). As a result, we can have hope (Rom. 5:1–5; 1 Pet. 1:3–5), even in the midst of the gloomiest circumstances (2 Cor. 1:8–11).

Jeremiah's eloquent expression of God's faithfulness and compassion is the basis for the contemporary hymn "Great Is Thy Faithfulness." If you know that hymn or have access to a hymnbook containing it, why not sing it now in praise of God's never-failing mercies?

Showing Mercy

Scripture shows the Lord to be a God of mercy (Deut. 7:9). But what exactly does it mean by "mercy"?

The Hebrew term for "mercy" (*chesed*) described not simply the emotion of pity, much less the ignoring, excusing, or indulging of wrongdoing. It implied that one could be counted on to faithfully carry out the promises made in a covenant or agreement. Thus God "[kept] covenant and mercy" with His people the Jews in terms of showing loyalty to them—even when they didn't deserve it.

In the same way, God calls those who fear Him to show mercy (*chesed*) in their dealings with others. For example:

- Governments show mercy when they diligently enforce laws that prevent oppression of the vulnerable.
- Husbands and wives show mercy to each other when they stick to their vows of marital faithfulness, love, and service despite all the pressures on the marriage from without and within.
- Employers show mercy when they keep employees on the payroll in accord with earlier agreements, written or implied, despite financial difficulties in the company.
- Employees show mercy when they give their employers their best efforts day in and day out, despite fatigue and competing demands on their attention.
- Businesses show mercy when they give their customers the quality of merchandise and service for which they have paid, even if it means reduced profit (Ps. 15:4).

To what extent does "mercy" define and describe your dealings with others? Can you be relied on to follow through on your word the way God does?

GOD'S POWER
Psalms of Power

Psalm 29 describes the awesome power of the Lord through the image of a crashing thunderstorm that sweeps the length of Canaan. The Book of Psalms talks about many demonstrations of power:

- Psalm 18: God uses His power to rescue and defend people of integrity from those who are committed to evil.
- Psalm 29: God is all-powerful and rules over nature.
- Psalm 52: The more one uses power corruptly, the more corrupt one becomes.
- Psalm 60: Sometimes God takes strong measures to correct and discipline His people.
- Psalm 66: The awesome works of God are available for all to see.
- Psalm 91: Because God is compassionate, His power is a refuge and comfort to those who feel weak and powerless.
- Psalm 93: The mighty seas are a great metaphor for the majestic, eternal power of God.
- Psalm 144: This psalm is the prayer of a soldier facing battle, who needs the Lord's powerful help for victory.

The Proper Measure

"What is man?" David asked in Psalm 8:4–6. He found his answer not by looking at man in himself, but *man in relation to God.* Five hundred years later, the Greek philosopher Protagoras took a completely different approach by offering, "Man is the measure of all things." Today, our culture tends to side with Protagoras.

But the Bible shows that God is the true measure of all things. Adopting that perspective is the beginning of humility, the doorway to all the other virtues.

Scripture constantly emphasizes the relative insignificance and transitoriness of humanity and the rest of creation in comparison to the greatness of eternal God. David asked, What is man in comparison to his Creator (Ps. 8:3–4)? What is man that he should merit God's attention and affection (Ps. 144:3–4)?

This lends perspective to so many of the idealistic, even utopian, plans to solve the problems of our world. There's nothing wrong with humans working cooperatively to solve problems. But it's a grave mistake to dismiss faith in God and rely instead on the omnipotence of a corporation, a state, or an international collective. To do so smacks of the same blind pride that brought judgment at the Tower of Babel (Gen. 11:1–9). It is cause for God to laugh (Ps. 2:1–4). If we as individuals are as fleeting as grass (Is. 40:6–7), then groups of us, no matter how large, are just as fleeting. We still need the wisdom and strength that only God can supply.

GOD'S PRESENCE

Comforted by God's Presence

The poetry of Psalm 139 celebrates the fact that God is present wherever David goes, or even imagines going (Ps. 139:7). First he looks up at the sky, then down toward the ground (139:8). Then he looks east toward "the wings of the dawn," and west toward the Mediterranean Sea (139:9). Wherever David thinks of going, he has the certainty that God will be with him in that place.

Are you comforted, as David was, by the presence of God? As you look around you, do you consciously think about the Lord being there, right where you are? Why not pause right now to thank Him for His ever-watchful care and concern?

God Among Us

The first fourteen verses of John 1 were probably a hymn for the early church. They remind us that Jesus is God's Word (John 1:1), "word" being a Greek term that means a thought expressed. Jesus is the human expression of God. He is light and flesh, to use

John's metaphors (John 1:4–5, 14). To see Jesus is to see God, and to know Jesus is to experience God's grace and truth.

It is no accident, then, that believers are called to practice community and witness publicly. The gospel is both what we say and how we live. Just as Christ became flesh and "dwelt among us," so we are to "flesh out" the good news about Christ in our everyday world.

Our Refuge, Strength, and Help

Psalm 46 is made up of three parts that expand on the theme established in the opening lines—that God is our refuge, strength, and helper:

- God's protection provides reassurance in a tumultuous world (Ps. 46:1–3).
- God's presence provides an immovable defense in a hostile world (Ps. 46:4–6).
- God's peace deserves worship and praise throughout the world (Ps. 46:8–10).

A Minority View

Perhaps you sometimes feel that you have no one to turn to with your stresses and struggles. It is not just a matter of having someone to understand, but of finding someone you can *trust.*

Micah must have felt quite lonely as he faced the proud, powerful people of Jerusalem. Like Elijah (1 Kin. 19:10), he probably felt as if he were the last faithful believer on the planet (Mic. 7:2). Wherever he turned, he seemed to find people who were bloodthirsty, corrupted, treacherous, and deceitful. Even the members of one's own family were not to be trusted (Mic. 7:2–6).

Faced with such a world, Micah found reassurance in the fact that God remains in control and takes care of His faithful children, no matter what others may be up to (Mic. 7:7). This truth can be a great hope for believers today, especially when we find ourselves in the minority, or even all alone among people who do not know or honor the Lord.

Knowing God Is with Us

Wherever God's people go, God goes with them. That was the comforting message that Ezekiel delivered to the Babylonian exiles (Ezek. 11:16). They were far from home and had no temple such as the one at Jerusalem, where God's presence was said to dwell. That same sense of isolation was going to be felt by the people of Judah when God scattered them throughout the ancient world. But the Lord assured His refugees that He would be their "little sanctuary" wherever they went. Furthermore, He promised to eventually bring them back to the land of Israel (Ezek. 11:17).

The promise of God's presence among His people can be a great comfort to believers today who find themselves alone among those who do not know or honor God. The Lord is with us wherever we go. We can call on Him no matter what the circumstances around us.

For more on this topic, see HEAVEN, "The Lord Is There—Forever!" page 196.

GOD'S PROTECTION

Under His Wing

One of David's favorite symbolic expressions was the word-picture of sitting in the shadow of God's wings (Ps. 63:7; compare Pss. 17:8; 36:7; 57:1; 61:4; and 91:4). The wings of a bird were a symbol of protection, defense, and refuge. For example, faced with a forest or range fire, a mother grouse or prairie chicken would gather her chicks together under her wings, settle down, and let the flames sweep over her. If necessary, she would die in order to save them. After the fire, the chicks would crawl out from under their mother's burnt body. They enjoyed life and safety because of her sacrificial devotion.

In a similar way, David was shielded from numerous attempts on his life, especially by King Saul and later by his own son Absalom. David knew by experience what it meant to have nothing standing between him and death but the gracious protection of God.

The Lord still offers the same refuge and protection today. For one thing, having voluntarily died on the cross for our sins, He can deliver us from the penalty of sin (Rom. 5:6–10). Furthermore, He watches over His children with diligent care (Heb. 13:5–6; 1 Pet. 5:7). Thus we can rely on a God who loves us and acts on our behalf when we cannot help ourselves.

The Angry Protector

It may be difficult to imagine God as being like a bird, but Isaiah did. He pictured God as an angry bird that dives, pecks, and claws in order to protect its young (Is. 31:5). In the same way, God pledged to protect Jerusalem from Assyria.

This image of God was frequently used in the Psalms. For example, David described himself as sitting in the shadow, or protection, of God's wings. Likewise, another psalmist offered the assurance that the Lord would "cover you with His feathers, and under His wings you shall take refuge" (Ps. 91:4).

In reading these texts, it is important to remember that God's loyalty and protection extend not only to individuals, but to entire cities and nations as well. When we look outside and observe birds darting about to protect their nestlings from cats, squirrels, and other predators, we are seeing a picture of the way God intervenes to defend and shelter people.

Taking It Personal

God so identifies with His people that when their opponents curse and taunt them, He takes it as an affront to His own character. That was Isaiah's message of hope to Hezekiah. The Assyrian Rabshakeh's defiant letter insulted Judah, but the Lord saw it as an offense against Himself (Is. 37:23).

A similar situation occurred in the early church when the Jewish elders and chief priests arrested and threatened Peter and John. Later, the believers recognized that persecution, while aimed at them, was actually an outburst against the Lord Jesus Christ whom they were following. God affirmed that perspective with a manifestation of His presence (Acts 4:23–31).

Like the ancient Israelites and the early Christians, we who are God's people today may face opposition and persecution. When we do, it is important to remember that ultimately the attack may not be directed at us, but at the God who stands behind us (1 Pet. 4:12–16). Knowing that can help us keep things in perspective and take hope in God's strength and help.

GOD'S SOVEREIGNTY

A Pagan Instrument

As human beings, we are prone to speculate about which governments and government officials God will or will not use, and for which purposes. But we need to remember that all governments and rulers serve at God's pleasure, and that the Lord can use virtually any means to accomplish His purposes. A good illustration of this principle was God's selection of the Persian king Cyrus to serve as His "shepherd" (Is. 44:28) and "anointed" (Is. 45:1).

In Isaiah's time, a king named Cyrus I ruled Persia, and some have speculated that he was known to Isaiah. But it was his grandson Cyrus II, also known as Cyrus the Great, who fulfilled Isaiah's prophecy.

Cyrus II came to power in 559 B.C. Under his rule, Persia became an empire that displaced Babylonia. His sympathetic policies toward the many peoples that the Babylonians had conquered and taken into exile made it possible for the Jews to return to Jerusalem and begin rebuilding the temple (2 Chr. 36:22–23). In this way, Cyrus II became a "shepherd" to God's people, leading them safely back home. He also became their anointed deliverer by overcoming their former captors (Is. 45:1; compare 2 Chr. 36:20).

God's use of Cyrus can serve as a powerful encouragement for believers today as we consider the governments of the world. Many seem utterly opposed to God, and others promote policies that appear to go against biblical values. But if God could work through pagan King Cyrus, even though he did not know the Lord (Is. 45:4), He can certainly work through leaders today, no matter how far from Him they may appear to be. That is one reason Scripture encourages Christians to pray for those in authority (1 Tim. 2:1–2).

God's Great Declaration

The latter chapters of Isaiah contain a number of declarations by God of who He is and what He has done. As He addresses the nations of the world with warnings of judgment and promises of redemption, the Lord states plainly that He alone is able to carry out these purposes. No other so-called god, no superpower on earth, no human being can match His sovereignty, authority, or power. As His declaration to the kingdoms of Egypt and Cush shows (Is. 45:21–22):

- God alone can say what will happen in the future.
- God alone is God.
- God is just.
- God is the Savior.
- There are no other gods beside the Lord.
- God is ready to save all people who live on the earth if they will look to Him.
- God is God.

Elsewhere in the same chapter, the Lord asserts that:

- He rules over great and powerful kings, such as Cyrus (Is. 45:1–7).
- He is the source of all righteousness (Is. 45:8, 19, 24).
- He is the Holy One of Israel (Is. 45:11).
- He is the Savior of Israel (Is. 45:15).
- He is against all false gods and idols in people's lives (Is. 45:16, 20).
- He is the Creator of the universe (Is. 45:18).
- He is the Lord to whom every knee will ultimately bow (Is. 45:23).

What is your response to this awesome God?

God Rules, Even in "Tragedy"

It is common to hear people rejoice (or sometimes even boast) that their material prosperity is a blessing from God. Yet have you ever heard anyone say, "My business failure was a blessing from God"? Why is it that only "good" things are seen as "blessings," while "bad" things are viewed as "tragedies"?

Human beings see things from a very limited perspective. What looks like a tragedy may be the best thing that ever happened, particularly when God's hand is superintending the outcome. For example, a poor youth whose family sold him into slavery may emerge later as a wiser person, fit to be king (Eccl. 4:13–14). That's essentially what happened to Joseph (Gen. 37–41).

God is sovereign over the things that happen to us. That does not mean that everything that happens to us is His responsibility. For example, He does not cause evil. Yet He may permit evil, as He did in Job's life (Job 1:6–19), for reasons that go beyond our understanding. God's sovereignty means that He is God and has the right to work out His own purposes in our lives.

We tend to be quick to judge whether what happens to us is fair or unfair. How might our perspective change if we took the view that Joseph had when he confronted his brothers: "Am I in the place of God? But as for you, you meant evil against me; but God meant it for good"? (Gen. 50:19–20; compare Rom. 8:28).

Agents Unaware

Who is the most treacherous, dangerous world leader you can think of? Who would you say is the greatest threat to world peace and stability today? Whoever it is, you probably cannot regard that person with greater suspicion and disdain than the people of Judah had for Nebuchadnezzar of Babylon.

Yet God described this pagan king as His own "servant" (Jer. 27:6; compare Jer. 25:9). That had to be unimaginable for the people of Jeremiah's day. To them, Nebuchadnezzar was a great evil. He ruled a ruthless superpower that was poised to overrun their lands and destroy their cities. How could he possibly be God's servant?

Interestingly, the description of Nebuchadnezzar sounds a lot like the description of Cyrus, the Persian king, given through Isaiah: "My shepherd" and "His anointed" (Is. 44:28–45:1).

Both of these rulers had power over vast territories in the ancient Middle East. Their decisions determined much of what happened in history at that time. From the human perspective, they were the ones in charge.

But the prophecies of Isaiah and Jeremiah show that ultimately they were not in control of the final outcomes. Whether they knew it or not, they were only finite human beings placed in positions of authority by the hand of God. As such, they were God's servants, God's agents. Through their decisions, they ended up serving God's purposes—even if they didn't realize they were doing so!

Yet it's a fact that even as these two men were unwittingly fulfilling God's will, He was seeking them. He wanted them to know and worship Him as their Lord. For example, God used Daniel to steer Nebuchadnezzar toward Him. It is even possible that believers will meet Nebuchadnezzar in heaven. Likewise, Cyrus may have been confronted by the Lord (Ezra 1:1), insomuch as he praised, worshiped, and obeyed God by issuing a decree that allowed the Jews to return to Judah and rebuild the temple (Ezra 1:2–4).

God is the King of all the kings—then and now. If that is so, then what does it say about the leaders of the world today? Perhaps the ones we dislike the most are in fact "servants" of the living God! And like Nebuchadnezzar and Cyrus, God seeks not merely to use them, but for them to know Him. Are you praying and working toward that end (1 Tim. 2:1–2)?

No God But God

Most Western-style democracies guarantee freedom of religion. For example, the Bill of Rights of the United States Constitution ensures that American citizens are free to practice whatever religion they choose (as long as they are not harming anyone). Perhaps because of this liberty, many people today assume that all religious beliefs or systems are basically the same. But that is not the case.

The God of the Bible insists that He alone is God. There is no other God besides Him (Is. 46:9). To modern ears, this may sound intolerant, or even arrogant. It certainly conflicts with certain fashionable beliefs today, which claim that more or less everyone and everything is God. But the Lord leaves no room for disagreement or compromise on the point: there is no God but God. One can either agree with Him or call Him a liar, but there is no middle ground.

Suppose we deny that God alone is God. That does not affect God in the least. He simply says that we are wrong, and reminds us that we are mere mortals, who will die. But God also warns us that our perspective is distorted, because we are stubborn-hearted sinners (Is. 46:8, 12). Who are we to decide who and what God is?

God refuses to be bound by our ideas of Him. That's why He declares the truth to us: "I am God, and there is no other."

The Limits of Evil

Given all the evil and suffering in the world, some people argue that God must not exist, or that if He does exist, He must not be in control. But the Book of Job affirms that not only does God exist, He sets limits on evil. For example, He told Satan that although he was allowed to touch Job's body, he could not

G

take his life (Job 2:6). Earlier, God had limited Satan's destructive power to Job's possessions (Job. 1:12).

God's sovereignty is a comforting thought as we contend with an increasingly chaotic world. God may allow evil in His world, but He does not allow it to take total control. He will permit it to spread only so far before He cuts it back. Ultimately He will do away with all sin and evil and those who promote it, handing over the rule of His perfect creation to His Son, Jesus Christ (1 Cor. 15:24–28; Phil. 2:9–11).

The Commander

Joshua was fearless when it came to facing enemies on the battlefield. So when he came upon a stranger outside the city of Jericho, he challenged him: was he friend or foe? Was he going to fight for the Israelites or against them? Neither, the Man replied. He had not come to fight, but to take over; He was the Commander of the army of the Lord (Josh. 5:13–14).

So it is today. God does not intend to be merely a foot soldier in our personal campaign, whatever it may be. He does not make His resources available to us so that we can accomplish our own agenda. He comes as the Lord, the Sovereign One, the supreme Commander. We serve Him. We fight in His army. We worship at His feet, for in His presence we stand on holy ground (Josh. 5:15).

Are you prepared to let Jesus give the orders in your life? Will you allow Him to determine the ultimate objectives? To give Him allegiance does not mean giving up all control or personal responsibility, but it does demand a conscious choice to deal with Him in terms of who He is—the Lord God, your Creator, Savior, and Commander.

For more on this topic, see **CIRCUM-STANCES,** *"Who Knows?" page 62.*

GOD'S WRATH

A God Who Hates?

We know from Scripture that God is a God of love who shows mercy to sinners (for example, Ps. 103:3; Matt. 9:12–13). Yet the Psalms declare that He "hates" people who commit iniquity and wickedness (Ps. 5:5; 11:5). How can we reconcile these seemingly contradictory pictures of God?

When the Bible speaks of "hatred," it does not mean the normal human reaction of retaliation or "getting even" for wrongs suffered. Nor does it mean a mad, irrational response to wrong or injustice. Rather, biblical "hatred" describes a studied expression of anger rooted in a commitment to justice. God *does* get angry at sin that injures and destroys His creation, especially human beings made in His image. He will not tolerate that which violates His "very good" work (Gen. 1:31).

But God's righteous indignation is not a fit of anger. It is rather a carefully considered application of a just disapproval and penalty against wrongdoing. It is godly wrath against evil (Ps. 2:5, 12).

Have you given God cause to "hate" you? If so, you need His forgiveness (1 John 1:8–10). And what about your own response to wrongs suffered? With the Lord's help, can you find ways to react that are more like God's way than the human tendency toward retaliation?

God's Anger Produces Peace

Critics of Christianity sometimes point to God's wrath as a contradiction in His supposedly loving character. "How can you say that God is a God of love when the Old Testament says that He is going to 'strike the earth with the rod of His mouth'?" (Is. 11:4) they scornfully ask.

One response is to observe that God's wrath is not exactly like the anger that human beings often display. People often vent their rage in vindictive, selfish ways that may dissipate emotion but do little to promote true justice. By contrast, God's wrath is based in His just and righteous character (Is. 11:5). When He judges people and nations, it is not because He feels hurt, but because wrongs need to be righted. His wrath comes against evil and wickedness.

Furthermore, God's anger results in a righteous outcome—peace (Is. 11:6–9). When human beings vindicate themselves, their wrath often leads to more violence, suffering, and bitterness. But God's judgments will ultimately produce peace on earth because they serve true justice and do away with those who are committed to injustice and unrighteousness.

Patient, but with Limits

Scripture is clear that God is patient, slow to anger and not willing that anyone should perish under His judgment (Ps. 103:8; Nah. 1:3; 2 Pet. 3:9). Yet even the patience of God has its limits. He will not allow sin to go unchecked forever. Sooner or later, He will deal with evil and those who commit it, and when He does, His wrath is likely to come rather swiftly (Gen. 19:24; 2 Pet. 3:10).

The wrath of God fell on Nineveh in about 612 B.C. when a coalition of Babylonians, Scythians, and Medes penetrated the city's seemingly impregnable defenses after sudden floods eroded the walls (compare Nah. 2:6–8). The invaders quickly turned Nineveh—which was second only to Babylon in size—into a mass of smoking rubble. This event came nearly a century and a half after Jonah was sent to warn the Assyrians of God's impending judgment (Jon. 3).

Initially the Ninevites repented from their wickedness and idolatry with sackcloth and fasting. They cried out to God for mercy, and the Lord stayed His hand. But this spiritual awakening was apparently short-lived.

The Book of Nahum points out the limits of short-term repentance. God leaves rebellious sinners unpunished only for so long (Ex. 34:6–7). His grace is free, but it is not cheap. It does not allow people to continue to do whatever they wish, without guilt and without consequence. The Lord will not allow lying, killing, violence, and idolatry, such as the the Assyrians practiced (Nah. 3:1–4), to go unabated or unpunished. Eventually He will act to put an end to them.

Having once experienced God's forgiveness as a result of Jonah's preaching, the people of Nineveh were that much more responsible. To whom much is given—or forgiven—much will be required (Luke 12:48). In the time of Jonah, Nineveh had been forgiven of enormous sins. Yet the Assyrians did not follow up their short-term repentance with long-term changes, especially in the public sector. Perhaps if they had, Nahum's woeful message might have been directed elsewhere.

God is a God of justice. He cannot just keep on overlooking the sins of people who have no interest in making a genuine break with evil. Nor can he turn His back on the cruel injustices of nations such as Assyria. To do so would be to ignore the prayers of the victims (compare Nah. 1:12, 15).

The Wasteland Ahead

Damage to the earth's environment seems to be on the rise today. Yet current ecological difficulties pale in comparison to what the world will experience someday under God's judgment. Isaiah envisions a virtual wasteland in which nothing remains untouched (Is. 24:1).

Why will the earth be plundered, polluted, burned up, and destroyed? Because it languishes under the curse of a broken covenant (Is. 24:5–6). Humanity has turned away from God, and the world must be destroyed before it can be made anew.

It will be made anew, but not before "the wine fails, the vine languishes, [and] all the merry-hearted sigh" (Is. 24:7). In other words, joy will be turned to gloom. Society will break down, as evidenced by boarded-up houses (Is. 24:10), a depressing sight already common in many cities today. Likewise, the city "gate" will be destroyed (Is. 24:12), meaning that urban life and commerce—indeed, everything the city stands for—will be ruined. The world will be left like so many war-ravaged areas today: without government, police, hospitals, and food; wracked by disease, desolation, and death.

This somber outlook for the world leaves little room for comfort. It assures us that in the end God will reign (Is. 24:23), but the point seems to be that our world is ultimately headed for judgment. If we are sobered and saddened by that message, then perhaps Isaiah's words have had their intended effect.

Why Israel Fell

Four times Isaiah repeats the phrase, "For all this His anger is not turned away, but His hand is stretched out still" (Is. 9:12, 17, 21; 10:4). What was it that caused this unending wrath on the northern kingdom, variously called Jacob, Israel, Ephraim, and Samaria (Is. 9:8–9)?

Isaiah cites five crimes of the Israelites:

- Pride and arrogance (9:9–10).
- Refusal to repent and return to the Lord, despite His discipline (9:13).
- The corruption of the nation's leaders (9:15–16).
- Widespread hypocrisy and wickedness (9:17).
- Unjust laws and policies that robbed the poor (10:1–2).

Because of these sins, which were practiced for generations, the Lord promised to bring enemies who would destroy the nation's cities (Is. 9:11–12), depose its leadership (Is. 9:14), kill the people (Is. 9:16–17; 10:4), and cause widespread famine and civil war. All of these prophecies came to their final fulfillment during the rule of King Hoshea (c. 732–722 B.C.; 2 Kin. 17:1–18).

As we look back on what happened from today's perspective, it is worth asking: which of the sins that led to Israel's downfall persist in our own society? No one knows exactly how God will deal with modern nations that continually disregard His ways. But it seems likely that where widespread sin is tolerated and even institutionalized, God may allow the same kind of profound judgment to fall. The alternative is to turn away from evil and develop a culture of honesty, purity, and justice.

Judgment and Hope

Jeremiah announces specific judgments that the Lord vowed to bring on nine nations (chs. 46–51). In reading these sobering words, it is important to remember two things:

1. *God's wrath was not without cause.* There was definite justification for God's wrath: every single one of the nations listed had turned away from their Creator to worship and serve false gods. Every one of them was guilty, and God's holy nature required judgment on their sin.

2. *God's wrath was not without remedy.* Even as the Lord had called Judah to repent of its sins throughout the years of Jeremiah's ministry, so He had called the nations to turn to Him and be saved. Tragically, they had refused God's gracious offer. Now they faced His wrath.

Yet even the Lord's judgment is redemptive in its purpose. He is willing that no one should perish (2 Pet. 3:9), and repentance is always available as an alternative to wrath,

right to the very end. There was always the possibility that the nations listed in Jeremiah 46–51, or even a handful of individuals in those nations, would fear the judgment of the Lord and turn toward Him.

GOOD AND EVIL

(*see* Evil)

GOVERNMENT

Derived Power

Psalm 2 is sending a similar message to that of Romans 13, which affirms the institution of government by asserting that "there is no authority except from God" (Rom. 13:1). Psalm 2 describes how far-reaching are the implications of this truth by showing that even raging nations and rebellious kings must answer to God, the great King who reigns from Jerusalem through His appointed servant (Ps. 2:1–6).

All governmental power is derived and delegated power. Ultimately it comes from God. Human governments are visible institutions and political agents that are accountable to and limited by Him.

This encourages political leaders to bow their knee in humble worship of the Lord and to serve Him with fear (Ps. 2:10–11). In the spirit of this psalm, they can show respect to God, who has placed them in authority and stands ready to help them govern with goodness and justice.

When a Ruler Sins

In most nations of the world today, government leaders are assumed to be fallible. In many countries they are known to be crooked. And in some cases they are regarded as just plain evil. That contrasts sharply with the ancient world, where many nations considered their rulers to be gods whose pronouncements were sacred.

But not Israel. By commanding a sin offering for rulers (Lev. 4:22–26), God made it plain that their leaders were not gods. Sooner or later, those human authorities were bound to fail morally and spiritually. Therefore, like everyone else, they needed atonement for their sins.

Perhaps there's a lesson here for Bible readers today. Scripture is sober and realistic about the humanity of leaders. Thus we need not be shocked when elected officials and governmental authorities fail. No one but Christ is perfect. The issue, as God pointed out to His people, is not *if* a ruler sins, but when.

The Kingmaker

The books of 1 and 2 Samuel tell about Israel's transition from the period of the judges to the rule of the kings. First Samuel 8 is a pivotal chapter in the account.

The people petitioned Samuel to appoint a king over them (1 Sam. 8:4–5). It was common in the ancient world for religious leaders to choose kings. A similar practice existed well into the Middle Ages, when popes crowned kings. Eventually, however, monarchs realized that the person who crowns the king is more powerful than the king himself. At that point they began to eliminate the concept of the church as kingmaker.

The Israelites would later rue the day when they cried for a monarchy. But in the days of Samuel, they wanted to be like neighboring nations (1 Sam. 8:5, 20). Their insistence amounted to a rejection of the theocracy, the form of government in which God was ultimately their King (1 Sam. 8:7).

Samuel felt angered by this rebellious appeal

G

GOVERNMENT

for a new form of government (1 Sam. 8:6). Yet despite dire misgivings, he gave them their wish, as God directed (1 Sam. 8:9, 19–22). At the same time, he gave them fair warning of all the ways in which their kings would oppress them (1 Sam. 8:9–18).

Nations today have forms of government that differ from that of the ancient Israelites. Yet a basic principle remains for God's people: God is the ultimate authority. Governments come and go, but He remains the One to whom believers owe final allegiance.

The Limits of Government

When Paul wrote to the Roman believers about governing authorities (Rom. 13:1), there was no question as to what authorities he had in mind—the imperial government of Rome, probably led at the time by Nero. According to this passage, even Rome's harsh, corrupt system was established by God and deserved the respect and obedience of Christians.

However, Rome's authority—and all authority—was merely delegated authority. Ultimate authority belongs to God, as Paul pointed out. But that raises a tough question for believers, then as now: If governments are subordinate to God and accountable to Him for what they do, then aren't there limits on the extent to which believers must submit to them? Aren't there times when Christians need to obey God rather than human officials? If so, shouldn't the church pay attention to whether any particular civil government is usurping God's power and undermining His purposes rather than carrying out its intended function?

The early church had to wrestle with these issues. Rome's government was far more tolerant of Christians when Paul likely wrote Romans 13 than in the 90s, when John penned Revelation. Within that span of some thirty years, believers changed their view of Rome from God's "minister for good" (Rom. 13:4) to a usurper of power that deserved to fall. In fact, the Book of Revelation is seen at one level as the story of Rome's fall.

Throughout church history, believers have struggled with whether to obey or resist evil governments. There are no easy answers. But one principle that Paul clearly affirms here is

that government itself is intrinsically good, having been established by God.

*For more on this topic, see **CHURCH AND STATE**, "State-Established Religion?" page 61; **CIVIL DISOBEDIENCE**, "A Case of Civil Disobedience," page 65.*

GOVERNMENT OFFICIALS

Shaping Future Leadership

How important is the character and quality of a nation's leaders? Extremely important, according to Isaiah. At the time when Isaiah 3 was given, the nation probably was prospering under the wise, godly leadership of King Uzziah (c. 792–740 B.C.) or his successor, King Jotham (c. 750–735 B.C.).

However, Isaiah foresaw a time when God would remove the better leaders (Is. 3:1–3), leaving behind mere "babes" who would have no experience in running the institutions of society and no respect for the wisdom of the past. As a result, these "children" would become selfish oppressors (Is. 3:4–5) who would run roughshod over the needs of the poor (Is. 3:14–15). That happened when Jerusalem fell to Babylon (586 B.C.; 2 Kin. 25:11–12, 22–26), though no one can say whether that exhausted the fulfillment of Isaiah's prophecy.

The lesson is that a leadership vacuum leads to public crisis. That being the case, we as God's people today do well to prevent that kind of vacuum from forming by:

- recruiting and appointing the best people available, leaders of high moral character and outstanding leadership skills;
- appropriately paying and rewarding people for their public service;
- supporting leaders and working together with them in their efforts to promote good government and prevent social, economic, and moral deterioration;
- praying for leaders as they exercise their authority; and
- raising up and training our children to be outstanding leaders for the coming generation.

God-Fearing Judges

In many Western countries today, political leaders can have a major influence on the ethical and moral fiber of their countries through the judges they appoint and the judicial policies they support and enforce. In a similar way, King Jehoshaphat brought reform to Judah by appointing judges and other legal officials and declaring specific policies to guide them (2 Chr. 19:5–7).

1. *Judges were to take the job seriously* (2 Chr. 19:6). Again and again, Jehoshaphat urged his legal officials to pay attention to what they were doing.

2. *Judges were accountable to God* (2 Chr. 19:6). As king, Jehoshaphat was responsible for the legal system. But ultimately the judges' authority and power derived from God. Thus they needed to serve in fear of Him (2 Chr. 19:7), "faithfully and with a loyal heart" (2 Chr. 19:9).

3. *Judicial character was to mirror God's character* (2 Chr. 19:7). Just as God was pure in His character, so the judges needed to judge with purity and equity. In practical terms that meant that they should avoid perverting justice by showing partiality or taking bribes.

4. *The judge's role was to warn and educate as well as decide cases* (2 Chr. 19:10). There was a preventive aspect to Jehoshaphat's conception of the judiciary. He expected judges to use disputes as a teachable moment to instruct the people in the Law and to warn them about violating God's commandments. If they failed to do so, they would be guilty before the Lord if the people fell into sin.

5. *Judges presided over certain areas of the law* (2 Chr. 19:11). Apparently the judiciary was organized in a way that handled both religious and civil matters. Two leaders were appointed as "chief justices" and consultants over these two areas respectively. Levites and others were appointed as peace officers to assist the judges.

Jehoshaphat's reforms, which probably had the effect of increasing centralized control of the justice system, had an immediate impact. Other nations had decided not to make war on Israel (2 Chr. 17:10), and those that did attack were defeated through God's miraculous help (2 Chr. 20:22–23).

Would Jehoshaphat's judicial policies make a difference in justice systems today? It is important to remember that Israel had a special relationship with God that governed its political life. Even so, modern nations, and especially people who work in the justice sys-

tem, could implement most of Jehoshaphat's principles. They serve as a broad outline of the godly basis on which true justice is founded.

Oath of Office

The expectations placed on government leaders have never been higher than they are today. Yet from the Bible's point of view, the key responsibilities are not political, social, or even moral, but spiritual. Psalm 101 lists the characteristics expected of Israel's leadership:

- To govern wisely, without compromising their integrity.
- To completely disassociate themselves from wicked schemes and those who promote them.
- To tolerate no slanderous talk and to dismiss subordinates who even appear to be using privileges to unfair advantage.
- To surround themselves only with people who are faithful to the Lord.
- To purge their administrations of deceivers and liars.
- To root out and destroy wicked people from the land.

Two observations are in order. First, kings were to put as much distance as possible between themselves and evil. There was to be no walking a fine line between right and wrong. Rather, they were to avoid temptation by surrounding themselves as much as possible with a clean environment.

Second, they needed to choose their advisors and assistants carefully. The spiritual quality of the people who served them would go far to determine the spiritual climate in which they governed.

Public servants today can only benefit by heeding this psalm. There is no question that politics tends to be a dirty business. But that only increases the need for officials who govern with a pure heart.

The Basis of Government

Political parties often formulate a platform to let voters know what their fundamental beliefs and values are, and where their candidates stand on issues. But what is the underlying "platform," or basis, for the institution of government itself? Scripture teaches that government ultimately derives from God's wisdom (Prov. 8:15–16).

For some, this truth may be hard to accept in light of widespread disillusionment with government today. The decisions of political leaders and government officials around the world sometimes look most unwise. Yet that does not change the fact that God established rule and authority, and that all leaders will ultimately answer to Him for their leadership. And as evil and foolish as governments sometimes are, the world would be in anarchy without them.

Proverbs challenges government leaders to fulfill their roles with godly wisdom. They can start by fearing the Lord (Prov. 1:7; 2:1–9). Then they can be wise about who they listen to and how they make decisions. If the wisdom of God has placed leaders in power, then it makes sense for them to wield power according to the wisdom of God. The Book of Proverbs is a good place to start acquiring that wisdom.

The Prayer Breakfast Movement

Paul urges prayer for "kings and all who are in authority" (1 Tim. 2:1–2). In that spirit, Christians today pray for presidents, cabinet members, legislators, governors, mayors, and judges. In fact, a modern prayer breakfast movement has developed, with events held annually in many major cities.

City-wide prayer for leaders recalls Abraham, who prayed for the doomed city of Sodom (Gen. 18:16–33). Abraham assumed that his prayers as a righteous man could preserve a city. In the same way, Paul affirms that believers ought to petition God for a "quiet and peaceable" community life (1 Tim. 2:2).

One interesting result of that peace—and a good reason for believers to serve in public office and/or to support in prayer those who do—is more effective evangelism (1 Tim. 2:3–7).

Who's Really in Charge?

The nature of sin is to defy God, and the strong tendency of people in power is to stay in power by any means possible—even if it means defying God to do so. Thus the rulers of the world often conspire together against the Lord (Ps. 2:1–2).

But what these leaders fail to realize is that the Lord's Anointed is King and Lord over all the nations of the world, including their own.

God has given Him the nations as an inheritance (Ps. 2:8).

God is sovereign even over nations that rage against Him. The psalmist realized that his own country was just a part of God's international reign. Do we understand the same truth about our own nations and governments?

For more on this topic, see **CITIZENSHIP,** *"Pledging Allegiance," page 64;* **CORRUPTION,** *"A Nation Sells Its Soul," page 91.*

GOVERNMENT SERVICE

Government as Ministry

The largest category of employment in many nations is government. That outrages some citizens, who see government as a massive, wasteful, scandal-plagued bureaucracy. But God takes a different view. If you work in government—as an elected or appointed official, a letter carrier, a police or military officer, a water-meter reader—you'll want to pay special attention to Romans 13:1–7.

Paul refers to governmental authorities as God's *ministers* (Rom. 13:4, 6), meaning "servants." It's the same word translated elsewhere as "deacons." The point is, if you work in government, you are ultimately God's worker. Your authority derives not just from the people, but from God Himself. (This is an amazing statement from Paul. He was not living under a democratically elected government, but under an imperial Roman system, probably headed by Nero!)

Government, then, is established by God. That doesn't mean that He approves of everything governments or their representatives do. But good or bad, He chooses to allow them to exist and have authority. He actually works through them to accomplish His purposes.

As a government employee, you are a "minister for good." In what way? This passage describes one important category of governmental authority—policing citizens by motivating them to pursue good and punishing those who do evil. Of course, your work in the system may involve very different tasks. Still, God wants you to be a "minister for good" by helping society function, by meeting the needs of people, by protecting the rights of people, or by defending your country from attack.

With authority comes responsibility and accountability. As a "minister of God" you will answer to Him for your decisions and actions. If God promises to avenge the evil that citizens commit, how much more will He avenge the evil that those in authority commit?

GRANDPARENTS

(*see* Family)

GRATITUDE

Let Us Give Thanks

Thanklessness is all too common among humans. Rather than being grateful for the good gifts we have received from God, we often act as if we had a right to far more. Sometimes we even complain about the privileges and blessings God has given us, and we go to great lengths to obtain more, even coveting what is someone else's (compare James 4:1–3).

The Psalms help to combat such selfishness by calling us to give thanks to the Lord (Ps. 136:1). They do that by:

- rehearsing what God has done for us in His mercy (Ps. 107; 136);
- challenging us to express gratitude for what we have (Ps. 92:1); and
- reminding us of the source of everything we have (Ps. 104).

And lest we minimize the importance of offering heartfelt thanks to God, Psalm 106 illustrates the dangers of forgetting. It reviews Israel's history of faithlessness, from unbelief in Egypt to idolatry in the Promised Land. The psalm ends with a plea for God to save His people in order that they might give thanks to His holy name. We can avoid great pain and loss by living thankful lives before the One who provides us with life and all that we have.

For more on this topic, see ABUNDANCE, "Celebrating Abundance," page 3; GIVING, "Saying Thank You," page 168; INGRATITUDE, "Where Are the Others?" page 222; MEMORY, "Never Forget!" page 260.

GREATNESS

Simple Obedience

Like Naaman, many of us expect God to require something "great" of us in order to satisfy His will (2 Kin. 5:13). But the insight of Naaman's servants was that God usually calls people to relatively "simple" obedience.

Naaman balked at washing in the Jordan. In the same way, many believers today balk at seemingly insignificant actions such as prayer, Bible reading, a kindness shown to a poor person, keeping one's word, and other uncelebrated behaviors that demonstrate compliance with God's will. Likewise, many unbelievers scorn God's "simple" requirement of confessing one's sinfulness and placing faith in Jesus' work on the cross for salvation. Surely God must require more than that (they assume)!

Yet God is not impressed by greatness; He looks for faithful obedience to what He has asked. What does it say, then, if we minimize His relatively easy demands as too "small" or too "lowly"? Jesus said that if we are unwilling to show faithfulness in routine, everyday matters, we can't expect to be given larger responsibilities (Luke 16:10).

Vying for Power

On the final trip to Jerusalem, something of a power struggle began to emerge among Jesus' disciples. James and John were the first to try to obtain positions of power in the coming kingdom (Mark 10:35–37).

Jesus rebuked them in an interesting way. He compared them to the leaders of the Gentiles that they so despised (Mark 10:42)—people like Pilate and Augustus and all their governors, tax collectors, soldiers, and centurions. The disciples detested those people as living only for themselves. Yet Jesus implied that this was the way His disciples were acting when they jockeyed for positions of power. The comparison must have challenged them to the core. Jesus was telling them, "You are no different than Gentiles!"

The Quest for Greatness

Is it wrong to desire greatness—to be a great salesperson, a great athlete, a great scholar, or a great performer? Shouldn't we all seek excellence in what we do? Does God not want us to experience great achievements?

Jesus' words to the disciples in Luke 22:24–30 touch on this complex issue. As He did so often, the Lord challenged the motives of His followers rather than their desires. He realized that they wanted greatness for its own sake, in order to lord it over others. They sought position and power as means to personal gain, not service to others.

*For more on this topic, see **VALUES**, "Confused About Greatness" page 411.*

GREED
Do-It-Yourself Religion

In a world where the motto often seems to be "do your own thing," people frequently develop self-styled religious beliefs and practices. For some this means taking a pick-and-choose, take-it-or-leave-it approach to established Christianity. For others it means coming up with outlandish ideas about God and eccentric ways of living. Either way, the ultimate authority seems to be the individual, who assumes the prerogative of ignoring any demand or discipline that feels too limiting or imposing.

A somewhat similar attitude seems to have characterized the Israelites as they prepared to enter the Promised Land. Apparently they were doing whatever was right in their own eyes when it came to religious observance (Deut. 12:8). Not that they were necessarily turning away from God, but the lack of a permanently located worship center seems to have brought about a degree of laxness in regard to the ritual obligations of the Law.

Moses warned them that that must change once they entered the land and God desig-

GREED

nated a site for worshiping Him (Deut. 12:13–14). They were to follow the detailed instructions of the Law concerning sacrifices, holy days, tithes and offerings, and other elements of religious life.

Is the same true for Christians today? In answering that question, it is important to note that the New Testament's instructions and descriptions of worship are not nearly as detailed as those given to Israel in the Old Testament Law. There seems to be a great deal more freedom given to individual believers and to their communities of faith.

However, that does not mean a do-it-yourself approach to religion. Scripture gives an objective set of truths to be believed and of behaviors to be lived. There may be latitude within those boundaries for cultural, ethnic, and geographic applications, but all believers fall into sin when they move outside the clear teaching of Scripture. In whatever manner we worship God, He still calls us to worship Him "in spirit and truth" (John 4:23).

What's Your Price?

Money has a way of revealing what really matters to a person. How about you? What would you do for the right price?

King Balak, fearful of the Israelites, twice offered a generous fee to Balaam, a reputed seer, if he would curse the people of God (Num 22:1–17). After consulting with the Lord, Balaam realized that he could not render services to Balak.

Yet the lure of money and new friends caused Balaam to waffle on his initial refusal. He tried to find a way to do business with Balak. As a result of his departure from God's clear direction, Balaam's own donkey was used by the Lord to force him to back off from the assignment (Num. 22:22–35).

Balaam's focus on money and power made it hard to deter him from opposing God's people. As a result, his name eventually became a byword for greed and avarice (2 Pet. 2:15; Jude 11). Indeed, to this day the term "Balaam's ass" is used to indicate stubbornness and foolishness.

Do you sometimes feel tempted to compromise your integrity for financial gain? Do you ever ignore the clear will of God because it might cost you something? If so, consider carefully the legacy of Balaam.

Watch Out for Greed!

Jesus gave a direct, unequivocal command to guard against *covetousness* (Luke 12:15)—longing for something we don't have, especially for what belongs to someone else. He was not telling us to watch for it in others, but in ourselves.

According to this verse and the following parable, covetousness, or greed, is based on the foolish belief that what matters in life is how much one has. It may be money (as is the case here), or status, power, intelligence, beauty, even spiritual blessings; it is possible to covet anything that can be acquired. The idea is that having that thing will make us content. But biblically, only God can—and will—satisfy our real needs, as Jesus goes on to show (Luke 12:22–31).

To covet is to be discontented with what God brings our way. Yet our consumer-oriented culture excels at stoking the fires of discontent. In subtle yet powerful ways, we come to believe that whatever we have, it's not enough. We need more, we need bigger, we need better.

So more than ever, we need to pay attention to Jesus' warning: *Watch out for greed!*

The Meaning of "Covet"?

Many people think of coveting as having wrong desires. The biblical word translated "coveting" often means that, particularly when it is a strong desire for anything that belongs to your neighbor (Ex. 20:17; compare Deut. 5:21). And coveting is not limited to someone else's property, either. One can covet one's own property by having an inordinate longing for or attachment to it.

It is also possible to commit the grievous sin of coveting what belongs to God. A man named Achan did this when the Israelites entered the Promised Land, by taking plunder from the ruins of Jericho, which God had said belonged to Him (Josh. 6:17–19; 7:20–21). This sort of desire amounts to idolatry. It means craving a certain thing so much that one values it more than God. Scripture warns us to "put away" that kind of covetousness.

However, the word used for "coveting" does not always mean a wrong desire.

G

Sometimes the Bible uses the word for a good desire. For example, God's judgments are to be "desired" more than gold (Ps. 19:10). Perhaps the key, then, as to whether one's longings are right or wrong depends on the object of one's affections. To love anything more than God is to fall into covetousness and idolatry.

GRIEF

A Father's Anguish

The tragic account of David's son Absalom is a story of . . .

- *appearance.* Apparently he was the most handsome man in all Israel. His most notable feature was his thick, long hair, which he cut annually. Its weight was said to be two hundred shekels, or several pounds (2 Sam. 14:25–26).
- *affluence.* As a son of the king, he enjoyed the benefits of a royal family whose empire was on the rise. For example, Hiram of Tyre had built David a palace of cedar (2 Sam. 5:11; 7:1–2). Absalom may have had his own home at Baal Hazor, several miles north of Jerusalem, where he employed sheepshearers (2 Sam. 13:23).
- *advantage.* He was next in line to the throne after his half brothers Amnon and Chileab. He also must have had a special place in his father's heart, for even after Absalom took Amnon's life, David longed to be with his son (2 Sam. 13:39).
- *anger.* When Amnon violated Absalom's beautiful sister, Tamar, Absalom took revenge by luring Amnon to his country home, where he had his servants kill him after dinner (2 Sam. 13:1–29).
- *ambition.* Reinstated after two years of exile, Absalom began building a power base among the people, right under the nose of David (2 Sam. 15:1–6). When the time was right, he launched a rebellion to depose his father and rule in his place (2 Sam. 15:7–18). His ultimate act of defiance was to violate his father's concubines, which in effect meant that he had assumed the throne (2 Sam. 16:20–22).
- *anguish.* Under the seasoned command of Joab, David's troops severely defeated Absalom's army and, through an odd set of circumstances, brought an end to Absalom's life (2 Sam. 18:6–15). Despite hav-

ing his throne restored, David mourned the death of his son in anguish and despair (2 Sam. 18:33–19:4). David's sin with Bathsheba had finally come to its tragic and painful outcome, just as Nathan had predicted (2 Sam. 12:7–12).

Lasting Scars

Following accidents and natural catastrophes in which property has been lost but people have been saved, survivors are often quoted as saying, "We're just glad everyone is safe. Things can be replaced, but people can't." How true that is.

That sense of the irreplaceable value of human life is important to remember in reading the closing verses of the Book of Job. After all of his trials and suffering, Job was blessed in his old age when the Lord restored to him twice the amount of property that he had lost (Job 42:10, 12), and by giving him ten more children.

However, as precious as those children must have been, they could never "replace" the ten who had perished in a windstorm (Job 1:18–19). The grief of that loss would remain. To be sure, the gift of a new family must have brought a measure of healing. But the wounds suffered earlier must have left lasting scars.

The Comfort of Presence

When we're facing severe trials and suffering, the last thing we need is a set of "Job's counselors," people who only tell us what they think we have done wrong. Rather than having people on our back, we would prefer people who are on our team, pulling for us as we wrestle with our problems.

Unfortunately, Job had to get through his trials without much support. Three of his friends came when they learned of his troubles (Job 2:11), but they are remembered more for their condemnation of Job than for their comfort.

Still, the three friends started out with good intentions. In fact, their actions serve as a useful pattern for intervening in the midst of a friend's distress. Notice that they:

- came as a group to be with their friend;
- agreed ahead of time that they should come to Job's aid;
- wanted to mourn with him and comfort him;

- openly wept for him when they could not recognize him in his disfigured body;
- tore their robes in anguish for him, a custom in that day;
- gave Job their silent presence for seven days, willing just to be with him;
- refrained from speaking until Job first began to share his heart with them; and
- listened patiently to Job's lament and frustration.

As we today seek to comfort people around us who are feeling deep pain and suffering, the initial response of Job's friends can teach us some valuable lessons. Just quietly being with hurting people can be a great help and encouragement to them. God can use our presence in their lives as a gift of His love.

For more on this topic, see BURIAL AND FUNERAL CUSTOMS, "The Mourners," page 40.

GROWTH

(see Spiritual Growth)

GUIDANCE

(see also Mentoring)

Divine and Human Guidance

The way that Moses led Israel through the wilderness serves as an instructive model for Christians seeking guidance in today's complex world. On the one hand, Moses invited a relative, Hobab, to act as a guide (Num. 10:29–31). On the other, he continued to follow the fiery cloud of the Lord's presence (Num. 10:34; compare Num. 9:15–23). Thus Moses used a combination of human and divine guidance to lead Israel to the Promised Land.

The fiery cloud, the tablets of stone, the Law, and other direct communications from God were the primary means of guidance, to be sure. But for many if not most day-to-day decisions, human judgment and wisdom—such as Hobab's knowledge of the wilderness—were required.

The appearance of Hobab at this point is interesting. Earlier, Moses' father-in-law had counseled him to appoint judges to assist him in leading the people (Ex. 18:17–23). Now Moses appealed strongly to Hobab to "be our eyes" (Num. 10:31). So in both cases Moses realized the value of human resources.

Actually, the text doesn't say whether Hobab gave in to Moses' insistent appeals. It may be that Hobab returned to his own land and people as he had intended (Num. 10:30). Yet even if he left, the combination of human and divine leadership remained, as Moses, Aaron, Miriam, and the leaders appointed earlier continued to make decisions.

This takes nothing away from God's leadership. Rather it demonstrates that God uses a variety of ways to lead His people—sometimes through a fiery cloud, just as often through people to whom He has given unique abilities. Thus as we seek guidance today, we need to pay attention to divine revelation—particularly to the Bible, God's written Word—but we also need to recruit, listen to, and follow those whom God has gifted with insight and leadership.

Going Ahead Anyway

What happens when we reject established authority and become our own authority? Quite often the result is disaster. It certainly was for the Israelites. Having rejected God's promise to help them take the land, they decided to go ahead and attack it on their own (Num. 14:39–40). Even after Moses warned them that their plans would fail, they still moved ahead. The outcome was disastrous.

This tragic episode challenges believers today to ask: Where have we resisted God's will and authority and then gone ahead and acted without His direction or power? How can we avoid such presumption in the future? Here are some suggestions:

- Search the Scriptures to find situations that are similar to those you are facing and then study how the people involved acted.
- Discuss your situation with a close friend who can give you godly counsel. Ask the person to really challenge your thinking, not just agree with everything you say.
- Ask yourself: What would be helped or hurt if I delayed acting until I were more certain of God's direction?

The Value of a Spiritual Mentor

Quite often, the difference between success or failure in a person's career is determined by whether that person has been guided and nurtured by a mentor. The same can be true in spiritual matters. The extent to which a person matures spiritually and stays that way is often determined by the presence or absence of a spiritual mentor.

King Joash is a case in point. As long as the godly priest Jehoiada was around to guide young Joash, the king ruled well and brought spiritual renewal to the land (2 Chr. 23:16–24:16). But after Jehoiada died, Joash turned to wickedness, allowing idolatry to creep back in (2 Chr. 24:17–18), and even killing Zechariah, the son of his mentor Jehoiada (2 Chr. 24:22). Joash eventually suffered a stunning military defeat and was murdered by his own servants (2 Chr. 24:23–25)—a tragic ending to what started out as a good reign.

Joash's apostasy reminds us that leaders today need spiritual mentors and religious guidance if they are to stay on course. If you are in a position of authority, who are you looking to for godly wisdom and counsel?

The Leading of the Lord

Do you ever wish that God would lead you the way He led Israel through the wilderness, with a miraculous pillar of cloud by day and a pillar of fire by night (Ex. 13:21; 14:19–20)? Those must have been very reassuring signs to the people that their God was present with them and actively intervening to lead them through the wilderness.

God adopted a kind of communication well known to large groups of travelers in the ancient world. When armies marched long distances, with their lines sometimes drawn out for miles, they needed a way for troops at the front to communicate with troops at the rear.

So the leaders lighted a brazier of burning coals to carry at the front of the march. At night, the flames provided a fire that could be seen for miles. During the day, water poured on the coals produced an easily recognized cloud of smoke and steam. When marching through unfamiliar terrain, the rearguard troops had only to march toward the cloud to stay on course.

In the case of Israel, God Himself was in the cloud and the fire, which He produced supernaturally. But how does He lead believers today? The most direct way is through the Bible, His written revelation to humanity. The vast majority of what we need to know about God's will is revealed in Scripture. If we keep aiming toward that, we'll tend to end up in the right spot.

Naturally, Scripture does not give us pinpoint directions for every detail of life, such as what job we should work at, or what city we should live in, or how many hours of sleep we should get. For that we have to use our heads, just as the Israelites had to make their own decisions about numerous details, such as how to cross a particular stream, or how much baggage to load on an animal, or how many layers of clothing to wear each day.

Does God lead His people today? Yes, He does. But we need not look to the skies for His will when we have it written right in front of us.

For more on this topic, see **GOD'S GUIDANCE** *"Reflecting on God's Guidance," page 169.*

H

HANDICAPS

Physical Limitations

The Israelite priests were required to reflect God as much as possible, both in conduct and character. One practical result of this standard was an exclusion of priests who had any physical defect from serving at the altar (Lev. 21:16–23).

This does not mean that God has a bias against people with physical defects and handicaps. It's important to notice several factors as we evaluate this prohibition:

1. There were numerous groups besides the handicapped that God excluded from the job of offering sacrifices: women, children, foreigners, anyone from a tribe other than Levi, even kings.

2. The list of "defects" that excluded a priest sometimes went beyond what we today normally think of as "handicaps":

- Blindness.
- An impaired limb.
- A marred face.
- An oversized limb.

- A broken foot or hand.
- A hunchback condition.
- Dwarfism.
- A defective eye, possibly including imperfect vision.
- Eczema.
- A scab.
- The absence of (or possibly damaged) genitalia.

3. Physical defects did not totally exclude a man from the priesthood, only from serving at the altar where sacrifices were made (Lev. 21:22).

4. Elsewhere in the Law, God demanded protection and fair treatment for those with physical limitations (Lev. 19:14).

Then why the prohibition? Because God is perfect, and to as great an extent as possible, He wanted the ceremonial life of His people to reflect that perfection.

The "no defects" policy reminded everyone that God was worthy of their best. It did not mean that only perfect people could gain access to God. If that were case, there would have been no priesthood, for even priests were sinners and had to offer sacrifices for their own sins (Lev. 16:11; Heb. 5:2–3).

HAPPINESS
Having—and Being Had

Do you own your possessions, or do they own you? Consider how many things you have that you could just as easily live without. Are you like the sinner described in Ecclesiastes, spending your entire life "gathering and collecting" (Eccl. 2:26).

Solomon devoted much of his life to the acquisition of great riches. "Whatever my eyes desired I did not keep from them," he said. Yet he concluded that this was nothing but "vanity and grasping for the wind" (Eccl. 2:10–11).

Here is a brief self-assessment to help you take account of what you own, and how important these things are in your life:

- Do you have specific possessions that you would never consider giving away to anyone?
- Do you have certain possessions that are important in establishing your identity among your friends and in your community?

- How do you define success? To what extent does a certain level of income or net worth enter into your definition?
- How many of your major decisions are calculated largely by their financial impact on you and your family?
- Is it easier for you to buy "luxury" items than it is to give money to your church, world missions, or a charity?
- Do you have any friends that could be considered poor? If not, why not?
- How do you measure self-fulfillment? How do you know when you are happy?
- How important is it for you to outdo your parents' level of financial achievement?
- Do you measure your progress in life by whether you made more last year than the year before?
- Do you think your financial success has any impact on the poor and needy in your community, or elsewhere in the world?

HATRED
Blinded by Differences

Heading south from Galilee to Jerusalem (Luke 9:51), Jesus traveled with His disciples through Samaria (Luke 9:52). Prejudiced against the Samaritans (John 4:9), Jews commonly bypassed this region by journeying down the east bank of the Jordan River. But Jesus deliberately chose the more direct route, as if to seek out conflict rather than avoid it.

Confrontation erupted at the first village. The Samaritans did not want Jesus or His followers there, nor did the disciples want to be there. Neither group could see past the other's ethnic identity. But the disciples turned exceptionally ugly. Insulted by the villagers' rejection of their Lord, they were itching to call down fire from heaven—with the justification (according to most manuscripts), "just as Elijah did."

Their response shows how terribly destructive centuries of hatred and bitterness can be. No wonder Jesus utterly rebuked this response. He realized that His followers were blinded by their presumption of religious and ethnic superiority. In rebuke, He reminded them of His mission: to save lives—even Samaritan lives—not to destroy them.

We as Jesus' followers today need to

consider this incident carefully. Who do we regard with condemnation rather than compassion? Is it someone of another race or a different ideology? Our differences may arise from legitimate concerns. But if we would just as soon see someone eliminated in order to reinforce our feelings of ethnic, racial, moral, theological, or spiritual superiority, then we need the rebuke of Jesus' words: "You do not know what manner of spirit you are of" (Luke 9:55).

As we read in John 3:17, "God did not send His Son into the world to condemn the world, but that the world through Him might be saved."

The Cycle of Prejudice

Anyone who has ever been hurt by a member of a different ethnic or racial group is at risk for developing an attitude of prejudice against all members of that group. Somehow age-old biases tend to be powerfully reinforced by even the slightest offenses. The incident between Israel and Edom (Num. 20:14–21) is a good illustration.

The king of Edom refused to open the King's Highway to Moses and his people. In all likelihood, this hostile act grew out of an attitude of prejudice whose roots could be traced back hundreds of years to two brothers: Jacob, the ancestor of Israel, and Esau, the ancestor of the Edomites. Jacob obtained Esau's birthright and cheated him out of their father's blessing (Gen. 27:36). Esau swore he would get even (Gen. 27:41–42).

Years later the brothers were reconciled (Gen. 33:4, 10–11). Yet Esau had married Canaanite wives (Gen. 36:1–8), and the Bible does not mention his descendants, the Edomites, again until this incident in Numbers 20. But apparently those descendants never forgot the wrongs that Jacob had committed against their ancestor. Now, with the Israelites struggling to make their way across the desert, the king of Edom perhaps saw an opportunity for "payback."

In turning down Moses' request, Edom made life much more difficult for the Hebrews. The incident with the fiery serpents (Num. 21:4–9) would likely never have occurred apart from Edom's discourtesy. But the worst result of the Edomites' act was that it perpetuated hostility between the two ethnic groups. Even though God explicitly commanded His people not to "abhor" an Edomite (Deut. 23:7–8), the people and their descendants nursed their feelings of hurt.

The attitude of prejudice boiled over many years later when Saul began harassing the Edomites (1 Sam. 14:47). David, during his reign, slaughtered thousands of them (2 Sam. 8:13–14, according to some manuscripts) and turned their land into a military possession. David's general Joab then carried out a campaign of genocide (1 Kin. 11:15–16).

The cycle of hate went on and on for centuries. Even the baby Jesus felt its impact: King Herod, who ordered the slaughter of infants at Bethlehem (Matt. 2:16–18), was descended from the Edomites.

Ethnic conflicts can have long-term consequences. The question that every believer of whatever race or ethnic group needs to ask is: How can I as a follower of Christ help to break the cycle of prejudice? If I've been offended or attacked by someone of another race or nationality, what can I do to keep from amplifying my pain into general mistrust and hatred of the other group? Can I resist creating stereotypes and instead reach out in love to seek a better understanding?

For more on this topic, see ENEMIES, "Love My Enemies?" page 126; "Upside-Down Values," page 127.

HEALING

(*see* Sickness)

HEALTH CARE

Preventive Health Care

God has a deep interest in both personal and community health. He cares not only about restoring people from ill health, but about preventing unhealth in the first place.

This becomes evident from the detailed laws of Leviticus 13, which have to do with detecting, examining, quarantining, cleansing, and restoring those who had leprosy, skin diseases, boils, burns, skin spots, sores, and other skin-related maladies. The fact that God would give these kinds of laws to His people shows His concern for their standard of health.

Earlier in the Law, we see dietary restrictions placed on the Israelites (for example,

Ex. 22:31; Lev. 11:1–47). The text does not mention the health-protecting qualities of these statutes. Nevertheless, we now know that a number of the requirements promoted good health.

The same is true for the instructions about the cleanliness of garments, as well as the walls, floors, and ceilings of houses—even the stones of which houses were built (Lev. 13:47–59; 14:33–53). We cannot read these and many other passages without concluding that the environment people live and work in, and the relationship between that environment and health, are important to God.

In light of this, it's worth taking a close look at the tradeoffs we often accept between certain environmental health hazards and the opportunity for economic gain. These are complex issues, to be sure. But knowing that God cares about good health, we might ask: What risks, both biological and financial, are worth taking? Someday we must give an accounting to God for our decisions and actions in this area.

Valuing Health Care Workers

When Job called his friends "worthless physicians" (Job 13:4), he was lashing out at his caregivers with an exaggerated statement that tells more about Job's pain than it does about his friends. Essentially he was saying that his three comforters were frauds, not that physicians as a class are worthless.

In general, the Bible seems to have a high

HEALTH CARE

view of physicians, nurses, midwives, and others devoted to health care. Compassion is an important product of faith, and physical health is something that God cares about. As a result, believers throughout history have had a strong record of providing health care and medical technology to people around the world.

The Bible honors these workers by including accounts of a number of people who tended the sick, helped those with physical needs, and generally promoted good health.

The Bible mentions more than forty specific diseases or disabilities and alludes frequently to sickness and health issues in general.

- Midwives were relatives of friends (Gen. 35:17; 1 Sam. 4:20), but sometimes professionals (Ex. 1:15–22), who helped women give birth to their babies.
- The physicians of Egypt were directed by Joseph to embalm the body of his father (Gen. 50:2), showing that a doctor's responsibilities continued even after death. The Israelites may have learned much of their medicine from the Egyptians.
- The Levitical priests were called to attend to a variety of medical needs as well as spiritual needs.
- Jesus devoted considerable time and teaching to health issues, healed the sick, and even raised the dead.
- Luke is described as the "beloved physician" (Col. 4:14) who traveled with Paul and others, no doubt caring for their physical needs—perhaps including Paul's "thorn in the flesh, " if it was a physical malady (2 Cor. 12:7).
- Elders in the early church were available on request to provide prayer and anointing with oil for Christians who were ill (James 5:14–15).

*For more on this topic, see **HOLISTIC MEDICINE**, "Body and Soul," page 199; **HYGIENE**, "Clean vs. Unclean," page 209.*

HEAVEN

Glimpses of Heaven

Popular culture tends to make a caricature out of heaven as a place where people sprout wings and become angels, wear halos, strum harps, and walk on clouds. St. Peter supposedly sits at heaven's gate, deciding who may enter. And heavenly choirs sing incessantly—not a bright prospect for those who have trouble singing or do not like to sing!

But what is heaven really like? The Bible does not give us a detailed description, but it does offer several glimpses, often using metaphors, about the nature of heaven:

- In the Old Testament, particularly the Psalms, heaven is sometimes understood to mean the sky, but it is also referred to as the place from which God rules creation (Ps. 103:19). (This is not to suggest that God is "located" in or confined to heaven. God is pure spirit who is infinite and everywhere present.)
- Heaven will be free from the curse of sin, lit by the brilliance of God, and the place where those who are saved will enjoy eternal life with God (Rev. 22:1, 3, 5, 17). These citizens will come from every people on the earth (Rev. 14:6–7).
- In heaven, there will be no more hunger and thirst (Rev. 7:16), nor tears (Rev. 7:17; 21:4), nor pain and sorrow (Rev. 21:4). All evil will be imprisoned forever in another place (Rev. 20:10; 21:8).
- Heaven will be a work of art and beauty in its construction (Rev. 4, 21).
- In heaven, people will have enjoyable, productive work to do.

Heaven is a wonderful place to think about, yet God has chosen not to tell us very much about it. He has let us know that it exists, and that someday His people will join Him there, and that is enough to give us hope (John 14:1–4).

But inasmuch as the Bible gives us limited information, it is futile to speculate on what heaven will be like. Instead, God wants us to concentrate our efforts on becoming Christlike people in the here and now. That will prepare us to eventually become citizens of heaven. As an old saying warns us, we don't want to become so heavenly minded that we are no earthly good.

The Lord Is There—Forever!

Scripture gives us only the barest glimpses of what heaven will be like. But one feature that we know for sure is that God will be there, and we will never be separated from Him again. With this bright vision of eternity, Ezekiel's book of prophecy draws to a close (Ezek. 48:30–35).

Just as the apostle John saw the New Jerusalem descending from heaven (Rev. 21), so Ezekiel envisioned the day when the city of God would finally be made perfect and complete in every way. Both prophets saw twelve gates facing the four corners of the earth (Ezek. 48:31–34; Rev. 21:12–13), an indication of accessibility for everyone. Inscribed with the names of the twelve tribes of Israel, the gates suggest inclusion, restoration, and fulfillment of all that God has promised His covenant people. In John's vision, this image is strengthened by the fact that these gates never shut (Rev. 21:25).

The name of this ideal city is "THE LORD IS THERE." This is a fitting climax, not only to the Book of Ezekiel, but to John's Revelation and to the Bible itself. It shows that a reversal has occurred during the course of history. Whereas Ezekiel had seen the Lord withdrawing from His temple because of the people's wickedness (Ezek. 10:18), now He has returned to a new temple to live among His people forever. Likewise, whereas fellowship with God was cut off through the sin in Eden (Gen. 3:22–24), it is made permanent in the New Jerusalem (Rev. 21:3).

This is a strong hope we can look forward to with great anticipation. Right now, we may sometimes feel distant from God, perhaps alone and confused and wondering whether He even knows who we are. The assurance of Scripture is that someday we will no longer wonder where God is; we will be with Him—forever!

HELL

The Valley of Hinnom

A deep, narrow ravine south of Jebus (later Jerusalem) called the Valley of Hinnom, or the Valley of the Son of Hinnom, was the boundary between the territories of Benjamin and Judah (Josh. 18:16). The location was unremarkable in Joshua's day, but came to have great significance later in Israelite history.

In the period of the divided monarchy, this valley was the site of a pagan altar, or "high place" (see Deut. 12:2), known as Tophet ("fireplace"). Parents sacrificed their children there to the god Molech. The Bible singles out Ahaz and Manasseh, kings of Judah, as having led the way in this grotesque ritual (2 Chr. 28:3; 33:6). But Scripture praises King Josiah for destroying this idolatrous altar during his reforms (2 Kin. 23:10).

Jeremiah, who was called as a prophet during Josiah's reign, foretold that God would judge the Israelites for committing the awful abomination of human sacrifice, among other evils. The Lord would cause such destruction that the Valley of Hinnom would become a cemetery known as the Valley of Slaughter (Jer. 7:31–32; 19:1–6; 32:35).

This prophecy began to be fulfilled when Jerusalem was destroyed by the Babylonians in 586 B.C. Later, the Valley of Hinnom became the city dump for Jerusalem. Fires continually smoldered there, as the site was used as a burning ground for refuse and the dead bodies of criminals and animals.

In time, the valley became so noxious that its name became a synonym for hell. The Hebrew phrase *ge* ("valley of") *hinnom* eventually became the Greek *Gehenna* (Matt. 5:22; Mark 9:43, 45, 47). At one time, Jewish tradition even held that the entrance to hell began at that valley.

For more on this topic, see SPIRITUAL WARFARE, "The Gates of Hell," page 378.

HERITAGE

Outgrowing Our Roots

In recent years, more and more people have shown interest in their "roots." They want to know where they came from and what sort of family they are descended from. Doing so may help them find clues about family traits and behaviors.

The sons of Korah had an infamous past on which to look back. Their ancestor Korah, of the tribe of Levi, led at least 250 of Israel's most important leaders in one of the worst rebellions against Moses and the Lord during the Exodus. God severely judged Korah's coalition by causing the earth to split open and swallow them and their possessions (Num. 16).

However, Korah's family survived (Num. 26:11), and years later his descendants were among the Levites appointed by David to oversee music in the worship of the Lord (1 Chr. 6:37). Their responsibilities included composing, arranging, and performing, and in this connection eleven of the psalms bear the heading, "of the sons of Korah."

The sons of Korah illustrate how a tragic legacy can be overcome. It need not determine the destiny of a family. By honoring the Lord, Korah's descendants became known, not for their ancestor's rebellion, but for their musical responsibilities.

Perhaps you can take hope from this talented family of Levites. Maybe your family has a tragic history, perhaps as a result of crime, alcohol abuse, emotional unhealth, racial prejudice, or some other evil. With God's help, you can overcome that legacy. God is greater than your family. He can give you the grace to emerge from the sin and shame of generations past into a life of health and holiness.

*For more on this topic, see **ANCESTRAL ROOTS**, "Genealogies—Records of God's Grace," page 18.*

HISTORY
Looking Back

Perhaps you have visited your school for a founder's week or homecoming celebration and listened to a keynote speaker review the history of the institution. Or perhaps your pastor gives an annual report of your church in which he points out some of the ways in which God has been faithful to the congregation over the previous year. In a similar way, Psalm 105 takes a look back at Israel's history in order to praise the Lord for honoring His commitments to the Hebrews' ancestor, Abraham.

The occasion for which this psalm was originally composed may have been one of the religious festivals, possibly the Feast of Tabernacles (see Lev. 23:33), but more likely the Festival of Weeks or Pentecost (Lev. 23:15–21). The former celebrated the Lord's help during the Israelites' Exodus journey, when they resided in tents (or "tabernacles"). The latter was to show thanksgiving to God for the annual harvest.

Psalm 105, along with other psalms recalling Israel's history (for example, Ps. 78, 106), encourages God's people today to formally celebrate the promises that He has made and

fulfilled for us. The habit of looking back at His gracious acts can stir up joy for today and new hope for the future.

*For more on this topic, see **FAITH**, "Despair vs. Confident Faith," page 142.*

HOLINESS
Holy Places, Holy People

For many people, the word *holy* brings to mind special places such as cathedrals and temples. It would be easy to limit our concept of holiness to such concrete examples, especially when we see so many such cases in the Old Testament. Certain monuments, the tabernacle, the temple, and even certain mountains, along with some of the leaders, the priests, and the prophets were designated as "holy," consecrated, or set apart to the Lord.

This pattern was continued in Ezekiel's vision of the new temple, access to which was to be highly restricted (Ezek. 44:1–19). Likewise, a certain "holy district" was to be established in the restored land (Ezek. 45:1–5).

So holiness was attached to certain places, but we shouldn't forget that the call to holy living is not confined to one place or another. All of life is to be holy, no matter where one is. Ezekiel pinpoints some very practical and even mundane dimensions of holiness:

- Stop the use of violence and oppression (Ezek. 45:9).
- Cease the pattern of evicting people (Ezek. 45:9).
- Restore honest dealing in business, using standards of value that have integrity and can be trusted (Ezek. 45:10–12).
- Donate a percentage of each business transaction to God, whether one is a prince or one of the common people (Ezek. 45:13–17).
- Mark all of life with monthly festivals and celebrations that include everyone (Ezek. 45:18–25).
- Restore the six-day work week, and protect the Sabbath rest, with the prince providing substantially for this observance (Ezek. 46:1–15).
- Follow careful guidelines in the matter of inheritances and boundaries, maintaining fair treatment of aliens and strangers (Ezek. 46:16–18; 47:13–23).

- Provide an area for the common people, for homes and common space (Ezek. 48:15–20).
- Name each of the commercial centers—the exits or gates of the city—after a portion of the citizenry (tribes) (Ezek. 48:30–35).
- Name the city itself "THE LORD IS THERE," reflecting a very inclusive view of holiness: everything that goes on there pertains to the Lord (Ezek. 48:35).

All of life is to be holy. One might be more reverent in certain settings and on certain occasions, but one is made neither more nor less holy by entering or exiting a particular place. Christ has already invited us into the most holy place there is, so that we will live as His holy people in everything we do (Heb. 9:11–15; 10:19–25).

The Holiness Code

Most of the religions of the ancient world made a distinction between the sacred and the profane. However, the gods of these pagan religions were usually seen as behaving little better than human beings, and often quite a bit worse. Furthermore, the religious rituals of many of these religions were often cruel, degrading, and dehumanizing.

God did not want His people Israel to practice those things. He was not a God to be worshiped in that way. So when the Israelites left Egypt, He gave them careful instructions for how they were to worship Him. Most of these religious laws are contained in the Book of Leviticus, which means "the book of the Levites." The Levites were the descendants of Levi who were called to be priests and religious leaders. Thus Leviticus could be said to be Israel's manual for worship and religious life.

Another term by which Leviticus is often known is the Holiness Code. It spells out what it means to worship and serve a holy God. Categories of instruction include:

- Worship through offerings and sacrifices (Lev. 1–7).
- The relationship between physical and biological matters and religious life (Lev. 11–15).

- The Day of Atonement, the annual occasion on which the nation's sin was dealt with (Lev. 16).
- The spiritual implications of day-to-day life (Lev. 17–24).
- The Year of Jubilee, involving the return of property and lands to their owners, and servants to their families (Lev. 25).
- The implications of obeying or disobeying the Law (Lev. 26).
- Vows (Lev. 27).

The letter of these laws applied only to ancient Israel, but the spirit of them continues to apply to God's people today. Like the Hebrews, we are called to holiness in every area of life (1 Pet. 1:14–16). In fact, Jesus said that the commandment of Leviticus to "love your neighbor as yourself" (Lev. 19:18) was second only to loving God with all of one's being (Matt. 22:37–39).

As you read Leviticus, you may find the strict and repetitive laws concerning blood sacrifices and other religious rituals to seem far removed from modern life. But they remind us—just as they reminded the Israelites—of the heavy penalty that sin exacts, and of the necessity for the atoning death of the Lord Jesus Christ. He is the Lamb of God whose blood made atonement for our sins. In fact, His death was anticipated by the sacrifices made on the Day of Atonement (Lev. 16:11–34; Heb. 9:6–28).

Recognizing this connection, we have great cause to praise and thank the Lord as we read Leviticus. Here we have a picture of what it cost Jesus to make us right with God. We also have a picture of what our response should be—a life of holiness.

For more on this topic, see ETHICS, "Be Holy, for I Am Holy," page 128.

HOLISTIC MEDICINE

Body and Soul

The connection between a woman's biology and the need for a sin offering (Lev. 12:6–7) is one of a number of laws in Leviticus that shows that Israel's priests had to pay as much attention to the body as they did to the soul. God made clear distinctions between "clean" and "unclean" (Lev. 11:29), and it fell to the priests to distinguish between the two.

As a result, the priests had to be concerned with women following childbirth (Lev. 12), actual, potential, and false cases of leprosy (Lev. 13–14), bodily discharges and emissions, including those related to reproduction (Lev. 15), dietary matters (Lev. 11), and the disposition of dead bodies (Num. 19:11–22).

Thus a priest was in a primary role to be aware of both physical and spiritual needs. He could not divorce the two in his mind. Practically speaking, the Law virtually forced him to keep them connected.

This suggests some important implications for modern-day Bible readers. In the West, work has become highly specialized. As a result, work related to the body (such as medicine and health) often has little in common with work related to the soul (such as ministry and religion). But there is no reason why workers in either field cannot "compare notes" with workers in the other field.

Along the same lines, health professionals have a strategic opportunity to raise spiritual issues; on the other hand, religious professionals can be sensitive to physical needs.

HOLY SPIRIT
Power

At the beginning of Acts, Jesus' followers appear confused and fearful. But by the end of the book they are well on their way to transforming the Roman world with the gospel. What accounts for this dramatic change? Acts 1:8 provides the answer: "You shall receive power." But notice:

1. *The power promised was not force or political authority.* Israel had enjoyed superiority under David and Solomon, but those days were a distant memory. Jesus was not indicating a revival of Jewish dominance. Instead, the word "power" means *ability* or capacity. Jesus promised that once the Holy Spirit came upon them, His followers would have a new ability.

2. *The ability had more to do with being than doing.* The believers would "be witnesses," not just "do witnessing." Evangelism is a process, not just an event. It involves a total lifestyle, not just occasional efforts.

3. *The power came from without, not from within.* The believers were not to manufacture their own ways of proclaiming the gos-

pel, but to look for supernatural ability from the Spirit to make them effective in gospel presentation. The power came when the Holy Spirit arrived, not before.

4. *The believers were to be witnesses to Christ, not to themselves.* They were to make disciples not to themselves but to the risen Lord (Matt. 28:18–20).

The Holy Spirit in the Old Testament

No clearer statement of the intimate interworking of the triune God—Father, Son and Holy Spirit—and especially of the Spirit's powerful role can be found in the Old Testament than in Isaiah's prophecy of the Servant of the Lord (Is. 42:1–9). The passage summarizes the redeeming work of all three Persons of the Trinity in the salvation of the lost. Thus it ties together in remarkable harmony both the Old Testament and New Testament understandings of God's grace. It also sheds light on our understanding of the Holy Spirit.

Some Bible readers assume that the Spirit's activity in Scripture is limited to the New Testament. But actually He is just as active in the Old:

1. *The Spirit participated in creation* (Gen. 1:2; Job 26:13; Is. 32:15).

2. *The Spirit gives life* to humanity and the other creatures (Ps. 104:29–30). It is interesting that when Genesis says God endows people with life by breathing into their nostrils the "breath of life" (Gen. 2:7), the word for "breath" is the same word translated elsewhere as "spirit"

3. *The Spirit strives with sinners* (Gen. 6:3), which is perhaps related to His work in convicting people of sin (John 16:8–11).

4. *The Spirit came upon certain judges, warriors, and prophets* in a way that gave them extraordinary power: for example, Joshua (Num. 27:18), Othniel (Judg. 3:10), Gideon (6:34), Samson (13:25; 14:6), and Saul (1 Sam. 10:9–10). However, the Spirit later departed from Saul because of his disobedience (16:14).

5. *The Spirit played a prominent role in the long span of Old Testament prophecy.* David declared that "the Spirit of the Lord spoke by me, and His word was on my tongue" (2 Sam. 23:2). Likewise, Ezekiel reported that "the Spirit entered me when He spoke to me" (Ezek. 2:2).

6. *The Spirit inspired holiness in Old Testament believers* (Ps. 143:10). And Scripture promised that someday God would put His Spirit in His people in a way that would cause them to live according to His statutes (Ezek. 36:27).

7. *The Spirit was crucial in helping God's people anticipate the ministry of the Messiah.* For example, Isaiah 11:1–5 is a trinitarian preview of the working of the Father, the Spirit, and the Son, who is the Branch of Jesse. Looking forward to the ministry of Jesus Christ, the Holy Spirit inspired Isaiah to prophesy: "The Spirit of the LORD shall rest upon Him" (Is. 11:2), inspiring God's Chosen One with wisdom, understanding, counsel, might, knowledge, fear of the Lord, righteousness, and faithfulness. Thus we come full cycle to the New Testament, where Jesus claimed to be the fulfillment of this prophecy (Is. 61:1–2; Luke 4:18–19).

The Promise of the Spirit

Joel described the time when God would pour out His Spirit on all flesh as "afterward" (Joel 2:28). He is believed to have been referring to the days of the Messiah, which were to follow the period of restoration (possibly from the exile; Joel 2:18–27).

Peter quoted Joel's prophecy of the Spirit in full and claimed its fulfillment at Pentecost (Acts 2:16–21). In a way of speaking, that makes Joel a spiritual "grandfather" of the church. Christians are now experiencing the Spirit in fulfillment of Joel's promise. However, the prophet also describes other events associated with the "day of the LORD," which it appears will not have their ultimate fulfillment until the end times.

Empowered for Ministry

If you've ever assumed that God's work in the world is accomplished primarily by ordained clergy, then you need to look carefully at Jesus' words to the hometown crowd of Nazareth. "The Spirit of the Lord is upon Me," He declared, applying an Old Testament prophecy to Himself (Luke 4:18–19; Is. 61:1–2). "Today this Scripture is fulfilled in your hearing" (Luke 4:21).

The promise fulfilled was that the Messiah had come and would do all of the things foretold in the ancient text. But the text went on to make more promises about what would

happen *after* the Messiah's initial work: "You shall be named the priests of the Lord, they shall call you the servants of our God" (Is. 61:6).

This would be a profound change. The tasks of "ministry" would no longer be done just by priests, rabbis, or clergy, but by all of God's people. Just as the Spirit of the Lord had come upon Christ, enabling Him to accomplish God's work, so the Spirit would enable Christ's followers to accomplish God's work, too.

If you are a believer in Christ, God has empowered you with His Spirit. Are you carrying out His assignments for you?

HOLY WAR

(*see* War)

HOMELESSNESS

Jesus—A Homeless Man?

Jesus was born poor and lived poor. His comment in Matthew 8:20 even suggests that He was homeless. He never celebrated poverty, but He did ask His followers to forsake the common belief that real security comes from having wealth (Matt. 6:19–34).

Does that seem too difficult for those of us living in a society that craves financial security and independence? If so, consider that Christ is not asking us to do anything that He did not do Himself. He wants us to learn to hold what we have very lightly.

HOMEMAKING

Jewish Homemaking

Mark recounts Jesus' visit to the home of two of His new followers, Simon and Andrew. There He healed Simon's mother-in-law, after which, the text says, "she served them." Her service likely involved far more than cooking a meal.

In Jewish homes of the day, work began at sunrise. After a simple breakfast of curds and bread, the women went to the nearist well or stream to fill their jars with fresh water for the day's needs.

Some of the water was used to make the daily bread. The women ground kernels of wheat or barley by hand on the family millstone, then added water and some of the previous day's dough that had yeast in it. Kneaded and left to rise, the dough was shaped into several large, flat disks and baked in the household oven. The oven was fueled by grasses and brush gathered by the women and their children.

Other chores included spinning wool, weaving, making clothes and linens, mending, washing, producing pottery and other utensils for cooking, and preparing food. Far more than hobbies, these tasks were absolutely necessary to the family's survival. In that pre-industrial society, each household had to rely on its own labor and skills. Women acquired these from their mothers and in turn passed them on to their children.

Perhaps for that reason, first-century Jewish women enjoyed a "seamlessness" in their lives between work and home: the two were not separate categories of life, but parts of an integrated whole. Caring for children and providing for essentials such as food and clothing were highly valued in Hebrew culture.

Nor was a woman's work confined to material needs. The wife provided essential leadership in the home, shaping the cultural and religious values of her children. Formal schooling was rare, so she tutored them in craft skills and literacy. She was also expected to help them follow the customs and faith of Israel. It was through her that her children's Jewish heritage was determined.

The woman was responsible for preparing the home for the Sabbath. She filled the lamps with olive oil, prepared Sabbath food and special treats, and collected an extra day's water. No wonder that on each Sabbath, as part of the evening ceremony, her husband would recite to her Proverbs 31:10–31, an acknowledgement of her vital and varied work.

HONESTY

Free to Be Honest

The foundation of a believer's witness must be honesty. If we can be open with God about our own sinfulness (Ps. 51) and our continuing struggle with sin (Rom. 7:14–8:1), we won't be prone to mislead others about sin and faith. God knows we aren't sinless and He calls us to be honest (1 John 1:8).

As Paul stood before the hostile Jewish council, he could honestly declare that he had a clear conscience (Acts 23:1). He said the

same thing later when he and his accusers appeared before Governor Felix (Acts 24:16). That gave him tremendous freedom and boldness, even though his powerful opponents were hostile and wrong.

Honesty and a clear conscience are not the same as perfection. Paul was by no means perfect, just honest about his failures. He apologized, for example, after lashing out in anger (Acts 23:5). But he was real. He didn't cover up in an attempt to look good as a Christian witness.

Jesus does not ask us to project an impossibly perfect image. That would be a lie. Instead, He challenges us to admit our failures. He also delights in forgiving us when we do (Mark 11:25). If we can be honest about ourselves with others, it can give them hope for their own failings and turn them toward our gracious God.

Helping God Out

Do you resort to scheming when faced with trouble? Do you ever try to "help God out" in solving thorny problems?

Jacob had a tendency to do that, as his experience with Laban shows. Laban must have been a difficult father-in-law at best. He constantly found new ways to cheat his son-in-law, whether it involved a "bait-and-switch" bride (Gen. 29:14–30) or manipulation in the family business (Gen. 30:25–36).

At times Jacob responded as a principled man. But at other times he resorted to treating Laban in kind, using his own style of deception and scheming.

Eventually God told Jacob to return to his homeland with the promise, "I will be with you" (Gen. 31:3). But instead of trusting God and making a clean break with Laban, Jacob began complaining to his wives (Gen. 31:4–16), with the result that the family stole away, taking some of Laban's property with them (Gen. 31:17–21). Pursued and caught by Laban, Jacob grew angry and attempted to justify himself (Gen. 31:36–42).

Much of this could have been avoided if Jacob had simply trusted and acted upon God's promise to be with him. Instead, he further complicated his troubled family by causing Laban's daughters to turn on their father in deceit and treachery.

Are you like Jacob when you find yourself frustrated? Do you create ways to avoid God's clearly revealed will, just because it may be hard to carry out? Do you run from conflict and hide from facing up to problems, or do you deal with them out in the open?

For more on this topic, see EVASION, "Is Evasion Ethical?" page 133; FRAUD, "What's Wrong with Dross?" page 162.

HOPE

A Promise of Hope

The Book of Joel describes a dark and frightening event known as the "day of the Lord" (Joel 2:1–2; see 1:15). The doom and gloom of that judgment are all-encompassing: fields and pastures are ravaged by locusts as if burned to the ground (Joel 2:3–5), death steals upon the cities (Joel 2:6–9), and even the cosmos itself trembles (Joel 2:10–11).

Yet all of this terror is intended to bring about repentance (Joel 2:12–17), which results in a renewal of the land and the restoration of its inhabitants (Joel 2:18–27). Thus signs of hope outshine all previous disasters (Joel 2:25). The creation will be in full bloom, the rains will fall again, the threshing floors will be full of grain, the vats will overflow with oil and wine, and households will be satisfied and ringing with praise. Ultimately, the world will experience a spectacular spiritual renewal (Joel 2:28–32).

God offers people hope. He remains opposed to the proud and will destroy the wicked, but He preserves the humble and shows grace to those who repent (Prov. 3:34). As you consider the state of the world today and its prospects for the future, lay hold of God's promise of hope. "Whoever calls on the name of the Lord shall be saved" (Joel 2:32).

Light-bearers

Today's world is full of pain and bitterness. So many groups feel deep disappointment. So many problems seem to defy solutions. A glance at the daily headlines reveals a tide of distrust, discord, and disharmony sweeping the planet. Can Christians be effective in such an environment? Not unless they recognize the pain and perplexities that abound wherever real people encounter the real struggles of everyday existence.

Jeremiah serves as a model for how to make a sober, realistic appraisal of human need. As he witnessed the devastation left in the aftermath of Jerusalem's fall, he reflected on the darkness and despair that covered the city (Lam. 3:1–18). Yet having looked that harsh reality in the eye, he then turned an eye toward God. He recognized that God was the only hope that remained for his people— hope in God's mercy, compassion, faithfulness, and goodness (Lam. 3:22–24).

Like Jeremiah, Christians today have a message of hope to offer the world—the hope that is in Jesus Christ. We do not have all the answers to today's needs and problems, but we have the Lord. He is the light of the world, and we are called to bring His light into this dark world (Matt. 5:14–16; John 1:4–5; 1 John 1:5).

God could have used angels or miracles or numerous other means to announce His message. Instead, He has chosen everyday people to carry His message. Working through ordinary people facing the ordinary issues of day-to-day life, God intends to let the world know that there is hope beyond the problems and frustrations of the here and now.

Are you fulfilling this calling in your life?

The Dream Lives On

Imagine a world without sin. No problem is too great to be solved. No one goes without food. Everyone's needs are met. People live in peace and prosperity. Justice reigns. There is no crime. Death is unknown.

Down through history, various groups have grasped at that utopian ideal. None has succeeded. Yet the dream lives on, and for good reason: that was God's original intention for His creation. He made a perfect world and placed humankind in it with a mandate to "be fruitful and multiply" (Gen. 1:28). Likewise, He has promised to someday restore His creation to its original purpose and perfection (Rev. 21:1–4).

In the meantime, humanity must live with the memory of what Eden was and the hope of what the new creation will be. God helps people keep alive that vision of life with Him—which sometimes seems more like a dream—by offering occasional glimpses of it:

1. Genesis describes what Eden was like (Gen. 1:1–2:25). The account tells of a world

that was "very good" as God determines "good" (1:31).

2. In the Law, God promises to bless His people Israel with a land of peace and prosperity if they uphold His commandments (Lev. 26:3). Life in the Promised Land would not be a return to Eden, but it would have much of the same character. For example, God promised to make the people "fruitful" and help them "multiply" (26:9). (Note that this was a covenant agreement.)

3. In the Psalms, the world as it is, even in its fallen condition, is full of the "possessions" of the Lord. He has not left it to fend for itself. He maintains the earth and its creatures and rejoices in His works (Ps. 104:24–30).

4. Isaiah foresees new heavens and a new earth. There will be no more weeping or, by implication, sin or death. God's people will build houses in a renewed Jerusalem and will do meaningful, satisfying work (Is. 65:17–23).

5. Paul also looks forward to the day when creation will be set free from its "futility," a day when God's people will finally be "delivered from the bondage of corruption" (Rom. 8:19–25).

God's people live in hope. They base their lives on the promise that God's original design and purpose will not be crushed under the terrible load of sin, rebellion, and condemnation. Instead, because of Christ, they look forward to the day when they will enter a new world to live with God forever.

HOSPITALITY
When and How to Disagree

We live in a day in which any and everything is tolerated. No matter how outlandish or how strenuously we disagree with what others cherish or embrace, we accept their right to their opinion. There seems to be no basis for saying "no" anymore. Ours is an age of "I'm okay, you're okay."

But that is just not true. It would be more honest to affirm, "I'm *not* okay and you're *not* okay. We both need help that we can count on."

The early church faced a similar predicament. After Jesus' death and resurrection, many claimed to know Him and His message, even though their versions of the story differed remarkably. For instance, Paul faced a

conflicting gospel in Galatia and at Philippi and vehemently challenged his opponents' claims (Gal. 1:6–9; Phil. 3:1–4). Likewise, John warned against those who distort the truth (1 John 2:18–29; 4:1–6; 3 John 9–11).

The recipient of 2 John, possibly a woman (2 John 1), was given to hospitality (2 John 10)—a wonderfully Christlike virtue. But John was concerned to help her become more discerning and not lend the reputation of her household to those who would distort the truth about Christ (2 John 7, 11). He knew that not all who claim Christ are true followers. So believers must develop discernment if they are to remain loyal to truth.

Do you know the basics of what the Bible teaches? Can you detect error in the statements of others? When you do, do you know how to lovingly disagree on major issues of faith and truth?

Rude Rejection

Jesus' parable of the king's wedding feast for his son (Matt. 22:2–14) turns on an important detail of Jewish marriage custom. Wedding hosts sent out two invitations for a wedding. The first was sent far in advance to let people know that a wedding was being prepared and they were invited. This was necessary because weddings were major events that could last as long as a week. Furthermore, it took time for the replies to come back.

When all the preparations were complete, messengers were sent out with a second invitation telling the guests that the feast was ready and it was time for the celebration to begin. To turn down that second invitation—which was the one the guests in the parable refused (Matt. 22:3)—was not merely bad manners. It was considered a rejection of the host family's hospitality and a complete insult to their dignity.

God had sent Israel an early "invitation" to His Son's wedding through the Old Testament Law and prophets. Now that Jesus had arrived, proclaiming the second invitation, the nation was rejecting Him—a perilous choice.

HUMAN RESOURCES
Three-stage Development

God has a three-stage "human resource development" program for believers (James

1:2–5). Stage one involves *trials*—as many as we need, as hard as they need to be. That leads to stage two, *patience*—waiting for God with trust and perseverance. The final result is stage three, *wisdom*, which is God's goal of growth for personnel in His kingdom.

Do you want wisdom? Be careful when you ask for it! You could get a healthy dose of trials that demand patience. Eventually the process leads to wisdom—*if* you let it work.

Making Human Resources Work

Hiram of Tyre's letter to Solomon (2 Chr. 2:11–16) offers strong evidence that *people*, not plans, cause things to happen. Plans can help people initiate, guide, and evaluate their work, but it is human beings who must use their God-given skills and abilities to actually get things done.

Huram the master craftsman (2 Chr. 2:13) became a key resource in Solomon's project to build the temple. Working from plans largely developed by David (1 Chr. 28:11–19),

he led an army of skilled workers (2 Chr. 2:14) in creating an architectural masterpiece.

This example of Huram provides a case study for managers today. It shows that an effective plan is one that makes the best use of people's talents and capacities, one that encourages people to do what they do best. It suggests that plans and job descriptions have no value in and of themselves, but rather derive their value from the extent to which they empower workers to do constructive work.

HUMAN RIGHTS

(*see* Civil Rights)

HUMANE TREATMENT OF ANIMALS

(*see* Animals)

HUMILITY

True Humility

By recommending "lowliness of mind" (Phil. 2:3), Paul fired a broadside at the

Philippian culture—and our own. Like us, the Greeks and Romans exalted the lifestyles of the rich and famous.

Lowliness of mind? Who would want that? A "lowly" (or humble) person meant a slave—a servile, groveling, wretched individual. And for Paul to associate the word "lowly" with "mind" was a laughable contradiction: everyone assumed that lowly people had no intelligence, and everyone honored higher thinking and self-conceit.

Paul was not talking about a groveling, abject demeanor. Biblical humility means not thinking of oneself more highly than is true (Rom. 12:3), but rather acknowledging what one is—with all of one's strengths and weaknesses, pluses and minuses, successes and failures. Far from self-loathing, real humility makes people so truthful that they don't hesitate, when necessary, to tell about even their good qualities.

Do you want true humility? It comes from seeing yourself in relation to God. No wonder, then, that this virtue ran counter to the Roman worldview. Their concept of a god was grossly similar to their concept of humanity, and the mythological Roman gods were hardly noble.

By contrast, Jesus praised the humble, "the poor in spirit," (literally, "the destitute," Matt. 5:3). Humility is not an option for us as believers—it's an essential if we want to walk with God. Over and again, Scripture insists that we either walk humbly with Him, or not at all (Ps. 138:6; Is. 57:15; 1 Pet. 5:5–7). In short, a biblical lifestyle knows nothing of looking out chiefly for "number one". Just the opposite. With John the Baptist we need to say, "He must increase, but I must decrease" (John 3:30).

Humility affects these crucial areas of everyday life:

- our view of ourselves;
- our attitude toward controlling our circumstances;
- how good or bad we think we are; and
- our perspective on status and power.

Three Spiritual Virtues

What does it mean to know God? What are the marks of true spirituality? Micah offers a summary by giving three primary virtues that are to characterize every one of God's people: to do justice, to love mercy, and to walk humbly with God (Mic. 6:8).

This three-sided approach to life is balanced, unlike many of the fads and fetishes of modern spirituality. For example:

1. To act with justice keeps one in the real world rather than getting bogged down in theoretical abstractions that actually ignore oppression and injustice.

2. To love mercy keeps one in touch with the grace of a faithful God rather than succumbing to the tyranny of results-oriented spirituality, which tends to produce legalism, weariness, and burnout.

3. To walk humbly with God keeps one dependent on God's resources rather than trusting in merely human solutions, which creates unrealistic pressure on individuals and institutions.

Micah's triad of spiritual virtues is the high-water mark in his book. However, it is important to notice the urban context in which these values are to be lived out (Mic. 6:9). It is not enough to do justice, love mercy, or walk humbly with God in merely a private way of isolated spirituality. The demands of public life, represented in the city, are ever before us. For example, justice requires honest weights and measures, wages and audits, and restitution for sin (Mic. 6:10–12). Clearly, godly values have tremendous implication and application to everyday life.

Is that true for your life? These three virtues are qualities that every believer needs not only to understand, but to practice. Therefore, they warrant extensive study.

The Humblest Man on Earth

Most of us would balk if someone claimed, "I'm so humble!" It would be a self-defeating statement, because by definition, humility doesn't allow for boasting. Yet Numbers, which was written by Moses, tells us that Moses was the humblest man on the face of the earth (Num. 12:3). What are we to make of such a statement?

There are several possibilities. One is that this comment was inserted by a later writer such as Moses' successor, Joshua. We know that someone besides Moses had to have written about his death and burial in Deuteronomy 34. Since Joshua is believed to have written the book that bears his name (Josh. 24:26), it is possible that he completed Deuteronomy and also added this editorial comment to Numbers.

Another possibility is that the word translated "humble" does not mean lack of pride, but has more to do with affliction, oppression, and harsh treatment. That certainly fits with the relentless complaints and attacks that Moses endured from the people of Israel, such that he was overwhelmed (Num. 11:14). In that case, Numbers 12:3 may be an honest statement of Moses' weariness as he faced yet another assault, this time from his own sister and brother (Num. 12:1–2).

In any event, Moses was indeed a humble man. He put up with a great deal of grief and rarely complained. No wonder he was remembered as the foremost of Israel's prophets (Deut. 34:10). His example challenges us to consider our own response to harsh treatment. Could we be considered humble in the way we deal with others who oppose us? Remember: God is opposed to the proud, but He gives grace to the humble (Prov. 3:34; James 4:6).

The Power of Humility

How difficult is it for you to accept and admit that others are mightier than you? If you regard strength as the power to dominate, you'll always be intimidated by those who seem to have more than you—more expertise, more experience, more energy, more intelligence.

John the Baptist held a different understanding of strength (Matt. 3:11). He saw it as a gift from God to be used for divine purposes. That gave him tremendous power in his community (Matt. 3:5). His humility gave him the capacity to serve and to welcome others—in this case, Jesus—as valuable associates.

The Way Up Is Down

Of all the virtues Christ commended in the Beatitudes, it is significant that the first is humility, being "poor in spirit" (Matt. 5:3). That underlies all the others.

You cannot mourn (Matt. 5:4) without appreciating how insufficient you are to handle life in your own strength. That is humility.

You cannot be meek (Matt. 5:5) unless you have needed gentleness yourself. Knowing that need is humility.

You cannot hunger and thirst for righteousness (Matt. 5:6) if you proudly think of yourself as already righteous. Longing to fill that spiritual appetite demands humility. In a parable that Luke recorded, a humble tax collector prayed, "God, be merciful to me a sinner!" He went away justified, unlike a proud Pharisee who boasted of his righteousness (Luke 18:13).

You cannot be merciful (Matt. 5:7) without recognizing your own need for mercy. Jesus said that it's the person who is forgiven much that loves much (Luke 7:47). To confess your sin and ask God and others for forgiveness takes humility.

You cannot be pure in heart (Matt. 5:8) if your heart is filled with pride. God promises to exalt the humble, not the proud (James 4:10).

You cannot be a peacemaker (Matt. 5:9) if you believe that you are always right. To admit your own fallibility takes humility. Peace results when both warring parties move toward each other.

Finally, identifying with Christ no matter what the reaction of others (Matt. 5:10–12) demands a certain death to yourself and a renunciation of your own rights. Standing up under persecution demands Christlike humility.

*For more on this topic, see **FAME**, "A New Style of Fame," page 146.*

HUNGER

Feeding "the World"

Joseph's well-executed strategy ended up feeding the entire Middle East during a seven-year famine (Gen. 41:57). His economic plans, which helped to revitalize cities and alleviate world hunger, appear as mere background details in the larger account of how he was reconciled to his brothers (Gen. 41:46—47:27). But his example as a ruler—and in effect a manager—invites believers today to work in and through corporate and political structures on behalf of human needs, particularly hunger.

Consider Joseph's accomplishment: he leveraged the massive institutions of a pagan government to develop two seven-year plans—one for a "budget surplus," the other for a "budget deficit." During the years of plenty, Egypt set aside twenty percent of its crops in preparation for the coming years of scarcity, thanks to Joseph's initiative (Gen. 41:34–36). When the seven years of famine finally came, as predicted, the "deficits" were unusually severe, yet Joseph and the people found creative, cooperative ways to beat hunger. He managed what today we would call a food cooperative, a world food bank, a land bank, and urban housing projects (Gen. 47:13–26).

Joseph's strategy utilized strong, centralized government control. However, the key was not the control but the effective planning, a result of God's hand upon Joseph, working through him to carry out His purposes.

What human needs, great or small, does God want to meet through your life? Whatever skills He has placed within you, He wants you to use them to carry out meaningful work in service to others. And given the account of Joseph, it seems clear that God wants at least some of His people involved in businesses and governments for humanitarian purposes, for a public witness, and for international impact.

Gleaning in the 21st Century

Allowing the poor to glean the fields (Lev. 19:10) was ideally suited to the agriculturally based society of ancient Israel. But what counterpart to gleaning is there in a modern, information-based culture? Is there any way for the poor to live off the excess of the land today?

We must be careful not to press the concept of gleaning too far in an attempt to draw parallels. Many modern nations are vastly different from ancient Israel. Systems to help the poor are often far more developed, and certainly more complex. Still, it seems that modern-day efforts fall far short of what is needed. Does the concept of gleaning offer any ideas for us?

Consider the "throwaway" nature of life today. Between homes, offices, factories, restaurants, hospitals, military installations, airports, and the like—to say nothing of farms—people leave lots of leftovers. If they did not, there would be no burgeoning flea market industry, no garage and yard sales, no used goods stores, no used car lots, no landfill crisis, and no movement for recycling.

Can any of those leftovers be directed toward the poor? The spirit of gleaning at least encourages us to think seriously about it. For example:

- How could programs, organizations, and establishments that give (or sell at thrift rates) used clothing and other goods to the poor be expanded and made more efficient?
- Is there an opportunity to enlist the poor in the nation's recycling efforts?
- In recent years, the distance between available jobs and the poor has often increased with migration to the suburbs, away from inner cities. Is there "excess transportation" that could be made available at low cost or no cost?
- What tax laws need to be considered (or reconsidered) that might make it easier for the poor to work at jobs related to household chores and lawn care?
- What projects and processes might intentionally use muscle power, rather than more "efficient" mechanical or electrical power, in order to put people to work?
- What partnerships could churches and denominations develop with industry to channel remaindered, returned, and used goods to the poor?
- How could the food industry cooperate with soup kitchens and homeless shelters to use leftover food rather than throwing it away?

HUSBANDS

(see also Male-Female Relationships; Marriage)

Portrait of a Husband

Many men struggle to define what it means to be a husband today. Perhaps Isaiah's description of God, the "husband" of Israel (Is. 54:5) can help. Isaiah's portrait suggests that a godly husband is one who:

- helps his wife find fulfillment (Is. 54:1–3);
- seeks to allay her fears (Is. 54:4, 14, 15);
- builds up her reputation (Is. 54:4);
- displays godly character toward his partner (Is. 54:5);
- does not allow prolonged conflict or lingering anger to keep him separated from his wife (Is. 54:6–8);

- replaces anger with kindness (Is. 54:9–10);
- brings comfort in the midst of stress (Is. 54:11–12);
- instructs the couple's children in spiritual matters (Is. 54:13); and
- protects his wife from dangers and threats (Is. 54:16–17).

God's relationship toward Israel is a picture of committed love. Husbands, imagine giving that sort of incredible gift to your wife! What can you do to get started?

HYGIENE

A Concern for Hygiene

Bodily discharges (Lev. 15:2–15) were not evil, but they did render a person "unclean" and therefore temporarily disqualified from approaching a holy God. The hygienic laws in Leviticus 15 and elsewhere were given primarily for this religious reason. However, God clearly was concerned about His people's health and hygiene.

Clean vs. Unclean

God's list of "creeping things" (Lev. 11:29) is among some one hundred "clean versus unclean" laws itemized in Leviticus 11–15. These laws had both a spiritual and a hygienic aspect to them.

As early as Noah, God designated certain animals as "clean" (Gen. 7:2), meaning that they were acceptable for sacrifice. Later, in the Law, God described certain practices and bodily functions as "unclean": for example, touching a corpse, menstruation, and eating the flesh of an "unclean" animal, among others. These things rendered a person ritually unfit to participate in religious ceremonies. However, there was no suggestion of moral defilement in them; they were not sins.

In Leviticus, however, God linked "clean" and "unclean" with food laws. In effect, this section of the Law formed the basis for Israel's national health policy. It not only addressed questions about food (Lev. 11), but also certain childbirth issues (Lev. 12), bodily functions (Lev. 15), contagious skin diseases, especially leprosy (Lev. 13–14), and related matters such as mildew and a toxic environment.

Of what relevance are these laws today? Since believers no longer live under the Mosaic system of sacrifices, the ceremonial implications of "clean" and "unclean" no longer apply. Still, "clean" and "unclean" reflected God's holiness (Lev. 10:10), and Christians need to pursue a holy lifestyle (1 Pet. 1:15). Furthermore, they need to look out for the conscience of others, for whom certain things remain "clean" and "unclean" (Rom. 14:14–19).

What about the hygienic dimension of these laws? Again, Christians are not under dietary laws. Nevertheless, it's important to note that these laws took into account the best interests of individuals and the community. Do ours? We have good precedent here to promote wise policies for the benefit of people's health, protection of the environment, and the control and cure of diseases.

HYPOCRISY

Bad Religion

Have you ever been disappointed or even angry with religion? Perhaps you've heard someone say that the church is full of hypocrites. Maybe you've even said that yourself! Isaiah rebuked Israel for practicing bad religion—religion that benefited no one and offended God (Is. 58:1–14). The prophet specifically zeroed in on fasting (Is. 58:2–5), pointing out ways in which the people misused this important spiritual discipline:

- They nagged God in the interests of their own personal gain.
- While seeking their own self-interests, they exploited their laborers.
- Their fasts became a source of strife, debate, and hostility toward others.
- They used severe fasting practices to call attention to themselves.

After challenging these practices, Isaiah described what true fasting ought to be like (Is. 58:6–13):

- It should result in bringing relief to the oppressed.
- It should result in feeding the hungry.
- It should result in the poor being taken into homes for shelter and clothing.
- Superior attitudes of finger-pointing and evil should decline and ultimately disappear.

- It should lead to repairing things, including damaged relationships.
- It should involve treating the Sabbath as a day to worship the Lord rather than continuing to work for personal gain.

It's easy to point the finger at others and criticize or ridicule their religious practices and spiritual life. But what about your own patterns of faith? How do they measure up to the Lord's description of true religion? If there are places where you need to change, find at least one other person who will hold you accountable for making the necessary reforms.

Jeremiah's Rebuke at the Temple

"Pure and undefiled religion," wrote James, involves caring for orphans and widows and keeping oneself morally pure (James 1:27). By that measure, the people of Jeremiah's day were practicing a religion that was anything but "pure and undefiled." According to the prophet (Jer. 7:5–9), they:

- failed to implement justice in their business dealings;
- oppressed the weak and disadvantaged, such as foreigners, orphans, and widows;
- committed manslaughter;
- practiced idolatry;
- stole from each other;
- committed adultery; and
- lied under oath and went back on their word.

Having committed these "abominations," the people then came to the temple, satisfied that God would continue to bless them (Jer.

7:10). They believed the lies of false prophets who assured them that their prosperity would be unaffected as long as they kept up a pretense of worshiping the Lord (Jer. 7:4, 8).

In response, the Lord told Jeremiah to stand in the gate of the temple and preach a sermon, denouncing the people's hypocrisy and warning them to change their ways (Jer. 7:1–3). Amended behavior was called for, not pious pronouncements or new laws. This was not a new demand, but the old command to love God and to love one another (Lev. 19:18; Deut. 10:12–13; compare Matt. 22:37–39).

Doing justice and preaching grace—that is the biblical model for God's people to follow, no matter when or where they live. If we say we are God's people, then we must not only "worship" Him with our rituals, but with our day-to-day lives.

A Good Day for Mercy

The incident in Luke 13:10–17 put the ruler of the synagogue and his fellow rabbis to shame. Jesus rebuked them for showing more concern for their animals than for a disabled woman. They grumbled about profaning the Sabbath, but Jesus pointed out that any time is appropriate to meet a genuine need; *any* day—even the Sabbath—is a proper day for acts of mercy.

Actually, of all the days on which the woman could have been given rest from her affliction, the Sabbath—a day of rest—was perhaps the most appropriate.

Jesus put a name on the legalists' attitude and behavior: hypocrisy. He wanted everyone to see that the outward appearance of righteousness often masks inner unrighteousness.

I

IDEAL SELF

Accepting Our Roots

Jesus' family tree hides nothing. His heritage was multiethnic and included several unattractive or embarrassing individuals. Indeed, the circumstances surrounding His own birth might have raised questions in the minds of some. But Jesus never denied His ancestry or allowed others to shame Him. If

we want to be like Him, we need to understand and accept our roots in terms of culture, race, gender, and reputation. Moreover, like Jesus we want to avoid demeaning anyone else's heritage.

Admitting Our Vulnerability

Matthew's inclusion of the temptation of Jesus is remarkable. It shows that the sinless Lord of the universe was tempted, just as we are (Heb. 4:15–16). If we want to be like Jesus, we must accept that temptation is real—as is the possibility of overcoming temptation. But we need to be open about our struggles. In doing so we honor God, recognize the power of sin, and encourage others to do likewise.

Affirm Others

Jesus invested Himself in the development of other people, particularly the Twelve. He gave them responsibility and authority, resisting the temptation to get the job done "right" by doing it Himself. In doing so, He accepted the risk that they might fail. Of course, He gave them adequate preparation before sending them out, and on their return He affirmed them on their successful completion of the mission. Jesus calls us to help others grow. If we want to be like Him, we will share the joys and risks of working together with our brothers and sisters.

Commit Ourselves to Other Believers

John the Baptist was not your average individual. He was an unexpected child. He lived in the wilderness—the "other side of the tracks" for that day. He wore strange clothing and ate strange food. He was pugnacious, even offensive at times. Yet he helped launch Jesus' career. In return, Jesus had nothing but praise for him (Matt. 11:7–15). If we want to be like Jesus, we must not pick and choose our brothers and sisters in God's family. We need to embrace other believers and demonstrate our unity in Christ, no matter how awkward or inconvenient.

Radical Change Needed

In His Sermon on the Mount, Jesus explained the values of the kingdom. Money, prayer, relationships, possessions, information, and power were a few of the categories He redefined from God's perspective. He showed that following Him will involve radical change for most of us. It may mean undoing the way we've always done things and rethinking traditional sources of wisdom from our parents and culture. To become like Jesus involves a tough-minded review of our values and a thorough change in our behavior.

Engaging the World's Pain

Jesus' entry into human life was fraught with awkward tensions and human dilemmas: a miraculous but nevertheless embarrassing conception, an earthly father who was considering a quiet divorce, an outraged king resorting to infanticide, an early childhood in a strange culture, and a return to a homeland that remained hostile and dangerous. We, too, are all born into some troubles and circumstances. If we want to be like Jesus, we need to face up to the world and remain very much in it, despite all its troubles.

The Word Plus the Walk

Jesus' life was not an open book, readable by all. To be sure, He lived a perfect, model life. But even that could not stand alone as an undeniable witness. His actions needed interpretation. So He supplemented His good deeds with good news. In the same way, we need to verbally declare our faith if we want to be like Christ. Certainly we need to back up our words with a Christlike lifestyle. But what we tell others gives meaning to our quiet walk and good deeds.

Serving Others

The Sermon on the Mount was immediately followed by "deeds in the valley." Christlike values lead to servant actions—and it was obedient action that Jesus cared about, not just sermonizing (Matt. 7:21–29). Jesus modeled how to do the will of God by actively serving more than twenty-five different people (Matt. 8–9). These included such undesirables as lepers, an officer of the Roman occupation troops, the sick, the demon-possessed, cave dwellers, tax collectors, and a diseased, outcast woman. If we want to be like Jesus, we need to befriend those who are weak, under oppression, or without Christ. Like Him, we need to become "a friend of sinners" (Matt. 11:19). He offered much more than religious information—He served them.

Time for a Checkup

How can we evaluate the quality of our faith? Are there any ways to assess spiritual progress and growth? Yes, Paul gives us a number of them in Ephesians 5.

Ephesians can be viewed as two halves of one big picture about giving and receiving faith. Ephesians 1–3 describe what God has done for us in Christ. Ephesians 4–6 describe what we are to do in response to what God has done for us.

We are called to live for God and to be imitators of God (Eph. 5:1), just as children follow after the patterns seen in their parents. Here are some of the patterns that a godly lifestyle would include:

- Living in love, which means giving of ourselves sacrificially for the benefit of others, just as Christ has done for us (Eph. 5:2).
- Forsaking selfish pursuits such as self-seeking immorality and ruthless greed (Eph. 5:3, 5).
- Replacing filthy talk, flippant chatter, and unkind jesting with communication rooted in thanksgiving to God and affirmation of others (Eph. 5:4, 20).
- Exercising discernment about what we are told so as not to be susceptible to trickery from others (Eph. 5:6–7, 15).
- Bowing out from situations where evil is the agenda (Eph. 5:11–12).
- Managing our time well (Eph. 5:16).

Perhaps you'll want to develop your own list of Christlike patterns from this passage and others. Consider asking a close believing friend to assess your progress over several days or weeks. Allow these patterns of godliness to affect your own life before using them to evaluate others (Matt. 7:1–6).

For more on this topic, see SERVICE, "Leadership with Humility," page 364.

IDENTITY
Comparisonitis Can Kill You

How do you establish your identity? Are you always comparing yourself to others? If so, you suffer from "comparisonitis," a malady that can kill you! Consider the Pharisee in Jesus' parable (Luke 18:9–14). He was so proud of himself that he started off his prayer with a comparison: "God, I thank you that I am not like other men."

Do you do that? Do you try to build up your self-esteem by looking down on others less fortunate or gifted than you? If so, you are standing on shaky ground because your identity becomes uncertain. You can never be sure about yourself on those terms. Sooner or later, someone is bound to come along who is better than you in some way. You also

risk loneliness, because no one cultivates friends by always finding fault with others in order to feel better about oneself.

In contrast to the Pharisee, the second man in Jesus' parable looked to God in order to see himself properly. Doing so exposed his sin, but it also brought about God's forgiveness and restoration. This man shows us the path to true identity. It is based on honesty about ourselves and becoming like Christ.

For more on this topic, see COMMITMENT, "God's Family Album," page 70; CONFIDENCE, "Crises of Confidence," page 82.

IDLENESS
(*see* Laziness)

IDOLATRY
A Sobering Object Lesson

Shiloh was a sobering object lesson for Judah. Once the center of Israel's religious life and the site of the tabernacle (see 1 Sam. 1:3), Shiloh lay in ruins in Jeremiah's day, and its people had been taken captive by the Assyrians. Why? Because the northern kingdom of Israel had turned away from the Lord to idols. Jeremiah warned that the same outcome awaited the people of Jerusalem—and for the same reason (1 Sam. 7:12–15).

Jeremiah's message of judgment must have sounded incredible. Jerusalem was the site of the temple, the magnificent house of worship that David had envisioned and Solomon had built to the glory of God (see 2 Chr. 5:1). How could God allow His temple and its city to be destroyed? Yet if anyone doubted Jeremiah's warning, all they had to do was travel a little more than twenty miles north to Shiloh.

Apparently, few people heeded the prophet's word, because Jerusalem fell to the Babylonians within a few short years. The temple was burned and most of the people were either killed or deported.

This tragic outcome challenges us to consider whether idols exist in our own lives. We don't bow down to images of wood and stone, but if we allow anything to take the place of God, then we are practicing idolatry. This can happen in our work, in our relationships, and, like the people of ancient Judah, even in our houses of worship. In that case, God may take away the thing that we hold so dear in order to redirect our attention and affection to where they belong—on Him. The first commandment is still in effect: "You shall have no other gods before Me" (Ex. 20:3).

Idolatry of the Heart

Perhaps you tend to think of an idol as a figure made from wood or stone to which primitive people pray and offer sacrifices. But the Lord defined what an idol is when he told Ezekiel that it is something that a person puts before him in a way that causes him to stumble into iniquity (Ezek. 14:4). Idols are not just the carved objects that sit in pagan temples; they are the godless cravings and commitments that rule in our hearts.

The people of Ezekiel's day set up these "idols of the heart," even as they continued to practice their religious rituals. Having committed themselves to ungodly purposes,

they came to the prophets expecting to find out what the Lord had to say. God promised to confound these hypocrites by telling them whatever they wanted to hear. Ultimately their idols would fail and judgment would come (Ezek. 14:4–5).

This is a sobering condemnation. Apparently it is possible to commit ourselves to things that are utterly opposed to God, and then expect God to bless us in our pursuit of those things! The worst thing that could happen would be for Him to bless us, for then we would be ensnared by our own worthless gods rather than liberated to find genuine goodness in the living God.

Modern-day Idols

Perhaps you think of idols as objects of wood, stone, or metal worshiped by ancient civilizations or primitive peoples. That perception is accurate, but from the Bible's point

of view, idolatry fundamentally involves allowing anything or anyone to stand in the place of God.

The ancient Babylonians fashioned many idols for both public and private worship (Is. 46:6–7). But the Lord ridiculed this practice, for the gods of Babylon were impotent: they had to be hand-carried, as they were unable to move on their own, they were mute, and they were powerless.

Yet as we read the Lord's rebuke in Isaiah, it's worth considering the extent to which people practice forms of idolatry today. For example, modern society has come to rely so heavily on technology and government to solve its problems that many people no longer feel a need for God. They seem to place as much faith in human ingenuity as the ancients placed in their carved images.

Likewise, certain psychotherapies practically do away with any need for the God of the Scriptures. Instead, they rely on their own principles and methods to deal with guilt and sin, and to make people healthy and whole. They hold out the promise that people can become all that they were meant to be *apart from God.*

A third form of modern idolatry is actually a relic of ancient idolatry. Many people today dabble in occult practices using physical objects such as Ouija boards, Tarot cards, and crystals to tell fortunes and receive supernatural messages. Likewise, horoscopes are as popular as ever, and those who promote them even boast in the fact that astrology, on which horoscopes are based, was heavily practiced in ancient Babylon.

Forms of idolatry such as these may be more sophisticated than the shrines set up by the ancient pagans, but they are idolatry just the same. They have been made to stand in the place of God.

The Lord will not allow those who practice these things to go unpunished. Consider His judgment on the Babylonians (Is. 47:10–15). Is there any reason why He would not pour out just as much wrath on idolators today? He still hates idolatry (Deut. 7:25–26). The first and second commandments are still there (Ex. 20:2–6). And the Lord is still who He declared Himself to be to the ancients: "I am God, and there is no other; I am God, and there is none like Me" (Is. 46:9).

Contemporary Pagans

Today's increasingly secular society may seem to have little in common with the world of Jeremiah's day. Yet the truth is that many people who disavow the traditional idea of God or gods nevertheless have a very similar mind-set to the pagan idol worshipers, or "Gentiles" (Jer. 10:2), of ancient times.

Jeremiah lived in a world of cultures based on idolatry (Jer. 10:3–10). His own nation, Judah, was quite given over to idols during the reigns of Manasseh and Amon, probably the period when Jeremiah was a boy (2 Kin. 21). In fact, the prophet observed that Judah had as many gods as it had cities (Jer. 2:28). Likewise, each society surrounding Judah worshiped its pantheon of gods. The Babylonians, for example, were said to be "insane with their idols" (Jer. 50:38).

Looking back on these religions from today's perspective, our tendency may be to think of an idol merely as an object crafted from wood or metal to whom superstitious, benighted pagans bowed down in hopes of receiving good fortune or avoiding misfortune. But that would be a superficial understanding. An idol is anything that is sacred to a person, in that it defines self-worth, becomes the controlling center of life, and takes priority over all other loyalties.

In light of that definition, what are some of the idols that people worship today? Certainly work and possessions would have to qualify for many people, especially given the addictive way in which they pursue them. What would be an idol for you? What do you hold "sacred" in the sense that it defines who you are, controls your life, and is the last thing that you would ever let go?

Jeremiah recognized the idols of his day for what they were—futile customs that supplanted the true God (Jer. 10:3, 10). Are you pursuing futility at the cost of knowing the living Lord?

The Counsel of Idols

Some managers make the mistake of gathering about them only those who see things as they do, and who depend on the managers for their jobs. As a result, these managers tend to hear only what people think they want to hear.

The people of Hosea's day made a similar mistake when it came to seeking advice in spiritual matters. They sought the counsel of idols (Hos. 4:12). But of course, since the idols were nothing but wood crafted by their own hands, the "advice" the people received invariably turned out to be whatever they wanted hear.

To what extent do you surround yourself with "yes-people"? Are you open to what others have to tell you, even if their perspectives are different from yours? If you tend to shy away from conflict or dismiss information that makes you uncomfortable, watch out! You may even find yourself avoiding direction from God because you know He may disagree with your thinking.

For more on this topic, see ADDICTION, "The Respectable Idol," page 7.

ILLEGAL SEARCH AND SEIZURE
Grasping for What Others Have

Imagine a society that allowed powerful citizens to seize property and lands whenever they wanted, especially from those who were too weak or poor to defend themselves. That was the situation in Micah's day. The wealthy and powerful of Judah were grabbing real estate that belonged to others, by force and even violence if necessary (Mic. 2:2; 3:10).

The prophet rightly decried this practice, which amounted to robbery and murder. The leaders of the country allowed it to go unchecked. Indeed, they not only denied justice to the poor, but essentially "skinned them alive" in order to enrich themselves (Mic. 3:3, 10; compare Prov. 22:16).

In seizing the lands of their countrymen, the powerful businesspeople of Judah were violating a key principle of the Law. They were stealing people's allotted portion of the Promised Land, in disobedience to the Ten Commandments (Ex. 20:13, 15, 17), the law of redemption (Lev. 25:23–28), and the law against changing landmarks (Deut. 19:14). For the breaking of these laws, the Lord promised to exact retribution in kind by allowing foreigners to seize the lands of Judah (Mic. 2:4).

The justice that the Lord expected in ancient Judah is the same kind of justice that He expects today, particularly among His people. The New Testament strongly warns believers against covetousness (Eph. 5:5; James 4:1–5). Longing for more can lead to longing for what belongs to others, which in turn can lead to injustice as we grasp for the things we want.

ILLEGITIMATE BIRTHS
Overcoming a Tough Start

What hope is there for a child born to a prostitute? Society tends to have low expectations—and sometimes downright hostility—for people born out of wedlock. Such was the case for Jephthah (Judg. 11:1).

The product of his father's dalliance with a prostitute, Jephthah was not only excluded but expelled from his more "respectable" family (Judg. 11:2). Like many rejects, he led the life of a criminal (Judg. 11:3), though he and his gang of raiders may have harassed the Ammonites more than the Israelites.

The irony of Jephthah's life was that when Israel faced war with Ammon, the leaders of his hometown came looking for Jephthah to deliver them! They offered no apology; they merely appealed for help. To his credit, Jephthah agreed to help them after negotiating his terms (Judg. 11:9–11), and God gave him the victory (Judg. 11:33).

Jephthah's life is a good illustration of the truth that God does not judge people on the basis of appearances (Deut. 10:17; 1 Sam. 16:7; Rom. 2:11). He can overcome any background and use any set of circumstances to accomplish His purposes.

IMMIGRANTS
Seizing an Opportunity

Sometimes God puts an opportunity in our way that could advance our career and bring prosperity. That's what happened to Jacob and his sons when they migrated to Egypt. Of course, they were hardly looking for a career move; mainly they wanted to escape the famine in Canaan, and they ended up relocating largely at the request of Joseph. But once they arrived, circumstances created a unique opportunity.

Joseph was faced with a bit of a problem: how to introduce his long-lost family to Pharaoh. Pharaoh had an extremely high regard for Joseph. But what would be his reaction when he learned that Jacob and his sons were shepherds and ranchers? Those occupations were an "abomination" to the Egyptians (Gen. 46:34), fit only for slaves. (One can gain some idea of how detestable they were by noting that when the brothers came on their second journey to Egypt, bringing Benjamin with them, they were forced to eat by themselves, away from the Egyptians (Gen. 43:32). Apparently Hebrews and shepherds were synonymous in the Egyptian mind.

But Joseph turned this potential embarrassment into an opportunity. He instructed his brothers to boldly claim their skills rather than downplay their occupation. He knew that Pharaoh probably would never change his opinion of shepherds, but most likely the ruler at least would to allow the family to live by themselves in the Goshen district.

That's exactly how the plan worked out (Gen. 47:1–6). But in addition, Pharaoh's respect for Joseph led to a request that the brothers have oversight over Pharaoh's own livestock. He still detested shepherds. But when it came to the care of his own animals, apparently he preferred to employ the kin of someone he trusted.

The assignment matched the skills and experience of the brothers. Like many immigrants around the world today, they were willing and able to do work that people in host cultures find unacceptable. As a result, they prospered in the land (Gen. 47:27; compare Ex. 1:7).

A Legacy of Resentment

Solomon's census of all foreigners living in Israel (2 Chr. 2:17–18) recalls David's census several years earlier. On that occasion, seventy thousand people died as a result of the king's foolishness (1 Chr. 21:1–14). Apparently God did not oppose Solomon's census as He had David's, but the count created long-term problems that came to a head under Solomon's successor.

Solomon's purpose in numbering the people was to conscript a labor force for his numerous building projects, beginning with the temple. The government could not gain much revenue by taxing these aliens, since foreigners could not own land. So forced labor was used as a form of taxation.

In addition to 153,600 foreign workers, Solomon contracted thirty thousand laborers "out of all Israel" (1 Kin. 5:13). Perhaps these were unskilled Israelites who could not pay the heavy taxes that the king levied on the rest of the Hebrew population (1 Kin. 12:4). These he sent to Lebanon in shifts, but the aliens he sent to the mountains under heavy supervision. Perhaps they might not have come back had they gone to Lebanon.

Later Solomon conscripted even more aliens to work on his palace complex and various storage cities around the empire (see 1 Kin. 9:19). These foreigners were descendants of the peoples Israel had conquered in the days of Joshua (2 Chr. 8:7–9).

Solomon's use of heavy taxes and forced labor allowed him to take Israel to its zenith as an empire. But it also left a legacy of resentment that boiled over when his successor, Rehoboam, determined to increase the burden (2 Chr. 10:1–19).

IMMORTALITY

Eternal Life

From beauty creams to vitamins to aerobics, many people today are pursuing a "fountain of youth." They want to avoid growing old, perhaps because it leads to the final, ultimate reality, death. That reality is so painful to most people that they won't even consider it. They make little or no preparation for their death and its aftermath.

John offers the one way that a person can actually do something about his or her death. He speaks of a revolutionary promise that God has made—we can live happily forever (1 John 2:24–25)! God makes that promise of eternal life for those who put their faith in Jesus Christ.

Have you chosen to act on God's promise? Are you trusting in Christ for your eternal life? If not, why not do so now? If you already have, then tell someone else about God's promise today.

Is There Life After Death?

Throughout history people have wondered whether this life is all there is. Is there a heaven or hell? Or does it all end here?

Job asked that same question as he contemplated his sufferings (Job 14:14). He believed that death would end his pain (Job 14:13); but would it also end his existence? Elsewhere Job described death as the "way of no return" (Job 16:22) and the "king of terrors" (Job 18:14). At times it appears that Job did not have a particularly positive outlook as he faced the end of life.

Yet in reading about Job's perspective on death, it is important to remember that he was working from a smaller knowledge base than God's people have today. He probably had no written portion of Scripture, and he was unfamiliar with the work of Jesus to deliver people from sin and death (Rom. 6:23; 1 Cor. 15:20–28).

Yet even without these important truths, Job had a certain confidence that he would see God after death. In fact, his stirring declaration of faith, beginning with the words, "I know that my Redeemer lives" (Job 19:25–27), has provided hope for generations of believers (helped in no small measure by George Frideric Handel, the eighteenth-century composer who set Job's lines to music as part of his masterpiece, "Messiah").

Whatever questions about death may have lingered from the days of Job, Jesus answered them when He declared, "He who believes in Me, though he may die, he shall live" (John 11:25). For that reason, Jesus' followers can celebrate even in the midst of grief and mourning over the loss of friends and loved ones. Jesus has promised eternal life to believers, free from all tears, sorrow, and pain (Rev. 21:4). That is why when it comes to death, Christians are a people of hope.

Set for Life—But Then What?

The parable in Luke 16:19–31 draws a stark contrast between the rich man and the poor beggar Lazarus. The key to understanding it is to notice who Jesus told it to—the Pharisees, whom Luke describes as "lovers of money" (Luke 16:14). Like the rich man, they were set for life, but not for eternity. They displayed an image of righteousness but were actually hypocrites (Luke 16:15). Careful to preserve the letter of a greatly expanded Mosaic tradition, they violated the spirit of the Mosaic Law. Worst of all, they rejected Jesus as the Christ (Luke 16:31).

So Jesus told the parable to rebuke them. He was not saying that all the poor will go to heaven and all the rich will go to hell. He was warning those who live as though this life were all that matters: they are playing with fire!

Clearly, it is a dangerous thing to have it made in this life. The insensitive rich man received his "good things" during his lifetime (Luke 16:25). He was like the men described in Psalm 17:14 who "have their portion in this life," but have no portion in the life to come. Likewise, Psalm 73 talks about the wicked who appear to have it all: They live above the everyday problems that everyone else faces. They wear their pride like jewelry. They have more wealth than they can possibly use. Yet they belittle those who live hand-to-mouth. With all of their status and power they strut through life, giving not a care for God. Who needs Him?

But in eternity, the tables turn, as the rich man discovers to his horror (Luke 16:23). The parable concludes on an ominous note. Jesus describes the hardness of people who are determined to reject God. Despite plenty of evidence to warn them that they are headed for ruin, they persist in their ways, just as the Pharisees did.

This grim parable moves one to ask: "What portion do I value most in life? Which am I more interested in: being set for life or set for eternity?" The writer of Psalm 73 made his commitment clear:

Whom have I in heaven but You?
And there is none upon earth that I desire besides You.
My flesh and my heart fail;
But God is the strength of my heart and my portion forever.

There's a Welcome Here

Perhaps you or someone you know feels hesitant about spiritual things. Matters of faith may feel forbidding, even scary. Religion may seem like nothing but judgment and condemnation.

Yet Jesus came not to condemn, but to save. His primary purpose was to offer life to dying people, inviting them to experience forgiveness, healing, and hope. "Come!" He says to those who are thirsty, "Whoever desires, let him take the water of life freely" (Rev. 22:17; see also John 7:37–38).

Centuries prior to Jesus' coming, a prophet foretold this invitation (Is. 55:1, 3):

Ho! Everyone who thirsts,
Come to the waters;
And you who have no money,
Come, buy and eat.
Yes, come, buy wine and milk
Without money and without price . . .
Incline your ear, and come to Me.
Hear, and your soul shall live.

This is a powerful invitation because the same Jesus who makes it wields the power to withdraw it from those who refuse His call and continue to live in rebellion and sin (Rev. 22:14–15, 18–19). Just as He has authority to welcome us into eternal life, so He has the authority not to welcome us. Yet in His grace He chooses to offer life to sinful people.

You may be confused about many issues of religion, but hear God's gracious offer: Jesus wants to forgive your sins and welcome you into new life. If you haven't already accepted His invitation, why not do so now and begin the exciting journey that leads to eternal life?

For more on this topic, see **DEATH,** *"Beyond Death," page 97; "Death Loses Its Power," page 97.*

IMPERFECTION

(*see* Perfection)

IMPRISONMENT

Paul's Roman House

Paul rented a house at his own expense (Acts 28:30), possibly in south Rome. Technically under house arrest, he spent his time in outreach to both Jews and Gentiles, but especially to Gentiles (Acts 28:28–29).

The restrictions under which Paul lived should have held back his efforts to proclaim the gospel, but they "actually turned out for the furtherance of the gospel" (Phil. 1:12). Confined to his lodgings and handcuffed to one of the soldiers who guarded him in four-hour shifts, he was free to receive visitors and talk with them about the gospel. The guards and the official in charge of presenting his case were left in no doubt about the reason for his being in Rome. The message of Christ

actually became a topic of discussion among them (Phil. 1:13). This encouraged Christians in Rome to become more bold in their witness to the faith than ever before.

For more on this topic, see **CIVIL DISOBEDIENCE,** *"Convicts with Conviction," page 66.*

IMPULSIVENESS

(*see* Maturity)

INCEST

(*see also* Sexuality)

Human Sexuality: Awesome Potential for Good or Evil

Sexuality is one of the most powerful dimensions of human life. Sexual union can create incredible bonds between a loving couple. It also can lead to the birth of a baby, producing another human being in the image of God. Yet sex can also bring horrible devastation when misused—for example, through the violence of rape, the out-of-control obsession of sexual addiction, or the tragic sexual abuse of another human.

God gave humankind the gift of sexuality, and He is very concerned that people understand its proper use. So He included clear warnings about its misuse (Lev. 18:6–30). The explicit tone of this teaching reflects the nomadic, tent-dwelling closeness that the ancient Israelite families experienced day in and day out. How should they conduct themselves toward each other living in such proximity? God gave them a number of principles to guide them.

The people were not to engage in incest. They were instructed not to "uncover the nakedness" of other members of the family, including one's father or mother (Lev. 18:7); stepmother (Lev. 18:8); sister or half-sister (Lev. 18:9, 11; 20:17); grandchild (Lev. 18:10, 17); aunt (Lev. 18:12–14; 20:19–20); daughter-in-law (Lev. 18:15; 20:12); sister-in-law (Lev. 18:16; 20:21), except in the case of a widowed sister-in-law (Deut. 25:5–10); and mother-in-law (Lev. 20:14).

Note that this opposition to incest was presented in terms of God's *holiness* being reflected in marriage. No appeal was made to the genetic dangers of inbreeding (though that is of concern). Others outside the family were to be respected as well, including a neighbor's spouse; such intercourse amounted to adultery (Lev. 18:20; 20:10).

Leviticus sounds a call to "holy sexuality" and "holy love" (Lev. 20:26). There is no nervousness about sexuality here. Rather, the commands are evidence that sex is a beautiful and powerful gift from God. He wants to restore its significance and preserve its dignity rather than leave it as a plaything for sinners who are prone to misuse it.

INDEBTEDNESS

(*see* Debt)

INDIVIDUALISM

You Are Unique

A fundamental truth of Scripture is that God has created people in His image (Gen. 1:26–28)—not only humanity in general, but every individual, including you (Ps. 33:15). The same God whose mind and power fashioned the stars, the seas, the animals, and all other human beings has carefully, intentionally, and individually crafted you. You are not just a collection of molecules thrown together by random chance. The Lord of the universe has called you into being.

This truth has profound implications. Consider three of the most important:

1. *You are unique.* Even though you share many things in common with other people, you are essentially one of a kind. No one else has been given exactly the same makeup as God has given you. Your face, your fingerprints, your voice, and your genetic makeup are matched by no one else's. Likewise, God

INDIVIDUALISM

has handcrafted you with your personality, your unique set of talents and motivations, and your special "bent" in life. This leads to the fact that . . .

2. *You have a unique purpose.* Not only has God made you, He has designed you for His special reasons. He has crafted you to carry out a unique purpose and mission in life—what the New Testament calls your "good works." (Eph. 2:10). God intended that your life would be aimed toward these special ends before He created you. For that reason, ultimate meaning in life comes from discovering and carrying out this unique purpose. That's why . . .

3. *You have a responsibility to your Creator.* God created you both to live with Him and to live for Him. Ultimately, you belong to Him (Rom. 14:7–8). Therefore, your life needs to center on Him. The great tragedy of many people is that they turn their backs on their Creator and live unto themselves. But everyone will give an account to the Lord for how they have lived their lives. He will ask whether or not they have used what He has given them to honor Him and fulfill His purposes.

For more on this topic, see ABORTION, "The Creator's Craftsmanship," page 1.

INFERTILITY

Barrenness

Sarah laughed at the thought of bearing children at such an advanced age (Gen. 18:11–12). But she may have laughed more out of pain than surprise, for in the ancient world, to be barren, as she was, was considered a curse (Gen. 16:2; 20:17–18; Luke 1:25). It was even considered grounds for divorce.

Several women in Scripture illustrate the predicament of the childless woman. Yet it's interesting that each of those named eventually gave birth to a child.

- Rebekah conceived after her husband Isaac prayed to the Lord on her behalf; gave birth to twins, Esau and Jacob (Gen. 25:21).
- Rachel, driven by despair, used her maid Bilhah to compete with the other wife of her husband Jacob, her older sister Leah; eventually gave birth to Joseph and

later Benjamin, whose birth caused her death (Gen. 29:31—30:24).
- Hannah prayed desperately for a son, whom she vowed to dedicate to the Lord; gave birth to Samuel, a judge of Israel (1 Sam. 1).
- Elizabeth conceived after her husband Zacharias was promised a son who would be the forerunner to the Messiah; gave birth to John the Baptist (Luke 1:5–25, 57–66).

From Barrenness to Bounty

Occasionally a couple who have tried for years to have children suddenly find themselves expecting twins or even triplets. Isaiah envisioned a somewhat similar situation for Israel. After years of barrenness following the exile, God's people would find themselves with so many offspring that they would have to expand their housing to accommodate the newborns (Is. 54:2–3).

Barrenness was considered a curse in the ancient world (see Gen. 18:11–12). A childless woman lived with shame and disgrace (Is. 54:4) and the sense that God Himself had abandoned her (54:6).

But God had not abandoned His people, at least not permanently. His "everlasting kindness" (Hebrew, *chesed,* Is. 54:8) meant that He would not only stand by them, but fulfill His promise to their ancestor Abraham and his barren wife Sarah to make their offspring as numerous as the stars of the heavens (Gen. 15:4–5).

In a sense, God's word to Abraham and Sarah and to the people of Isaiah's day is now being fulfilled spiritually in Christ. As people come to faith in Him, they join the ever-growing family of God. By the time the Lord returns to claim His own, that family will have reached the size foretold to Abraham: "a great multitude which no one could number, of all nations, tribes, peoples, and tongues" (Rev. 7:9).

Pleading for a Baby

Isaac's earnest prayer for the Lord to help his wife conceive (Gen. 25:21) was probably motivated by many factors. He himself was the result of a promise (Gen. 18:10–14), and he knew that God had promised to bless Abraham with descendants as numerous as the sands of the seashore and the stars in the sky (Gen. 15:5; 22:17). Furthermore, Isaac deeply loved his wife Rebekah (Gen. 24:67), and he grieved that she was childless, because barrenness was considered a curse in that day. Yet it was a condition that many women in the Bible experienced (see Gen. 18:11–12).

INFLUENCE

Using Our Influence for God

The more status some Christians gain in their career and community, the less vocal they become about their faith in Christ. As a result, these believers often squander the excellent opportunities God gives them to influence others toward the gospel.

By contrast, David committed himself from the beginning of his reign as king of Israel to making God's name known among neighboring kingdoms. Psalm 18 was composed at the time when David realized that the kingdom was his. He felt humbled and amazed at the position God had given him. Realizing that foreign nations would follow his leadership, he was determined to tell them about the great God who had delivered him from the hand of Saul (Ps. 18:43–45). By giving thanks to the Lord and singing His praises, David hoped to influence his neighbors so that they, too, would fear and follow God.

God wants you to have a similar kind of witness with the people who live around you. Are you willing to speak up for the Lord wherever God has placed you—in work, in your neighborhood, and in the community?

Leaders Leverage Their Power

Management has been defined as the ability to get things done through other people. However, that can happen only if the people involved are in a position to get things done. Thus leaders must use their influence to get people of means participating in their efforts.

Nehemiah followed this principle in his plan to rebuild Jerusalem. He was in a key position of influence as the cupbearer to Artaxerxes. He had the king's ear, and he leveraged his proximity to power for the advantage of his people. He requested and was granted a leave of absence (Neh. 2:5–6), letters of reference (Neh. 2:7), and a government grant for building materials (Neh. 2:8).

Today, the ability to leverage power is an indispensable requirement of leadership, especially for those who work in community development and urban ministry. There are plenty of resources to help the poor, but it takes wise and disciplined leaders to align themselves with the powerful on behalf of the powerless. Tasks such as grant-writing, resource development, and asset distribution require careful cultivation of relationships with those in the networks of power.

If you are in a position of leadership, what is your relationship to the powerful? Do you know how to befriend those to whom God has given authority and influence, so that you can enlist them appropriately in your efforts for good? Or do you resist or resent them, thereby alienating yourself and those you lead from vital resources that could help you accomplish your goals?

Insider Opportunity

God often places His people in strategic positions in order to accomplish His purposes. To bring about the reconstruction of the wall at Jerusalem, God used Nehemiah, a man who was perhaps closest to and most trusted by Persian king Artaxerxes I.

As the king's cupbearer (Neh. 1:11), Nehemiah held one of the most important assignments a courtier could have in the ancient world. Cupbearers tasted a ruler's food in order to test its safety and ensure against poisoning, whether intentional or accidental. In the Assyrian, Babylonian, and Persian courts, which were notorious for political intrigue and assassination, the job of cupbearer carried enormous responsibility.

Usually foreigners, cupbearers often became trusted confidants of the rulers they served. Given the nature of their position, they tended to enjoy unusual political privilege and prestige. It was in a ruler's self-interest to keep his tasters happy, so their requests were listened to carefully and their wishes frequently granted.

This situation worked to Nehemiah's advantage. Unburdening himself to the king concerning the situation at Jerusalem, he requested and received a leave of absence and letters of authority to go and rebuild the city (Neh. 2:3–8). Later, when his adversaries at Jerusalem threatened to falsely accuse him of rebellion (Neh. 6:5–9), Nehemiah must have been comforted by the fact of his close association with Artaxerxes and the trust that his years of service had earned.

Where has God placed you in order to accomplish His purposes? What position and responsibility do you hold that might be useful to bring about good? Like Nehemiah, are you in prayer about what God is doing in the world? And are you prayerfully considering ways to leverage your influence to bring about His will?

For more on this topic, see **ETHICS,** "Standing for God," *page 129.*

INGRATITUDE
Where Are the Others?

Jesus chose a route that made it likely that He would encounter Samaritans (Luke 17:11). And once again Luke's account has to do with the tension between Jews and Samaritans.

It's easy to see why Jesus would ask, "Where are the nine?" (Luke 17:17). He was amazed at their lack of gratitude. But why did He call the one man who did return a "foreigner"? Luke singles out the fact that he was a Samaritan. That meant that he and Jesus were divided by a cultural wall that was virtually impenetrable. In fact, it was said to be unlawful for a Jew even to associate with a "foreigner" (compare Acts 10:28). Yet Jesus openly violated that taboo as He marveled at the Samaritan's thankful heart.

What of the other nine? Were they not Samaritans as well? Possibly, since this incident was taking place in or near Samaria. But is it not equally possible, given Luke's comment and Jesus' remark, that the other nine were not Samaritans, but Jews who had been driven away from the Jewish community to the Samaritans because of their leprous condition?

If so, their ingratitude was inexcusable. There was no racial wall separating them from Jesus. The only barrier had been their leprosy—and Jesus had removed that. They had every reason to turn in faith toward the Lord, but instead they turned away.

By contrast, a man who had every reason to stay away from Jesus returned and gave glory to God. As a result, he received what the other nine—and most of the rest of Israel—did not: spiritual healing, and not just physical.

INHERITANCE
God's Heirs

In the ancient world, conquering rulers often made a gift of conquered territories and other property to their children or to valued servants (Luke 19:12, 14, 17, 27). Such treasures formed an "inheritance" (Matt. 21:38). A similar idea appears in Ephesians 1:18, where Paul speaks of God's "inheritance in the saints."

God is preparing an inheritance, a kingdom, for His Son, Jesus Christ. It will include people from throughout history, people the Bible calls "saints," or true believers. These are people that God has called and chosen to be His children. Paul wanted the Ephesians—and us—to know that believers in Christ will be part of that joyful crowd.

God didn't have to do things that way. When sin entered the world He could have started all over again and created new and perfect creatures to present to His Son. But He chose to gather from the fallen, broken hordes of humanity a people for Himself. By telling us that we are going to be part of His inheritance, He's making a promise: the renovation that has started in our lives will continue until we are perfected and ready to be presented to Christ.

Birthrights

When Jacob asked Esau to sell him his birthright (Gen. 25:31), he was looking to obtain a position that had both legal and spiritual benefits.

In Bible times, the firstborn son enjoyed a favored position, which was his by right of birth (hence birthright). He was privileged to inherit a double portion of his father's assets (Deut. 21:17) and could expect to receive a special blessing before the father died. After his father's death, a firstborn son became the head of the family, carrying on the family name and even acting as the family priest.

The inheritance rights of the firstborn were protected by law; a father could not give his benefits to a younger son (Deut. 21:15–17). However, the firstborn himself could lose, forfeit, or sell his birthright. Jacob's son Reuben lost his favored position because he committed incest with his father's concubine (Gen. 35:22; 1 Chr. 5:1–2). Likewise, Esau sold his birthright for a stew of lentils (Gen. 25:29–34), or "one morsel of food" (Heb. 12:16).

In doing so, Esau committed a grave sin. It was bad enough to squander his inheritance for a single meal. Far worse, he was throwing away the blessing of God, who he knew had promised to make a great nation of Abraham (Gen. 22:15–18).

In this way, Esau serves as an example to believers today to hold on to what God has promised.

Issues Call for Answers

Often when vast new resources become available, new rules must be written to manage the distribution of those resources. Sometimes new systems are required to ensure fairness and mediate among competing interests.

Israel faced such a situation as it prepared to enter the "land of milk and honey." The daughters of Zelophehad (Num. 27:1) had listened while Moses reviewed the laws for inheritance (Num. 26:53–56). These laws must have been of keen interest to every family, for soon each one's inheritance would include a portion of the Promised Land.

The rule of thumb in settling an estate was to divide the land among the sons of each clan (Deut. 21:15–17). This kept land within the family throughout the generations. Daughters, who were more likely to marry outside the clan, were not included in the settlement of the estate. This was true not only of the Hebrews but also of the surrounding Near Eastern cultures. Instead of inherited land, daughters received dowries at the time of marriage (for example, Judg. 1:13–15; 1 Kin. 9:16).

However, the daughters of Zelophehad brought an appeal to Moses because their father had died without leaving sons to inherit any land that would have come the family's way. They pointed out that fairness demanded that they be given their father's allotment (Num. 26:33–34; 27:4).

Moses enacted a new law and the daughters received land. Thus new opportunities and new resources led to a reexamination of old values and revised legislation.

This incident challenges us today to consider where there might be a need for change in light of new developments. We live in a rapidly changing world, so there is a constant need to look at old patterns and evaluate whether they remain fair.

Getting What's Coming to You

The man we read of in Luke 12:13 appealed to Jesus for justice. He wanted to make sure that he was going to get his inheritance. But Jesus turned the issue from the material to the spiritual. He was far more concerned about the man's covetous spirit than his family's estate.

The Old Testament, which governed Hebrew life, had a great deal to say about family estates and the succession of land and property. Sometimes Christians have understood such teaching as merely foreshadowing the spiritual inheritance of New Testament believers. But our earthly, material estates are not to be treated as insignificant. An inheritance is a responsibility that God wants both parents and children to view and manage properly.

Here, Jesus showed grave concern that the man did not view his physical inheritance properly, but rather with a greedy attitude—a major problem because it threatened his spiritual inheritance, his eternal destiny.

The Lord's response and the parable following it (Luke 12:16–21) challenge us to ask: What is our perspective on the inheritance coming to us in this world? Will it be a blessing and a resource to be managed responsibly before God? Or, like this man and the man in the parable, are we trying to fashion a life out of the abundance of our possessions? If so, we need to pay attention to Luke 12:20–21.

INITIATIVE

(*see* Laziness)

INJUSTICE

It's Not Fair!

Are you suffering at the hands of an unjust superior? Are you paid unfairly, or have you been cheated out of a raise? Have you been loaded down with more than your fair share of work? How should Christians react to injustices in the workplace?

Healthy confrontation may be called for. There's a time to claim one's own rights or stand up for the rights of others. Scripture provides many examples and guidelines. For instance, Jesus gave instructions on how to deal with a believer in sin (Matt. 18:15–17), and Paul appealed to Caesar when he realized that justice was being withheld from him (Acts 25:8–12).

On the other hand, there is also a time to quietly suffer injustice as a matter of testimony, as Peter indicates (1 Pet. 2:18–21).

Jesus told His followers the same thing (Matt. 5:38–42), and Paul discouraged lawsuits among believers for the sake of their testimony (1 Cor. 6:7).

Either way, Christians should never just ignore injustice. We may decide to quit if our employer is grossly unjust. But we should do so not out of cowardice or an unwillingness to endure hardship, but to honor Christ or else to find a constructive, godly alternative elsewhere.

Why Don't Things Change?

Have you ever felt frustrated by problems in society that just seem to go on and on? Perhaps you've lamented, "Why doesn't someone do something? Why don't things ever change?"

The composer of Psalm 94 appears to have felt that way. Looking around at the injustices of society, the writer cried out to God, the righteous Judge, to do something, yet also wondered how long wickedness would continue (Ps. 94:1–3). This psalmist's frustration compares with an urban pastor who appeared in housing court one day, where many of his poor parishioners were having their cases decided. The minister sat for hours, witnessing one case after another. In every verdict, the judge was siding with the rich and powerful, even when the facts seemed to overwhelmingly favor the poor.

Finally the pastor could take no more of what he saw as blatant injustice. Shaking with outrage, he leaped to his feet and cried, "Your Honor, if it please the court, I have a question."

The judge stopped his proceedings and acknowledged the pastor. "Yes, Reverend, what is it?"

"Your Honor, I've been watching all day long as case after case after case has gone against these poor people. Where is the justice in this court?"

Immediately the judge replied, "Reverend, you don't understand. This is not a court of justice. This is a court of law. If you want justice, go change the law."

The judge's point is well taken. When evil triumphs in society, or when justice is not served, it could be the result of an imperfect system or institution "which devises evil by law" (Ps. 94:20). In such cases, things will change if the righteous engage in reforming the system, with God's help.

Sometimes the real question is not *Why don't things change?* but *Why don't believers change things?*

Will Evil Ever Get Its Due?

Anyone who pays attention to today's headlines is likely to wonder whatever happened to ethics and justice. Sometimes it seems like fairness never happens in matters of business, government, the law, and world affairs. But for those who long to see justice reign, the Bible offers powerful hope.

God will not turn His back on injustice. His character demands that He give people what is coming to them. Moreover, Scripture promises that He will deal with evil in absolute, final ways. John's vision foresees that triumphant accomplishment:

- God will bind evil and cast it into a bottomless pit (Rev. 20:2–3).
- He will place a seal on the source of evil (Rev. 20:3).
- He will administer judgment and restore believers who have been killed unjustly (Rev. 20:4).
- He will deal finally with Satan after allowing him one last attempt to deceive (Rev. 20:7–9); the devil's punishment will include eternal torment (Rev. 20:10, 14).
- The dead will stand before God and be judged (Rev. 20:11–15).

This picture offers tremendous hope to anyone concerned about the injustices of our world today. As we seek to deliver God's righteousness into our communities, workplaces, and families, it's a relief to know that no human being—no matter how impartial and objective or biased and corrupt—is the final judge. Ultimate justice will someday be administered by One who can be thoroughly trusted—God, through Christ.

For more on this topic, see **ILLEGAL SEARCH AND SEIZURE,** *"Grasping for What Others Have," page 215;* **SOCIAL REFORM,** *"Justice in the Gate," page 376.*

INSTITUTIONALIZED EVIL

(*see* Evil)

INSTITUTIONALIZED OPPRESSION

(*see* Oppression)

INTEGRITY

Ten Tests of Integrity

Psalm 15 lists ten marks of integrity. How does your life compare?

The person of integrity . . .

- walks uprightly. What is your basic ethical commitment? Are you out to honor the Lord or to serve yourself?
- works righteousness. What is the end result of your work? Are you promoting good in the world—or evil?
- speaks the truth. Are you in the habit of telling "little white lies" when it is necessary or convenient?
- does not backbite. Do you tear down others behind their back?
- does no evil to a neighbor. What is your policy on office politics? Do you believe in "doing unto others before they do unto you"?
- does not take up a reproach against a friend. How loyal are you? When everyone is down on a colleague, do you jump on the bandwagon, or do you offer support and seek fair play?
- honors those who fear the Lord, not the ungodly. What is the character of your best friends? What is their attitude toward God and the things of the Lord?
- keeps his word, even when it is costly. Are you trustworthy and reliable? Is your word your bond, or is there always a question whether you will follow through?
- does not practice usury. Do you make it harder or easier for poor people to gain the resources necessary to support themselves?
- does not take bribes. What would it take to get you to compromise your integrity?

Ethics and Character in Psalms

Over and over the Book of Psalms reminds us that what ultimately matters to God is the quality of our character (Ps. 37:27–29). The following psalms merit careful study if we want to pursue ethical decision-making and godly behavior:

- Psalm 26: Integrity is a reasonable basis for seeking the Lord's protection.
- Psalm 101: This psalm expresses some of the high ideals that the person of character will pursue.
- Psalm 119: God's Word provides clear guidelines for living with integrity.
- Psalm 141: This psalm is a prayer for help to maintain integrity when one is tempted to compromise.

Out of Sight, Out of Mind

In a sense, the chief butler owed his life to Joseph, who had correctly interpreted his dream (Gen. 40:9–13). All that Joseph asked in return was to be remembered once the butler was reinstalled in his position. The account implies that the butler agreed to do so. But like so many people, he forgot his promise once he was out of trouble (Gen. 40:23). It was not until two full years had gone by (Gen. 41:1) and Pharaoh happened to have a dream of his own that the butler remembered his commitment, apparently with some guilt (Gen. 41:9).

The incident stands as a reminder to us all: When was the last time we agreed to do something? Have we followed through on our commitment? Or have we slipped into the common pattern of "out of sight, out of mind"? God wants us to be people of our word (Matt. 5:37).

Risk and Responsibility

An inheritance can be a blessing to a family, but it can also be a terrible curse that divides family members. A lot depends on who manages the disbursements of the assets and how well they do their job.

When Israel divided Canaan, it was Joshua's job to act somewhat like a trustee of an estate, making sure that each tribe received the lands to which it was entitled. It was a delicate job that required him to act with great integrity. Otherwise he might be charged with being unfair in assigning boundaries or with neglecting commitments previously made by Moses.

Joshua handled his responsibility by seeking the welfare of the twelve tribes first before asking for land himself (Josh. 19:49–50). In doing so, he ran the risk of having to settle for a leftover, second-best portion of Canaan. But he avoided any question of impropriety.

This policy was in marked contrast to that of the Canaanite and Amorite kings of the city-states that the Israelites were inheriting. The pagan kings generally lorded it over their people, choosing for themselves the first and the best. Joshua took the posture of a "servant-leader," forsaking greed and self-interest in order to seek the highest good for his people (see Matt. 20:25–28).

Joshua's example is worth emulating today. As we accept responsibilities and make decisions that affect others, our challenge is to do the right thing by seeking justice, trusting God to work out the details of our own welfare.

For more on this topic, see **HONESTY,** *"Free to Be Honest," page 202.*

INTELLECTUALS

Apostle to the Intellectuals

At Athens the gospel collided with a centuries-old culture rooted in intellectualism and discourse. Certainly Paul had encountered Greek philosophy elsewhere; indeed, he had grown up with it in Tarsus. But his visit to Athens brought him into direct contact with the inheritors of the city's celebrated intellectual tradition (Acts 17:18).

Was Paul intimidated by the arrogance and cynicism of the leisurely Epicureans and Stoics (Acts 17:18–21)? Some believe that he was (based on passages like 1 Cor. 2:1–5). Yet even though he might have felt more apprehen-

sion addressing them than any other audience, Acts gives no hint that he felt inferior. On the contrary, he addressed them at their own forum, the Areopagus, building on common ground by discussing their altar "to the unknown god" and citing one of their poets (Acts 17:28).

Was Paul's strategy effective? If judged by the number of converts, no. Only a handful believed. The rest dismissed him immediately or else postponed judgment pending later discussion—which apparently never came, as Paul departed.

On that basis, some believe that the apostle was wrong for ever going to Athens. In fact, some contend that Paul was so disillusioned by the experience that for a time he left the ministry to make tents at Corinth (Acts 18:1–3).

Supposedly, his words in 1 Corinthians 1:18—2:5 denouncing philosophy as so much "foolosophy" reflect that view. As a result, some conclude that it is a waste of time to offer the gospel to intellectuals.

Luke doesn't tell us exactly why Paul left Athens, but nothing suggests disillusionment. He never "left" the ministry, just as he had never abandoned his trade, tentmaking. While working with Aquila and Priscilla at Corinth, Paul continued to preach in the synagogue and in the house of Justus (Acts 18:4, 7), a ministry that lasted more than eighteen months (Acts 18:11). Later in Ephesus he followed the same pattern for two years (Acts 19:8–10).

Paul's approach to the Athenian intellectuals should encourage believers today to actively participate in universities and other centers of learning. Those that God calls to work within the academic disciplines have an outstanding model to follow—Paul, God's apostle to the intellectuals.

INTELLIGENCE

(*see* Education)

INTERCESSION

(*see* Mediation)

INTERRACIAL MARRIAGE

Too Many Wives?

Why was it wrong for Solomon to marry "many foreign women" (1 Kin. 11:1)? Was it a problem of . . .

• *ethnicity?* Perhaps Solomon erred by marrying outside of Israel. The Law prohibited Hebrews from intermarrying with the Canaanites (Deut. 7:1–5; compare 1 Kin. 11:2).

Yet elsewhere the Law permitted Israelite men to marry women captured in warfare, so long as they were not Canaanites (1 Kin. 20:14–18). Moses himself had a wife from Ethiopia (Num. 12:1). And Ruth, who married Boaz and was the great-grandmother of David, was a Moabite.

• *gender?* As some would see it, the main failing in Solomon's marriages had something to do with the inherent nature of woman. Just as Eve caused trouble for Adam (Gen. 3:6), Delilah for Samson (Judg. 16:6–21), and Bathsheba for David (2 Sam. 11:1–5), so Solomon's many wives weakened his resolve to follow the Lord and led him into sin, according to this view. Yet woman was created equally with man and shares responsibility for the creation (Gen. 1:26–27). And Scripture presents many examples of women who showed spiritual insight, sensitivity, and obedience to the Lord: for example, Jael (Judg. 4:17–24; 5:24–27), Ruth (Ruth 1:6–18), Abigail (1 Sam. 25), and Lydia (Acts 16:14–15).

• *polygamy?* Perhaps the real problem for Solomon was that he practiced polygamy. After all, the Law warned the kings of Israel not to "multiply wives" (Deut. 17:17).

Yet the Hebrew patriarchs all had more than one wife, as did Moses, Gideon, and David. That does not mean that God encouraged the practice, but neither can one say that it was the primary cause of Solomon's downfall.

Ultimately, the Lord disapproved of Solomon's many marriages because his wives, who worshiped idols, turned his heart away from the true God (1 Kin. 11:4–10). God's anger was not about intermarriage, but about Solomon's idolatry. It was a spiritual issue, as the Law concerning kings reveals (Deut. 17:19–20).

This is an important point for modern readers of Scripture to grasp. God's main concern, then as now, is with a person's heart attitude. Is there faith and obedience? Other issues are relevant to that question to the extent that they either aid or impede one's walk with God.

An Interracial Marriage

The marriage celebrated in the Song of Solomon appears to have been a match between two members of different ethnic groups. The groom, presumably Solomon, is described as "white and ruddy" (Song 5:10), while the bride is "dark" like the black tents of Kedar. If these descriptions indicate skin color, then Solomon was evidently marrying a woman from a different ethnic background.

Marriages across ethnic and racial lines were not uncommon in the ancient world (for example, Num. 12:1; Ruth 1:4; 1 Kin. 11:1). Today, however, they pose a problem for some. Yet it is important to note that whatever reasons people may have for opposing interracial unions, the Bible neither condemns them nor prohibits them. Israelites were forbidden to marry Canaanites, Ammonites, or Moabites (Deut. 7:1–4; 23:3), but these prohibitions were not based on mere ethnicity, but had to do with religion, morality, and geopolitical considerations.

God created a diversity of races on the earth. Differences in background and skin color may be hard for people to accept, but not for God. He Himself reaches out to all the peoples of the world, so it is not surprising that His Word may celebrate a marriage between two people from different ethnic groups.

Intermarriage Issues

Some segments of the modern-day church around the world, especially those in inner cities and developing countries, struggle with issues related to intermarriage between races and ethnic groups. For these believers, Ezra's reaction to the intermarriages of many of the Jews who had returned from the exile (Ezra 9:2) might prove instructive.

As a scribe (see Ezra 7:6), Ezra knew the Law extremely well. He knew that intermarriage with the Canaanites and other peoples of Palestine (Ezra 9:1) was explicitly condemned (Ex. 34:12–16; Deut. 7:3–5). He also was familiar with the prophets' denunciation of the practice (compare Jer. 3:1–9; Mal. 2:10–16). Thus Ezra was beside himself with remorse when he learned of the people's sin (Ezra 9:3–4). After all, violation of the laws concerning intermarriage was one of the reasons that God had sent His people into exile in the first place (Ezra 9:10–14).

The scribe's solution to this problem was swift and decisive: he ordered a mass assembly for the confession of sins and the immediate dissolution of all intermarriages (Ezra 10:3–5, 11–17). However, Ezra's prayer (Ezra 9:6–15), the people's confession (Ezra 10:2–4, 12–14), and Ezra's systematic and carefully recorded mass divorce proceedings (Ezra 10:16–44) all served to highlight a key issue that affects how we apply this Scripture today: God did not forbid interracial marriage, but rather interreligious marriage.

Interracial unions took place often in the Old Testament. For example, Moses married an Ethiopian woman (Num. 12:1), Salmon married Rahab, the harlot of Jericho (Matt. 1:5), and Boaz married the Moabite Ruth (Ruth 2:10; 4:13). Nevertheless, God generally cautioned His people against marriage to foreigners because their allegiance to idols and foreign gods would dilute the Israelite's allegiance to the one true God. As Nehemiah pointed out twenty-five years after Ezra, that was the undoing of Solomon (Neh. 13:26).

This is a principle worth keeping in mind today as pastors and church leaders try to help believers wrestle with issues of intermarriage. The main question to consider is not that of ethnicity, but spirituality: what solution best enables Christians to follow God?

Ezra took a somewhat radical approach when he immediately dissolved the intermarriages of his people. When Nehemiah confronted a similar problem several years later,

ISOLATION

he took a slightly less strident posture by exhorting the people to prevent future intermarriages. (Read Neh. 13:23–27.)

Ezra's model for dealing with interreligious marriages stands in contrast to Paul's approach. This is because the Jews of Ezra's day were turning away from God by intermarrying, whereas the Christians Paul wrote about were already married when they became believers. Paul counseled these people to remain in their marriages to still-unbelieving spouses if at all possible.

INTERRUPTIONS

Holy Interruptions

How full is your schedule? Is it booked so tightly that only an act of God seems able to force an adjustment?

Jesus certainly had a demanding task with lots of responsibility. God sent Him to earth to gain salvation for all and to launch the church—and gave Him little more than three years to do it! Yet somehow Jesus' value system allowed for what we would call interruptions. People barged into His presence, even when His associates tried to prevent them.

Such was the case for a blind beggar by a roadside near Jericho (Luke 18:35–38). The man called out to Jesus as He and his leadership team were on their way to major events in Jerusalem. Then as now, well-traveled roads were cluttered with such inconveniences. Some tried to ignore the beggar, or at least keep him away. But amazingly, Jesus stopped and met the man's needs.

It's interesting that Jesus' very next encounter, with a known government crook, was also an interruption (Luke 19:1–10). Yet again, Jesus set aside His travel plans and turned aside to Zacchaeus' home to talk with him and meet his family and friends.

Do you have room for others in your life, especially the "little people" such as your children, an entry-level employee, a visitor to your church, or someone poor? When Jesus took time to serve a forgotten castaway, it caused everyone nearby to give praise to God (Luke 18:43). Watch out for God's holy interruptions!

INTROSPECTION

Avoiding Morbid Introspection

Paul wisely recognized that even our most conscientious attempts to maintain pure motives fall far short (1 Cor. 4:3–5). Indwelling sin taints everything we do. But Paul didn't allow that to discourage him from aiming at high motives. Neither did he despair of doing anything good. He was content to do his best in life and let God be his Judge.

Are you free from the chronic worry that your motives are not always perfect? Are you living under the grace of God?

ISOLATION

Cocooning

One of the major developments in modern Western society is the phenomenon of "cocooning"—people pulling in, living private lifestyles in which they shut out the world and its concerns. Cocooners have interest only in what touches them, and they set up their environment so that they control what touches them.

Unfortunately, cocooning has subtly invaded the church, contributing to the "pulling in" of Christian faith. It shows up, for instance, in overemphasis on the relationship of the individual to Christ and what He can do for each person, to the neglect of what Christ wants to do among communities of His people, including their corporate responsibilities to each other and the larger society.

The book of Hebrews speaks to the danger of cocooning as it describes Christ's work on our behalf (Heb. 4:14–16):

1. *Christ chose to get involved.* He did not remain in His privileged position with the Father, but "passed through the heavens" (Heb. 4:14) to come to earth, becoming poor in order to make us spiritually rich. We can't imagine what that move cost Him.

2. *Christ faced reality.* He is no stranger to real life. He never walled Himself off from what people go through every day (Heb. 4:15).

3. *Christ empowers people.* He gives His people sufficient power to deal with life. One rationale for cocooning is the attitude, "When I'm done with work, I'm worn out. I can't be bothered with people's problems. I can hardly manage my own! If anything, I need

to be a receiver of grace, not a dispenser of it." Result: the many take comfort, help, and peace from the few who give.

But Hebrews 4:16 challenges believers—individually and corporately—to "come boldly to the throne of grace." Why? In order to obtain mercy—a personal need of every individual—and "grace to help in time of need." Notice: grace to help. God's help relieves some of our cares and allows us the freedom and strength to "pass it on" by helping others.

J

JEALOUSY
Are You the Older Brother?

If you grew up in the church or have been a believer for many years, it's worth looking carefully at the prodigal son's older brother (Luke 15:25). He's one of the most intriguing characters in all of Jesus' parables—a case study in what can happen to people who have been around religion for a long time.

In contrast to the father, who shows nothing but mercy to his long-lost son who has finally come home, the older brother sneers at the joy and celebration heaped on his brother. He is not merely jealous, but outraged at what he perceives as injustice. How could the father kill the fatted calf just because his wayward, ne'er-do-well son had come back, while seeming to neglect the faithful, diligent loyalty of his other son (Luke 15:29–30)?

That was the attitude of the Pharisees who were among those listening to this story (Luke 15:2–3). And in a larger sense, it would become the attitude of Jews in general as the gospel spread to the Gentiles (for example, Acts 11:1–3). How could Jesus be so friendly toward known sinners, such as the tax gatherers, and so distant from people like the Pharisees who carefully practiced the finer points of the Law? How could God be compassionate toward Gentiles, while the Jews, who had been His people for generations, were passed by?

Have you ever felt that way when someone came into the faith? Have you ever felt that more attention is paid to new converts than to those who have followed biblical teaching all their lives? If so, Jesus' parable contains a comfort and a challenge. The comfort is that God never forgets who His children are and has great treasures stored up for them (Luke 15:31). The challenge is to maintain a proper perspective—the perspective of compassion and mercy that is at the heart of the Father (15:32).

Perils of Being a "Straight Arrow"

Being a responsible employee and a person of character will not always make you popular with coworkers. Sometimes people who have little integrity themselves mock those who do. They may even try to trip you up if you are conscientious, setting you up for failure and throwing obstacles in your way. And should you receive praise and preferment because of your reputation and character, they may even launch a jealous campaign to "knock you off your high horse," as they see it.

That was what happened to Daniel. Daniel's proven history of integrity and leadership resulted in his advancement when his "company," the kingdom of Babylon, changed "owners" (Dan. 5:30–6:3). As a result, his rivals plotted against him (Dan. 6:4). But the only "dirt" they could find was that he was too faithful to God (Dan. 6:5)!

Could your coworkers charge you with being too faithful to God where you work? Is your reputation above reproach? Or are your character and track record so bad that they would bring shame on the name of Christ if people knew you were a Christian? Integrity may incite some people to jealousy, but hypocrisy incites them to scorn and unbelief. Which would you prefer?

JOY
Joy on the Way to Jail

Jail seldom produces joy. The condemnation of society and the grim realities of incarceration bring many reactions, but rarely happy ones. However, when the cause is just

(Acts 28:25–28), the conscience clear (Acts 23:1; 24:16; 26:19), and friends loyal (Acts 28:15), imprisonment can take on a new dimension.

As Paul neared the end of his journey to face trial, believers from Rome and its environs welcomed him along the Appian highway from Puteoli to Rome (Acts 28:13–15). He had written them three years before, describing his deep longing for them (Rom. 1:9–15; 15:22–29). Even his chains and the prospect of prison could not cloud the joy of connecting with those fellow believers.

Can Christians today surprise their culture by becoming true friends to those in jail?

For more on this topic, see CELEBRATION, "Let's Celebrate!" page 47; RULES, "Rules That Lead to Joy," page 352.

JUDGING OTHERS

Judge Not!

What was Jesus calling for when He ordered His followers to "judge not" (Matt. 7:1)? Did He want us to close our eyes to error and evil? Did He intend that managers forgo critical performance reviews of their employees? Or that news editors and art critics pull their punches? Or that juries refrain from judgment? Should we decline any assessment of others, since none of us is perfect?

No, those would all be misapplications of Jesus' teaching. In the first place, He was not commanding blind acceptance, but grace toward others. Since all of us are sinners, we need to stop bothering with the failings of others and start attending to serious issues of our own (Matt. 7:3–5). His words here extend His earlier exposé of hypocrisy (Matt. 6:1–18). Don't blame or put down others while excusing or exalting yourself, Jesus was saying.

Is there room, then, to assess others, especially when we know we are not perfect? Yes, but only in Jesus' way: with empathy and fairness (Matt. 7:12), and with a readiness to freely and fully forgive (Matt. 6:12, 14). When we are called upon to correct others, we should act like a good doctor whose purpose is to bring healing—not like an enemy who attacks.

For more on this topic, see DOUBLE STANDARD, "A New Standard for Judgment" page 115.

JUDGMENT

Averting Judgment

Why does the Bible so often speak about judgment? Page after page of the Old Testament seems to be filled with sobering descriptions of terrifying wrath and punishment—ultimately brought about by God. Why the emphasis on judgment?

The short answer is because the judgments of God are real. The Bible is straightforward about the Lord's wrath against evil and sin. God hates evil (Ps. 45:7) and condemns it whenever He sees it. Ultimately He will do away with it (Rev. 21:4–5).

But in reading the judgment passages of Scripture, it is important to notice that a warning of the Lord's judgment always leaves room for repentance. For example, Joel's spine-tingling description of the "day of the Lord" (Joel 2:1–11) is followed by a call to turn to the Lord "with all your heart, with fasting, with weeping, and with mourning" (Joel 2:12).

God wants no one to fall into condemnation and come under His judgment (2 Pet. 3:9). He warns people ahead of time so that they will recognize their sin and experience the "godly sorrow" that leads to repentance (2 Cor. 7:10). The God of judgment is also the God of mercy, "slow to anger, and of great kindness" (Joel 2:13).

Tough Love May Require Judgment

If you've ever spent much time around a courtroom, you know that a constant tension is at play there between judgment and mercy. At issue is the determination of justice. What extenuating circumstances should be taken into account? What sort of punishment fits the crime? When should judges show mercy, and when should they "throw the book" at a criminal?

In thinking about these matters, it is commonly assumed that judgment and mercy are irreconcilable opposites. But even though we as humans may see them that way, that does not mean God does. From His standpoint, judgment and mercy need not be reconciled because they are not opposed in the first place.

Human beings tend to think of mercy as ignoring, excusing, indulging, or even approving of wrongdoing. God never does that.

Indeed, He is "of purer eyes than to behold evil, and cannot look on wickedness" (Hab. 1:13). Thus when He withholds punishment, it is not because He is indulgent, but because He is patiently waiting for repentance, allowing people ample time to change their ways (Is. 30:18; 2 Pet. 3:9, 15).

However, if repentance from sin never comes, the Lord's very mercy—or *chesed*, a word often translated "mercy" but with the fundamental sense of loyalty to the people with whom one has a covenant, and loyalty to the covenant itself—moves Him to enforce justice (Deut. 5:9; 7:9–11).

Perhaps a modern way of describing this response is the term "tough love." Genuine love means genuine commitment to the welfare of another. Thus love must sometimes act punitively in order to bring about, if possible, the best in and for the beloved. God loves us too much to let us drown in our own sin. His infinite love sometimes moves Him to judgment when we refuse to seek His best.

The Legacy of Lost Cities

Throughout Scripture and in countless extrabiblical works, Sodom and Gomorrah and the other cities of the plain (Gen. 13:12) stand

as a symbol of divine judgment for collective wickedness. What was once a well-watered, fertile region is today barren, full of tar pits, mounds of asphalt, and marsh. These ill-fated cities show that God not only judges sinful individuals, such as Lot's wife (Gen. 19:26), but also entire cities and their surroundings.

However, the story is not all bad news. After the tragic end of Sodom and Gomorrah, "God remembered Abraham" (Gen. 19:29). When we remember the patriarch's righteous example, several lessons of the story become clear:

Prayer makes a difference. Abraham shows us that it is legitimate to pray for cities, as he did (Gen. 18:22–33). We may not always be able to go to a city, but we can still pray for it. Abraham prayed persistently for an entire city, believing that nothing was too hard for the Lord (Gen. 18:14). Are we praying for cities today? What are we asking God to do? Save the city—or judge it?

People count. Ten believing persons living in Sodom could have saved it (Gen. 18:32). The presence of righteous persons acting as salt and light can preserve places where evil runs rampant. He spared Zoar, for the sake of one righteous person—Lot (Gen. 19:16–22; 2 Pet. 2:6–7). As God's people, are we living righteously in the places to which He has called us?

God is sovereign. God's decision to destroy four cities of the plain but to preserve the fifth, Zoar, shows that He is ultimately in control. God does not want to destroy cities or their people (2 Pet. 3:9); but He can—and will. He decides when, where, and how judgment will fall. On the other hand, God can rescue people from evil places when and if He wishes. Do we live with a perspective that God is ultimately in control? Do we act as though we are accountable to Him?

Pride goes before a fall. Sodom was destroyed not only because of sexual sin (Gen. 19:1–17; Jude 7), but because it had pride and a surplus of wealth, yet failed to care for its poor and needy (Ezek. 16:48–50). What are we doing with the resources God has put under our control?

Fleeing from the city does not avoid sin—it only spreads it around. The behavior of Lot and his daughters after fleeing from Sodom shows that sin is not confined to the city; they exported Sodom-like immorality to the hinterlands (Gen. 19:19–22, 30–36). Are we running from the city in order to "escape" its problems and evils? Is it possible that God wants us to stay and live as His representatives of righteousness?

JUDICIAL OFFICIALS

(*see* Government Officials)

JUSTICE

Balancing Mercy and Justice

In showing Himself to Moses, God revealed more than His appearance; He revealed His character as well. He declared Himself to be a God of mercy, grace, patience, and goodness (Ex. 34:6). Yet at the same time, He executes justice on wrongdoers (Ex. 36:7).

If one ever needed evidence that there are not two Gods in Scripture, but one, this incident provides it. These two "sides" to God's moral character—the merciful and the just— in no way contradict each other. In fact, they complement one other. For God to be merciful, He must right the wrongs that people do; that calls for justice. On the other hand, to be fully just He must allow for the weakness and limitations of His creatures; that demands mercy.

In a similar way, God's people need to balance mercy and justice in their dealings with others. Their mercy must not give way to indulgence, nor must their justice degenerate into vengeance.

Is God Fair?

Fires. Floods. Earthquakes. Famine. So many people seem to suffer from "acts of God" that strike without warning. Like Job, they appear to be relatively innocent of wrongdoing that might explain their pain. People wonder, "Is God fair to let these things happen?"

This was one of the questions with which Job and his friends wrestled. Calamity struck Job and his family for no apparent reason. Why? His friends took the view that God was punishing him, that he must have done something wrong to deserve such evil. Job disagreed, not only because he felt certain of his own integrity, but because the wicked actually seemed to prosper, not suffer (Job 12:6).

Yet that only brought Job back to the original question: Is God fair? If the wicked prosper, where is justice in the world? Job concluded that the seemingly easy life of the wicked is very temporary; sooner or later it will all fall apart (Job 27:13–23). In the end, Job maintained, God will humble the proud, those with integrity will inherit their possessions, and justice will be served.

Ultimately God is indeed fair (Job 36:6; 37:23–24)—a fact for which we can be thankful, because life is not fair. In this life, people do not always get what they deserve. But this life is not the end of the story. God Himself will write the final chapter.

When Laws Collide

Whenever new laws and statutes are enacted, there's a need to evaluate their impact. Sometimes the new laws are struck down because they do not uphold fundamental principles. Other times the new statutes replace existing ones, and in that way a nation's body of law evolves.

The Law for Israel was given by God and in that sense was absolute. Yet from time to time, cases arose that required special consideration. The division of the Promised Land created such a moment. The daughters of Zelophehad brought a complaint that their family would receive no land because their father had died without leaving sons. After Moses deliberated with God, the women won an important concession by receiving land.

Now, however, that decision was revisited when relatives of Zelophehad from the tribe of Manasseh pointed out that the law of the Jubilee Year could cause the tribe to lose land (Num. 36:4). In the Jubilee Year, lands were to be returned to the families to which they were originally given. But ownership of the land was determined through male heirs. Thus, if women born to Zelophehad's daughters married outside the tribe, the lands would be lost.

This was a complex legal problem. Three parts of the Law were in tension: the division of the Promised Land, the laws of inheri-tance, and the law of the Jubilee. As before, Moses consulted God and a compromise was struck: Zelophehad's daughters could keep the land by marrying only within the tribe (Num. 36:6–9). It was an acceptable decision that preserved the Law.

The solution of this technical matter may seem like an odd way to end the book of Numbers. It may also seem irrelevant to modern-day Bible readers. But the decision is a good reminder that God cares about justice and fairness. He listens when people bring difficult matters to Him. By inference, we can conclude that those who pay attention to the details of codes and legislation do a tremendous service to everyday citizens by protecting their rights and working out conflicts among the competing interests of the law.

Avoiding Empty Religion

God never allows formal religious observance to take the place of practical, everyday godliness. As He pointed out through the prophet Zechariah, spiritual disciplines such as fasting, as important as they can be, make little impression on God if at the same time one's lifestyle lacks justice, mercy, and compassion (Zech. 7:5, 9).

In Babylon, the people had imposed two fasts on themselves. One occurred in the fifth month (Ab, or July-August) to commemorate the destruction of the temple (2 Kin. 25:8–9). The other occurred in the seventh month (Tishri, or September-October) to commemorate the assassination of Gedaliah, the appointed governor of Judah after the Babylonians destroyed Jerusalem (Jer. 41:1–3). Neither of these fasts was required by the Lord, but that was not why the Lord rebuked the people.

The Lord challenged the returnees for substituting empty religion—whether through fasting or feasting—for true spirituality (Zech. 7:5–7). Like their forebears (Is. 58:1–9), they followed the forms of religious ritual without the substance of a godly lifestyle.

The same challenge exists for believers today. Attendance at church, Bible reading, prayer, sharing one's faith—as crucial as these are—need to be matched by a lifestyle of integrity and Christlike character, especially in one's dealings with others. Otherwise, they become empty rituals that leave one open to self-deception and hypocrisy.

What the Curse Tells Us About God

A snake made to crawl on its belly (Gen. 3:14–15). A woman whose birth pangs will be multiplied (Gen. 3:16). A man whose work will turn into toil (Gen. 3:17–19). These curses would be a blast of vindictive retaliation from the mouth of someone less than God. But when God pronounces these words, He reveals something important about His character: He is a God of justice who takes seriously matters of right and wrong.

As sinful humans we may look the other way when moral issues are at stake. But God is holy and righteous. He does not wink at sin. In the curse He shows us that sin has consequences. Those consequences are a sad outcome for what was declared no less than seven times to be a good creation (Gen. 1:4, 10, 12, 18, 21, 25, 31).

However, God did set limits on the effects of the curse. For example, after Cain killed Abel, God marked him for protection and set up a deterrent against anyone killing him (Gen. 4:10–15). Later, Christ established final and absolute limits on sin's consequences by taking the curse and its penalties on Himself (Gal. 3:13). Eventually, after its purposes are complete, the curse will be removed from the earth and lifted from God's people forever (Rom. 8:18–25; Rev. 22:3).

God doesn't enjoy the curse any more than those of us who suffer under it. In fact, from the outset, He knew that His judgment would ultimately fall on His own Son (Eph. 1:4–10). Yet His very character demanded that justice be satisfied.

We may grieve over the outcome of Adam and Eve's disobedience. But we can also be thankful that their sentence (and ours) was set by a God of justice who is also a God of love.

For more on this topic, see **INJUSTICE,** *"It's Not Fair!" page 223; "Will Evil Ever Get Its Due?" page 224;* **PEACE,** *"A Vision of Peace," page 293;* **SOCIAL REFORM,** *"Justice in the Gate," page 376.*

JUVENILE CRIME
Juvenile Offenders

In light of our modern-day justice system's overload of juvenile offenders, it is interesting to consider the ancient Israelites' method of dealing with a chronically stubborn young man: "stone him to death with stones" (Deut. 21:21). Does the capital punishment of a juvenile show the Hebrews to have been a violent, mean-spirited society? Notice several points about this law:

1. *It prescribed an extreme punishment to an extreme situation.* It was talking about a thoroughly incorrigible youth—probably a teenage or young adult male, certainly not a child—who engaged in repeated, steadfast rebellion. Despite the vocal correction of both parents and despite their discipline (Deut. 21:18), he has not heeded them. He has turned his back on them.

2. *It assumed intact families with parents exercising responsibility and leadership.* Parents were accountable to God for how they raised their families. Thus, by turning his back on his parents, a rebellious son was in effect turning his back on God. Likewise, by turning to the elders of the community, the parents were admitting that they had given up hope. Now, if they were to honor God, they had no recourse but to turn their son over to the community.

3. *It assumed community participation in both the judgment and the punishment.* The parents were not to pass sentence on their son. That was up to the elders of the community (Deut. 21:19–20). Assuming that they confirmed the charges against the youth, "[All] the men of the city" were to stone him to death (Deut. 21:21). The father was not asked to initiate the punishment; it was a shared responsibility.

4. *It assumed the independence and will of the individual.* The Law recognized that young adults make their own choices. They may be under the authority of their parents, but sooner or later they must decide what sort of life they will lead. Parents had responsibility to teach their children God's ways; they could not force them to accept them.

It is unclear how much this remedy for rebellion was enforced by the ancient Israelites. What application can be drawn from it by parents today? First, this law by no means gives parents license to abuse their children or punish them by death or any life-threatening means. Such behavior goes totally against Scripture, and our society rightly enforces laws against it.

On the positive side, this instruction reminds parents that they have responsibility for the spiritual and moral training of their children (compare Eph. 6:4). It also implies that society at large and the community of believers especially have a responsibility to help parents fulfill their parental role and to back them up with resources, encouragement, and community support.

K

KINDNESS
Blessings for the Unbelievers

What is your attitude toward people who might be called committed unbelievers—people who have made up their minds that they will ignore or have nothing to do with God? Are you tempted to treat them with anger and animosity? If so, consider Abraham's example in Genesis 14. He not only showed a great kindness toward his unbelieving neighbors, but actually placed his life and property at risk to do so.

The battles mentioned in Genesis 14 came about as a result of the expansionist plans of the Elamites. Under Chedorlaomer, the Elamites made a raid into Canaan, capturing Lot, Abram's nephew (Gen. 14:11–12).

That's when Abram moved into action. He mustered his own servants, along with a group of Amorite neighbors who had survived the Elamite invasion. The combined forces probably numbered no more than a thousand or two thousand men. But God enabled the little militia to launch a surprise attack against Chedorlaomer's army and send his troops running for their lives out of Canaan (Gen. 14:14–15).

Abram's victory accomplished several objectives. It rescued Lot and his family from almost certain slavery. But it also delivered the Canaanites from Elamite control. This is significant in light of the fact that the Canaanites—both those in the cities of the plain, as well as those living elsewhere in Canaan, such as the Amorites—were pagan idolators whose wickedness would eventually result in their destruction (Gen. 18:20–21; 19:13, 24–25).

God could have used Chedorlaomer to destroy Sodom and the rest of the Canaanites. Instead, He blessed these godless people by stirring up Abram to chase away their enemies. Perhaps the Lord was giving the Canaanites an opportunity to repent. Certainly Abram's behavior modeled grace for them. Even though he was an immigrant from Ur, he became highly respected as their friend. In fact, his rout of Chedorlaomer may be a reason why Abraham, Isaac, and Jacob lived in relative peace with their neighbors for the next two hundred years.

Are you a model of grace to your unbelieving neighbors and associates? They may be hardened in their resolve to reject the Lord. Nevertheless, God wants to bless them through you. Are you willing to be a source of blessing, even to those who will never respond to God?

KNOWING GOD
Knowing About God vs. Knowing God

Many people have knowledge about religion, Christianity, and the Bible. But as the writer to the Hebrews warns, intellectual knowledge is not the same as vital faith. Knowing about God is not the same as having a personal relationship with Him.

This is clear from everyday relationships. Reading books on marriage is not the same as spending time with one's spouse. Knowing someone's phone number is a far cry from enjoying friendship with that person. Knowing who one's customers are is not the same as dealing with a specific customer.

In the same way, *knowing* God involves far more than knowing *about* Him. Information alone does not produce tangible faith. To be sure, right thinking is involved in faith, but faith is more than mere knowledge. For example, the recipients of Hebrews knew quite a bit about the faith, such as the basic teachings about Christ, the need for repentance and for faith in God (Heb. 6:1), and the meaning of baptism, ordination, resurrection, and judgment (Heb. 6:2).

Nevertheless, without the constant work of cultivation (watering, weeding, fertilizing, pruning), spiritual weeds soon sprout and in time take over, producing thorns rather than good fruit or grain (Heb. 6:7–8). In that case, the crop (faith) is worthless and destined for burning. To avoid that outcome, diligent tending and development are required (Heb. 6:11–12). Perseverance is crucial: we must never "coast" on past experience or former tidbits of knowledge.

This part of Hebrews is a stern warning and a loving appeal for renewed commitment to Christ. Are you in need of spiritual renewal? What disciplines might help you get started on making your faith vital once again? Perhaps you might:

- Establish a small group with other believers in your workplace, industry, neighborhood, or family to meet regularly for prayer and discussion on how Christ enters into everyday situations.

- Volunteer for a program to serve the needy through your church or a community service agency.

- Speak out on workplace policies, decisions, or practices that you know to be unethical or harmful to others or the environment.

- Begin a regular habit of Bible reading and study in order to apply God's Word to your life.

- Get to know people in international missions work.

- Begin patterns of prayer such as: prayer for people with whom you live and work—even those you may not like; prayers of thanksgiving for the things God has done for you and for the responsibilities He has given to you; prayers of confession and repentance for sin or areas of neglect in your life; prayers that meditate on God and His Word; prayers that express your innermost feelings and thoughts to God.

- Keep a journal of developments and changes in your life.

- Take on a task that uses ability with which God has gifted you, especially if

K

that ability is unused or underused elsewhere in your life.

- Consider whether you have ignored, offended, or hurt someone and need to repent of your error and apologize to that person.

The point is that faith works best when it is the central unifying factor in one's life. Christ must never be just one more thing to occasionally acknowledge; rather, He must be the Lord of life and be brought into every area of life. Hebrews 6 urges us to take our faith beyond only knowing to being and doing.

KNOWLEDGE

(see Education)

L

LAITY

Can Laity Get the Job Done?

Are you surprised by Jesus' choice of His leadership team? A close reading of Luke 9 suggests that the Twelve were not exactly prize recruits for a new spiritual movement. They showed some embarrassing traits that might cause a manager to wonder, "Who hired these people? How can they possibly get the job done?"

Jesus delegated real power and authority to them to get the job done (Luke 9:1). When they reported back from their first assignment (Luke 9:10), He took them aside for a "performance review." From that point, the Twelve made many mistakes that we might be tempted to assume would disqualify them from leadership:

- They acted from a short-sighted vision. When their retreat was interrupted by a crowd eager to meet Jesus, all they could see was their limited resources in a desert place (Luke 9:12–13).
- Some of them fell asleep at a moment of great opportunity. When Jesus met with Moses and Elijah, two of the greatest leaders in Israel's history, Peter, James, and John were caught napping (Luke 9:28–32).
- They tried to preserve the status quo. Peter wanted to hang on to a good experience and build monuments to it (Luke 9:33–36).
- They gave way to fear of the unknown. Jesus healed an epileptic boy, but then fear caused the Twelve not to ask questions when they were confused (Luke 9:43–45).

- They competed to see who would be top dog. The disciples argued over greatness and privilege rather than concern themselves with serving others (Luke 9:46–48).
- They dallied in partisan politics. Encountering a rival teacher, the disciples tried to claim exclusive rights to God's activity (Luke 9:49–50).
- They plotted a dirty-tricks campaign. When their ethnic enemies proved inhospitable, the Twelve turned vicious. Jesus replied by issuing one of His strongest rebukes (Luke 9:51–56).
- They bit off more than they could chew. As they traveled, Jesus' followers overstated their commitment; in the end they failed to deliver what they promised (Luke 9:57–62).

In spite of their shortcomings, Jesus kept the Twelve on His team. He showed that undeveloped rookies can be developed into servant-leaders—over time. The Lord's hopes were rewarded, but only after His death and resurrection. The outcome can be found in Acts, where God used empowered laypeople like the Twelve to do His work.

Can we as laity do the work of God? Absolutely! But as we do, we need to take a serious look at ourselves and ask God to help us purge out those mistaken attitudes that we share with Jesus' early leaders.

From Refugee to Royalty

When society turns on you, doubts about your worth and significance can abound. This was the case for the Jewish followers of Christ to whom Peter was writing. Scattered throughout the Roman Empire, they were suffering as persecuted refugees (1 Pet. 1:6;

2:11–12; 4:12). Both the Roman government and synagogue leaders were harassing them.

In the midst of their troubles, Peter reminded these believers of what it means to belong to Jesus Christ. Instead of seeing themselves as virtual nonpersons in a hostile culture, they needed to focus on their standing in Christ, who had called them out of darkness into His marvelous light (1 Pet. 2:9). They were:

- *A chosen generation.* They were among the elect of God, chosen according to His foreknowledge and born again to a living hope (1 Pet. 1:2–5). God had called each one of them out of sin, to be a part of His redeemed people.
- *A royal priesthood.* These believers were part of the fulfillment of God's plan to prepare a kingdom of priests for Himself (Ex. 19:6; Is. 61:6; Rev. 1:6). They were to serve and worship God not by offering up the bodies of animals, but by presenting their own bodies as living sacrifices, available for His purposes (Rom. 12:1).
- *A holy nation.* Like the God who had called them to Himself, these people were to be holy (1 Pet. 1:16; compare Ex. 19:6). Their lifestyles were to reflect the very character of God, and their identity as His people was to be expressed in their character.
- *A special people.* They were called to a special, intimate relationship with God and each other. As a community, they were the people of God, with unique access to Him (Eph. 2:18).

These affirmations needed to be heard by believers who lack confidence about their significance and competence as children of God. Otherwise, too many modern-day pew-sitters may hold on to their low self-esteem, not unlike Peter's persecuted readers. They may remain spectators in the cause of Christ, watching from the sidelines and occasionally cheering while a handful of professionals carry out the contest.

Surely that is not what God wants. He has given His people eternal citizenship in His kingdom, complete equipping for His service, the opportunity of working on His behalf, and full and free friendship with Him. We are no longer refugees, but sons and daughters of the King, with all the rights and blessings of family membership.

Is Your Church Upside-Down or Right Side Up?

The believers at Thessalonica became something of a model church by embracing the gospel with unreserved commitment and sincerity (1 Thess. 2:13; 1:8–9). What does a model church look like? We can gain some idea by looking at the New Testament's many glimpses of the early church worshiping the Lord, relating to one another, and effectively reaching out to its surrounding culture with the gospel.

It's interesting that the first believers apparently did not rely on hired staff to carry out most of the church's work, nor did they occupy many formal church buildings until the fourth century A.D. Nevertheless, they were very successful at carrying out the Lord's command to be His witnesses "to the end of the earth" (Acts 1:8). At Ephesus, for example, Christian outreach was so effective that "all of Asia [Minor] heard the word of the Lord" (Acts 19:10).

If we compare the pattern that seems to emerge from the New Testament with the way most churches in the West are structured today, we can see two models for describing church life.

The first model shows a chain-of-command, pyramid-like structure. At the top are the professional, "full-time" clergy who make up perhaps one percent of any local congregation.

A second level near the top are the "paraclergy," volunteers who are particularly active in congregational life. Their dedicated service within the programs and structures of the church is greatly appreciated by the clergy and is often used as a measure of their Christian commitment.

Next are the "activists," some of whom may be among the paraclergy. These believers take a special interest in matters requiring action and the taking of a position. For example, they may advocate for a certain public policy, lead programs of social outreach, or lobby within the church to influence a particular decision.

That leaves a majority of the church's faithful worshipers available for ministries out in the world among unbelievers. They are the "church scattered" as they live and work in the world, representing Christ. They should be affirmed, equipped, and supported to impact the world for Christ.

The New Testament description of the early church includes all of the groups mentioned above. However, they are organized and deployed for service more like an inverted pyramid—"upside down" from the first model—or "right side up," depending on your viewpoint. In this model the whole congregation sees itself as the people of God, agents of Christ in the world. The pastors, teachers, and paraclergy function to equip the saints "for the work of ministry" (Eph. 4:12).

Actually, both the "gathered" and "scattered" dimensions of a church are important. God's people are called out of the world and into the "church gathered," which functions as a home for safety, a hospital for restoration, a school for development, and an orchestra for worship.

In its "scattered life," however, the church looks outside itself to fulfill Christ's Great Commission (Matt. 28:18–20) in the world. Thus the "church scattered" becomes an army overcoming spiritual opposition, a social agency to meet the needs of hurting people, an agent of justice promoting righteousness in the community, and a communications company proclaiming the good news of salvation.

The church—gathered for equipping, scattered for service. Both dimensions are crucial. Where does your church place its emphasis? What ways can you think of to strengthen its internal growth and external outreach?

Workers for the Kingdom

Do you ever wonder what your life contributes to the work of God in the world? If you are in a "secular" occupation, you may conclude that the only way to further the kingdom is to pray for and contribute financially to those who are in "full-time" Christian work. But are those your only options?

Paul described Aristarchus, Mark, and Justus as "fellow workers for the kingdom" (Col. 4:11), indicating that they may have been vocational Christian workers. However, there is no way to say whether they were employed in that work as a full-time occupation. In fact, if they followed Paul's example, they probably had other jobs through which they made their living.

The point is that drawing a paycheck for doing "ministry" is not the criterion by which to judge whether someone is a worker for God's kingdom. Kingdom work involves promoting the values, beliefs, and lifestyle of the kingdom. That may involve professional employment such as pastoring a church or serving on a mission field. But kingdom workers are also found among doctors, accountants, engineers, painters, salespeople, auto mechanics, and homemakers. Wherever believers are furthering the goals and objectives of Christ, they are working for His kingdom.

How does your life promote the purposes of God? Do you use your skills and abilities toward that end, whether or not pay is involved? Or have you given up and concluded that because you are not a vocational Christian worker, you aren't really serving the Lord with your life and career? If so, you'll want to reconsider what it means to be a worker for Christ's kingdom!

*For more on this topic, see **CALLING**, "All Believers Are 'Ministers,'" page 42; **VOCATION**, "Called to a New Purpose," page 414.*

LAND USE

(*see* Conservation)

LAW

God's Law

Paul's reference to "law" (Rom. 2:12) has to do not with laws in general, but with the specific code of rules and regulations that God gave to Moses on Mount Sinai. The Law was part of the covenant that set Israel apart as God's people. It governed their worship, their relationship to God, and their social relationships with one another. The Ten Commandments form a summary of that Law.

Israel was not the only nation to have a law code. Indeed, such collections were common in the ancient world. Most of them began by explaining that the gods gave the king power to reign, along with a pronouncement about how good and capable he was. Then came the king's laws grouped by subject. Finally, most of the codes closed with a series of curses and blessings.

What set the Mosaic Law apart from these other codes was, first of all, its origin. The Law was given by God Himself. It issued from His very nature; like Him it was holy, righteous, and good. Thus, all crimes in Israel were crimes against God (1 Sam. 12:9–10). He expected all of the people to love and serve Him (Amos 5:21–24). As their final judge, He disciplined those who violated the Law (Ex. 22:21–24; Deut. 10:18; 19:17), though He also held the nation responsible for insuring that justice was carried out (13:6–10; 17:7; Num. 15:32–36).

Furthermore, God ruled over Israel, in effect, as the nation's King. Ancient kings often enacted laws to try to outdo their predecessors in image, economic power, and political influence. God, however, gave His Law as an expression of love for His people, to advance their best interests (Ex. 19:5–6).

The Law can be divided into three categories—moral laws, ceremonial laws, and civil laws. The latter regulated in great detail matters having to do with leaders, the army, criminal cases, crimes against property, humane treatment, personal and family rights, property rights, and other social behavior.

The ceremonial laws contained specifications regarding public worship and ritual, giving high priority to the concept of holiness. Because God is holy (Lev. 21:8), Israel was to be holy in all its religious practices.

The Law was given specifically to Israel, but it rests on eternal moral principles that are consistent with God's character. Thus it is a summary of fundamental and universal moral standards. It expresses the essence of what God requires of people. That's why when God judges, He can be impartial. Gentiles will not be judged by the Law (Rom. 2:12), since it was not given to them, but they will still be judged by the same righteous standard that underlies the Law.

For more on this topic, see CIVIL DISOBEDIENCE, "A Case of Civil Disobedience," page 65; INJUSTICE, "Why Don't Things Change?" page 224.

LAWSUITS
Suing for Damages

The Law was given to an agricultural society. Thus we find codes concerning goring oxen and open pits (Ex. 21:28–36). Nevertheless, the principles of care for human life and safety and for awarding restitution for personal injury carry over into any society and any work environment.

God took a strong interest in preventive health care (for example, Lev. 13:1–59), and that involved safety in the workplace and community. When an injury occurred, the injured party was due restitution in an amount and to a degree that was appropriate to the case. The Law provided penalties for injuring another human being to an extent that would approximate the loss suffered by the injured party (for example, Ex. 21:23–24; Lev. 24:17–22).

It's interesting that nothing in Scripture suggests that injured persons should profit from their losses. Nor do we find anything about damages for pain, suffering, fear, psychological stress, or similar emotional conditions.

As Christians living in a society prone to lawsuits, we do well to carefully consider the Old Testament's prescriptions for settling property and injury cases. We are not bound by these codes, but they do show us the spirit with which we should seek restitution.

For more on this topic, see ARBITRATION, "The Scandal of Litigating Christians," page 24; VIOLENCE, "A New Way to Respond," page 411.

LAZINESS
No Work? No Eat!

Paul urged that those who would not work should not eat (2 Thess. 3:10). He may have been dealing with the laziness and idleness of those who thought there would be no tomorrow because they expected the immediate return of the Lord. Two thousand years later, we still anticipate the Second Coming. But it's interesting that nowadays people generally work as if there will be a tomorrow without a return.

It's worth noting that these Macedonian believers, if they were the same ones that Paul referred to in 2 Corinthians 8:2, lived in abject poverty. It is common in poor communities—where jobs are few and many of those that do exist pay too little to support even the basics—for some to grow discouraged and give up all attempts at finding employment. That could also explain the "disorderly" behavior Paul rebuked (2 Thess. 3:6).

For more on this topic, see **DILIGENCE**, *"Laziness—The Path to Ruin," page 105.*

LEADERSHIP

Watchmen Who Don't Watch

Even as Isaiah spoke of God's salvation that would be available to all people (Is. 56:1–8), he warned about a group of blind watchmen who would be found sleeping on the job (Is. 56:10).

In ancient Israel, watchtowers were erected in fields, pastures, and vineyards to enable watchmen to keep a lookout for wild animals, thieves, and other hazards. The security of the crops, animals, or property depended on these watchmen, so the blind watchmen described by Isaiah were not only derelict, they were dangerous.

Who were these sightless guards? They may have been the numerous false prophets and religious leaders of Isaiah's day, along with rulers and government officials who were foolish, incompetent, lazy, greedy, or irresponsible. However, the denunciation of derelict watchmen may also refer prophetically to the corrupt leaders of Jesus' day, who stood staunchly opposed to God's Son (Matt. 23:16–17).

Whoever these leaders are, they stand condemned before God, having failed in their responsibilities. It is a warning to those of us in leadership today—especially in positions of spiritual leadership—to stay alert, keeping an eye out not for our own gain or personal welfare, but for that of the people among whom God has placed us to serve.

It's Windy at the Top!

Moses had many occasions to learn what countless leaders down through history have discovered: it's windy at the top! Lacking water, the people complained bitterly to their leader, as if he had caused the situation or had the power to fix it (Ex. 17:2).

Perhaps you've been through a similar experience of being in charge, knowing that you are doing the right thing, or at least the best that you can, only to hear complaints from the people following you because things are not going so well.

If so, this incident from Moses' life is a reminder that just because you exercise authority correctly, you will not necessarily be treated favorably by others. Often the one in authority must make a real tradeoff between being faithful and being popular.

A Performance Review for Leaders

Much has been written in recent years about effective managers focusing on customers, markets, trends, quality, succession, marketing, teamwork, and commitment. These and other factors are important, sometimes vitally so. But Ezekiel's prophecy concerning the leaders of Israel (Ezek. 34:1–2) points out one more critical factor: if the people are neglected or suffering, the leader's qualifications to lead are in question.

The "shepherds" of Israel received a "performance review" from God, and it was not good. The leaders were spending most of their energies feeding themselves instead of the flock (Ezek. 34:2–8), and they were giving them nothing but leftovers (Ezek. 34:18–19). Not only were they neglecting the least powerful and most vulnerable among the people—the weak, the sick, the broken, and the refugees—but they were actually taking advantage of them (Ezek. 34:4–6, 21). There was only one remedy for this situation—to remove the leaders from leadership (Ezek. 34:9–10). God Himself would heal the hurting, restore the scattered, and feed His flock (Ezek. 34:11–16).

Centuries later, Jesus prescribed "shepherd leadership" for one of His followers (John 21:15–19). As the Good Shepherd, Jesus had modeled this approach by laying down His life for His sheep (John 10:11–17).

Security, safety, sufficient supply of necessities, and shared outcomes: these are some of the essentials that good leaders provide for their followers. If you are in a position of leadership in your work, home, church, or community, ask yourself how well you are providing these essentials for the people following you. In what ways could they be better served by you as a leader?

Missing Out on the Payoff

Imagine starting a business and working long and hard for many years to make it successful. The enterprise struggles at first, but eventually it stands on the brink of a major breakthrough in which all your efforts will pay off handsomely. Yet at virtually the last instant before you hit it big, you learn that the fruits of your labor will go to someone else.

That, essentially, is what happened to Moses after leading the Israelites to the brink of the Promised Land. Despite a lifetime of leadership, he would pass the reins of control to Joshua, who would take the people into the land (Deut. 3:28).

Under the circumstances, Moses accepted the transition with remarkable goodwill. How can we account for that? Perhaps it was because he was a humble man (Num. 12:3) who never assumed that the authority and position he enjoyed were his to keep. He saw them for what they were—temporary gifts from God to be held in trust during his brief life on earth.

How about you? Do you find yourself clinging to your possessions, power, or position, ever suspicious that God might take them away? Or do you hold them with a light touch, mindful that whatever you have is a gift from God, given to you to manage, not own (see 1 Cor. 4:7)?

*For more on this topic, see **ADVISORS**, "David's Folly," page 9; **BURNOUT**, "Jethro Performs an Intervention," page 40; **INTEGRITY**, "Risk and Responsibility," page 226.*

LEARNING

(*see* Education)

LEGALISM

Jesus Confronts the Legalists

A pleasant day's hike through the grainfields turned sour when Jesus and His disciples ran into some Pharisees (Luke 6:1–2). Ever on the lookout for infractions of their traditions, especially by Jesus and His followers, these legalists objected to the disciples "harvesting" grain in violation of the Sabbath. Never mind the group's hunger. For that mat-

ter, never mind that they were obviously snacking: after all, a handful of tiny heads of wheat or barley could hardly make a satisfying meal.

But the Pharisees would take Scripture out of context or add to it in order to condemn people for normal, God-given behavior. They ignored God's love and the freeness of His grace.

The Pharisees had lost sight of the intent of the Law and had taken upon themselves the impossible task of earning God's favor through moral perfectionism. The more they labored to "keep the Law," the more they wrapped themselves in an ever-expanding cloak of man-made rules and regulations. Worse, they judged everyone around them by their impossible standards.

Jesus challenged them by using the very Scriptures they claimed to honor (Luke 6:3–4). Furthermore, according to Matthew's account of this incident, Jesus questioned their basic attitudes, which seemed to have more to do with ritual than with the mercy that God values (Matt. 12:7).

Yet the critics only seemed to harden in their legalism, continuing to dog Jesus' steps on another Sabbath, when He visited one of their synagogues (Luke 6:6–7).

Legalists may be the hardest people to reach with the message of God's love. Jesus never won the Pharisees over as a group. But neither did He allow their abuse of Scripture or people to go unchallenged.

The Letter and the Spirit

The Sabbath-day controversy (Luke 14:1–6) shows a tension between the letter of the Law and its spirit. The Old Testament was clear about keeping the Sabbath holy by resting from work (Ex. 20:8–11). But Jesus was known for doing the "work" of healing on the Sabbath (Luke 13:10–17). Was He breaking the Law or not? The lawyers and Pharisees couldn't say (Luke 14:6).

Jesus let them stew over the issue, but clearly He was convinced that He was acting well within the Law. If He appeared to break it, it was only because His enemies paid more attention to superficial, external ways of "keeping" the Law than to its underlying moral spirit. Furthermore, over the centuries their predecessors had heaped up countless traditions on top of the Law, creating a mammoth set of expectations that no one could fulfill.

In our own day, even believers sometimes try to live by a rigid set of dos and don'ts that go beyond the clear teaching of Scripture. Like the Pharisees, we are tempted to be more concerned about the externals of the faith than the larger principles of "justice and the love of God" (Luke 11:42). Given His treatment of the self-righteous Pharisees, what would Jesus say to us?

LEISURE

(*see* Rest and Recreation)

LIBERTY

(*see* Freedom)

LIFE AFTER DEATH

(*see* Immortality)

LIFE IN THE FAST LANE

(*see* Burnout; Rest and Recreation)

LIFE PLANNING
Building a Life by the Blueprints

No reliable contractor would start work on a skyscraper without first consulting the architect's plans. Yet how many of us try to build something far more complex and significant than any high-rise—our own lives—without bothering to check the plans that God has drawn up for the project?

While Solomon was building the temple, the most significant architectural achievement of his reign, God reminded him of the spiritual foundation that undergirded the project as well as life itself (1 Kin. 6:12). Just as plans were developed for the building (1 Kin. 6:37–38), so God's statutes, commandments, and judgments formed the blueprints for Solomon's life and the lives of his people.

God's Word also forms the guidelines by which we need to build our lives today. As we "walk in them," God can be relied on to fulfill His promises and purposes in us. Are you checking your life against the divine blueprints on a daily basis by reading and studying Scripture? If not, you are putting up a structure that is ultimately going to collapse (Matt. 7:24–27).

LIMITATIONS
Hemmed In?

No one likes freedom to be limited and restricted, yet boundaries and limits are often the wisest and most compassionate safeguard there is. Job complained that God had hemmed him in so much that he felt shackled and chained (Job 13:27).

Job could not see what God saw. All he knew was that his freedom was limited. But he had no idea of what perils might have awaited him if God had given him total latitude over his life.

You may feel hemmed in by the limitations that are placed on your life. For example, at work you may face policies that restrict your movement and limit your options. But look carefully at the underlying reasons behind those boundaries. Perhaps they are set for reasons of:

- safety—for example, restrictions on what cannot be worn on a factory floor;
- security—for example, who can and cannot gain access to confidential files;
- prudence—for example, specifications about bidding procedures for suppliers; or
- people development—for example, necessary training in order to develop and promote people into higher positions.

You may not like the restrictions that are placed on you. But consider them as safeguards against potential problems. Doing so can help you accept a small loss of freedom in exchange for greater good that you may not always be able to see.

*For more on this topic, see **MATURITY**, "Learning from Peter's Impulsiveness," page 258.*

LITIGATION

(*see* Lawsuits)

LOANS
Co-Signing for Loans

A common policy among lending institutions today is to require people with risky credit to have someone co-sign their loan. The cosigner must be able to make good on the note if the principal borrower defaults on repayment. In effect, the risk in the transaction is being transferred from the lender to the cosigner. However, Proverbs warns would-be cosigners that the risk is too great to accept, even for a friend (Prov. 6:1–5; 17:18).

There are many reasons why:

- Guaranteeing debts will sooner or later result in loss (Prov. 11:15).
- Co-signing lessens the incentive for the principal borrower to pay back the loan, and thus may encourage irresponsibility.
- We are accountable both to God (Matt. 25:14–30) and to our families and heirs (Prov. 13:22) for how we manage our property. We are supposed to use our resources to the glory of God and for the benefit of others (1 Pet. 4:10), not risk them unnecessarily.
- If we cannot afford to lose what we pledge, then we may jeopardize the security of our family and heirs, a form of irresponsibility that Scripture strongly condemns (1 Tim. 5:8).
- If we co-sign for a friend or family member, and he fails to pay the debt, we risk the loss of the relationship.

Are there circumstances under which cosigning a note is permissible? Yes. Scripture does not flatly prohibit suretyship. In fact, it offers several examples which indicate that guaranteeing a loan can be a form of service to others, and even a testimony of love and the self-sacrificial spirit that lies at the heart of the gospel:

The patriarch Judah volunteered to be "collateral" for his younger half-brother Benjamin (Gen. 43:8–9). Joseph was overwhelmed by this willingness of Judah to place himself at risk (Gen. 44:32; 45:11). Judah was demonstrating the kind of self-sacrifice that Jesus later urged His followers to practice.

Paul became surety for the runaway slave Onesimus (Philem. 10–13, 18–19). Paul did not incur this risk foolishly. He knew Onesimus quite well (Philem. 12). Nonetheless, Paul's act was a marvelous display of the grace of Christ.

Christ became surety for us as sinners when He obtained eternal redemption for us (Heb. 7:22; 9:12). By His atoning death, He "wiped out the certificate of debt with its requirements against us" (Col. 2:14; compare 1 Pet. 1:18–19).

In light of these models, there may be times when guaranteeing a note not only makes sense, but gives us an opportunity to demonstrate in concrete terms the redeeming work of Christ. For example, a wise and financially able believer could offer to become surety for someone who needs help in buying equipment or tools to earn a living. He could explain in the process that what he is doing is analogous to what Jesus has done for us. Thus the cosigner would not only be sharing the gospel, but showing the gospel as well.

*For more on this topic, see **BANKING**, "Charitable Loans to the Poor," page 29; **DEBT**, "Freely You Have Received, Freely Give," page 98.*

LORD'S DAY

Observing the Lord's Day

John's reference to the Lord's Day (Rev. 1:10), generally regarded as referring to Sunday, suggests that to first-century Christians the first day of the week was particularly significant. That raises the question of whether Sundays are special today.

We know that the early church gave special honor to Sunday, the first day of the week, as the day on which Jesus was raised from the dead. Every week on that day they celebrated His resurrection and met for worship and instruction (1 Cor. 16:2). This observance of a special day was both a parallel and a contrast to the Jewish Sabbath, or day of rest, at the end of the week. The Sabbath celebrated God's rest from creation.

Some Jewish Christians continued to observe the Sabbath, as well as the Jewish festival days. But many Gentiles in the church did not. Apparently this created tension, especially when the observance of Jewish practices began to be linked by some to salvation. A council of church leaders at Jerusalem did not include a demand for Sabbath observance in its decision regarding Gentile converts (Acts 15:20, 28–29).

Likewise, in writing to the Romans, Paul urged everyone to decide for themselves whether one day should be esteemed above another; but by all means, no one should judge another for his convictions.

It's interesting that the phrase "the Lord's Day" occurs only this one time in Rev. 1:10. In Asia Minor, where the churches to which

John was writing were located, people celebrated the first day of each month as the Emperor's Day. Some believe that a day of the week was also called by this name. Thus, by calling the first day of the week the Lord's Day, John may have been making a direct challenge to emperor worship, as he does elsewhere in the book.

LOVE

Love Is a Choice

Popular culture often describes love in terms of passion, sexuality, or blind devotion. By this measure, love is little more than an uncontrollable attraction toward another person that ebbs and flows unconsciously. This sort of "love" looks only for its own gain and can walk away if its demands and needs go unmet or unsatisfied.

By contrast, God called Hosea to pursue a radically different kind of love, one based on a conscious choice to be committed to someone else for her benefit, regardless of her response to that gift (Hos. 3:1–3). That was how God was committed to Israel. Hosea's marriage was an illustration of God's marriage to the spiritually adulterous nation of Israel.

Lessons on True Love

Are you in love with love? Solomon was intoxicated with the love of his bride (Song 4:10). What is your understanding of this powerful force in human life?

Unlike our own culture, the Bible exalts genuine love. It invites us to discover love's true nature by portraying love from many angles. The Song of Solomon describes in vivid imagery the sights, sounds, and sensations of romantic love. This poem is one of several major treatments of love in Scripture. Other passages from which we can learn a great deal are:

- Moses' call to the Israelites to learn and practice the love of God toward all (Deut. 10:12–11:22; 30:6–20).
- Psalm 45, a "Song of Love" that praises the marriage relationship.
- The Book of Hosea, in which God calls the prophet Hosea to seek out, rescue, and lovingly restore his adulterous wife.
- Jesus' teachings on love, including: loving our enemies (Matt. 5:43–46), loving

the Lord (Mark 12:30–38), and the love of God the Father and the practice of that love among believers (John 13:34–15:19).
- Paul's teaching on love between neighbors (Rom. 13:8–10), love among fellow church members who are experiencing competition and conflict (1 Cor. 13:1–7), and love among spouses, families, and other believers (Eph. 5:25–6:24).
- John's teaching concerning love among believers and how that love should operate in a hostile world (1 John 3:1–5:3).

The Bible invites us to discover what love really is. The love that our world promotes tends to be a distortion. People use it to make money, to hurt others or oppress them, and to gratify themselves. But following the love of Christ opens up a whole new world as we receive God's love for us, learn to love our neighbors, and obtain a healthy love for ourselves.

Love Is Tough Work

First Corinthians 13 has been called the Love Chapter because of its powerful description of love. However, in reading this passage, keep in mind that it's easy to talk about love; it's much harder to do the tough work of living it. Love as God intended it is more than just passion, romantic feelings, or sentimental expressions. It involves commitment, sacrifice, and service—the kind of things that benefit both the giver and the receiver.

Here is a summary of the characteristics of godly love:

- Does not rival for attention ("envy").
- Does not brag on itself ("parade").
- Does not inflate its self-view ("puffed up").
- Does not tread on another's feelings ("rude").
- Does not take another's things ("seek its own").
- Does not take offense easily ("provoked").
- Does not keep a record of wrongs suffered ("no evil").
- Does not make unrighteousness its object of rejoicing ("rejoice in iniquity").
- Does celebrate others' achievements in righteousness ("rejoIces in the truth").
- Does keep all things in confidence ("bears all things").

- Does know what God can do ("believes all things").
- Does hold out holy ambitions for others to achieve ("hopes all things").
- Does survive under every condition ("endures all things").

Where do we learn to love like this? John wrote, "We love . . . because He first loved us," referring to Christ (1 John 4:19). We receive this magnificent kind of love from Christ Himself. Would you like to be loved as 1 Corinthians 13 describes it, and then be able to love others in the same manner? It starts by accepting Christ's love for you, and then committing yourself to expressing that kind of love in your life and relationships.

Ways to Love

Are you ever in doubt about what you should do in a given situation? One rule of thumb that always applies is, Do unto others as you would have them do unto you (Matt. 7:12).

This "golden rule" is universally recognized. It summarizes the principle of love as an ethical cornerstone for life. In fact, Jesus taught that the greatest commandment was to love God with all of one's heart, soul, and mind, and the second greatest was to love one's neighbor as oneself (Matt. 22:37–39). Likewise, James called love the "royal law" (James 2:8), and Paul wrote that of faith, hope, and love, love was the greatest; it never fails (1 Cor. 13:8, 13).

We also see this in Hebrews. Having summarized the vast changes brought about by the coming of Christ, the book's final chapter begins with a clear statement about one thing that has not changed, love. Love among believers must continue (Heb. 13:1). The writer goes on to list several ways in which that can happen:

- Hospitality toward strangers; in our day these might include immigrants, the homeless, and people of a different race than we are (Heb. 13:2).
- Remembrance of prisoners; it would be just as easy to forget them, but the principle of love says we ought to treat them as if chained with them (Heb. 13:3).
- Faithfulness to our marriage; this goes beyond sexual fidelity to active enrich-

ment and development of our partner (Heb. 13:4).
- Contentment regarding money and possessions; this is a severe challenge in modern culture (Heb. 13:5–6).

Christlike love is very practical. It seeks expression toward a wide variety of people. Is that love "continuing" in your life?

The Power of Love

Human history and literature is filled with stories of the challenges and failures of people in love. Love has produced great tragedies, as well as great achievements. The Bible speaks extensively about the great power of love:

- It can be "better than wine" (Song 1:2).
- It is "as strong as death" (Song 8:6).
- It is greater even than faith or hope (1 Cor. 13:13).
- It is the root of great evil when its object is money (1 Tim. 6:10).
- It "covers all sins" (Prov. 10:12).
- Perfect love "casts out fear" (1 John 4:18).
- The love of Christ "passes knowledge" (Eph. 3:19).
- It is the only debt we ought to owe each other (Rom. 13:8).
- It "does not envy" (1 Cor. 13:4).
- It makes believers capable of blessing those who curse them, and doing good to those who hate, spitefully use, or persecute them (Matt. 5:44).
- It is the essence of the commandments of God (Rom. 13:9; Gal. 5:14; James 2:8).
- Its absence is evidence that one does not know God (1 John 4:8, 12, 20).
- It empowers people to give their lives for someone else, even as Christ did (John 15:13–17; Eph. 5:25–28).

God is the source of love. Sinful human beings have often twisted and abused it, and even reduced it to destructive fits of passion and lust. But God wants to help us rediscover love, so that we bring restoration and healing to ourselves and everyone we touch. This is basic to the message of Christ.

The Test of Love

A key test of our commitment to Christ is our love for other believers (John 13:31–35). It is not just our words that express our love,

L

but our attitudes and actions as well. Jesus did not say that others would know we are His disciples by what we say, or how we dress, or what we know, or the label of our denomination. He said, "as I have loved you" (John 13:34). Shortly afterward, He laid down His life for those first believers.

What Kind of Love Is This?

"Love" is a very confusing concept these days. People use the word "love" to describe very different relationships: people "love" their dog . . . a certain type of car . . . a brand of pizza . . . a sexually intimate partner . . . another person for whom they have deep feelings. What can "love" possibly mean if it applies equally well to dogs, machines, food, sex, or close companions?

The Bible is not confused or vague about the powerful concept it calls love. Greek, the international language of Jesus' day and the language in which the New Testament was written, had four distinct words for love, each with its own shade of meaning:

- *Eros* denoted the relationship between male and female, including physical desire, craving, and longing. That word for love is not used in the New Testament.
- *Stergos* described affection and was applied especially to the mutual love between family members. It is not used in the New Testament either.
- *Philos* reflected the care and concern that friends have for each other, what we would call brotherly love. Peter spoke of this kind of love when he and Jesus discussed his future task of serving others (John 21:15–17).
- *Agape* described a unique type of supreme love involving a conscious and deliberate choice to do good for another, a commitment based on the willful choice of the lover, not the qualities of the person receiving the love. Agape love is perhaps best seen in God's love for the world (John 3:16) and in the love that God calls believers to display (1 Cor. 13:1–13).

When Jesus recalled the greatest of the commandments, both of which had to do with love (Matt. 22:34–40), He was calling for agape love, a sustained and conscious choice to gra-ciously serve God, neighbor, and self, expecting nothing in return. Followers of Christ learn this kind of love as God loves them first. He then commands us to live in the same way toward others (1 John 3:11–24). God's love empowers us to love by choice rather than just emotion or senses, and to sustain our love even in the face of hostility or rejection.

God wants to deliver a new kind of love—agape love—to families, workplaces, and communities through His people. Who around you needs that kind of intentional touch of compassion and grace?

For more on this topic, see **RELATION-SHIPS,** *"Love God, Love People," page 335.*

LOYALTY

Known for Our Commitment

Commitment is in jeopardy these days. Some even call it the "C" word, as if to shame it as something we won't even acknowledge. After all, the demands and costs are too great. Today, convenience usually wins out over the sacrifice involved in being committed to someone or something.

The situation was no less confused in Jesus' day. As He began to unveil a new way of life for His followers, critics appeared and challenged Him on the difficulties of keeping the marriage commitment (Matt. 19:3, 7). Even His disciples quivered as they perceived the costs of maintaining one's marriage vows (Matt. 19:10). Later, they wanted to send away some bothersome children in order to deal with more "important" things (Matt. 19:13). It seems that Jesus was surrounded by men who were a little unsure about domestic matters.

The discussion of divorce followed appropriately on the heels of Jesus' remarks about the merits of boundless forgiveness (Matt. 18:21–35). What better way to lead into the topic of commitment? Jesus didn't ignore the problems and failures of human relationships. Those very shortcomings are what make forgiveness—and commitment—crucial.

Those lessons were reinforced in Jesus' next encounter, with a rich man who wanted to ensure his possession of eternal life (Matt. 19:16–30). The man proposed rule-keeping as the standard by which he should be judged, but Jesus countered with an appeal for service (Matt. 19:21). True wealth involved a higher commitment—serving the Lord and others rather than the idol of material gain (Matt. 19:23, 29).

Followers of Christ need to be known for their commitment—to marriage, to family, to community, to work, above all to Christ. Such loyalty often means messy obedience, but it is the way of Christ. How desperately that is needed in a day when people make vows of convenience rather than commitment.

*For more on this topic, see **STING OPER-ATION,** " 'Stings' Expose Loyalty to God," page 384.*

LUST

(*see* Sexuality)

LUXURY

(*see* Affluence; Prosperity)

LYING

Led Astray by Lies

Have you ever tried to minimize the guilt of telling a lie with the attitude, "Of course I lied. Doesn't everybody? What's the big deal?"

Part of the "big deal" is that if you assume you're joining the crowd by using deception,

LYING

then who can you trust ultimately? How can you ever be sure that you are hearing the truth from anyone? Maybe everyone else has taken the same attitude you have: "Everyone lies. What's the big deal?"

Amos warned the people of his day that lies would always lead them astray; deception would always cause trouble. In fact, they were already in trouble largely because they followed the lies of their fathers (Amos 2:4). The prophet's statement and the history of Israel show that generations can suffer tragically from patterns of deception.

Yet people try many ways to deceive themselves about the true nature of lying. For example, we use euphemisms such as "shading the truth," "telling a little white lie," or "skirting the issue." We also try to justify lying by suggesting that it is normal, and even inevitable, as if sooner or later we have to lie.

Yet the worst tragedy about this way of living may be that we end up telling lies and believing lies about God (Rom. 1:25), and about ourselves (1 John 1:10).

Lying is not an inescapable fact of human nature. God does not lie (Num. 23:19; Titus 1:2), and He tells us not to lie in the Ten Commandments (Ex. 20:16). Likewise, Paul exhorted believers not to lie to one another (Eph. 4:25; Col. 3:9). So it is possible to speak and live with honesty. But it is self-defeating to practice deception. In the long run, there is no integrity in the habit, and sooner or later one begins to distrust everyone—including oneself.

Lying Leads to Trouble

Is honesty *always* the best policy? Or are there times when it may be best to lie? Ethicists may debate whether certain circumstances justify deception, but Scripture seems clear that lying leads to trouble. Deceit turns on its source, exacting a high price in the long run.

For example, Hananiah the prophet misled the people of Judah by denouncing Jeremiah's prophecy and then giving a prophecy of his own, preceded by the words, "Thus says the LORD." But in fact, the Lord had not spoken to him (Jer. 28:10–11). That kind of false prophecy was a grievous sin, punishable by death (Deut. 13:1–5). Not surprisingly, the

Lord called Hananiah to pay for his deception with his life (Jer. 28:15–17).

The Bible gives numerous other examples to show that "he who speaks lies shall perish" (Prov. 19:9), and that the Lord hates dishonesty (Prov. 6:16–17):

- Sin and death were introduced into the world because a lie was told and believed (Gen. 3:1–7; 1 Tim. 2:14).
- Cain tried to lie his way out of accountability for killing his brother Abel. The result was a lifetime of running from others (Gen. 4:1–16).
- Rebekah engineered a lie for her son Jacob to tell his father Isaac in order to gain the family blessing. The result was estrangement in the family and generations of hostility between the offspring of the two brothers (Gen. 27:5–17, 41–46).
- Joseph's brothers lied to their father about selling the boy to slave traders, resulting in profound heartache for their father (Gen. 37:28–35).
- Potiphar's wife crafted a lie to frame Joseph with attempted rape, resulting in an unjust prison sentence (Gen. 39:7–20).
- David practiced a gruesome form of deception by arranging for the murder of Uriah to cover up his affair with Bathsheba. Through Nathan the prophet the lie was exposed. Bathsheba's child died, and a lifetime of painful relationships ensued in David's family (2 Sam. 11–12).
- Peter denied that he even knew the Lord when asked by several bystanders in the courtyard of Caiaphas' house, resulting in great shame and sorrow (Matt. 26:69–74).
- Ananias and Sapphira lied to the early church and the Holy Spirit about a financial gift, which brought about their untimely death (Acts 5:1–11).

Jesus spoke clearly about the nature of lying when he declared that lies are of the devil (John 8:44). By contrast, Jesus is the source of all truth, and those who speak and practice the truth show that they belong to Him (John 14:6; 1 John 3:19). Are you a person of truth and integrity, or is lying a way of life with you?

Peter and a Servant Girl

Fear of the truth and its consequences can lead even the strongest among us to hide behind lies and half-truths. So it was for Peter, the stouthearted fisherman and leader among the apostles. No doubt fearing for his life as he sat in the courtyard of the high priest's house, Peter denied to a servant girl that he had any connection with Jesus (Luke 22:56–57).

Normally Peter would have paid little attention to the young woman, who was merely a doorkeeper in Caiaphas's household (John 18:15–17). But having watched his Master's arrest and perhaps having learned from John, who gained him access to the courtyard, about the events taking place inside, Peter told an outright lie. Apparently he feared what the girl might say or do if he admitted to being one of Jesus' followers.

It's interesting to contrast this situation with Peter's later encounter with another doorkeeper, the servant girl Rhoda (Acts 12:1–17). On that occasion, it was not Peter who was afraid of the servant girl, but the servant girl who was astonished and overjoyed at seeing Peter, who had been miraculously delivered from jail. By that point, of course, Peter had repented of denying Jesus and had received the Holy Spirit, who filled him with power and boldness to stand before not only the high priest (Acts 4:5–6, 18–21), but King Herod as well.

What place in your life is so vulnerable that you would tell an outright lie—even to someone that you would normally regard as inconsequential—rather than reveal the truth? Like Peter, are you afraid of the consequences of being identified with Jesus? If so, you need a dose of the Spirit's power to give you the courage to be honest (see Acts 1:8).

For more on this topic, see DECEIT, "Playing Games with God," page 99.

M

MAGIC

(*see* Occult)

MALE FRIENDSHIPS

A Solid Friendship Between Men

Many men today have numerous acquaintances but few friends, lots of associates but few companions. As a result, a man can feel lonely, isolated, and misunderstood. Even if he is married to a supportive wife with whom he has good communication, he can feel an emptiness inside, because no one knows his soul "man-to-man."

David and Jonathan shared a rare and valuable friendship. Their bond serves as a model for men today who need and seek healthy relationships with other men.

Perhaps the key, as in any relationship, is trust and loyalty. That was the basis of David and Jonathan's companionship. Why else would a child of royal privilege risk friendship with a rural shepherd boy who was an enemy of the family? Jonathan's family had experienced what today we would call severe dysfunction (1 Sam. 19:1–17). Perhaps insecure and troubled, he was drawn to the commoner David because he recognized him as someone who would be true and faithful. As the two young men got to know each other, they formalized their commitment to each other. Then they honored that pledge during a time when their relationship was severely tested (1 Sam. 18:1–4; 20:1–4).

If you are a man, are you prepared to enter into this kind of profound trust and loyalty with another man? It may mean sacrifice, just as Jonathan ultimately lost his relationship with his father Saul in order to fulfill his pledge to David (1 Sam. 20:32–33). But some things are worth paying dearly for. A solid friendship that lasts through the years is one of them.

MALE-FEMALE RELATIONSHIPS

(*see also* Husbands; Marriage)

A New View on Marriage

In a great many pagan marriages of the first century, the husband was much older than his wife. He frequented other partners for sex, taking on a wife only to father legitimate children. Thus a girl of thirteen or fourteen entered an arranged marriage, frequently against her will and often with a man she had never previously met. There was little communication, cooperation, or affection—or expectation of these.

But new life in Christ called for new patterns in marriage (Eph. 5:21–29). Paul instructed the husband to love his wife and seek her personal development—a radically new idea in that culture. The wife was to respond with commitment and loyalty. Her submission was not subordination but a wholehearted response to her husband's love.

Every Man King

Fear of women learning to assert themselves is nothing new, as the account of Esther shows. Queen Vashti's refusal to parade her beauty at her husband's men-only, week-long drinking-fest (Esth. 1:5–12) was officially interpreted as nothing less than an act of rebellion against male authority (Esth. 1:16–17). As a result, King Ahasuerus fired off a decree intended to reinforce the mastery of every male in the empire over the women in his household (1:22).

It would be perilous to try to judge ancient cultures and customs against modern-day understandings of gender issues. Nevertheless, it seems clear that some of the men of Persia felt threatened by Vashti's self-will. Perhaps they feared the social chaos that might result if women refused to comply with their husbands' wishes, no matter how degrading those wishes might be.

Many men today display similar fears about assertive and independent women. The Book of Esther can help by showing the value of a woman with strong character. Vashti's successor, Esther, also showed assertiveness by not waiting to be called by Ahasuerus, but entering into his presence on her own initiative, at the risk of her life (Esth. 4:11; 5:1–3). As a result, she saved her people the Jews from genocide.

Esther is hardly the Bible's last word on the subject of authority in male-female relationships. But it seems to encourage women to speak their minds and assert their wills to combat evil and promote good.

A New Role for Women

The discounting of women by men is a pattern that has persisted throughout history. Jesus' male disciples found it easy to dismiss Mary Magdalene, Joanna, Mary, and the other women when they reported the empty tomb and a conversation with the risen Lord (Luke 24:11).

The news should have been encouraging, given the confusion that dominated the group after their Master's cruel death. But the men rejected the words of these women. It didn't seem to matter that the women had followed Jesus just as closely and in fact had stood by Him through His ordeal rather than betray Him (as Judas had), or deny Him (as Peter had), or run away in fear (as all the men had).

Male skepticism of women's testimony raises questions about the masculine mind. Why are some men so insecure that they must exalt themselves over the other sex to feel significant? Can true companionship survive that kind of distrust? Sooner or later, men can expect to pay for that kind of abuse, especially since both male and female are created in God's image and vested with authority and responsibility together (Gen. 1:26–31; 2:18–25).

If you're a man, are you growing in your appreciation of woman as God's creation? Do you esteem the women God brings your way? Are you learning to listen to them, partner with them, and even follow their lead toward godliness?

For more on this topic, see **SUBMISSION**, *"A Lifestyle of Submission," page 386.*

MANAGEMENT

A Reputation for Trustworthiness

One of the hardest challenges for employers and business owners today is to find trustworthy employees—especially managers. With millions of dollars of investment at risk, companies search high and low for people they can depend on to protect their interests.

Things were no different in Daniel's day. When Darius the Mede conquered Babylon, he needed experienced, trustworthy people to manage the province for him. He was looking for leaders who could maintain civil order, collect taxes, and stimulate trade and commerce. So he selected one hundred twenty provincial governors known as *satraps*, which means "protectors of the kingdom" (Dan. 6:1). Over these he placed three governors, including Daniel (Dan. 6:2).

Why Daniel? "Because an excellent spirit was in him" (Dan. 6:3). That is, he was trustworthy. His reputation was above reproach. He was known to be above bribery and extortion, which were common among officials of that day. In placing him in a senior position, Darius had confidence that he would "suffer no loss" (Dan. 6:2). Indeed, Daniel's ethical character so distinguished him from the other officials that Darius intended to place him over the whole realm (Dan. 6:3).

Are you characterized by an "excellent spirit," a reputation for trustworthiness and ethical integrity? If managerial responsibility has been entrusted to you, are you honoring that trust by faithful, conscientious service? Consider Daniel as a model for your life, and work hard at emulating his godly "workstyle" (see Titus 2:9–10).

Practical Principles for Exercising Authority

Leadership has become a popular topic among business and professional people today, and for good reason: the effectiveness of any organization is largely a function of effective leadership.

The Bible offers many models to help leaders serve their people more effectively. Moses' conversation with Jethro (Ex. 18:13–23) is one of the most significant. Notice a number of principles that flow from this exchange:

1. *Moses, himself a man of authority, respected the authority of Jethro (Ex. 18:7, 24).* Moses could have become defensive and protected his own political "turf" when Jethro offered advice. But he showed him respect and then listened and responded willingly to the counsel of his father-in-law. If you're a leader, can you expect those under you to respect your authority if you do not respect the authorities over you?

2. *Authority has a way of becoming intoxicating (Ex. 18:14–15).* Moses apparently knew little about delegation of responsibility. This may explain why he was overburdened. When Jethro asked him why "you alone sit, and all the people stand before you," he re-

plied that "the people come to me to inquire of God." Does this statement reflect the intoxicating allure of being in charge? Fortunately, Moses seemed eager to give up some of his centralized control. How about you? Do you find yourself reluctant to share power because of the boost it gives your ego to have others dependent on you?

3. *Authority should be invested in others prudently (Ex. 18:21).* Jethro was not suggesting that Moses fill a handful of leadership positions, the way so many people do, with relatives and cronies. Rather, he described job qualifications based on proven character. Delegation is a privilege, not a right. A leader ought to consider the quality and ability of prospective appointees.

4. *Authority is a resource to be invested in others (Ex. 18:22–23).* By delegating authority to subordinates, Moses would unleash incredible energy that would take the people much further as a community than if he retained centralized control. Authority is a resource to be used to empower others to act more effectively.

5. *Effective leadership increases the health and longevity of an organization and its people (Ex. 18:22–23).* Moses probably prolonged his own life and ensured the progress of the nation by appointing effective judges. No organization can survive for long if only a handful of its workers are involved in the task. By giving each member a stake in the outcome, leaders can bring more resources to bear on complex decisions. Is your organization set up for maximum effectiveness?

Solomon's Administrative Districts

King Solomon organized Israel into twelve administrative districts, with a governor over each district (1 Kin. 4:7). A primary job of the governors was to "provide food for the king and his household" (1 Kin. 4:7, 27). They must have needed to collect plenty of taxes, as Solomon's expansive household needs (1 Kin. 4:22–23), large military (1 Kin. 4:26, 28), and vast building projects (1 Kin. 6:37–7:12; 9:15–19) required a great amount of money and other resources.

The districts were generally identified by their principal cities (1 Kin. 4:8–19). Notably absent from the list was the territory of Judah. Apparently Solomon regarded his own tribe as distinct from the rest of Israel (1 Kin. 4:20) and may have even exempted it from taxation.

Solomon's administrative plan was an efficient way of governing. But perhaps Solomon's outlays exceeded what his governors could bring in. That could be why he gave twenty cities in Galilee to King Hiram of Tyre (1 Kin. 9:10–14). The heavy taxes also left a bitter legacy, as Solomon's son, Rehoboam, would find out (1 Kin. 12:1–19).

*For more on this topic, see **EXCELLENCE**, "Modeling Excellence," page 138; **HUMAN RESOURCES**, "Making Human Resources Work," page 205; **ORGANIZATION**, "Organizing for a Big Project," page 285.*

MANIPULATION
Retaliation Foiled

When highly competitive people are overshadowed or intimidated they often resort to ugly tactics to try to regain their superiority. An unhealthy need for importance, success, and power can bring out the worst in anyone. Have you noticed this pattern among coworkers, family members, or yourself?

As community leaders saw Jesus once again gaining popularity and influence, they schemed to ensnare Him (Luke 20:9–19). They even enlisted agents for their plot (Luke 20:20). Unfortunately, there always seems to be a ready supply of help for evil designs.

But Jesus refused to stoop to their methods (Luke 20:23–25). As they tried to undo Him, He foiled their plans with grace and truth.

Do you know how to respond to trickery or evil when it is intended for you?

*For more on this topic, see **DECEIT**, "Trick Questions," page 99.*

MANSLAUGHTER
Places of Refuge

In today's society, a person charged with manslaughter is likely to call a lawyer to defend himself and stay out of jail. In ancient Israel, such a person would probably flee to the nearest of six cities designated as "cities of refuge" (Num. 35:11). The cities of refuge combined issues of urban planning, justice, and religion in some interesting ways.

After the Israelites entered the Promised Land, they set apart forty-eight cities as Levitical cities in which members of the priesthood and their families lived (see Josh. 21:1–3). Of those forty-eight cities, six were declared cities of refuge for the protection of "the manslayer who kills any person accidentally" (Num. 35:11). It is important to note that refuge was given only in cases of unintentional death. Willful murderers were executed (Num. 35:30).

The six cities of refuge were strategically located for accessibility: three to the east of the Jordan River, including Bezer, Ramoth Gilead, and Golan (Deut. 4:41–43; Josh. 20:8), and three to the west, Kedesh in Galilee, Shechem, and Kirjath Arba (Hebron; Josh. 20:7).

Refuge from revenge was necessary because Hebrew custom gave next-of-kin the right, if not the obligation, to avenge a person's death. If a manslayer was able to enter a city of refuge, he was safe from immediate harm. However, the elders of the manslayer's hometown were to investigate the matter and let the "congregation" decide whether the killing had been done intentionally. If the person were found guilty of murder, he was brought back and delivered over to the avenging blood relative for execution (Num. 35:24; Deut. 19:11–12).

Otherwise, the manslayer was granted asylum in the city of refuge, but he had to remain there until the death of the high priest (Num. 35:25). This kept him safe from revenge but did not let him totally off the hook. Many years might pass before the high priest's death, so that his prolonged stay in the city of refuge became something of an exile, little better than living under house arrest.

MARRIAGE
Betrothal

Betrothal (Luke 1:27) was a mutual promise or contract for a future marriage (Deut. 20:7; Jer. 2:2). Not to be entirely equated with the modern concept of engagement, betrothal followed the selection of the bride by the prospective husband. The contract was negotiated by a friend or agent representing the bridegroom and by the parents representing the bride. It was confirmed by oaths and was accompanied with presents to the bride and often to the bride's parents.

Betrothal was celebrated by a feast. In some instances, it was customary for the bridegroom to place a ring on the bride's finger as a token of love and fidelity. In Hebrew custom, betrothal was actually part of the marriage process. A change of intention by one of the partners after he or she was betrothed was a serious matter, subject in some instances to a fine.

Betrothal was much more closely linked with marriage than our modern engagement. But the actual marriage took place only when the bridegroom took the bride to his home and the marriage was consummated in the sexual union.

Connecting Separate Lives

Perhaps the area where people squander their greatest opportunity for companionship is their marriage. Instead of growing together as God intended (Gen. 2:18, 23–24; Eccl. 4:11), they grow apart and develop separate lives. As a result, neither spouse ever really knows the other.

Here are three suggestions for increasing

communication, intimacy, and companionship in your marriage:

1. Find at least one interest you have in common and build on that. This may be something as simple as a walk, a sunset, a piece of music, or even a memory. Tell each other what you like about that thing. Describe what it means to you. How would you feel if that thing were taken away? What else can you find in common?

2. Set aside at least one time every day to stop what you are doing, shut out the rest of the world, and have a conversation with your spouse. Let one partner talk a while as the other listens—really listens! Then let the other partner talk for a while as the first one listens—*really* listens! If necessary, start with just five or ten minutes, but do it *every* day. Don't let anything interrupt—children, the phone, television, or anything else. Devote that time to each other.

3. Pray with your spouse. If you're too far apart to pray together every day, start by praying together once a week. If you're not ready to pray out loud together, just pray silently side by side. If you're not already in the habit, the hardest thing may be just getting started. So why not start right now?

Marriage Within Family

Abraham was so concerned about the racial heritage of his son's prospective wife, whoever she might be, that he sent his servant to Haran and made him swear that he would find a bride there among "my country and . . . my family" (Gen. 24:3–4). This sort of marriage between related persons was common in the ancient world.

Even though marriage between relatives was accepted in the ancient world, incest of the sort that occurred between Lot and his daughters (Gen. 19:30–35) was strongly condemned. When the Law was given to Israel, it extended the prohibition against sexual relations within the family to a man's mother, sister, aunt, granddaughter, sister-in-law, daughter-in-law, stepmother, stepsister, stepdaughter, or stepgranddaughter (Lev. 18:6–18).

Marriage Issues for New Believers

Have you ever listened in on half of a telephone conversation, trying to figure out what the whole conversation is about? That's what we have in 1 Corinthians 7—half of a very important conversation on marriage between Paul and the Corinthian believers. But we can glean many practical lessons from this passage, for marriage was undergoing profound changes then just as it is today.

Some of the believers in the early church had married before they became Christians. They wondered whether they should divorce their unbelieving spouses in order to remarry Christians and live more wholeheartedly for Christ.

An argument could be made for that. After all, if people's primary loyalty were now to Jesus, shouldn't that invalidate their pre-conversion marriage vows? (Of course, it would also provide them with a convenient excuse to escape bad marriages.)

But Paul didn't recommend that. He viewed the abandonment of one's family as a very serious matter (1 Cor. 7:10–11), arguing that the believer should stay in the marriage as long as possible (1 Cor. 7:12–13). However, God desires peace in relationships (1 Cor. 7:15), and that may not be possible in a family where Christian values are not shared. If the unbeliever wants to leave, he or she should be allowed to do so (1 Cor. 7:15).

Many churches in different cultures around the world today are faced with very similar circumstances. For example:

- The new believer who wonders what to do, since her husband isn't interested in church or religion.
- The inner-city congregation that has members who live in common-law marriages. What should the church tell them?
- The recent immigrant who tells his pastor that he has two families, one in each of two countries. "Should I get rid of one or both of those families?" he wonders.
- A tribal chief who wants to join the church—along with his five wives. What should he do with the wives? Divorce them all? Keep one? If so, which one?

Paul offers no simple solutions for any of these situations, but he does share one piece of very good news: it is possible for one believer to "sanctify" a family, that is, to be an agent of God's love and grace, and perhaps to eventually bring other family members into the faith. No matter how unconventional the situation might be, Scripture doesn't counsel sudden changes. God may have work left to do in that family, and He may use the believer to do it—if he or she stays.

The Bride-Price

The bride-price (Ex. 22:16) was the price paid to a bride's family to acknowledge the financial loss created by the woman's marriage. Since a woman became part of her husband's family, her family of origin was impoverished by the marriage. The bride-price repaid at least a token of the family's loss of a productive worker. It was often a gift of substantial value.

In a few instances, the Bible reports that brides received gifts from their families when they married. For example, Laban gave maids to his daughters Leah and Rachel when they married Jacob (Gen. 29:24, 29). Caleb gave springs of water to his daughter (Josh. 15:19). And when the daughter of Pharaoh married Solomon, she was given an entire city to bring to the marriage (1 Kin. 9:16).

A High View of Marriage

Newlyweds bring a variety of expectations to marriage. But what are God's expectations for the marriage relationship? He designed the institution. What did He have in mind when he established it?

One window on God's perspective comes from His own "marriage" to Israel. The prophet Isaiah portrays the relationship between the Lord and His people as a marriage (Is. 62:1–5). Notice what God as the Bridegroom does for His bride:

- He protects and purifies her.
- He honors and values her.
- He identifies Himself with her, as signified by giving her new names.

Centuries later, Paul echoed Isaiah's bridal portrait of God and Israel when he described the marriage between Christ and the church (Eph. 5:21–33). Once again, the Bridegroom shows His love by protecting and purifying His bride, honoring and valuing her, and identifying Himself with her. Paul exhorted Christians to build their marriages on a similar basis.

Is this how you view marriage? Do you see it as a high and holy calling to serve your partner in the ways described? This is the heart of a *biblical* foundation for marriage. There can be no greater love and commitment expressed between two people than to exhibit the character that God has shown toward Israel and that Christ has shown toward the church. Furthermore, this is an important reason for a believer to marry a believer, knowing that one partner holds himself or herself accountable to God for the other's well-being.

For more on this topic, see **MALE-FEMALE RELATIONSHIPS,** *"A New View on Marriage," page 251.*

MASCULINITY

The Tears of Men

Some men today rarely if ever cry. But is that healthy? Tears can be a genuine and appropriate way to express feelings. An inability to shed tears may be symptomatic of a problem.

Unlike many men in certain cultures today, the men portrayed in the Bible seem to have had little if any shame about weeping. They apparently felt free to express pain and grief, as well as joy and gladness, through their tears. For example, Jeremiah wept bitterly over the terrible plight of his people after Jerusalem fell to the Babylonians (Lam. 2:11; compare Jer. 9:1).

Following are some other men in Scripture who came to tears and the occasions that brought them to it. As you consider these men, ask yourself: What moves you to tears? If you never cry, why not?

- David and Jonathan cried together as they parted company after Saul's vicious attacks (1 Sam. 20:41–42).
- Elisha wept as he foresaw the cruel evils that Hazael's troops would commit against Israel's women and children (2 Kin. 8:11–12).
- King Hezekiah wept bitterly when he was told he would not recover from a sickness (2 Kin. 20:3).
- Israelite elders in the time of Ezra broke down in tears when the foundation for a new temple was laid (Ezra 3:12).

M

- Ezra wept over the disobedience of the Jewish men who had married pagan wives (Ezra 10:1).
- Nehemiah was moved to tears on hearing a report of conditions at Jerusalem (Neh. 1:4).
- Job poured out his tears to God after the painful loss of his goods, family, and health (Job 16:20).
- Jesus was moved to tears at the tomb of His friend Lazarus (John 11:33–36).
- Peter wept with bitter shame after he realized that he had betrayed his Lord (Matt. 26:75).
- Paul acknowledged that he was sometimes moved to tears in his work (Acts 20:18–19).

MATERIALISM

(*see* Affluence; Money; Possessions)

MATURITY

Learning from Peter's Impulsiveness

Are you impulsive? Are you quick to step forward with a plan of action? As the exchange between Peter and the Lord in Matthew 16:22–23 shows, there were times when Peter liked to take charge quickly and set the agenda for himself and others. But just as often he found himself in over his head:

- When Jesus came walking on water to a storm-tossed boat that held His terrified disciples, Peter demanded that He show that it was He by bidding Peter also to walk on water. After a few steps, Peter noticed the wind and the waves and promptly sank, requiring Jesus to rescue him again (Matt. 14:22–32).
- He overstated his commitment to Christ, claiming that "even if I have to die with You, I will not deny You!" (Matt. 26:35). Yet only a few hours later he denied having any association with the Lord (Matt. 26:69–75).
- He took charge of defending Jesus against Roman soldiers when they came to arrest Him—even though he had failed to "watch and pray" with Christ as had been requested (Matt. 26:36–46; John 18:1–11).

- He refused to allow Jesus to wash his feet at the Last Supper, then called on Him to wash his hands and his head as well (Matt. 13:5–11).

Eventually Peter's leadership skills were captured in a more controlled spirit and he became a significant figure in the early church. Despite many false starts as a result of Peter's impetuous nature, Jesus enlisted this impulsive but loyal follower to "feed My sheep" (Matt. 21:17).

Have your personality and skills become more mature and thoughtful? Or are you still in the raw stage, ready to jump at the first idea that occurs to you?

MEANING AND PURPOSE

Dark Reflections on Life

Ecclesiastes opens with a poem on the endless cycles of life (Eccl. 1:3–11). Observing nature, the book observes that nothing in the world really develops, nothing changes, "there is nothing new under the sun" (Eccl. 1:9). How does your view of life compare with this one?

The book has already stated that all of life is "vanity"—futility or frustration. Why? Because no individual is immortal. We work for rewards that we cannot enjoy. Generation follows generation, the earth turns (Eccl. 1:4), the sun rises and sets, the wind blows this way and that (Eccl. 1:5–6), the rivers empty into the sea but never fill it (Eccl. 1:7), and nothing ultimately satisfies (Eccl. 1:8). There is nothing new. No one learns from history, so all are condemned to repeat it (Eccl. 1:9–11).

This is a sobering outlook on life, particularly when we read it in our day, when technologies promise unprecedented opportunities. But Ecclesiastes insists that in the end the same basic patterns of life continue.

What about your own life? Perhaps this poem rings true for your experience. Consider the following questions:

- In what ways, if any, have you broken out of the mold of what people have been doing for generations?
- What have you done that will have significance beyond your death and the passing of your family name?

- What motivates you to continue the daily patterns at work and home?
- What rewards do you expect for your labor? Are they lasting and permanent, or will they fade away in a day, a week, or a few years' time?

As a further way to reflect on your life, read the entire Book of Ecclesiastes in a single sitting—it will probably take less than a half hour. Be sure to get to the resolution that the book brings to this dark and sometimes bitter view of life (Eccl. 12:13–14). When you have finished, consider what changes in your beliefs, values, attitudes, and activities might be in order for you to "fear God and keep His commandments."

An Invitation to Life

If you listen carefully to public discourse today, you hear the recurring theme that modern society is in moral and spiritual decline. Having heaped up incredible material affluence, Western civilization is believed by many to have lost its soul.

That makes the message of Isaiah as timely as ever. To those who "spend money for what is not bread," and wages for "what does not satisfy" (Is. 55:2), the Lord offers a compelling invitation: "Come to Me . . . and your soul shall live" (Is. 55:3).

This marvelous call of God is extended to the whole world. He invites nations who do not even know of Israel to come to Him. *Anyone* who is thirsty can drink of His waters of grace (Is. 55:1, 5).

This same invitation is still in effect today. In the Book of Revelation, the Lord says, "I will give of the fountain of the water of life freely to him who thirsts. . . . And let him who thirsts come. Whoever desires, let him take the water of life freely" (Rev. 21:6; 22:17).

Have you personally responded to God's gift of life through faith in Jesus Christ? Are you still dying of thirst? The Lord invites you to come and drink!

Short-Term Pleasure, Long-Term Despair

"Go for the gusto." "You only go around once in life." "Look out for number one." "Whatever turns you on." All of these slogans represent commonly accepted concepts of the good life. But these attitudes fail to take into account the long-term dimension of life, and they certainly ignore the life hereafter. Pleasure-seeking has its thrills, but it offers little if anything that will last into eternity.

Solomon might have fit right into the modern world with his commitment to enjoying pleasure, gratifying his flesh, enlarging his works, acquiring more possessions than his predecessors, achieving greatness and excellence, and getting for himself whatever his heart desired (Eccl. 2:1–10). If anyone ever "went for the gusto" and "took care of Number One," it was Solomon. He achieved the ultimate in short-term pleasure and instant gratification.

Yet eventually, he grieved over the outcome of his life (Eccl. 2:11, 17–21). His pursuits left him longing for something else.

That "something else" is God. Faith in God moves us out of a self-centered pursuit of life by introducing us to something bigger: we have been created to serve God and other people, not just ourselves. Through service we find significance for the long term. As Moses transmitted and Jesus repeated, the greatest commandments are to love God and to love other people (Deut. 6:5; Lev. 19:8; Matt. 22:37–39).

If we spend our lives exalting ourselves, we will become enslaved to our own appetites and never find the fulfillment we seek. Pleasure can be a delightful servant—if it is dedicated to God—but it makes a horrible master.

Which master do you serve? What drives you? Are you squandering your future on short-term delights? Or are you building for eternity?

MEDIATION

The Go-Between

Perhaps as you look at some of the tragedies of the world—the armed conflicts, the political breakdowns, the crimes of injustice or indifference, the ethical compromises—you wonder why some good and strong person cannot be found to lead the way out of the trouble.

The Lord wondered the same thing as He surveyed wicked Judah. Having enumerated the sins of the people, He told Ezekiel that He had searched in vain for someone who could

M

"stand in the gap" between their guilt and His righteous wrath (Ezek. 22:30). No worthy go-between could be found.

This search recalls Jeremiah's futile attempt to locate even one righteous person whose presence would save the city. Neither among the poor nor the leaders was there a single individual who was not guilty of departing from God's ways.

Ultimately, only Christ is righteous enough to serve as the go-between to connect a holy God and sinful humanity (1 Tim. 2:5; Heb. 9:15). Apart from Him, none of us would be free of God's wrath, for all of us have sinned (Rom. 3:21–26). However, because Jesus took on Himself the judgment for our sin, we can have unimpeded access to God.

We can also act as go-betweens in the troubles around us, "standing in the gap" to bridge chasms of indifference and oppression. We can do what we can to stem the tide of evil and tell others of the opportunity to know God through Christ. And we can intercede for others in prayer.

MEDICINE

(*see* Physicians; Sickness)

MEMORY

Never Forget!

A visitor to the world headquarters of a major corporation was ushered into the office of the company's founder and chief executive officer. The guest marvelled at the magnificent view from the window, the expensive works of art on the walls, and the plush furniture in the room where the man worked. One detail seemed out of place, however. Prominently located on the executive's finely polished mahogany desk was a dusty, dirty black rock.

Noticing the visitor's curiosity about it, the successful businessman explained, "That's a lump of coal. I keep it there to remind me of my roots. It came from the coal mine where my father worked for forty-five years. I never want to forget that I am were I am today because of where he was when I was a boy."

As the Israelites were about to enter the Promised Land, Moses urged them never to forget how they had gotten to the new land and who had provided it for them. Over and over he reminded them that the land was a gift from God (Deut. 27:2–3). One way to remember that was to set up large memorial stones with the Law written on them.

Stop for a moment to consider what God has done for you. Reflect on His grace in providing salvation in Christ. Think about the blessings He has provided at work, at home, at church, or in your community: the people He has brought your way, the livelihood He has provided, the achievements He has enabled you to accomplish. How can you keep from forgetting that it is God who has brought you to this point? Consider setting up your own "memorial stone" (or lump of coal) as a reminder of His provision.

MENTORING

(*see also* Discipleship; Guidance)

Barnabas—A Model Mentor

Barnabas's example serves as a textbook case in kingdom-style mentoring. This model mentor . . .

- Befriended Saul (Paul) as a new believer (Acts 9:26–27).
- Recruited a forgotten Saul from his home in Tarsus to help him stabilize a new group of multiethnic believers at Antioch, a year-long project (Acts 11:25–26).
- Helped organize an international team of leaders in prayer, fasting, and decision-making. Result: he launched out with Paul to bring the gospel to peoples in the western empire (Acts 13:1–3).
- Moved Paul to the forefront of leadership. "Barnabas and Saul" (Acts 13:7) became "Paul and his party" (Acts 13:13).
- Contended with ethnic hostility, personal attacks, and idol worship (Acts 13:46–14:20).
- Resisted well-meaning but misguided attempts at Lystra to make him and Paul into gods of Greek culture (Acts 14:8–18).
- Took the lead with Paul in defending Gentile believers before the Jerusalem church council (Acts 15:1–4, 12).
- Stood up to Paul over a negative assessment of young John Mark (Acts 15:36–38). Notice: Encouragers like Barnabas need not avoid conflict.

• Gave John Mark a second chance, taking him with him to Cyprus (Acts 15:39). He was vindicated several years later when Paul described John Mark as "useful to me for ministry" (2 Tim. 4:11).

Mentoring, Kingdom-style

Paul describes the powerful process of mentoring in 2 Timothy 2:2. Just as he had helped Timothy during a formative stage in his development, he challenged Timothy to mentor others, who in turn could become mentors and keep the reproductive cycle going. Christians today need to recover this pattern of older believers working with younger ones, which dates to the earliest days of the faith. Here are a few examples from the New Testament:

Priscilla and Aquila with Apollos. Manufacturers of mobile living units (tents), Priscilla and Aquila drew alongside gifted but confused Apollos, tutoring him in the faith and then sponsoring his ministry (Acts 18:1–3, 24–28).

Paul with Timothy. Pioneering leader Paul recruited young Timothy and built on the foundation laid by the young man's mother and grandmother (2 Tim. 1:5). Enlisting him as a fellow-traveler and tutoring him in the faith, Paul guided him in his first major assignment, the multiethnic start-up at Ephesus (Acts 16:1–3; Phil. 2:19–23; 2 Tim. 1–4).

Paul with Philemon. Paul helped Philemon, a wealthy leader in Colosse, deal with a runaway slave who had broken the law. He recommended full acceptance—even as a brother in the family—rather than insisting on the usual retribution.

For more on this topic, see **DISCIPLESHIP,** *"Discipleship—or Mentoring?" page 109; "Passing On the Mantle," page 110;* **GUIDANCE,** *"The Value of a Spiritual Mentor," page 191.*

MERCY

Mercy to the Repentant

God's forgiveness has always required repentance on the part of sinners. It did in ancient times; it still does today.

In Ezekiel's vision of Jerusalem, the Lord commanded angelic executioners to place a special mark on the foreheads of those who were moved to repentance over the "abominations" being committed in the city. The rest were to be slain (Ezek. 9:4–7). The justification for this slaughter was that the sins of the wicked—bloodshed and perversity (idolatry)—were "exceedingly great" (Ezek. 9:9). By contrast, citizens who demonstrated a deep concern for holiness were shown mercy.

This vision recalls a similar judgment in Egypt, in which the Lord killed the firstborn children of the Egyptians, but spared the Hebrew households that had marked their doorposts with blood (Ex. 12:1–36). In both cases, God marked out those to whom He would show mercy on the basis of their heart attitude toward Him.

It is interesting to note that the "mark" referred to by Ezekiel is the Hebrew letter *taw,* the last letter of the Hebrew alphabet. Today, *taw* is the equivalent of "T," but in Jeremiah's day it was written like an "X" and was often used as a signature (Job 31:35). Early Christians pointed out the similarity between Ezekiel's "mark" and the sign of the cross. Both indicated God's mercy and redemption of sinners.

The judgment foreseen in Ezekiel's vision applies to people today. It demonstrates that God shows mercy, but He always looks for repentance. Those who resist Him and remain committed to sin can expect His wrath. But those who "sigh and cry" over their own sins and the sins of others will know His comfort and forgiveness (compare James 4:8–10).

Taking It to Extremes

Did Christ intend for us to take what He said in Luke 6:27–36 literally? It sounds noble to love our enemies, bless those who curse us, and pray for those who spite us. But what about physical abuse, robbery, or endless appeals for help (Luke 6:29–30)? Surely He didn't mean those words the way they sound. Or does Christianity encourage people to run to dangerous extremes?

It's legitimate to notice that Jesus often used hyperbole and stark contrasts in His comments. So when we read Jesus' words today, it's easy to set up all kinds of exceptions and qualifications to soften them. But in the process, do we miss His point? Do we distort His message?

M

Jesus was not calling here for unhealthy responses, nor setting forth a political or social agenda, nor offering a statement of public policy, nor constructing a model for business and finance. Instead, He posed a tough challenge to His followers—to those "who hear" (Luke 6:27): What difference does our faith make in the way we respond to people in need? That's the key—our response to human need. That shows the true condition of our hearts. Do we respond to people as God Himself does, with mercy (Luke 6:36)?

The test comes when we are faced with extremes. As Jesus pointed out, it's easy to love those who love us (Luke 6:32). It's easy to give when we know we'll get back (Luke 6:34). But God loves people who do not love Him, and gives to those who will never even thank Him, let alone give back to Him (Luke 6:35).

Even God's enemies have needs that only He can meet. In His mercy, He meets those needs. Do we? When faced with people in genuine need, do we look only at their character, and base our response on that alone? Or do we look at their needs and do what we can to meet them?

We may question how far Jesus wants us to go in the various situations described in Luke 6:29–30. But we need never question how far God is willing to go to show mercy. That's what we need to take literally and imitate practically.

*For more on this topic, see **GOD'S MERCY,** "Showing Mercy," page 175; **JUSTICE,** "Balancing Mercy and Justice," page 233.*

MILITARISM

Nimrod and His Legacy

Like a storm cloud on the horizon, the name Nimrod (Gen. 10:8) signals the coming of trouble. As subsequent history shows, the people and empires descended from Nimrod—particularly the Assyrians and Babylonians—became ruthless conquerors who vexed and vanquished many of their neighbors in the ancient world, including the Israelites.

Nimrod was the grandson of Ham, whose first three sons, Cush, Mizraim, and Put (Gen. 10:6), are believed to have settled in the Nile River area of Africa. Ham's fourth son and Nimrod's uncle, Canaan, settled in the land

of Canaan along the eastern shore of the Mediterranean Sea. Thus the descendants of Nimrod, who settled in southern Mesopotamia, had connections to groups in Africa such as the Egyptians and Ethiopians, and in southwestern Arabia such as the Sabeans, and to the Caphtorim (or Philistines) and the Canaanites (Gen. 10:7, 13–20).

Nimrod established two kingdoms, one in the "land of Shinar," the other in Assyria (Gen. 10:10–12). These areas correspond to the Tigris and Euphrates valleys, and the beginnings of the Sumerian, Babylonian, Akkadian, and Assyrian empires are traceable to Nimrod. In fact, Assyria came to be called "the land of Nimrod" (Mic. 5:6).

Some believe that the name Nimrod means, "we will revolt," implying that this "mighty one on the earth" and "mighty hunter before the Lord" (Gen. 10:8–9) was actually a mighty leader in rebellion against the Lord. Certainly his descendants turned away from God (Is. 47:1, 10–15; Nah. 3:1–7).

Yet as crucial a role as Nimrod played in history, his identity remains uncertain. Some suggest that he was (or was similar to) King Sargon the Great, whose kingdom of Akkad was flourishing around 2300 B.C. Sargon proclaimed himself "King of Universal Dominion" while building an empire that stretched from the Mediterranean coast and Asia Minor to Persia.

After the Akkadians, other empires rose and fell in Lower Mesopotamia during the next two thousand years, but all of them could be traced to Nimrod. It was not until Alexander the Great that the political and economic might of the Sumerian-Akkadian peoples was broken.

Despite its eclipse, the culture that was fathered by Nimrod left a rich legacy in the history of civilization:

The spread of language began at Babel, on the plain of Shinar (Gen. 11:1–9).

The Akkadians and their descendants created military empires which brought political, economic, and social organization from the Mediterranean Sea and Asia Minor to the Persian Gulf. These superpowers reflected a major transition from small city-states which were more common in the ancient world.

Sumerian-Akkadian culture and technology spread throughout the ancient Middle East.

Restraints on Urban Warfare

God's policies of urban warfare (Deut. 20:10–15) presupposed that Israel would someday be attacked from the outside, since certain besieged cities included in the policy would be far from the boundaries of Israel (Deut. 20:15). The cities of the Canaanites, which God was giving to His people, were to be utterly destroyed (Deut. 20:16–18). But this "scorched earth" policy did not apply outside the borders of the Promised Land.

God did not intend for Israel to become an ever-expanding empire like Assyria or Babylon, which devoured foreign territories, demolished their cities, and deported their people. Instead, the Israelites were to occupy the land given to them and generally remain within the borders assigned for that land (Num. 34:1–12). As far as possible, they were to live in peace with their neighbors.

Nevertheless, there would be times when Israel would be threatened or attacked. Staging a counteroffensive against these foreign enemies might require Israel's army to travel into enemy territory, where it would encounter walled cities. When that happened, the Israelites were to sue for peace (Deut. 20:10). Depending on the response, they were either to spare the city or besiege it (Deut. 20:11–12). Yet unlike the policy in Canaan, foreign cities were to be treated with a measure of mercy and restraint (20:14).

For more on this topic, see **CENSUS,** *"A Temptation to Trust in Numbers," page 48.*

MINISTRY

A Church That Defies Market Research

The population of the United States is becoming increasingly diverse. Can the church prosper in a pluralistic society? Yes, judging by Acts. In fact, the response of the council at Jerusalem to an influx of Gentile believers (Acts 15:22–35) suggests that Christians must allow for cultural differences if they want their churches to thrive.

The collections of people who responded to the gospel and banded together in the first century defy much of modern market research and ideas about church growth. Modern thinking holds that groups of people with similar sociological backgrounds ("homogeneous" groups) grow more quickly than ones with different backgrounds ("heterogeneous") because like attracts like. Therefore, churches should target people of the same race, demographic profile, socioeconomic status, and so forth.

But the untidy collection of Acts believers seems to contradict that model. Churches sprouted up spontaneously in response to God's grace more than through social marketing.

- They came from all classes of society, from the wealthy and privileged to destitute beggars, slaves, and even criminals.
- They represented the many cultures of that day—Roman, Greek, Hebrew, African, Arab.
- They varied widely in their political allegiances and power, from government, military, and civic leaders to reactionaries, revolutionaries, and displaced refugees.
- Their leadership was male and female, old and young.
- They came from all manner of religious traditions—pagan sorcery and mystery cults, Greek and Roman mythology, idol worship, and Judaism.

The early church was a diverse, grassroots, from-the-ground-up movement that drew people together in surprising ways. It turned them inside out, toward one another in service and love. Its example challenges believers today to ask: How are we allowing for cultural differences in our pluralistic society?

A "Praise March" Captures a City

When Joshua and the Israelites besieged Jericho, they used a tactic still employed by people of faith today—the praise march (Josh. 6:3). The biblical text simply calls it a "march," but it is interesting to consider the elements of praise involved.

Joshua's army marched around the city for seven days. The only sound allowed was the blowing of the priests' trumpets as they preceded the ark (Josh. 6:9–10). By the seventh day, the warriors' pent-up emotions must have been at a fever pitch, so that when

Joshua signaled them to shout (Josh. 6:16, 20), a mighty roar erupted, perhaps exceeded only by the crashing of the walls.

Joshua was assured that God would win the battle because he was waging a "holy war." A holy war is a war that God declares, takes responsibility for, and brings to its proper resolution. The call to a holy war was perhaps unique to Israel, not to be repeated in our day. Even so, many churches today are finding the idea of a praise march similar to Joshua's a useful tactic in urban witness:

1. Some groups have organized marches and demonstrations in support of or opposition to a particular policy or proposal. The point is to stand up and be counted publicly as one of the Lord's people.

2. Sometimes groups take a somewhat quieter approach that is more of a *prayer walk* than a praise march. The members of a congregation may covenant together to pray for designated parts of their parish or community. This increases their compassion for and knowledge of the community.

3. A third model for "praise marching" is the long, determined marathon of community development. Nehemiah serves as a good example. He began by praying for Jerusalem in response to distressing news. Then, when he arrived at the city, he quietly inspected its walls, devised a plan, recruited personnel, and gathered resources to accomplish a major task of reconstruction. It was a long, tough process of community development in which many obstacles had to be overcome. But by committing himself to a long-term process, he was able to finish by saying, "This work was done by our God" (Neh. 6:16). It was a work of praise.

The tool kit for ministering in the city today is vast and varied. What is your strategy for impacting your city?

What Does It Take to Serve God?

It's interesting to notice how Moses prepared Aaron and his sons for the priesthood (Lev. 8:2–3). According to God's command, he assembled them in front of the tabernacle. There he initiated their ministry with sacrifices to atone for their sins (Lev. 8:14–36).

The prospective priests also had to be trained in the elaborate rituals detailed in the

Law. But the text makes it plain that neither special ability nor even the good fortune to be born into the tribe of Levi fully qualified a man to serve as a priest to the Lord. A man was fit for service only after his sins had been forgiven.

What is required to serve in the professional ministry today? Various qualifications might be mentioned. But chief among them is still the requirement of being cleansed from sin (2 Tim. 2:1, 20–21).

*For more on this topic, see **HOLY SPIRIT**, "Empowered for Ministry" p. 201; **LAITY**, "Is Your Church Upside-Down or Right Side Up?" page 239.*

MINISTRY SUPPORT

Don't Fleece the Flock!

Several flagrant abuses by prominent ministers, involving hundreds of millions of dollars, were exposed during the 1980s. As a result, many people adopted a general distrust of Christian ministers and ministries, and giving declined. The situation makes Peter's words to overseers (1 Pet. 5:2) required reading for all vocational Christian workers and their supporters. Clergy need to maintain the utmost integrity when it comes to finances.

Peter speaks here of dishonest gain, literally "filthy" or "shameful" money. What brings shame is not the money but the greed, which is nothing less than idolatry (Col. 3:5). No wonder Paul strenuously warned church leaders to beware of using ministry as a pretext for gain (1 Tim. 3:3, 8; 6:3–5; Titus 1:7).

Of course, it is not inevitable that ministers should fall to greed. Peter refused Simon's offer of a bribe in exchange for the power of the Holy Spirit (Acts 8:18–20). Likewise, Paul frequently refused the financial support to which he had a right as an apostle (1 Cor. 9:7–15).

Do you make your living in the ministry? If so, are you doing so willingly and eagerly, as Peter indicates? If not, why are you in the ministry?

"I Have Not Coveted"

Paul's emotional farewell to the Ephesian elders ended with a significant disclaimer: "I have [not] coveted" (Acts 20:33). Paul seems to have been at pains to emphasize that he was not a deadbeat while among them, sponging off their generosity. Rather, he worked as a tentmaker, first in order to provide for himself and his companions, and second, to "support [help] the weak" (Acts 20:34–35).

These words merit our attention. First, they reveal a biblical work ethic that forsakes greed in favor of hard, honest labor and a trust in God to provide for basic needs. Then, as God blesses, a worker's abundance should overflow into generosity toward others in need. This pattern recurs throughout the New Testament (for example, Matt. 6:24–34; Luke 16:9–13; Eph. 4:28; 2 Thess. 3:6–15; 1 Tim. 6:6–10, 17–19).

However, Paul's statement also bears upon the reputation of churches and ministries today. A growing number of people regard Christian work and workers with skepticism, as little more than fundraising vehicles for a greedy clergy. Apparently Paul faced similar attitudes, and therefore chose to support himself during his stay in Ephesus. Is there any reason why modern Christian leaders shouldn't at least consider that as an option today?

But Paul's words also present a stiff challenge to "laypeople." What about our attitudes toward work, income, and material things? How would we rate on a scale measuring greed versus generosity?

Paul goes beyond saying that generosity is just a nice virtue. "You *must* support the weak," he urges (Acts 20:35, emphasis added), because it is the very thing that Christ taught. What must that have sounded like to people from the extraordinarily affluent city of Ephesus? It certainly is a powerful exhortation to us today. But it is backed up by two powerful examples—Paul (a tentmaker) and Christ (a carpenter).

Paul's "Real" Job

Though the ministry today is viewed as a full-time profession, some of the first gospel workers earned all or part of their living through other occupations. Paul was a tentmaker (Acts 18:3), a trade he may have learned as a boy in Tarsus.

That kind of "bivocationalism" is worth considering in today's world. Many pastors in both urban and rural settings work at second and third jobs, since their churches cannot support them financially. And in developing countries, "secular" skills are desperately needed in supplying food, shelter, and economic development. In some countries, anti-Christian governments refuse to admit Christian workers unless they make a "secular" contribution to the society.

Paying Vocational Christian Workers

How much should pastors, missionaries, and others who work in churches and ministries be paid? Or should they be paid at all? Paul's example with the Corinthians offers some insight.

In Paul's day, philosophers traveled from city to city, teaching publicly for a fee. The more prestigious the teacher, the larger the fee. However, Paul charged the Corinthians *nothing* when he came and delivered the gospel message. As a result, some were criticizing him, asserting that he must not be an authentic leader of the church if he was rendering his services for free.

In reply, Paul explained himself (1 Cor. 9). First, he insisted that those who labor spiritually should be supported materially by those with whom they work. He pointed to five familiar examples to support his position:

- Roman soldiers drew pay for their service (1 Cor. 9:7).
- Vintners enjoyed the fruits of their vineyards (1 Cor. 9:7).
- Shepherds received food from their flocks (1 Cor. 9:7).
- The Old Testament Law affirmed the right of laborers to receive fair compensation (1 Cor. 9:8–10).
- The Law also allowed temple priests and attendants to live off of the sacrifices that the people brought (1 Cor. 9:13).

Paul also explained that the Lord Himself allowed those who preach the gospel to make their living from that occupation (1 Cor. 9:14). Elsewhere the apostle wrote that church elders who rule well are worthy of "double honor" (1 Tim. 5:17–18). The context shows that Paul had payment in mind. In short, effective vocational Christian workers should be paid fairly for their labor.

M

Yet Paul refused payment in Corinth. Why? Because He felt that he owed it to God to communicate the gospel for free. When he considered his past and how God had saved him, the "chief of sinners" (1 Tim. 1:15), it was payment enough to be able to tell people about Jesus (1 Cor. 9:18).

Should workers in churches and ministries be paid? This passage insists that they have a right to a fair wage, and Christians today do well to pay attention to Paul's words here in light of the many workers who are leaving the ministry because of inadequate support. On the other hand, Paul's example opens the door to an alternative—the idea of carrying out ministry for free while supporting oneself through other means. That is also a model worth considering in a day when, for a variety of reasons, an increasing number of churches and ministries are strapped for funds.

MINORITIES

Cultural Assimilation

We live in a time of heightened ethnic conflicts the world over. On every continent, groups vie with each other to maintain cultural identities, and sometimes to establish cultural dominance. The Bible speaks to these issues particularly through the Old Testament books of Ruth and Esther. Ruth, a woman of Moab, assimilated into Hebrew culture by forsaking her ethnic roots and marrying Boaz. By contrast, Esther held onto her Jewish ways and remained identified with her people, despite her marriage to the Persian king Ahasuerus.

Which of these two approaches should God's people adopt? This has long been a difficult issue to decide. The fact that the Jews of Esther's time didn't assimilate into Persian society may have had something to do with the racial discrimination evidenced by Haman's plot against the Jews. After the plot failed, the feast of Purim (Esth. 9:26–28) became a permanent expression of Jewish identity.

Purim is from the word *pur*, meaning "lots," which were cast to determine the day on which the extermination of the Jews was to take place (Esth. 3:7). This feast celebrated God's deliverance of His people within a dominant culture—in this case, Persia. By contrast, the feast of Passover celebrated God's deliverance out of a dominant culture, Egypt (see Luke 22:7).

Feasts and fasts such as these became some of the means by which the Jews maintained their cultural identity over the centuries. These traditions became invaluable when the people no longer had a land to live in, or a temple at which to worship, or priests. By keeping the feasts, especially Passover and Purim, they were able to remember who they were when there were no more familiar landmarks to point to or shrines to visit. Passover reminded them that God could liberate His people by bringing them out of an oppressive setting. Purim reminded them that even if He left them in an oppressive setting, He would still be with them.

Similarly, Christians have two seasons that honor the Lord Jesus Christ in a special way—Advent, which leads to the holiday of Christmas, and Lent, which leads to Easter. The one season celebrates the birth of Christ, the other His death and resurrection. Both provide tangible reminders of the salvation He has brought us, and of our hope in Him.

Jesus and Race Relations

Jesus' encounter with the Syro-Phoenician woman (Mark 7:24–30; Matt. 15:21–28) seems to raise some troubling questions about racial and ethnic attitudes. His treatment of the woman seems to be a contradiction of His image as the international Christ, the Savior of the whole world.

The woman came in sincerity and with great respect, yet Jesus rebuffed her with hard words. Why would He do that? Does God want us to relate to people from other races and ethnic groups like that?

Perhaps the key is that Jesus' words were intended less for the woman's ears than for His disciples'. Maybe it was to them, not the woman, that He said, "I was not sent except to the lost sheep of the house of Israel" (Matt. 15:24). They wanted Him to heal her daughter and send her away, but He refused—by appealing to their own national pride and exclusivism.

Jesus may have turned this incident into a living parable to show His disciples how hardened they were in their attitudes against Gentiles. Tyre, the setting for this story, was only fifty miles from the Galilee region where most of the Twelve had grown up. But it was an entirely different culture, dominated by Greek influences and populated almost exclusively by Gentiles. Many of them had already come south to learn more about Jesus (Mark 3:8). Now Jesus was taking His followers north on a crash course in cross-cultural awareness.

So upon encountering the woman, perhaps Jesus treated her the way His disciples would have treated her. Perhaps He wanted to illustrate that despite rejection, Gentiles like the woman deeply hungered for God's grace and power. In the end, Jesus' high praise for the woman's faith and the healing of her daughter repudiated the notion that God was concerned only with Israel.

How would Jesus have to treat someone today to illustrate prejudice among His followers?

MIRACLES

Miracles—On God's Timetable

The parting of the Red Sea (Ex. 14:21) is one of the most well-known examples in the Bible of what are called miracles. Miracles are supernatural interventions by God into the natural order of the world in a way that accomplishes His purposes and brings glory to His name.

God usually seems to allow nature to operate according to the principles or laws with which He originally created it. Thus, for example the normal course for the Red Sea would be to obey the laws of gravity and remain unparted. But God caused the waters to temporarily "disobey" the normal principles of gravity, and the Israelites were able to cross on dry ground.

A study of the miracles in the Bible shows an interesting pattern: most of them appear to be clustered around four key periods in biblical history:

1. *Early in Israel's history.* During the Exodus from Egypt and the initial conquest of the Promised Land, God performed many miraculous acts. These are recorded in Exodus, Leviticus, Numbers, and Joshua.

2. *During the prophetic ministries of Elijah and Elisha.* God raised up the prophets Elijah and Elisha to warn His people against their sinful ways. Numerous miracles are recorded in 1 and 2 Kings as having taken place during the ministries of Elijah and Elisha.

3. *In connection with Jesus' earthly life.* When Christ came to provide salvation through the Cross and to make known the kingdom of God, miracles were among the most important signs that authenticated His ministry. The four Gospels record dozens of miraculous events in Jesus' ministry.

4. *In the early church.* As the Spirit of God filled and mobilized the early church to take the gospel to all peoples, another cluster of miracles took place, especially through the movement's founding leaders. Peter's ministry included several miracles or visions, as did Paul's.

Without question, God performs miracles. He can intervene in the world whenever and however He chooses. But the biblical record of miracles, showing clusters of miraculous events during times of emerging new eras in spiritual history, should inform our expectations. On the one hand, we should avoid any attempt to get God to serve us; on the other, we should never say "never" to the surprising works of God.

The Healing Miracles of Jesus

Jesus devoted considerable time and teaching to health issues, provoking many questions in the process. The most challenging aspect of His work was the miracles of physical healing that He performed. They were as troubling to those who saw them first-hand as they are to us today.

The Gospel writers make it clear that Jesus' first-century witnesses had no problem believing that He actually healed the sick and even raised the dead. They never accused Him of charlatanism. Apparently they accepted the miracles as miracles. But what they struggled with profoundly was the source of His power to perform them and the resulting implications. The curious wondered whether He might not be the Messiah (John 7:31); His enemies accused Him of being in league with the devil (John 8:48; 10:19–21; Matt. 9:34).

M

What most troubled people was that the miracles signaled the arrival of the kingdom of God. It was not the healings themselves that they anguished over, but what they were going to do with the One who claimed to be the Christ on the basis of those healings. Was He or wasn't He? And were they ready to receive Him or not?

Today our culture challenges the credibility of the miraculous itself. Capable of accomplishing many physical feats once thought to be "impossible" (flying, curing leprosy, seeing inside the body noninvasively), and lacking many (some would say any) current examples of miracles, skeptics look for some "rational" explanation. "Perhaps Jesus knew more about the body than the average first-century Jew and cleverly manipulated physical forces in a way that people assumed were miraculous," some say. "Perhaps He only appeared to heal, duping the simple like so many modern-day pretenders. Perhaps the miracles never really occurred; they were simply imagined by later believers eager to embellish the myth of a God-man."

Other explanations have been put forth in the last two centuries. They all reflect the skepticism of our age. Yet in the end, one comes out at the same place as those who originally challenged the authority of the miracles: "If I cast out demons by the Spirit of God, surely the kingdom of God has come upon you" (Matt. 12:28). In other words, is it really the possibility of miracles that troubles

MIRACLES

moderns? Or is it the staggering probability that the One who performed them is in fact God Himself?

Miracles and the Super-natural

Miracles trouble some people, and for that reason are dismissed as fables—or worse, as frauds. Others take a more accommodating but nevertheless patronizing view. They explain away miracles as merely surprises of life and nature that seem out of the ordinary, and therefore are difficult (but not impossible) to explain. According to this theory, reports of "miracles" are really just the aberrant perceptions of primitive, superstitious people, and therefore should be ignored.

But the Bible treats miracles as matters of fact. For example, the healing of King Hezekiah, including the reversal of the sundial's shadow, is told in a straightforward way (Is. 38:1–9). Is this myth—or mystery?

The possibility of miracles is easy to accept if one starts where the Bible starts—with the premise that the entire world and all its systems, including human life, are the creation of a powerful and ever-working God who oversees it all (Gen. 1–2; Ps. 104; John 1:1–3). That's why the biblical writers can speak of creation and miracles in the same context. For example, the psalmist describes creation alongside Israel's miraculous escape from Egypt, treating both in the same manner (Ps. 135:5–9; 136:1–16).

Likewise, the amazing systems that God has placed in our bodies are cause for us to praise Him. We call them "natural," but are they really any less "miraculous" than God being present in the deepest darkness or the highest heavens (Ps. 139:7–18)? The point is, what we often describe as "nature" does not exist in and of itself. Nature has been created and is sustained by God. Thus exceptions to the way things "naturally" operate must be seen in the larger picture of God ruling all. If everything belongs to Him, then exceptions to the normal are His prerogative.

The Widow's Oil

In the days immediately following the departure of Elijah, God empowered Elisha to perform a number of miracles. One of them was the increase of oil for a poor widow (2 Kin. 4:1–7).

This incident confirmed Elisha as a true prophet of God and the successor to Elijah. In fact, the increase of oil recalled the miracle that Elijah performed for the widow of Zarephath (1 Kin. 17:8–16).

But in addition to what the miracle revealed about Elisha, it illustrated an important aspect of God's character: His concern for the poor and disadvantaged. Both Elijah and Elisha dealt with kings, commanders, and other powerful leaders. But they also helped the powerless. In this case, the widow was about to lose her sons to pay for a debt left by her late husband. That meant that she would be left with no means of support. God provided for her needs through the intervention of Elisha (compare Ps. 68:5).

In the New Testament, James reminds us that true religion involves action, such as caring for "widows in their trouble" (James 1:27). Thus Elisha was a true prophet practicing true religion.

MISSIONS

An Amazing Promise

How would you feel toward an adult who lured a young person into a life of crime? Imagine the adult teaching a youngster how to break into houses and steal, so that the adult can obtain stolen property at very little risk to himself. Then imagine the juvenile being caught and punished, while the adult remains free. Wouldn't you feel a sense of outrage at this injustice, and want to see the adult put away for a long, long time?

A somewhat similar situation to this occurred in the ancient Middle East, as the Israelites' neighbors recruited them into the evils of idolatry (Jer. 12:14, 16). The surrounding pagan cultures taught the Lord's people to "swear by Baal," that is to worship and serve the gods of their lands. This idolatry broke the covenant that Israel had with the Lord, and as a result, God's people were taken into captivity.

It is unclear whether these "evil neighbors" (Jer. 12:14) were the remnants of the old Canaanite tribes that the Israelites had dispossessed, or the nations who went into captivity along with Judah—Moab, Syria, and

M

Ammon—or the Babylonians, to whose lands the exiles were deported. At one time or another, the Israelites imported and worshiped the gods of all three of these groups.

But whoever these treacherous neighbors were, God extended to them an amazing promise: He would show compassion to them by allowing them to learn about Him, the Israelites' God, even as they had taught the Israelites about their gods (Jer. 12:15). Rather than just wiping them from the face of the earth—which they clearly deserved in light of the grievous sin they had introduced among His people—the Lord would give them an opportunity to turn from their worthless idols and serve Him, the true God.

This was truly amazing grace. This gesture shows God's heart of compassion for all the people of the world. It demonstrates the truth that Peter would later express, that the Lord is "not willing that any should perish, but that all should come to repentance" (2 Pet. 3:9).

Israel—Chosen for Service

In what sense was Israel a "chosen" nation (Is. 44:1–2)? As Isaiah makes plain, God chose the Israelites to carry out a mission. His choice was based on sovereign purpose and strategy.

Israel's assignment was twofold: to serve as the family through whom the promise and blessing of the Messiah would come (compare Gen. 12:1–3; 15:5–7; 17:4–8), and through Him to be a spiritual light to the other nations of the world (Is. 42:6–7; 44:8; 49:6).

The Hebrews, beginning with Abraham, were given a missionary task to live in the light of what God had revealed to them. He placed them in a strategic locale, and enabled them to build a house of prayer for all nations (see 1 Kin. 8:41–43). Grateful obedience and faithful witness were the proper responses to God's call.

The Gentiles Called by God's Name

Amos offers a wonderful ray of hope in an otherwise unhappy book of prophecy when he alludes to all the Gentiles who are to be called by the Lord's name (Amos 9:12). This is a hope to all who are not descended from Jacob. It is not just a possibility, but a promise, that those outside of Israel will have access to God. Even as His judgment was

coming upon Israel and the nations of the ancient world, God promised that out of the chaos and calamity He would raise up a place of worship for all who will come to Him.

This promise was fulfilled in Christ, who broke down the wall of separation between Jew and Gentile, so that everyone may enter into the grace of God (Eph. 2:14–22).

*For more on this topic, see **CHURCH**, "Are We Still a Light to the World?" page 57; "Isaiah's Vision, the Church's Mission," page 59.*

MONEY

A Shrewd Manager

What is the point of the parable in Luke 16:1–13? Was Christ commending the manager (or steward) for cheating his boss (Luke 16:8)? No, He was merely observing that people go to great lengths to secure favorable treatment when they are in legal or financial trouble. They may cheat others or pervert the law to do it, but in a way their conduct reveals a certain wisdom, a prudent concern for oneself. If only they took similar pains with their eternal destiny (Luke 16:9–12)!

Luke 16:9 speaks of "unrighteous mammon." Jesus was not implying that money (mammon) is inherently evil, only that material wealth is temporal in nature and will not go with us into eternal life. It will "fail." Therefore, we should use our wealth wisely in this life. In fact, we should "make friends" with it—that is, use it in a way that brings others into the kingdom of Christ (Luke 16:8–9).

Jesus' words in Luke 9:10–11 make it plain that He is not denouncing money. On the contrary, our level of responsibility in His kingdom will depend on how we manage the resources that God gives us in this life. In fact, we might ask: What condition are our finances in? Are we overseeing our material resources prudently and faithfully?

The "bottom line" of this passage is found in Luke 9:12–13. All our earthly goods ultimately come from God and belong to Him. They are not really ours; we only manage them on His behalf. Any other outlook leads to a divided mind. We can't serve God if we're convinced that our money and property belong to us. We'll inevitably end up serving them.

Christians, Money, and Contentment

Paul ridicules the idea that God is in the business of dispensing material gain in exchange for spiritual cooperation (1 Tim. 6:5). That launches him into a discussion of money that modern believers would do well to study carefully, given the emphasis on money in our culture.

Paul warns us strongly against "the love of money" (1 Tim. 6:10). But let's be sure we interpret his words correctly. He does not say that money itself is evil. Neither does he say that money is the fundamental root of evil, or that money lies at the root of every evil. Rather, the love of money (something inside people, not money itself) can be a root (but not the only root) of all kinds of evil (but not of all evil).

But don't let those qualifications soften the blow: people who love money are vulnerable to all kinds of evil, the worst of which, Paul points out, is straying from the faith. Given this danger, believers should avoid greed.

Paul offers the alternative to greed, or covetousness, as contentment (1 Tim. 6:6–8). However, his description of contentment—food and clothing—sounds incredibly spartan in our own culture that extols self-made millionaires. Are believers required to take vows of poverty like Franciscan monks?

No, but Paul does remind us in this passage what poverty really is: lack of food, clothing, and shelter adequate for survival where one lives. If we have these, we ought to be content. Is it really possible in our society to be content with the basics—food, clothing,

and shelter? Paul should know. He experienced firsthand the wealth and privileges of prominence in the Jewish community and of Roman citizenship. Yet he also suffered extraordinary hardships in his work. Through it all he learned a secret that helped him maintain contentment. What was it?

Paul's example was especially important to Timothy, his protégé in the faith. He challenges the young pastor to pursue a lifestyle that values character over cash (1 Tim. 6:11). The words are addressed to Timothy, but they apply to anyone who wants to honor God in life. Timothy needed to watch out for greed just like any other believer.

What should people with money do if they want to honor God? Paul says they should start by examining their attitudes. Money has incredible power to create feelings of pride, superiority, and self-sufficiency (1 Tim. 6:17). So people of means have to learn to look beyond their money to God—the ultimate source of wealth.

But attitude is only half the battle. Sooner or later rich Christians need to take conscious, decisive action with their wealth. They need to put it into the service of God and others (6:18).

What is your deepest desire? Is it to be rich rather than righteous? If so, beware! Longing for wealth leads to many dangers—even to death. God wants you to grasp something far more permanent and satisfying—eternal life (1 Tim. 6:12, 19).

Managing Your Money—
Some Biblical Principles

Money is a wonderful servant but a horrible master. The love of it can cause a person to exploit others (Mal. 3:5) and rob God (3:8–9). Like Malachi, Paul warned believers concerning the seductive power of money (1 Tim. 6:10).

Here are some basic lessons from the Bible about money:

- Do not set your heart on riches, and especially be on your guard against oppression and robbery (Ps. 62:10; James 5:1–6).
- God calls us to be contented with what we have rather than coveting what others have (Ex. 20:17; Heb. 13:5).

- If we place so much importance on money that we start loving it, we are liable to unleash all kinds of evil and sorrow (Ps. 52:1–7; Matt. 13:22; 1 Tim. 6:6–10; Rev. 3:17).
- Give God praise and thanks for any and all resources that you have, and honor Him by giving freely to others (Deut. 8:11, 17–18; Prov. 3:9–10; Matt. 10:8; Acts 20:35).
- Building your reputation around money is false; it can lead to dangerous and devastating results, as was the case for one couple in the early church (Acts 5:1–11).
- Wealth is a gift from God and should be received with thanksgiving, generosity, and stewardship (1 Tim. 6:17–18; 2 Cor. 8–9).

Wealth—Hold It Lightly

Whether we own land, buildings, things, or cash, wealth is tricky to handle. How we hold these assets speaks volumes about our values. If we hold them too tightly, the results will likely be possessiveness, stinginess, manipulation, and elitism.

Barnabas converted some land that he owned into a cash gift for needy believers (Acts 4:36–37). Notice how he *let go* of the money, laying it at the apostles' feet to be administered by them. By contrast, Ananias and Sapphira practiced a similar transaction for the same need, but lied about it (Acts 5:1–2). Apparently they wanted to look good among the believers, but they also wanted to secretly hold on to some of their money from the sale.

God calls us as believers to hold our resources lightly. After all, everything that we have comes from Him. He gives it to us as a trust to be managed—not a treasure to be hoarded.

For more on this topic, see GIVING, "Giving with Compassion and Integrity," page 168; GREED, "What's Your Price?," page 189.

MONOTHEISM
God Above All Gods

Some people today object to Christianity's claim that its God is the one true God. But the Bible states emphatically that the Lord is above all other gods, which are idols (1 Chr. 16:23–27). He alone deserves worship, for He is the Creator and Sustainer of life.

Most of the cultures in the ancient world worshiped many gods, almost all of which were associated with nature. For example, the gods of the Canaanites were part of what was essentially a fertility cult designed to increase their harvests and the birth rate of their women. The Hebrews were virtually unique in their belief in one supreme God.

Today, things are not much different. Around the world, people worship and serve a variety of gods, as well as a variety of often conflicting ideas about God. Meanwhile, the belief that there is one supreme God seems to be less and less popular, especially in an age that holds tolerance and pluralism to be among the highest of values.

Yet God has not changed. He still invites—indeed, commands—all the families of the world to give Him the glory due His name (1 Chr. 16:28–30). Doing so need not be a statement of intolerance, simply a response to what is true.

The Lord Is One

The Hebrews were unique among the peoples of the ancient world in their belief in only one God (Deut. 6:4). All of the surrounding cultures were polytheistic; they worshiped numerous gods. For example, the Canaanites had at least seventy deities. Likewise, the Egyptians had a pantheon, or collection, of gods, and the Pharaohs themselves were considered gods. Most cities throughout the Middle East had their own local god or gods.

The Israelites were different. Abraham originally lived in the city of Ur with his father and family (Gen. 11:27–30). Ur was dedicated to the moon god Sin and the goddess Nin-gal. But in the midst of this polytheistic society, the Lord spoke to Abraham, instructing him to leave the country (Gen. 12:1–3; Acts 7:2–3). From then on, it appears that Abraham essentially believed in only one God—the God who continued to reveal Himself over many years to Abraham and his descendants. In fact, by Moses' day, the Lord referred to Himself as the God of Abraham, Isaac, and Jacob (Ex. 3:15).

The distinction between monotheism and polytheism is not simply the number of gods (one versus many), but their very nature.

The Israelites had a monotheistic religion, but at times they still lapsed into idolatry.

Ironically, doing so only confirmed the Lord as supreme God alone, because each time they turned away from Him, He reasserted Himself in a way that exposed the futility of the idols and established His sovereignty.

MOTHERHOOD

A Mother's Influence

If you are the mother of a child growing up in today's world, you may sometimes wonder how much of an impact you are having on your child's life. At times, the influences of teachers, peers, television, video games, and even the government may seem to outweigh your own.

But consider the example of Jochebed, the mother of Moses. She lived in extremely difficult times, and had limited say over what would happen to her son. Yet she used what opportunity she did have to affect his growth and development. First she exercised bold faith by refusing to put him to death (Ex. 1:15–16; 2:2–4). God honored her faith not only by preserving the baby's life, but also by arranging circumstances that allowed Jochebed to serve as his nurse—and mother (Ex. 2:5–10).

The history of Moses' life makes it apparent that Jochebed helped to shape her son's character. The fact that as an adult he unashamedly identified with the Hebrews and the God of Israel, despite his connections to the royal court, is a testimony to Jochebed's influence during those formative years (Heb. 11:24–26).

As a mother, you probably have much more opportunity than Jochebed to influence your child. Are you taking advantage of those few short years of your young one's childhood to make a positive, lasting contribution, to the glory of God? Or are you allowing the prevailing culture to have the dominant impact on your child's development?

A Pushy Mother

Overzealous mothers are not exclusive to the twentieth century, as the incident in Matthew 20:20–23 makes clear. The mother of Zebedee's sons would have claimed that she only wanted what was best for James and John.

But when Jesus found out what she was seeking, He gave her and her sons a warning. He knew that suffering had to come before

M

glory. Could James and John endure that suffering? The two men were quick to promise that they would. Jesus assured them that they would have the chance to back up their words.

Perhaps later James and John regretted making such bold promises. But how often are we like them—eager to promise whatever we have to in order to get what we want? Perhaps worse, how often do we push our children into things based on our own needs for pride and significance?

A Mother's Legacy

Eunice (2 Tim. 1:5) was Jewish, but apparently her father was not very orthodox: he violated one of the clear commands of the Law in arranging a match for his daughter with a Gentile (Acts 16:1). Later, when Timothy was born, he wasn't circumcised (Acts 16:3). So it seems that neither Eunice's father nor husband were observant of Judaism.

But Eunice was. Paul praised her for her "genuine faith," which she shared in common with Lois, her mother (2 Tim. 1:5). Eunice imparted that faith to her son, Timothy, and more than anyone else equipped him for a lifetime of usefulness for God.

Eunice is an encouragement for every woman faced with the daunting task of nurturing the spiritual life of her children, especially if she can't count on the help of a strong male. Eunice may have had no formal religious education and little encouragement from her family, except for Lois. But she had two crucial things going for her that offer hope for mothers today—the inherent power of being a mother and the dynamic power of a loving God.

MOURNING

(see Burial and Funeral Customs; Grief)

MUDSLINGING

(see Smear Tactics)

MURDER

Family Chaos

Many Christians today have high expectations for what their families should be like, and the Bible offers a great deal of help toward building healthy family relationships.

But Scripture also helps us keep our expectations realistic by showing us the world's first family, which was far from idyllic (Gen. 4:1–16). The murder of Abel is a sobering reminder that a family is made up of sinners who frequently reveal that side of their character.

Murder on the Job

Why do mediocre workers often resent excellent workers? Why do people who lie to and steal from their employers and customers resent honest coworkers? Why does the person who cuts corners on the job feel ill-at-ease with someone who gives an honest day's work? Because the unrighteous hate the righteous, as John shows (1 John 3:11–13). They can't stand someone who has integrity. That person's honest lifestyle exposes their evil and wrongdoing, like a light that penetrates moral darkness.

The reference to Cain (3:12) is sobering. Cain killed his brother, Abel, out of resentment (Gen. 4:3–8; Heb. 11:4). In the same way, a worker with a poor attitude and substandard work usually resents a coworker whose work ethic and performance are consistently higher. Like Cain, he may "murder" his nemesis in his mind and heart, simply by begrudging his conscientious efforts.

The warning is clear: Pay attention to feelings of resentment against coworkers who outperform you. Consider what happened to Cain!

*For more on this topic, see **SELF-DEFENSE**, "Killing in Self-Defense," page 361.*

MURPHY'S LAW

(see Troubles)

MUSIC

Praise the Lord!

Here's an exercise to try with young children, to help them carry out the exhortation of Psalm 150 to praise the Lord (Ps. 150:1).

Begin by telling them that God deserves to be praised:

- He is our Creator, who made the world and all its animals and people.
- He is our Lord, who is ultimately in control, even though people sometimes do things that cause a great deal of trouble.
- He is our Savior, who forgives us for the wrong things we do because Jesus paid our penalty on the Cross.

• He loves all the children of the world—and their parents, too!

Explain to the children that one way to praise the Lord is with musical instruments. Talk about the instruments mentioned in the psalm. Then provide the children with "instruments" that correspond to the instruments mentioned: for example, a kazoo for the trumpet, a ukelele for the stringed instruments, a tambourine for the timbrel, and cookie tin lids for the cymbals.

Finally, have them play their instruments as they march around the room singing "Jesus Loves the Little Children," or some other appropriate tune. Be sure to tell them that when they shout "Hallelujah!" they are saying, "Praise the Lord!"

New Songs for the Lord

Six times the psalms encourage God's people to worship Him through a "new song" (Ps. 98:1; compare Pss. 33:3; 40:3; 96:1; 144:9; 149:1). This exhortation fits with the fact that during Israel's monarchy, and especially during the reigns of David and Solomon, a torrent of new music flowed from the musicians at Jerusalem.

What does this imply for God's people today? For one thing, it strongly suggests that the church encourage and support believers to whom God has given musical ability. These brothers and sisters can use their gifts to lead others in worship and to create new expressions of praise for God. Indeed, without them, the church will be hard-pressed to fulfill the instruction to sing new praises to God.

This is not to suggest that old hymns and musical compositions be forgotten. They have great value in that they remind modern-day believers of the great heritage from which we have come. But even as Christians down through the centuries have honored Christ by composing music in the forms available and meaningful to their cultures, so Christ's people today can praise Him with "new songs."

MUTUALITY

(see Cooperation; Teamwork)

N

NATIONAL DEFENSE

In God We Trust

All currency in the United States is stamped with the motto, "In God we trust." Thus whenever they exchange money, American citizens have a small but ever-present reminder that the foundation of life is the Lord, not money.

Psalm 33 offered a similar reminder to the ancient Israelites. The foundation of their society was the Lord, not the size or strength of their defenses (Ps. 33:16–17). This was an important point to keep in mind in that day, because the ability of a nation to defend often determined its continued existence. In fact, the history of the land of Canaan is a history of invading armies from the north and south. Thus it would be natural to rely on the military for protection, rather than God.

The point of Psalm 33 is not to diminish the need for either a strong defense or a stable income, but to urge people to place their ultimate confidence in the Lord (33:18–22).

Things like money and the military are merely means to an end. What ultimately matters is whether we fear the Lord and trust in Him to meet our needs.

Prayer: The Best Defense

Some people think of prayer primarily as a last resort, an act of desperation to try when all else fails and one is faced with overwhelming odds. But the example of Asa shows while prayer ultimately is the best defense, it also is the best offense, a discipline that should be practiced long before trouble strikes.

Faced with an army more than three times the size of his own three hundred thousand-man force, Asa cried out to God for help. He humbly acknowledged that the Lord, not military might, was his ultimate defense (2 Chr. 14:11). The Lord responded by defeating the Ethiopians (2 Chr. 14:12–15).

This incident showed that what matters in battle is not the size of the armies, but trust in the Lord. As always, what counts with God is faith.

Yet Asa's trust in God was not just a "fox-hole faith," motivated by fear. He was able to pray as he did because he had been praying, worshiping, and honoring the Lord for years (2 Chr. 14:3–7). In fact, his reign had reversed many of the sins initiated by his great-grandfather Solomon.

Less than two decades earlier, Solomon's successor Rehoboam had been defeated by Egyptian forces, which included Ethiopians. The invaders from the south overran Judah and captured Jerusalem with far fewer military resources (2 Chr. 12:1–12) than the army which Asa saw crushed. This emphasizes the point that when the people of God made worship and prayer their first priorities, God was faithful to take care of them. But when they turned away from the Lord and made other things such as wealth and prestige their top priorities, then God allowed them to fail.

So it is with spiritual warfare today. God wants to see whether we respond in faith when circumstances overwhelm us. But He also is interested in the quality of our faith before tragedy strikes, when things are going well. Either way—in calm or in crisis—we need to pray to the Lord in faith (1 John 5:4).

NATIONS

A Vision That Includes All Nations

The prophecies of Isaiah are remarkable in light of the time in history when they are believed to have been given (about 740–681 B.C.). The northern and southern kingdoms of Israel were in political and national decline. The glory days of David and Solomon were only a distant memory. Assyria was the reigning superpower, and no nation could effectively challenge its might or authority. In the midst of this chaos, God called Isaiah to speak on His behalf.

But Isaiah's writings do not focus solely on the Hebrew kingdoms of Israel and Judah. The prophet also presents a vision of God's love and concern for all nations (Is. 2:2). Isaiah is overwhelmed by the greatness of God, who stands as a firm foundation amid the chaos of war and moral decay. For that reason, he is able to offer hope rather than de-

spair. Yet it is a hope with its eyes wide open to the reality of sin and its consequences.

In 722 B.C., the tragic consequences came to pass for the northern kingdom. Israel was captured and its people carried away into exile by the Assyrian army. Then, a few years later, Jerusalem was surrounded by the same mighty army. The end seemed near for Judah, and it appeared that nothing could be done.

Isaiah, however, was able to look through the smoke and debris of the present to a vision of God's glory and control over all that was taking place on the earth. He also revealed God's glorious heart of love for all peoples. For Isaiah, a loving, just, and sovereign God was in control of history.

Isaiah foresaw that history would eventually culminate in a day when the temple at Jerusalem would serve as a worship center for all the nations of the world (Is. 2:2–3). The peoples would flow like a river from all over the earth to see and know the living God. The Lord would judge the nations (Is. 2:4; compare Matt. 25:31–46; Rev. 20:11–15), wars would end, and God's peace would rule the world (compare Is. 11:1–10).

So for Isaiah, God is an international God. He is Lord of all the nations. He is also the Savior of the world. His offer of life is for all. People and nations that refuse to repent and receive His life will be judged (Is. 2:10–11, 19, 21).

The Ruler of All Nations

Psalm 33 is international in its scope, calling the whole earth to worship the Lord (Ps. 33:8). Why should the peoples of the world "stand in awe" of this God? Because the Lord's purposes supersede the counsels of the nations, and He blesses those nations that honor Him (Ps. 33:10–12). Furthermore, God's watchful eye is on all nations (Ps. 33:13–15), not just one's own country.

Given this perspective, the world's nations and their leaders enjoy only limited sovereignty. But by honoring God's rule and authority, they can have unbounded hope. He blesses nations that pursue righteousness and justice and make God their Lord.

NATURAL DISASTERS
Sudden Calamity

Almost by definition, disaster usually strikes suddenly and without warning. Even though people know that earthquakes, famine, accidents, and death are bound to occur, they are still shocked when they do.

The tragedies that claimed Job's possessions and family (Job 1:13–17) came suddenly and without warning. In hindsight, we can guess that Job surely knew of the ever-present risks under which he and his family lived: bands of Sabean raiders (Job 1:15), lightning (the "fire of God," 1:16), bands of Chaldeans on the prowl for fresh camels (Job 1:17), and windstorms (Job 1:19). Yet even though he must have known that sooner or later he would probably confront dangers like these, Job was still thunderstruck when news of their occurrence reached him (Job 1:20).

In this way Job and his family were like most people, then and now: conscious of risks, but living out their lives in day-to-day routines. Then when calamity strikes, their world is turned upside down.

Jesus warned that the condition at the end of the ages would be similar. People would be going about their routines—eating and drinking, marrying and giving in marriage—forgetful of the fact that the Lord is returning; no one knows when (Matt. 24:38, 42). Would you be ready to meet the Lord if He were to come today? Jesus urged us as His followers to "be ready" by faithfully going about the responsibilities that He has entrusted to us (Matt. 24:44–46).

There is no shame in being taken by surprise by natural disasters, as were Job and his family. But is there any excuse for being shocked at the Lord's return, when He has already told us that He is coming?

NATURAL RESOURCES
(see Environment)

NATURE
(see Environment)

NEGOTIATION
(see Conflict Resolution)

N

NEIGHBORLINESS

Getting Involved

How easy it is to excuse ourselves when we see someone in need by thinking, ''There's no reason why I should get involved. Those people are strangers, and I have no obligation to them.''

But Scripture doesn't let us off that easily. Obviously we can't help every needy person we come across. Or can we? We can at least pray! At any rate, the lawyer's restatement of Leviticus 19:18 (Luke 10:27) and Christ's response (Luke 10:28) show that in fact we do have an obligation to strangers—even though we've made no commitments to them.

As Jesus goes on to show in the parable of the good Samaritan (Luke 10:29–37), we who intend to follow Him have a responsibility to everyone in the human race, because everyone is our neighbor. We are to demonstrate ''mercy'' to all (Luke 10:37). Or, as Paul later wrote, ''do good to all'' (Gal. 6:10).

NETWORKING

A Networking Disciple

In addition to working in his family's commercial fishing enterprise, Andrew followed the teaching of John the Baptist and was considered one of his disciples (John 1:35–40). Thus he heard John declare that Jesus was

NATURAL DISASTERS

the Lamb of God—a clear reference to Him as the Messiah. Eager to know more about this new Teacher, Andrew pursued Jesus, prompting an invitation to spend an evening with Him. The meeting convinced Andrew that he had indeed met the long-awaited Christ.

The text is quite clear that the first thing Andrew did after coming to this conclusion was to find his brother, Simon, and tell him the extraordinary news: "We have found the Messiah!" He then brought his brother to meet Jesus (John 1:41–42).

Later, after Jesus called both of the brothers to follow Him as His disciples, Andrew and the others found themselves on one occasion confronted by thousands of people. Jesus asked His disciples where they could buy food for the crowd to eat, a proposition that staggered them. But Andrew had made the acquaintance of a boy with a handful of barley loaves and a couple of fish. He brought this meager supply to the attention of the Lord, who then multiplied it to feed the entire crowd of about five thousand (John 6:4–14).

Shortly before Jesus' arrest, certain Greeks desired to meet Him. Once again, Andrew acted as a go-between, carrying their request to his Teacher (John 12:20–22). All of these incidents suggest that Andrew was a networker, a man who liked to put people together—and especially to put them together with Jesus. He serves as a model for believers today in bringing others to Christ.

Tradition holds that Andrew devoted the later years of his life to spreading the news about Jesus to Scythia, the region north of the Black Sea. Some say that he was martyred at Patrae in Achaia by crucifixion on an X-shaped cross.

The Christian Network

Computer networks have become important systems in today's competitive marketplace. They enable teams of workers in different offices, at regional sites, and even from around the world to join together on tasks that would otherwise be difficult if not impossible.

One way of setting up a network is to use a central computer to handle the main programming, storage, and communication functions, with remote workstations for individual input and retrieval. This is similar to the situation that Jesus described in His image of the vine and the branches (John 15:1–10):

1. *Jesus is the key (John 15:1).* Like the central processing unit of a computer system, Jesus provides the life, the direction, and the commands for His followers, those of us "on-line."

2. *To be effective, believers must maintain their relationship with Jesus (John 15:4).* In order to use the features of a network, a user must remain attached to the network. If one "signs off," there is no more access to the central computer or to others in the network. Likewise, if we allow sin to disrupt our walk with Christ, we lose fellowship with Him and with other believers (1 John 1:6–7).

3. *Jesus wants His followers to be productive (John 15:5–8).* Companies install computer networks so that their employees can get their work done. The systems cost too much to be treated as toys or to be underutilized. Correspondingly, the relationship that believers have with God was purchased through Christ's blood, so we need to take it seriously. Christ wants us to enjoy walking with Him, but He also wants us to accomplish His purposes.

4. *To love Jesus is to follow His commands (John 15:9–10).* Occasionally network users receive an "error message" indicating that they have not followed the instructions of the program correctly. By the same token, Jesus has given us commands to follow, and the only way to experience His life and power is to obey those commands. To do so is not only practical, but an expression of our love for the Lord.

Are you "on-line" with Jesus, drawing on His resources and obeying His commands? Is your life productive, accomplishing the tasks and responsibilities that He has assigned to you?

NOSTALGIA

Remember the Past, but Face the Present

Many churchgoers in the inner city today glory in, yet are discouraged by, the greatness of their church's past. Perhaps they gather in the cavernous, unheated sanctuary of a historic old church that is now but a shell of what it once was. The handful of senior members who still attend can remember when it was a great and prestigious congregation. But no more.

These faithful members have a lot in common with some of elderly citizens among the people of Jerusalem to whom Haggai was sent. As a new temple began to take form in the place where the old one had stood, some of the old-timers could remember the "former glory" of the first temple (Hag. 2:3). They remembered its beautiful cedar paneling, gold overlay, and other magnificent furnishings. By comparison, the new temple seemed "as nothing" in their eyes.

The Lord did not discourage them from honoring this gilded, glorious past, but He did exhort them to turn their eyes toward the present. He challenged the leaders and the people: "Be strong and work; for I am with you" (Hag. 2:4). The new structure might not bring back the days of Solomon, but it would at least be a building of which they could be proud.

Scripture often encourages us to remember and honor the past, but it also urges us to face the reality of the present. God is at work *today*, just as He was at work yesterday. His Spirit remains with us (Hag. 2:5; John 14:16–17), just as He was with believers in times past. If we cooperate with what the Spirit is doing, we may bring even greater glory to God and accomplish even greater ministry than has yet been seen.

The Good Old Days

Do you ever find yourself wishing for the "good old days"? Job did (Job 29:1). As his trials and tribulations lagged on, and as the "counsel" of his friends wore him out, he began to look back on more prosperous times.

There's nothing unusual in that. But let's look at several of the issues with which Job was dealing. We might phrase them in the form of tough questions:

1. If we are meeting with success, is that necessarily a sign that God is with us (Job 29:2–6)? Conversely, if we are experiencing hard times, does that necessarily mean that God is against us? In the end, Job discovered that external circumstances are not necessarily evidence of God's work in and through one's life.

2. To what extent is the admiration of others important to us (Job 29:7–11)? Should we interpret the words and actions of other people as indications of God's favor or opposition in our lives? Job eventually decided against doing so. His former associates in the marketplace had turned away from him, yet he knew he was innocent of wrongdoing. His three friends harshly criticized him, yet in the end he was vindicated by God Himself (Job 42:7–8).

3. When are we closer to God—when we can function as the source of strength and support for others (Job 29:12–17), or when we are weak and broken down, and must depend on others (Job 30:9–15)? Job seemed to honor God both in prosperity (Job 1:1–3) and adversity (Job 1:22; 2:9–10).

For more on this topic, see CHANGE, "Old-timers' View of Change," page 50.

O

OBEDIENCE

Benefits of Obeying God's Word

Psalm 119:2 promises blessings for obeying God's Word (or "testimonies") and seeking the Lord with one's whole heart. The psalm goes on to mention or allude to a number of these benefits:

- Avoiding sin and pursuing godliness (Ps. 119:3, 11, 36, 102, 133).
- A motivation and basis for praising God (Ps. 119:7, 171).
- A pure lifestyle (Ps. 119:9).
- Readjustments in our priorities (Ps. 119:14, 92) and values (Ps. 119:16, 20, 37, 48, 72, 103, 111, 127).

- Insight into our purpose on earth (Ps. 119:19, 32, 125).
- Avoiding and learning from God's rebuke (Ps. 119:21–22, 67, 71, 75, 118).
- A basis for evaluating criticism and opposition (Ps. 119:23, 41–42, 51, 61, 69, 84–88, 98, 161).
- A source of wisdom and guidance for day-to-day life (119:24, 66, 105, 130, 176).
- Encouragement, hope, and comfort (Ps. 119:25, 28, 41, 49–50, 52, 55, 61, 81–83, 114, 166).
- Something valuable with which to occupy our minds (Ps. 119:27, 55, 62, 97, 147–148) and conversation (119:46, 164, 172).

• A basis for truth, honesty, and integrity (Ps. 119:29–30, 99–100, 104, 163).
• A sense of freedom (Ps. 119:45).
• A source of new songs (Ps. 119:54).
• An accurate basis for self-examination (Ps. 119:59).
• Fellowship with like-minded believers (Ps. 119:63, 79).
• A solid foundation for our faith (Ps. 119:66, 89–90).
• Protection and peace (Ps. 119:114, 165).
• The ability to discern right from wrong (Ps. 119:136, 138–139, 158).
• A motivation and basis for prayer (Ps. 119:169–170).
• The Lord's help (Ps. 119:173–174).

Obeying Begins by Listening

The English word "obey" (2 Chr. 30:12) comes from a Latin word meaning "to hear." Thus the old proverb is literally true: to hear is to obey.

An exasperated parent asks a child who comes late to the dinner table, "Why didn't you come when I called you?" The child responds, "I didn't hear you until the third time!" Thus we see that obedience involves an informed choice.

Do you know how to obey (listen to) God? It helps if you allow your familiarity with God's interests and values to grow through some regular form of Bible reading. As you do so, carefully ask yourself: What is God telling me to do as a result of His Word?

For more on this topic, see **DUTY,** *"Doing Your Duty," page 117;* **LOYALTY,** *"Known for Our Commitment," page 248.*

OBSTACLES

Overcoming Obstacles—with the Lord's Help

Planning is a valuable prelude to almost any endeavor. But too often plans fail to produce results because they do not take into account four significant obstacles. David's advice to Solomon (1 Chr. 28:20–21) points out these barriers, and also shows some ways around them:

• Lack of strength—the inability to do what is necessary to get the job done. David promised God's help to strengthen Solomon's hand, and also the resource of skilled workers who could supply the competencies needed for the temple project.
• Lack of courage—the failure to stay the course when the task looks discouraging or the problems overwhelming. David promised that God would be with Solomon throughout the project; therefore, he need not be afraid or dismayed.
• Lack of follow-through—the inability or unwillingness to translate good intentions into effective activity. To this David had one response: "Do it!"
• Lack of faith—the decision not to acknowledge, trust, or make use of God's perspective, power, and presence. This was a choice that only Solomon could make. God stood ready to help him, but only he could respond to God's help in faith and obedience.

OCCULT

Condemning the Occult

There is today a growing interest in occult beliefs and practices, such as fortune-telling, witchcraft, and astrology. But John reveals the true nature of the occult when he writes that the sorcery of Babylon has deceived all the nations (Rev. 18:23).

Occult practices were common among the pagan nations of the ancient world. But attempts to contact or control evil spirits were expressly forbidden to the Hebrews, and the prohibition extends to believers today. Among the practices that Deuteronomy 18:10–12 calls "an abomination to the LORD" are:

• child sacrifice (making one's son or daughter "pass through the fire");
• witchcraft;
• soothsaying, a form of divination which may have been similar to tea leaf reading or astrology;
• interpreting omens;
• sorcery;
• conjuring spells;
• consulting mediums;
• spiritism; and
• calling up the dead.

In the New Testament, the gospel exposed two sorcerers, Simon (Acts 8:9–25) and Elymas (13:6–8). They may have been something like the "itinerant Jewish exorcists," also mentioned in the Book of Acts (19:13), who attempted to drive evil spirits out of people in the name of Jesus.

The New Testament word translated "sorcery" comes from the same Greek word as our English word "pharmacy." Obviously this has to do with drugs; a more relevant and contemporary application could hardly be found. The denunciations of Revelation 9:21; 18:23; 21:8; and 22:15 apply to those who use drugs to bring on trances during which they claim to have supernatural knowledge or power.

Dangerous Delusions

From time to time, newspapers carry stories of drought-ravaged farmers who hire professional rainmakers and "water witchers." Some of these "experts" use divining rods, others try rain dances. Their occultic efforts are often portrayed as a noble, last-ditch effort to try to save the crops when all else has failed.

There were apparently droughts in Judah after the exile (Zech. 10:1), and some of the people were turning to diviners and false gods for help rather than the Lord (Zech. 10:2). This was utterly foolish in light of the fact that Judah's exile had been a judgment for exactly these kinds of practices (compare Jer. 14:1–10).

The Lord condemns all forms of divining, fortune-telling, and sorcery. Practices such as rain dances, consulting the stars, seances, casting charms and spells, and the use of items such as divining rods, tarot cards, Ouija boards, and crystals are far from innocent. These arts and objects engage demons that are in opposition to the one true God. Their leader is a liar (John 8:44), and his strategy is to deceive people (2 Cor. 11:3–4).

The way of true wisdom is to be found in a relationship with God, not through dabbling in the occult.

False Forecasting

When modern-day weather forecasters miss a forecast, and it rains rather than shines, or snows a blizzard rather than turning out clear and cold, the public outcry is often severe, especially if property or lives have been placed at risk as a result of the inaccurate information.

Imagine, though, if the forecasters knowingly broadcast lies about the weather! That's what God charged the false prophets of Judah with doing (Jer. 14:14), only their forecasts were not about the weather, but about political and spiritual matters. Rather than listening for a word from the Lord, these charlatans resorted to divination, attempting to tell the future through such means as astrology or examining the entrails of ritually slaughtered animals.

Scripture strongly denounced this practice, along with other forms of the occult arts.

Official Magicians

Many cultures in the ancient world had occult practices, but the Babylonians distinguished themselves by institutionalizing the magical arts as part of their government (Dan. 2:2). They were particularly known for their extensive use of astrology. This is among the reasons why God severely condemned Babylon. Scripture repeatedly warns God's people against the "abominations" of the occult.

The Abominations of the Canaanites

Recent years have seen an increase in occult practices and Satanic rituals. But these things are nothing new. Somewhat similar rites were taking place in Canaan at the time when Israel left Egypt. God referred to the Canaanite practices as "abominations" for which "the land vomits out its inhabitants" (Lev. 18:25–26).

The historical context of Leviticus 18 shows that God's concern had to do with religious as well as sexual purity. The chapter opens and closes with warnings to avoid the ways of the Canaanites (Lev. 18:3, 30).

The practices mentioned—incest, adultery, fornication, intercourse during a woman's menstrual flow, child sacrifice, sodomy, bestiality—were all acts committed as part of the Canaanite religion. That religion was essentially a fertility cult. Worshipers appealed to their gods to help their women reproduce and to make their lands fertile. Thus sexual intercourse played a major role in the worship.

There were other "abominations" involved, such as idolatry and the use of mediums and witchcraft. For all of these things, the Lord promised to drive the Canaanites out of the land. In their place He planned to install His people living according to His ways and worshiping according to His holy practices.

The Seduction of Spirits

It is often said that "curiosity killed the cat." One curiosity not worth risking one's life over is the mystery of magic and the spirit world. God's Law spoke very clearly about the attraction of divination, witchcraft, mediums, oracles, and soothsayers: it called them "abominations" (Deut. 18:9–12).

Magic was practiced by every one of the cultures surrounding Israel. Scripture specifically names the Egyptians (Ex. 7:11), the Assyrians (Nah. 3:4), the Babylonians (Dan. 2:2), and the Canaanites (Deut. 18:14) as resorting to magical arts, and usually condemns the practice when it mentions it.

Yet there is no denying the strong seduction of magic and the occult. A longing for power or significance can create tremendous interest in the real or apparent use of supernatural forces working on one's behalf.

Perhaps that's why Israel often succumbed to the seduction of magic later in its history. Despite the strong warnings of Deuteronomy and other passages, the nation and its leaders turned to sorcerers and other spiritists during several times of crisis (2 Kin. 17:17; 2 Chr. 33:6; Mic. 5:12).

God does not resort to magic and other occult arts to make His will known or to exercise His power. His people have no need to resort to any sort of magic, witchcraft, astrology, horoscopes, Ouija boards, tarot cards, mediums, seances, divining rods, fortunetellers, "spiritual advisors," crystals, potions, drugs, or any element of the occult.

If we want to engage in true spirituality, we can find it clearly presented through the Scriptures and, ultimately, in the person of Jesus Christ, who is God among us. "God is Spirit, and those who worship Him must worship in spirit and truth" (John 4:24). We should be aware of spiritual evil but not be seduced by it, lest we be like moths drawn to a flame that kills.

*For more on this topic, see **ADVICE**, "Bad Advice," page 9; **ASTRONOMY**, "The Failure of the Stars," page 26.*

OLD AGE

(*see* Aging)

OPENNESS

Discerning the Truth

Discerning truth from falsehood is a continuing challenge for those in authority (Prov. 29:12). There are several reasons for this:

- Subordinates often have a personal agenda. They do not so much "lie" as tell the boss the things that will further their agenda.
- Subordinates are generally reluctant to tell their superiors bad news.
- Subordinates are generally reluctant to voice ideas or opinions with which they think their bosses are likely to disagree.
- People often see the same thing in different ways.

Given these realities, perhaps the leader's greatest challenge is to create an atmosphere in which truth and openness are respected, encouraged, and rewarded. If you are in a position of authority, can you list three ways in which you encourage the people under you to be honest? Or do you just assume they will be? Do they see honesty demonstrated in your treatment of them?

OPPORTUNITY

An Opportunity to Speak Up

When God is at work, people will marvel. The people in Jerusalem marveled at the healing of a lame man (Acts 3:11). People today may be just as surprised by social or personal changes that God brings about. Often that makes them ready and even eager to hear believers as we explain the message of Christ. Curiosity opens an opportunity for us to speak up. We can help "open the eyes" of others to see God's hand behind what they have observed, the way Peter did (Acts 3:12–26).

Of course, like Peter and John we may also trigger a hostile reaction from some (Acts 4:1–4). Our explanation might confront the anger or confusion that often accompanies conviction—the realization that one has offended God. But belonging to God means that we speak the truth anyway, no matter what the outcome.

For more on this topic, see **FAILURE,** *"A Wasted Opportunity," page 139.*

OPPOSITION

Faithful Living Can Trigger Opposition

Caring for others, speaking the truth, and living with integrity are not always rewarded in this broken world. God's grace often exposes the sin and guilt of people, sometimes triggering hostility. Believers can become a convenient target of anger.

Paul experienced that from the Jewish leaders in Jerusalem (Acts 24:1–26). Notice the varied forms of opposition they mobilized against him before Felix:

- They enlisted a skilled orator, Tertullus, who flattered the governor as he represented them in their case against Paul (Acts 24:1–3).
- They trumped up a variety of accusations that amounted to little more than name-calling (Acts 24:5–6). On a previous occasion, Jason of Thessalonica had experienced similar treatment for merely entertaining Paul and his team (Acts 17:5–9).
- They arrested Paul, and though they accused commander Lysias of violence, it was they who had been on the verge of a riot (Acts 23:7–10; 24:6–7).
- They engineered the testimony of others against him (Acts 24:9).
- They demeaned the entire Christian movement, describing it in loaded terms like "plague" and "sect" (Acts 24:5, 14), not unlike some today who use sweeping negative generalizations and caricatures to dismiss religious activity.
- They apparently played politics with Felix, who was obviously used to settling disputes through bribes and other deals (Acts 24:26; 25:9).

Recognizing this pattern can help us to avoid the mistake of personalizing all attacks on our faith. These responses are more often rooted in our opponents' sense of guilt or fear of judgment than in any justified assessment of our character or conduct.

Leaders Adapt to Adversity

Many people run from adversity; wise leaders cheerfully expect it! Wherever change and progress are underway, competing interests inevitably rise to challenge them. At that point, leaders must decide whether they will accept the challenge and meet it, or turn tail and let their opponents set the agenda.

Nehemiah's adversaries were a group of Jews from racially mixed backgrounds and Gentiles who had a vested interest in seeing that Jerusalem remained unprotected (Neh. 4:7). During the seventy years of Judah's exile, they had established dominance over those left behind. Therefore, Nehemiah's plan to rebuild the walls and revitalize the city threatened to end their monopoly on control.

Nehemiah responded to their opposition with resolute faith and prayer and measured resistance. Rather than escalate a touchy situation, he defended against attack and kept on working. Thus he adapted to adversity rather than run from it or overreact to it. God eventually rewarded Nehemiah's perseverance with the completion of the wall (Neh. 6:15).

If you are in a position of leadership, how do you respond to opposition and adversity? Do you bend but not break, strengthened by your faith and confident that God will see you through? Do you respond to the opposition in appropriate ways, taking practical steps to ensure that the task goes forward, even as others try to shut it down?

OPPRESSION

Deliverance from Oppression

God is a God of justice. Therefore He takes notice when people are oppressed and abused by governments, bosses, and others in power. As the ultimate Judge, He can be counted on to right the world's wrongs, if not in this life, then in the life to come. Exodus is the story of what God did when He heard His chosen people Israel crying out for justice and deliverance (Ex. 3:7–10).

The theme of deliverance is developed through hundreds of biblical passages about the poor and oppressed. Many of those passages remind us that such people ought to receive justice and reform, not just mercy or relief. The biblical teaching suggests several models of deliverance:

- Geographical deliverance. Seen in deliverance of the Jews from Egyptian bondage (Ex. 5:1; 7:16; 8:1; 9:1).
- Social and political deliverance. Seen through Queen Esther working within the structures of pagan society to save an oppressed minority from genocide (Esth. 1–10).
- Deliverance by pagan political leaders. The result of a sovereign God appointing Cyrus of Persia to accomplish his purposes (Is. 45:13).

God still takes notice of the poor and oppressed. What are we doing to help people find freedom—both spiritually and practically?

Equality vs. Slavery

Some people have criticized Paul and the early church, claiming that they did not call for an end to slavery. But Paul wrote the believers in Colosse, "There is neither . . . slave nor free, but Christ is all and in all" (Col. 3:11). Similarly, Galatians 3:28 reads, "There is neither slave nor free . . . you are all one in Christ Jesus."

In Christ, societal divisions and distinctions become immaterial, and practices that degrade and devalue people are condemned. It is true that first-century believers didn't actively campaign for an end to slavery, as far as we know. They never petitioned the government or urged slaves to rebel.

Yet in Philemon we have a clear case of a believing slave owner being asked to put into practice the Christian ideals cited above. Philemon and Onesimus had an opportunity to demonstrate the gospel's power over slavery.

This was one of a number of cultural divisions that early believers broke down, such as:

- Hellenists and Hebrews (Acts 6:1–7).
- Samaritans and Jews (Acts 8:5–8).
- Gentiles and Jews (Acts 8:26–40; 10:1–48).
- Women and men (Acts 16:14–15; 18:1–4, 24–28).

Our society has formally done away with slavery. But there are systems still in place that abuse or oppress people. From the standpoint of the gospel, the issue is not whether they are legal, but whether they treat people as God would want them treated. If Paul were writing today, what would he challenge us as believers to do? What does "one in Christ" mean for the systems we participate in from day to day?

ORGANIZATION

Organizing for a Big Project

How do you break a large job down into manageable parts? One good way is to organize teams around specific tasks. That's how God instructed Moses to handle the mammoth task of moving Israel's house of worship, the tabernacle. It was a delicate but important job. Notice the work teams assigned to the task:

Aaron and the priests carefully prepared the ark, lampstands, utensils, and furniture for the move. Each piece had specific wrapping requirements (Num. 4:5–16).

The Kohathite division was assigned transportation of the items that Aaron and the priests had packed. This team could not go to work until the tabernacle's holy things were completely wrapped and ready to be placed on the carrying poles (Num. 4:15).

The Gershonite unit then collected and carried all the hangings, screens, and remaining utensils. Their work was carried out under strict supervision (Num. 4:21–28).

The Merarite group loaded and carried all the bases, pillars, bars, cords, and pegs under the supervision of the priests, who were careful to name each worker assigned to carry each individual item (Num. 4:29–33).

This kind of careful precision can be continued today among believers as they serve God. For example, Paul taught a cooperative model of the church when he used the image of the body of Christ functioning according to each member's nature and ability (1 Cor. 12:4–26). By working together, planning systems and assignments carefully, and overcoming tendencies toward competition and conflict, Christians can rise to the challenge of managing projects in a way that honors the Lord.

ORPHANS

Protect the Widows and Orphans!

In the New Testament, James wrote that part of "pure and undefiled religion" was to "visit orphans and widows in their trouble" (James 1:27). Perhaps he had in mind the Law's prohibition against mistreating in any way those without husbands or fathers (Ex. 22:22–24).

Widows and orphans (along with aliens, Deut. 27:19) were more likely to be oppressed by the wicked because they lacked anyone to protect them. They also tended to lack the ability to seek legal recourse for the wrongs they suffered, even though systems were in place to provide such protection.

That's why God's people were commanded to pay special attention to these disadvantaged persons. The community was to ensure not only that they were not oppressed, but also that they were not left without provisions because of their situation (Deut. 14:29; 16:11–14; 24:19–21; 26:12–13).

As believers, we also have a responsibility to care for those who have been left without a breadwinner (for example, Gal. 2:10; 1 Tim. 5:3–7). Of course, that responsibility begins with caring for our own relatives who may be in distress (5:8).

OVERCONFIDENCE

Warning: Danger Ahead!

One mark of the fool is overconfidence about being able to avoid evil (Prov. 14:16). "It can't happen to me" is his motto. "And if it does, I can handle it," he boasts. But the Bible says he is tragically mistaken.

"Let him who thinks he stands take heed lest he fall," the New Testament warns (1 Cor. 10:12). And Jesus told His disciples, who insisted that they would never deny their Lord even if it cost them their lives, "Watch and pray, lest you enter into temptation. . . . The spirit indeed is willing, but the flesh is weak" (Matt. 26:35, 41).

Overconfidence about one's own moral and spiritual strength is perilous. It shows that one has no appreciation of the nature and power of evil. If people such as Moses, Samson, David, and Peter were tempted and fell into sin (Num. 20:2–13; Judg. 16; 2 Sam.

11; Matt. 26:69–75), what chance do the rest of us have if we fail to respect sin's power?

For that reason, Proverbs counsels that we depart from evil (Prov. 14:16), that we turn our backs on temptation and refuse to toy with sin. For one person that might mean finding a new set of friends; for another, changing jobs; and for someone else, canceling a magazine subscription.

Whatever tempts you to sin, you are wise if you do whatever it takes to turn your back on it, and turn toward "righteousness, faith, love, peace with those who call on the Lord out of a pure heart" (2 Tim. 2:22).

OVERPOPULATION

(*see* Birth Control)

OWNERSHIP

A Tenant Mentality

Are we owners of possessions like money, houses, land, cars, clothing, TV sets, and so forth? Our culture tells us that we are. In fact, many messages tell us that significance is determined by how much we own and how much what we own is worth.

But the parable of the vineyard owner (Luke 20:9–19) challenges that way of looking at things. Jesus tells of tenants or workers who scheme to steal a vineyard from its owner rather than return its produce to him. They value the land, the trees, and the fruit more than people—they beat the owner's representatives (Luke 20:10–12)—and even more than life itself—they kill the owner's own son (Luke 20:14–15).

In the same way, the community leaders among Jesus' listeners harbored the same desire to kill Him (Luke 20:19). At that point they were prevented from acting by the rest of the people. But eventually they would have their way. Just as their forebears had rejected the prophets that God had sent, so they would now reject God's own Son in a futile effort to keep the nation under control. But they would only succeed in bringing down God's judgment.

This parable challenges us to consider what God has entrusted to our care, and what He expects from us. No matter what He has given us, we are like tenants; the true Owner of all things is the Creator God. He has loaned us our lives, our families, our skills, and all our resources. He calls us to manage those gifts in a way that honors Him.

That means that we must resist getting so tied to our possessions that we are tempted to resort to evil or even violence to keep them. We must hold things with the attitude of tenants, keeping in mind who really owns them—God who loaned them to us for His glory and the service of others.

Do We Really Own Anything?

Do you own your possessions, or do they own you? The Lord told Israel, "I have *given* you a land" (Josh. 24:13, emphasis added; compare Josh. 1:3, 11, 15). That indicates that the land ultimately belonged to God; Israel took possession of it as a gift from His hand, a resource to be treasured and managed wisely.

Elsewhere, Scripture affirms that all of our possessions as human beings ultimately come from a good God:

- The earth itself, with all of its resources, is a gift from God (Gen. 1:29–31; 2:15; 9:2–3; Ps. 8:6–8).
- The ability to work and earn a living is a gift from God (Deut. 8:18).
- The capacity to enjoy the basic elements of life—food, family, work—is a gift from God (Eccl. 3:13; 5:19).

However, these gifts do not come without condition. Like everything else in this world, God's gifts are temporary. Someday we will give an account for what we have done with and to them (Gen. 9:5; Rom. 14:12; 2 Cor. 5:10).

Like Israel in Canaan, all of us are called to a life of thankful dependence on God and stewardship of the resources He has given us. What are you doing with God's gifts to you? Are you serving Him and serving other people with equity and compassion at home, on the job, and in the community?

P

PAGANISM

(*see* Idolatry)

PARENTHOOD

A Father's Final Instructions

A farewell charge like the one that David gave to Solomon (1 Kin. 2:1–9) was a fairly common way for fathers in the ancient world to pass on a legacy to their successors. David's last words provide a useful model for parents today to give final instructions to their children. David's charge contained several elements:

- A blunt recognition and acceptance of death (1 Kin. 2:2).
- A challenge to Solomon to act responsibly (1 Kin. 2:2).
- A review of God's covenant with the nation of Israel (1 Kin. 2:3) and with the house of David (1 Kin. 2:4).
- Instructions about serving justice and honoring David's commitments (1 Kin. 2:5–9).

If you are a parent, what charge would you want to leave to your children before you die? What challenges would you want to set before them? What aspects of God's nature and character would you want to fix in their memory? Is there unfinished business that you need to ask them to complete? Are there promises you have made that you want them to honor?

No Guarantees

Most Christian parents hope to see their children turn out to be followers of Christ and model citizens. Yet while Scripture offers a great deal of practical advice for raising children, there are no guarantees.

Aaron, the high priest and leader of Israel's worship, is a prime case. First, his two older sons, Nadab and Abihu, violated God's commands by offering "profane fire before the Lord" (Lev. 10:1). It's interesting that this occurred immediately after the ceremony initiating the sacrificial system, at which their father had presided (Lev. 9:22–24). Whatever the reason for their disobedience, they died as a result (Lev. 10:2).

Shortly after this, Aaron's two remaining sons, Eleazar and Ithamar, also violated the sacrificial code, and Moses had to discipline them (Lev. 10:12–18).

These incidents raise questions about Aaron as a father. We know from the incident with the golden calf at Sinai that he had a tendency to waffle under pressure (Ex. 32). But quite apart from Aaron's parenting skills, the account suggests that none of us can be certain of how our children will turn out. Even the "best" families can produce rebels. Scripture shows that sinners often make sinful choices.

Rebellious Children

While Scripture urges parents to raise their children "in the training and admonition of the Lord" (Eph. 6:4), it makes no guarantees about how one's children will turn out. Parents can point their children in the right direction, but once young people become adults, they determine which way they will go.

That helps to explain why some godly parents have children who are spiritually rebellious. By the same token, people of great faith and compassion have been known to come from homes where God was dishonored or even unknown.

Josiah was a man of faith and a conscientious ruler of Israel (see 2 Chr. 34:1). Never-

PARENTHOOD

SOLOMON, MY SON, BE STRONG, LOVE GOD, AND BE A WISE MAN, NOT A WISE GUY.

theless, all three of his sons, including Zedekiah (Jer. 37:1–2), turned away from God and paid a tragic price as a result.

Here are some other fathers in the Bible who generally honored the Lord, but whose sons largely departed from His ways:

- Aaron helped lead the people of Israel during the Exodus and was consecrated as the nation's first high priest (Ex. 28:1). But his sons Nadab and Abihu dishonored the Lord in their official duties by offering "profane fire" before the Lord (Lev. 10:1–3).
- Gideon obeyed God's call to lead the Israelites in a successful rout of the Midianites (Judg. 6:11–14; 7:19–22). His son Abimelech hired assassins to murder his seventy brothers and led a treacherous assault on Shechem (Judg. 9).
- Manoah worshiped the Lord during a period of great spiritual darkness (Judg. 13). Samson, his son, dishonored his parents' Nazirite vow, visited prostitutes, and gave little indication of fearing the Lord until the end of his life (Judg. 14–16).
- Samuel judged Israel with integrity and anointed its first two kings (1 Sam. 3:19–21; 9:27–10:1; 16:11–13). His sons Joel and Abijah accepted bribes and violated justice in their positions as judges in Beer-sheba (1 Sam. 8:1–5).
- Hezekiah enacted numerous reforms and remained faithful to the Lord during a siege of Jerusalem by the Assyrians (2 Kin. 18–20). But his son Manasseh thoroughly reversed his father's reforms, reinstituted idolatry, and ruled by violence (2 Kin. 21).

The Blessing

Can you recall a time in your life when your parents told you how special you were to them? Were you ever handed down a family treasure that had special significance and value? Has someone ever praised you and wished you a prosperous future? Gifts of goodness like these are examples of a *blessing,* not unlike the blessings that the elderly Jacob gave to his twelve sons (Gen. 49:28).

In Old Testament times, it was common for an Israelite father to pronounce a formal blessing on his children, and especially on the firstborn son. The pronouncement was intended to bestow goodwill, and sometimes carried prophetic significance and the weight of responsibility. Jacob himself had received his father Isaac's blessing on the firstborn (Gen. 27:26–29). Jacob also gave a blessing to two of his grandsons, Ephraim and Manasseh (Gen. 48:8–20). Centuries later, the baby Jesus and His earthly parents received a blessing from an aged man named Simeon (Luke 2:25–35).

The blessing was a cultural rite rather than a religious obligation. The Law did not mandate that parents pronounce a blessing. Yet there was great value in doing so, and believers today do well to continue this ancient custom. Our children and other loved ones will benefit from hearing formal declarations of their value and receiving formal statements wishing them well in life. A blessing can be a great way to pass on a godly heritage, because it reminds a young person of his connections to family and to God.

Can you think of ways to give your children the gift of a blessing?

For more on this topic, see **CHILDREN,** *"Rearing Children with Discipline," page 53; "Pass On the Story," page 54; "The Problem of a Difficult Child," page 55;* **EXAMPLE,** *"Faith at Home," page 136;* **FAMILY,** *"Learning at Home," page 148.*

PARENT-YOUTH RELATIONSHIPS
Affirming Your Parents

If you come from a home background that left painful memories of childhood, you may find it hard to think kindly toward your parents. Yet Proverbs urges us as children to respect our parents, faulty though they may be. We need not like or approve of everything our parents did (and do), but only a fool despises his parents (Prov. 15:20).

It is important to add that the Bible sees parenting as a partnership between both the father and the mother, in which both are committed to each other and to the child's welfare. That is the ideal, and a child tends to thrive in that kind of home. But whether or not our parents have come even close to fulfilling their biblical responsibilities, they deserve a measure of respect and affirmation.

P

Proverbs includes a number of principles about how we and our parents ought to relate:

- We have life through the union of father and mother (Prov. 4:3; 23:25).
- As children, we have a significant impact on how our parents view their lives and evaluate their significance (Prov. 10:1; 15:20; 17:25; 23:24).
- How we treat our parents displays our values and attitudes (Prov. 19:26).
- Disrespect for our parents can have terrible implications for our own life (Prov. 20:20).
- As our parents grow older, we should give them the gifts of listening and caring (Prov. 23:22).
- By pursuing wisdom, we not only benefit ourselves but can bring great joy to our parents (Prov. 23:25; 29:3).
- By pursuing evil and folly, we can be a destructive force in our parents' lives (Prov. 28:24; 29:15).
- We will suffer greatly if we show no respect for our parents (Prov. 30:11, 17).

Which of these principles do you need to apply right now? What gifts can you give to your parents in light of their parenting of you? Can you think of ways in which they were good for you? Have you thanked them?

An Age-old Battle

One of the greatest battles being fought today is between generations. Workplace opportunities, public policy, government funding, and community priorities turn more and more on the question of age.

But the battle is as old as the days of Job (Job 30:1). In the time of his prosperity, Job was a highly esteemed elder in his community. Younger men paid him deference, and his peers treated him with respect (Job 29:8). But after his reversal of fortune, Job became an object of mockery among the young (Job 30:1, 9–10). Do we sense a twinge of jealousy toward youth in Job's complaint? On the other hand, might some of Job's younger associates have used Job's troubles as an opportunity to "pay him back" for petty grievances in the past?

Regardless, the struggle between old and young is a problem on which every believer today needs to reflect. For example: How do you react to people older than yourself? Or younger than yourself? Do you feel threatened by the "young lions" who at times may seem reckless and irresponsible? Likewise, do you see older people as out of touch or "over the hill"?

Honoring Parents

Giving equal honor to both father and mother (Mark 7:10) was a requirement of the Law (Ex. 20:12). Indeed, the Law decreed stiff punishment for those who cursed their parents (Lev. 20:9). According to Jewish wisdom literature, only a fool would disobey his mother or mock his father (Prov. 30:17).

Nevertheless, the scribes and the Pharisees of Jesus' day had found a way around these commands, at least in part (Mark 7:11–12). Their man-made tradition was more important than keeping the Law. No wonder Jesus called them hypocrites (Mark 7:6).

Growing up in a dysfunctional or abusive home environment can make it hard to respect your parents. Yet the Bible urges us to honor who they are, if not what they do.

"It's My Parents' Fault"

Perhaps you are among the many people today who find a way to blame most of their problems on their parents. Whenever trouble strikes, many are prone to complain, "It's all my parents' fault! They caused me to be this way."

There's little doubt that parents can have a profound and lasting influence, for better or for worse, on their children's development and outlook on life. That's why the Bible strongly exhorts parents to raise their children according to godly values and principles. But Scripture seems to refrain from holding parents completely responsible for the ultimate state of their children. Sooner or later, the children must assume responsibility for their own choices and actions.

Ezekiel recognized the tendency to blame parents. Actually, given their situation, the children of Ezekiel's day had much about which to complain. After all, they were coming of age as exiles in a foreign land because their parents and grandparents had forsaken the Lord. So they kept alive a popular saying about children's troubles coming from their parents (Ezek. 18:2).

But God declared that His people should stop talking that way (Ezek. 18:3). He spoke at length about the fact that sin and righteousness are not inherited. One reaps what one sows. Individuals will be held responsible for their choices and behavior in regard to matters such as idolatry (Ezek. 18:6, 12, 15), sexuality (Ezek. 18:6, 11, 15), the use or abuse of money (Ezek. 18:7–8, 13, 16–17), and treatment of the poor (Ezek. 18:7, 12, 16–17).

Wrongdoing in areas like these cannot be blamed on anyone but the perpetrator. Thus the Lord warned that those who did these things would pay the penalty (Ezek. 18:4, 13, 18). On the other hand, those who honored Him would be rewarded for their righteousness (Ezek. 18:21–29). Responsibility would not be determined by whether or not one had good parents.

The same principle holds true today. No matter how bad a start you may feel that your family has given you, God calls you to accept responsibility for your own life. Even with a troubled background, you can share in the Lord's forgiveness, healing, and righteousness. God delights in fresh starts, and He invites you to make one in Him.

Treating Parents with Respect

Think about your relationship with your parents. Have you ever tried to divide them, or set one against the other? Do you favor one over the other? Scripture says that showing disrespect for our parents is a shameful thing (Prov. 19:26), and urges us to honor them instead (Ex. 20:12). The Book of Proverbs warns us several times against mistreating our parents:

- How we live affects both of our parents, for better or worse (Prov. 10:1; 15:20).
- Our lives can be destructive to our parents (Prov. 19:26).
- Disrespecting our parents causes damage to us (Prov. 20:20; 30:17).
- As children, we are to learn from both of our parents, and pay respect to both of them all of our lives (Prov. 23:22, 25).

- We are not to enrich ourselves at our parents' expense (Prov. 28:24).

Even if our parents fall short of the ideal, God has used both of them to bring us into the world and make us into the people we are. So we do well to honor them for giving us life. Have you learned to recognize and appreciate the ways in which God has used your parents in your life? Have you ever expressed gratitude for their efforts to raise you?

PAST

(*see* Nostalgia)

PATIENCE

Getting It Now—Or in God's Time

Many people in modern society have been raised without being taught to wait for anything. They were spoiled as children by parents and others who regularly gave in to their demands in order to stop their begging or crying. As a result, we now live in a culture that thrives on instant gratification, whether it be food, sex, travel, fun, or achievement. We not only want everything and feel entitled to everything—we want it right now!

However, the Book of Proverbs opposes this sort of attitude when it tells us that the impatient craving of the lazy person is fatal (Prov. 21:25). Other cautions along these lines include:

- Quick, illicit sex will result in long-term penalties (Prov. 5:3–6).
- Dishonest wealth cannot compare with the benefits of gain through hard work (Prov. 13:11).
- Deferring our hopes may feel awful, but doing so leads to ultimate satisfaction that is like a healthy tree (Prov. 13:12).
- Quick fixes and fast answers are described as "folly and shame" (Prov. 18:13, 17).
- Good advice may be difficult or irritating at first, but ultimately it yields blessings (Prov. 19:20).
- Righteousness may seem to leave you far behind in this life compared to others who lie, cheat, and steal, but God's justice in the next life will show that you have made the right choice (Prov. 23:17–18).

- Intoxication with alcohol seems satisfying at the time, but later you pay a heavy price for that brief moment of enjoyment (Prov. 23:29–35).

Delayed gratification is the road less traveled, but it offers rewards that others will never enjoy. Quite often, the quick payoff is the "way that seems right to a man, but its end is the way of death" (Prov. 16:25). That's why the New Testament urges believers to be "rejoicing in hope, patient in tribulation, continuing steadfastly in prayer" (Rom. 12:12). Likewise, Scripture assures us that the "testing of your faith produces patience," in order that "you may be perfect and complete, lacking nothing" (James 1:3–4).

Have you learned to wait for good things, or do you have to have everything right now? Consider, for example, whether you are an impulsive buyer. Can you try to see past immediate jolts of pleasure to more significant, lasting benefits later? Scripture teaches us to be discerning and farsighted, separating ourselves from anything that would destroy us (Prov. 27:12).

Job's Patience and God's Compassion

Job's devotion to God in the face of overwhelming adversity (Job 1:22) has become proverbial today. People speak of the "patience of Job" to indicate unusual perseverance and longsuffering. Yet Scripture indicates that the outcome of Job's life is a testimony not only to Job's patience, but to God's compassion and mercy (James 5:11).

Some may not see much kindness in God allowing Job to go through the tragic loss of his family, possessions, and health. Given Job's integrity, his sufferings seem unfair. Yet the book itself teaches that none of us knows all that we would need to know to pass judgment on the situation, let alone to challenge God (Job 38:1–3; 42:3).

We cannot say why Job went through what he did, but we do know that God responded with compassion. For example, He limited Satan's attacks (Job 1:12; 2:6); He answered Job (even if His questions went beyond Job's understanding; Job 38–41); He vindicated Job before his friends (Job 42:7–9); and He restored Job's losses (Job 42:12–17). Thus, in response to some of the worst that life had to offer, not only did Job prove himself faithful, his God likewise proved Himself trustworthy and kind.

Preparing for a Purpose

Have you ever felt as if you've been spending your life getting ready for something important, but have never quite arrived at doing it? Perhaps you're a college or graduate student, an apprentice, an entry-level employee, or a junior executive. You may feel impatient and frustrated in a lower level of responsibility, wondering whether your life is stuck in a permanent holding pattern. Every effort at advancement seems to be met with the words, "Not yet!"

If so, you might benefit from considering the example of Moses and several other people in the Bible. They illustrate the value of preparation and the truth that God never wastes a person's time. He is always leading us toward a purpose—if we are willing to be led:

Joseph had God-given abilities in leadership and management, as well as wisdom to interpret dreams. But he spent a number of years as a household servant and an unjustly sentenced inmate in prison before being given responsibility as Pharaoh's second-in-command (Gen. 39:2–4; 41:37–39).

Moses spent two-thirds of his life being shaped for the last third. During the first third, he was growing up in Egypt, where Scripture says he was learning "all the wisdom of the Egyptians" and becoming "mighty in words and deeds" (Acts 7:22). Apparently Moses thought that this training and experience was enough to qualify him for leadership of his people, the Israelites. But his first attempt at taking charge ended in disaster (Ex. 2:11–15). He was not yet ready to assume the responsibilities that God had in mind for him. His second third, spent as a desert shepherd, taught him humility as well as survival skills.

Daniel submitted to a course of study that included "the language and literature of the Chaldeans." As a Hebrew, he probably found much of this curriculum to be opposed to his upbringing. Yet he experienced it without succumbing to the pagan Babylonian culture. Over the years he rose higher and higher in the government, until he was advising the kings of empires (see Dan. 1:19).

Paul grew up under the tutelage of a rabbi named Gamaliel (Acts 22:3). He had extensive training that made him an outstanding member of the Pharisees (Phil. 3:5), one of the leading religious and political groups of his day. After his conversion, he spent many years developing his faith in private before becoming a public leader in the early church (Gal. 1:14–2:2).

No matter where you are in life, God has purpose and direction for you. Right now, things may seem slow, perhaps even boring. But as a follower of Christ, you have reason to make today count. Today is the foundation on which tomorrow will be built. What a tragedy it would be if, when opportunity knocks, you were found unprepared to accept it because you had squandered the time of preparation.

For more on this topic, see **DISCIPLINE,** *"Tightening the Screws—Carefully," page 111.*

PEACE

A Vision of Peace

The Book of Isaiah seems to be largely about God's judgment—His wrath on Judah (Is. 5), Israel (Is. 7:1–10:4), and Assyria (Is. 10:5–23). The Lord promises to cut down these arrogant kingdoms as a logger cuts down the massive cedars of Lebanon (Is. 10:33–34). But after the crash of timber comes a comforting vision of peace (Is. 11:1–10).

God promises to raise up a Rod and Branch out of the stump and roots of His people (Is. 11:1). Ultimately this refers to Christ, who will lead His people into the state which the Lord intended for them all along. (It has also been suggested that the prophecy was partially fulfilled when God preserved a remnant out of the ruins of Israel.)

The peaceable kingdom involves transformed relationships, places, and societies, as symbolized by peace between animals that are normally enemies (Is. 11:6–7). Moreover, the Spirit and fear of the Lord will help leaders rule with justice, righteousness, and faithfulness (Is. 11:2–5).

Ultimately, this vision cannot come about completely until Christ Himself assumes power. But even today it can serve as an ideal for God's people to pursue as they live and work in the world's societies, systems, and institutions. Renewal is God's work, but God's people can make a difference, especially if they are Spirit-led and fear the Lord (Is. 11:2–5). By promoting justice for the poor and equity for the meek, they can bring something of God's peaceable kingdom to pass. The world desperately seeks peace, but as Isaiah shows, peace is largely the fruit of a just society.

"Perfect Peace" for the City

Some Bible readers are prone to claim as personal promises certain phrases and statements from the Old Testament without regard for the biblical context. This often happens with Isaiah's two prophecies in Isaiah 26:2–3.

In reading these verses, it is important to remember that they are describing events that will take place "in that day" (Is. 26:1), presumably the day when the Lord Himself will return to reign. Furthermore, they clearly pertain to the institutions of a "strong city" which God upholds (Is. 26:1), as opposed to the "lofty city" which He brings low (Is. 26:5). The "walls and bulwarks" suggest fundamental systems on which the strong city is built, such as its buildings, government, commerce, transportation, food, and health care. All of these aspects of the city's "gates" will be saved by God so that His righteous people may enter in (Is. 26:2).

It is in that redeemed city that "perfect peace" is to be found (Is. 26:3). The peace is not so much a promise as a description of what the person who enters into the city will find there. His mind will be at rest because he is confident that God is upholding the city.

The irony of Isaiah's prophecies is that they were given to urban people whose neighboring cities were being captured by the Assyrians and whose own city would soon be overrun by the Babylonians. Thus they had a real need for a "strong city." As we read what God promised them, we might ask: What is our real need today? What things genuinely threaten us for which our only hope is God?

For more on this topic, see **CIRCUMSTANCES,** *"Seeking the Peace of the City," page 61.*

P

PEAK PERFORMANCE

(*see* Excellence)

PERCEPTIONS

Challenging Our Perceptions

Many of us find it hard to accept thoughts and ideas that contradict our own point of view. The Old Testament prophets had the task of confronting people with realities that were sometimes hard to take. Yet as messengers of God, it was their duty to present the truth, even if it challenged their listeners' perceptions. For example, Zechariah presented a word from the Lord to the governor Zerubbabel that confounded accepted ways of thinking. He said that:

1. Ultimately, brute force is not the way that God accomplishes His work. God's Spirit is the empowering agent of His activity (Zech. 4:6). Human energy, creativity, planning, and thinking have value, but they count little without spiritual strength (compare Ezek. 37:1–14).

2. Grace can move the biggest mountains one faces, reducing them to easily traveled plains (Zech. 4:7). Zerubbabel saw examples of this in his own day when God graciously removed a number of obstructionists who stood in the way of the temple's completion (Ezra 4:1–6:12)

3. Small things can be just as much an evidence of God's work as great accomplishments (Zech. 4:9–10). The temple that Zerubbabel and his people were rebuilding was a far cry from the magnificent structure of Solomon's day. Yet the project was significant because God was in it.

4. True standards, like straight buildings, are ultimately determined by God (Zech. 4:10). Like a carpenter using a plumbline, the Lord evaluates the whole earth. Zechariah's word was similar to Amos' description of God measuring His people's worship and integrity (Amos 7:7–9; compare 2 Kin. 21:13).

The words of the prophets, along with the rest of Scripture, are revelation from God, part of His disclosure of truths that we would otherwise not know because of sin which has blinded us (Job 42:3; Rom. 1:16–20; Heb. 1:1–2). By nature, God's Word challenges—and corrects—our perceptions. Are you willing to hear those kinds of realities? It takes humility to accept that God is right and that we are often wrong, but accepting His truth leads to life (Prov. 3:5–8).

PERFECTION

Nobody's Perfect

It's common today for people to excuse their faults with the attitude, "Hey, nobody's perfect!" True enough. People can only be expected to be human—and that means fallible.

Unfortunately, though, few people take that reality seriously enough. Indeed, when it comes to their standing before God, all too many take a different stance: they may not be perfect, but they're "good enough."

The question is, Are they good enough for God? Romans says they are not. That's what Paul means when he writes, "all are under sin" (Rom. 3:9) and then cites a number of Old Testament passages to back up his claim (Rom. 3:10–18).

It's not that people are evil through and through, or that they never do any moral good. Quite the contrary. People are capable of impressive acts of courage, compassion, and justice. But in light of God's holy (morally perfect) character, which is the ultimate standard against which people's goodness is measured, people are indeed far from perfect. Their good behavior turns out to be the exception rather than the rule.

The good news that Paul writes about in Romans, however, is that God has reached out to humanity despite its imperfect ways. His attitude has not been one of rejection, as if to say, "They're not good enough for Me," but one of grace and compassion that says, in effect, "I will make them into good people—people as good as I AM—by means of Christ My Son."

PERFORMANCE REVIEW

Celebrate Quality

Good work deserves to be acknowledged. After the tabernacle's organizers and its work force had completed the project according to the Lord's exacting specifications, Moses *blessed* them (Ex. 39:42–43, emphasis added).

A "blessing" is a sign of approval that can be as refreshing to the recipient as fresh rain or dew that renews faded grass (Ps. 133:3).

And a thorough performance review or quality check can bring tremendous blessing to a worker who has done a good job.

Is there someone where you live or work who needs the refreshing gift of a blessing?

The Ultimate Performance Review

People often joke about standing before God and having their lives examined. But the picture Paul paints in 1 Corinthians 3:9–15 is anything but funny. He is deadly serious about a day of accountability for believers. Most of us are familiar with performance reviews on the job. Paul describes the ultimate performance review—the moment when we stand before God and He evaluates the worth of our lives on the earth, not for salvation but for reward or loss.

Paul uses the image of metal being purified in a refining fire (1 Cor. 3:13–15). The fire burns away the worthless impurities, leaving only what is valuable. Based on the values set forth in many passages of Scripture, we can imagine the kinds of things that constitute "gold, silver, [and] precious stones": acts of charity and kindness; ethical decision-making; the pursuit of justice and fair play; keeping our word; courage and perseverance in the face of opposition and persecution; humility; communicating the message of Christ to co-workers; honoring our marriage vows; working diligently at the work God gives us; trusting God to keep His promises. Whatever is left when the fire burns down, Paul says, God will reward us for it (1 Cor. 3:14).

Conversely, we can envision what sorts of "wood, hay, [and] straw" will burn up: the lies we've told; ways we may have cheated

customers; abuse heaped on family and relatives; manipulation of situations to our advantage; selfishness of all kinds; the squandering of income on trivial luxuries; turning a deaf ear to the poor; damage allowed to our environment; the systems created to lock ourselves into power and lock others out; the arrogance of self-sufficiency; lack of faith.

When the smoke clears, what will be left of your life?

PERSECUTION

The Cost of Commitment

Are you prepared to be *hated* because of your commitment to Jesus Christ? Perhaps you expect to be misunderstood occasionally or even chided by associates for "going overboard" on religion. But Jesus used strong words in John 15:18–25: "hate" and "persecute." He indicated that our true commitments will be made clear when they start to cost us something.

What has your faith cost you? A promotion or some other career opportunity? Criticism or even ostracism by coworkers or family? Legal action? Or nothing at all? Sooner or later, following Christ has a cost, and those who think they can get by without paying it are misguided. In fact, if there's no cost, is there really any genuine commitment? Jesus' words suggest not.

However, it's also possible for our actions or words to cause offense because they are inappropriate. In that case, the hostility we may receive is not persecution. Like Jesus (John 1:14), we are called to be people of grace and truth, not obnoxious and rude. True persecution involves unmerited hostility for doing good works in the pattern of Christ (1 Pet. 2:12–21).

Welcome to Stressful Living

For many people in the world today, tension, conflict, weariness, and suffering have become commonplace. Nevertheless, some offer the vain hope that life's troubles can be done away with, that we can somehow get to the point where things will always be great. They suggest that faith in Christ will deliver us into a state of serenity and ease and bring prosperity, health, and constant pleasure.

However, that was neither the experience nor the teaching of early Christians such as Paul, James, or Peter, and certainly not of their Lord Jesus. Paul described the life of a servant of God in terms of tribulation, distress, tumult, and sleeplessness (2 Cor. 6:4–5). But he also linked these stress producers with rich treasures that money cannot buy: purity, kindness, sincere love, honor, good report, joy, and the possession of all things (2 Cor. 6:6–10).

So as long as we live as God's people on this earth, we can expect a connection between trouble and hope. That connection is never pleasant, but our troubles can bring about lasting benefits:

- Jesus told us that if we want to follow Him, we must deny ourselves and take up a cross. If we try to save our lives, we will only lose them. But if we lose our lives for His sake, we will find them (Matt. 16:24–25).
- The writer to the Hebrews encouraged us that our troubles are often a sign that we are legitimate children of God, who lovingly disciplines us to train us in righteousness (Heb. 12:8–11).
- James encouraged us to rejoice in our various trials, because as they test our faith, they produce patience, which ultimately makes us mature in Christ (James 1:2–4).
- Peter knew by personal experience the kind of pressure that can cause one's allegiance to Christ to waiver. He warned us that "fiery trials" are nothing strange, but that they actually allow us to experience something of Christ's sufferings so that we can ultimately experience something of His glory, too (1 Pet. 4:12–13).

We can count on feeling stress if we're going to obey Christ. But we can take hope! That stress is preparing us for riches we will enjoy for eternity.

For more on this topic, see **DISCIPLESHIP,** *"The Price of Discipleship," page 110.*

PERSISTENCE

Keep On Keeping On

Do you intend to overcome evil? If so, make sure to replace it with good or else, as Jesus warns, the evil may return with its friends, producing more evil than ever (Matt. 12:43–45).

This teaching warns us to persevere in the journey of faith. That can be hard to do when everything in us wants to quit, the way an exhausted long-distance runner wants to drop out of a marathon. Besides (we reason), look how far we've already come!

Yes, but God's goal is not just to make us nicer people or better people, but to make us Christlike people. That won't happen completely until we're with Him. For now, He wants us to keep growing in that direction. Stopping short can bring disaster. In a warning similar to Jesus' words here, the writer of Hebrews urges us to "go on to perfection" and describes in sobering words the fate of those who "fall away" (Heb. 6:1–12).

Fortunately, God lends us help to prevent us from falling back. As Hebrews also says, He disciplines us for our good. His stern efforts can feel harsh, but they are the loving protection of a caring Father (Matt. 12:3–11).

Living by Faith

Few phrases of Scripture have had as far-reaching an impact as the Lord's declaration to Habakkuk that "the just shall live by his faith" (Hab. 2:4). If you are a Protestant today, this verse is an important part of your spiritual heritage: Martin Luther adopted it as his watchword during the Protestant Reformation of the early 1500s.

However, Habakkuk probably had little idea of the explosive truth contained in God's statement. It came as part of a prelude to a taunting song that the prophet was instructed to give against Babylon (Hab. 2:1–6). The Lord was explaining why the Babylonians would be judged. Fundamentally, they were a "proud" people in the sense that they had no fear of God. By contrast, the "just" person—the individual deserving of God's approval and blessing—would find favor because of his "faith" in God.

Actually, the Hebrew word used for "faith," *emunah,* means "steadfastness" or "faithfulness." An Israelite who faithfully pursued the covenant by following God's Law was considered a "just" or righteous person (Ps. 15). The issue was not one's ethnicity as a Jew, but obedience to God. Thus the problem for the Babylonians was not that they were Gentiles, but that they were committed to a lifestyle of wickedness and idolatry. They arrogantly lived as if their own self-interests were all that mattered. For that reason, the Lord would humble them according to the five "woes" pronounced by Habakkuk (Hab. 2:6–20).

In the New Testament, Paul picked up on the idea of the just living by faith (Rom. 1:17; Gal. 3:10–12). Because of the coming of Christ, he was able to deepen the understanding of this phrase. "Living by faith" does not mean outward observance of the Law, as many of the Jewish leaders of his day had come to assume. Rather, it involves a heart commitment to the Lord and a recognition that Christ alone is able to make one righteous before God. This does not take away the need for "faithful," godly living; if anything, it establishes a proper basis for it.

It was this perspective of Paul's that Martin Luther reclaimed for the church in the sixteenth century. People had forgotten the place of faith and obedience toward God. Instead, their religion boiled down to empty ritual, legalistic standards, and attempts to buy God's favor and forgiveness with money. Luther cut through all of that with the powerful truth that God announced to Habakkuk: the just shall live by faith—faith alone!

In our own day, the advantage of "living by faith" is that we can put into perspective the troubles of the world around us. Despite appearances to the contrary—when evil forces appear to have the upper hand, or when economic woes, ill health, or family circumstances appear to be doing us in—we can trust that God remains in control and that His sovereign purposes are being worked out. We need not fear that life will come undone; indeed, we need not fear death itself. We know that God has said: "The just shall live by faith."

Persistence Pays Off

Jesus took His disciples to the seacoast towns of Tyre and Sidon (Matt. 15:21), probably to rest (Mark 7:24). As far as we can tell, He had no intention of preaching or healing in that area. But as so often happens when one has no intention of being available, someone interrupted His vacation. Today, phone calls prove to be the major source of interruptions. But in ancient times it was worse:

interruptions arrived at one's doorstep and stayed until someone answered.

In this instance, a woman who supposedly had no claim on Jesus' attention begged Him to deliver her daughter from demons. She had probably already tried to heal the girl and failed. In ancient societies, women usually tended the sick and nursed the dying.

Jesus hardly encouraged this woman. As He pointed out, she had no ethnic or religious claim on Him. But somehow she recognized that He was capable of doing what she could not—heal her daughter. In the end, her courage, faith, and sheer persistence won out.

How persistent are you in crying out to God for people who matter a lot to you? Like the woman, will you keep coming back to God in faith?

Unfinished Business

Spiritual growth is often likened to a journey. A person comes to faith and then begins walking with God, step by step, year by year, traveling into ever-higher regions of spiritual maturity. However, for many people, the journey seems to peter out along the way. Perhaps they feel that it has become too difficult. Perhaps they get sidetracked by distractions, or detoured by sin. Perhaps they feel that they have reached a dead end and can go no further. Whatever the case, their spiritual life remains at a standstill. The journey is incomplete.

The people of Jerusalem in Haggai's day had an unfinished project. Around 538 B.C. they had returned from Babylon and had enthusiastically laid a foundation for a new temple with great fanfare. Yet two years into the project, the work came to a standstill. The reasons why may or may not have been legitimate, but for sixteen years nothing more was done. The people went about the rest of their lives, making a living, establishing families, building houses, setting up businesses—but the temple remained unfinished.

Finally the Lord sent the prophet Haggai to tell the people to consider their ways and get back to work (Hag. 1:6–7). They needed to complete what they had started. Not only did their spiritual lives depend on it, but their physical lives as well (Hag. 1:9–11).

Perhaps like the temple, your spiritual life has become unfinished business. Perhaps you have stopped growing as a believer, for whatever reason. If so, "consider your ways!" You can take steps to get back on track. Perhaps you need to repent of long-term sins. Perhaps you need to reestablish contact with fellow believers who can encourage you and hold you accountable. Perhaps you need to renew some of the spiritual disciplines that foster growth, such as Bible reading, prayer, and fasting.

Whatever steps are needed, Scripture encourages you to finish the journey (Heb. 6:11)! God is ready to help you (Phil. 1:8), but He cannot do your walking for you. Only you can take the steps of faith and obedience that lead to maturity in Christ.

For more on this topic, see **FAITHFUL-NESS,** *"Finishing Well," page 146.*

PERSUASION

(*see* Conflict Resolution)

PHYSICAL FITNESS

Aerobics for the Mind and Spirit

Do you work out regularly to keep your body trim and fit? Perhaps you exercise at an aerobic level, keeping your heartbeat quite a bit higher than normal for several minutes every few days. If so, then you have a healthy pattern to follow for another kind of conditioning—the exercise of your mind and spirit.

Bodily exercise can yield tremendous benefits. Consider, then, how much more benefit you can derive from a regular regimen of "spiritual aerobics"! It has implications not only for this life, but for the life to come (1 Tim. 4:7–8). That is why the writer of Psalm 119 was intentional about personally getting into God's Word on a regular basis and putting it into practice. It was a discipline that meant life itself (Ps. 119:93).

This lengthy psalm has twenty-two stanzas, arranged according to the letters of the Hebrew alphabet. We see eight words used in this translation to describe God's truth. We can consider these terms as eight different kinds of spiritual "exercises" through which to strengthen ourselves.

- *Law.* Of the eight terms, this is the one used most often in Ps. 119 (for example, 119:1, 18, 92). It reminds us that God's truth is to be obeyed (compare James 1:25).
- *Testimonies.* God's Word is a witness and a warning against sin and disobedience (Ps. 119:31, 152; compare Deut. 31:26).
- *Precepts.* This word conveys the idea of an overseer looking at life and attending to it much as a shepherd does with sheep (Ps. 119:4, 15; compare Jer. 23:2).
- *Statutes.* Like statutes, God's Word is enduring and obligatory (Ps. 119:8, 12; compare Is. 30:8).
- *Commandments.* This word reinforces the idea that God's truth is to be obeyed (Ps. 119:10, 47). It is authoritative for all of life.
- *Ordinances.* Scripture provides the standard for our dealings with each other and for our duties in life (Ps. 119:43, 91; compare 1 Sam. 10:25).
- *Word.* God has spoken, and we are to hear and respond (Ps. 119:11, 16–17; compare Ps. 33:4, 6).
- *Judgments.* God is the one who best discerns right from wrong and good from evil (Ps. 119:75).

What is your discipline for exercising your heart, soul, and mind in God's Word? If your physical heart needs so much healthy exercise so many times a week, perhaps a similar schedule would be in order for your inner life. One suggestion for getting started would be to read one psalm each day, or one chapter of Proverbs each day.

By regularly placing ourselves under the instruction of God's Word, we are promised great peace and security (Ps. 119:165).

For more on this topic, see **DIETING,** *"The Value of Fasting," page 103.*

PHYSICAL IMPAIRMENT

(see Handicaps)

PHYSICIANS

Priests as Medical Professionals

Leprosy, or skin disease, was frightening and had to be dealt with quickly and thoroughly, lest others become contaminated.

The Bible gives no indication that Israel had medical professionals. Instead, priests were called to do the work we associate today with physicians (Lev. 13:2–3).

In the case of leprosy, the priests' job was to:

1. *Diagnose the disease.* The word "examine" is used numerous times in Leviticus 13–14, the main passage in the Law dealing with leprosy. Great care was taken to distinguish which disease was being treated, and the instructions that God gave were exacting. This suggests that the priests were to show great care and concern for the victims of leprosy. Early detection was important in order to prevent, if possible, the disease from doing its terrible work on the individual.

2. *Prescribe treatment for the patient.* The main "treatment" for the disease was to isolate the infected person (for example, Lev. 13:21; 14:30). Isolation was crucial to protect others from the dreaded contagion. The text describes intricate processes to counter the ravaging effects of the sickness.

3. *Contain costs.* An important fact behind the precise details given for the clothing and housing of infected persons is that during this era, many Hebrews were relatively poor. God had a concern that they not lose all of their possessions through the sanitizing process. Thus a leper's clothes were carefully purged and cleaned so as not to destroy what might be his or her only possession (Lev. 13:47–59). Similarly, the person's house was to be carefully purged if possible, rather than totally destroyed (Lev. 14:33–57).

4. *Sanitize the environment.* Concern about the spread of the disease is shown in the careful process of cleaning the clothes and the residence of the patient and rechecking it to be sure of its condition (Lev. 13:47–58; 14:34–47).

For more on this topic, see **HEALTH CARE,** *"Valuing Health Care Workers," page 195.*

PLANNING

A Change of Plans

Somehow there's a certain comfort in knowing that Paul's plans did not always work out (Rom. 1:13). Paul was a great visionary. He intended to take the message of Christ to Rome, and from there to Spain (Rom.

P

15:28). To that end he laid plans and made decisions, and God guided and directed his efforts.

But Paul was also willing to go wherever God opened doors for him, even if that meant scrapping a carefully organized agenda. For example, he made a complete, one-hundred-eighty-degree turn at Troas in obedience to a vision from God, taking the gospel west rather than east (Acts 16:6–10).

Does that mean that planning is pointless, that we should wait for the "leading" of the Lord before making any moves? Not if we judge by Paul's example. He understood that it's better to adapt and change one's plans than to have no plans at all.

Preparations for Those Who Follow

What are you doing that will enhance the effectiveness of those who follow you? As he neared the end of his life, David made extensive preparations to allow his son Solomon to build the temple (1 Chr. 22:5). In fact, even though the structure was commonly known as Solomon's temple, it could just as easily have been called David and Solomon's temple, for the site, design of the architecture, collection of materials, and even worship format and instruments were largely prepared by David prior to his death (1 Chr. 21:25–26; 22:1; 28:11–21; 2 Chr. 7:6).

David's astute planning encourages us to ask, what sort of preparations are we making for our successors? What kind of legacy are we leaving behind? At home, do we lead a life that will make it easier or harder for our children to understand and follow God's ways? Do we lead by example and mentor other believers in understanding and following biblical principles? In our work, are we leaving behind a history of character and quality on which others can build?

Principles of Planning

The Bible affirms ten principles of planning:

1. *God makes plans.* God not only knows the future (the "future" from a human point of view; God lives in eternity, beyond time, and hence beyond a "future"), He can make the future by choosing what will happen (James 4:13–15). For example, in creating the world, He planned or determined much of the world's future by the way in which He created it. His planning manifests both clear purposes and orderly processes (Rom. 1:20).

2. *God encourages and empowers people to plan.* People, who are made in God's image (Gen. 1:26–28) are created with a consciousness of time (Eccl. 3:11). We are aware of the connections between past, present, and future, and how causes shape effects (Ps. 90:12; Eph. 4:16).

3. *All planning involves a value-based perspective.* The processes of establishing goals and priorities, joining ends and means, and linking "what is" with "what ought to be" are based on assumptions about what is of value and what is not. In that sense, no planning is morally neutral in either its process or its effects. This principle frequently lay behind the choices that people in Scripture were called to make (Josh. 24:15; 1 Sam. 8:4–7; 1 Kin. 18:21).

4. *Effective planning tends to involve more than one person.* No one except God has all wisdom. Therefore, consultation in the formulation of plans and collaboration in carrying them out can be invaluable. This is not only common sense; it is a principle of godly wisdom.

5. *Planning is a powerful yet fragile process.* By pinpointing goals, marshalling resources, and initiating action, the process of planning can empower people to get things done. Yet planning is also subject to the weaknesses of people, such as being blind to reality, narrow in vision, and mean-spirited in motives. For example, the Tower of Babel was a well-planned project; nevertheless, it was condemned by God (Gen. 11:1–9).

6. *Planning and prayer should be intimately related.* Through prayer, our plans are expanded with God's wisdom, ennobled by God's holiness, and empowered through God's providence. Planning that honors the Lord needs to be based on a prayerful recognition of God's grace, sovereignty, and resources (Phil. 4:6–7).

7. *Planning by its nature is based on faith.* When we plan, we exhibit certain beliefs and assumptions—for example, faith in the process of planning, faith in our capacity to bring our plans into reality, or faith in the justice of the ends we seek. But all planning involves

commitment to things hoped for in the future, based on the evidence of things visible in the present (Heb. 11:1).

8. *Planning does not determine the future—it can only direct the present.* At best, the future will only partially reflect our intentions and efforts. Like Paul, we "see in a mirror dimly," and "know in part" (1 Cor. 13:12). Thus the future lies outside our grasp. All we can do is make choices and take action today in light of how we suppose those decisions and activities might affect tomorrow.

9. *Planning is only partly rational.* The process involves not just our heads, but our hearts and hands as well. This is as true in formulation, where intuitive insight can be just as important as analytical processes, as it is in implementation, where people must be motivated and organized as well as informed.

10. *Planning often motivates by pointing attention and effort toward a hopeful future.* Planning can shift people's attention from problems to solutions, from limitations to possibilities, and from despair to hope. It can also galvanize people for action by highlighting needs, rallying opinion, and pointing the way.

Spirit-Filled Planning

In today's world, planning is often thought to be a valuable skill possessed innately by born leaders or developed over time in experienced managers. But Scripture describes a further dimension to planning—the wisdom of God's Spirit (1 Chr. 28:11).

As David crafted plans for the temple, he was apparently given insight into what the Lord wanted. His description of the planning process is interesting: "The LORD made me understand in writing, by His hand upon me, all the works of these plans" (1 Chr. 28:19). It was as if God had given David a blueprint for the project.

This was not the first time that the Lord had provided people plans for construction. Noah was told to build a boat and given details for its design and use (Gen. 6:13–21). Likewise, Moses was given exceedingly detailed plans for the tabernacle (the precursor to the temple, Ex. 25–31) and the worship to take place in it (Lev. 1–7).

Does God reveal plans like that to people today? Perhaps not in quite the same way. Nevertheless, the Holy Spirit is available to every believer for help in planning and preparation. Based on what we know about the Spirit's work, especially from the New Testament, we can identify at least three characteristics of Spirit-filled planning that apply to most situations:

1. *Spirit-filled planning focuses on revealing and glorifying God's character.* Jesus said that one important aspect of the Spirit's work is to bring glory to Jesus by revealing the things of Jesus (John 16:14). Thus as we plan with the Spirit's help, He enables us to arrange things in a way that honors the Lord and His values.

2. *Spirit-filled planning prepares the way for others to succeed.* David's preparations for the temple enabled Solomon to successfully complete the project. While it would be a mistake to say that God always wants His people to succeed in terms of success as the world measures it, He does want His people to accomplish meaningful, productive work (Eph. 4:12). Thus Spirit-filled planning seeks to help people meet needs and serve the Lord with their abilities and resources, and not just benefit themselves.

3. *Spirit-filled planning has breadth (vision) and depth (detail).* In other words, God cares about the entirety of a project. He is as interested in our means as our ends. He not only wants us to honor Him in the big picture, but in the nitty-gritty as well. As we plan, the Spirit wants to help us achieve God's ultimate objective, the "praise of His glory" (Eph. 1:12), and also carry out His will in specific, measurable ways (Eph. 5:1–21). The Spirit is not limited by our needs, experiences, or desires.

The Value of Strategic Planning

A missile without a guidance system is a dangerous thing: all power and no direction. In the same way, leaders who don't know where they are going can wreak havoc. That's why it pays for people in leadership positions to gather the right kind of information, so that they can make wise choices about which path to pursue.

Before he launched his plan to rebuild the walls of Jerusalem, Nehemiah conducted careful research about the task at hand. He quietly walked around the city by night, without fanfare, surveying the extent of the problem and perhaps formulating some tentative strategies (Neh. 2:11–15).

Nehemiah's low profile was especially appropriate given that he was a new member of the community. As a representative of the king, he could have come in with trumpets blaring and declared what his expectations were. Instead, he kept his thoughts to himself and avoided attracting attention until he had formulated a plan.

If you are in a position of leadership, do you take pains to gather the kind of information you need to make decisions? Are your decisions informed and based on reality? Or do you assume that the power of your position alone is all that is required to bring about the results you seek?

What Good Is Planning?

If the Lord frustrates the plans of the nations and their peoples (Ps. 33:10), and only His plans remain forever (Ps. 33:11), then what's the point of planning? Wouldn't it make more sense to just live with a carefree attitude, letting what happens happen?

By its nature, planning is a somewhat paradoxical process. It looks toward the future, yet it tends to be grounded in the past. It is fundamentally about change, yet in and of itself it changes nothing. It tries to respond to anticipated future events, yet it also contributes to future events. Almost everyone agrees that it is crucial for success, yet people and organizations sometimes succeed without planning, and also fail even with the best planning.

For people of faith, the paradoxes of planning are even more acute. We inevitably try to plan for the future, yet we know that ultimately the future is in God's hands. God calls us to wait patiently for Him (Ps. 27:14; 37:7), yet He also admonishes us to act and initiate (James 1:22; 1 John 3:18). Scripture encourages us to seek God's wisdom before we act (Prov. 3:5–6; James 1:5), yet we must often act in faith without answers to many of our questions.

What, then, should be our attitude toward planning? A careful study of biblical passages on the subject shows that God encourages us to make plans, yet always with an awareness that He has plans of His own. Our plans may or may not fit into His plans, and ultimately, His will and purposes will be accomplished.

PLEASURE

Self-Indulgent? Who, Me?

Is your lifestyle focused on peace and pleasure, comfort and convenience? The affluent people to whom Amos was speaking lived a lifestyle of luxury that many modern-day Westerners would recognize (Amos 6:3–7). But the prophet pronounced woe on them for allowing their easy living to lull them into spiritual slumber (Amos 6:3). Their self-indulgence completely deadened their sensitivity to the Lord.

Could your lifestyle be described as self-indulgent? Is it designed around making yourself feel good and satisfying your own desires, with little thought of the needs of others or the values and concerns of God?

To help you think about these issues, carefully read Amos' description of the Israelites' lifestyle, then reflect on the following questions. The point is not that having material things is a cause for guilt, but to think carefully about what Jesus called the "deceitfulness of riches" (Matt. 13:22), which can strangle your spiritual life.

- Do you view a forty-hour maximum work week as a right to which you are entitled?
- What kind of home do you live in? Would others in our society be envious? Is your home a benefit to anyone else?
- Do you spend more on clothing each month than you give to your church or to charity in a year? Who benefits materially from your disposable income?
- How much do you spend on personal grooming—for example, on such things as hair care, manicures, pedicures, facials, massages, cosmetics, or perfume?
- Have you ever had plastic surgery other than to correct a medical problem? Describe your motivation in doing so.
- What percentage of your income do you donate to your church, religious organizations, or charities? Has that increased or decreased in the past three years?

How much is your giving determined by tax advantages?

- Do you aspire to be rich? How do you define "rich"? What would you consider to be "enough" for you in financial terms? Could you live on ten percent less income than you have now? Thirty percent? How about fifty percent?
- Do you own a second home or vacation home?
- How do you spend your leisure—the time that is not taken up with work and family obligations?

How would you fare under Amos' scrutiny? What kind of a steward are you with God's resources?

PLURALISM

A Competition of Gods

Religious pluralism—the idea that everyone's religion should be tolerated—has become widely accepted in many countries today. But the history of the world reflects the fact that religions do compete for people's allegiance. In a sense, the gods of various cultures could be said to have battled each other for supremacy.

For example, in the ancient Middle East, a victorious army often subdued conquered people by destroying their religious shrines and taking their idols and relics back to the shrine of their own gods (1 Sam. 4:10–11; 5:1–2). This was to allege that the gods of the invaders were more powerful than the gods of those invaded.

Following this tradition, the Babylonian King Nebuchadnezzar looted the Israelites' temple following the siege of Jerusalem. He took untold riches back to Babylon, including the costly implements used in Hebrew worship (2 Kin. 25:13–17). Years later, many of these spoils—which the Israelites had carefully set apart for use in only the holiest rituals of worship and sacrifice—were brought out at the request of drunken Belshazzar and used as expensive tableware at a drinking party (Dan. 5:2–4). Like his predecessor Nebuchadnezzar, Belshazzar apparently thought he had won the game of "competitive gods" (Dan. 5:23).

But God turned the tables on this foolish king. As Daniel predicted, that very night Belshazzar's city was captured, its mighty ziggurats pulled down, its gods removed, and its king killed (Dan. 5:30).

There is only one true God (Deut. 6:4; 1 Tim. 2:5). Nations may choose to serve another god or permit many gods. But in the end, the God of heaven will prevail. He will win the game of "competitive gods." He has said, "My name shall be great among the Gentiles" (nations; Mal. 1:11).

Does It Really Matter What You Believe?

Peter describes the exclusiveness of Christianity by claiming that "there is no other name" that can save (Acts 4:12). That doesn't play well in our pluralistic society where tolerance is a chief virtue. Indeed, many people feel that an exclusive commitment to any one religious system is pointless, since they assume that all religions are basically the same.

But they are committing themselves to a deception. The assumption that we are all looking for God and will find Him in the end is false both to the nature of people and to the nature of God.

In the first place, we are not all looking for God. Many people today have absolutely no interest in God or religion. They are not atheists, just committed secularists. Moreover, there are far more motives behind the practice of religion than a search or desire for God. Political power, tradition, standing in the community, a desire for increased fertility or wealth, even sexual gratification are among the forces driving countless people back to their centers of worship. Looking for God? Hardly.

Nor is there any guarantee that people will find Him in the end. If there is a God at all, He obviously lives in realms beyond us. Otherwise all of us would already know Him from birth. But the religions of the world, including today's New Age systems, recognize that people do not naturally and instinctively know God, which is why they promise their followers access to Him. The problem is, they offer competing and often conflicting versions of who God is and how we can know Him.

P

Christianity is unique in that it claims that instead of people gaining access to God, God has made Himself known to people. His ultimate self-disclosure was in Jesus Christ. No longer is He the unknown God. Although "no one has seen God at any time," Jesus "has declared Him" (John 1:18).

So does Christianity claim that all other religions are totally wrong? Of course not. Most have some measure of truth in them. Islam and Judaism in particular have a great deal of truth in them. They are like candles that bring a bit of light into a very dark world. Nevertheless, all religions pale into insignificance at the dawn that has come with Christ. He fulfills the hopes, the aspirations, the virtues, and the insights of whatever is true and good in all faiths.

Pluralism at Pentecost

What happened at Pentecost began to reverse what happened at ancient Babel (Gen. 11:1–9). At Babel God confused the languages of the peoples and dispersed the nations abroad in order to stop their evil from multiplying. At Pentecost He brought Jews from many nations together in Jerusalem. Once again there was confusion (Acts 2:6), but this time it came from the fact that everyone heard ordinary men and women, filled with the Holy Spirit, speaking in the various languages of the ancient world. Then an international, multilingual church was born when the onlookers heard the gospel preached and believed it.

For more on this topic, see ETHNIC DIVERSITY, "The Antioch Model," page 130; SECULARISM, "The Gospel in a Pluralistic Society," page 359.

POLITICAL INFIGHTING

Political Intrigue

Anyone who laments the state of politics and government today might pay careful attention to the account of Adonijah's bid for the throne of Israel (1 Kin. 1:5). With a dynasty in the making, the question was, who would succeed David? Adonijah enjoyed popular support, but David named Adonijah's half-brother, Solomon, as heir to the throne (1 Kin. 1:11–14, 28–30, 38–39).

Solomon extended grace to Adonijah (1 Kin. 1:50–53), but the older brother refused to accept a lesser role. Desperate to maintain a foothold in the power structure, he enlisted Solomon's mother, Bathsheba, in a ploy to marry David's mistress, Abishag (1 Kin. 2:13–18). The marriage would have implied to the public that Adonijah was the rightful heir to the throne, since a king's harem normally went to his successor. Solomon saw through the scheme and called for Adonijah's execution (1 Kin. 2:22–25).

Times have not changed much since Solomon's day. Political power brokers still scheme to protect their turf. So we need not be shocked when public officials are found to be involved in scandal and intrigue. From ancient times, the lust for power has driven people to commit all kinds of evil. Rather than placing matters in God's hands and then faithfully carrying out their role, whatever it may be, the power-hungry have always tried to force through their agenda, even if it means opposing God's will. At times they may appear to succeed. But ultimately, God accomplishes His purposes—and destroys those who oppose Him.

POLITICAL INVOLVEMENT

(*see* Community Service)

POLITICAL SCANDAL

Scandal and Cover-Up

The account of David's adulterous affair with Bathsheba (2 Sam. 11:2–5) makes a point of the fact that David stayed at home in Jerusalem while his armies went to battle. That suggests that the affair occurred because David was neither where he should have been nor doing what he should have been doing.

However, regardless of why David fell into sin, most of the biblical account of it is devoted to the cover-up that David attempted once Bathsheba conceived (2 Sam. 11:6–27). David tried three plans to cover his sin (or so he thought):

1. Plan A was to make the pregnancy look like the result of normal relations between Bathsheba and her husband, Uriah. But as a man of conscience, Uriah would not allow himself a privilege that was denied the rest

of David's troops (2 Sam. 11:6–11). In that way, loyal Uriah put unprincipled David to shame.

2. Plan B was based on the assumption that drunkenness would lower Uriah's well-guarded principles so that he would sleep with his wife. But again Uriah resisted the impulse (2 Sam. 11:12–13).

3. Plan C called for neither coercion nor deception, but outright murder. Uriah was to be sacrificed to the enemy in a way that would make his death appear to be a casualty of war. Then David could respond to the grieving widow by embracing her as his wife (2 Sam. 11:14–27).

Plan C might have worked, except that David was not some pagan king but the Lord's anointed (2 Sam. 12:7). In violating Bathsheba and arranging Uriah's death, David had "despised the commandment of the Lord" (2 Sam. 12:9). Thus the Lord sent Nathan to expose his sin and pronounce judgment (2 Sam. 12:9–12).

David admitted his sins (2 Sam. 12:13) and repented of his wrongdoing, turning to God for forgiveness and the renewal of his spiritual walk (Ps. 51). God forgave him (2 Sam. 12:13), but the child died. Once David was right with God, his union with Bathsheba was blessed with another child, Solomon (2 Sam. 12:24). Nevertheless, despite his cleansing from the Lord, David was permanently affected by this scandalous episode.

The sins of adultery and murder are grievous offenses before the Lord (Lev. 20:10; Deut. 5:17–18). But just as hateful in his sight are attempts to cover up one's sins rather than come clean (Ps. 51:17; Prov. 6:16–19; 1 John 1:8–9).

POLITICS

A Shrewd Politician

Whatever fear Gideon may have felt prior to the battle with the Midianites, he displayed shrewd political instincts when he dealt with the men of Ephraim. His allusion to gleaning after a quality harvest (Judg. 8:2) was designed to soothe the Ephraimites' resentment that they had not been mustered for the main battle, but only given the mop-up operation (Judg. 7:24–8:1).

Gleaning was a custom of Israelite law that required landowners to leave a portion of their harvests in the fields or on the vines for the benefit of the poor. After the harvesters had completed their work, the poor were allowed to go through the fields and vineyards to gather what was left.

Thus Gideon praised the men of Ephraim by saying that the gleanings, or leftovers, of their vineyards was superior to the firstfruits of his own clan of Abiezer. This was quite a compliment, since the Valley of Jezreel, where the Abiezrites lived, was one of the most productive vineyard regions in all of Israel.

Political Conflicts

The exchange between Balak and Balaam is one of the most unusual in all of Scripture. It contains a great deal of intrigue, irony, and humor. Among its many interesting points is the political struggle between Balaam, a non-Jewish prophet, Balak, the Moabite king, and God, the Lord of Israel. Balaam was caught between the other two. He had little choice but to bless Israel according to the Lord's command, rather than curse the nation as Balak wanted (Num. 23:11–12).

Perhaps you have found yourself in a similar situation. Where you work, for example, perhaps you have been asked to discredit someone else to serve political ends. Or maybe you've been asked to deliver a sales pitch that misrepresents another product or firm. Or maybe you've been told to discriminate against someone because of race or gender.

Balaam realized that he could not violate God's charge to him (Num. 22:12). How will you honor the Lord's authority over your life in the situations you face?

Political Marriages

In the ancient world, rulers used marriage as a way to seal treaties, alliances, and other covenants. David's marriage to Michal, the daughter of Saul (2 Sam. 3:13–14), had been largely a political marriage.

The relationship began when Saul saw his influence waning as David's was rising. Saul assumed that David would want to increase his standing by marrying into the king's family. So Saul offered his older daughter Merab to David, on one condition—that David vanquish the Philistines. Saul's real plan was to

P

have David killed in battle, but the pretense was based on the prospect of a political marriage (1 Sam. 18:12–17).

David declined Saul's offer (1 Sam. 18:18–19). But Saul's younger daughter Michal loved David, so Saul tried the strategy a second time (1 Sam. 18:20–25). This time David agreed, and after David returned from battle unharmed, the two were betrothed (1 Sam. 18:26–27).

Either they were never actually married, or else Saul caused his daughter to commit adultery when he later gave her to a man named Palti (Paltiel) as his wife (1 Sam. 25:44; compare 1 Sam. 19:11–17). In any case, as David came into power, he demanded the return of Michal as a condition of his covenant with Abner (2 Sam. 3:12–14).

David formed other political marriages (2 Sam. 3:2–5), as did his son Solomon (1 Kin. 11:1–3), in violation of the Law (Deut. 17:17).

From the standpoint of the Bible's overall teaching on the institution of marriage, political marriage seems hard to justify. It corrupts marriage into a political tool instead of honoring it as the holy union between a man and woman that God originally ordained (Gen. 2:21–24). It also demeans the woman, making her little more than an item in a transaction. After all, a male ruler who marries solely for political purposes is unlikely to serve his wife in the way that God intends (compare Eph. 5:25–33).

Today, political marriage may seem like a relic of the past, since few ruling monarchies remain. Yet marriage is still sometimes used as a way to bind together powerful families and organizations. However, the account of the tragedies that resulted from political marriage should give pause to anyone who fears God. Marriage is a holy institution, and God will not leave unpunished those who corrupt it.

Using Religion for Political Gain

Mixing religion and politics can be a problem if not done correctly. In Jeroboam's northern kingdom, the abuse of religion to further political ends was a recipe for disaster.

The Lord had promised Jeroboam that if he followed Him and walked in His ways, the Lord would be with him and would build for him "an enduring house" (1 Kin. 11:38). Yet when Jeroboam came into power, he apparently distrusted this word and feared that the kingdom would revert to the house of David (12:26–27).

To prevent that, Jeroboam disregarded God's instructions and set up two idolatrous shrines, one in the south of his kingdom at Bethel and the other in the north at Dan (1 Kin. 12:28–30). He also broadened the class of priests to include people from every tribe, not just Levi (1 Kin. 12:31), a capital offense against the Law (Num. 3:10). And he instituted his own rival system of feasts and holidays (1 Kin. 12:32–33).

As a result of these sins, the Lord judged Jeroboam by cutting off his family rather than establishing it as a dynasty (1 Kin. 14:7–16). The king squandered his unique opportunity through fear, lack of faith, and the corruption of the religious system.

Subversion of religion for political ends is still possible today. A public figure can project an image of religiosity that plays well with voters. But as always, while people may look at the outward appearance, the Lord looks at the heart (1 Sam. 16:7).

POLYGAMY
Giving Birth to Trouble

Many people today have found that success in a career does not necessarily translate into success in personal and family life. David is an illustration of that fact. While the "house of David (his position and stature as king-designate) grew stronger and stronger" (1 Sam. 3:1), his family life was headed for serious trouble.

Evidence for that can be found in the list of David's six sons born at Hebron (1 Sam. 3:2–5). Each was born to a different wife, which indicates that David was strengthening his political ties through marriage, a common practice for ancient kings. But we see that in David's case it was a foolish practice.

Not only did David's polygamy violate the Law (Deut. 17:17), it led to enormous problems as he tried to to blend his various families together. For example, David's son Amnon violated his half-sister Tamar, then was killed by her avenging brother, Absalom. That led to a bitter estrangement between Absalom and his father that resulted in the treason and, ultimately, the death of Absalom—all to David's great regret (2 Sam. 13–18).

David's polygamy also set a poor example for his successor, Solomon, who expanded his kingdom while marrying seven hundred wives and three hundred concubines. Just as the Law had predicted, these women turned his heart away from the Lord to idols (1 Kin. 11:3). The Lord judged him for that sin by allowing the kingdom to be divided after his death (1 Kin. 11:9–13).

David demonstrates the biblical principle that the sins of the parents extend "to the third and fourth generations" (Ex. 20:5). The choices that we make in order to further our professional lives can sometimes do lasting damage to our immediate families and even our descendants. We may succeed brilliantly in our field, but is it worth it if we wreak havoc on those closest to us?

For more on this topic, see **INTERRACIAL MARRIAGE,** *"Too Many Wives?" page 226;* **SURROGATE MOTHERS,** *"Concubines," page 390.*

PORNOGRAPHY

The Power Behind Porn

Pornography exposes more than skin. Jude connects the illicit sex in Sodom and Gomorrah (Jude 7) with demonic powers (Jude 6). The real evil behind porn is not that it is so shameful or unfulfilling, though it is, like "clouds without water" (Jude 12–13). Nor is the evil that the peddling of raw sex and lustful pleasure makes someone else rich, though it does (Jude 11). Jude hints at the real sources of power and profit behind the porn market: demonic evil that traffics in human sex.

POSSESSIONS

A Man Who Almost Had It All

He was young, well-mannered, well-educated, and well-off. He was sincere, honest, and above reproach. Maybe he also had an engaging personality and a winsome smile. Certainly Jesus found him likable; He even tried to recruit him (Mark 10:21). He was the man who had everything—except eternal life. And he could have had that, too. All he had to do was get rid of his money and follow Jesus.

But it wasn't to be. Elsewhere Jesus had said that no one can serve both God and money (Matt. 6:24). Here was living proof of that principle. In coming to Jesus, the rich young ruler came to a fork in the road. He had to choose which one he would serve—money or Jesus. Apparently he chose money.

Jesus never condemned people for being rich. Nor does Scripture condemn the possession or the accumulation of money. But Jesus warned people about what He called "the deceitfulness of riches" (Mark 4:19). He understood the powerful but ultimately fatal attraction of money as a substitute for God.

Jesus perceived that tendency in the rich young ruler. The man was placing far too much value on his wealth. So Jesus told him to give it away, to free himself from its entanglements. It's worth noting that Jesus did not give that same advice to every other rich person He encountered. But it was a requirement for this young ruler.

There are many rich young rulers today, people who have or are well on their way to having relatively sizable assets. Some are Christians and some are not. But sooner or later they all must answer the question that this man asked Jesus: "What shall I do that I may inherit eternal life?" (Mark 10:17).

Jesus' response is still the same: there's nothing you can do; only God can give eternal life (Mark 10:27). But He gives it freely and graciously to those who follow Him (Mark 10:29–30). However, that's especially hard for the rich (Mark 10:23). They have a competing offer, and it's very attractive.

Naked Before God

It is easy to forget that ultimately we will stand naked before God (Job 1:20–21; 26:6). We can surround ourselves with clothing, houses, cars, and other possessions that hide our true condition. Yet in the end all of that will slip away, and then we must consider: What will we have left?

The author of Ecclesiastes faced that issue. Like Job, he was one of the wealthiest and wisest men who ever lived. Yet after taking his kingdom to the height of its prosperity, he wrote, "As [a person] came from his mother's womb, naked shall he return" (Eccl. 5:15). An Arab proverb offers a similar perspective: "There are no pockets in a burial shroud."

P

So if we cannot rely on our possessions when we stand before God, what will we present? At least Job had his integrity and righteousness (Job 27:2–6). How much of that will we have when we stand before God? Ultimately, our standing must be determined by Christ's work on our behalf (Phil. 3:9). Nevertheless, God will evaluate our character and how we have lived our lives—either to His glory or to our shame (1 Cor. 3:9–15; 2 Cor. 5:1–11). Which will it be for you?

Rich in . . . Faith?

James notes the tension between wealth and faith (James 2:5–6). None of us is exempt from the distracting and distorting effect of growing affluence. God does not condemn wealth, but He clearly warns us that we can't pursue wealth or trust in it and also pursue God and trust in His faithfulness (Matt. 6:24–34).

Those of us who have wealth might consider several tough questions:

- What plans do we have for giving money away? Are we giving away more in the name of God now than we did last year or the year before?
- What is our intention—to move to an even higher level of luxury, or to hold steady where we are, or even simplify our lifestyle and give away the excess?
- Can we name any ways in which our increased wealth has brought us closer to God?

*For more on this topic, see **HAPPINESS**, "Having—and Being Had," page 193; **STEWARDSHIP**, "The Rest of Your Paycheck," page 383.*

POVERTY

An Economic Safety Net

In developed nations today, economic assistance for the poor is generally handled by a network of government agencies and nonprofit organizations. In ancient Israel, private citizens themselves were expected to help the poor. One of the primary means for that was gleaning (Deut. 24:19–21).

Gleaning allowed the poor to go through a field, orchard, or vineyard after the main harvest and gather whatever the harvesters had missed or intentionally left for them. The Law encouraged landowners not to be overly zealous in gathering produce from their fields, but to purposely leave some behind for the poor. The point was not to hand the poor a free meal but to provide them a way to keep from starving. Thus gleaning was an economic safety net.

Deuteronomy named three types of people who were likely to be poor: the stranger, the fatherless, and the widow. Strangers, or "sojourners," were non-Jews who came to live in Canaan for a period of time. Although foreigners enjoyed numerous privileges among the Hebrews, they did not own land. Thus they tended to live in poverty.

The fatherless and widows also tended to be poor since they lacked a male to work the land, provide for their needs, and look out for their rights.

The Israelites' welfare system was not like ours, but it did address the needs of poor people through laws such as the law of gleaning. That fact provides a strong argument for helping the poor today. We may debate the means by which that help is delivered, but there can be no debate about the ends involved: to see that people's basic needs are met when they would otherwise have no way to meet them.

God, Defender of the Poor

The God we worship is deeply concerned that the poor and needy receive justice, deliverance, and vindication (Ps. 35:10). These issues deserve to be high on the agenda for any nation or public servant seeking to honor God and receive divine blessing.

The psalms mention "the poor" more than twenty-five times, usually either in terms of what the wicked are doing to them or what God is doing for them. Thus, to be on the side of God is to take up the cause of the poor. Doing so rescues the perishing (Ps. 35:17), silences unjust critics (Ps. 35:19–25), and magnifies the Lord (Ps. 35:18, 27–28)—assuming that the spirit behind one's efforts is a genuine concern for justice and righteousness.

Institutionalized Poverty

Anyone who takes the attitude that poor people's poverty is all their own fault needs to consider Isaiah's prophecy concerning the poor of Israel (Is. 10:1–4). The passage is clear that a poor person's greatest enemy is often "the system." The powerful can institutionalize injustice in ways that take advantage of the powerless.

This does not remove individual responsibility, but it does create social and corporate responsibility for how communities treat the poor. It speaks to a host of social issues and institutions: housing, lending practices, zoning laws, education, jobs, crime prevention, the courts, the prisons, the creation of political districts, voting, and many more.

Two principles in particular emerge from Isaiah's warning:

1. *God pays attention to what societies do to the poor.* The Lord does not look the other way when policymakers "decree unrighteous decrees" that "rob the needy of justice" (Is. 10:1–2). He sees how their system operates and calls it what it is: robbery.

2. *God promises to bring justice to the poor, and to judge those who mistreat the poor.* God is a God of justice, and He promises a day of punishment for the unjust (Is. 10:3–4). Isaiah describes a reversal in which the poor are raised up and the powerful are brought low.

In light of who God is, those who fear the Lord today do well to study the legal, regulatory, and social systems of their community or country. In what ways do systems promote institutionalized injustice against the poor? Furthermore, what should be done about them? What changes could God's people help to implement?

Israel's Systematic Relief Program

One of the most difficult public policy issues for any nation to face is what to do about its poor people. One view says to let the poor fend for themselves and not become a burden on society. Another view holds that humane governments have a responsibility to help all of their citizens, and especially those who are unable to provide for their own needs. Is there a place for government-sponsored assistance to the poor, according to the Bible?

The question is not easily settled. But it might help to consider what the Lord told the Israelites to do (Deut. 14:28–29). The Law assumed that certain classes of people would be at an economic disadvantage in Hebrew society: Levites, "strangers" or non-Israelite foreigners, orphans, and widows.

To help these groups, the Law said that a tithe (or ten percent) of every third year's produce should be set aside for their use. It was to be stored "within your gates" (Deut. 14:28), indicating that the aid should be collected and administered by towns and cities, not by individual households. Thus the third-year tithe was a form of community charity.

However, the system was designed to prevent chronic dependence or laziness. The poor were welcome to eat what they needed from the supplies. But by storing up the food, a city could prevent inappropriate distribution. In addition, the beneficiaries of this aid were to be those living "within your gates" (Deut. 14:29). In other words, they were citizens of the city and neighbors of those doing the tithing. Thus it would not be possible for someone to travel from town to town freeloading.

The regularity of the third-year tithe, which was to be collected and distributed in the third and sixth years of every seven-year cycle (Lev. 25:4), made this a systematic, not a haphazard, program of relief. Its infrequency ensured that no one could take advantage by shirking all work and eating only what came through charity.

Nothing but the Clothes on Their Backs

God takes a special interest in the plight of the poor (Ex. 22:25). But it's important to note that when Scripture speaks of material poverty, it has in mind destitution.

Here, for example, God describes the poor person as one who has so little that if his garment is taken as pledge for a loan, he will suffer from cold in the night (Ex. 22:26–27). Apparently he has nothing more than the garment to keep him warm. He is in dire straits indeed. He literally owns nothing more than the clothes on his back.

Are there any people like that around you? How do you respond?

Notice that God says He will hear the cries of a poor person who is oppressed (Ex. 22:27). That means not only that God will come to the person's aid, but that He will exact vengeance on the oppressor (compare James 5:1–6).

Who Are the Poor?

By comparison to the many modern Christians who live in affluence, the Corinthian believers would appear poor. Yet Paul described the Christians of Macedonia as living in "deep poverty" (2 Cor. 8:2), so they were much poorer even than the Corinthians. What does Scripture mean, then, when it says that God "has given to *the poor*" (2 Cor. 9:9, emphasis added)? And what does that mean for believers today who are relatively affluent?

The word for *poor* (2 Cor. 8:9) described someone who toiled for a living, what we would call a day laborer. Such persons were distinct from the truly destitute. The former may have had a difficult life, but at least they were in no danger of losing it. By contrast, the truly poor were in immediate danger of perishing if they didn't receive charitable aid.

Paul described God as dispersing to the poor, the day laborers, not food for survival but seed that they could sow to raise a crop (2 Cor. 8:9–10). He indicated that God would aid the Corinthians so that they, in turn, could aid the completely destitute believers in Jerusalem.

So what does that mean for us as Christians today if we work at relatively stable, well-paid jobs, own our own homes, and manage to salt away at least some money for retirement? Paul would doubtless identify us as rich. We may work hard, but we have disposable income that most first-century Christians could have only imagined. God will hold us accountable for how we dispose of it.

For more on this topic, see **DEBT,** *"Freely You Have Received, Freely Give," page 98.*

POWER

"Give Me Power!"

Simon's request (Acts 8:18–19) was motivated by the same illusion of power that drives so many in today's business, political, and entertainment arenas. Popular culture invests actors, sports figures, and other celebrities with the appearance of unusual significance. Even among Christians there exists a strong tendency to create power figures out of preachers, singers, writers, and parachurch leaders. But God's power has little or nothing to do with outward appearances or worldly acclaim.

Simon had adopted the world's perspective on power. Showered with uncritical adulation (Acts 8:9–10), he became obsessed with himself and his supposed importance. Tragically, he viewed others through the same distorted lens.

What about you? Have you succumbed to the illusion of power? Consider:

- How much time and energy do you devote to fantasizing about how great you could become?
- Do you pay attention only to those who stroke your ego? Or do you listen to those who aren't impressed with your status and will level with you about weaknesses?
- How much do status and position define who you are? Suppose you were to lose it all—what then?

The Power Behind the Power

Pilate assumed that he had more power than Jesus because he had authority to condemn Him to death (John 19:10). But Jesus knew that all power ultimately comes from God, even the power of the state (John 19:11; Rom. 13:1). Indeed, one of the reasons Jesus could submit to the injustices of His trial was that He was submitting to God's will (John 18:11). Pilate and those under him were merely exercising limited authority. Meanwhile, God's purposes were being fulfilled.

What sort of power do you have—in your work, at home, in your community? Do you recognize that your authority ultimately comes from God, and that you are ultimately accountable to Him for the use of that power?

The Right Kind of Power

Business, government, nonprofit organizations, and churches all feel the impact of people pursuing and defending power. Here in John's vision of God triumphing over evil, God holds the ultimate power (Rev. 11:17).

What does the New Testament teach about power?

- There is tremendous power in humility. It gives us strength that is a gift from God to be used for His purposes.
- Forgiveness is powerful and liberating and is a power that Jesus has delegated to His followers.

- When others observe us and the way we use power and authority, they ought to see Jesus.
- Like fire, power can be used to accomplish good. But always lurking in its shadow is the temptation of abuse.
- Jesus described the power that He supplies as the right and ability to lay down one's life for others.
- All power ultimately comes from God, and we are ultimately accountable to Him for how we use power.
- Jesus gives His followers a unique kind of power to accomplish His tasks.
- God's power has little or nothing to do with outward appearances or worldly acclaim.
- Paul was competent in and comfortable with the powerful Roman judicial system and its procedures, even when he faced officials who dealt in bribes and political favors.
- The message of Christ is powerful enough to transform lives.
- The gospel appears foolish to many people. Yet the irony is that it is far more powerful than even the strongest players in our culture can imagine.
- Sometimes we give away the control of our lives to things like status and possessions. When we do, they overpower us: we no longer possess our possessions—they possess us!
- Our world prizes strength and power, but Scripture puts a new twist on the notion of strength: weakness can make a person strong.

Do you have what it takes to "make it" in life? Scripture teaches that God's power gives us what we need to experience real life in a way that pleases Him.

Three Misuses of Power

Like fire, power can be used to accomplish good. But always lurking in its shadow is the temptation of abuse—to use power for self-centered gains that harm others, and to avoid accountability for that harm. Responding to the Roman soldiers who policed Jerusalem (Luke 3:14), John raised three issues in regard to the abuse of power:

1. *Intimidation.* We can use our power to push others around, especially those who are too weak or afraid to push back. Using power in that way is ungodly and harmful. Ultimately such power users destroy themselves, for their subordinates serve them without loyalty and with increasing resentment.

2. *False accusations.* We can use our power to make snap decisions and judgments. But power used in that way keeps us in the dark, since others will be too afraid to tell us when we're wrong. When things go awry, it's all too easy to start blaming people under us and around us.

3. *Discontent.* If we use our power in self-centered, hurtful ways, we'll tend to increase our appetite for power and seek more, perhaps by pressuring superiors or by cheating and stealing.

For more on this topic, see **HOLY SPIRIT,** *"Power," page 200;* **LEADERSHIP,** *"Missing Out on the Payoff," page 243.*

PRAISE
Cheering for God

Anyone who has ever attended an event where a large crowd of people was gathered—a sports contest, a parade, a concert—knows how thunderous the applause and shouts of an audience can be. Thousands of people acting together can generate a lot of noise, because there is tremendous power in the collective voice of a crowd.

Psalm 47 envisions the whole world clapping and shouting in praise to the Lord (Ps. 47:1). Imagine what a deafening din that would be! God (and God alone) deserves that kind of honor, for He is the Lord Most High, the great and awesome King who rules over all the earth, over all its peoples and nations (Ps. 47:2–3).

Do you give God the respect and praise to which He is entitled?

Praise Rather than Pride

How do you handle success or achievement? Do you automatically expect to receive credit, acclaim, or acknowledgement for all that has been accomplished, and even engineer ways to ensure that you get them?

David celebrated his victory over his enemies' oppression by praising the Lord for deliverance, not by claiming that he himself had achieved it (Ps. 18:46–50). He gave the glory to God.

David had been severely persecuted by King Saul, who was eaten up with fear that David was out to capture the throne. Saul's vengeful and vicious campaign drove David into hiding, fearing for his life (1 Sam. 18–24). So when the Lord delivered David from this mad campaign against his life, he responded by composing this psalm of praise. David had no illusion that somehow his own ingenuity had delivered him. Only God had preserved his life.

Are there situations in your world that tempt you to take all the credit for outcomes rather than giving glory to God? In what ways might you give Him a gift of praise or thanksgiving?

PRAYER

God Answers Fervent Prayer

Do you ever feel as if your prayers bounce off the ceiling rather than reaching God? If so, consider carefully the prayer of Daniel for the release of his people from captivity (Dan. 9). It is a testimony to the fact that God answers prayer—in His time and according to His purposes—as the angel Gabriel announced (Dan. 9:24–25).

However, God does not answer any and every prayer as the one praying would like. Why, then, did He respond to Daniel's? Here are some observations:

1. *Daniel's prayer was the result of his study of Scripture.* The timing of Daniel's prayer is highly significant. It came "in the first year of Darius," around 539 B.C. (Dan. 9:1). That was

PRAISE

the year in which Babylon fell to the Persians, a truly astounding event that must have sent Daniel back to the Scriptures to search for understanding.

As he studied the Law, he found the reasons for Judah's exile (Dan. 9:11–13; compare Lev. 26; Deut. 27–28). He also found a promise of restoration—if the people repented of their sins (Lev. 26:40–45).

2. *Daniel confessed and repented of his people's sins.* By all appearances, Daniel was a godly man of faith who lived a life of utmost integrity, both before and after being deported to Babylon. Yet despite his own personal innocence, he confessed to numerous sins as a member of God's wayward people. Four times he told the Lord, "We have sinned" (Dan. 9:5, 8, 11, 15). This is a powerful example of corporate confession, in which one accepts personal responsibility for the sins of one's people (see Lam. 1:18).

3. *Daniel fasted and prayed for a period of time.* The Bible does not say exactly how long Daniel's prayer of confession lasted, but it was probably more than a day, as he refers to fasting (Dan. 9:3). He also demonstrated his remorse for sin in a very tangible way by wearing sackcloth and smearing himself with ashes. Clearly he wanted God to know that he was sorry for the sins of his people.

Only after this prolonged period of confession did Daniel ask the Lord for mercy (Dan. 9:16–17). He did not even raise the possibility of restoration, despite God's promise in the Law and his awareness of Jeremiah's prophecies (Dan. 9:2). He asked only that the Lord would act on behalf of His own interests (Dan. 9:18–19).

James said that "the effective, fervent prayer of a righteous man avails much" (James 5:16). Daniel's prayer seems to be a case in point. Not long after Daniel prayed, Cyrus issued a decree allowing the Jews to return to Jerusalem and begin rebuilding the temple (2 Chr. 36:22–23). Was there a connection between Daniel's prayer, Cyrus' decree, and Jeremiah's prophecies? Gabriel indicates that there was (Dan. 9:23–25).

Prayer is not a gimmick by which we charm or coerce God into giving us what we want. Prayer is a sober-minded acknowledgment of our true situation before the Lord

and an admission of our need for His divine help. Are you prepared to pray like Daniel?

Learning to Pray Like Moses

Prayer is a scary, awkward proposition for many people. It's the kind of activity that they would just as soon leave to the religious "professionals." But Scripture encourages us with numerous examples of people who demonstrate that prayer is an everyday activity for everyday people. Moses, who asked God for a successor (Num. 27:15–17), is a case in point.

Moses was a hard-working man. He went through at least three different careers—privileged ruler in Egypt, forgotten shepherd in Midian, and national liberator and leader of the Israelites. Throughout these pursuits, Moses regularly turned to God in prayer. Consider the following conversations that he had with God:

- He debated with God about his fitness to lead Israel out of Egypt (Ex. 3:11–4:17; 6:28–7:7).
- He interceded on behalf of the Egyptians (Ex. 8:9–13).
- He asked for water for his thirsty nation of refugee people (Ex. 15:24–25).
- He pleaded with God about the sinful Hebrews and what God would do to them (Ex. 32:11–13, 31–34).
- He interceded with God concerning his sister's leprosy, after she exhibited prejudice against Moses' foreign-born spouse (Num. 12:4–15).
- He prayed for the transition of leadership to Joshua (Num. 27:15–17).
- He appealed to God to allow him to join his people in their entrance to the Promised Land (Deut. 3:23–25; 34:1–4).

Moses demonstrated the often forgotten truth that God is more than ready to hear our complaints, appeals, and frustrations. Are you willing to approach God in prayer about the problems that vex you? Why not pause to do so right now?

Nehemiah's Model Prayer

Nehemiah's prayer (Neh. 1:4–11) offers several important lessons for believers today for how to practice the discipline of prayer:

1. *Nehemiah's first response was to turn to God in prayer.* Prayer was not something that

Nehemiah engaged in after he had exhausted all other alternatives. He did not approach it as a last ditch effort, with the attitude, "What have I got to lose?" Instead, his immediate, instinctive response to the news of trouble back home was to fast and pray (Neh. 1:4).

2. *Nehemiah recognized and affirmed God's sovereignty.* He realized that the Lord had first and primary claim over all nations and people, whether they were Israelites or Persians. He saw himself and his people as being in the hands of God, dependent on His grace.

3. *Nehemiah identified with his people.* He used the pronoun "we" in his prayer. Rather than blame others, he accepted corporate responsibility for his people's sin.

4. *Nehemiah recognized the whole of God's promises and commandments.* In praying to God, it is easy to focus on what one wants from God, but ignore what God asks and expects from His people. Nehemiah knew what the Scriptures said about the Lord's covenant with Israel, and he accepted the responsibilities of the covenant, not just the privileges.

Overcoming Obstacles to Prayer

Do you find prayer intimidating? Have you ever said, "I don't know how to pray"? If so, you may be surprised to learn that there is no "right" or "wrong" method of prayer. Nor is prayer reserved for a handful of religious professionals. If the wicked king Manasseh could cry out to God and be heard (2 Chr. 33:12–13), surely there is hope for the rest of us.

Which of the following characterizes your situation?

- You feel deep guilt for willful sin that perhaps has even ruined your own or someone else's life. See David's prayer after he committed the sins of adultery and murder (Ps. 51).
- You feel scared by responsibilities that seem totally beyond your skills and ability. Read Moses' "argument" with God (Ex. 3:1–4:17).
- You feel frustrated and angry as you read about local, national, and international conditions, wondering why God doesn't seem to be doing anything. Study the Book of Habakkuk.

- You are afraid of a family member's hostility over wrongs that you have committed. Hear Jacob calling out to God for safety from his brother Esau (Gen. 32:9–12; for the outcome, see Gen. 33).
- You have been threatened by a superior who thinks you are out to take over his power and position. Listen as David cries out to God while fleeing from Saul (Ps. 57, 142).
- You have experienced prejudice and even persecution for your religious convictions. Look at the prayer for boldness that the early church prayed after its leaders had been jailed and threatened (Acts 4:13–31).
- Your child is terribly afflicted and you feel powerless to help. Consider the Syro-Phoenician woman's appeal to Jesus for mercy (Matt. 15:21–28).
- You are troubled by a chronic physical malady and have not experienced healing. Read about Paul's three appeals to God to remove his ailment (2 Cor. 12:7–10).

There is no single method for expressing oneself to God. The Lord is not only completely able to hear our arguments, pleas, and pain—He wants to! He also delights to hear our joys, praises, and ecstasies. So open your heart to God. Then give yourself to patient listening for His response.

Persistence in Prayer

Do you ever feel impatient with God? Does He seem late in answering your requests or meeting your needs?

Jesus spoke to the issues of how to pray, how long to pray, and how long God might take to respond. One day His disciples asked Him to teach them to pray (Luke 11:1). He told a story about someone with a need who was very persistent in asking a neighbor for help (Luke 11:5–8).

The story makes it clear that our ability to ask does not equal God's response or its timing. God is not a celestial bellhop waiting at our beck and call. Neither does He rely on us to define our needs, outline solutions, or say when or how He should act. No, God does those for us—which is just as well since He is all-wise.

God delights in His children developing the habit and freedom of asking Him for help (Luke 11:9–10). But He won't leave us trapped in our limited perception of the situation (Luke 11:11–13). Sooner or later He will answer our prayers, but in His own time. He asks us to trust Him to know what is needed and when.

Our calling, then, is to ask—even persistently—and to grow in the process. One of the surprising benefits of praying is how much we change. Sometimes, that in itself is the answer to our prayers.

Prayer and Temptation

Temptation is tough. It's a test. It's an enticement to do wrong. It may involve great pleasure, a chance to escape risk, or illegitimate gain. Whatever the offering, it's usually attractive.

But Scripture calls giving in to tempting opportunities "sin". It even warns us that repeatedly giving way to temptation can result in falling away permanently, with a total loss of interest in returning to God (Heb. 6:6–8, according to one interpretation). Clearly we need God's strength, and wisdom to flee (1 Cor. 6:18; 1 Tim. 6:11).

As Jesus and His closest companions faced great danger, they were afraid and tired (Luke 22:42–45). Jesus knew how vulnerable and confused that condition can make a person. He urged His followers to join Him in prayer so that they would not fall into temptation (Luke 22:40). They could not face the trials to come without new strength from God.

Earlier Jesus had taught His followers to ask the Father not to lead them into temptation (Matt. 6:13). There is no sin in being tempted. In fact, temptation is a sign that our spiritual lives are strong enough to recognize values that conflict with godliness. But giving in is sin. That's why it's crucial to take time to declare to God our weakness, weariness, and need for help in the midst of testing.

It may also help to have others pray with us, just as Jesus did in His hour of need. Do you have others you can turn to for prayer in times of difficulty? Are you available when others have that need?

For more on this topic, see **FRUSTRATION,** *"Bitter Prayers," page 165.*

PREJUDICE

A History of Enmity

Sin involves more than just personal misdeeds. It can extend into family histories and become incorporated into public policy and cultural systems. The enmity between Haman and Mordecai (Esth. 3:2–6) showed that principle at work.

At first glance, the hostility between the two men appears to be a simple case of disrespect on Mordecai's part (Esth. 3:2)—possibly for religious reasons, although the text does not say—and racial prejudice on Haman's (Esth. 3:6). However, further investigation reveals that the encounter outside the palace of Ahasuerus was not the first time that the people of Haman and the people of Mordecai had met.

The Book of Esther emphasizes that Haman was the son of Hammedatha the Agagite (Esth. 3:1, 10; 8:3, 5; 9:24). Tradition holds that the Agagites were descendants of Agag, the Amalekite king whom Saul, Israel's first king, had failed to kill, disobeying the Lord's instruction (1 Sam. 15). The Amalekites stood under the permanent judgment of God for attacking the Israelites during their journey from Egypt to Canaan (Ex. 17:8–13; Deut. 25:17–19).

Now, with Haman's rise to power, the Amalekites were in a sense threatening once again to destroy God's people. But this time, the Lord used Mordecai to frustrate the plan. Ironically, Mordecai was descended from Kish (Esth. 2:5)—the same family of Benjamites from which Saul had come (1 Sam. 9:1). Thus, in the end, Mordecai carried out what Saul had failed to accomplish (Esth. 7:10; 9:4–5, 13–15).

Perhaps neither Mordecai nor Haman knew about the long-standing enmity between their two peoples. Nevertheless, their conflict illustrates that personal sin can be passed on to one's children, and in turn to their children. Over the years, it can become imbedded in the very life of a culture. That legacy of sin may lie dormant for generations, then suddenly flare up, as it did in Haman's case, in institutionalized evil (Esth. 3:9).

For that reason, it is not enough just to live a good life personally, as important as that is. To root out evil requires the renewal of systems. That may involve new laws that honor godly values or the repeal of bad laws that work against godly values. In either case, the point is that we cannot be too careful when it comes to sin. The seeds of sin that we fail to root out today may spring up in later generations and yield a harvest of evil.

Acting Like a Neighbor

The parable of the good Samaritan (Luke 10:30–37) is one of Jesus' most popular. It reduces an abstract theological question, "What shall I do to inherit eternal life" (Luke 10:25), to a simpler, more practical challenge: "Go and do likewise [i.e., show mercy]" (Luke 10:37).

The story begins with the lawyer's self-justifying question, "Who is my neighbor?" But Jesus turned the question around: "Which of these three do you think was neighbor to him who fell among the thieves?" What matters, Jesus implied, is not identifying needs, but meeting them. The question is not *Who is my neighbor?* but rather *Am I a neighbor to others?*

What makes the story so poignant, however, is the contrast between the Jewish priest and Levite who avoid the half-dead victim, and the Samaritan who shows him compassion. Jesus was playing on the deep-seated animosity that existed between the two groups. He knew His listeners would find it hard enough to show mercy, but unthinkable that a Samaritan would illustrate how. Prejudiced people find it almost impossible to think that their ethnic enemies might be compassionate human beings.

Jesus' challenge to "go and do likewise" is a test for us as we consider the many racial and ethnic divisions in the world today. God is interested in mercy, not maintaining prejudice.

Confronting Ethnic Prejudice

Success never means the end of problems; it just means a new set of problems. The community of believers in Jerusalem discovered this truth as they experienced significant development in their life together. Their group was constantly growing and changing (Acts 1:15; 2:41, 47; 4:4, 32; 5:14). There was amazing agreement among them (Acts 2:46; 4:32;

5:12). And their material needs were being met through sacrificial generosity (Acts 2:45; 4:34, 36).

Nevertheless, a situation developed that threatened to fracture this successful movement (Acts 6:1). The immediate problem had to do with the daily distribution to widows, but the underlying issue was ethnic tension between the *Hebrews*, Jews born in Judea and Galilee, and the *Hellenists*, Greek-speaking Jews born outside of Palestine. The clash could have destroyed the church or divided it into two Christian ethnic communities. Notice how the apostles responded (Acts 6:2–6):

- They met face-to-face with the Hellenists (the powerful with the powerless).
- They listened to the complaints and acknowledged their legitimacy.
- Together with the Hellenists, they devised guidelines for godly leaders and chose seven with names that suggest they were from among the Hellenist minority.
- They approved and commissioned the new leaders through the laying on of hands and committed themselves to work with them.
- They gave the new leaders authority over the distribution.
- They shared power and resources and affirmed the dignity of the newly chosen leaders.

Result? "The word of God spread, and . . . multiplied greatly in Jerusalem" (Acts 6:7).

What problems do you or your church confront as a result of success? What steps are you taking to manage those problems in a way that serves people and honors God?

Getting Along in the New World

According to Isaiah, God will someday bring together people from every nation to live together under His lordship (Is. 66:20). Considering the tensions that exist today between people of different races, colors, customs, and cultures, one can only marvel at the fact that somehow everyone will get along.

Perhaps the key to surmounting differences will be the realization that ultimately all peoples have been brought into being by God and are called to live under God (Is.

66:19; compare Gen. 10). Isaiah's vision of international blessing and worldwide unity echoes the promise made to Abraham and Sarah, that through them "all the families of the earth shall be blessed" (Gen. 12:2–3). It also anticipates John's vision of people from "every tribe and tongue and people and nation" worshiping and serving the Lord (Rev. 5:9–10; 7:9).

Given this bright promise of cross-cultural peace and harmony, it makes sense that people might start trying to get along right now. We can experience a taste of heaven on earth as we learn to communicate with, understand, and trust others who differ from us in ethnic background, language, culture, gender, age, tradition, or other ways that often divide. This will involve hard work, but the effort is worth it. It not only improves our world today, but prepares us for eternity with God—and all His other children!

Perpetual Enemies of Israel

The Edomites and Israelites were descended from Isaac's two sons Esau and Jacob, respectively. Yet despite this kinship, the two peoples feuded repeatedly throughout biblical history:

- Edomites denied the Israelites access to the King's Highway during their journey to Canaan (Num. 20:14–21).
- Edomites opposed Saul under Hadad, a member of the royal family who had escaped Joab's massacre (1 Kin. 11:14–22).
- Edomites rebelled against Judah's control during the reign of Joram (2 Kin. 8:20–22).
- Edomites invaded Judah and took captives while Judah was being attacked by Pekah of Israel and Rezin of Syria (2 Kin. 16:5–6; 2 Chr. 28:16–17).
- Edomites rejoiced over Jerusalem's fall to the Babylonians (Ps. 137:7).

For more on this topic, see ETHNIC DIVERSITY, "Jews, Gentiles, and Jesus," page 132; HARTRED, "The Cycle of Prejudice," page 194.

PREPARATION

(*see* Planning)

PRIDE
A Case Study in Humbling the Proud

Numerous times, Scripture makes the point that God brings about a reversal in people's prospects, depending on how they respond to Him. The proud and the wicked who defy Him will be brought low, while the poor and the meek who honor Him will be raised up. A man of Isaiah's time offers a case study in this principle.

Shebna (Is. 22:15) was a high government official under King Hezekiah of Judah. He was among the leaders who went to meet with the Assyrian Rabshakeh when he came against Jerusalem (Is. 36:2–3). Isaiah predicted that God would pull this man down because of an extravagant tomb that he had built for himself (Is. 22:16–19).

The problem with Shebna's sepulcher was that it typified the careless attitude of God's people (Is. 22:12–13). Shebna was not merely planning for his death; he was building himself a grand monument. When he should have been on his knees, crying out to the Lord for mercy, he was puffing up his own image and pride. Therefore, God assured him that he would never use the elaborately carved tomb, but would die in a foreign country. Meanwhile, another official named Eliakim would inherit Shebna's position (Is. 22:20–23).

God still humbles the proud (James 4:6). For that reason, God's people do well to take personal inventory to see whether they are arrogantly ignoring what He has asked them to do, or whether they are fulfilling His will with humility and obedience.

For more on this topic, see AMBITION, "Pride Goes Before a Fall," page 18; SELF-RELIANCE, "Self-Reliance," page 362; SHAME, "From Honor to Shame," page 366.

PRIORITIES
First and Foremost

To what do you give your first and best efforts? When the Israelites eventually entered the Promised Land, God told them that the first thing they needed to do was to worship Him by bringing before Him some of the produce of their first harvest (Deut. 26:1–2).

What might this imply about the priorities of modern-day believers? Is there one thing we should put first above all others? Actually, Christians have no reason to arrange the various areas of their lives in a hierarchy, since Jesus is Lord of all of life. Yet because that is true, Jesus Himself becomes the priority. Whatever we do, we need to honor Him and put Him first.

So what might putting Christ first look like in the different responsibilities of daily life? For example . . .

- In our work, how might we honor Christ in the way we do our jobs, the way we deal with customers and coworkers, or what we do with the money we earn from our employment?
- At home, how might putting Christ first affect how we communicate with our spouse, how we resolve conflicts, or how we spend time with our children?
- In the community, how might we honor Christ in issues of public policy: the way we allocate resources, the projects on which we spend money, the treatment of people, the justice shown toward the powerless and disadvantaged?

One can tell a lot about people by what they put first in life. If someone audited your life, what could be concluded about your first and foremost priorities?

First Things First

"I'll pay more attention to religion as soon as my schedule lightens up." "I'll get back into a daily time of prayer and Bible reading as soon as I finish the project I'm working on." "One of these days I'll get around to helping that mission to the poor I've been thinking about."

If you've ever made comments such as these, then you have some idea of the situation in postexilic Judah. The people had started to rebuild the temple, but stopped after a year or two of work. They got involved in other commitments, and before they knew it, sixteen years had gone by. The temple was still incomplete. "We'll get around to it," they apparently said. "It's just not time yet" (Hag. 1:2).

However, God rebuked them for that attitude. Their priorities were distorted. They were putting God at the tail end of their com-

mitments, rather than honoring Him as the Lord of their lives. The neglect of the temple was essentially a neglect of God.

Perhaps, in light of God's word to the Jewish returnees, you'll want to rethink your priorities. If your spiritual life has been slipping, maybe it's time to put first things first and place God back at the center of your commitments.

Solomon's Dissatisfaction

Thanks to the Lord's help, Solomon apparently became the wealthiest and wisest man of his era (2 Chr. 1:1). No one, it seems, accumulated or accomplished as much as he did (Eccl. 2:1–9). Yet by his own admission (assuming that Solomon wrote Ecclesiastes), his life was far from satisfying (Eccl. 2:11, 16).

Solomon is a case study in how a person can be successful in terms of power, wealth, and prestige, yet lack the true success that comes from knowing and honoring God the way someone should.

Solomon wasn't all bad, but his life shows us that great achievements and success—whether in business, government, academia, or any other field—pale in comparison to being faithful to God. Do you need to restructure your priorities in order to focus more on loving and serving Him? Or are you so driven by success as the world defines it that you have little if any interest in the things that God cherishes?

Taking Stock

In Philippians 3, Paul takes stock of his life to determine what he has done that counts and what doesn't. His list of qualities and the conclusions he draws offer some important guideposts to help us assess our motives for and definitions of success:

- What does success look like to you? How have you arrived at that definition? What or who has influenced your vision of a successful life? What role, if any, have God's perspectives and purposes been given in your definition?
- What have you given up or sacrificed in order to pursue success?
- What have you determined to be worth your investment of time, energy, and/or money?

- How have your priorities and loyalties changed over time? Why?
- In what ways do you think God and His purposes are served by the life you are pursuing?

For more on this topic, see **FAITH,** *"Staying Focused," page 143.*

PROBLEMS

A Cause to Pause

Sometimes it's worth stopping to reflect on what is happening in one's life. Aaron had reason to do some serious thinking. He realized that the misbehavior of his sons raised serious questions about his fitness for ministry (Lev. 10:19).

Aaron provides an instructive lesson in the painful fact that good people have weaknesses, shortcomings, and a sinful, dark side. Like all of us, his failures were the outcome of separation from God and bondage to evil.

Aaron was not a worthless individual. He was a good speaker, which was one reason why God called him to assist his brother, Moses, in leading Israel out of Egypt (Ex. 4:14). He and his descendants were also appointed by God to be the priests over Israel's worship (Ex. 28:1–4).

But the biblical account shows that Aaron struggled with some major problems that led to serious problems on several occasions:

- Even though he was aware of God's jealous love and holiness, he gave in to the people at Sinai and led them into idolatry (Ex. 32:1–4). Later, he avoided taking responsibility for his appalling lapse of leadership (Ex. 32:21–25).
- He joined his sister, Miriam, in speaking against Moses because of Moses' possibly interracial marriage to an Ethiopian woman. God judged them harshly, so that Aaron pleaded for forgiveness (Num. 12:1–16).
- Though the text does not explicitly comment on Aaron as a parent, the back-to-back incidents involving all four of his sons raise serious questions about his effectiveness as a family leader (Lev. 10:1–3, 16–20).

No one can completely avoid failure and sin. Fortunately, God does not make us His children on the basis of our own ability not to commit sin, but on Christ's ability to deal with it. Every one of the "greats" in the Bible fell short of God's holiness. Yet they could find forgiveness and restoration through repentance. Aaron is a good example of a frail, very human servant of God who found favor with the Lord through serious reflection, repentance, and recovery.

"Problem" People

Nearly everyone has at least one person in life with whom it's hard to get along. The Israelites shared the Promised Land with entire nations with whom they were in constant conflict (Judg. 3:1–4).

Israel was supposed to displace these groups as it took possession of Canaan (Deut. 7). But for various reasons, many Canaanites were left. During the period of the judges, God used them to challenge His people, to punish them for violating His laws, and to turn them back toward Him.

As you think about people in your life with whom you frequently run into conflict, is it possible that God may have placed them in your path to challenge your faith and open your eyes to areas where you are not following Him? Perhaps it's an unreasonable supervisor, an unreliable employee, an unusually demanding customer, or an unbelievably insensitive relative. Could it be that these so-called "problem" people are not really problems but God-given opportunities for you to grow?

Turning Pain into Prayer

Perhaps you deal with problems caused by your background or upbringing. Or maybe you live with unchangeable circumstances that affect your life in a major way. If so, it's easy to feel like a victim and complain to God. But consider the example of Jabez (1 Chr. 4:9–10).

In the books of 1 and 2 Chronicles, many little people of faith loom large, even to the point of overshadowing some of the kings. Jabez is one of those little people. He stands out because he was a person of prayer.

Jabez's name means "pain" or "misery." His mother bore him in pain, which may mean that she had a difficult childbirth, or

P

that the circumstances of her family were distressing. Whatever the case, Jabez turned pain into prayer, asking God for territorial gain and spiritual blessing. He didn't use his name or background as an excuse with God. Instead of complaining about his lot, he prayed for increased responsibility and an enlarged place in the Promised Land.

If you feel like a victim, you can follow Jabez's example by praying to God. Instead of irresponsibly allowing the circumstances of life to overwhelm you, you can begin to take charge of your life by asking God for the power to make changes.

PROGRESS

Which Way Are You Headed?

Faith is not a one-time, sensational event in one's life, neither is it a state of moral and spiritual perfection to which a handful of super-saints attain. Faith is a dynamic, lifelong journey that each believer is on. At any given moment, we are either moving toward God or turning away from Him.

The people of Jeremiah's day stood under God's judgment because they turned away from Him—they "went backward and not forward" (Jer. 7:24). Rather than cultivate a growing relationship with the Lord based on sustained, faithful obedience, they went their own way and followed the "dictates of their evil hearts" (Jer. 7:23–24).

May that not be true of you! The only way to make progress in your journey of faith is to keep moving toward God as best you know how. You may fail and fall at times, but the main thing is to keep turning back toward God, not away from Him. Paul described this dynamic in his own spiritual experience: "Forgetting those things which are behind and reaching forward to those things which are ahead, I press toward the goal for the prize of the upward call of God in Christ Jesus" (Phil. 3:13–14).

PROJECT MANAGEMENT

(see Management)

PROMISES

He Remains Faithful

Have you ever reneged on a business agreement? Or skipped out on an appointment? Or gone back on your word to a co-worker? Or missed a crucial deadline on which everyone was counting? Have you ever broken promises to your spouse or children?

Fortunately we can count on God to keep His commitments. Even though we as humans are frequently faithless, He remains faithful to His word (2 Tim. 2:13).

If we want to develop godly character, then one of our main objectives should be to honor our commitments. Psalm 15 describes a person who is moving closer to God as one who "swears to his own hurt and does not change." His word is his bond.

Honoring Promises

Do you believe that God can be depended on to honor His promises? Abraham did (Rom. 4:20–21).

All of us rely on the promises of others in our daily lives and work. Vendors promise to deliver products in specified quantities and qualities. Project groups promise to deliver results by certain dates. Companies promise to stand behind their products with "satisfaction guaranteed." If we can believe the promises of fallible human beings, how much more can we trust the promises of God, who never fails?

Of course, if we are one of God's people, we need to live and work with the same trustworthiness and reliability. When we give our word, we need to fulfill it. When we make a commitment, we need to honor it. When we enter into a contract, we need to abide by it. Otherwise, we bring discredit to God.

Keeping Commitments

Many people today have grown skeptical of the campaign promises of politicians. Often the electorate's hopes have been dashed by people who make appealing claims while running for office, yet fail to deliver when elected.

Scripture presents David as a leader who kept his promises. David had sworn that he would show "kindness" (Hebrew, *chesed*, "devotion") to Jonathan's descendants (1 Sam. 20:11–16, 42). So once he was installed as king, David asked whether any of Saul's descendants (and therefore Jonathan's relatives) remained alive (2 Sam. 9:1). Jonathan's son Mephibosheth was found, and David kept his promise (2 Sam. 9:7–13).

This incident stands as a challenge to God's people today to follow through on their promises and covenants. Sometimes it's easy to rationalize a way out of keeping faith, especially when circumstances and relationships change. Yet David kept his commitment, even though Jonathan was dead, and even though Jonathan's father spent years trying to take David's life. David knew that God took the covenant between him and Jonathan seriously. So David determined to follow through.

David's example also challenges parents and grandparents to uphold commitments made by earlier generations. To do so is a marvelous legacy to pass on to one's children. It reflects the truth that we serve a promise-keeping God.

Making Promises to God

Talk is cheap. It's easy to make impressive promises when we need someone's help. But how about when it comes time to deliver on those commitments? Do we waffle and make excuses, or do we fulfill our word?

God warned the Hebrews to honor their commitments, both to Him and to others (Num. 30:2). He reminded them that whatever came out of their mouths was binding. The Lord knows better than anyone how empty promises can be. After all, He probably hears more vows from desperate people than anyone else does: "If only You'll help me, God, then I'll do this or that." Scripture has some strong cautions to make about making promises:

1. *Watch what you say.* It is possible to swear an oath thoughtlessly, unaware of the commitment. But God says we are responsible for what we have said (Lev. 5:4–5; Prov. 20:25).

2. *Deliver on your promise.* It is no sin to abstain from making promises, but once made, a promise must be kept—and kept right away. To delay is to sin. It would be better to avoid making promises or vows at all (Deut. 23:21–23).

3. *Be careful of excessive devotion.* It is possible to feel so excited and happy before the Lord that we say foolish things that we cannot live up to. Rash talk, delayed fulfillments, and hasty promises are described as the "sacrifice of fools" (Eccl. 5:1–7). The mouth can be a cause of sin and a source of destruc-

tion in our lives, so it's worth heeding the warning, "Let your words be few" (Eccl. 5:2).

4. *Words are cheap; actions are what count.* We don't have to be Old Testament believers paying vows of animals and lands to fall into the sin of broken promises. As Christians, we can "talk a good game" of faith, yet live in a way that contradicts our words. Instead, we can "put feet on our faith" by such actions as caring for the poor and disadvantaged and showing fair treatment to others (James 1:27–2:26).

Promises Made Before God

In our day, guarantees and promises often mean nothing. Frequently the bold claims of advertisers and salespeople are more sizzle than steak. Likewise, a company's grandiose commitments about servicing the customer can suddenly vanish after one has taken home the product. And for some, marriage vows are little more than a formality, easily discarded when a more tempting prospect comes along.

Yet while many people may live by the motto that "contracts were made to be broken," God takes a different view when it comes to the commitments we make. He expects people to fulfill their vows and promises, especially the ones made before Him (Deut. 23:21–23). As the Law pointed out, there is no sin in not making promises in the first place (Deut. 23:22). But once we commit ourselves, we need to follow through. Otherwise we sin against God Himself.

Keeping our word is more than just good business; it is responsible living as a believer. Are you living up to the promises you have made in your marriage, family, work, and other areas of life?

*For more on this topic, see **SUPERVISION**, "Stick to Your Word," page 389.*

PROPERTY

How Much Is All?

When Jesus recited the greatest of the commandments (Mark 12:29–30), He repeated the word "all" four times. How much of "all" is *all?* When does a person "love the Lord God" as Jesus commanded? Is this limited to what one does for an hour or so on Sunday morning? If so, then worship takes up a mere 3,900 hours, or 0.9 percent, of one's waking life—assuming that one goes to church every Sunday for seventy-five years!

Christ is Lord of all of life—not just Sunday mornings, but weekdays, too, including time at work. Furthermore, He is Lord not only of our time, but of our money and possessions as well. Unfortunately, many Christians in the West have developed some dangerous attitudes in these areas that push God to the fringes of life.

One myth is that one-seventh of our time belongs to God. Some Christians speak of Sunday as "the Lord's day," a day for religion. And so it might be if Christians worshiped from sunup to sundown. But for most people Sunday worship means an hour-long service before an afternoon of televised sporting events. Thus the "day of worship" is reduced to less than one-twentieth of the week.

That was never what God intended. Originally, the seventh day or Sabbath rest was viewed as the completion of the week, not a break or separation from the work week. It was a time for review, celebration, and restoration. Yet by Jesus' day the Sabbath had become a day of legalistic ritual. Jesus sought to restore it as a day of compassion and worship (Luke 6:1–11; John 5:1–18).

Another myth is that ten percent of our money belongs to God. Some Christians believe that God expects them to give a flat ten percent of their income to church and other ministries. The reality is that on the average, American believers give only 2.3 percent of their income to religious or charitable causes of any kind.

The underlying principle that needs to be considered is that God has given us the ability to earn money, so actually all one hundred percent of our earnings belong to Him. We are called to manage our money—not just what we give away, but what we keep, too—according to His values. Tithing was never intended to replace obedience to all of God's commands (Matt. 23:23–24).

Paul says that "all things were created through Him and for Him" (Col. 1:16). Even our bodies are temples of God (1 Cor. 6:19). God calls us to serve Him in *all* that we do (Col. 3:17).

*For more on this topic, see **OWNERSHIP**, "A Tenant Mentality," page 286.*

PROPERTY RIGHTS
Property Security

Occasionally we injure people or damage their property unintentionally. What should we do when that happens? The laws concerning reckless injury to a neighbor's property (Ex. 22:5–6) set forth a principle of restitution that we do well to heed.

Of course, our modern situation is somewhat different because of our systems of insurance and other forms of financial aid. But the point remains that Scripture offers strong support for people's right to security in their lives and property.

PROPHECY
An Everlasting King from Bethlehem

Having denounced Judah's leaders (Mic. 3:1–12), Micah announced good news: an ideal, eternal king would someday rule over the land (Mic. 5:2). This unique hope offered a glimmer of light in the midst of the gathering darkness (Mic. 5:1; 7:8).

However, Micah's encouraging word also presented a bit of a puzzle. The hometown of this mighty prince would be tiny Bethlehem. Could this really be the place that would give birth to God's Chosen One?

Yes, as even the names employed by Micah reveal. The everlasting Ruler would come from Ephrathah ("Land of the Fruitful"), an ancient name for the land surrounding Bethlehem ("House of Bread"). We know from the New Testament that Jesus the Messiah was born at Bethlehem (Matt. 2:1; Luke 2:4–6), fulfilling Micah's prophecy (Matt. 2:6; compare John 7:42).

On the surface, Micah's prophecy seems to imply that the ruler was coming right away. Actually, seven centuries separated the prophet from the Ruler whom he was heralding. Yet in terms of God's timetable, the Messiah's appearing was just around the corner. Samaria would fall (c. 722 B.C.), and Jerusalem would soon follow (c. 586 B.C.). Decades later, Jews would begin returning to Palestine. Then the next major event in the Lord's plan would be the birth of Jesus in Bethlehem. He would bring everlasting salvation, not only to the people of Israel, but to the whole world (7:7, 18–20).

Beyond the Rivers of Ethiopia

If you are a Christian and of African descent, you may be interested in Zephaniah's prophecy that the Lord would restore His "dispersed ones" from "beyond the rivers of Ethiopia" (Zeph. 3:10). This was a remarkable promise, given the map of the world in Zephaniah's day.

As far as we know, Ethiopia represented the southwestern limits of Judah's knowledge of the world. The interior of Africa, "beyond the rivers of Ethiopia," was literally "off the map" for the ancient Israelites. It was uncharted territory for them.

To what, then, was Zephaniah referring? The context shows that he was anticipating the day when the Lord would bring people from the ends of the earth to form a holy people who would worship and serve Him with true hearts (Zeph. 3:9, 12–13). Among them would be people from "beyond the rivers of Ethiopia."

The prophet called this new people "the daughter of My dispersed ones" (Zeph. 3:10) and "the remnant of Israel" (Zeph. 3:13). Thus Zephaniah's vision seems to tie in with Jeremiah's predictions of a scattering of the Jews throughout the world, followed by an eventual restoration (Jer. 30:10–11, 18–22; 31:1–40).

Beginning in the sixth century, many Jewish colonies were established along the Nile and the Mediterranean coast of Africa. In fact, some have suggested that Zephaniah's prophecy pertains to the Jewish community in northern Abyssinia.

However, the prophecy may look beyond a strictly Jewish restoration. It seems to correspond with a prediction by David that Ethiopians would someday "stretch out [their] hands to God." Likewise, Isaiah envisioned a day when distant lands which had not heard of God would be recruited to send representatives to the Lord at Jerusalem—a vision that appears to correspond with the mission of the church.

As far as we know, Zephaniah himself had no idea of the vast tribes of people living "beyond the rivers of Ethiopia." But every time one of their descendents turns to faith in

Christ, Africa adds one more member to the "peoples [of] a pure language" who are called to serve the Lord "with one accord" (Zeph. 3:9).

Responding to Prophecy

Modern-day readers of the Bible have a variety of reactions to the prophetic passages of Scripture. Some find them fascinating and revealing, others puzzling and enigmatic. Some regard them as a clearly marked roadmap for the future, others as writings whose meaning generally remains hidden and mysterious. For quite a few, the question is, what difference do these prophetic passages make?

In thinking about an appropriate response to biblical prophecy, it helps to understand that the prophets were less concerned with prediction than with revelation. That is, whether or not a prophecy pertains to the future, it is significant because it reveals something that the Lord wants His people to know. It has been said that prophecy is not just foretelling the future, it is forthtelling the Word of the Lord.

Daniel's response to the prophecies of Jeremiah is instructive. When the kingdom of Babylon was taken over by the Persians, Daniel recognized that more than political change was involved; he perceived the hand of the Lord. Apparently he had access to Jeremiah's prophecies (Dan. 9:2). Perhaps he had a copy of the letter that Jeremiah sent to the exiles in Babylon, telling them to expect a seventy-year captivity (Jer. 29:10).

As Daniel reflected carefully on this information, he was moved to repentance (Dan. 9:3–7). This is a remarkable response, given other reactions that one might expect. For example, he could have hailed the fall of Babylon as the prophetic event signaling the end of Judah's captivity. He could have taken the information to Darius and demanded his people's immediate release, in the style of Moses. He could have become complacent in his duties, figuring that he was on his way home.

Daniel did none of these things. Instead he repented. His focus was not on dates and timetables, but on his own heart attitude toward the Lord. He was less concerned with how soon the captivity was going to end than with why it had to happen in the first place.

P

The question for him was not When are we going to return? but Are we ready to return?

Perhaps Daniel's response is worth emulating today. Prophecy can be a fascinating study, but the point is not to solve riddles; it is to hear what God has to say and respond accordingly. Daniel shows that one of our first responses to God's revelation should be repentance and remorse for sin.

The Purpose of Prophecy

Perhaps you think of prophecy as having mainly to do with predictions about the future. That's understandable, since prophets in Bible times sometimes foretold what would happen in the future (for example, Is. 7:14–17; 45:1–7; Jer. 28:12–17). However, the purpose of prophecy goes beyond merely informing people about things to come. There are at least two additional reasons why God spoke through the Old Testament prophets:

1. *To show that God is God.* A god who cannot reveal himself to human beings is unlikely to command much respect. But through prophecy, the Lord has made Himself known in compelling ways. For example, He demonstrated His omniscience by revealing to the Israelites what would happen in the future, something no pagan idol could do (Is. 48:5). He also demonstrated His power through the prophets in ways that left no doubt about who He is (1 Kin. 18:36–39).

2. *To proclaim God's Word.* Closely related to God's revelation of Himself through prophecy is His communication of truth that He wants people to know. Prophecy is often referred to as the "word of the LORD" (Is. 1:10; 28:14; 38:4); in fact, it is often prefaced by the words, "thus says the Lord GOD" (Is. 7:7; 10:24; 22:15). Thus prophecy is revelation from God. It brings to light things that would otherwise remain unexpressed.

The point of these revelations is not merely to inform, but to declare what is true, and then to tell people how they should live in light of what is true. Sometimes prophecy helps to warn people about the consequences of their actions, sometimes it encourages them when circumstances appear to be desperate. But whatever its effect on people, the purpose of prophecy is to proclaim God and His Word.

For more on this topic, see OCCULT, "False Forecasting," page 282.

PROSPERITY
Success and Prosperity

Who among us does not want to succeed in life and prosper in performing tasks? Joshua certainly did. As he prepared to lead his people into Canaan, God told him of a way to have success and prosperity (Josh. 1:8). Is there a secret to success here for all of us?

Some believe that God wants His children to prosper, especially materially and financially, and turn to Bible verses such as Joshua 1:8 to support their claim. But a careful reading of the text shows us some important qualifications:

1. *God made a conditional promise to Joshua and Israel.* Imagine opening someone else's birthday presents and claiming them. That's exactly what we would be doing with the promises that God made to His people Israel if we were to claim those gifts for ourselves.

God's words to Joshua are a case in point. The Lord was commissioning General Joshua to take the Promised Land. As part of His instructions He gave Joshua a condition followed by a promise: *If* you hold unswervingly to the Law, *then* you will succeed—succeed in terms of conquering Canaan and settling the land. It was a specific promise for a certain occasion.

2. *The emphasis was on the blessing that comes from obedience.* Still we might be tempted to use Joshua 1:8 in a general way to claim that God blesses people who obey Him. Thus success and prosperity would be claimed as rewards for good behavior.

But the emphasis of the passage is not on the blessing but on the doing of the Law. That is, following God's ways are inherently good for us. They are themselves the reward (Deut. 29:9).

For example, loving one's neighbor as oneself (Lev. 19:18) means having a neighbor to love. Not committing adultery (Ex. 20:14) means stability and trust in one's home life. The benefits come in the doing itself, not in some "payoff" that God gives for good behavior.

3. *The Bible does not promise earthly riches.* When we consider what the Bible has to say

about success and prosperity in general, we find no support for the idea that God has promised them to His children. Actually, we are discouraged from seeking material prosperity as an end in itself. God may allow us to have health and wealth, but we ought not to expect them (Eccl. 7:14).

If there is any "secret to success" in Joshua 1:8, it is this: true success means faithfully following God in the places where we find ourselves. Joshua's responsibility was to lead Israel into the land. What responsibilities has God given you?

Working Hard—For What?

As more than one financially successful person has discovered, it is quite possible to be materially wealthy but spiritually bankrupt. Likewise, many people have worked themselves to the bone their entire lives—for what? What do they have to show for all their labor? A nice home? A fancy car? The means to travel or spend all day playing golf? As one quickly discovers, possessions and prosperity by themselves are ultimately empty and unsatisfying. Unless a person's soul is alive and well, life is spiritual poverty, no matter how "well off" that person may be.

This was the truth with which the prophet Haggai challenged the Jews who had returned from Babylon (Hag. 1:6). They had started out like many people do in the aftermath of a tragic war—poor and lacking basic resources. At first they concentrated on rebuilding the temple. But within a year or two, they gave up on that project and became distracted with their own material needs. For the next decade and a half, they poured themselves into reestablishing an economy.

To a large extent they succeeded. They began to build paneled houses (Hag. 1:4), a sign of wealth. They replanted their fields and set up their vineyards again, which required a great deal of hard work. Yet Haggai pointed out the fundamental futility of all of their busy activity (Hag. 1:6). It was not that the work itself was wrong, but that it was inappropriate, given the disrepair of the temple. The people's priorities were all wrong. They were prospering materially, but starving spiritually.

There is a lesson here for people today, especially those who live and work in an afflu-

ent society. Jesus asked, "What will it profit a man if he gains the whole world, and loses his own soul?" (Mark 8:36). The problem is not gaining the world, but doing so at the cost of one's soul. That is too big a price to pay.

So in the midst of your hard work, are you building up your soul as much as you are your retirement account?

For more on this topic, see AFFLUENCE, "A Chicken in Every Pot," page 11.

PROSPERITY THEOLOGY

The Dangers of Prosperity Theology

Susan is a sales representative. She can make a big sale, but only if she mildly deceives the customer. She decides to tell the truth and she loses the sale. Should she expect God to honor her integrity by helping her make an even bigger sale in the future?

A contractor is deciding whether to award a job to Allen's firm or to another company. Allen really needs the business. So he prays at length that he will get the contract, and asks others to pray, too. Should he anticipate that God will somehow make the contractor award him the job? If not, should he expect God to arrange for other work to come along soon?

John and Joan are reviewing their finances. John has recently received a small bonus from his company, and they're wondering what to do with it. They finally decide to give ten percent of it to their church, and another ten percent to a mission. Can they expect God to bring them more money as a result?

Does God reward godliness with material blessing? Not according to 1 Timothy 6:5. In fact, Paul describes those who teach that as being "destitute of the truth." They are guilty of fostering a "prosperity theology." That's a dangerous view:

1. *It encourages perverted motives.* God wants us to seek Him for His own sake, not for a "payoff" of physical well-being or financial gain. The reward of loving obedience is a closer relationship to God (John 14:15–18, 21–23). He also wants us to be content with what He provides us, not greedy for more (John 6:6).

2. *It misinterprets God's deepest concerns for us.* If God wants us to have abundant material benefits, if He sees that they would be

in our best interest, then we can trust Him to supply them. Otherwise, such "blessings" would be harmful. God loves us too much to destroy us with what we don't need or can't handle.

3. *It misrepresents God's promises in Scripture.* The Old Testament offers plenty of promises about material prosperity and blessing. But for the most part, those benefits were offered to the nation of Israel, not to individual believers.

Furthermore, God's promises are always offered to those who truly love Him, seek His will, and obey Him from a pure heart. The Lord Himself is always the end to be sought; material benefits are never an end in themselves.

A final note: God has established certain "moral laws" that benefit anyone who adheres to them. (The Proverbs are filled with prudent advice that rewards those who keep them.) For example, paying taxes avoids the trouble, fines, prison terms, and public censure associated with nonpayment. In this sense it "pays" to obey the law. But we shouldn't expect special blessing for doing what God wants us to do anyway (Luke 17:7–10).

PROSTITUTION

Prostitutes in the Ancient World

Prostitutes like the woman whom Samson visited at Gaza (Judg. 16:1) were common in the ancient world. In fact, prostitution has been a part of religious rites since at least 3000 B.C.

In Babylon, Syria, Canaan, Arabia, and Phoenicia, intercourse with a temple prostitute was believed to induce fertility among humans, animals, and crops. The historian Herodotus tells of a Babylonian custom that required every woman to sit in the temple of the goddess Ishtar until chosen by a stranger for sexual relations. A desirous man would toss a coin in a woman's lap. If she accepted the coin and his sexual advances, she would have paid her obligation to the goddess and be free to return to her normal life.

In Israel, however, ritual prostitution was forbidden (Deut. 23:17). Laws existed to prevent priests from marrying prostitutes (Lev. 21:7), and income from prostitution could not be used to pay vows in the temple (Deut. 23:18).

Nevertheless, commercial prostitutes practiced their trade rather freely in Hebrew society. They were easily recognizable by their hairstyle, head ornaments, or perhaps a special mark on their foreheads. Their clothing and jewelry signaled their availability, and like streetwalkers everywhere, they frequented particular locales well known as meeting spots. Payments were accepted in money, grain, wine, or livestock. It was even common to accept a pledge until the payment could be fulfilled.

Samson retained his God-given strength and even used it to escape from the Philistines after spending the evening with the prostitute (Judg. 16:3), but that does not mean that God overlooked his immorality. Samson's next choice—to take up with the woman Delilah (Judg. 16:4)—was a poor decision that ultimately led to his betrayal and capture (Judg. 16:18–21). Samson's morality had reached a low point when he visited the prostitute at Gaza, and he soon was paying the consequences of ignoring God.

The Price of a Dog?

The Law's prohibition against offering "the price of a dog" for a vow (Deut. 23:18) raises two questions: Why would money from the sale of a dog be unacceptable, and why is this included in a passage dealing with ritual prostitution (Deut. 23:17)?

The answer to both questions becomes obvious when we learn that "dog" was a figure of speech for a male temple prostitute. The Canaanites routinely practiced prostitution as part of their religions, which were essentially fertility cults.

Despite God's commandment, the Israelites eventually engaged in ritual prostitution. For example, during King Rehoboam's days, centers of idolatry were set up and Scripture tells us that there were "perverted persons" in the land, a well known reference to male temple prostitutes (Hebrew, *qadesh;* 1 Kin. 14:24; compare 1 Kin. 15:12; 22:46; 2 Kin. 23:7).

As for actual dogs, they were not kept as pets by the Hebrews. Wild dogs roamed in packs outside the cities, waiting for refuse to be thrown out. However, other cultures such as the Egyptians held dogs in high honor and used them for hunting.

For more on this topic, see **GOD'S LOVE,** "Prodigal Wife, Prodigal People," page 174; **ILLEGITIMATE BIRTHS,** "Overcoming a Tough Start," page 215.

PUBLIC HEALTH

Public Health

When Israel entered the Promised Land, its priests functioned somewhat like a department of public health by examining suspected cases of "leprosy" in the community (Lev. 14:33–53). Many of the dietary restrictions in the Law make sense from the standpoint of modern public health. Even though these laws were ultimately religious in nature, they reveal God's concern for the health and safety of His people.

For more on this topic, see **HEALTH CARE,** "Preventive Health Care," page 194; **HYGIENE,** "Clean vs. Unclean," page 209.

PUBLIC OFFICIALS

(see Government Officials)

PUBLIC OPINION

Not Like Everybody Else

Many of us put a lot of effort into being like others around us. We also follow the thoughts of "opinion leaders" and the styles of celebrities. But God challenges His people not to be like everybody else.

In the Old Testament, God instructed Israel not to pattern itself after the nations around it. Instead, He called the Israelites to consecrate themselves (or set themselves apart from others) and be holy, for He, the Lord their God, was holy (Lev. 11:44–45).

One of the main ways that Israel was to be different was in its worship. Worship in the surrounding cultures included many rituals that Israel was not to follow. These forbidden practices were based on values that were not holy or rooted in a high view of God, people, or creation. Among them were:

- divination or magic;
- frenzied, chaotic dances;
- self-mutilation;
- ritual prostitution;
- sensuality and orgiastic fertility rites;
- human sacrifices; and
- sacrifices for the dead.

By contrast, Israel's worship was measured against God's holiness and defined the nation as God's people. There was no need to compete with other nations, cultures, or religions. The closing song at the end of Leviticus, Israel's manual for ritual and worship, says: "I will walk among you and be your God, and you shall be My people" (Lev. 26:12).

This promise became a watchword for Israel (for example, Hos. 1:9–10; 2:23; Jer. 31:33; Ezek. 36:28). Later, the church also came to define itself as belonging to God first and foremost, with a responsibility for holy worship and living (1 Pet. 1:13–16; 2:9–10).

Do you tend to conform to surrounding trends and pressures? Ask God for strength to be like Him, not like everybody else.

Standing for the Truth

Opposing popular opinion in favor of godly wisdom can make a person very unpopular. It is easier just to "go along to get along," especially when it seems as if everyone else is in agreement. It can be terribly hard to stand against the crowd. Yet Scripture shows that it is better when God's people honor His truth rather than the shifting winds of public opinion.

Four times God called Ezekiel to go against the popular wisdom of his day:

- In a vision, he was told to stand against twenty-five elders of Jerusalem who seem to have counseled the inhabitants of Jerusalem that the city would never be taken (Ezek. 11:2–4).
- He was told to denounce false prophets whose lies were rarely exposed because of a popular saying in Israel to the effect that all prophecies should be ignored because no one lived long enough to see them come to pass (Ezek. 12:21–25; compare Deut. 18:22).
- He was told to rebuke the people of Israel because they dismissed his prophecies as having to do with the end times rather than the imminent fall of Judah (Ezek. 12:26–28).
- He was told to oppose a popular point of view which held that the present generation was innocent, and that whatever troubles were coming were the fault of past generations (Ezek. 18:2).

P

Ezekiel's listeners were deluding themselves. False but attractive opinions had taken on the aura of truth. But Ezekiel spoke out against these delusions in the same manner that Peter spoke against the scoffers of his day who ridiculed the promise of the Lord's return (2 Pet. 3:3–13).

Telling people a hard truth includes the risk that they may reject you as a messenger, as well as your message. But is it truly loving to just go along with others, knowing full well that they are mistaken?

PUBLIC SCHOOLS
A Secular Education

Christians face increasingly difficult choices in the education of their children. Public policy in some nations has mandated that public education be secular. As a result, Christians who want their children to learn in an environment that honors biblical beliefs and values often wonder what to do with the public schools.

There are no simple answers to this issue, but the educational experience of Daniel may offer insight. As a young noble, he was deported to Babylon and placed in a program to learn the "language and literature of the Chaldeans" (Dan. 1:4). This curriculum exposed him to a number of practical skills such as mathematics and glassmaking. However, it also involved many things that were utterly opposed to God: casting spells, sorcery, astrology, and other occult arts (compare Dan. 2:2); myths, legends, and lore from ancient Chaldea; and prayers and hymns to the numerous gods of the Babylonians. It was a system of study based on a worldview that was polytheistic and, from the standpoint of the Jewish Law, idolatrous.

The purpose of this three-year program was to prepare Daniel for a lifetime of employment in a pagan government. Daniel is a model for how Christian young people today should prepare to live and work in a secular society. Notice the following important points about his experience:

1. *Daniel grew up in a godly Jewish home.* This suggests that education in the ways of God must begin in the home. Formal education may or may not support and expand on that foundation, but it can never replace it.

2. *Daniel had God-given abilities of intelligence and discernment.* The Bible makes it clear that Daniel was a bright person with a superior intellect (Dan. 1:4). Perhaps this says to parents today that they should take into account the talents and God-given bent of their children as they choose among educational alternatives. The morals and values of the educational environment, important as those are, are only one consideration among many.

3. *Daniel's Babylonian education was secondary, not elementary.* Daniel was probably about fifteen or sixteen years old when he was deported to Babylon. Thus his training in the king's service was preparation for a specific career, not unlike many vocational, college, and graduate programs today. Daniel brought a worldview with him to Babylon— one that had been formed on the basis of the Hebrew Law. This foundation enabled him to evaluate what he learned by comparing it against God's absolute truth.

4. *Daniel was exposed to Babylonian culture, but he did not succumb to that culture.* He was able to maintain his distinctive beliefs and values. Even after a lifetime in the service of pagan kings, his faith was as rock-steady as ever (Dan. 6:4–5, 10, 22). The challenge for Christian young people today is to remain *in* the world, yet not become *of* the world (John 17:15–16). There can be no modern-day Daniels if Christians compromise their fundamental beliefs as soon as they are exposed to competing worldviews.

5. *Daniel did not reject Babylonian culture out of hand.* While Daniel objected to eating the king's food (Dan. 1:8), he apparently did not object to reading the king's books, listening to the king's instructors, or thinking about the king's ideas. It seems that Daniel was able to reject what was unworthy while retaining what was useful. Clearly he not only survived, but thrived.

6. *Daniel did not function alone.* Three other youths of like-minded faith shared the disciplines and challenges of the Babylonian captivity (Dan. 1:6). Going against the grain is easier to do in partnership with other believers than by oneself.

These observations encourage Christians

today to participate in the culture, even though many aspects of it may be opposed to God. While much is worthless, much is not. Wise believers will learn to discern the difference and act accordingly.

For more on this topic, see CHILDREN, "Protecting Your Heritage," page 52.

PUBLIC SERVANTS

(*see* Government Officials)

Q

QUARANTINE

Leprosy

Leprosy (Lev. 13:12) was one of the most feared diseases in the ancient world. Lepers suffered from a slowly progressing, ordinarily incurable skin disease that was believed to be highly contagious and therefore greatly feared. As a result, anyone who appeared to have leprosy, even if the symptoms were caused by some other condition, was banished from the community.

True leprosy is caused by a bacterium that spreads across the skin, creating sores, scabs, and white shining spots. The most serious problem, however, is a loss of sensation. Without the ability to feel, lepers injure their tissue, leading to further infection, deformity, muscle loss, and eventual paralysis. Fortunately, modern medicine has all but eliminated the disease.

The Old Testament Law was quite detailed in its instructions regarding recognition and quarantine of leprous persons. Priests became the central figures for diagnosis, care of patients, and taking sanitary precautions to protect the rest of the community. The Law required that a leper be isolated from the rest of society (Lev. 13:45–46). Infected persons were required to wear mourning clothes, leave their hair in disorder, keep their beards covered, and cry "Unclean! Unclean!" so that others could avoid them. Any contact would defile the person who touched a leper.

Sometimes lepers were miraculously cured, as in the case of Moses (Ex. 4:7), his sister Miriam (Num. 12:10), and Naaman (2 Kin. 5:1, 10).

In the New Testament, Jesus intentionally healed lepers as a sign to vindicate His ministry. On one occasion He healed ten of them, but only one returned to thank Him (Luke 17:11–15).

R

RACISM

A Radically Changed Worldview

In Galatians 1:13–17, Paul recounts his dramatic confrontation with Christ on the Damascus road and his subsequent conversion (Acts 9:1–30). Imagine the emotional strain that placed on Saul (as he was called at the time): Jesus was alive! What members of the Way (the early Christians) had been saying about Him was all true! And Saul had killed many of them! What a shattering experience for one "advanced in Judaism" and "exceedingly zealous for the traditions" of his fathers (Gal. 1:14).

Perhaps that's why God made Saul blind for three days. He had a lot to sort out after

meeting the risen Lord. It's not easy for someone to suddenly revise the entire theological basis on which he's been living, especially as a respected leader. No one wants to admit he's been wrong. No wonder Saul spent much of the time in prayer.

But God not only intended to change Saul's theology; He was determined to transform his bigoted view of the world. At the root of Saul's intense hatred of the Christian movement might well have been a belief that it would destroy Judaism by mixing it with foreign, Gentile elements.

Imagine Saul's shock, then, when Ananias came to tell him that God had chosen him to bear His name to the Gentiles (Acts 9:15; 22:14–15; 26:16–18)! Unthinkable! Jews like Saul, who were utterly committed to holy living by all the laws and traditions of Judaism, had nothing to do with Gentiles (Acts 10:28). No wonder it took Saul years to reevaluate his perspectives and bring them in line with the heart of God for the world (Acts 9:26–30; 22:17–21).

Paul's experience forces us to ask: What attitudes of prejudice keep you from recognizing God's heart for the whole world? What attitudes of bigotry operate where you live or work? Do you in any way challenge that thinking, or do you just keep silent—or worse, go along with it or even promote it? Would God be able to use you to bear His name to people from a different ethnic heritage?

"No Dealings with Samaritans"

Hatred between Jews and Samaritans was fierce and long-standing. It dated to the fall of the northern kingdom of Israel in 722 B.C. The victorious Assyrians deported 20,000 Israelites, mostly from the upper classes, and replaced them with settlers from Babylon, Syria, and several other nations. These foreigners introduced pagan idols and intermarried with the Hebrews, creating an ethnically mixed population.

When the Jews of Judah returned from the Babylonian captivity, they met resistance from the Samaritans as they tried to rebuild the temple, Jerusalem, and the rest of their society. They looked down on their northern cousins because of their mixed marriages and idolatrous practices. Soon, permanent walls of bitterness had been erected by both sides. By Jesus' day, the hostilities were so severe that the woman at the well was astonished that Jesus would even speak with her. As John explained, "Jews have no dealings with Samaritans" (John 4:9).

There are countless modern parallels to the Jewish-Samaritan enmity—indeed, wherever peoples are divided by racial and ethnic barriers. Perhaps that's why the Gospels and Acts provide so many instances of Samaritans coming into contact with the message of Jesus. It is not the person from the radically different culture on the other side of the world that is hardest to love, but the nearby neighbor whose skin color, language, rituals, values, ancestry, history, and customs are different from one's own.

Jews had no dealings with the Samaritans. With whom do you have no dealings?

Reaching Out to All

By the time Paul wrote his letter to the Christians at Rome, Gentiles were probably becoming a majority of believers throughout the church. Jews had less and less influence theologically, culturally, or politically. Gradually—and tragically—the attitudes of pride and prejudice with which Jews had looked down on Gentiles were coming back to haunt them, as Gentile believers began to turn away from their Jewish brothers.

In Romans 9–11, Paul pleaded with his Gentile readers to remember that God has not forgotten Israel. God made promises to the nation that He cannot forsake (Rom. 11:29). Furthermore, Gentiles have no room for arrogance: they were not originally included among God's people, but were allowed in, like branches grafted onto a tree (Rom. 11:17–18).

Paul saw the possibility of a church divided, with Jewish and Gentile believers going their separate ways. If that happened, Gentiles would ignore the Jewish community altogether rather than show compassion and communicate the gospel so that Jews could be saved. That's why here, as elsewhere, Paul challenged believers to pursue unity in the body of Christ and charity among the peoples of the world.

Are we as believers today carrying out that exhortation? Unfortunately, the legacy that we've inherited is not encouraging. Had the church wholeheartedly embraced Paul's teaching, it would not have kept its tragic silence or participated in some of the great evils of the past two thousand years. In fact, many of them probably could have been avoided, or at least resisted, had Christians paid careful attention to Romans 9–11.

We need to ask: What are the current challenges to the ethnic, racial, and cultural attitudes of believers? What tragic evils are currently operating that we need to be aware of and actively resisting? God's desire is clear—to have mercy on all (Rom. 11:32). Does that describe our heart?

For more on this topic, see **ETHNIC DI-VERSITY,** *"Jews, Gentiles, and Jesus," page 132;* **PREJUDICE,** *"A History of Enmity," page 315; "Acting Like a Neighbor," page 316; "Perpetual Enemies of Israel," page 317.*

RAPE

Supposed Safety in the City

Popular opinion today tends to assume that cities by nature offer a lower quality of life than do suburbs, small towns, or rural areas. In fact, some people have made getting out of the city a goal of their lives. But the Bible does not endorse the idea that cities are inherently evil, or that life is necessarily better away from the bright lights of the urban landscape.

Actually, Scripture seems to hold cities to a higher standard of justice and morality than rural areas. For example, the Old Testament Law held that if a woman was raped in the country, the man who raped her was liable for death (Deut. 22:25–27). But if a woman was raped in the city, she, too, was liable (Deut. 22:23–24).

The logic behind this seeming double standard was based on the assumption that a woman in the city must have consented to the sexual act, since she could have (and should have) called for help. In the city, with neighbors all around, such a call was expected to be heard and heeded. Thus the law of rape assumed that city neighbors were beneficial and responsive. They were to stand up for the laws of God.

Are you standing up for godly ways where you live and work? Are you a good and godly neighbor to people around you who call out for help, protection, and justice? Whether you live in a highly populated metropolitan area or a quiet little town, God wants you to fill that place with His presence. He wants you to do something about evil, not just walk away and let it destroy people whom He loves.

Unbridled Sexual Passion

Personal pleasure makes a good slave but a poor master. When our primary focus is on self-gratification, the results can be destructive, not only for us, but for everyone around us (Titus 3:3; James 4:1–4). Scripture makes it clear that living for our own pleasures is both unacceptable and unhealthy.

The outcome of Shechem (Gen. 34:2) illustrates this point. When young Shechem saw the beautiful girl Dinah, he allowed his lust to rule his behavior, and raped her. Like an animal, he let his hormones run his life, so sexual gratification became more important than Dinah's dignity as a person.

By contrast, Scripture challenges God's people to exercise control over their sexuality (1 Thess. 4:3–4). This often means delayed gratification, which is good because waiting helps to set things in perspective. As humans we are not just a bundle of physical urges that have to be satisfied. Granted, biological needs such as food, sex, and sleep are important. But when we allow these to run our lives, they tend to become vicious addictions that destroy us.

Two great poems in Scripture address the theme of love—the Song of Solomon and 1 Corinthians 13. In the Song of Solomon, the writer repeats three times the wise words, "Do not stir up nor awaken love until it pleases" (Song 2:7; 3:5; 8:4). The message seems to be: Wait!

Like a free-spirited horse, sexual passion can be powerful and beautiful, but to keep it from running away it needs to be fenced in by commitment, discipline, and service toward one's mate. Our sexuality is not our own; it is a gift from God to be treasured and used for His glory (1 Cor. 6:18–20).

REBELLION

Foghorns Ignored

Along the seacoasts in many parts of the world, foghorns bellow day and night, warning approaching ships away from dangerous rocks and reefs. Remarkably, seagulls frequently build their nests on these loud, moaning alarms, seemingly unperturbed by their monotonous blasts.

In Zephaniah's day, the people of Judah had grown deaf to the periodic warnings of the Lord concerning the imminent shipwreck of their nation. Occasionally He took extreme measures to shake them out of their complacency, to no avail. For example, He "cut off" entire nations and cities (Zeph. 3:6), including Israel, as an example of the judgment waiting for them. He felt that perhaps this would cause His people to "receive instruction" before it was too late (Zeph. 3:7).

Yet despite the Lord's every effort, Judah remained stubbornly "rebellious and polluted," refusing to receive correction (Zeph. 3:1–2). Princes, prophets, judges, and priests persisted in their evil ways, oblivious to God's urgent warnings of danger ahead (Zeph. 3:3–4).

Is this a picture of your life? Do you willfully ignore the "foghorns" through which God speaks—the circumstances He brings your way, the calamities that befall you and others around you, and above all the clear, straightforward instruction of Scripture? Many people today—even entire nations—turn a deaf ear to the warnings of God. But they do so to their peril. In the end, the Lord will have His way (Zeph. 3:9).

For more on this topic, see **EVIL,** *"God Limits Evil," page 134.*

RECKLESSNESS

(*see* Foolishness)

RECOGNITION

The Lord Knows

Some people spend their whole lives working in obscurity, with little to show for their efforts despite years of toil. The Hebrews fit that profile after trudging through the wilderness for forty years (Deut. 2:7).

The nation's decades-long detour on the way to the Holy Land resulted from a crisis of faith at Kadesh Barnea. Everyone twenty years of age and older was condemned to die in the wilderness, except for Joshua and Caleb (Num. 14:29–30). Thus, many who had been children when Israel came out of Egypt were now in their forties, fifties, and perhaps even sixties. Yet what had they done with their lives but "wander" through desert wastes, waiting for their parents' generation to expire?

Thus Moses' word that "the LORD your God . . . *knows* your trudging through this great wilderness" (Deut. 2:7, emphasis added) must have come as a tremendous encouragement. God had not forgotten this new generation. He was mindful of the "work of [their]

hand," which amounted to the task of surviving the wilderness journey.

In the same way, God is mindful of you if you have been toiling away for years with little or no recognition, through tough times and good times. He knows what you have been through and, whether you have been recognized or not, has been there with you every step of the way.

RECONCILIATION

Payback

Sometimes good happens to us when we least expect it. Sometimes we receive far more good than we deserve.

When Jacob learned that Esau was approaching (Gen. 32:6), he was terrified. Here was his older twin brother—the brother that he and his mother had cheated out of his rightful portion of the family inheritance (Gen. 27:1–29)—coming toward him with four hundred men. Jacob assumed the worst. He cried out to God for mercy and deliverance (Gen. 32:9–12) and sent his own extended family and his possessions to his brother's "welcoming committee" (Gen. 32:13–23).

Yet to Jacob's surprise, Esau ran to him, embraced him, kissed him, and wept (Gen. 33:4). This kind of grace was completely unexpected. It proved disarming to Jacob, and he could only respond by pressing his gifts on Esau, perhaps as a small remuneration for the lost inheritance (Gen. 33:8–11).

Like Jacob, we, too, were extended grace and forgiveness when we least expected it—or deserved it. In providing salvation through Christ, God offers unmerited favor to people who actually deserve judgment (Rom. 3:23–25; 5:15–17; James 4:1–6).

Jacob insisted on paying back his brother, and Esau finally accepted. But we can never pay back God for what He has done for us. However, we can respond to His gift of love by showing that same kind of love to others, especially as God teaches us how (1 John 3:11–17).

We Are Family!

In Galatians 3:28, Paul emphasizes that three major social distinctions no longer matter in Christ:

- Ethnicity: "neither Jew nor Greek."
- Socioeconomic status: "neither slave nor free."
- Gender: "neither male nor female."

First-century culture was deeply divided along these lines. So was the church. But Paul stressed, "You are all *one* in Christ Jesus" (emphasis added).

Christians have become children of God through faith, which means we are all in the same family. We are no longer divided by ethnicity, social status, or gender, but have become brothers and sisters in God's family.

One powerful symbol of that new unity is baptism (Gal. 3:27). As part of the baptismal ceremony, a believer affirms the lordship of Christ and his or her commitment to a new way of life. Paul is possibly quoting from a first-century baptismal creed (Gal. 3:28) to remind us of our promise to "put on Christ," not in word but in deed.

In the early Christian communities this meant that both Gentiles and Jews could exercise their spiritual gifts. Both slaves and masters could pray or prophesy. Both women and men could enjoy full membership in the body. "Christ [was] all and in all" (Col. 3:11). The breaking down of traditional barriers wasn't just a future hope. The early church worked to make it a reality.

Which brings us to the question: What walls of ethnicity, status, or gender divide believers today? Are we willing to model reconciliation between different and even antagonistic groups? If not, then is our church truly a sign of God's kingdom, or merely a human institution?

REFUGEES

Blessings of a City

Among other ways, God has aided His people by providing them with a city (Ps. 107:4–7, 36). For the Jewish refugees coming out of Babylon, a city to dwell in meant a steady supply of food, water, and other "goodness" from the Lord.

Modern-day refugees in places around the world are likewise inclined to give thanks to God for cities in which to dwell. To them, the city represents a job, shelter, food, medical aid, and political protection, among other "goodnesses."

The city is a blessing of God. Can you think of ways in which the city has been God's gift to you?

Jesus, a Refugee

Have you ever thought of Jesus as an intercontinental political refugee? He was, according to the Christmas story in Matthew 2:13–15. Through His parents, the Asian-born Jesus sought political asylum in Africa, avoiding the infanticide ordered by King Herod, the ruthless ruler of Palestine.

The text doesn't say where the family stayed. Perhaps they were absorbed into the one million Jews estimated to have lived in Alexandria at that time. Wherever they ended up, we know that Jesus, perhaps close to two years old at the start of the journey (Matt. 2:16), spent at least some of His formative years in Egypt, displaced from His homeland. And when the family migrated back to Palestine (Matt. 2:22–23), they did not settle in a privileged neighborhood, but in Nazareth in rural Galilee.

Jesus can identify with the many migrating peoples of the world today. He is an international Savior who knows the pain of forced migration. That is indeed good news for those who have been displaced by natural disasters, famine, or political unrest.

Songs of the Refugees

Psalm 137 summarizes the question that perplexed not only the exiles of Judah in Babylon, but all of the Jews who were quickly being dispersed throughout the ancient world: How can we worship and serve the Lord in a foreign land? (Ps. 137:4).

Cut off from their homeland, they were without their magnificent temple. They had no king to guide them, no high priest to offer sacrifices, no ark of the covenant to signify God's presence. Spiritually speaking, they were cast adrift in the world without their familiar landmarks to guide them.

No wonder the people of Judah sat down and wept by the rivers of Babylon (Ps. 137:1). Asked by their captors to sing songs of Zion, all they could think about was how their beloved city was now laid waste (Ps. 137:3). Consequently, they sang a song—but not one that

R

was expected. They sang a sorrowful, vengeful song calling for curses on the Babylonians who had destroyed Jerusalem (Ps. 137:8) and on the Edomites who had celebrated the city's fall (Ps. 137:7).

However, despite the sentiments expressed in this psalm, several positive things resulted from the Jews' dispersion. Lacking a temple, they invented the synagogue (see Mark 1:21). They also collected their writings, which eventually led to the canonization of the Old Testament. And because they were forced to learn new languages and adapt to foreign cultures, they eventually translated the Old Testament from Hebrew into Greek, the common language of Christ's day.

Thus necessity became the mother of invention for the Hebrews. Many such gifts from the Lord came into the world because God's people were forced to "sing the Lord's song in a foreign land."

The Problems of Repatriation

The return of refugees to their native lands is a growing problem for many modern nations, including Israel. Some of the displaced would like to resettle in their homelands, but cannot; others are reluctant to return at all, for a variety of reasons. The latter was a problem that Ezra and the other Jewish leaders faced as they led their people back to Palestine (Ezra 2:1).

No one knows exactly how many inhabitants of Judah were carried into exile in 586 B.C. A census in Uzziah's time counted 310,100 men of military age (2 Chr. 26:12–13), so the actual population of Judah under Uzziah, including women, children, elderly, and the priests and Levites, was probably in the millions and likely remained so until the time of the exile.

The Babylonians killed thousands of Jews during their successive campaigns against Judah, but they probably took tens if not hundreds of thousands back to Babylon. However, of those exiles, only 42,360 returned under Sheshbazzar (Ezra 1:11; 2:1, 64). Apparently many if not most of the Jews preferred to remain in Babylon.

And why not? After seventy years of captivity, many probably had grown accustomed to life in Mesopotamia. If they had been young

or unborn at the time of the exile, they had few emotional ties or memories of the homeland. Even the few adults who could remember Judah knew that their capital lay in ruins, its temple was destroyed, and the fields of their parents had either run wild or been taken over by others.

Sheshbazzar, Zerubbabel, Ezra, Nehemiah, and the other leaders had to contend with these kinds of psychological barriers to repatriation. The fact that they succeeded in rebuilding the temple, repairing the walls of Jerusalem, and resettling the land is a tribute to their perseverance and steadfast faith.

The Reluctant Refugee

Terrified of the Babylonians after the fall of Jerusalem, and fearful of the Ammonites after the assassination of the appointed governor Gedaliah, the survivors of Jerusalem made preparations to flee to Egypt (Jer. 41:16–18). Before departing, however, they made a pretense of asking Jeremiah for a word from the Lord (Jer. 42:1–3).

Despite Jeremiah's warnings to remain in the land (Jer. 42:9–22), the people insisted on leaving (Jer. 43:1–7). Apparently Jeremiah and his secretary Baruch were compelled to go along, reluctant though they were. Jeremiah may have spent his final days in Egypt, for there is no record that he returned to Jerusalem.

*For more on this topic, see **RESETTLEMENT**, "God Has His People Everywhere," page 339.*

REJECTION

A Response to Rejection

As believers called to proclaim the message of Christ, our role is not to change people; that's a job for the Holy Spirit (John 16:8). Instead, we need to give a full and careful disclosure of what God has done for us, realizing that it might result in rejection.

Paul knew very well that following Christ would lead to hostility and rejection (Acts 28:19). But in responding to criticism and defending himself legally, he made sure that his judges had the benefit of a full explanation, even though it took a special meeting that lasted all day (Acts 28:23). Yet even that careful effort did not completely set the record straight or convince all of his hearers (Acts 28:24, 29).

Scripture records a long tradition of God-sent messengers whose words fell on deaf ears. For example:

- Isaiah, who was told ahead of time that he was being sent to people who would not listen to him (Is. 6:9–12);
- the Lord Jesus, who also came to those who would not receive Him (John 1:11; 12:37–43);
- Barnabas and Paul, who turned to the Gentiles at Pisidian Antioch after Jews rejected their message (Acts 13:44–46);
- Paul, who turned to the Gentiles at Corinth after Jews rejected his message (Acts 18:5–6) and who grieved over his countrymen's rejection of the gospel (Rom. 11:7–10).

How should we respond to rejection? The key issue is to make sure that we give our hearers a chance to consider Christ. We must offer them as faithful and convincing a presentation as possible. It may mean hostility and personal cost, but should we expect to suffer any less than Christ did (Phil. 1:29–30)?

RELATIONSHIPS

Love God, Love People

Jesus said that the entire Law rests on two preeminent commandments: loving God and loving one's neighbor as oneself (Matt. 22:36–40; compare Deut. 6:5; Lev. 19:18). The Ten Commandments (Deut. 5:6–21), which summarize the Law, show how this is true and speak to ten practical ways in which the duty to love God and others is fulfilled.

The first four commandments (Deut. 5:6–15) speak to loving God:

- no other gods before me,
- no carved images to worship,
- no taking the name of the Lord in vain, and
- observe the Sabbath.

The last six commandments (Deut. 5:16–21) speak to loving other people:

- honor your father and mother,
- no murder,
- no committing adultery,
- no stealing,
- no bearing false witness, and
- no coveting.

Loving God and loving others are interdependent. We can't do one without doing the other (James 2:10). The more we love God, the more involved we must become in serving the needs of others. And if we want to love others, we need to ground that love in the love of God.

Down through history, Christians have often tended to emphasize one side or the other—sometimes even to the virtual exclusion of the other. But the Ten Commandments do not allow for an either/or appoach to love. God's people must love Him *and* love others. The two cannot be separated (1 John 4:7–16; 5:2–3).

Wisdom Through Relationships

Perhaps you are wondering how you can develop the kind of wisdom described in Proverbs. The place to start is by cultivating friendships with wise people (Prov. 13:20). Wisdom is not a set of facts to be memorized, but a set of life skills to be mastered. Relationships are the key to making that happen.

A beautiful illustration of this principle can be found in the relationship of Moses with his father-in-law Jethro. Moses was heading toward burnout when Jethro took him aside. He not only warned the younger man that he was in imminent danger of collapse, but wisely counseled him to delegate authority (Ex. 18:17–27). As a result, Moses developed an organizational structure that enabled him to lead Israel for the next forty years. That system might never have come about had Moses not had a relationship with a wise man like Jethro.

But it is not enough to choose wise friends. Proverbs also warns us about friendships with those described as "fools". The point is not to try to avoid all contact with foolish people, which would be impossible. Rather, knowing that the company we keep can have a profound influence on us, we should avoid becoming overly familiar with unwise people. We should not listen to their advice or emulate their habits.

As you reflect on your network of relationships, whose friendship are you cultivating?

R

Are they people who possess wisdom? Or are you building relationships with those who scoff at and reject God's ways? Be careful, because the wrong set of friends can lead to disaster (13:20).

For more on this topic, see COMMUNITY, "God Is a Community," page 74; FRIENDSHIP, "Kindred Spirits," page 164; PROBLEMS, "'Problem' People," page 319; RESPECT, "Attention and Respect," page 340.

RELICS

(*see* Symbols)

RELIGIOUS ROOTS

Researching Your Religious Roots

The Book of Hebrews shows that God uses history to bring people to Himself. In the case of the Jews, God used generations of people and centuries of political events and religious symbolism to prepare the way for Christ. If you are Jewish, you have much to celebrate as you ponder God's sovereignty and grace in using your ancestors the Hebrews to bless "all the families of the earth" (Gen. 12:3; 22:18; Acts 3:25–26; Gal. 3:8).

However, God's participation in history extends far beyond the Jews. In fact, every believer is indebted to God's grace for superintending the circumstances that brought the gospel to him or her.

Have you ever traced the path between Jesus' proclamation of the gospel in the first century and your reception of it today? Do you know the religious roots of your own family and ancestors? Why not examine that heritage, either on your own or with a small group of believers? Doing so will help to personalize the gospel to your own life and experience. Here are some suggestions for getting started:

Begin by collecting as much information as you can about your genealogy. Widespread interest in genealogical studies in recent years has made this process easier. Many books, articles, libraries, data bases, organizations, seminars, and other resources exist to help you. In addition, you'll want to talk with your parents, grandparents, or other relatives who might have information about your family and its heritage.

As your knowledge about your ancestry grows, you can begin to piece together some idea of your religious heritage. Be careful not to jump to conclusions or make too much of sketchy details. You probably won't be able to come up with any definitive answers, but you can at least gain an appreciation for how God has worked in your past and what it took for Him to bring you to faith.

Of course, you may discover elements of your family's religious history that run counter to the gospel. But that, too, is important to know. You need not agree with what others believed or did in the past, but it's worth understanding the bolt of cloth from which you've been cut.

As you evaluate your data, consider these questions:

- Is the gospel recent in your family's history, or has there been a long legacy of participation in the faith?
- If Christianity has been a part of your cultural or religious roots, what distinguishes your family's expression of Christianity from other traditions within the faith? Why? Where did that tradition come from, and how and why did your family identify with it?
- What beliefs and practices among your religious roots would you disagree with or even denounce? Why?
- What has been the reception of your family to your personal faith in Christ? Why? How might the past contribute to their response?
- How might your understanding of the past affect the way in which you present the gospel to any unbelievers among your relatives?
- What is the story of how the gospel traveled from the apostles in the first century to your life today? What response can you make to God for superintending this process?

For more on this topic, see ROOTS, "Playing Ethnic Games," page 352.

RENEWAL

Starting Over

People and organizations periodically need revitalizing in order to gain fresh, new insights and momentum. Things are no different when it comes to faith. For believers, the process of starting over is sometimes called reformation, renewal, or revival. Starting over is a major theme of Judeo-Christian history. Some examples of spiritual renewals and revivals recorded in Scripture are:

1. *Jacob (Gen. 35:9–15).* After Jacob was reunited with his estranged brother Esau, one of Jacob's daughters, Dinah, was raped by a Canaanite (Gen. 34). The incident and the revenge that followed shocked Jacob into realizing how far his family had departed from loyalty to God. So he led them back to Bethel for repentance and renewed worship of the Lord (Gen. 35:1–4). In the process, God gave Jacob a new name—*Israel* (''God strives,'' Gen. 35:9–15). Thus Jacob and his family made a fresh start as God's people.

2. *Josiah (2 Kin. 22–23).* Josiah, the boy king of Judah, followed the reigns of his father Amon and grandfather Manasseh, two of the southern kingdom's worst kings. Nevertheless, Josiah initiated powerful reforms that included repairs to the temple (2 Kin. 22:1–7). During the process, workmen found the Book of the Law, possibly a portion of Deuteronomy. When it was read to Josiah, he tore his clothes to indicate his sorrow over how far his people had fallen away from the Lord. That led to a major program of purging Judah of its idols and restoring true worship in the temple (2 Kin. 23:1–27).

3. *The Early Church (Acts 11:26).* As faith in Jesus spread among first-century Jews, some of the new believers arrived in Antioch, where they did something new: they offered the gospel to a group called the Hellenists,

RELIGIOUS ROOTS

WOW! ONE OF MY ANCESTORS WAS BABY JESUS' CRADLE!

ROOTS

JONNY HAWKINS

R

Greek-speaking Jews not originally from Palestine (see Acts 6:9). The result was a multi-ethnic church that led the way in sending messengers throughout the Roman world with the good news of God's grace (Acts 13:1–5). However, concerns were raised by some Jewish Christians who were worried about non-Jews coming into the church. Eventually a major summit meeting was held to look into the issue, and a statement was produced that opened the church to all who believe in Christ (Acts 15:1–35). Thus the church, which was itself a new movement, experienced a new beginning as a result of expansion outside of Judea.

How about you? What patterns in your personal life, family, work, church, or community have grown dull or perhaps even sinful with the passage of time? Do you need to reinvent, reform, or renew certain habits, relationships, or systems in order to make a fresh start that would honor God and benefit people? How might you bring about needed change?

REPUTATION

Skeletons in the Closet

Some people go to great lengths to hide their background. They feel ashamed of certain details about their origins which they regard as "skeletons in the closet," ugly facts that they feel would harm their reputation if brought out into the open.

God rebuked the people of Jerusalem and the surrounding country by revealing three "secrets" about their past that called into question their proud self-image. The Lord said that:

- They were born to Canaanite parents (Ezek. 16:3). The Lord was insulting the people of Judah by suggesting that their culture was as sinful and given over to "abominations" as that of the Canaanites, whom their ancestors had dispossessed (Lev. 18:24–30; 2 Kin. 17:7–19).
- They were abandoned at birth (Ezek. 16:4–5). The point of this image seems to have been that the Hebrews were not descended from a great and mighty nation, such as the Egyptians or Babyloni-

ans. When they came into existence, no one really wanted them but God.

- They were adopted (Ezek. 16:6–7). In His sovereign grace, the Lord chose Israel as His people. God revealed Himself to Abraham, a native of the Sumerian city of Ur in southern Mesopotamia (see Gen. 12:1), and He appointed Abraham and Sarah to be the ancestors of a people through whom He would bless "all the families of the earth" (Gen. 12:1–3).

Someone with backgrounds like these would have been considered by the Israelites as having a checkered past. These facts would have raised questions about the person's qualifications as a Hebrew. But the Lord was raising these issues to challenge His people's arrogant self-righteousness.

The humiliating facts about Jerusalem's past are basically no different from the "skeletons in the closet" of any Christian today. We, too, were born outside the family of God. We, too, were once lost apart from His grace. We, too, have been adopted in God's family. Therefore, we, too, need to evaluate our lives and consider whether we are living with humility and gratitude, and honoring the Lord with our attitudes and behavior. Otherwise we raise questions as to whether we really belong to God.

For more on this topic, see ETHNIC CLEANSING, "A Legacy of Genocide," page 129.

RESENTMENT

Change Brings Out Resentment

Nehemiah faced growing opposition as progress on the wall of Jerusalem moved forward (Neh. 4:7). Who were these opponents and why were they so upset?

1. *Sanballat* (Neh. 4:1, 7; 6:1) was probably descended either from a family of Israelites that had been left behind when the northern kingdom was captured by Assyria (722 B.C.), or from the racially mixed Samaritans that resulted from Assyria's resettlement of the area (2 Kin. 17:24).

2. *Tobiah* the Ammonite (Neh. 4:3, 7; 6:1) is referred to as an "official," which may mean that he was a Persian appointee or possibly Sanballat's deputy. Apparently he was

joined by other Ammonites in opposing the reconstruction.

3. *Geshem* the Arab (Neh. 6:1) is known mostly from extrabiblical records. These suggest that he was the king of Kedar, a nation of nomads in northern Arabia. He and his people (Neh. 4:7) served the Persians by controlling the caravan routes between Palestine and Egypt.

What all of these people had in common was that they had remained in Palestine during the period of Judah's exile. This helps to explain why they were so angry (Neh. 4:1, 7). For decades they had lived in the political, cultural, and spiritual wasteland that the Babylonians created in Judah. The best and brightest of the Jews had either been killed during the capture of Jerusalem, or else deported to Babylon. That left only the poorest and least capable people behind (2 Kin. 24:14–16; 25:11–12).

Thus it was natural that over the years, strongmen such as Sanballat, Tobiah, and Geshem would come to dominate the region. The Persians used these bureaucrats to maintain order, but did little to help redevelop the territory. Then Nehemiah entered the picture. Unexpected and uninvited, he represented change being imposed from the outside. His bold plan to rebuild the wall offered long-term benefits, but it also threatened the immediate interests of the local bosses.

People who live in ghettos and other "throwaway" communities often feel seething resentment against those who have left them behind, those who oppress them, and those who are supposed to protect them but don't. When an outsider comes in with sweeping plans and promises, that resentment can boil over into outright hostility and even violence. Nehemiah offers a case study in how community developers might go about working with people—adversaries as well as advocates—to effect lasting change that actually benefits residents.

For more on this topic, see **JEALOUSY**, *"Are You the Older Brother?" page 230;* **MURDER**, *"Murder on the Job," page 274.*

RESETTLEMENT
God Has His People Everywhere

As you look at the world today, you may feel that the tide of evil is rising, while the number of people committed to godly faith and righteousness is on the decline. It may seem to you that control of things has slipped into the hands of those of have no fear of God. But in evaluating the state of the world, consider this: God has His people everywhere, in places and positions that most of us would never imagine.

That was true for the Jews deported to ancient Babylon. Most of them were resettled along the Chebar River, a canal northeast of the city of Babylon. It is probable that they were conscripted for labor on Nebuchadnezzar's vast building projects in the nearby city.

This left the Jews free to live in their own communities, but dependent on the Babylonians for work. In other words, it left them poor. Nor did they have much reason to hope for a change in their circumstances. They lived in ghettos with few freedoms, limited resources, and few advocates with the government.

But Daniel was one of those advocates. We do not know how much contact he had with the Jewish exiles. They may have been unaware of him; but he was not unaware of their situation. Perhaps he had them in mind as he urged Nebuchadnezzar to change his ways by "showing mercy to the poor" (Dan. 4:27). In doing so, the king would be showing mercy to Daniel's own people, who were also God's people. Thus God was at work on behalf of the Jews, even though they were completely unaware of it.

Daniel's strategic placement is a reminder that God never leaves Himself without a means of accomplishing His purposes. He has a way of placing the right person where we would least expect it. This is cause for God's people to have hope. No matter what "hot spot" in the world we may point to, the likelihood is that God has a believer or two strategically placed in the center of it. They may have limited control over what happens, but their presence can promote much good and avoid much evil in ways that we can hardly imagine.

R

*For more on this topic, see **COMMUNITY DEVELOPMENT**, "The Ten Percent Solution," page 75.*

RESPECT

Attention and Respect

Perhaps what people want more than anything else from those in authority is attention and respect. Abigail got both from David, who heeded her words and respected her person (1 Sam. 25:35).

Abigail was a wise woman. Anticipating trouble because of her husband's foolish words, she seized the initiative by going to David herself as an intermediary (1 Sam. 25:18–31). She took along a peace offering, admitted that her husband was wrong, and pointed out what David stood to gain or lose by the course of action he was pursuing. She commanded attention and respect, and David had to take her seriously.

The king was wise in doing so. He could have ignored her counsel in his determination to pay Nabal back for his discourtesy. Likewise, David could have disregarded Abigail because she was a woman. But he proved himself to be an honorable man by hearing her out, evaluating her words carefully, and then heeding her advice. Furthermore, he rightly praised her for doing him a favor by coming to him.

The exchange between David and Abigail holds important lessons for relationships today. If we want others to pay attention to us, we need to act and speak in a way that commands respect. On the other hand, as others approach us, we need to listen to what they have to say and heed their counsel when it is wise.

RESPONSIBILITY

Chosen for Responsibility

God told the Israelites that He was driving out the Canaanite nations from the Promised Land (Ex. 34:11), but it's important to interpret this promise in light of the covenant that preceded it (Ex. 34:1–10).

The covenant established the Israelites as God's chosen people. However, chosenness did not imply natural superiority. As Moses pointed out, Israel was "a stiff-necked people" who needed pardon from iniquity and

sin (Ex. 34:9). Indeed, God chose the Hebrews not because of anything special about them, but because of His own love and sovereign will (Deut. 7:7–8).

Then why were the Israelites told to drive out the Canaanites from the Promised Land, and in some cases to destroy them entirely? Because "chosenness" in the Bible means responsibility. Israel's God-given responsibility was to establish the reign of God in the land. Thus, exterminating the "enemy" was a religious campaign, not a war of "ethnic cleansing." The point was to remove the Canaanites' idolatry and pagan practices. Canaanites who submitted to the God of Israel and surrendered were to be spared, as Rahab was (Josh 2:8–13; 6:17).

Given the racial and ethnic strife in the world today, often arising from religious roots, it's important to understand what it means to be "chosen" by God. To be "chosen" does not make one better than one's neighbors, but more responsible to treat them as God would treat them.

Shared Responsibility

There is an interesting tension in the relationship between God and His people. One the one hand, we human beings are fully responsible and accountable for planning, organizing, and directing our lives. Yet on the other hand, we need to be fully aware that God is accomplishing His purposes in, through, and sometimes despite our plans and efforts (Prov. 16:9).

Scripture often affirms this shared responsibility between us as human beings and God as the sovereign Lord of the universe. For example, the New Testament exhorts us to "work out" our salvation—that is, to make responsible choices on a day-to-day basis in light of our eternal salvation; yet it adds that God is at work in us "both to will and to do for His good pleasure" (Phil. 2:12–13).

Are you fulfilling your part of your relationship with God? Are you making wise choices based on what He has said in the Bible? Are you trusting Him to fulfill His part?

*For more on this topic, see **AUTHORITY**, "A Symbol of Authority and Responsibility," page 27; **EXCUSES**, "Aaron's Excuses," page 138.*

REST AND RECREATION
A Day of Rest

When God "rested on the seventh day from all His work which He had done" (Gen. 2:2), He was modeling for humanity His intention for a weekly day of rest. Clearly He did this for the sake of Adam and Eve (and for us), because God Himself does not tire or need to "rest," as people do. In what sense, then, did He "rest" from His labors, and in what sense should we "rest" from ours?

The term *Sabbath* has the root meaning of "cessation." On the seventh day God ceased His work of creating the world (Ex. 20:8–11). However, He did not cease His work of sustaining and maintaining the world (Ps. 145:15–16; Col. 1:17). This distinction helps to clarify the significance of the Sabbath, a day which God set aside (or sanctified) and blessed. His clear intention was that people would emulate Him by pausing from their labors—the exercise of their dominion over the creation (Gen. 1:28–31)—for one day out of seven.

Was this day of "rest" given merely as a day off? No, one of the most important purposes of the Sabbath was to provide a day for believers to worship and focus on God, as individuals and communities (Is. 58:13–14). It is not that we are free to ignore God on the other six days; *every* day belongs to Him. But by designating one day as a special opportunity to come before the Lord, we demonstrate our dependence on Him as Creator and our obedience to Him as Lord.

This means that the Sabbath—or in New Testament times, the Lord's Day—was not intended simply as a "day off" to catch up on chores or pursue leisure activities. Not that these are wrong, but the point of the day is to "stir up love and good works, not forsaking the assembling of ourselves together, as is the manner of some, but exhorting one another" (Heb. 10:24–25).

There is an obvious tension here regarding how we should treat the Lord's Day as a Christian Sabbath. In deciding the issue, it is worth remembering that Jesus pointed out that God established a day of rest for the sake of people, not the other way around (Mark 2:27). Sabbath observance is not to become a legalistic obligation. In fact, conditions occasionally require work on the Sabbath: an ox can get stuck in a ditch, and must be gotten out (Luke 14:5). Likewise, human beings have basic needs even on Sundays. Of course, the spirit of Sabbath observance implies that we should take steps to prevent finding ourselves routinely stuck in the ditch with the ox on the Sabbath, and that we use our abilities on the other six days to meet the needs of people.

When God rested on the seventh day and set it aside, He did not intend to turn Sabbath-keeping into a strangling rule. The Sabbath was meant to provide true freedom—freedom from turning work into tyranny, and freedom to enjoy fellowship with God, our neighbors, and our loved ones.

Slow Down

Fast food. Fast-forward. Fast lane. HOV lane. Laser lane. Jet plane. Instant coffee. Instant photos. Instant gratification. We live in the Culture of Now. We want what we want *right now*. In fact, we want it yesterday.

Job's world was not quite so hectic. Still, his life had been full of family, festivities, worship, and work until he lost it all, along with his health. After lengthy suffering and deep depression, he heard God through his friend Elihu, saying, "Stand still and consider the wondrous works of God" (Job 37:14). It was a much-needed pause for reflection.

God beckoned David to the same kind of reflective rest stop in the midst of chaos and turmoil. Even as "nations raged" and "kingdoms were moved," the Lord entreated the king to "come behold the works of the LORD," and to "be still and know that I am God" (Ps. 46:6, 8, 10).

Maybe you've heard the old adage, "Stop and smell the roses." There is great gain in taking notice of something which you had part in making, owning, or using. It can remind you that you are part of something much larger your own life. By appreciating the wonders of this world, you can begin to revel in the amazing truth that you are loved by its Creator.

So slow down if you are moving so fast that you're about to disintegrate! Wouldn't it be wonderful if your epitaph could read, "He (or she) cared!" rather than fulfilling Bildad's

R

ominous warning: "The memory of him perishes from the earth, and he has no name among the renowned" (Job 18:17).

Take a Year Off!

Perhaps you dream of taking an extended time off from your job. Imagine the entire country putting work on the shelf for twelve months! That's what God told Israel to do every seven years (Ex. 23:10–11). All work on the land was to be suspended during the sabbatical year. The people were to rest from their ordinary work. Bondservants were to be set free (Ex. 21:2–3; Deut. 15:12–18), and debt payments were to be suspended (Deut. 15:1–3).

How would the people survive during that twelve-month holiday? God promised to bless their harvest during the sixth year, making it produce enough for three years—enough to last until the harvest of the eighth year. However, that gift would be given on one condition: that Israel had to faithfully follow the sabbatical year regulations (Lev. 25:18–22). We have no record that they ever did.

The Law's emphasis on rest from work challenges the nose-to-the-grindstone lifestyle of today's compulsive workers. What do your patterns of work and rest say about your trust in God's provision for you? If you had been an Israelite in Old Testament times, would you have lived as if you believed God's promise to provide, even if you rested one day each week (Ex. 23:12) and one year out of every seven?

The Human Machine

The Law made provision for people and animals to have one day of rest each week (Ex. 23:12). God knew the makeup of His crea-

FISHING VACATION

tures. Neither human nor beast was capable of working endlessly like a machine.

Yet today, when more people work with machines than with animals, there's a tendency to start seeing people as machines rather than human beings with a need for rest and refreshment. This trend is accelerated by a common view of the world that reduces everything to the material and ignores the spiritual side of life.

The Law's amplification of the fourth commandment, which concerns the Sabbath (Ex. 20:8–11), reflects not only a godly view of work, but a godly view of humanity. We are more than just sophisticated pieces of technology. We are living souls made in the image of God (Gen. 2:7). Therefore, as He rested from His work, so should we.

Weekly Liberation

The commandment to keep the Sabbath holy (Deut. 5:12) doesn't mean that the other days of the week and their activities were not holy. The Sabbath was to remind Israel that human beings are finite, dependent creatures of God.

As people, we have a strong tendency to exalt ourselves and our accomplishments. Indeed, sometimes we practically turn them into gods—or idols, to borrow an Old Testament expression. In today's terms, we might say that our pursuits easily become addictions.

For the Israelites, the Sabbath enforced a day of rest and worship in the weekly cycle to keep their focus on the Lord rather than on themselves and their accomplishments. In a similar way, the weekly observance of Sunday as the Lord's Day can help Christians set boundaries on who and what we worship and make central in our lives.

Do you allow God to liberate you each week from the bondage that work so easily becomes in our society?

Why Not Rest a While?

When the Twelve returned from their preaching tour (Mark 6:7, 12, 30), Jesus took them aside for a bit of rest and relaxation (Mark 6:31). In doing so, He modeled a principle that many of us today could stand to practice more—the principle of rest.

Rest may seem to be the last thing we need, given industry's obsession with productivity and our culture's reputation as a "leisure society." But God wants us to adopt His values, not the values of our culture. One thing He values is leisure. He values work as well. But rest is something God Himself does (Gen. 2:2), which means that rest is good in and of itself. In fact, God actually commanded His people Israel to rest (Ex. 20:8–11).

Have you determined how much time you actually need to spend at work? Have you carefully considered how to balance your time and energy between workplace commitments and your family? Are you perhaps working too much, not because the job demands it, but because you won't trust God to supply your needs through a reasonable amount of work? Perhaps you need to take Jesus' advice: "Come aside . . . and rest a while."

Wisdom at Work and Play

Proverbs personifies wisdom as a companion and associate of the Lord when He created the heavens and the earth. Wisdom was both a master craftsman and a delightful colleague in enjoyable, even playful work (Prov. 8:30–31).

It is easy to see wisdom's mastery as a worker. Every aspect of creation reveals infinite insight and genius (Prov. 8:27–30; compare Ps. 19:1–4; 104:24). But wisdom is not all work; it has a playful side as well. At the creation, wisdom was God's daily delight, always rejoicing (literally "playing") before the Lord. Apparently God enjoyed both the product (Gen. 1:31) and the process of creation. Like any act of creativity, forming the universe was play as well as work.

RESTITUTION

Making Restitution

Some modern lawmakers, educators, and others concerned with human behavior often make proposals based on the idea that people are basically good. In Leviticus, we see that God held a more realistic view.

For example, He knew that there would be cases of dishonesty among His people. So instead of excusing the offenses as the result of bad upbringing and proposing more education as a preventative, He instituted a system of sacrifices for the sin of the offender and restitution to the offended party (Lev. 6:1–7).

It's easy to see why such laws were needed. Israel was a refugee nation traveling through a desert. Every day the people faced limited resources, so they may have found it easy to rationalize theft and deception, just as some people today regard poverty as an excuse for breaking the law. Then as now, temptations were many, and sooner or later people succumbed.

To address this problem, God called sin sin and devised a guide for forgiveness and restitution. If someone deceived another in a transaction, the perpetrator was required to sacrifice a ram and to repay the loss with twenty percent interest.

The guiding law behind restitution was that of loving one's neighbor as oneself (Lev. 19:18). Centuries later, Christ reaffirmed this as the guiding principle for moral and social issues (Matt. 5:43–44; 19:19).

For more on this topic, see **CRIME,** *"A Law for Criminals—and Their Victims," page 95;* **STEALING,** *"The Starving Thief," page 382.*

RESTRICTIONS

(*see* Limitations; Maturity)

RESULTS

A Craving for Results

Authority figures often see their main task as making things happen and—above all—getting results. Indeed, many leaders want results so badly that they sacrifice other important values in a mad scramble to "get it done."

Saul lost his kingdom because of his craving for results. He wanted to defeat the Philistines so much that he offered a burnt offering, which it was not his place to do (1 Sam. 13:8–14). He was determined to do things in his way and according to his timing rather than God's. So God found a man "after His own heart" (1 Sam. 13:14), a man who would get results, but do so by following God's plans.

Actually, getting results is not a leader's main job. The primary task is to create a climate where others can make things happen and accomplish goals. That climate has a variety of dimensions: technical (task-oriented), behavioral (relationship-oriented), political (power-oriented), and spiritual (God-oriented).

If a leader concentrates on the immediate task at the expense of the other dimensions, the outcome may be short-term results but long-term losses. Saul could have avoided the loss of his kingdom by waiting for Samuel, trusting God to defend him and his warriors against the chariots and horses of the Philistines.

RETALIATION

(*see* Revenge)

RETIREMENT

A Spiritual Retirement Account

One of the most well-known investments today is the individual retirement account (IRA). By investing tax-free money over several decades, one can amass a tidy sum by the time of retirement. One of the keys to this strategy is the principle of compounding: profits from the investment are reinvested so that what starts as a small balance grows at a steadily increasing rate.

Proverbs says that a spiritual IRA is available to us—the advice of wise counselors. By heeding their suggestions, we can arrive at our "latter days" with a wealth of wisdom (Prov. 19:20).

For more on this topic, see **AGING,** *"From Success to Significance," page 13.*

REVELATION

Aha!

Have you ever puzzled over a difficult problem, only to have a sudden flash of insight? "Aha!" you may have exclaimed with a sense of satisfaction. Job came to the end of his trials with an "Aha!" experience (Job 42:1–6).

Job's moment of insight came after God plied him with questions to which Job had no answers (Job 38–41). God's point was not to humiliate Job, but to reveal Himself as the all-powerful, all-wise God whose ways are unimpeachable. It was when he finally "saw" God (Job 42:5) that things suddenly began to make sense for Job. He felt a sense of wonder after having a dazzling encounter with the living God.

This is clear from the language Job used to describe his reaction. After hearing from God, Job realized that he had been uttering "things too wonderful for me, which I did not know." The Hebrew word translated "know" suggests intimate knowledge of the sort that comes by personal experience. Job was admitting that all of his high-sounding talk had been so much blabber; he hadn't really known what he was talking about. He had been pontificating on things that only God could understand (compare Ps. 139:6).

Job's response to this unexpected encounter with God was a sense of utter and absolute humility (Job 42:5–6). The words, "I abhor myself" might be translated, "I reject what I have spoken"; "I cast away my words"; "I despise or disdain them." It's as if Job had written a journal or a book to detail and interpret his experience (Job 19:23–24), or a legal brief to make his case before God (Job 31:35–37). But upon realizing who God was, he threw the book away.

Job gave up his pretensions to wisdom and comforted himself "in dust and ashes," a common symbol of mourning or humility. He was satisfied with the humble knowledge that his sufferings were all part of the purposes of God—even if he could not understand those purposes with his finite mind.

Perhaps you are encountering a problem in life that seems to make no sense. Like Job, may you have something of an "Aha!" experience with God. It is comforting to know that some day, all mysteries will find their meaning in Him. Right now, such knowledge may be "too wonderful" for us to grasp.

"If Only I Could See Him"

How many times have you heard people say words to the effect that "I'd believe in God if only I could see Him"? According to this common excuse, a person's unwillingness to put wholehearted trust in God is actually God's fault: He hasn't revealed Himself plainly. If He would, such people would instantly believe in Him and start following Him.

But the experience of the people of Israel at Mount Sinai gives the lie to this sort of reasoning. If ever there was an occasion on which God revealed Himself to human beings, it was at Mount Sinai. For many days,

God's presence descended on the mountain, producing a spectacular display of thunder, lightning, trumpet sounds, and smoke. In fact, the sight was so overwhelming that the people trembled with fear (Ex. 19:16; 20:18). Clearly they were convinced that they were standing before God Himself.

Yet did that cause them to believe in Him? No, it may have verified His existence for them, but it did not change their hearts. In fact, while the Lord's presence was still hovering over the mountain, the Israelites fashioned an idol and began worshiping it in riotous abandon (Ex. 32:1–6)! What an incredible rejection of God!

History contains ample evidence of God's revelation of Himself to humanity. The creation reveals His existence (Ps. 19:1–4; Rom. 1:19–20), the Bible reveals His will (John 5:46–47), and Jesus Christ has revealed His Person (John 1:14; 14:7–11). If these and countless other attesting signs are not enough to persuade someone to turn to the Lord in faith and obedience, probably nothing else will—not bolts of lightning, not the thunder of His voice, not even someone rising from the dead (Luke 16:31).

Learning from Every Angle

Our understanding of God comes from three levels of His self-disclosure: the general revelation of Himself through nature, which He created (Ps. 19:1–6); the special revelation of His Word (Ps. 19:7–11); and the particular work of God in one's individual life (Ps. 19:12–14). After looking first at the firmament of God's world and then at the Word which is the foundation of that world, David focuses on his own infirmities in his inner world.

Psalm 19 is typical of many psalms that look back and forth, up and down, outward and inward (compare Ps. 139). David realized how much he needed God to provide an integrated understanding of life. We can gain similar insight by using these multifocused psalms first to consider God's glorious universe, then to apply the spiritual disciplines of confession, Bible study, and prayer to our own lives, and finally to bear public witness to what we have come to know, see, and experience of God above, God around us, and God within.

The Glory of the Lord

God is spirit (John 4:24) and therefore has no body and is invisible to the human eye (John 6:46; Col. 1:15). How then can God make His presence known? In Old Testament times, He often revealed Himself by showing His "glory" (Hebrew, *chabod;* 2 Chr. 7:1).

The "glory of the LORD" was a term that the Hebrews used to describe the way in which God showed that He was present through visible signs such as thunder, lightning, clouds, or fire (for example, Ex. 3:1–6; 19:16–19; Num. 12:5; 2 Chr. 5:13–14). Keep in mind that the Hebrews were not responding to natural phenomena like these by calling them God, as some suppose. Rather, the invisible God was revealing Himself through means that humans could perceive.

When Christ was transfigured, He revealed God in perfect human form. Thus John could write that "the Word became flesh and dwelt among us, and *we beheld His glory,* the glory as of the only begotten of the Father" (John 1:14, emphasis added). And when the Holy Spirit came upon the first believers in the Upper Room, He revealed His presence through tongues of fire and other signs (Acts 2:1–4).

Two other ways that God reveals His glory are through the creation (Ps. 19:1) and through His people (Eph. 1:12; Col. 1:27). As believers in Christ, we are temples of God, and He wants to fill us with His glory (1 Cor. 6:19–20).

REVENGE

Overcome Evil with Good

Scripture is straightforward: no believer should avenge himself on others (Rom. 12:19). Why? Because God has reserved vengeance to Himself.

What, then, can you do to those who hurt you? You must do them good, not evil (Rom. 12:21). If you do them evil, you will yourself be overcome by evil. You can't be too careful when it comes to vengeance. One of Satan's favorite tactics is to lure someone into doing evil by providing a "good" excuse for it. And retaliation feels so appealing.

But Scripture challenges you to overcome evil, both in yourself (the will to retaliate) and in those who harm you (by doing them good). Doing so will "heap coals of fire" on the heads of your enemies (Rom. 12:20). In other words,

you may magnify their sense of guilt when they see that their evil against you is met by your good toward them. Indeed, their guilty conscience may drive them to repentance.

For more on this topic, see MANSLAUGH-TER, "Places of Refuge," page 254.

REVERENCE

(*see* Fear of God)

REVOLUTION

A Tax Revolt

Complaints about high taxes are nothing new. In ancient Israel, the tax burden became so great that the citizens of all but one tribe revolted, killing the chief tax collector and forcing King Rehoboam to flee in haste (1 Kin. 12:18–19).

Actually, many factors led to the division of the kingdom. But the crisis that touched off rebellion was Rehoboam's decision to add to the people's already high taxes (1 Kin. 12:13–14). Under Solomon, heavy taxes were required to pay for his numerous building projects and lavish lifestyle. While Israel's international trade was brisk and aliens were conscripted for relatively cheap labor, the Israelites themselves apparently lived under a heavy yoke (1 Kin. 12:4).

Rehoboam, perhaps intending to outdo his father, rejected the advice of his father's counselors (1 Kin. 12:6–8) and raised taxes. As the account makes clear, this was all part of God's plan to judge Solomon and the people for turning to idolatry (1 Kin. 11:9–13, 29–39; 12:15). The kingdom was split, and eventually both parts were carried away into exile.

What do we learn from this incident? Certainly it illustrates what can happen when government places excessive tax levies on its people. It also shows what can happen when a nation turns away from the Lord.

Jesus told His followers to give Caesar his due (Matt. 22:17–21), and Paul explicitly urged Christians to pay their taxes (Rom. 13:6–7). However, believers can get involved in efforts to make government more responsive to its citizens, more efficient in the use of its revenues, and more responsible in its fiscal policies. By doing so, God's people today can help to head off the kind of anger, frustration, and injustice that led to Israel's downfall.

*For more on this topic, see **CONSPIRACY**, "Plots and Coups," page 87.*

REWARDS

Establish the Ground Rules

God clearly defined rewards for obedience (Lev. 26:3–13) and punishments for disobedience (Lev. 26:39). (He also promised to remember His people when they repented from disobedience, Lev. 26:40–45). In doing so, He modeled two important principles for the effective use of authority:

1. Leaders need to establish and clearly communicate what they expect others to do and to refrain from doing; and

2. Leaders need to clarify the consequences for fulfilling or not fulfilling those expectations.

If you exercise authority over others, have you made it clear to them what you expect? Have you been consistent in rewarding and punishing in accordance with those expectations?

What's in It for Me?

Do you ever wonder what you're going to get out of following Christ? Peter and the other disciples wondered. "We have left all and followed You," Peter told Jesus. "Therefore what shall we have?" (Matt. 19:27). In other words, "What's the payoff? What's in this for me?"

Paul describes some of the "payoff" for believers in Ephesians 1:3–14. Because so much of it lies in the future, in another mode of existence, the language is strange and hard to understand. But in Ephesians 1:11 he mentions an inheritance that is coming to us. What is it that we are going to receive "in Christ"?

Simply this: all that God has prepared for Christ in "the fullness of the times" is going to be ours as well (Rom. 8:15–17). This includes salvation from sin (Heb. 1:14), everlasting life (Matt. 19:29), and the kingdom of God (Matt. 25:34). In fact, we will inherit God Himself.

Is this just wishful thinking? No, God is already giving us glimpses of that inconceivable future. The Holy Spirit lives inside us as a guarantee of things to come (Eph. 1:14). He "seals" us, assuring that we remain in God's family and do not lose our inheritance. And while we move toward that day, He works within our lives to make us like Christ. Paul describes what that looks like in Ephesians 4–6.

*For more on this topic, see **COMMITMENT**, "Do You Fear God for Nothing?" page 70; **DUTY**, "Doing Your Duty," page 117; **LEADERSHIP**, "Missing Out on the Payoff," page 243.*

RICHES

(see Wealth)

RIGHT AND WRONG

Made in His Image

Human beings are a distinctive creation. We are unlike all other creatures because we were created in the image of God (Gen. 1:26–30; 5:1; 9:6; compare Eph. 4:24; Col. 3:10). Scripture never describes any other creature or being as bearing God's image.

This fact—that we are like God in a unique way—has extremely important implications, among them:

- That as humans we can have a true knowledge of God—a knowledge that transcends mere information about God to actually *knowing* Him and *relating* to Him as a Person (John 17:3).
- That we can understand meaning and purpose in life in light of His nature (Ps. 89:15; Eccl. 12:13–14; Col. 3:10).
- That we are moral beings with the capacity to do what is right or wrong—right or wrong as defined by God's own nature and according to His expressed will (Rom. 1:17–18; Eph. 4:24).
- That we are capable of being holy—that is, separated from evil—if we truly know God and obey Him (Eph. 4:24; 2 Pet. 1:3–4).

Two Paths to Consider

Poet Robert Frost wrote of having to choose between two roads that diverged in a yellow wood. Frost wrote that he did well to choose the less frequently traveled road. About three thousand five hundred years ago, the psalmist wrote something similar as he described two paths on which one could live life: the way of the ungodly and the way of the righteous (Ps. 1:1–2). The way one chooses makes all the difference.

Psalm 1 is like much of the wisdom literature in the Old Testament in that it draws a

R

sharp contrast between good and evil, right and wrong, godliness and ungodliness. The choice is one or the other; there can be no middle ground. Thus Psalm 1 presents a proverbial fork in the road in which we must make moral choices today that have long-term (indeed eternal) consequences.

The way of the ungodly will not withstand judgment, while the way of the godly is blooming and productive, resilient, and prosperous. The question is, which road are you taking? If you find yourself

- paying more attention to the advice of those who do not believe in God than of those who fear Him;
- behaving pretty much as unbelievers do; or
- making cynical statements about God and the things of God,

then beware! You may already be far down the road of unrighteousness. If so, then do whatever it takes to turn back, because the end of that road is destruction.

For more on this topic, see **CONVICTION,** *"Values in the Workplace," page 90.*

RIGHTEOUS INDIGNATION

(*see* Anger)

RIGHTS

Rights

We live in a time when it seems that everyone is concerned about exercising their "rights." Indeed, society has become somewhat polarized as various groups form around their perceptions of rights that they feel they are being denied. The more intense the struggle to achieve those rights, the more social conflict seems to escalate.

Paul indicated to the Galatians that before God, no one has any rights; whatever rights humanity once had have been forfeited as a result of sin. To bring this situation home to his readers, Paul used the metaphor of a slave (Gal. 4:1–3), an image that the Galatians probably knew well, as the Roman Empire depended heavily on slave labor (see Rom. 6:16).

The Galatians had become children of God, but before that they were in bondage to sin, to the "elements of the world" (Gal. 4:3; compare Col. 2:8, 20). As slaves to sin, they had no rights before God. He owed them nothing. They belonged to sin, which they were forced to serve. Emancipation from that position had to come from a source other than their own power, ingenuity, or morality.

Such is the plight of all sinners before God—helpless and hopeless (Rom. 3:23, John

RIGHTS

3:19–20). But just as God gave life, resources, and responsibility to humanity in the beginning (Gen. 1:26–2:4), so now He has given Christ His Son to rescue or "redeem" people from sin and grant them all the privileges of adoption into the family of God (Gal. 4:4–7). No one deserves that, which is why receiving Christ's new life and the rights therein is truly a gift.

If as believers we have received these treasures from God, then we ought to let others know that the same opportunity is available to them.

RIOTS

Cities on Fire

Next time you see a city going up in flames, consider the word of the Lord through Isaiah. The prophet warned the people of his day that the real cause of cities on fire (Is. 1:7) is not politics, but sin (Is. 1:4).

The cities of Judah were going to burn, Isaiah said, not just because they would be invaded by an aggressive superpower, Babylon, but because sin covered the nation from head to toe (Is. 1:6). The heart and soul of God's people were sick with sin. For example, the people had turned their backs on orphans, widows, and other down-and-outers (Is. 1:16–17, 21–23; 3:13–15). That kind of proud, oppressive behavior would bring about punishment (Is. 1:8; 3:9).

Was there any way to avert economic and military disaster? The issue was a spiritual one; therefore, what was called for was not more sacrifices (Is. 1:11–15), but true, nationwide repentance (Is. 1:18–20). In addition, moral leadership was needed, because genuine renewal and reform could happen only if the nation's leaders honored God's ways.

Isaiah's vision of burning cities was intended as a wake-up call to Judah. But it also serves as a warning to societies today. Ultimately, the potential for our cities to explode and burn down does not come from outside forces, but from an internal enemy—sin. Scripture challenges all of us—city residents, government leaders, even disinterested bystanders—not to remain indifferent to the evils in our society.

RISK

Here We Go Again

How easy it is easy to forget the lessons of the past. As Israel again came up to the Promised Land, two of the twelve tribes made a proposal to Moses. They wanted to settle right where they were—in the verdant pasture lands east of the Jordan river—rather than enter the Promised Land. But Moses rebuked them (Num. 32:6–15).

The memory that burned in Moses' mind was the incident at Kadesh Barnea forty years earlier (Num. 13–14). At that time, the Israelites had resisted the challenge of entering the land. They listened to the timid report of the ten spies and determined to either die where they were or return to Egyptian slavery (Num. 14:1–4). Only two of the spies saw opportunity in the call of God to enter the land and dispossess the Canaanites.

As a result of this lack of faith, Israel spent forty years wandering in the Sinai wilderness until all of those who had rejected God's promise had died.

In reminding Reuben and Gad of this history, Moses seemed to be shaming them into sticking with their brothers, as if to say, "Here we go again! You are just like your forefathers, resisting God's opportunity" (Num. 32:6–8). Fortunately, the two tribes listened to him and a compromise was arranged (Num. 32:16–24).

Risk-Takers

Do you have a built-in resistance to risk? Many people do. Settling down in comfort seems to have a lot more attraction than venturing out in faith, for faith often involves risk. Yet Scripture is full of examples of God blessing risk-takers who trusted His promises:

- Abraham and Sarah left Ur to go to an unknown land. As a result, their descendants were greatly blessed (12:1–9).
- Ruth joined her mother-in-law in returning to Israel, where Ruth's ethnic heritage would be a drawback. Yet she ended up marrying well and even became the grandmother of Israel's most famous king and an ancestor of the nation's Messiah (Ruth 1–4).
- Elizabeth and Mary endured the problems of awkward pregnancies and gave

R

birth to John the Baptist and Jesus, respectively (Luke 1–2).

• Ananias was told to pay a visit to the chief enemy of the Christian movement. Because of Ananias' obedience, Saul, the persecutor of believers, became Paul, the apostle to the Gentiles (Acts 9:1–22).

The lives of the heroes of the faith challenge us not to miss out on great opportunity just because the end is not guaranteed and safety is not assured.

Taking a Professional Risk

Personal crises can cause us to break with our peers and cultural traditions in order to seek help. Jairus (Mark 5:22) risked his job as the ruler of the synagogue by turning to Jesus. This leader was well known in his town, and his actions were carefully watched by people. But he was desperate to save his daughter's life, so he went to Jesus as a last resort.

Jesus was a controversial rabbi. Some Jews followed Him, but many others took great offense at His teaching (Mark 3:6). So when Jairus fell at Jesus' feet, he must have known that some in his synagogue would sharply criticize him.

When Jesus arrived at Jairus's home, He took the daughter by the hand. In doing so, He risked a violation of Jewish custom. By touching her dead body, Jesus was making Himself ritually unclean. Moreover, by touching a woman, He was doing something that Jewish men, and particularly rabbis, were told not to do.

Jairus risked his secure, prestigious job because he loved his daughter more than his career. Jesus risked His reputation as a teacher in order to bring the daughter back to life.

Whom do you love enough to risk your career for?

For more on this topic, see **FAILURE,** *"Go Ahead and Try It," page 139.*

RITUALS

Documentation

Most computer programs come with a set of printed operating instructions and technical information known as the "documentation." The materials are supposed to explain what the different functions of the program are and how the user can make them work.

The Book of Leviticus is like "documentation" for Israel's worship. It spells out in extraordinary detail the policies and procedures of the nation's religious life—right down to such concerns as how a bird should be sacrificed: split at its wings but not divided completely (Lev. 1:17). The book told the people of Israel what they needed to know about worshiping God, including:

• *Who.* It emphasized who was to bring the sacrifices (the people), and who was to actually offer the sacrifices (the priests, Aaron and his descendants).

• *What.* It described details such as the required quality and cost of the sacrifices and the elements involved in the different events.

• *When.* It laid out an order and sequence for the various offerings and the seasons or times of the year when the sacrifices were to be made.

• *Where.* It located the place in or around the tabernacle where the different rituals were to be performed.

• *How.* It explained the procedures required for proper worship, such as methods for slaughtering animals and the preparation of materials.

• *Why.* It gave reasons for worship, one of the most important being: "You shall be holy, for I the Lord your God am Holy" (Lev. 19:2).

Modern-day readers sometimes find the religious laws of Leviticus to be tedious. Why bother with all of these ancient rituals. Aren't they "irrelevant" for today?

Perhaps it will help to consider that apart from the computer program for which it is written, most documentation makes for pretty boring reading. But to the users of the program, it can be invaluable. Similarly, the Book of Leviticus was invaluable to the ancient Israelites. Christians, of course, need not practice the rites outlined here. Even so, we can gain a great deal of insight into what worshiping and serving God is all about by looking carefully at this "manual" for Israel's worship.

The Value of Rituals

Anyone who has ever participated in a wedding, attended a funeral, or even sung "Happy Birthday" has taken part in one of the oldest and most pervasive aspects of human culture—ritual. Every known society has developed its unique ceremonies and rituals. Rites of passage into adulthood, the inauguration of leaders, the celebration of holidays, and victories in sport or war have become deeply ingrained patterns for nearly every culture.

The first five books of the Bible, known as the Pentateuch, invite us into the rituals of a struggling people, the Hebrews. Through their God-given regulations for worship, instructions for the building of the tabernacle, rules regarding offerings and sacrifices, and prohibitions concerning daily life, we can learn a great deal about values as well as the nature of ceremony. We can also meet a righteous God who cared for His people.

Like the ancient Hebrews, we today participate in rituals, often without even thinking about the minute precision assumed in each one. Consider, for example, how your family works its way through births, weddings, deaths, holidays, and reunions. Can you detect well-established patterns and habits that are not only repeated, but may even carry penalties if violated?

The books of Moses teach us the importance of passing on our traditions to succeeding generations. Unless their elders explain and enforce the meaning and significance of rituals, young people may forget their heritage and become "cultural vagabonds." What's worse, without proper understanding, people can turn ritual into thoughtless exercises, or even pervert the tradition.

What are some of your cherished memories of family, church, work, and community life? Do you need to rekindle old rituals or perhaps even develop new ones to reinforce basic values and to celebrate milestones, accomplishments, and blessings?

ROLE MODEL

Always an Example

People in authority *always* set an example—be it good or bad. Nadab and Abihu (Lev.

10:1) were judged severely by God not only because they had offered "profane fire" to the Lord, but also because in doing so they had dishonored God before "all the people" (Lev. 10:3).

God was well aware that people tend to follow leaders not on the basis of what those leaders say, but on what they do. The same is true for Christians who have been called to act as light in the world (Matt. 5:14–16). As followers of Christ, we are under particular scrutiny, especially by people who do not share our faith. Such a "fishbowl" existence may feel burdensome at times. But God wants us to take seriously the privilege of representing Christ in our community and workplace.

Sarah . . . and Her Daughters

Sarah (1 Pet. 3:6) was no doubt well known to the Jewish believers to whom Peter was writing. Just as Jewish men valued their connection with Abraham (compare Matt. 3:9; John 8:39; Acts 13:26), so women regarded themselves as daughters of Sarah. Peter affirmed that connection by describing what it would mean for Christian women facing severe persecution: doing good and not giving in to fear.

The Book of Genesis does not record Sarah calling her husband "lord," but the term was commonly used by members of a clan to show esteem to the head of the clan. By using such a title of respect, Sarah was honoring Abraham and demonstrating her submission to God by following her husband's leadership (1 Pet. 3:1, 5).

Sarah exerted some leadership of her own by arranging for her servant Hagar to bear Abraham a son (Gen. 16:2–4), and later by urging him to send Hagar and her son Ishmael away (Gen. 21:10–14). It's interesting that God instructed Abraham to listen to (obey) Sarah, even though Abraham was displeased with her plan.

In holding up Sarah as a model, Peter emphasized her good works and courageous faith (compare Heb. 11:11). She followed Abraham into some risky situations where courage and righteous living were required (Gen. 12:15; 20:2). In a similar way, Peter's readers were undergoing "fiery trials" as a result of their faith in Christ (1 Pet. 4:12). The key to their survival was not to capitulate to cultural standards of worth, but to develop a Christlike inner character, which is both beautiful and enduring (1 Pet. 3:3–4).

For more on this topic, see EXAMPLE, "God's Name on the Line," page 136; "Models of Faith," page 136.

ROOTS

Playing Ethnic Games

Jesus must have made the woman at the well very uncomfortable when He spoke with such detailed, personal knowledge of her past (John 4:17). Perhaps that's why she began to play ethnic games with Him, falling back on her religious roots (John 4:19–20).

Samaritans were good at that. Nearby was Mount Ebal, where Joshua had renewed Israel's covenant with God (Josh. 8:30–35). According to the Jewish Torah (Deut. 27:4–6), Mount Ebal was also where Moses built an altar to celebrate the Israelites entering the Promised Land. But the Samaritans held that Mount Gerizim, also nearby, was the only true place of worship. The Samaritans built an altar there in 400 B.C., but the Jews destroyed it in 128 B.C. That only added to the historic enmity between the two groups— and provided ammunition for the woman to challenge Jesus.

Today, many people still play ethnic games with their religious roots. In Mexico City, for example, some churches are located on top of Aztec or Mayan shrines. Some Mexicans, seeking to recover their Indian roots and throw off their Spanishness, literally dig deep into their past to promote paganism and reject Christianity. Similar behavior can be found among other groups exploring and recovering their roots. Like the Samaritans in Jesus' day, they want to affirm who they are as a people.

Jesus understood this woman's need for ethnic identity and security. But He challenged her and her neighbors with a deeper issue—their need to turn to God and become true worshipers of Him. He refused to play ethnic games when there was a matter of eternal life and death at stake.

For more on this topic, see ANCESTRAL ROOTS, "Jesus' Roots," page 18; "The Three Sisters," page 19.

RULES

Rules That Lead to Joy

Most parents expect obedience from their children as a sign of loyalty and trust. In a similar way, God expects His children to follow His commandments (1 John 2:4–5). In fact, when we obey God and act like Him, we show ourselves to be His (1 John 2:6).

We can be thankful that God has established rules and standards. Without such boundaries, we would not experience freedom but chaos. After all, we no longer inhabit Eden, but a broken world of sinners. We need moral safeguards that protect people's rights, delay gratification, enforce commitments, define relationships, ensure privacy, and demonstrate a respect for life.

Furthermore, we can be thankful that God is the One who has defined moral absolutes. Sinners could not be trusted to define goodness or justice.

God's original desire was for humans to have authority over all creation (Gen. 1:26–31). But sin and rebellion made us incapable of carrying out that responsibility (Gen. 3:22–24; Rom. 1:18–32). However, Christ has opened the way for us to reestablish our relationship with God and assume once again the responsibilities for which He created us:

- He has provided for the forgiveness for our sins (John 3:16–19).
- He has provided renewal for all of our life (2 Cor. 5:16–21).
- He empowers us to carry out His work (Acts 1:6–8).
- He has established guidelines for proper conduct (1 John 2:7–17).

When we follow God's commandments we experience true liberty. As His obedient children we can be fulfilled, fruitful, and joyful as we look forward to the promise of eternal life (1 John 2:17).

For more on this topic, see DISOBEDIENCE, "Disobedience Has a Price," page 112.

SABBATH REST

(*see also* Rest and Recreation)

A Day of Worship

For most Christians, Sunday is a day for going to church. However, once an hour or two of formal church attendance is over, Sunday often becomes little more than a day off from the routine of the week. People use it for recreation and entertainment, or to catch up on chores and errands. Is that what it means to "give to the Lord the glory due His name," and to "worship the Lord in the beauty of holiness" (Ps. 96:8–9)?

True worship means focusing on the Lord rather than ourselves. The Israelites were commanded to devote one day out of seven to focus on God (Ex. 20:8–11). To do that, they were told to cease from their normal labors, just as God ceased, or paused, from His work of creation on the seventh day (Gen. 2:1–3).

Christians are not bound to keep the Sabbath, but they are commanded to worship the Lord together (Heb. 10:19–25), and traditionally this has occurred on the first day of the week (1 Cor. 16:2).

The point of making Sunday an anchor in the weekly rhythm is to remind us of who we are in relation to God. Worship and cessation from labor help to redirect our focus from ourselves to God. Used for these purposes, Sunday reminds us of our dependence on God for the gift of life, the skills by which we work and live, and the privilege of using all that God has given us as resources on loan.

Practically speaking, we can use Sunday for its intended purpose by:

- ceasing from our work and getting away from the routines of labor;
- pausing to reflect on what has happened during the previous week, and interpreting our experience through the eyes of faith;
- engaging in activities that help to restore and nurture our inner life;
- praying through the many areas of our life, focusing on God rather than just on ourselves, by making extensive use of Scripture as we form our prayers; and

- joining together with other believers to worship the Lord, praise His name, and celebrate life together.

Keep It Holy

What was God's will for the Sabbath (or "day of cessation," as the term literally means)? The fourth commandment is straightforward: "keep it holy" (Ex. 20:8). But what does it mean to keep the Sabbath "holy"?

The prologue to the Ten Commandments (Ex. 20:2 provides a clue. All ten laws rest on the close relationship that God has to His people:

- He is their sovereign Lord.
- He is their Almighty God.
- He is their Deliverer.
- He is their Savior.
- They are His children.

If God's people keep in mind their relationship to the Lord and value it in their hearts, they will exhibit the kind of behaviors outlined in the Ten Commandments. For example, they will set aside one day of the week, the "day of cessation," in order to consciously emulate what their Lord did on the seventh day of creation.

God "rested" or ceased from His creative labors on that seventh day. He did not stop sustaining, maintaining, and redeeming the world, but He did cease from creating, shaping, and forming it. And that is what He asks His people to do, to set the day apart for Him, in order to do whatever He loves and desires—everything except the routine labors that are normally carried out on the other six days of the week.

Christians today have a degree of latitude in how they fulfill God's intentions for the Sabbath. But the spirit of "keeping the Sabbath holy" still means to honor God, to focus on the needs of others rather than ourselves, and to pursue fellowship, unity, and concern for other believers.

The Sabbath as a Metaphor

How would you explain the gospel to Jews living in the first century? How would you describe what it means to trust in Christ's work on the cross rather than working to merit it by strict observance of the Law? The writer of Hebrews found a useful comparison in the Sabbath (Heb. 4:1–13).

When God completed His work of creation, He rested. He stopped. It wasn't that He was tired and needed a break; He no longer needed to work because His work was finished. Creation was complete (Heb. 4:4; Gen. 2:1–2). In the same way, people don't need to work for salvation because in Christ salvation is finished. The way to God is open. We can rest from slavish adherence to the Law in an attempt to make ourselves acceptable to God. We need only trust in Christ's finished work on our behalf (Heb. 4:3; Rom. 10:4).

The writer knew that nothing would dramatize what Christ accomplished like the Sabbath. Every seven days the Jews ceased from their work. They didn't just take a day off to catch up on chores or go to the lake, as many modern people do on Saturdays. They put an emphatic pause in life for an entire day. Society came to a screeching halt to remind everyone of what God had done (Ex. 20:8–11).

So when Hebrews equates rest in Christ with Sabbath rest, it draws on the heart of Jewish culture. Jesus is God's Sabbath rest when it comes to the work of salvation.

Every culture has powerful metaphors and symbols to describe its life. As you consider how to communicate Christ to people in your culture, what are some useful metaphors that you could use? How could you communicate the "old, old story" in "new, new" ways?

Harnessing Our Work, Freeing Our Spirit

How hard is it for you to take a break from work? Can you give it up for a day, or are you always trapped in constant toil? One way to find out is whether you feel anxious when you're not getting something "accomplished."

Work is a gift from God and is essential to our nature. Even so, work was never intended to define our identity. God does not measure our worth by our productivity. He loves us for who we are—the way He has made us to be.

One indication of that is the Sabbath. By establishing a day of rest each week, God put work in its proper perspective. (For the Israelites, that day was Saturday, the seventh day of the week. Most Christians observe Sunday

as their day of rest, that having been the day of Jesus' resurrection.) This break in the routine cycle of productivity reminds us that:

- work has limits and does not totally define who we are (Ex. 20:9–10; Ps. 127:1–2);
- God has created all things and gives us the gift of life (Ex. 20:11; Ps. 104); and
- God delivers His people from bondage (Deut. 5:15; Heb. 4:1–11).

The weekly day of rest was intended for our good. It allows us to restore our mind, body, and spirit from the demands of our labors. It also gives us time to celebrate what has been accomplished during the week, as well as in times past, as we gather with other believers to worship the Lord. If we ignore the sabbath principle, we may lose our health, become addicted to our work, and develop an inflated sense of self-importance.

Have you ever viewed a day off as God's gift to you? He wants you to use that gift in ways that benefit yourself, your family, your work, and your faith.

For more on this topic, see REST AND REC-REATION, "Weekly Liberation," page 343.

SACRIFICE

Relative Value

What did Jesus mean when He said that the widow had put more money into the treasury than anyone else (Mark 12:43)? Clearly, He was indicating that economic value is relative. The widow's contribution would have been nothing but spare change to the rich who preceded her. But to her, two mites represented enormous value. It was "*all* that she had, her *whole* livelihood" (Mark 12:44, emphasis added). Replacing it would be difficult, if not impossible; as a poor widow, she was probably unemployable. Giving it to God meant that she could not use it to buy her next crust of bread.

But Jesus indicated that God placed moral rather than economic value on her tiny offering. Her gift showed that she was giving herself entirely to God and trusting in Him to meet her needs. Her use of money disclosed the moral and spiritual condition of her heart.

The Costs of Following Jesus

Following Jesus has its privileges—but also its costs, as Luke 14:25–33 reveals:

- The cost of *service.* Jesus' followers must serve Him before all others (Luke 14:26).
- The cost of *sacrifice.* Jesus' followers must subordinate their own interests to the interests of Christ (Luke 14:27).
- The cost of *self-assessment.* Jesus' followers must be fully in touch with who they are and how Christ has equipped and empowered them to do what He asks (Luke 14:28–30).
- The cost of *strategy.* Jesus' followers must think through the issues and have the courage to act in the face of uncertainty (Luke 14:31–33).

The Power of Self-sacrifice

What does power look like in the lives of people you know? Does it mean aggressively making things happen? Does it mean political or financial muscle? Jesus described His power as the right and ability to lay down His life for others (John 10:17–18).

For whom or what would you lay down your life? Is there a cause so noble or people so dear that you would willingly let go of life itself? The world may not view that kind of self-sacrifice as power. But we who follow Christ can know the profound power of love—looking out not only for our own interests, but also for the interests of others (Phil. 2:4).

For more on this topic, see GIVING, "Amount vs. Attitude," page 167; GOD'S LOVE, "He Did It for You!" page 172.

SANCTITY OF HUMAN LIFE

(*see* Worth of Persons)

SANITATION

Sanitation and the Sacred

Most people probably would not connect sewage and sanitation with religion and things sacred. But God did. He gave instructions to the Hebrews to properly dispose of their waste. It was not for public health reasons but for a spiritual one: "the LORD your God walks in the midst of your camp . . . therefore your camp shall be holy" (Deut. 23:12–13).

It is interesting to consider this law in light of other health-related laws, such as those covering diet, leprosy, skin diseases, boils, burns, spots on the skin, and sores. Even though none of these laws was given specifically for reasons of health, they all contributed to health in Hebrew society. Thus it would be reasonable to conclude that anything that threatened the health and safety of a person was a concern to God.

Likewise, such things should be a concern to God's people today. Issues such as waste disposal, clean air and water, acid rain, toxic chemicals, and other potential hazards deserve our careful attention and management.

SARCASM

The Biting Edge of Sarcasm

Nothing takes the heart out of a person quite like biting sarcasm from an authority figure. It can be hard enough just to get up the courage to approach a powerful leader. But if that figure responds with derision, even the bravest can lose hope.

Pharaoh used the tactic of sarcasm with Moses and Aaron when they came to warn of the plague of locusts (Ex. 10:10). There is no clear indication that they were disheartened by the ruler's taunts. But given Moses' fears before returning to Egypt, perhaps he and his brother were not exactly rejoicing as they went out from Pharaoh's presence.

There are at least three ways to handle biting sarcasm, especially when it is directed against a person's faith:

1. *Know who your God is, and why He has sent you.* If you don't have much confidence in God to begin with, it won't take much to knock out your "faith." Likewise, if you don't know what God's purpose is for you, it will be easy for a sarcastic comment to make you forget why you are doing what you are doing.

2. *Know yourself—your strengths as well as your weaknesses.* What is the worst that someone could say to you, or about you? To what sort of comments would you be most sensitive and vulnerable?

3. *Know your enemy.* What does your opponent stand to gain by turning you aside? Or lose if you prevail? Most importantly, do you know who your real enemy is?

S

SATAN

Meeting and Beating Satan

Who is Satan (Zech. 3:1–2)? Scripture instructs us about the nature and activity of this evil, fallen angel, who is ceaselessly opposed to God, God's creation, and God's people. God wants us to be aware and be alert so that we are not caught off guard by his schemes.

1. He is called "the devil," which means a false witness or malicious accuser. (This terms occurs thirty-five times in the New King James translation of the Bible, always in the New Testament). Satan regularly accuses believers before God, seeking to tear down their sense of well-being and wear down their strength through guilt (Job 1:6–11; Eph. 4:27; 6:11; Rev. 12:10).

2. He specializes in deceit (Gen. 3:1–7), sometimes masquerading as an "angel of light," as though he were representing God (2 Cor. 11:14). Jesus called him the father of lies (John 8:44). Paul and John further illuminate this characteristic deception (1 Tim. 3:6–7; Rev. 20:10).

3. He is a tempter, seeking to draw people into activities that are disobedient to God and destructive to them (Matt. 4:1–11; 1 Cor. 10:13; 1 Thess. 3:5).

4. He has a great deal of influence on this world. Three times Jesus described him in Scripture as the "ruler of this world" (John 12:31; 14:30; 16:11). Paul used similar expressions (2 Cor. 4:4; Eph. 2:2).

How, then, should we as believers respond to this dangerous enemy?

1. We need to remind ourselves that Satan has been defeated by the death and resurrection of Christ, and therefore we need not submit to him or fear him (Heb. 2:14–15; 1 John 3:8; Rev. 20:10). Our Lord Jesus is familiar with his enticements and has met him head on— and won (Luke 4:1–13; Heb. 4:15).

2. We need to remember that Satan's power and impact are limited by God. Ultimately he is not free to do whatever he wants (Job 1:7–12; 2:6; John 14:30–31; 2 Thess. 2:7–8).

3. We are to stand opposed to Satan at all times. He will flee when we do (1 Pet. 5:8–9; James 4:7).

4. We are to equip ourselves for this constant battle (Eph. 6:13–18).

5. We need to lean on God, who gives us the power to escape Satan's various temptations and enticements (Eph. 6:11; 1 Cor. 10:13).

6. We must maintain a healthy respect for the power of the evil one and for the constant battle that he wages against us. This is not a game; it is a life-and-death struggle in which there will be casualties (1 Tim. 3:7; 1 Pet. 5:8; Jude 9).

The Sons of God

The term "sons of God" (Job 2:1; compare Job 1:6; 38:7) refers to the angels, heavenly beings who are superior to humans in power and intelligence. According to the Book of Job, these beings would periodically present themselves before God, though we know little about the gatherings.

It may seem odd to find Satan mentioned as one of the "sons of God." Elsewhere Scripture describes him as an angel who was cast out of heaven for rebelling against God. Now he seeks to undermine the cause of righteousness in the world. In fact, the name Satan means "adversary." So in what sense is Satan a "son of God"?

The Hebrew word for "son," *bar,* can refer not only to an immediate male offspring, but to a member of an entire class or category. For example, the Old Testament speaks of the "sons of Israel" (Ex. 28:9) to refer to the descendants of Israel (Jacob), the Israelites. Likewise, the "sons of Asaph" (1 Chr. 25:1) refers to the temple musicians descended from Asaph, King David's principal musician.

In Job, the term "sons of God" is a descriptive term meaning "from or made by God," in the sense that angels, fallen or not, are spirits and inhabit the supernatural realm.

*For more on this topic, see **EVIL,** "Blaming Satan?" page 134.*

SATANISM

(*see* Occult)

SCHOOLING

(*see* Education)

SCIENCE AND RELIGION

The Truth About Science and Christianity

The people of Jesus' day demanded miraculous signs as a condition for belief (John

4:48). Yet even though Jesus performed astonishing miracles, His Jewish brothers and sisters by and large rejected Him as their Messiah (John 1:11). Today many people reject Christianity on similar grounds. We live in a natural world, they say, a world that can be explained by science. Since Christianity relies on faith, it no longer applies in our modern, scientific world. In fact, Christianity and science conflict.

The interesting thing is that while many top scientists do not make this claim, many untrained people do. They have bought into a number of myths, including the following:

1. *Science can be proved; Christianity cannot.* The truth is that both science and Christianity deal with evidence. Science examines evidence about our world from things that we can see, touch, measure, and calculate. Christianity is based on evidence about our world from the life, teaching, death, and resurrection of Jesus.

Of course, it is a misconception that science can be "proved." The heart of the scientific method is to allow the evidence to lead one where it will. But in that case, one cannot "prove" a scientific hypothesis, but only support it with evidence.

2. *Science is progressive; Christianity resists progress.* There is some truth to this—but only some. At certain times in history, Christianity has opposed ideas that seemed to challenge its worldview. Yet at other times Christians have been (and still are) on the vanguard of scientific progress. Indeed, modern science is largely the product of inquiring believers.

3. *Science is logical; Christianity involves a leap of faith.* Without question there is a logic and an order in scientific inquiry. But the same is true for the philosophical, historical, ethical, and theological disciplines of Christianity. Our faith is not opposed to reason. At points it may go beyond reason. But it is a reasonable faith. It hangs together logically.

At the same time, science demands an element of faith. In science, one must commit oneself to the belief that the world we see and touch is real, that nature is uniform, and that it operates according to the principle of cause-and-effect. Without these prior "leaps of faith," reasonable though they are, one cannot undertake science.

4. *Science deals with the laws of nature; Christianity thrives on miracles.* If science involves a closed, physical universe with fixed, unalterable laws, then the concept of miracles, which involve the local, temporary suspension of natural laws, will prove intolerable. But that is a nineteenth-century view of science. Few scientists of stature today support such a view.

Moreover, the so-called "laws of nature" are not prescriptive but *descriptive.* They do not determine what may happen; they describe what normally does happen. Therefore, science can legitimately say that miracles do not usually occur in nature. But it would be illegitimate to claim that miracles are impossible. Such a claim speaks outside the limits of science. If God has really come into this world in Christ, is it so surprising that He would perform miracles, as the Gospels report?

Science is not in conflict with Christianity. To be sure, some scientists are. But other scientists are passionately committed Christians, just like people in other walks of life. There are reasons why people choose for or against Christ, but those reasons are found elsewhere than in science.

For more on this topic, see **MIRACLES,** *"Miracles—On God's Timetable," page 267.*

SECOND CHANCE
A New, Improved Contract

Are you losing hope in your current situation? Do you long for a better arrangement? Perhaps you need a fresh start at work, in your family, your friendships, or your personal life. For too long you've felt trapped in old patterns.

Hebrews addresses those kinds of circumstances. Thousands of years of Jewish history were built on God's covenant with Israel. But Christ came to rewrite the script of history. He offers a superior covenant rooted in better promises and without fault (Heb. 8:6–7). As the prophet Jeremiah had foreseen, under the new arrangement wickedness will be forgiven, sins will be forgotten, and the old covenant will fade into the shadows before vanishing altogether (Heb. 8:12–13; Jer. 31:31–34).

What an amazing message! We can have a fresh start. Bondage to old, seemingly unbreakable patterns can be broken and replaced. But first we must confess our condition and

S

accept God's provision, which includes His agenda for change (1 John 1:8–10). Therein lies the fresh start for our lives.

The same pattern of newness holds true for relationships. Owning our responsibility and admitting our faults open the door to new ways (see Acts 19:18–20; James 5:16).

Have you learned the joy of confession, apology, and repentance? Do you need some breakthroughs among your peers, friends, or associates? Take the risk to speak the truth to them about your failings and seek a renewal in the relationship.

Forgiveness Unlimited

Do you ever feel hopeless regarding your faith? Do you doubt God's willingness to forgive you over and over again?

Peter (John 12:15) might easily have felt that way. He had risen to a position of leadership among Jesus' followers. He had even been given the "keys of the kingdom" (Matt. 16:19). And he had positioned himself as the defender of Christ when Roman soldiers came to arrest Him (John 18:10). But when he felt the heat of a national trial, conviction, and death, Peter denied three times that he even knew Christ (John 18:15–18, 25–27) and afterward disappeared. What Jesus had predicted about him came true (John 13:31–38).

So when Jesus engaged Peter in a conversation on the shore (John 21:15–23), Peter might easily have felt that he was already disqualified from further service for the Lord. After all, as we would say, three strikes and you're out. But Jesus reconnected with Peter and called him to genuine love and the continuation of His work.

Second and third chances are not often available in families, communities, or workplaces. All you have to do is fail once too often, and you're gone. But Christ offers tangible love and boundless forgiveness—to those who own up to their failures and repent (Luke 7:47). Can we offer anything less to our co-workers, families, and friends?

Second Chances

Peter asks us to consider Sodom and Gomorrah, which God did not spare (2 Pet. 2:6; Gen. 19:24). This and fifty other biblical references to those twin cities make two things clear: they could have been saved in spite of

their evil, and God wants future generations like ours to avoid their mistakes.

For more on this topic, see RENEWAL, "Starting Over," page 336.

SECULARISM
Sulfa Drugs and Street Lights

Following Christ goes far beyond private spirituality. It also involves a believer's public life, particularly through work and participation in the community. Jesus used two metaphors to describe that dynamic: salt (Matt. 5:13) and light (Matt. 5:14–16). In Jesus' day, salt was used to preserve foods like fish from decay. In the same way, believers can help to preserve society from moral and spiritual decay. Of course, in our culture, salt has given way to chemical preservatives (many of which have come under attack in recent years for their alleged role in causing cancer). So Jesus might use a different metaphor if He were speaking today.

Perhaps He would talk in terms of an infection-fighting drug, such as an antibiotic like penicillin, or the sulfa drugs developed in the 1940s that have proved so valuable in fighting meningitis and pneumonia. Christians can help to ward off spiritual infections and diseases in the larger society. One of the most powerful arenas for influence is the workplace, particularly jobs that affect values, laws, and public opinion. That's why believers need to pursue careers in education, government, and journalism, among many others. They may not be able to transform the entire society, but they can use whatever influence they have to promote Christlike values and hinder evil.

Jesus also called His followers "the light of the world" (Matt. 5:14), an image that fits perfectly into modern society. The Lord's first-century listeners would be astonished at the availability and importance of light in our culture. We use it not only to illuminate but also to communicate. Thus, Jesus wants us as His followers to shine, to be visible and attractive, not to bring attention to ourselves, but to bring people to God (Matt. 5:16). Again, our vocations are one of the primary means we have to reflect Christ to others.

Jesus' teaching here challenges us as His followers to ask: How are we engaging our society? What spiritual infections are we fighting to overcome? What positive changes are we trying to promote? What impact for God are we having through our work? Have we lost our saltiness (Matt. 5:13)? Are we standing like burned-out street lights, ineffective and waiting to be removed? Or are we shining brilliantly with the love and truth of Christ?

The Gospel in a Pluralistic Society

Jesus' nighttime meeting with Nicodemus (John 3:1–21) and His midday encounter with the Samaritan woman (John 4:5–42) show two of the many different ways in which He dealt with people. Whether it had to do with a respected urban leader like Nicodemus or a hardened, street-wise loner like the woman of Samaria, Jesus approached people on their own terms, as individuals with unique concerns. He modeled for us what it means to live, work, and communicate the gospel message in a pluralistic society.

Nicodemus was an upper-class Jew, a Pharisee from one of the prominent families of Jerusalem. He approached Jesus, alone, at night. The Lord confronted him with his need to be "born again," then let him go away to think things over. The next time we see him, he is defending Jesus on a procedural matter (John 7:45–52). But Nicodemus apparently didn't openly identify with Jesus until after the crucifixion, when he helped prepare His body for burial (John 19:39).

The Samaritan woman, on the other hand, had lived a scandalous lifestyle with a succession of husbands and then with a live-in companion. As a result, her community despised her. She also probably came from mixed ancestry, for which the Jews despised her. She was spoken to by Jesus in broad daylight, in public, first by herself but later in the company of others. He told her of "living water" and the need to worship in spirit and truth. She responded much more quickly than Nicodemus. Furthermore, hers may have been not so much an individual choice as a clan decision (John 4:39–41).

John went on to record many other ways Jesus dealt with people, and many ways they responded to Him. Some became believers after they were fed (John 6:4–14), others after they were healed (John 9:1–38), and others after they had seen the resurrected Christ

(John 20:24–29). Some responded to the Lord's miracles, others to His teaching. There was no one kind of response to Jesus.

We as believers today must present the gospel in an increasingly pluralistic world. Like Jesus, we need to use many different approaches. What are some of the creative means you can use to influence friends and coworkers for Christ?

For more on this topic, see **PUBLIC SCHOOLS,** *"A Secular Education," page 328;* **SKEPTICISM,** *"Minority Status" page 370.*

SECURITY

A False Sense of Security

It's a normal human tendency to flee from danger by running to places of safety. However, real peace and security do not come from gates, guards, or guns. Ultimately, they come from God.

The people of Jeremiah's day lived in an increasingly dangerous world. The Assyrian Empire was in decline, creating political instability in the Middle East. Seizing the opportunity, the Egyptians began to stage offensive campaigns from the south. Meanwhile, Babylon was emerging as a new superpower.

Yet in the midst of these danger signs, false prophets in Judah comforted the Israelites with words of peace (Jer. 8:11). The citizens took comfort in their walled cities, assuming that these defenses would be a safe haven against hostile forces (Jer. 8:14). But they were merely denying their true condition. The gravest danger the residents of Judah faced was one that they had created themselves, and one that they brought with them into their cities: they had turned their backs on God (Jer. 8:5, 8–12).

In our own day, many people have sought refuge from urban crime by moving to the suburbs. In fact, some new developments have taken a step back toward the days of walled cities by building gated communities. Such attempts to curb violent crime are understandable, but evil is not so easily excluded (Jer. 8:15). It cannot be controlled merely by controlling the environment. Ultimately, evil is a matter of dealing with sin, whether personal or institutional, and that means repentance and turning toward the Lord (Jer. 25:4–7; 35:15; Matt. 11:28).

S

What are you trusting in for peace and security? There's nothing wrong with wanting to protect yourself and your family from harm. But inner peace cannot come just from shutting out evils from the outside; it also takes rooting out evils from the inside.

Security Comes from God

God will impose justice on a corrupt society. He warns that His judgment will fall like a plague of devouring locusts (Is. 33:3–4), disrupting the "business-as-usual" complacency of His people (Is. 33:7–8). He will assert Himself among those who have assumed that He either does not care about their wrongdoings or is too weak to act (Is. 33:10–13).

Yet even in the midst of judgment, there is hope for the righteous. As in some of the Psalms, which contain questions and answers regarding the conditions for admittance to worship (for example, Ps. 15; 24), Isaiah describes those who will escape punishment and dwell with the Lord in safety (Ps. 33:15). They are those who:

- live lives of righteous behavior;
- speak only what is right and true;
- turn away from oppressing powerless people in order to make money;
- make it plain that their integrity cannot be bought with a bribe;
- won't even listen to suggestions for eliminating competitors and opponents by resorting to violence; and
- won't tolerate evil in their presence.

The comfort of this passage is that those who pursue a godly character will be eligible to enjoy the Lord's protection (Is. 33:16). He will make their lives secure when He comes to reside in and rule over Jerusalem. He will fill the city with justice and righteousness. Little wonder, then, that refugees from the rural areas will seek refuge there (Is. 33:20).

The occasion for this psalm may well have been the Assyrian invasion of 701 B.C., when the forces of Sennacherib captured numerous cities in Judah and besieged Jerusalem (Is. 36:1–2). Isaiah's prayer seems to invite people from the countryside to flee to the city for protection. However, real safety comes not from strong walls and strategic preparation, but from honoring the Lord.

As you read this psalm, you probably do not have an invading army bearing down on your property, but there may be other dangers from which you long for protection. As you seek refuge and security, are you pursuing a lifestyle that honors God, like the one described above? Or are you like the hypocrites (Is. 33:14) who spurn God's ways, yet feel entitled to His protection?

Confidence and a Clean Conscience

Would you feel free to welcome others to attempt to assassinate your character? Would you even help them? Jesus did. He had such a clean conscience and a secure trust in God that justice would ultimately prevail, and that His enemies could do no lasting harm, that He actually aided His accusers. He welcomed them (John 8:4), identified Himself for them (John 8:5, 8), and even protected them from retaliation by His own loyalists (John 8:11). Jesus demonstrated grace in the face of hostility.

Jesus' innocence did not protect Him from suffering, pain, or death. But it gave Him a confidence rooted in a larger reality than life on earth. Because He answered to God's judgment (John 12:23–33; 14:1–4), He was free to suffer, even unjustly. He left justice up to God and did not resort to retaliation.

Trusting in God's Provision

War is often the result of people living in fear of being attacked or robbed. When people feel defenseless, their possessions—whether weapons for protection or food sources—often take on an inflated value. Nearly all of their energies are taken up with holding on to what little they have left.

Micah offered words of hope to the frightened people of Judah. He envisioned a time without war or the weapons of war (Mic. 4:3), a time of peace and security when everyone would have plenty of food (Mic. 4:4). Actually, this was God's original design for the world (Gen. 1:27–31). It was humanity's sinful rebellion that brought about the struggle for material well-being that so often leads to armed conflict (Gen. 3:17–19; 4:3–14). But according to Micah's prophecy, the Lord will ultimately resolve the issues of war and access to adequate resources. Then humanity will live in peace and abundance, and in the joy of God (compare Rev. 21:1–5; 22:1–5).

Micah's encouraging vision offers hope to us as God's people as we journey through this life. Are you trusting God for safety, food, and the future? In turn, are you a source of hope to others by telling them of God's promises, and by seeing to their basic needs?

SELF-CONFIDENCE

(*see* Confidence)

SELF-DEFENSE

Killing in Self-Defense

The Law explicitly permitted the defensive use of lethal force by private citizens—but not in all situations. At night, one could kill an intruder (Ex. 22:2), but after sunrise, one could not (Ex. 22:3). Why this difference? Was a homeowner supposed to allow an attacker to have his way during daylight, but be able to kill him in darkness?

No, the point was that at night a homeowner could not tell whether an intruder was a thief or a murderer. In daylight, it would be easier to discern an intruder's intentions. If he was merely a thief threatening property, then the homeowner could not kill him, because life was more valuable than property. But if he was a murderer, and thus a threat to human life, the homeowner was allowed to kill him in self-defense.

It was important to note that this part of the Law dealt expressly with theft, not murder. One could kill a potential murderer at any time if he threatened a person's life. One could also kill a thief if it appeared that the thief intended murder or mayhem as well.

But a person could not kill a thief solely to protect property, for no property was as valuable as a human life. Instead, citizens were to depend on the authorities of the community to capture the thief and restore stolen property, plus a penalty for the theft.

*For more on this topic, see **VIOLENCE**, "A New Way to Respond," page 411.*

SELFISHNESS

I, Me, and My

The words *I, me, my,* and *myself* appear more than forty times in Ecclesiastes 2:1–11! This says a lot about the lifestyle that the writer

was pursuing. He seems to have been focused on the gratification and glorification of himself.

Does this self-centered outlook sound familiar? Many people today are using their skills to attain a lifestyle that is built around their own comforts and convenience. The needs of others hardly matter to them.

But Ecclesiastes shows that this approach to living is ultimately empty, futile, and passing; it is "vanity and grasping for the wind" (Eccl. 2:11).

Is there a better way? Yes, the book goes on to say that real value in life can be found in fearing God (Eccl. 12:13) and honoring Him in the simple, basic "stuff" of life, such as work and family (Eccl. 2:24; 3:22; 5:18–19; 8:15).

One way to evaluate ourselves in this regard is to ask: In the midst of all our pursuits, whose life is enhanced by what we are about? If the only answer is "me," then we are already on the perilous road of self-indulgence.

The Delusions of Affluence

Just as overeating can make a person sick and too much insulation in a home can trap toxic air inside, too much wealth can be dangerous to the moral and spiritual health of an individual, a city, or a nation. In fact, Jesus warned about the "deceitfulness of riches" (Matt. 13:22). Luxury can easily delude us into spiritual carelessness, greed, and ultimate ruin.

Such is the case of Babylon in John's vision of her fall (Rev. 18:2–3, 7–8). Historically, Babylon achieved wealth, power, and dominance through constant warfare, oppression, and deception. It was known throughout the ancient world for plundering others for its own gain. Here in Revelation, Babylon is probably a symbol not only of Rome, but of a world system that operates in open rebellion against God.

But there is a heavy price to pay for the self-indulgent lifestyle that Babylon's people live, and for the injustices they resort to in maintaining it. Cruelty and deception do not go unanswered:

- The city becomes a dwelling place for demons (18:2).
- Her patterns of luxury become addictive, similar to alcoholism, sexual excess, and a lifestyle of greed (18:3).
- Insulated from pain, she lives in denial of her true condition (18:4–8).

S

- Her economic systems are taken away and her trading partnerships are dissolved (18:11–18, 22–23).
- All of her possessions disappear, and ultimately she is left desolate (18:19).

What happens to Babylon is instructive for those of us who follow Christ, especially as we live in a culture of affluence. Is there a note of warning in this text for us?

For more on this topic, see MEANING AND PURPOSE, "Short-Term Pleasure, Long-Term Despair," page 259; PLEASURE, "Self-Indulgent? Who, Me?" page 302.

SELF-RELIANCE

Self-Reliance

The "pride of Jacob" which God abhorred (Amos 6:8) refers to Israel's smug self-reliance. Their "palaces," or fortresses and strongholds, were symbols of dependence on military defense. The capital of Samaria, for example, was built on a hill three hundred feet above the surrounding valleys, which made it virtually impregnable (see 1 Kin. 16:24). In fact, it took three years of siege for the Assyrians to finally capture it (about 722 B.C.).

God hated the self-sufficiency of the Israelites, who were supposed to rely on Him. Their mentality was misguided and doomed to failure.

SELF-UNDERSTANDING

Healing for the Spirit

How can we remove the cancers of our spirit, the aspects of our character that destroy our integrity? David the psalmist declared that he would guard his ways "lest I sin with my tongue; I will restrain my mouth" (Ps. 39:1).

What a great intention! If only we could carry it out. Yet the reality is, "no man can tame the tongue. It is an unruly evil, full of deadly poison" (James 3:8).

No wonder, then, that as David attempted to restrain himself, he felt ready to burst— and finally did (Ps. 39:1–3). Yet instead of dumping emotional and spiritual poisons on his enemies, he gained insight into himself and his condition as a frail human being (Ps. 39:4–6). This realism enabled David to cast himself upon God for help and deliverance from his sinful patterns (Ps. 39:7–13).

Perhaps like David you need some new understandings of yourself in order to diagnose the true condition of your soul. Why not ask the Lord to perform spiritual healing on you? He alone "forgives all your iniquities" and "heals all your diseases" (Ps. 103:3).

SENIOR CITIZENS

(*see* Aging)

SERVANT-LEADERSHIP

A Model of Servant-Leadership

When Jesus washed His disciples' feet (John 13:3–5), He demonstrated a fundamental principle that He regularly stressed to His followers: To lead others, one must serve others. This is as true in public life and the business world as it is in the church. No number of corporate memos or rah-rah speeches exhorting workers to commit themselves to an organization or its clients will have as powerful an impact as a person of authority modeling consistently and clearly the attitude of a servant. A servant-leader will place others' needs before his own, commit himself to doing concrete things to meet those needs, and look for neither favors nor reciprocity from the people he serves.

Leadership 101

Leadership is often understood in terms of power, manipulation, assertiveness, and ambition. The literature of the work world is cluttered with "how to" books that profile the famous and successful who have fought and won by these cruel values. In the first century, the Roman Empire was dominated by very powerful and manipulative family dynasties riddled with competition, violence, greed, and dirty tricks.

But Jesus modeled a different way of leadership. Throughout the New Testament we are shown glimpses of His life and character. In them we discover a stark contrast to our world's soap opera of abuse and distortion.

Hebrews 5 is one such picture. It describes a true leader as a priest who is . . .

- focused on people and how they connect with God (Heb. 5:1);
- compassionate with the weak and ignorant (Heb. 5:2);

- required to face sin head-on (Heb. 5:3); and
- not self-appointed, but rather called by God into his role (Heb. 5:4).

Jesus was the perfect priest (Heb. 5:5–10). The writer admits that this portrait is hard to grasp (Heb. 5:11–14). However, those who seek to grow into Christlike maturity need to consider it carefully. Jesus provides for those who seek His help. All we need to do is ask (Heb. 4:14–16).

Who are your heroes when it comes to leadership? Why? Do you aspire to a leadership style that lacks the character of Christ? Why not ask peers or friends what patterns they see in you? Use the evaluations of others to rewrite your agenda for growth.

Servant-Leaders

Responding to a controversy among the disciples (Matt. 20:25–28), Jesus revealed a unique style of authority—servant-leadership. What does it mean to be a "slave" in order to become great (Matt. 20:27)? What does it mean to define leadership in terms of servanthood? Jesus suggested that both involve seeking the highest good for others—good as evaluated from God's perspective.

In light of Jesus' own example—particularly in giving up His own life as a "ransom for many" (Matt. 20:28)—we can observe that servant-leadership means:

- seeing ourselves as called by God to serve/ lead others;
- knowing intimately the people we serve/ lead;
- caring deeply about the people we serve/ lead; and
- being willing to sacrifice our own convenience to meet the needs of the people we serve/lead.

SERVICE

Getting or Giving

Do you feel that your life would be better if only you were wealthy? Would your friends describe you as generous? These two issues were at stake in the encounter between Jesus and the rich young ruler (Luke 18:18–30). The young man was wealthy enough for this life, but he wanted to know about eternal life. He was confident that he was living a clean life, but he was fearful of his destiny and came seeking security for his future.

Jesus did not challenge the young ruler's claims about his life, but rather focused on what was most important to him—his wealth. *Was it available for others?* was the probing question. Jesus made service to others the indication of fitness for eternal life. Real wealth involves following Jesus, living not to be served, but to serve others and to give one's life for others (Matt. 20:28).

This episode poses a challenge: Where is your attention focused, on accumulation or servanthood?

The Focus of Leadership

Some people regard leadership primarily as the art of getting results. Great leaders, they say, are those who get the job done. It matters very little how they operate, as long as they achieve their goals. But when we examine the great leaders of Scripture, we find that they not only accomplished much, but served people in the process.

Nehemiah illustrates the point rather well. His project of rebuilding the wall of Jerusalem was never an end in itself. The ultimate objective was to revitalize the people of Israel and return them to their covenant with God.

To that end, after the wall was completed, Nehemiah turned the city's management over to local government leaders (Neh. 7:1–2). He did not create dependency on his own skills, nor did he use the project to gain wealth or fame for himself (Neh. 5:18). Instead, right from the start, Nehemiah began the process of turning over management of Jerusalem to others.

Nehemiah also helped the people trace their roots by reviewing the census taken twenty-five years earlier in Ezra's time (Neh. 7:5). That set the stage for repopulating the city (Neh. 11:1–2) and continuing the initiative of urban revitalization.

If you are in a position of leadership, what is your posture toward the people you lead? Are you concerned about the task alone, or do you see people as the ultimate beneficiaries? If so, in what ways might you serve those who work with you, over you, or for you, so

S

that they gain from the process even as they carry out the work?

Leadership with Humility

Are you in a position of leadership in your job, in government, in your family, or in your church? In Luke 22:24–27, Jesus shows that biblical leadership starts with humility, by *serving* others.

The autocratic, authoritarian leadership style has fallen out of favor among many today. Yet a subtle, far more powerful approach has appeared, characterized by manipulation and selfish ambition. Masking their true intentions, many new-style "leaders" pretend to offer a "win-win" arrangement, but they have no real concern for others, except insofar as others can help them achieve their objectives.

Both styles are out of the question if we want to lead with Christlikeness. He asks us to take the posture of a *servant*—to genuinely concern ourselves with the rights, the needs, and the welfare of those we lead. Christ Himself has provided the example of true servant-leadership: not to be served, but to serve and to give (Matt. 20:28).

Paul encouraged believers to develop the same attitude that Christ had (Phil. 2:5–8).

Whom Do You Serve?

When God commanded Pharaoh to "let My people go" (Ex. 8:1), His intent was not that they would then be free to do as they pleased but "that they may serve Me." Clearly, God doesn't liberate people from slavery—either to Pharaoh or to sin—to make them libertines, but to make them His children. He doesn't emancipate them; He buys them for Himself to make them His valued servants. In this we find our significance, because we are created in God's image and likeness (Gen. 1:26–27).

What is your view of "redemption," that is, your liberation from sin? Do you assume that it makes you free to do whatever you wish? That is not God's perspective. Biblical freedom obligates us to a life of obedient holiness, serving God by living as He would have us live and doing what He would have us do (Rom. 6:15–22). Does your life reflect that?

From Worship to Service

What is your concept of *worshiping* the Lord? Attending a church service at which you sing hymns, read Scripture, recite prayers, listen to a sermon, and partake of holy communion? All of these practices can lead to worship, but Isaiah shows that true worship goes beyond that (Is. 58:6–7, 9–10).

In Isaiah's day, there were apparently plenty of religious people, but not many responsive people. They "afflicted their souls" with fasting, "delighted" to know God's ways, inquired about "the ordinances of justice," and enjoyed their worship services (Is. 58:2–3). Little if any of their piety translated into action, yet they expected God to answer their prayers and bless them.

Through Isaiah, God said that true worship is not just a weekly ritual, but a daily lifestyle. It may begin in a house of prayer, but it ends up in the public square.

What might that "public-minded" worship look like in today's world? What would it mean for believers as they respond to the hungry, the homeless, the prisoner, the wage-earner, the debtor, the poor, and the hopeless? There is no easy answer, but one thing is clear: as Isaiah told the people of his day, God cannot be expected to shower good things on His people as long as they withhold good things from others (Is. 58:8–9, 11–12).

So what starts with worship ends in service. Today that means that the church gathered for worship on Sunday becomes the church scattered for service on Monday through Saturday. Building believers leads to believers rebuilding their communities. Worship and service form a seamless robe.

For more on this topic, see **FOOT-WASHING,** *"The Order of the Towel," page 160;* **VALUES,** *"Confused About Greatness," page 411;* **MINISTRY,** *"What Does It Take to Serve God?" page 264.*

SEXUAL INTERCOURSE

Is Sex Unholy?

What was it about sex that caused Moses to warn the men of Israel, "Do not come near your wives" as they prepared to meet God at Sinai (Ex. 19:15)? Was this a roundabout way of suggesting that there was something sinful or dirty about intercourse?

After coming down from the mountain, Moses "sanctified" the people (Ex. 19:14); that is, he made them ritually clean to prepare them to stand before God. Part of this ritual cleansing meant abstinence from sexual relations for a period of three days.

So doesn't that imply that sex is unholy? After all, if intercourse makes one ritually unclean, then doesn't that say something about the nature of sex? No, because ceremonial uncleanness is not the same as moral uncleanness.

Notice that part of the ceremonial cleansing involved the washing of clothes (Ex. 19:14). Are dirty clothes unholy? Of course not. But which way would you rather meet God: in a dirty, smelly outfit, with disheveled hair and dirty fingernails, or in a fine set of new clothes with carefully groomed hair and manicured nails?

Actually, it didn't matter which way the Hebrews preferred to meet God, because He gave them clear instructions about how He wanted them dressed when they came before Him (for example, see Ex. 28). So to be ceremonially clean in that regard meant dressing according to the Lord's instructions.

In a similar way, Moses instructed the people to refrain from sex as they prepared to meet God. No one knows exactly why. Perhaps the idea was to help them focus their minds and hearts on the important event that they were about to witness.

But one thing is for sure: sex is not unholy. The Bible teaches that intercourse between married partners is not only natural and expected, it's a sacred act that God has blessed (1 Cor. 7:1–5; Heb. 13:4).

Biblical Love Waits

We live in a day when human sexuality is seemingly in chaos. Sexually transmitted diseases are epidemic. Teenage pregnancies are skyrocketing. Distinctions between genders have become confused. The merits of teaching abstinence are debated. The consequences of not teaching abstinence are dire. Virginity is commonly mocked.

In the midst of this confusion, the Song of Solomon declares a foundational principle for lovers. Three times it gives the exhortation: "Do not stir up nor awaken love until it pleases" (Song 2:7; 3:5; 8:4). In this way, the poem recognizes that the erotic passions of youth can be aroused before a relationship of true commitment has been established.

In biblical relationships, there is no room for a "love 'em and leave 'em" mentality. Biblical love demands commitment. It delights in the gift of sexual pleasure, but the sexual relationship takes place in the only context worthy of it—marriage, a bond in which both parties are growing together and being enriched emotionally and spiritually, as well as physically.

Sex, then, is a jewel that must await the right setting. As our culture shows, it is perilous to awaken passion before that setting has been provided.

If you are a single young person, Scripture encourages you to let sexual intercourse wait until marriage. Society may tell you that it is impossible to practice self-control, but that is a lie. With God's help you can remain chaste. You can hold onto one of your most precious gifts until the right time, with the right person, in the right relationship.

SEXUALITY

A New View of Sexuality

In an era when Greek women were often deprived both emotionally and sexually, Paul insisted that the Christian husband should recognize and fulfill the needs of his wife (1 Cor. 7:3–6). He declared that marriage partners have authority over each other. That means that both husband and wife were forbidden from using sex as a means of control, but were to enjoy mutuality in that aspect of their marriage.

The gospel required a different understanding of sex and marriage than the first-century culture's. Two thousand years later, it still does.

Accountable for Lust

Job's sufferings caused him to make a sweeping inventory of his inner life. One of the areas he evaluated was his attitude toward women and how he handled his own sexual drives (Job 31:1).

Job openly acknowledged the power of sexual appetites. He catalogued the steps of lust from "looking upon a virgin" (Job 31:1), to allowing one's heart to follow one's eyes (Job 31:7), to finally allowing oneself to be enticed

S

by a woman and then scheming to have her (Job 31:9).

Some may see this progression as normal, natural, or unavoidable. But Job viewed lust as a serious moral failure (Job 31:11). He spoke of it in the same context with:

- falsehood and deceit (Job 31:5);
- oppression of slaves (Job 31:13–15);
- mistreatment of the poor (Job 31:16, 19–20);
- abuse or neglect of widows (Job 31:16, 18);
- taking food out of the mouth of starving orphans (Job 31:17–18, 21);
- rejoicing over the misfortunes of others, even if they are one's enemies (Job 31:29–30);
- trusting in wealth (rather than in God, Job 31:24); and
- hypocrisy (Job 31:33–34).

Lust is a serious sin! So it's worth asking, how are you doing with God's gift of sexuality? Have you allowed it to become a consuming drive that craves others for your own pleasure? Or are you guarding your thoughts, eyes, and steps so as to remain pure and blameless before the Lord?

For more on this topic, see **INCEST,** *"Human Sexuality: Awesome Potential for Good or Evil," page 218.*

SHAME

From Honor to Shame

Scripture is quite clear that God is opposed to the proud (James 4:6). The Bible offers numerous examples of people whose pride was brought low through the discipline of God—Pharaoh (Ex. 14:26–15:10), Samson (Judg. 16:21–24), David (2 Sam. 12:7–15), Herod Agrippa I (Acts 12:21–23).

The people of Judah were brought low because of their arrogant, rebellious attitude toward God. Lamentations describes their humiliation by likening Jerusalem to a woman who has been put to shame. Notice the reversals that the Lord's judgment has brought about:

- From a wife to a widow (Lam. 1:1).
- From a princess to a slave (Lam. 1:1).
- From friends to enemies (Lam. 1:2).
- From honor to shame (Lam. 1:8).
- From respectability to prostitution (Lam. 1:9).

The Israelites, who were intended to enjoy the honor of being God's people, become dishonored and despised among the nations because of their sinful ways. Likewise today, a similar reversal can sometimes be seen in the lives of people who sin against God. When their wrongdoings are exposed, they fall from a place of honor and prominence to a place of shame and disrepute.

The same reversal can happen with nations. Not that any country today enjoys the kind of covenant relationship that God had with ancient Israel. But when a government openly defies God and establishes laws that oppose His truth and values, we can expect that sooner or later He will bring that government down.

God *will* be honored. He will not allow people to ignore Him forever.

SHARING

Sharing Things in Common

The first Christians were extraordinarily generous. In fact, "they had all things in common" (Acts 4:32–35), an ideal that pure communism advocated but never achieved. So were these first believers in some sense communists?

No. In the first place, they were not setting up an economic system here, but simply responding to each other with gracious, Christlike compassion. Such behavior was one powerful result of the outpouring of the Spirit (Acts 2:1–4). Unfortunately, not all New Testament believers demonstrated that kind of concern (Acts 5:1–11; 1 Cor. 6:8; James 4:1–2).

Furthermore, Scripture never mandates an equal distribution of goods, nor does it call for the elimination of property or ownership. This passage (along with Acts 2:44–45) is a historical account, not a doctrinal treatise. It documents the work of God in building the early church.

In that day, as in ours, there were both rich and poor Christians (2 Cor. 8:2; 1 Tim. 6:17–19). And when the New Testament does address issues such as wealth, care for the poor, work, equality, widows, slaves, and public justice, it inevitably calls believers to compassion and generosity. It does not, however, recommend asceticism, the idea that one can become more godly through self-denial and renouncing worldly wealth. In fact, Paul warns against that (Col. 2:18–23). The Bible condemns the love of wealth, not its possession, as a root of all kinds of evil (1 Tim. 6:9–10).

Reading about these early Christians, modern believers are challenged to consider: Do we, with our much higher standard of living, show the same commitment to compassion and generosity as these first believers? If we, too, are filled with the Spirit of Christ, then we ought to respond to the needs of people with the love of Christ.

SIBLING RIVALRY
Family Crisis, Leadership Crisis

Some families seem destined to leadership. The family of Moses, Aaron, and Miriam was such a family. Yet a crisis developed when the two older siblings turned on their younger brother Moses (Num. 12:1–2).

The text suggests that the root of the problem may have been racial intolerance toward Moses' Ethiopian wife. Ethiopia, sometimes referred to as Nubia or Cush, was a region south of Egypt. The ancient history of its dark-skinned African population (Jer. 13:23) was often intertwined with that of the Egyptians.

SHAME

So it may be that Moses met the woman during his years in Egypt. Or perhaps she was among the "mixed multitude" that accompanied the Israelites out of Egypt (Num. 11:4). Or perhaps the term used in Numbers 12:1, "Cushite," refers to Cushan, another name for Midian. In that case the Ethiopian woman could be Zipporah (Ex. 2:21).

But was the attack of Miriam and Aaron solely a racial issue? Was it possibly also a case of sibling rivalry, such as Cain and Abel experienced (Gen. 4:1–16)? Were the older brother and sister competing for leadership over Israel, much like James and John argued over who was closest to Jesus (Mark 10:35–44)?

This seems likely, because even though Miriam and Aaron apparently shaped their opposition in racial terms, the result was a crisis of authority. Together they criticized their brother's right to speak for God.

God was thoroughly displeased with this rupture in leadership (Num. 12:9). He made it clear who was ultimately in charge—He was, and He would communicate with whomever He chose (Num. 12:6). His chosen representative was Moses; Miriam and Aaron were secondary.

Miriam immediately became a leper, apparently as punishment for her part in this rebellion. The fact that Aaron did not may indicate that she was the primary instigator. In any case, the entire nation halted in its journey until she was restored (Num. 12:15).

Jealousy, power plays, and racism are ugly

SIBLING RIVALRY

sins of which God strongly disapproves. Yet they occur among even the best and brightest of us. What tendencies do you see in yourself in these areas? How can you resist acting on those impulses? Failure to resist could bring harm on you and your coworkers, as well as offend the Lord.

SICKNESS
Health and Disease in the Bible

When Jesus' disciples asked Him whose sin had caused a man's blindness (John 9:2), they were reflecting a common perception about health and disease in the ancient world. In their minds, physical maladies and suffering were the result of sin and/or God's judgment.

Viewed from our perspective two thousand years later, their question seems quaint and simplistic. Yet was it really? Even with all of our culture's medical technology, we still wrestle with the same issue: what is the ultimate cause of sickness and death? We may understand the scientific explanations and even know how to prevent or cure countless ills. But we still look for a larger meaning behind physical health and disease. We still ask, "Why did this happen to me?"

The Bible mentions more than forty specific diseases or disabilities and alludes frequently to sickness and health issues generally. It seems to accept that concerns about physical health are universal, inescapable, and problematic.

For more on this topic, see AIDS, "What Does Leprosy Have to Do with AIDS?" page 14.

SIGNIFICANCE
Little Things Mean a Lot

Do you tend to be impressed by bigness? Do you measure something's significance by whether it's bigger than anything else? Have you noticed the impact of little things, like the usefulness of a pinhead or the danger of a little bit of electricity in the wrong place?

Jesus described the kingdom and faith as starting out small, but ultimately having a big effect (Luke 13:18–21; 17:6; compare Matt. 13:31; 17:20; Mark 4:31). He likened the kingdom to a small seed that grows into a tree-like plant, just as today we speak of the acorn becoming an oak tree. He also borrowed an image from the baking industry, likening the kingdom to leaven, a piece of fermented dough that was added to a new batch, causing it to rise.

In our own culture, where people tend to equate significance with magnitude, these parables remind us of the power of small but potent faith and of simple but solid kingdom values. Paul listed these lasting things: love, joy, peace, patience, kindness, goodness, faithfulness, gentleness, and self-control (Gal. 5:22–23). None of them can be easily quantified.

God's challenge to us as His people is not to be impressed by power, success, or super-achievement, but to give ourselves to the so-called little things, the things of His kingdom. Therein lies ultimate significance.

For more on this topic, see ACHIEVEMENT, "A Kingdom Perspective on Significance," page 5.

SINCERITY
Being Sincere Is Not Enough

Have you ever heard people say things about God that are clearly untrue? Yet these lapses are often excused with the saying, "They may be wrong, but at least they're sincere." It's as if truth were inconsequential; what matters is whether one's heart is in the right place. However, God's words to Eliphaz (Job 42:7–8) show that He will not accept "folly," or wrong thinking, about His nature and character.

Job's friends Eliphaz, Bildad, and Zophar, were sincere, but they were sincerely wrong. Not totally wrong—their speeches in the Book of Job contain many accurate statements. But these men who knew so much about God did not speak of Him in a completely accurate way as they interacted with Job.

The book does not spell out for us how their comments were deficient. Clearly they were grappling with difficult issues as they tried to find an explanation for Job's troubles. But somehow in talking about God, they failed to say what was right. Perhaps they were just trying to sound authoritative, to be seen as wise and powerful men, rather than simply admitting that they had no answers and then caring for Job in his grief and agony.

Whatever their misstatements, their folly was unacceptable. God instructed them to have Job offer a sacrifice to atone for their sin of misrepresenting Him.

This is instructive for believers today. It cautions us to pay careful attention to what we

S

believe about God, and to how we represent Him to others. We need to make sure that our doctrines are true and accurate. How can we be sure? By examining them in light of the Bible, to see whether they square with what God has told us about Himself (compare Acts 17:11). And then we need to stay humble about areas where there is disagreement among those whose commitment to scriptural authority is equally strong.

SINGING
A Song for Young People

Psalm 136 is well-suited for a creative exercise that can help young people "give thanks to the LORD" (Ps. 136:1, 26). The key to this exercise is the repetition of the refrain, "For His mercy endures forever."

Begin by talking about God's mercy. Have the group discuss questions such as:

- Why do people need mercy today?
- How have you experienced mercy—for example, from a teacher, coach, or parent?
- Psalm 136 says the mercy of the Lord is enduring—it lasts. Can you think of situations where you need to "hang in there" with people and remain committed to them, even if they have let you down?

Conclude the discussion by quickly reviewing some of the historical background of the psalm—the Israelites' exodus from Egypt, crossing the Red Sea, and the defeat of enemy kings (Num. 21:21–35). Point out that throughout the journey, God's enduring mercy was showered on His people.

Next, have the group make up their own music for the chorus, "For His mercy endures forever." If someone can play the guitar or piano, encourage them to take the lead in this exercise by trying out chords and suggesting a melody line.

When the group feels that it has something that will work musically, pick one or two lead singers to handle the first part of each verse, and let the rest of the group reply by singing the chorus, "For His mercy endures forever." Or, go around the group in succession and let each person have a turn at singing the lead for one verse.

The point is to turn Psalm 136 into a song that young people enjoy singing, so that they will never forget: the Lord's mercy endures forever!

*For more on this topic, see **CELEBRATION**, "Let's Celebrate!" page 47; **FAMILY**, "Learning Faith Through Songs," page 148.*

SINGLES IN MINISTRY
The Four Daughters of Philip

In his Pentecost sermon, Peter declared that the words of the Old Testament prophet Joel were coming to pass: "Your sons and your daughters shall prophesy" (Acts 2:17–18). The four virgin daughters of Philip later became proof that it was so (Acts 21:9).

In the first century, prophets were recognized (not appointed) through the exercise of their God-given gifts, which they often displayed during worship, bringing a word from the Lord. (The New Testament had not yet been written.) The role was highly esteemed by Paul (Eph. 4:11).

Philip's daughters broke the cultural norm of being wives and mothers, perhaps choosing to remain single in order to carry out their prophetic work.

SKEPTICISM
Minority Status

Does you feel lonely at times because your faith and values seem out of step with the society around you? Perhaps you feel like you're always swimming against the tide when it comes to religious beliefs and moral choices in your family, community, or workplace. Perhaps you feel like a member of an oppressed minority, even if in other respects you are part of the majority in your culture.

If this is your experience, you have plenty of company! The Bible describes numerous followers of God who were assigned minority status because of their faithfulness and spiritual integrity. In the Old Testament, Micah and other writers refer to these faithful few as a "remnant" (Mic. 5:3, 7–8).

Technically, the term "remnant" describes survivors who remain after a devastating calamity and form the nucleus of a new community. Applied to Israel, the remnant were those who held onto their faith despite opposition at home and persecution abroad. Thanks to them, the faith was preserved until Jesus came into the world.

The Bible has much to say about believers living in the minority, and about the preservation of a godly remnant:

1. Moses warned the Israelites that they would be scattered among the nations if they disobeyed God. However, the Lord would not utterly abandon His people. He would still hear their prayers when they finally turned to Him; He would not forsake His covenant with them (Deut. 4:27–31).

2. Isaiah foresaw a day when a remnant of Israel would finally learn to depend on the Lord rather than alliances with pagan superpowers (Is. 10:20–23).

3. Amos urged the people of his day to change their ways, particularly in the marketplace, because that might cause the Lord to be "gracious to the remnant of Joseph" (Amos 5:14–15).

4. When Jesus announced the kingdom of God and began the training of His disciples, He warned that those who followed His ways would encounter opposition and persecution (Matt. 5:1–16).

5. Peter, writing primarily to Hebrew Christians who were living in cultures that did not share their beliefs or values, reminded them of their calling to holiness, and pointed out that they were "sojourners and pilgrims" (1 Pet. 1:15–16; 2:11–12). In a second letter, he said that "the Lord knows how to deliver the godly out of temptations," and used the examples of Noah and Lot—two people of faith living in corrupt societies—to support his point (2 Pet. 2:4–11).

6. Paul described the church as a "remnant according to the election of grace," not unlike the seven thousand faithful Israelites in Elijah's day (Rom. 11:2–5). He urged the Philippian Christians not to be terrified by their adversaries as they suffered for the sake of Christ, but to maintain conduct worthy of the gospel (Phil. 1:27–30).

Following God will often mean trials and testing at the hands of those who do not know Him. Are you experiencing that kind of opposition? If so, you can take heart in the fact that this is part of your calling in Christ (Phil. 1:29; 2 Tim. 3:12; 1 Pet. 2:19–24).

For more on this topic, see **DOUBT,** *"Skeptics Welcome," page 115.*

SKILLS

Gifts from God

Did you ever stop to think that God knows every worker by name? Here, He mentions two that He had made to be craftsmen (Ex. 31:2, 6). This implies that God knows your name in connection with the skills and tasks He has assigned to you.

That may be hard to imagine. But God is the Author and Enabler of every human ability. He has given talents to people because He wants to see certain work done in the world. In the construction of the tabernacle, for example, He filled people like Bezalel and Aholiab with wisdom, understanding, and knowledge by His Spirit, enabling them to carry out specific artistic and functional tasks.

This shows that God took a strong interest in the beauty, craftsmanship, materials, artistry, design, function, colors, and other specific details of the work. He didn't leave the results to chance. Instead, He gave detailed instructions to Moses about how the tabernacle should be constructed (Ex. 35:25–35; 36:1–8; 38:22–23; 39:3–27).

All of this has profound implications for our understanding of personal abilities and work habits. It shows that they are specific gifts from God. They are not to be taken for granted, viewed with pride, or looked down on when compared with others' abilities (1 Cor. 4:7; 2 Cor. 10:12). Every human ability—whether playing the flute in a high school band or composing great music; laying a straight line of bricks or driving earth-moving equipment; cooking, drawing, problem-solving, comprehending—is designed by God and matters to Him.

Do you know what skills God has given you? Are you using them to His glory?

Native Talent and Supernatural Ability

The statement that "God gave" the four young men unusual intellectual and spiritual abilities (Dan. 1:17) raises the question of whether we should pray for unusual talent that we do not ordinarily possess. Consider three examples:

1. A top salesman is unexpectedly promoted to the job of sales manager, in which he has responsibility over a large sales force. Even though he is excellent in sales, however, he

S

has never demonstrated management ability. Should he expect that, with enough prayer and faith in God, he will turn into a satisfactory, if not an outstanding, sales manager?

2. A student is doing poorly in a subject in which she has never excelled. Should she pray for knowledge and wisdom, and then expect her grades to noticeably and even dramatically improve?

3. A businessman comes to faith in Christ. In his enthusiasm about the gospel, he decides to quit his successful business and become a preacher, even though he has no ability as a public speaker or teacher. Can he expect God to suddenly make him powerful and persuasive in the pulpit?

One answer to these questions is that God can do whatever He chooses to do. Furthermore, Scripture records cases of people whose faith produced unexpected results. For example, frightened people trusted God, and "out of weakness were made strong" (Heb. 11:34).

In general, however, unusual abilities said to be given by God seem to be consistent with the general "bent" of the person and make use of abilities and talents already present. Daniel and his friends are a case in point. God gave them unusual wisdom and insight, even to the point of being able to interpret visions and dreams (Dan. 1:17). But they had always been intellectually bright and quick to learn (Dan. 1:4).

This correlation between native talent and supernatural ability is consistent with the fact that each of us is individually designed by God from the womb. He has handcrafted us with a unique set of talents and motivations in order to carry out His special purpose for our life.

So how should we focus our prayers? Should we ask for abilities for which we have never shown any talent, interest, or motivation? The example of the four Hebrew youths suggests that it is more reasonable to expect God to make use of what He has already given us. If we pray and apply our faith in those areas, we are more likely to be "surprised" by unusual—even supernatural—results.

Pray *and* Work

When faced with a problem, which is more important—to pray and have faith or to work and use one's skills? Hezekiah apparently es-

caped that tension as he faced growing threats from an expanding Assyrian empire (2 Chr. 32:9). He did both.

Hezekiah had demonstrated faith and total commitment to the Lord by destroying the idolatrous shrines that his father Ahaz had built (2 Chr. 28:22–25). Ahaz's idolatry was probably the result of foolishly allowing himself to become subject to the Assyrians by not trusting in the Lord (2 Chr. 28:16–21; compare Is. 2:6–9). By contrast, Ahaz's son Hezekiah renewed the covenant with the Lord (2 Chr. 29:10). His dedication went so far as to personally destroy a favorite relic of the people, the bronze serpent that Moses had fashioned in in the wilderness (Num. 21:4–9). Hezekiah was determined to show that God alone is worthy of worship.

However, Hezekiah's faith was as practical as it was devoted. For example, he wisely took steps to protect the city's water supply by constructing a tunnel to the spring of Gihon. Sennacherib's troops besieged the city, but they were unable to prevail, even though official records claimed that Sennacherib had shut up Hezekiah "like a bird in a cage."

Still, Jerusalem's survival was due to more than Hezekiah's foresight. Surrounded by well trained assault troops who tried to use letters of propaganda to dismay his people (2 Chr. 32:9–19), he trusted solely in God rather than turn to foreign allies (2 Kin. 19:14–19)—the exact opposite of what his father had done. The Lord honored Hezekiah's faith with the miraculous departure of the Assyrians (2 Kin. 19:35–36).

Is it more important to pray or to work? When faced with problems should we exercise faith or use our intelligence? Hezekiah's example strongly suggests that in any and every circumstance, we do well to serve God with both our devotion and our skills.

For more on this topic, see **TALENT,** *"A World of Talent," page 391;* **TEAMWORK,** *"A Project Management Team," page 397;* **TIME,** *"Working Smarter, Not Harder," page 399.*

SLANDER

Standing Up to Slander

When public figures and companies face accusations of wrongdoing, they often respond with a lawsuit. The point is to vindicate their names and demolish their accusers, or at least to force them to back down. But what happens when there is no legal recourse? What if someone has little if any power in society, or if the issue cannot be argued in a court of law?

Psalm 119 may have been written under those kinds of circumstances, during the Babylonian captivity. It was a time when the Hebrews had few rights and many opponents. They were strangers in an alien world (Ps. 119:19) and the victims of slander and harassment from wicked political rulers (Ps. 119:23). They were struggling under great affliction (Ps. 119:50, 61, 67). Yet in the midst of these trials, they learned to survive by hoping in God's Word—a constant theme for all 176 verses of Psalm 119.

The psalm includes passages decrying problems from within and dangers lurking without. Evil princes and tragic events beyond anyone's control are ready to undo the psalmist, so the fear is valid. But the antidote for that fear is the Torah, or Law, which applies to the full range of life—from Aleph (Ps. 119:1–8) to Tau (Ps. 119:169–176), from A to Z.

The idea is that nothing—no crisis, no conspiracy, no horrible affliction—is beyond the scope of Scripture's teaching.

This is instructive for believers today. Psalm 119 challenges us to live a principled, disciplined life based on the Word of God. That way, we have a foundation from which to contend with whatever comes against us. The lesson of the psalm is that a person of integrity, meditating on God's Word, will prevail. Such was the case for Joseph, Daniel, Nehemiah, and Esther. God's Word has power in moral battles.

SLAVERY

No Freedom for Female Slaves

The Law commanded that a man who had become a slave to pay his debts should be freed in the seventh year of his service (Ex. 21:2). However, no such law was given for setting free female debt slaves. Why? One reason might be that female slaves often became concubines of their master (see Gen. 30:9). Once a woman had been a concubine, she would have been unlikely to find a man willing to marry her. Yet without marriage, she would have had little means of surviving on her own.

The culture of that day was not conducive to anyone—male or female—living as a single person. Thus the Law may have assumed that a female slave would permanently remain in her master's household.

Slavery in Bible Times

Paul uses a powerful image when he pictures one's relationship either to sin or to obedience as slavery (Rom. 6:16). The Roman Empire was heavily dependent on slaves to take care of its hard labor and menial tasks. In fact, many of Paul's Roman recipients may have been slaves, since perhaps half the population or more were under servitude by one historian's estimate.

Slaves were taken from the many nations that Rome conquered. Those assigned to the empire's widespread construction projects or to its mines had a hard lot. Fed a subsistence diet, they were worked to exhaustion. Injuries and disease were common, and once they were too sick to work, or in rare cases too old, they were abandoned.

Household slaves, however, enjoyed better conditions. Nearly every Roman home owned at least two or three servants, and some had hundreds. They assisted the women in maintaining their homes and raising their children. Slaves with occupational expertise proved particularly valuable in the workplace, and some businesses were entirely dependent on these imported, cheap laborers.

Slavery existed long before the Romans, of course. The Bible records several different forms of slavery in ancient times: domestic slavery, as illustrated by Hagar (Gen. 16:1); state slavery, as illustrated by the Israelites under Egypt (Ex. 5:6–19; 13:3); and temple slavery, as illustrated by the slaves of the Levites for temple service (Num. 31:25–47; Josh. 9:21–27).

Curiously, the Bible does not directly condemn slavery as an institution, though it contains warnings about the practice of slavery (Amos 1:6–9; Rev. 18:13). The Old Testament Law did regulate Israel's treatment of slaves (Ex. 21; Deut. 15). Repeatedly, the people were instructed not to rule over a fellow Israelite harshly (Lev. 25:39; Deut. 15:14). If a master beat a slave or harmed him, the law provided that the slave could go free (Ex. 21:26–27); and the killing of a slave called for a penalty (21:20).

In the New Testament, slaves were advised to obey their masters (Eph. 6:5; Col. 3:22; Titus 2:9). Paul appealed to Philemon to receive back Onesimus, a runaway slave who became a Christian and therefore a brother. This was an illustration that in Christ, social distinctions such as slavery no longer apply (Gal. 3:28; Col. 3:11). As believers, we have been freed from sin, and in fact are now owned by God. We are now free to serve God.

For more on this topic, see CHANGE, "Token Gestures or Genuine Change?" page 50; OPPRESSION, "Equality vs. Slavery," page 285.

SMEAR TACTICS

Dirty Tricks

Having failed to intimidate Nehemiah into stopping the work of rebuilding Jerusalem's wall, Sanballat and his cronies tried smear tactics to shut the project down (Neh. 6:5–7). Frustrated opponents often resort to that approach when other methods have proven useless.

The Bible does not explain why Nehemiah so easily dismissed their accusations (Neh. 6:8) and apparently took no steps to prevent their letters from reaching the king. However, it seems plausible that he was relying on his years of trustworthy service as the king's cup-bearer. He might have known that he had the full trust of King Artaxerxes, who would quickly see through the deception of anyone who accused Nehemiah of sedition. He also knew the process by which letters such as those Sanballat had written would be read and evaluated.

In short, Nehemiah had a clear conscience and an impeccable reputation. Therefore, no amount of "mud" could cause him to lose heart. He knew that none of it would stick.

It is worth noticing that Nehemiah did not resort to slinging mud himself. He probably could have come up with plenty of counter-accusations against his adversaries. But rather than waste time on a verbal exchange that would have distracted him from the wall, he prayed and ignored the politics swirling outside the city.

If you are in a position of leadership, are you resistant to the dirty tricks of your opponents? Do you maintain your integrity, so that there can be no ground for accusation against you? Do you resist the temptation to "fight fire with fire" by resorting to political games and dirty tricks yourself?

SNAKES

Deadly Snakes

Jeremiah's prophecy likened the invading armies of the Babylonians to deadly snakes (Jer. 8:17). This recalls an incident that

JUST BECAUSE YOU'RE EARTHBOUND IS NO REASON TO HAVE A HISSY FIT!

SNAKES

occurred in the wilderness, when the Lord sent fiery serpents among His people to punish them for complaining against Him and Moses (Num. 21:6).

Moses fashioned a bronze serpent on a pole in order to heal those who were bitten (Num. 21:8–9). But the "serpents" that the Lord was bringing to Jerusalem in Jeremiah's day would be "vipers which cannot be charmed." In other words, nothing would be able to turn away Nebuchadnezzar's troops.

Snake charmers were common in the ancient Middle East. Cobras were especially popular, and charming them was one of the occult arts. In fact, snake charming and snake worship may have been among the "abominations" practiced in Jerusalem in its waning days (2 Chr. 28:2–3; Ezek. 8:9–10). But the snake charmers would be unable to tame the Babylonian "vipers."

It is interesting that generations earlier, the Lord had threatened to send the "poison of serpents" against His people to punish them for unfaithfulness (Deut. 32:24). Now God was using the the Babylonians to fulfill that promise.

SOCIAL REFORM

Justice in the Gate

There is a long tradition in Christian thinking for the idea that social reform comes about through spiritual regeneration. That is, people will change the ways in which they live and treat others after they have experienced inner change as a result of salvation in Christ. In effect, grace leads to justice.

But another approach is possible. The ancient Israelites were challenged by the prophet Amos with the concept that justice might lead to grace. That is, if they changed their society into one that was more just and loving, God might change His plans to destroy their society (Amos. 5:15).

Consider the threefold formula for change: "hate evil, love good; establish justice in the gate." The "gate" was the place where civic and commercial matters were handled, the ancient equivalent of City Hall (Ruth 4:1; Esth. 2:19–21; Prov. 31:23). Therefore, to establish "justice in the gate" meant to set laws, do business, and conduct other public transactions in ways that honored God and served people.

The Israelites were doing quite the opposite. They loved evil, hated good, and instituted injustice in their public life (Amos 2:6; 5:11–12; 8:4–6). No wonder God pledged to destroy them!

As Christians consider their influence on society today, they do well to consider the impact that public justice might have on people's openness to God's grace. There can be no question that grace leads to justice, that a person transformed by Christ will treat others with Christlikeness. Zacchaeus is a case in point (Luke 19:1–10). On the other hand, it also seems clear that when Christians work for social justice, they give people hope and win a hearing for the message of Christ's love.

SOCIAL SERVICES

God's Safety Net

People today sometimes speak of a "safety net" of social services that is supposed to catch cases of need and neglect before they lead to disaster. The Book of Psalms describes the ultimate safety net that God provides for the poor and needy (Ps. 12:5). This divine help is described in a variety of ways:

- support (18:18);
- broad place (18:19);
- secret place (27:5; 31:20);
- higher place or rock (18:2; 27:5; 40:2; 61:2);
- hiding place (27:5; 32:7);
- fortress (18:2; 91:2);
- shield (18:2); and
- wings (17:8; 61:4; 91:4).

Clearly, God's concern for the needy fills and flows out of this book of worship. The Psalms go beyond merely private or theological issues. They constantly encourage intercession for a class of people who are poor and frustrated, who often fall through the cracks of the world's "social safety nets." By praying through the Psalms, we can infuse our prayers with the concerns of those whom God has pledged to help.

SORCERY

(see Occult)

SPEECH

(see Talk)

SPIRITUAL DISCERNMENT
Judge All Things?

Paul's claim about judging all things (1 Cor. 2:15) sounds rather presumptuous. Is he urging believers to become moral policemen, passing judgment on everyone and everything around us?

Yes and no. Paul was challenging the spiritually immature believers at Corinth to grow up by applying spiritual discernment to the world around them. In this passage he mentions three categories of people:

- *natural*—those without Christ, still living in the lost condition in which they were born (1 Cor. 2:14);
- *spiritual*—believers in Christ who have been born of the Spirit and in whom the Spirit of God lives and is producing growth (1 Cor. 2:15); and
- *carnal*—believers who remain immature in the faith because they don't allow the Spirit to work in their lives (1 Cor. 3:1).

Spiritual people "judge" all things that come their way (1 Cor. 2:15) in the sense of scrutinizing, examining, and investigating spiritual value and implications. This is not something that we should do merely as individuals, but also corporately with other believers. For example, in the workplace Christians in various occupations need to band together to explore how the faith applies to particular vocations. By analyzing work situations in light of Scripture, we can discern what the issues are and how we might respond with Christlikeness.

"Judging all things" has nothing to do with damning others, but with recognizing and doing what God would want. Instead of pride, it calls for humility, since God will be the final Judge of everything we do (2 Cor. 5:10).

SPIRITUAL GIFTS
Gifts and Vocations

Does a hierarchy of gifts (1 Cor. 12:28–31) mean God values some jobs more than others? Judging by popular opinion, one might conclude that He does. In fact, for centuries Christians have subscribed to a subtle yet powerful hierarchy of vocations.

In our culture, that hierarchy tends to position clergy (missionaries and evangelists, pastors and priests) at the top, members of the "helping professions" (doctors and nurses, teachers and educators, social workers) next, and "secular" workers (business executives, salespeople, factory laborers, and farmers) at the bottom.

So what determines the spiritual value of a job? How does God assign significance? The hierarchy assumes sacred and secular distinctions, and assigns priority to the sacred. But does God view vocations that way? Note these lessons from Scripture:

1. *All legitimate work matters to God.* God Himself is a worker. In fact, human occupations find their origin in His work to create the world (Ps. 8:6–8). Work is a gift from Him to meet the needs of people and the creation.

2. *God creates people to carry out specific kinds of work.* God uniquely designs each of us, fitting us for certain kinds of tasks. He distributes skills, abilities, interests, and personalities among us so that we can carry out His work in the world. That work includes "spiritual" tasks, but also extends to health, education, agriculture, business, law, communication, the arts, and so on.

3. *God cares more about character and conduct than occupational status.* Paul's teaching in this passage is about gifts, not vocations. At the time Paul wrote it, there were few if any "professional" clergy in the church. Paul himself was a tentmaker by occupation, along with his friends, Aquila and Priscilla (1 Cor. 16:19; see Rom. 16:3–5). Other church leaders practiced a wide variety of professions and trades. God may assign rank among the spiritual gifts, but there's no indication that He looks at vocations that way.

Furthermore, Scripture says there is something more important than gifts, "a more excellent way" (1 Cor. 12:31). Chapter 13 reveals it to be the way of Christlike love and character. Implication: If you want status in God's economy, excel at love, no matter what you do for work. Love has the greatest value to God (13:13; Matt. 22:35–40).

SPIRITUAL GROWTH
One Day at a Time

How much do you understand about the faith? Do you wish you knew more? Perhaps

S

others intimidate you with their knowledge and familiarity with Scripture.

If so, Jesus' work with His disciples (Mark 4:33–34) can lend some helpful perspective. Just as our biological lives unfold slowly, so do our spiritual lives. God offers us what we can understand as soon as we can handle it, but not before. Most parents would consider explicit lessons on sexuality to be premature for preschoolers. Likewise, driving lessons for first graders would be inappropriate. And some athletic activities can cause great damage if children engage in them too early in their development. In the same way, God holds back certain lessons until we're mature enough to handle them.

Jesus called the disciples to follow Him one day at a time (Luke 9:23). But He also promised them that the Spirit would come later and lead them into truths that they could not handle then (John 16:12–16). Like those first disciples, we as Jesus' modern-day followers are not to know the end from the beginning, but to learn something from Him every day, applying it to our lives. Faith is not a badge to be worn or knowledge to be flaunted, but a little seed to be nurtured (Mark 4:26–32).

Paul in Perspective

The Bible offers many examples of people who struggled as they tried to live for God. Their stories are meant to encourage us. But sometimes comparing ourselves to the "heroes" of the faith only intimidates us. Paul, for instance, was a learned scholar, a fervent evangelist, a compassionate pastor, a competent businessman, and a diplomatic statesman. So when he tells us to follow his example as he follows Christ's example (1 Cor. 11:1), it sounds a bit unrealistic. How could we ever emulate a super-saint like Paul?

But Paul didn't start out as a super-saint. Nor did he end up that way. In fact, he never saw himself that way. On the contrary, he grew in the faith with some difficulty. Notice how his view of himself changed over time (dates given are estimates):

- About A.D. 55: "I am the least of the apostles" (1 Cor. 15:9).
- About A.D. 57: "I know that in me . . . nothing good dwells" (Rom. 7:18).
- About A.D. 60: "[I am] less than the least of all the saints" (Eph. 3:8).
- About A.D. 63: "Jesus came . . . to save sinners, of whom I am chief" (1 Tim. 1:15).

It sounds as if Paul was perhaps more "average" than we often think. In fact, look carefully at some of the highlights (and lowlights) in his life. If one changes a few particulars and develops the wholehearted commitment to God that Paul had, then his story could well be anyone's. That's because Paul was as human as any of us. His life challenges us to ask whether we are growing, struggling, and changing as he did. If so, then there's hope for us!

For more on this topic, see **PERSISTENCE,** *"Unfinished Business," page 298.*

SPIRITUAL WARFARE
"The Gates of Hell"

Jesus referred to "the gates of Hades" (hell) in His bold statement to Peter (Matt. 16:18). For Matthew's original readers, the word "gates" held special significance.

Ancient cities erected walls to protect themselves from invaders. Here and there along the walls they inserted massive gates to allow traffic in and out. In times of trouble, they could close the gates against attacking armies or bandits.

City gates, then, tended to be thoroughfares through which communications and commerce passed with frequency. Not surprisingly, bazaars and forums tended to congregate around a city's gates, so that they became an important arena in a town's public life. Goods were traded there and decision-makers gathered to hear news and deliberate on events of the day. Such gates exist to this day in some cities of the world.

Given this phenomenon, "gates" became a metaphor signifying the economic and political life of a walled city. The influential and powerful did their business "in the gates." For example, the husband of the virtuous woman of Proverbs 31 is "known in the gates, when he sits among the elders of the land" (Prov. 31:23). Boaz, the intended husband of Ruth, went to the gate to buy a marriage license (Ruth 4:1–12; also Deut. 25:7). War plans were devised and military treaties signed in the gates (Judg. 5:8, 11). Kings sat in the gates to address their people (2 Sam. 19:8). Even conspirators against kings hatched their plots and were exposed in the gates (Esth. 2:19–23).

So when Jesus spoke of the gates of Hades, He was drawing on a powerful image. Matthew's original readers would have seen it as a political metaphor, the way we use the terms *City Hall, the White House,* or *the Capitol* today. For them, the gates of Hades were not just a spiritual abstraction but actual forces of evil at work among human sys-tems—the Roman government, for instance. While not evil in and of itself, first-century government was quickly becoming corrupted and also anti-Christian.

Jesus was alluding to a spiritual warfare of cosmic proportions. His followers are pitted against the powers of hell itself, which not only attack individual believers but seek to corrupt institutions, enlisting them in their campaign against Christ. Satan's guises can take many forms, as a look at any day's news will attest.

Fortunately, Jesus also promised that in the end the gates of Hades would not succeed. That offers great hope to believers who live in difficult places and contend for good against powerful entities that, in ways known and unknown, are backed by spiritual forces of wickedness. In the midst of the fight Jesus has declared: "I will build My church!"

SPORTS

The Games

Paul's use of running, boxing, and other athletic feats (1 Cor. 9:24–27) as metaphors for spiritual discipline was suited perfectly to the Corinthian culture. Corinth hosted numerous athletic events, including the prestigious Isthmian Games, one of four major athletic festivals of the Greeks.

The Isthmian Games were held every other year and attracted athletes from all over Greece. The competitions were between individuals, not teams, who vied more for glory than for tangible prizes. At the Corinthian games, victors were crowned with pine-needle garlands, the "perishable crown" to which Paul referred (1 Cor. 9:25).

However, when the heroes returned home, their cities might erect statues in their honor, have a parade, and write poems celebrating their feats. Sometimes a champion was even exempted from paying taxes, given free meals, and placed in the seat of honor at public events.

One of the important institutions associated with these athletic contests was the *gymnasium*, where young men were educated by the philosophers and trained in various physical routines. The name derived from the fact that the athletes trained and performed naked (*gumnos*, "naked"). That and the fact that gymnastic activities were closely tied to Greek culture made the institution repulsive to most Jewish people. But Paul's Corinthian readers were no doubt well acquainted with this prominent part of Greek life.

STANDARDS

Life Is Not Fair

"It's not fair!" That is the oft-heard cry of people who feel cheated because things did not happen the way they wanted them to. One can hear it in families, courtrooms, athletic contests, businesses—even international pol-

itics. Ezekiel heard it from the people of his day. Reacting to the prophet's words concerning God's determination of guilt and innocence, they sang the sad song of injustice: "It's not fair!" (Ezek. 18:25, 29).

Their protest revealed the human tendency to establish right and wrong on the basis of what happens to one personally. Yet how can justice be administered for all if personal satisfaction is the standard? A "me first" way of thinking is not a sound basis for uniform, just, or totally fair treatment.

That is why God, who gives us the gift of life with all its choices, also gives us standards such as the Ten Commandments against which to measure justice. Personal, subjective standards cannot define absolute truth. Only through God's objective, holy standards can true and ultimate justice be obtained.

We can see this principle illustrated throughout Scripture. The great people of faith such as Noah (Gen. 6), Deborah (Judg. 4), and Daniel (Dan. 1) answered to God's standards, not those of the surrounding culture. By contrast, the greatest moral failures occurred when people set their own standards—for example, Korah (Num. 16), Samson (Judg. 13–16), and Jezebel (1 Kin. 19, 21).

Ultimately, every person must answer to God for his or her personal response to the Lord's absolute standards. Ezekiel offered three case studies to demonstrate this point:

1. *A person who lives righteously and serves others justly (Ezek. 18:5–9).* There were not many people left in Judah that fit that description, but recent memory could look back on such righteous figures as King Hezekiah (2 Chr. 29:1–2) and the faithful prophetess Huldah (34:21–22).

2. *A person who is born to righteous parents but grows up to live in wickedness (Ezek. 18:10–13).* Plenty of people in Judah fit into that category—for example, Hezekiah's son Manasseh (2 Chr. 33:1–2) and Josiah's son Jehoahaz (2 Kin. 23:31–32).

3. *A person who is born to wicked parents but grows up to live righteously (Ezek. 18:14–18).* Again, few people matched that description, but Manasseh's grandson Josiah (the son of Amon) did (2 Chr. 34:1–2).

If we just want things to always go our way, life will probably seem very unfair. But if we are truly concerned with justice, then we will submit to objective and absolute standards that ensure it. We have some experience of that in dealing with principled judges who run honest courtrooms, unbiased referees who keep things even on the playing field, and even-handed regulators who see to it that businesses abide by the law.

In a far more perfect way, God has established absolute standards of justice and love. By living according to His ways, we pursue what is truly fair and good for all people.

Needed: A Definitive Standard

"You can believe anything you want." "We each have to determine what is right for ourselves." "That may be true for you; I have my own truth."

The frightening thing about these modern viewpoints is that those who believe them become the definers of truth and reality. They leave no room for objective truth or absolutes. Yet if there are no absolutes determined by a Source that is higher than and above us as human beings, then we are all gods; or else no truth exists, and we have nothing to bind us together or define how we should treat each other.

God did not leave His people Israel in such a philosophical morass. He clearly spelled out moral and spiritual absolutes, and warned His people to seek ultimate truth from Him, not from other sources (Lev. 20:6–8).

We who live today do well to pay attention to God's unchanging Word. Apart from Him, how can we co-exist? By what standards will we define issues such as community, honesty, ethics, truth, morality, crime, and justice? Apart from His help, we are on a destructive path in a world where everyone is always right and no one is ever wrong.

One Standard for All

In 1 Timothy 3:3, Paul outlines the criteria that qualify people for leadership in the church community. All of the items mentioned have to do with character. God seems far more concerned with the personal integrity of leaders than with their education, eloquence, or charisma.

Without question, the standards are high, but that doesn't imply a higher standard for church leaders than "ordinary" Christians.

All believers are called to these same high standards of Christlikeness. Paul is not creating a class of the spiritually elite here. He is simply indicating that the church should select its leadership from among people who are generally living up to the ideals of the gospel.

Passing the Big Tests

If your school days are behind you, think back on them. Remember taking tests? How do you respond to the stress of life's testing situations? Do they cause you to increase your preparation, or do they paralyze you?

We don't earn salvation like a diploma. That's a free gift. But God tests His people (Ps. 11:5). His purpose is not to intimidate us or trick us into "wrong answers." Instead, He intends to strengthen us through stress, and teach us to depend on His council and guidance (James 1:2–8). In addition, His testing sometimes applies divine justice to our lives.

The Book of Psalms helps us see the standards by which God "grades" our performance. One way that we could be said to "pass" is when we act as a source of justice for the weak, the orphan, the lowly, the destitute, and the needy (Ps. 82:1–4; compare Matt. 7:12, 21). Another "passing" grade is given for trusting the Lord with unreserved confidence (Ps. 37:3–6; compare Job 13:15). But God will certainly "fail" us if we turn away from Him and treat others with evil.

Are you passing or failing the tests that God gives you?

What a Difference God Makes!

The commands of God always flow out of the character of God. Thus the numerous commands in Leviticus 19 are commands related to holiness, because "I the Lord your God am holy" (Lev. 19:2). Here are a few of the standards that a holy God enacted on His people:

- respect for parents (Lev. 19:3);
- keeping the Sabbath (Lev. 19:3, 30);
- forsaking idolatry (Lev. 19:4);
- concern for the poor (Lev. 19:10);
- honesty and integrity in business (Lev. 19:11–12, 35–36);
- protection of the physically challenged (Lev. 19:14);
- justice and truth in speech (Lev. 19:16);
- loving one's neighbor as oneself (Lev. 19:18);

S

- five years without harvesting a fruit tree for food (Lev. 19:25);
- dignified mourning (Lev. 19:28);
- forsaking magic and witchcraft (Lev. 19:31);
- respect for the elderly (Lev. 19:32);
- loving treatment of aliens (the "stranger," Lev. 19:34); and
- keeping the whole Law (Lev. 19:37).

Does a holy God make a practical difference in people's day-to-day lives? He certainly does! Notice the single reason given for all of the preceding statutes: "I am the LORD your God!"

For more on this topic, see PERCEPTIONS, "Challenging Our Perceptions," page 294.

STARS

(*see* Astronomy)

STARTING OVER

(*see* Renewal; Second Chance)

STARVATION

Starvation—The Great Leveler

There were five ways to capture a walled, fortified city in the ancient world. The least hazardous but most protracted was for the attacking army to surround the city, cutting it off from supplies and reinforcements, and then wait. Sooner or later, either the water supply or food supply would give out. Then the city would surrender or else fall rather easily when it was finally assaulted.

This was the strategy that the Babylonians used in the final siege of Jerusalem. The invaders arrived in late 589 B.C. and, except for a brief retreat the following summer (Jer. 37:5), remained encamped around Jerusalem for two years (2 Kin. 25:1–2). There was little danger of the city running out of water, thanks to King Hezekiah's foresight prior to an Assyrian siege in 701 B.C. But there was no such reservoir of food.

By the "ninth day of the fourth month"—perhaps of the continuation of the siege—the food supply was gone (2 Kin. 25:3). Jeremiah describes the severity of the situation by painting a before-and-after picture of a group known as Nazirites (Lam. 4:7–8). These may have been individuals who had taken what was known as a Nazirite vow (see Num. 6:2),

a sign of devotion to the Lord. Or they may have been certain nobles.

In either case, these Nazirites normally appeared in public wearing carefully laundered clothing, and were accorded an elevated status. But as a result of the siege, their robes, which had been "brighter than snow" (Lam. 4:7), were now "blacker than soot" (Lam. 4:8). Now they went unnoticed in the streets, not because they had lost their status, but because they looked no different than anyone else: they had the same emaciated, wrinkled look.

In other words, the famine conditions affected the entire population of Jerusalem, from the greatest to the least (compare Lam. 4:16). It was exactly the result that the Babylonians had planned, and it meant that the end was drawing near. For those inside the city, it meant desperation. They were forced to watch each other slowly die (4:9)—or worse, resort to cannibalism (Lam. 4:10).

STEADFASTNESS

(*see* Persistence)

STEALING

The Starving Thief

Suppose someone steals your car, your wallet, or your stereo. Later the thief is caught and found guilty of the crime. What sort of penalty would you impose on the offender if it were up to you?

Under the Old Testament Law, a thief was ordinarily required to make restitution of twice the value of the loss (Ex. 22:4). However, Proverbs indicates that if someone stole because he was hungry, he had to repay sevenfold, even if it meant losing his house and property (Prov. 6:30–31). What accounts for this higher penalty?

The answer may be that the Law made numerous provisions to prevent poor people from starving. These included:

- The third-year tithe (Deut. 14:28–29).
- Gleaning (see Lev. 19:9–10). (Significantly, the gleaning provision is followed in verse 11 by the command, "You shall not steal," perhaps in recognition that the poor, for whom gleaning was instituted, are especially vulnerable to the temptation to steal.)

- The release of debts in the sabbatical year (Deut. 15:1–3).
- The temporary sale of real property (Lev. 25:23–34).
- Mandatory charity loans (Deut. 15:7–11) at zero interest (Ex. 22:25).
- Voluntary indentured service (Lev. 25:39–55).

In light of these policies, there was no excuse for someone to steal in order to eat (unless the society failed to carry out these policies).

However, it is worth noting that each of these provisions involved a form of charity, and many people resist accepting charity for a variety of reasons such as pride, embarrassment, or a desire for independence. Perhaps the penalty of sevenfold restitution was intended to punish this prideful rejection of help.

A similar (and far more serious) situation concerns those who know about the saving grace of God, yet reject it out of pride and self-sufficiency. Their rebellion makes them subject to condemnation and eternal punishment (Heb. 2:1–4; 6:4–18; 10:29–31).

For more on this topic, see ILLEGAL SEARCH AND SEIZURE, "Grasping for What Others Have," page 215.

STEWARDSHIP

The Rest of Your Paycheck

Most Christians are well aware of their responsibility to financially support the work of the church. However, once they have fulfilled that obligation, many assume that the rest of their income is theirs to use as they please. But God is as interested in what we believers do with the money we keep as He is with the money we give away. It is from that perspective that Scripture exhorts us to honor the Lord with our possessions (Prov. 3:9–10).

The ancient Israelites gave to God the "firstfruits," the firstborn of the flocks and the first crops gathered at harvest time. These were dedicated to God by formally presenting them at the temple on the day of Pentecost (Num. 28:26). Giving to God the first and the best of one's harvest indicated a recognition that everything belonged to Him.

Included among the possessions that the Israelites owned were the means of production—land, animals, tools, mills, looms, potter's wheels, carts, boats, and the like. Therefore, honoring the Lord with one's "possessions" went far beyond a weekly or monthly check in the offering basket or a year-end contribution to a charity. In essence, it meant that all of one's work was to be dedicated to God.

According to Proverbs, the outcome of such a lifestyle would be prosperity (Prov. 3:10). It is tempting for modern-day Christians to read this as a promise of financial gain in exchange for obedience to God. However, the Proverbs are not so much promises to be claimed as they are observations about the way life tends to work. In the main, people prosper as they honor God in their work and with the income derived from their work.

We also have to remember that the Israelites had a special covenant relationship with God in which obedience to God's Law was directly related to abundance in their land (Deut. 28:1–14). God has made no such arrangement with Christians today. In fact, the New Testament cautions us against expecting God to reward us with material blessings for pursuing godliness.

Yet like the Israelites, Christians are challenged to honor God in their work and finances. Is that what you are doing? Do you approach your work with the conviction that Christ is the Lord of what you do and how you do it? Do you in some way give to the Lord "the first and the best" of your income? And what about the money you keep? Do you use it in ways that reflect God's character and purposes?

Robbing God, Robbing the Poor

As modern-day churches set budgets and allocate financial resources, it is worth noting that in the Old Testament, the Israelites were commanded to give tithes ("a tenth part") of their produce or income for three reasons: to celebrate the abundance of the Lord's provision (Deut. 14:22–26), to support the Levites (Deut. 14:27; Num. 18:20–24), and to provide for the poor (Deut. 14:28–29).

In Malachi's day, the postexilic Israelites were withholding their tithes and offerings (Mal. 3:8–10). Apparently they preferred to keep more for themselves rather than give what God asked. In doing so, they were not only robbing from God; they were in effect robbing from the Levites and the poor.

Could the same be true among believers today? Malachi tried to reawaken a sense of corporate responsibility for the poor and for public worship. He knew that obedience to God was more than just private religion; there are social implications to one's relationship with God. One of those implications involves giving away a portion of one's income to those who need it.

Tithing Today?

Jesus' words to the Pharisees (Matt. 23:23) raise the issue of tithing. Should Christians today pay tithes? Or are we free from that practice? For that matter, what is a tithe? The word means "a tenth part." In the Old Testament, God commanded the Israelites to give tithes—one-tenth of their produce or income—for one of three reasons:

1. To support the Levites, who were responsible for the tabernacle and worship.

2. To support various feasts and sacrifices.

3. To establish a pool of resources to help the poor, orphans and widows, and strangers in the land.

In the New Testament, neither Christ nor the apostles gave any explicit instructions about tithing. However, Jesus clearly endorsed it, as He did all the Law (Matt. 5:17–20; 23:23). So what is the place of tithing for believers today? Several principles might be considered:

1. As Christians, our allegiance is not to the Old Testament Law, which was primarily given to Israel, but to Christ.

2. Our giving needs to spring from a love of Christ, not a slavish obedience to a percentage standard. Throughout Scripture, loving God and worshiping Him are at the heart of tithing.

3. All of what we have ultimately belongs to God—not just what we give away, but also what we keep. So He has total claim on one hundred percent of our income, not just ten percent.

4. Ten percent makes a great starting point for giving. However, studies indicate that, as a group, Christians in the United States give nowhere near that much of their income away—to ministries or charities of any kind. In fact, while per capita income has in-

creased, church members have actually *decreased* their contributions to churches.

5. Vocational Christian workers have a right to financial support from those to whom they minister (1 Cor. 9:13–14; Gal. 6:6). Likewise, many churches assist the poor, orphans and widows, and strangers. So it seems legitimate to expect believers to donate money to those causes.

6. No matter how much we give or to whom, our first priority should be to ensure that justice is carried out around us, that we show mercy to our "neighbors," and that we practice our faith and not just talk about it. It is through our obedience that Jesus increases our faith.

*For more on this topic, see **GIVING**, "Amount vs. Attitude," page 167; "Giving with Compassion and Integrity," page 168; **OWNERSHIP**, "Do We Really Own Anything?" page 287.*

STING OPERATION
"Stings" Expose Loyalty to God

News headlines today often feature tales of scandal and exposé, especially when law enforcement officials set up a "sting" operation to catch offenders in the act. The stories gain especially wide publicity when those caught are among the high and mighty, particularly if their crimes are lurid or large in scope.

In ancient Babylonia, officials conducted a "sting" operation of sorts that caught three provincial governors in a clear violation of Nebuchadnezzar's command. What was their heinous crime? Failure to bow down to a ninety-foot-high, gold-plated image (Dan. 3:8–12). This act so outraged the king that he immediately passed sentence on them, and they were thrown into a super-heated furnace (Dan. 3:19–23). The three men had committed a brazen act of disloyalty to the king; but it was a courageous act of loyalty to the Lord.

A similar incident occurred years later in the time of Darius. Informers exposed Daniel for violating a decree against prayer to any god or ruler but the king (Dan. 6:6–13). The outcome was similar: Daniel was thrown to the lions (Dan. 6:16).

On both occasions, God delivered His faithful followers from death (though not from the threat of death). Moreover, their courageous stand for Him influenced others to fear God, and also resulted in the suppression or removal of troublemakers (Dan. 3:26–29; 6:21–27).

What would it be like if government "stings" today exposed believers practicing their faith? Imagine if the only way to entrap you would be to "catch" you being loyal to God (Dan. 6:4–5)! Would there be enough evidence to convict you?

STRESS

Quiet Living in a Hectic World

If any one word characterizes life in the modern world, it may be the word hectic. The rat race. The grind. The fast lane. Things seem to move faster and faster, and anyone who can't keep up is in danger of being left behind.

For that reason, Paul's exhortation to "lead a quiet life" (1 Thess. 4:11) seems out of step with contemporary culture. How can one lead a quiet life when technology accelerates change and increases complexity? When television and other media bring the world into our homes and broadcast private lives to the world? When a global economy makes everybody's business our business?

The challenge to lead a quiet life in a hectic world is considerable, but as believers we can take decisive steps that will benefit us personally and spiritually. Actually, Paul gives us an important first step in the exhortation to "work with [our] own hands." The focus is not on "hands" but on "your own": it was not manual labor that Paul insisted on, but self-support.

As far as quiet living, Paul was probably not objecting to noise and sound as such, but to needless distraction. One way that most

NEB'S HEATING AND COOKING HOTTER

NEED A FIERY FURNACE? CALL US!

STING OPERATION

people could bring a little more peace and quiet into their homes would be to cut their television viewing in half. Imagine the time left for family members and neighbors, personal reflection, and prayer!

However, the real thrust of this passage is not so much for believers to lower the noise level around them as to live peaceably with others, without disturbance or conflict (compare Rom. 12:18; Heb. 12:14). Minding our own business and working for ourselves are both means to that end, the end of "[walking] properly toward those who are outside [the faith]" (1 Thess. 4:12).

How can we live peaceably? By avoiding quarrels and complaints (Col. 3:13); by refusing to take offense when others hurt us (Matt. 5:7–12); by not getting entangled in the affairs of others (Prov. 6:1); and by humbly accepting the circumstances that God sends us for our good, rather than grumbling (Rom. 8:28; Phil. 4:11–12).

For more on this topic, see **PERSECUTION,** *"Welcome to Stressful Living," page 296.*

STUBBORNNESS
Stiff-necked to the End
One would have thought that after all that Azariah and his fellow citizens had been through—years of watching their leaders being deported to Babylon, the hardships of a three-year siege of Jerusalem, the city's eventual fall and sacking, and the assassination of their governor—they would have heeded Jeremiah's warnings against their proposed flight to Egypt. After all, the prophet had accurately predicted most of these calamities and more. Not one of his prophecies had ever failed.

Yet the frightened survivors denounced Jeremiah as a liar (Jer. 43:2). Like their neighbors who had been taken into exile, they remained obstinate in their rejection of God's counsel. They not only went to Egypt, but began worshiping idols there. They flatly told Jeremiah, "We will not listen to you! But we will certainly do whatever has gone out of our own mouth" (44:16–17). To the very end they insisted on having their own way.

Do you do that? Do you continue to reject God's word, even as it proves true time and time again? God will not force you to accept His ways, but neither will He protect you from the consequences of rejecting them. He is opposed to the pride of the person who is determined to ignore His truth (James 4:6).

For more on this topic, see **FREE WILL,** *"Did Pharaoh Have a Chance?" page 162.*

STUDENTS
(*see* Education)

SUBMISSION
Authority Is a Two-way Street
The way some people describe it, the success or failure of any venture rests almost entirely on good leadership. Yet at Mount Sinai (Ex. 32:7–8) we find that even the ultimate Leader—God Himself—experienced the disappointment of a mission gone awry. For authority is a two-way street. It involves not only the exercise of the superior's *authority*, but also the subordinate's *acceptance* of that authority. Israel declined to accept God's leadership, not only here, but on numerous other occasions.

Have you ever wished that your boss were more assertive and in control? Perhaps you can help by being more submissive to the authority he does exercise. Accepting his authority is a kind of investment you make in your superior. Effective leaders always must have those who are willing to follow.

A Lifestyle of Submission
A popular slogan in recent years has been "peace through strength." But James might change that to "peace through humility." After all, wars and fights arise from "desires for pleasure" (James 4:1). Our cravings lead to friendship with the world and enmity toward God (James 4:2–4). Thus, peace in the world depends upon peace with God, and that requires humility (James 4:6).

The way to show humility before God is to submit to Him (James 4:7). In fact, the New Testament calls believers to a lifestyle of submission. The fact that Christ submits to His Father shows that submission need not carry a sense of inferiority. In fact, it shows that submission—in the ways that Scripture indicates—is a Christlike behavior, and worthy of honor (Phil. 2:1–11).

It's worth mentioning that submission is only half the equation. For example, the church is called to submit to Christ, but Christ also has responsibilities toward the church: to love her, to give Himself up for her, to make her pure, to nourish and cherish her, to love her as He loves Himself (Eph. 5:25–33).

For more on this topic, see EQUALITY, "What Is Headship?" page 127.

SUBURBIA
Sisters and Daughters

Ezekiel called Jerusalem, Sodom, and Samaria "sisters" (Ezek. 16:55) because all three were notorious for their godless ways. However, the idea of sister and daughter relationships between cities is more than a metaphor. The cities and towns of the world have important links that are worth paying attention to, especially for urban Christians who are called to bring Christ to the issues and needs of the city.

Many cities today are linked together through ethnicity. As a result of the United States' history of immigration, the cities of the United States in particular have more ties than many realize to cities in Europe, the Middle East, Africa, Central America, the Caribbean, and Asia. Some family members live in North America, but others remain in the "old country." Likewise, many cities in the northern states and in California have ties to the Deep South through the migration of African Americans during the first half of the twentieth century.

One implication of this for the church is that North American Christians need not necessarily travel "over there" to reach a particular group with the gospel. It may be far more effective to begin with representatives of that group who already live "over here," and then let the gospel travel the "relational highways" overseas.

Ezekiel also speaks in terms of cities having "daughters." In the ancient Middle East, a major, walled city usually had smaller, unwalled neighbors nearby, forming a city-state of mutually dependent communities. Today we call these daughter cities "suburbs," and are becoming keenly aware of just how important it is that center cities plan and govern with a view toward the impact on their suburbs.

In turn, suburbanites, and especially suburban Christians, neglect their core cities at their peril. Ezekiel pointed out that one of the

reasons for Sodom's fiery judgment was its arrogant neglect of the poor in spite of its incredible wealth (Ezek. 16:49). The same was true for Jerusalem (Is. 3:13–15). Is there any reason why God should not chastise His people today if they are guilty of the same sin?

SUCCESS
Praying for Success

How many young people have prayed a prayer similar to that of Abraham's servant— for the Lord to give them success in finding the right spouse (Gen. 24:12)! In fact, from finding a partner to finding a job, from building a business to building a life, people frequently pray for God to bless their efforts with success. Is that prayer legitimate for God's people?

In a success-driven society, people of faith often struggle with the place and pursuit of success. Some believe that material success by its nature represents a compromise of spiritual convictions. Others, however, feel that success is actually a sign that God is pleased with them. Still others claim that they are not interested in success, yet this claim seems to be an excuse for their poor performance in the marketplace. What does success mean for people who want to honor God in their lives?

There are no simple answers to these questions. The issue of success is complex and charged with emotion. But perhaps the following three observations will prove helpful as you devote thoughtful consideration and public discussion to the subject:

- Success always implies striving to meet or exceed some set of standards established by some person or group.
- The pursuit of success is always a personal choice. No one can make someone else pursue success.
- Obtaining success always exacts a cost— it takes our time, ability, and resources.

In light of these principles, ask yourself three questions as you pursue, or refrain from pursuing, success: Who is determining what success means for me? What am I choosing by my pursuit of success? What price am I paying to achieve success?

Remember Where You Started

The lore of American business celebrates rags-to-riches success stories—the shipping clerk who rises to the position of CEO, the immigrant who founds a financial empire, the ghetto youth who ascends the political ladder. But with success always comes the danger of forgetting what one has left behind—the drudgery of the shipping room, the difficulties of learning a new culture, the fear of wondering whether anyone believes in you.

In Deuteronomy, Moses repeated a phrase again and again to keep the Israelites from forgetting their humble past: "remember that you were a slave in the land of Egypt" (Deut. 15:15; compare Deut. 5:15; 16:12; 24:18, 22). Given that history, the Hebrews had every reason to show compassion and equity to their own slaves and servants (Deut. 15:12–14).

From where have you started out? Have you forgotten what it was like to be an underling or underdog? How might your background influence the way you treat other people today? Thinking back, how would you have liked to have been treated? How do you treat others?

For more on this topic, see **AFFLUENCE,** *"The Dangers of Success," page 12;* **PRIORITIES,** *"Solomon's Dissatisfaction," page 318;* **PROSPERITY,** *"Success and Prosperity," page 324.*

SUFFERING

(*see also* Troubles)

A Time to Take Stock

Times of great loss or suffering can provide a valuable opportunity for reflection and self-examination. For example, the loss of a loved one often brings back vivid memories that give insight into the meaning of the person's life. In a similar way, Ezekiel's vision of the new temple appears to have been intended as a reminder of Solomon's temple, which had been the center of Judah's spiritual life and cultural identity. For centuries, that temple had stood as a powerful symbol of God's abiding presence. Now it was gone.

Yet God did not leave His people without hope. Through Ezekiel, He told them that He had plans for an entirely new temple. He described these plans in the most exacting detail (Ezek. 40–42). What was the point of this elaborate description? It seems to have been meant to help the people rehearse their failure as the people of God and to recognize

how much they needed His help. In effect, they were to measure themselves with the same level of precision with which God was designing the new temple (Ezek. 43:10–11).

The same principle applies to believers today. In our darkest moments, in times of great loss or fear, God would have us pursue insight and self-examination. We can harness our thoughts and feelings, much as the exiles of Judah were challenged to do through Ezekiel's description of the temple.

Insight from New Sight

The sixth sign miracle featured in John's Gospel reveals Jesus as the Light of the World (John 9:5). He was also unique among the prophets in that none of them had cured blindness (John 9:30–33).

The healing of the blind man speaks to the problem of human suffering. Then as now, sickness was often assumed to be divine punishment for someone's sin. Like Job's counselors (Job 4:7–9; 8:2–8; 11:4–20), Jesus' disciples asked, "Whose sin caused this man's blindness?" (John 9:2). But Jesus replied with a radically new truth: God can use human suffering to reveal His glory (John 9:3). Jesus immediately showed what He was talking about by healing the man's blindness, thereby revealing Himself to be the Son of God.

Questioning God

Some people believe that human beings should never question the ways of God. Some even feel that it borders on sin to ask God, "Why?" But the Book of Habakkuk counters that idea. It is filled with a prophet's perplexing questions—and the Lord's penetrating answers. God never seems to reproach His servant for asking two fundamental questions:

- Why does the Lord seem so unresponsive to the injustice and violence that Habakkuk sees around him? (Hab. 1:2–3)?
- How can God use the vicious, oppressive, idolatrous Babylonians (Chaldeans) to judge His people (Hab. 1:12–17)?

Habakkuk was not unlike many people today who are troubled by the world around them. They sometimes wonder: Where is God? Why doesn't He do something about all the pain and suffering, the injustice and oppression, the wars and diseases that destroy humanity? If He is there, why doesn't He speak? If He is powerful, why doesn't He act? If He is loving, why doesn't He intervene? Habakkuk shows that questions like these are as old as the seventh century B.C.

So are the answers. God may not explain everything to our satisfaction—nor are we capable of understanding everything He has told us. Yet He assures us, just as He assured Habakkuk, that His ways are just and righteous, and furthermore, "the just shall live by faith" (Hab. 2:4). This truth applies universally, as Paul and other writers of the New Testament realized (Rom. 1:17; Gal. 3:11; Heb. 10:38). In the end, the ultimate answer to our questions is to *trust* God.

Asking "Why?"

Faced with sudden tragedy, such as the loss of health, wealth, or a loved one, the natural question to ask is: Why? Why did this happen? Why did it happen to me? Why now?

Job struggled with questions of "why" as he tried to make sense of his sufferings (Job 7:20–21). So did Jesus' disciples when they came upon a man who had been born blind. "Who sinned?" they asked Jesus. "This man or his parents?" (John 9:1–2). They were asking why in the sense of *causality:* What was the reason for his blindness? They assumed that somehow sin must have been involved.

Yet on another level, the disciples were asking why in the sense of *purpose:* What was the significance for the man's blindness? In reply, Jesus borrowed an answer from Job. He assured His disciples that through the man's blindness, the glorious works of God would be made evident (John 9:3–5). Then He fulfilled that claim by healing the man on both a physical and spiritual level.

Job, too, eventually realized the awesome glory and grace of God as a result of his sufferings (Job 42:1–6). That should offer some comfort to those of us today who face seemingly senseless tragedy. The pain is real and must not be denied. But someday we will see the glory of God, even in the things that we suffer. We have the assurance of Job and Jesus on that.

For more on this topic, see **EVIL,** *"God and the Problem of Evil," page 133; "Blaming Satan?" page 134.*

SUPERVISION
Stick to Your Word

One of the most difficult tasks that anyone in authority faces is to take disciplinary action against people for violating organizational standards. Whether the discipline involves a mild verbal warning or a career-ending firing, there is no way to make it easy. But in God's severe discipline of a blasphemer (Lev. 24:13–14), we can see two important principles that may help to make discipline more consistent and effective:

1. *Enforce standards from the beginning.* God had already told His people that He considered blasphemy a capital offense (Ex. 20:7). This case involving Shelomith's son (Lev. 24:10–12) was the first major test of that law. God followed through on His warning by instructing Moses to carry out a sentence of stoning. In effect, God was making an example of the young blasphemer.

The principle here is to make expectations clear and then start tough. There's no point in letting improper behavior slide, hoping it won't happen again. It invariably will. But if people can see that there are definite consequences for noncompliance, they are likely to think twice before violating the policy.

2. *Hold everyone to the same standard; don't play favorites.* The fact that the text names the offender's father as an Egyptian (Lev. 24:10) is significant. Perhaps some among the Israelites thought that the severity of the man's punishment was due to his racially mixed background: he was the son of a foreigner; he had cursed Israel's God; so of course he would be punished by stoning.

But God made it clear that there would be no double standard: "*Whoever* curses his God . . . *whoever* blasphemes the name of the LORD . . . the stranger as well as him who is born in the land" would be punished (Lev. 24:15–16, emphasis added). God had no intention of playing favorites.

How consistent is your discipline, if you are in authority? Justice for all means justice for each one. Certainly there are times for mercy and taking into account extenuating circumstances. But fairness demands that even these be exercised evenly.

S

The Godly Use of Power

Because history includes many cases of people in authority abusing their power, some people are skeptical about the nature of power. They have concluded that power by its very nature is corruptive. But while the Bible is realistic about the tendency of sinners to abuse power, it also gives examples of rulers who used their authority wisely and with godly integrity.

Although it is generally believed to refer prophetically to the Messiah, Psalm 72 also sets forth principles for a godly use of power. The piece was composed either by or for Solomon, who exercised more power during his reign than any of the other Israelite kings, including his father David. Psalm 72 suggests a number of practical ways a ruler can use power:

- To judge with righteousness and justice.
- To bring peace to the people, and to restrain crime and violence.
- To bring justice to the poor and the children of the needy, and to allocate resources in a way that is compassionate.
- To undo the work of oppressors, and to prevent the powerful from hurting the little people.
- To gain the respect and support of his citizens.

That is how a ruler can exercise power. On the other side of the power equation are those affected by the leader's use of power. They include:

- The people of the nation, who will respond with respect and admiration.
- The poor among the people.
- The children of the needy, who have little stake in the community.
- Those who oppress others, who will be hindered in their abusive tendencies.
- Neighboring nations, who will pay respect.
- Many areas of life are affected:
- Nature and agriculture.
- Human relationships.
- The economy.
- International relations.
- The future.

If you are in a position of authority and power over other people, consider the influence you have, and how you can use it in ways that honor the Lord. Are there changes you need to make in the way you exercise authority? Are you living up to the godly ideals of Psalm 72?

*For more on this topic, see **ENCOURAGEMENT,** "Encouraging the Boss," page 124.*

SURROGATE MOTHERS

Concubines

Leah and Rachel, the wives of Jacob, used their maids to compete with each other for their husband's favor by having them bear his children (Gen. 30:3–13). Thus the maids, Zilpah and Bilhah, became secondary wives or "concubines" to Jacob.

The practice of "marrying" concubines, a form of polygamy, was known throughout the ancient Middle East. A concubine was usually a female slave with whom the leading male of the family was free to have sexual relations. She was not considered an equal to his "full" wife (or wives), but she could not be sold if the man lost interest in her. However, rights varied from culture to culture.

One of the main justifications for keeping a concubine was to give birth to children, particularly a son and therefore an heir. The wives of the patriarchs particularly used concubines for this purpose, as the following examples show:

- Hagar, concubine of Abraham. She functioned as a concubine at Sarah's insistence; gave birth to Ishmael (Gen. 16).
- Keturah, concubine of Abraham. She bore Abraham six sons (Gen. 25:1; 1 Chr. 1:32).
- Timna, concubine of Eliphaz. She gave birth to Amalek, the father of the Amalekites (Gen. 36:12).
- Esther, concubine of King Ahasuerus of Persia. She was selected from the king's harem to becone queen, a position from which she helped to save her people the Jews from genocide (Esth. 2:13–16).

SYMBOLS

The Danger of Relics

Jesus said that God is Spirit, and those who worship Him must worship in spirit and truth (John 4:24). That means that we worship and serve a God whom we cannot see with our eyes, but must believe with our hearts. As a result, God is a bit of an abstraction for some people. One way that they have tried to make Him more real and present is through artifacts that they have associated with Him.

Yet as understandable as the veneration of relics may be, it is a dangerous practice. It can easily tempt people to worship the object, rather than the God whom the object is supposed to point to. In essence, the relic becomes a focus of idolatry.

That happened with a number of items that the Israelites venerated, including the bronze snake that Moses had made during the Exodus journey (2 Kin. 18:4). Originally, the serpent on the pole served as a means of healing for snake-bitten people, by causing them to look to the Lord for help. But after the people settled in the Promised Land, they apparently turned this standard into an idol, as if the bronze snake itself had power to heal. They burned incense to it and even gave it a name, Nehushtan.

In a similar way, the Israelites turned a ceremonial robe, or ephod, that Gideon made from the spoils of his victory over the Midianites, into an idol (Judg. 8:25–27). Later they tried to use the ark of the covenant as a charm against the Philistines, with disastrous results. And in Jeremiah's day, the citizens of Jerusalem cared more about their temple than they did about the Lord of the temple.

These examples show the dangers of making too much of objects and places that have had a close association with the work of God. As human beings, we live in the natural world, but we worship a supernatural God. Therefore, we need to treat shrines and relics merely as means toward that end, never as ends in themselves.

The Value of Symbols

A symbol can be a powerful thing, whether it be a tangible, visible sign such as a corporate logo, or an intangible ceremony or event. The erection of a monument on Mount Ebal (Deut. 27:4) was part of an elaborate set of symbols designed to impress on Israel that following the Law was a life-and-death matter.

Like the successors of Moses, leaders today have a responsibility for the symbols their groups use to communicate meaning and values. Symbols can help organizations achieve several objectives:

- celebrating the history of the organization, the values and people that have shaped it into what it is;
- orienting new people into the corporate culture by showing them what matters and why;
- communicating core values by emphasizing, explaining, and enacting the fundamental beliefs and principles on which the enterprise is built; and
- providing a frame of reference through which all members of the organization can establish their identity in the group, evaluate their progress, and enforce accountability.

What are some of the symbols in the groups of which you are a part—your company, community, church, family, and so on? What do those symbols say about what matters to the group? If you are a leader in the organization, what symbols have been allowed to wither that need to be revived? Which ones may need to be reconsidered in light of change, or perhaps even allowed to die? What new, creative expressions need to be developed to communicate basic beliefs and values?

T

TALENT

A World of Talent

The world has never lacked for talented people. God has placed among humans a marvelous diversity of gifts and skills to accomplish meaningful work in the world. The experience of Israel in the wilderness is a testimony to this fact.

First, God gave Moses to Israel as a gifted leader. However, when it came time to construct the tabernacle, Moses did not have the skills required. He was not a craftsman in the building trades.

But God had already provided among the people migrating from Egypt skilled workers such as Bezalel, Aholiab (Ex. 36:1), and countless unnamed others such as the women who wove yarns and fine linen (Ex. 35:25–26) and those who gave freely and worked hard (Ex. 35:10, 21, 29; 36:3–7). All of these worked according to the abilities that the Spirit had given them.

In looking over God's instructions to Moses concerning these workers, one notices that he was to (1) identify them as skilled people, (2) affirm them in their responsibilities in the task, and (3) free them to do their jobs under the supervision of others who knew the trades. In carrying out this delegation of the work, Moses had a good example to follow in God, who delegated responsibility to people at the beginning of creation. He declared, "I have given it to you," and "It shall be yours" (Gen. 1:29; 9:2–3; 12:7; 13:15–17).

TALK

Talk Is Cheap!

Some people have a comment to make on virtually every subject. They never say, "I don't know," or just listen in order to learn something. They just spout off their uninformed opinions to any willing listener. Proverbs calls such persons fools (Prov. 18:2).

Talk is cheap partly because it is easily available. The Book of Proverbs offers some principles to help us evaluate the worth of our words:

- Sometimes the wisest course is to keep quiet. We need to weigh our thoughts and words carefully if we intend to be helpful (Prov. 11:12; 17:27–28).
- The one thing we never want to talk about is a confidence with which we have been entrusted (Prov. 11:13).
- If we know how to use words, we can accomplish noble ends—for example, defusing a heated situation (Prov. 15:1–2).
- We need to watch what we say. Our mouths can get us in deep trouble (Prov. 18:6–7).
- If we give our opinion on a matter before hearing the facts, we will tend to bring shame on ourselves (Prov. 18:13).
- Talk is cheap, but easy talk can be expensive. Saying the wrong thing at the wrong time can lead to unfortunate consequences (18:21).

For which are you known—lots of talk and self-important opinions, or the ability to listen and words of wisdom? To find out, you may want to ask others for an honest opinion. Another way is to ask, "When was the last time someone came to me and asked for counsel?" It may seem risky and even painful to learn the truth about yourself in this area, but you will be much better off if you know your errors and can change them (Prov. 12:1; 15:32).

The Dangerous Tongue

Has your tongue ever gotten you in trouble? Perhaps you have said something that you wish you had not. Or perhaps you have been on the receiving end of a biting or thoughtless comments, and have felt wounded or slandered. If so, you probably can appreciate the great damage that can come from from an uncontrolled tongue (Prov. 10:18–21). Hatred, slander, and wickedness thrive because of words we speak.

Jesus' brother James recognized this destructive pattern in the early church. He realized how easy it can be to blurt out comments without weighing the value of what is said, and he warned first-century Christians about lack of restraint when it comes to the tongue:

- He urged them to be quick to listen but slow to speak (James 1:19).
- He cautioned them not to think themselves religious if they could not control what they said (James 1:26).
- He told them not to claim to have faith unless their deeds matched their words (James 2:14–24).
- He wanted them to understand that the tongue boasts great things despite its tiny size (James 3:5).
- He warned them that the tongue is "a fire, a world of iniquity" (James 3:6), "an unruly evil, full of deadly poison" (James 3:8), and a fountain of grumbling (James 5:9).
- He pointed out that speech can be an unpredictable source of either blessing or cursing, like a spring that gives either fresh water or bitter, or a fig tree that bears olives, or a grapevine that bears figs (James 3:10–12).
- He noted that some were using speech as a means of maligning one another (James 4:11).

• He challenged believers about making promises and oaths that were inconsistent (James 5:12).

As we reflect on the teachings of Proverbs and James concerning the tongue, it becomes evident that we need to pay attention both to what we say and to how we say it. We may need to make changes in our patterns of speech in order to avoid the outcomes of the foolish (Prov. 10:21).

The Impact of Words

People tend to be known by what they say. Words may strike fear in others, they may reveal the speakers to be foolish, or they may

TALK

be a source of help or comfort to other people.

In a passage that probably pertains to the coming Messiah, Isaiah said the Lord's Anointed would "know how to speak" by receiving instruction from God (Is. 50:4). As a result of this divine tutelage, He would be able to speak appropriately to the weary.

How much more do the rest of us need help in knowing what to say, given our sinful condition. Scripture repeatedly warns us about the power and danger of our words. As Scripture frequently shows, they can:

- cut like a sword (Ps. 57:4; 64:3);
- be as dangerous and poisonous as a snake (Ps. 140:3);
- convey lies with the impact of a bow (Jer. 9:3);
- strike down other people like an arrow (Jer. 9:8); and
- curse and demean others (Hos. 7:16).

What is the impact of your words on other people? Does what you say build others up or tear them down?

For more on this topic, see **PROMISES**, *"Making Promises to God," page 321.*

TAXES

A Remedy for Tax Fraud

Luke describes Zacchaeus as a tax collector (Luke 19:2). His first-century readers would have understood that to mean that Zacchaeus was a cheating, corrupt lackey of the Roman government. In fact, he was a *chief* tax collector, which probably meant that he was "public enemy number one" to the Jews in Jericho, even worse than the notorious bandits on the city's main highway.

But Jesus reached out to the curious Zacchaeus, prompting him to change his ways. In fact, Zacchaeus came up with his own formula for making restitution on the tax fraud he had practiced: a four hundred percent rebate to those he had knowingly cheated, plus half of his net worth to go to the poor (Luke 19:8). By paying restitution, he showed a new respect for the Old Testament Law (Ex. 22:1). Giving away his possessions was not a requirement of the Law, but it revealed his change of heart.

Imagine a corrupt public official or shady corporate financier today following that formula. Imagine a pastor challenging a businessperson in his congregation to repay four times what was made on a crooked deal. It sounds simplistic. But Zacchaeus was truly repentant. He was like the tax collector Jesus had recently mentioned in a parable who cried out, "God, be merciful to me a sinner!" (Luke 18:13).

A Ten Percent Tax

How much is ten percent of your income? If you had lived in ancient Israel, you would have been obligated to pay that amount every three years in order to provide material assistance to two classes of people—the Levites and the poor (Deut. 26:12). Neither group owned any land, which meant that they had no access to the means of production. The tithe was one way to provide for their needs (compare Deut. 14:28–29).

It is interesting that after presenting the tithe, the Hebrews were to declare before the Lord that they had fulfilled their obligation (Deut. 26:13). In exchange, God had committed Himself to blessing their land with abundance (Deut. 26:15). Thus ideally a cycle of obedience and blessing was to be established in which no one would ever lack for their needs.

At ten percent paid every third year, the system was a bargain. Yet over the centuries countless details were added to the law of the tithe, with the result that by Jesus' day, tithing had become not only a bothersome burden but a corrupted ritual that bore no resemblance to the original law (Matt. 23:23–24).

Jesus and Taxation

The odd episode in Matthew 17:24–27 turns out to be a subtle and winsome reminder that Jesus claimed to be God. It's also a lesson in the proper exercise of moral liberty.

The temple tax of half a shekel was assessed annually on all Jews twenty years old and above. It paid for the support of the temple system (Ex. 30:13–15). Apparently Jesus and Peter had not yet paid their taxes, though Peter's response to the tax collectors indicated that they soon would.

The irony, however, is that the temple tax collectors were demanding taxes from the Messiah Himself! How ludicrous—as Jesus pointed out in His question to Peter about who is taxed by a ruler (Matt. 17:25). As God's Son, Jesus was the Lord of the temple; technically, He was exempt from taxation.

God put His stamp of approval on Jesus' reasoning with the miracle of the coin (Matt. 17:27). Peter found "a piece of money" (a stater, a four-drachma coin) in the fish's mouth—the exact amount needed for the two of them. The collectors were satisfied, and the transaction cost Peter and Jesus nothing.

But consider: Jesus voluntarily paid the tax to avoid offending the religious leaders that the collectors represented (Matt. 17:27). In doing so, He demonstrated something about how His followers should live.

We as Christians are properly free in many areas because of our relationship with God. We are not bound by legalistic rules about eating, drinking, or special observances. Nonetheless, we must be careful not to use our liberty in a manner that offends other people. If the Son of God paid a voluntary tax in order to avoid offending those who did not understand who He was, how much more should we, as God's children, bend over backwards at times to avoid offending those who do not understand our liberty?

Taxation had been a troublesome issue for the Jews for generations. In fact, centuries before Jesus' time, the heavy taxes that King Solomon levied to pay for his many construction projects contributed to a revolt and the division of the kingdom under his successor Rehoboam.

Scripture offers help for believers in

handling the "gray" areas of life in which God has prescribed no specific behavior.

A History of Taxes

Feelings of resentment over taxes ran deep among the Jews, who had endured a history of heavy taxation for centuries. In Egypt, Joseph warned of seven years of famine after seven years of abundance. Pharaoh then put him in charge of raising revenues. He collected a twenty percent tax to store up food and buy land for Pharaoh (Gen. 47:20–26).

During the Exodus, Moses asked for voluntary contributions to construct the tabernacle (Ex. 25:2; 35:5, 21). The Law prescribed that every male over the age of twenty was to give half a shekel for the service of the tabernacle (Ex. 30:11–116).

Under David and Solomon, several taxes were established: a ten percent tax on the produce of land and livestock (1 Sam. 8:15, 17); import duties (1 Kin. 10:15); and tribute paid by subject peoples (2 Sam. 8:6; 2 Kin. 3:4). The taxes became so oppressive under Solomon that they contributed to the split of the kingdom after his death (1 Kin. 12:4).

During the days of the Persian Empire, rulers collected taxes for their own provinces, from which they paid a fixed amount into the royal treasury. Revenues were derived from tribute, custom, and toll (Ezra 4:13). A tax was also collected for maintenance of the governor's household. Again, the taxes were crushing. Many people were forced to mortgage their fields and vineyards, and some even sold their own children into slavery (Neh. 5:1–5).

During the period between the Old and the New Testament, the Jews were first under the Egyptian Ptolemaic rule (301–198 B.C.) and later under the Syrian Seleucid rule (198-63 B.C.). Under the Ptolemies, taxing privileges were farmed out to the highest bidders. People came to Alexandria from the various provinces to bid for the privilege of collecting taxes from their own people. Contractors would tax their people up to double the amount required by law in order to make a handsome profit. These tax collectors were even given military assistance to enforce their demands.

The same type of system probably continued under the Syrians. A poll tax, a salt tax, and a crown tax were enforced during this time. The Syrians taxed as much as one-third of the grain, one-half of the fruit, and a portion of the tithes that the Jews paid to support the temple.

When the Romans captured Jerusalem in 63 B.C., a tax of ten thousand talents was temporarily imposed on the Jews. Julius Caesar later reformed the system by reducing taxes and levying no tax during the sabbatic years. But soon the Herods came to power.

The Herods instituted a poll tax and a tax on fishing rights. Customs were collected on trade routes by men like Levi in Capernaum (Matt. 9:9; Mark 2:14; Luke 5:27). The city may have also been a place for port duties and fishing tolls. Some items sold for one thousand percent above their original prices because of all the taxes. There may have been a sales tax on slaves, oil, clothes, hides, and furs.

Over and above these taxes were religious dues, generally between ten and twenty percent of a person's income before government tax. As a result, during Jesus' time, the Jews were probably paying between thirty and forty percent of their income on taxes and religious dues.

No wonder the Pharisees asked, "Is it lawful to pay taxes to Caesar, or not?"

Those Tax Collectors

Tax collectors (Matt. 9:10) were agents or contract workers who collected taxes for the government during Bible times. Some translations incorrectly call them "publicans," but publicans were wealthy men, usually non-Jewish, who contracted with the Roman government to be responsible for the taxes of a particular district. They were often backed by military force. By contrast, tax collectors were employed by publicans to do the actual collecting of monies. They were Jews, usually not very wealthy.

Tax collectors gathered several different types of taxes. Depending on the kind of rule in a given Jewish province, Rome levied a land tax, a poll tax, even a tax for the operation of the temple (Matt. 17:24–27). Some provinces, like Galilee, were not under an imperial governor, so their taxes remained in the province rather than going to the imperial treasury at Rome. Perhaps these inequities prompted the Pharisees in Judea (an imperial province) to ask Jesus, "Is it lawful to pay taxes to Caesar, or not?" (Matt. 22:17).

As a class, tax collectors were despised by their fellow Jews, and were generally associated with "sinners" (Matt. 9:10–11; Mark 2:15). They often gathered more than the government required and pocketed the excess amount—a practice that John the Baptist specifically preached against (Luke 3:12–13). But tax collectors were also hated because their fellow citizens viewed them as mercenaries working for the Roman oppressors.

For more on this topic, see **REVOLUTION,** *"A Tax Revolt," page 346.*

TEACHING
How We Need Teachers!

To invest in the future of another person is a praiseworthy activity. God especially calls parents to invest in the lives of their children (Prov. 1:8; 4:1), but others also play a vital role. Teachers, coaches, and other adults can have a lasting influence in the development of young people (Prov. 4:11–13).

Several notable teachers are mentioned in the Bible:

- Bezalel and Aholiab were two master craftsmen who were gifted and called to teach others in the construction of the tabernacle (Ex. 35:3—35).
- Samuel, the last of Israel's judges before the monarchy, taught the people "the good and the right way" (1 Sam. 12:23).
- Ezra, a scribe and priest, was committed not only to keeping the Law himself but to teaching it to others (Ezra 7:10).
- Jesus was a master teacher whose insights revealed the mysteries of the kingdom of God and the good news of salvation (John 13:13; Eph. 4:20–21).
- Paul, perhaps the church's most gifted teacher, was known to have taught throughout the Roman world, notably at Antioch (Acts 13:1) and the school of Tyrannus at Ephesus (Acts 19:9).
- Priscilla and Aquila were two believers who taught the way of God to a talented young orator named Apollos (Acts 18:26).

Who have been some of your most valuable teachers? What did you learn from them? Have you ever thanked them for the impact they have had on your life?

For more on this topic, see **CHILDREN,** *"Pass On the Story," page 54; "The Faith of Our Children," page 55;* **EXAMPLE,** *"Faith at Home," page 136.*

TEAMWORK
(*see also* Cooperation)

A Project Management Team

Moses pulled together a trio to form a leadership team for the complicated project of building the tabernacle:

- Ithamar, the youngest son of Aaron and Elisheba (Ex. 6:23). He functioned much as a comptroller or accountant might, keeping track of the many articles and resources collected for the building (Ex. 38:21). Later, he also supervised two priestly families of Levites (Num. 4:21–33).
- Bezalel, the son of Uri of the tribe of Judah. He was essentially the designer or architect of the project, providing designs and giving instructions for all the various craftspeople working in stone, metal, wood, and weaving (Ex. 35:30–36:1; 38:22).
- Aholiab, the son of Ahisamach of the tribe of Dan. He was a skilled artisan who provided instruction in the crafts needed for the project, especially in engraving, design, and embroidery (Ex. 35:34–36:1; 38:23).

Their final performance review showed that they and their workers "did according to all that the Lord had commanded Moses" (Ex. 39:32, 42)—the ultimate stamp of approval! No wonder Moses was pleased (Ex. 39:43).

Believers today have also been designed to function in their communities, where various temperaments, skills, resources, and strengths are needed to produce products and services of benefit to others. Are you employed in a way that makes the best use of your gifts?

For more on this topic, see **COMPETITION,** *"Who Gets the Credit?" page 80;* **CONFLICT,** *"From Conflict to Cohesion," page 84;* **COOPERATION,** *"United for the Work," page 91.*

T

TEMPTATION

Pay Attention to Temptation!

Paul's warning to "take heed lest [you] fall" (1 Cor. 10:12) is as necessary today as it has ever been. For we, like all who have gone before us, are fallen, temptable, and subject to thinking and doing what is wrong. Few teachings of Scripture have more practical implications for day-to-day living.

Opportunities for temptation are almost endless. And since human nature is not getting any better, nor is any of us immune to the corrupted appetites of the flesh, we need to take Paul's warning seriously and watch out for temptation, or we will surely fall. Yet Scripture offers several alternatives for dealing with temptation as we find it:

1. We should *avoid* temptation whenever possible. Proverbs 4:14–15 urges us, "Do not enter the path of the wicked, and do not walk in the way of evil. Avoid it, do not travel on it." Often we know beforehand whether a certain set of circumstances is likely to lead to sin. Therefore, the obvious way to avoid sin is to avoid those circumstances. Paul described a "way of escape" from temptation (1 Cor. 10:13). Often the escape is to stay away from the place or the people where temptation lurks.

As believers, we can help others in this regard. We can avoid setting up situations that encourage people to do wrong. Teachers, for example, can help students avoid cheating by making assignments, giving tests, and communicating expectations in ways that reduce the need or incentive to cheat. Likewise, business owners and managers can devise procedures that don't needlessly place employees in a position where they might be tempted to steal cash, inventory, or equipment. It's not that a teacher or employer can't trust students or employees, but that no one can trust human nature to be immune from temptation.

2. We should *flee* from powerful temptations. Earlier in this letter, Paul warned the Corinthians to flee sexual immorality (1 Cor. 6:18). Here he warned them to flee idolatry (1 Cor. 10:14). Elsewhere he warned Timothy to flee the lust for material possessions and wealth (1 Tim. 6:9–11), as well as youthful lusts (2 Tim. 2:22). The message is clear: don't toy with temptation. Flee from it!

3. Chronic temptation is something we need to *confess* and offer to Christ, and ask for His cleansing work. Some temptations are powerful inner struggles, with thoughts and attitudes that graphically remind us of how fallen we really are. What should we do with that kind of temptation? Rather than deny it or try to repress it, we should bring it to Christ. He alone is capable of cleaning up the insides of our minds.

4. Finally, we must *resist* temptation until it leaves us. When Christ was tempted by the devil, He resisted until the devil went away (Matt. 4:1–11). James encouraged us to do the same (James 4:7). Resistance begins by bathing our minds with the Word of God and standing our ground. We have the promise, after all, that the temptations we experience will never go beyond the common experiences of others, or beyond our ability to deal with them (1 Cor. 10:13). That is great news!

Under the Circumstances

In addition to the substance of what was happening when Satan tempted Jesus, we see an environmental aspect in this passage as well. Jesus was tempted in three very different settings:

1. *In a barren desert (Luke 4:1–4).* In the ancient world, deserts were believed to be inhabited by spirits that engaged in never-ending warfare. In fact, some of the early church fathers went into desert caves as a way to engage in spiritual warfare and develop spiritual disciplines. Unfortunately, they sometimes lost contact with the everyday world in which life has to be lived.

Centuries earlier, Israel had run into major problems in the desert, rebelling against God and wandering for forty years before entering the promised land (Num. 14:29–35).

2. *On a mountain (Luke 4:5–8).* A mountain setting may seem an unlikely environment for temptation. But in the ancient world, many religious shrines were carved or carried into mountains, where they became sources of idolatry and superstition. Today, mountain retreats, even those owned and operated by religious organizations, can become like shrines that tempt people to run away from problems. It's easy to prefer an exciting, memorable "mountain-top experience" to

the grinding reality of day-to-day life in the "valley." Retreats and vacations can be valuable, but they also can become a vain religion if they are used to avoid reality.

3. *In Jerusalem, a city (Luke 4:9–13).* Like us, Jesus was tempted to take command of a city. Any city—especially "the holy city"—can sorely tempt a person with power. Power itself is morally neutral, but like fire it has grave potential to destroy people when mishandled. One has only to review the political history of cities like New York, Chicago, Hong Kong, or Beirut to appreciate that grim reality.

Jesus' temptation touched the environment in three different ways. What environments pose temptations—and opportunities—for you? . . .

"You Don't Understand!"

How often we hear someone dismiss the implications of faith for day-to-day life with the retort, "You don't understand! I live in the real world, where things are tough. They play by a different set of rules there. Christianity is all well and good, but isn't it a bit simplistic when it comes to real life?"

The account of the temptation in Matthew 4:1–11 offers a response to that sort of thinking. It shows that Jesus does understand real life. He faced real temptations—the same temptations that show up every day in the "real world."

Some people think that because He did not give in to what was offered, He must not have been "really" tempted; therefore, He can't "really" understand our situation. But that won't do. Scripture affirms that Satan's devices were real temptations that really tempted Him. And because He was able to resist them, He is able to help us do the same (Heb. 2:18). He completely understands our feelings—and how to do what is right in spite of them.

TENTMAKING

(*see* Ministry Support)

THANKSGIVING
Passing On the Blessing

God's goodness to us is not solely for our own benefit and pleasure. He wants us to pass along the good gifts He brings our way.

Psalm 67 supports this principle by bringing together the twin themes of thanksgiving and worldwide evangelism.

The psalm begins with a prayer for blessing (Ps. 67:1); in fact, the prayer itself is a form of a blessing. But the prayer is more than a petition. It explains the *purpose* of asking for God's blessing: that the Lord's ways might become internationally known (Ps. 67:2). The psalmist recognized that the destiny of the nations was wrapped up in God's blessing of Israel. Ultimately they would praise and fear the Lord because of what He was doing for His people.

This psalm offers strong evidence that God wants salvation for *all* peoples, for the *whole* earth (Ps. 67:3–7). His purposes have been fulfilled through Jesus Christ. The Messiah came as a branch out of Israel and offered Himself as a blessing to all the peoples of the world.

What blessings has God brought your way? Whatever they are, He wants you to share His good gifts with the people around you. He especially wants you to share the gift of the gospel, the message of salvation in Christ. Think of someone right now who might be open to receiving the blessing of eternal life, and then *pass it along!*

For more on this topic, see **GRATITUDE,** *"Let Us Give Thanks," page 187;* **PRAISE,** *"Praise Rather than Pride," page 311.*

THEFT

(*see* Stealing)

TIME
Working Smarter, Not Harder

We often hear about the value and rewards of hard work. But how hard is work supposed to be? When faced with a difficult task or heavy volume of demands, how do you respond? Do you think through how to accomplish more with less effort and fewer resources, or do you just grit your teeth and exert more effort?

Proverbs suggests that our work need not always be toilsome labor and sweaty pain. It confirms the fact that God's original design was for work to be good—in fact, "very good" (Gen. 1:31). It was only after Adam and Eve's sinful rebellion that work came under the curse, with the result that laborers suffer from sweat and toil (Gen. 3:17–19). But as much as possible, God wants our labor to be a significant, satisfying activity.

Proverbs offers counsel on how that can happen, and how we can work "smarter, not harder":

- We are wise if we honor God in our work and with the pay that we receive from work (Prov. 3:9–10; 16:3).
- It is smart to learn and practice diligence and avoid the pitfalls of laziness (Prov. 6:6–11; 13:4; 19:15; 20:4; 21:25).
- Taking responsibility for our work and carefully planning it will yield enormous benefits (Prov. 12:11, 14, 27; 14:23).
- We will avoid much pain and find much joy if we do our work with ethical integrity (Prov. 16:11; 20:10, 17, 23).
- It is natural for us to want to provide for ourselves, and we are wise to use that motivation by showing initiative (Prov. 16:26; 20:13).
- It is smarter to work for long-term outcomes than for short-term gains (Prov. 20:21; 21:5; 24:3–7).
- The path to success is to develop excellence in our skills and performance (Prov. 22:29; 24:3–7).

*For more on this topic, see **PROPERTY**, "How Much Is All?" page 321.*

TIMING

Knowing When to Start and Stop

An important part of exercising authority is telling the group one leads when to start and when to stop. As God led Israel through the wilderness, He used the cloud of His presence to indicate starts and stops (Num. 9:15–23).

Today believers have the Word of God to guide them through life. Yet even so, we still need wise leaders who have a good sense of timing for when to get something started and when to bring an activity to a halt.

Nowhere is this more true than in the workplace. Every organization is on a journey. To successfully surmount the ups and downs of organizational survival and growth, business leaders need sensitivity to timing:

when to press forward, when to pull back, when to stay put.

Likewise, each of us as individuals needs to be sensitive to timing in our own professional and personal lives: when to look for a new job or career, when to stay put where we are, how long to keep working, when to stop and rest.

God was the Israelites' guide. Is He ours? Do we follow the basic guidelines of His Word and then make wise, responsible choices?

What to Do, When, and How

Decisions in organizational settings require much more than supposedly "right answers" and "yes sir" responses. Rulers are generally looking for people who can solve problems, not present them with new ones. Therefore, effective leaders rely on wise advisors known for their timing and judgment (Eccl. 8:5). This means a sensitivity and insight into *what* needs to happen, *when* it needs to occur, and *how* it can be accomplished. Often, the crucial difference between success and failure is timing and method.

TITHES AND OFFERINGS
(*see* Stewardship)

TONGUE
(*see* Talk)

TRADITIONS
The Value of Traditions

For some people, the term "tradition" conjures up ugly images of maintaining the status quo, adhering slavishly to a distant past, or trying to keep alive dead rituals. But traditional celebrations and routines can serve good purposes. For example, the Passover was intended to help succeeding generations of Jews grasp in a small way what God accomplished in bringing Israel out of Egypt (Ex. 12:26–27, 42).

In a similar way, the best religious traditions remind us that we are a dependent people. All that we are and have we owe to God's grace. We need reminders of that, because in a society that has so much, it's easy to forget God's intervention and blessing.

And if we ever forget God, then our offspring will forget Him, too. By adhering to the disciplines of tradition, we can remind our children of things they may not have personally experienced, but still need to honor.

So like the ancient Hebrews, we as believers today need to work at remembering God's work among us (Deut. 24:9–22; 1 Cor. 11:26). That's what the Lord's Supper is for. Furthermore, we can use celebrations, symbols, music, and other memorials to point out what God has done for our ancestors and for us. For this reason, some Christian churches have detailed, year-long calendars of festivals and holy days for their worshipers. Others have periodic observances and commemorations that are less formally established.

How do you celebrate God's work in previous generations?

Tradition and Values

Tradition. Is it the bedrock of intelligent change or the stumbling block to any change? Should leaders embrace and personify traditional values, or should they be mavericks, breaking with tradition and striking out in new directions?

Jesus rebuked the scribes and Pharisees for allowing their rabbinic traditions to actually supersede the express commands of God (Matt. 15:3). The specific issue here was a tradition about ritual washings connected with the preparation and serving of food. Not only must one's hands be washed, but also the bowls, cups, pitchers, and other utensils.

In modern American culture we do not follow the rigid pronouncements of a priestly class. Yet there are numerous traditions and expectations—most of which are unspoken—that govern our behavior in powerful ways. This creates tension for believers in the workplace, particularly managers. They are called upon to be both sustainers and breakers of tradition. There are no simple formulas to help one decide how to respond to tradition, but it might help to reflect on questions such as:

- What values and principles does the tradition seek to embody? How do those square with the values of Christ?
- Why does the tradition exist? Why is it maintained? Are there any major objections to it?

- In maintaining a tradition, who benefits and who suffers? If it changes, who might be helped or hurt? How would the organization be affected?

Tradition can preserve important values and beliefs for future generations. Tradition is an important area in which faith impacts the world.

*For more on this topic, see **RITUALS**, "The Value of Rituals," page 351.*

TRAVEL

Travel in the Biblical World

As they set off on their travels for "the work" to which God had called them, Barnabas and Saul traveled through Seleucia (Acts 13:3–4), the seaport for Antioch. The city was important to the Romans because it provided access to one of the major east-west land trade routes of the Mediterranean region, the Way of the Sea.

The Way of the Sea. The Way of the Sea (Is. 9:1) was the most important international highway throughout the biblical period. Originating in Egypt, it ran north along the coast to a pass over the Carmel ridge, through the Valley of Jezreel to Hazor, and eventually to Damascus. From there one could either head north through Syria toward Asia Minor, or east toward Mesopotamia, eventually linking up with the Euphrates River, which the highway followed to the Persian Gulf.

Many of the most important political and commercial centers of the ancient world were located along this road and its branches. Citizens thrived on supplying the needs and security of the many caravans traveling east and west.

However, it was the strategic military value of this roadway that ancient empires prized the most. By controlling a key city like Damascus or the passes at Megiddo and Hazor, an army could effectively shut down the Way of the Sea—or keep it open for its own troops or merchants. As a result, Palestine became a major factor in international politics and trade.

The King's Highway. A second major highway in the region was the King's Highway (Num. 20:17; 21:22). The King's Highway ran north and south along the length of the Transjordanian Highlands, near the desert to the east of the Sea of Galilee, Jordan River, and the Dead Sea, and linked Damascus (and the Way of the Sea) with Elath on the Gulf of Aqaba.

This route provided a secondary road to Egypt and access to the spice routes of Arabia. It was often controlled by semi-nomadic people who prevented the founding of settlements along its length. In certain periods, however, the route was guarded by a network of fortresses.

Secondary Road Systems. Within the region of Palestine, an internal system of roads provided communication between the various regions of the country. For people of means or position, such as the Ethiopian treasurer (Acts 8:26–28), travel along these roads might be by chariot or by portable chairs (Song 3:6–10). For most people, however, the only way to get about was on foot or donkeyback. Foot travelers could average about sixteen miles a day. Thus under normal circumstances, the trip that Joseph and Mary took from Nazareth to Bethlehem (Luke 2:1–7) probably took at least five days.

Sea Journeys. For long distances, ship travel was common (Jon. 1; Acts 13:4; 27:1–44). Cargo ships usually had little room for passengers, though occasionally they carried voyagers on the open deck or in the hold with the cargo (Jon. 1:5). Paul sailed on such a vessel on the last leg of his trip to Rome (Acts 28:11).

Despite his earlier shipwreck (27:13–44) and his allusion to the various "perils" of travel (2 Cor. 11:26), travel in Paul's day was relatively simple and considerably safer than in earlier times. The establishment of Roman control over the Mediterranean put an effective end to piracy and highway robbery in the region. Furthermore, the well-maintained Roman road system linked every corner of the empire and made travel much easier.

TREASON

A Traitorous Prophet?

The complaint that the princes of Judah brought against Jeremiah (Jer. 38:4) was nothing less than a charge of treason. If the prophet were found guilty, their request for the death penalty would have been justified.

The case against Jeremiah was considerably strengthened by a damaging piece of evidence, albeit a circumstantial one. Around 589 B.C., the Babylonians besieged Jerusalem in response to a rebellious alliance of which King Zedekiah was a part. However, the siege was temporarily lifted when the Babylonians heard rumors of an approaching army of Egyptians (Jer. 37:5).

During the lull in the fighting, Jeremiah made the mistake of traveling north toward his hometown in Benjamin to take care of personal business. This must have been the route that the retreating Babylonians had taken, for when Jeremiah arrived in Benjamin, he was arrested and charged with attempting to defect to the Babylonians. He was returned to Jerusalem and imprisoned (Jer. 37:11–15).

When the siege resumed, Jeremiah continued to urge surrender rather than resistance (Jer. 38:1–3). So in addition to defection, Jeremiah's enemies charged him with aiding and abetting the enemy. Again, a case could be made against him based on appearances.

There were five ways to take a walled city (see 2 Kin. 25:1–4). The least violent and costly way was by trickery. Apparently Jeremiah's enemies were convinced that the prophet was an agent of Nebuchadnezzar, and that his words concerning the certainty of Jerusalem's fall were a ruse to convince the city's defenders to lay down their arms and open the city gates.

Only through the intervention of the eunuch Ebed-Melech (Jer. 38:7–13) and the private doubts of King Zedekiah (Jer. 38:14–26) was Jeremiah spared. In the end he was vindicated when Jerusalem fell in 586 B.C. (Jer. 38:28–39:2; 2 Kin. 25:4).

TRICKERY

(*see* Deceit; Manipulation)

TRINITY

Trinitarian Support

One of the most important teachings of Christianity is the concept of the Trinity, the belief that God is one God, but exists in three Persons—Father, Son, and Holy Spirit. However, the Bible does not offer an explanation of this concept so much as a presentation of it. It assumes a triune God but does not try to "prove" the Trinity.

In 2 Thessalonians, Paul seeks to enrich

his readers' understanding of their new life in Christ by telling them about works done on their behalf by all three Persons of the Godhead. These same benefits are ours as believers today:

- The Father has selected us for salvation, loves us, and gives us consolation and hope (2 Thess. 2:13, 16).
- The Son shares His glory with us and provides comfort and stability in the faith (2 Thess. 2:14, 16).
- The Spirit purifies ("sanctifies") us and develops our faith (2 Thess. 2:13).

As believers, we have a powerful, caring, active God working on our behalf. For the first-century Christians at Thessalonica, that was a distinct contrast to the many gods of the surrounding Greek and Roman cultures that were often passive, sometimes capricious, and terribly self-absorbed. Likewise in our own day, our God is infinitely more powerful and personal than the vague "higher power" to which many people allude.

The doctrine of the Trinity may be difficult to comprehend, but as always we see in a dim mirror when it comes to ultimate truth (1 Cor. 13:12). Nevertheless, we can obediently respond to what we know clearly and not dwell on things that are cloudy. One thing we know for sure: our God is for us in every way!

TROUBLES

(*see also* Suffering)

A Plague of Your Own

God cares about the personal needs of each believer. Solomon's prayer of dedication is a passage of Scripture that especially supports belief in a personal, loving God.

Solomon realized that the temple at Jerusalem was a place of prayer—not only a place *in* which people would pray, but also a place *toward* which people would pray (1 Kin. 8:38, 41–42). The temple would be a representation of God's presence on earth. So when people prayed toward Jerusalem, they would be doing so in order to pray to the Lord.

When would people be likely to lift up their prayers? Surely when they experienced trouble—famine, pestilence, blight, and other plagues and sicknesses (1 Kin. 8:37). But it was not just general calamity that would move a person to turn to the Lord, but one's personal needs as well, "the plague of his own heart," as Solomon put it.

It's an intriguing thought—a plague of one's own, the point at which the trouble, pain, and sorrow of a fallen world intersect with a person's own heart and life. In that moment, when one "spreads out his hands" toward the Lord, God hears.

What is the plague of your heart? What trouble binds your soul so that you have nowhere else to turn but toward God? Are you willing to lift up your prayers to Him? His presence is abiding, and He has promised to hear your cry. Why not enter into His presence right now (Heb. 10:19–22)?

All Things for Good?

Romans 8:28 is easy to quote to someone else. But what about when it's your turn to suffer? Is there comfort in this passage? Notice two important things as you consider Paul's words here:

1. All things work together *for* good but not all things *are* good. The loss of a job, a tyrannical boss, physical illness, or family troubles are not good *per se*. In fact, often they are the direct result of evil. That's important to observe. Believers are never promised immunity from the problems and pains of the world. Every day we must put up with much that is not good.

2. Nevertheless, good can come out of bad! This verse promises that God uses all the circumstances of our lives—both the good and the bad—to shape outcomes that accomplish His purposes for us. And His purposes can only be good, because He is good by definition (James 1:17).

So how can you make this verse work for you as you face tough, troubling times?

- Affirm your trust in God's presence.
- Align your goals with God's purposes.
- Accept the reliability of God's promises.

Brokenhearted or Hardhearted?

Job was a broken man (Job 17:1). He not only lost his family, possessions, and health, he was stripped of whatever pride he might have had. Yet because he was brought low, he was able to reaffirm his faith and dependence on God (Job 19:25–27).

The Bible tells us that God is opposed to the proud, but gives grace to the humble (Prov. 3:34; James 4:6). It also provides numerous illustrations of people who at times fit into one category or the other.

Which side are you on? Do you stubbornly resist God? If so, be forewarned that hardheartedness can become a chronic condition, leading to spiritual bankruptcy (1 Cor. 10:1–13; Heb. 3:7–4:11). On the other hand, developing a tender heart toward God can only lead to greater intimacy with God. Trials and difficult times may break us down, but in the end God uses them to build us up—if we let Him (James 1:2–8).

By Water and by Fire

The history of ancient Israel was framed by flood and fire—the "flood" of the Exodus from Egypt and the "fire" of the Babylonian exile. Isaiah combines in parallel, poetic fashion these twin themes of exodus and exile that are so central to Israel's self-understanding (Is. 43:2).

The "waters" suggest the Red Sea, which the Lord parted so that the nation could cross and escape from Egypt (Ex. 14:21–22). Likewise, the "rivers" recall the Jordan River, which the Lord also parted in order for the people to enter Canaan (Josh. 3:14–17). The "fire" reflects the siege fires that burned Jerusalem (2 Kin. 25:8–10), and, symbolically, the seventy years that the people of Judah spent in Babylon.

Perhaps you have been through experiences of flood or fire, either literal or symbolic. In what ways was God with you? How did He preserve you? Or are you still in the midst of trial? If so, tell a fellow believer about your need, and ask for prayer that God will supply you with the resources to meet the challenge.

The Original Murphy's Law

An old adage called Murphy's Law states that "If something can go wrong, it will." The Book of Job states the matter a bit more poetically: "Man is born to trouble as the sparks fly upward" (Job 5:7). Eliphaz, Job's friend who gave this piece of wisdom, was probably misguided about some things, but on this point he was absolutely right: life in a fallen world is by its very nature marked by trouble and disappointment.

Usually we don't have to go looking for that trouble; it seems to find us on its own. Not that the struggles most of us face are anything like those that Job confronted. But we still have plenty of reminders that life is less than perfect: illnesses, heartaches, breakdowns in our relationships, disappointments in our careers, the death of friends and loved ones, natural disasters, wars. If we live long enough and remain honest, sooner or later we are compelled to reach the same conclusion that Job, Eliphaz, and their companions came to as they sat around Job's ash heap: "Man is born to trouble as the sparks fly upward."

Have you accepted that reality? Or do you deny it, believing that this is the best of all possible worlds, or should be? Some people go to great lengths to avoid pain. Job encourages us to accept the troubles of life, face them squarely, and turn to God in the midst of them. And if we should be fortunate enough to bypass some of the worst evils in the world, then the most appropriate response is thankfulness, as well as compassion for those with a more common experience.

For more on this topic, see **PROBLEMS,** *"Turning Pain into Prayer," page 319;* **SUFFERING,** *"A Time to Take Stock," page 388.*

TRUSTWORTHINESS

A Badge of Integrity

Told by the angel Gabriel that he and his wife would have a son, Zacharias expressed doubt (Luke 1:18) based on their advanced age. But implicit in his comments was a lack of trust in Gabriel himself. The angel responded with the simple statement, "I am Gabriel, who stands in the presence of God." No appeal to evidence; no attempt at persuasion—just a simple declaration of his position before God. That alone was enough to ensure that the messenger was absolutely trustworthy.

Were Gabriel a liar, God would have banished him long before. But his continued presence before God indicated that he must have been truthful, as none but the truthful can stand in God's presence.

Consider the implications of that for the character of believers today. If we know God, we are to be like Him (2 Pet. 1:3–4; 1 John

3:2). As He is faithful and true (Rev. 3:14; 19:11; 22:6), we must be faithful and true. Wouldn't it be something if the claim "I am a Christian" were enough to establish one's integrity!

Yet that is far from the case today. For example, how many "Christian businesspeople" bring disrepute to the name of Christ by failing to pay their bills, abusing contracts, performing sloppy work, or making excuses rather than fulfilling commitments? Even some churches and Christian ministries cheat vendors, shortchange visiting speakers and musicians, misrepresent their finances, or pay employees far below a fair wage for their work.

What a tragedy! If Gabriel's confident statement is any indication of the integrity that should mark God's workers, then it ought to be that one need only be identified as a Christian to erase all doubt. Of all people, Christ's followers should pursue an unimpeachable reputation for integrity.

God, the Model Shepherd

We often hear that the Lord is our shepherd (Ps. 23:1), but what does that mean? In David's time, good shepherds were devoted to the care, feeding, and protection of sheep. In modern terms we would say that they were

A SHEPHERD AND HIS STAFF

counted on to manage the resources of the sheep owner.

In doing their job, good shepherds sometimes took great risks to retrieve a stray or threatened animal (1 Sam. 17:34–35; Matt. 18:12). They did so not only because they were dedicated to the task, but because they were accountable for any lost sheep (Gen. 31:39).

In addition to David, two other men in the Old Testament are singled out for praise as good shepherds. Moses led the Israelites like a shepherd through a very tough journey from Egypt to Canaan (Is. 63:11–13). Later, God used King Cyrus of Persia to "shepherd" His people in the rebuilding of the temple at Jerusalem (Is. 44:28).

However, Scripture also mentions some bad shepherds—the selfish leaders of the divided kingdom who enriched themselves at the expense of their flock, the people (Ezek. 34:1–16; compare Jer. 25:34–38). God charged these wicked shepherds with ignoring the weak and the sick, failing to search out and bring back any wanderers, using coercion and cruelty to motivate the flock, carelessly failing to protect it from dangerous predators, and generally neglecting their responsibilities. As a result, the Lord promised to severely judge these leaders for their unacceptable work.

God offers Himself to us as a model Shepherd, a picture of faithful, trustworthy service. To whom can we become reliable shepherds in our family, community, and workplace?

TRUTH

Proclaiming God's Truth

In today's age of acceptance and tolerance, it is not easy or popular to disagree with others. It seems that the one truth everyone must bow to is that everybody has the right to their own beliefs, and what's true for one may not be true for another. To suggest that someone else could be wrong, or worse, to claim that there is such a thing as ultimate, absolute truth, is highly offensive in our culture.

But how can everything be true? That seems to be a contradiction in logic, if we agree with Webster that truth can be defined as "fact, the state of something being the case," or as "actuality, the body of real things, events, or facts." Jesus claimed to be *the* truth, not just *a* truth (John 14:6). He regularly

spoke of telling the truth to his listeners (for example, Matt. 5:18, 26; Mark 10:15, 29; Luke 21:3, 32; John 3:3–11; 16:7–23). So what God communicated through Christ is extraordinarily important and must not be compromised.

But as Jude demonstrates, not all who begin to follow God's truth finish well:

- When Israel fled from Egypt, some disbelieved—and died (Jude 5; Num. 14:26–45).
- Some angels turned away from God and were banished from their positions (Jude 6; Matt. 25:41; 2 Pet. 2:4).
- Sodom and Gomorrah stand as evidence that sin can bring about destruction (Jude 7; Gen. 13:10–19:28).
- Cain chose selfishness, greed, hatred, and murder (Jude 11; Gen. 4:3–8).
- Balaam gave in to error and lost his clarity regarding the truth of God (Jude 11; Num. 22–24; 2 Pet. 2:15–16).
- Korah mistakenly opposed God's leaders and paid for it dearly (Jude 11; Num. 16).

God's people are not called to be bigots who flaunt their connection with the truth. But we are called to be loyal to the truth of Christ, and we should challenge people to avoid anything less than what God offers (Jude 17–23). We're not to be a "truth squad," inflated with our own importance. But neither are we to be Milquetoasts who will agree to anything for the sake of peace. No, we must proclaim God's truth with mercy (Jude 22) to those who will perish without it (Jude 23).

Sorting Out the Truth

It seems as if everybody has one thing or another to sell. Even teachers try to persuade us to accept their ideas and claims about what is true. But when it comes to matters of faith, it's wise to remain slightly skeptical, especially if someone claims to be God's special envoy to you.

Paul warned young project leader Timothy about exactly that sort of activity—false doctrines, myths, and endless genealogies (1 Tim. 1:3–4). Here and in other passages, Paul gave guidelines for sorting out and testing what people say about faith issues and practices:

- Do they call for the practice of love (1 Tim. 1:5)?

- Are they ambitious, striving for esteem and acclaim through their teaching (1 Tim. 1:6–7)?
- Does their message promote internal moral standards that produce good behavior (1 Tim. 1:8–10)?
- Is there evidence of a radical change for the better because of their walk with Christ (1 Tim. 1:12–14)?
- Do they offer humble thanksgiving to God for what they have received (1 Tim. 1:15–17)?
- Does their position build on the wisdom of predecessors (1 Tim. 1:18–20)? (Paul contrasts those who called Timothy with two others whom he condemns.)

When people make claims about spiritual things, weigh their words carefully against standards like these. Others around you may criticize any form of doubting, questioning, or evaluation. If so, they need to consider Paul's teaching in this passage. Scripture invites careful examination of statements about spiritual things so that we will distinguish what is from God and will last.

*For more on this topic, see **OPENNESS**, "Discerning the Truth," page 283; **STANDARDS**, "Needed: A Definitive Standard," page 381.*

U

UNBELIEF

(*see* Doubt; Faith)

UNBORN CHILDREN

(*see* Abortion)

UNDERCLASS

(*see* Disadvantaged Persons)

UNDERSTANDING

An Understanding Heart

If you were assured that God would grant you your greatest wish, what would you ask for? Money? Health? Happiness? Solomon asked for "an understanding heart." The request itself showed remarkable wisdom, but it also made a great deal of sense given the circumstances in which Solomon found himself.

He was following in the footsteps of a remarkable man (1 Kin. 3:6) He was young and perceived himself to be inexperienced (1 Kin. 3:7). He was saddled with the responsibility of leading God's people (1 Kin. 3:8), a people who had shown themselves on frequent occasions to be stubborn, rebellious, and hard on their leaders.

He also had just emerged from a messy fight over succession to the throne (1 Kin. 1–2). Most of his enemies had been eliminated. But could he ever forget the intrigue surrounding those events? Likewise, could he ever forget the many attempts that had been made on his father's life? And what about the circumstances surrounding his own birth (2 Sam. 11–12)? Given Solomon's heritage, he had many reasons to ask for the ability to "discern between good and evil" (1 Kin. 3:9).

The Lord was delighted with his request, as He always is when people show purity of heart (Matt. 5:8). Consequently, God granted him wisdom beyond any measure that Solomon had anticipated (1 Kin. 3:12). Then He added gifts that Solomon had not asked for but that most rulers would want to have: long life, honor, and great wealth (1 Kin. 3:13–14).

Solomon's gift of an understanding heart was put to immediate use as he judged between two mothers (1 Kin. 3:16–27). Thus the nation was blessed with another king determined to fear God and follow His Law in rendering judgment (1 Kin. 3:28).

However, the ability to discern between good and evil is not the same as the ability to do the good and reject the evil. Despite the gift of wisdom, Solomon did a foolish thing by entering into hundreds of political marriages (1 Kin. 11:1–2; see 2 Sam. 3:13–14), a sin against the Law. His wives turned his heart toward idolatry, and as a result the kingdom was eventually torn in two (1 Kin. 11:9–13).

What would you ask for if you could have anything? If God answered your request, how would you use His gift? And what sort of person would you turn out to be?

U

UNITY

(*see* Cooperation; Teamwork)

UNWANTED PREGNANCIES

(*see* Abortion; Birth Control)

URBAN LIVING

Following God in an Urban Society

Many readers of the Bible may assume that Canaan was just a pastoral land of farms, forests, and wilderness when Israel moved into it. But the land that Israel inherited already had numerous "large and beautiful cities" (Deut. 6:10) which were said to be "great and fortified up to heaven" (Deut. 1:28)—that is, they had strong, high walls. In fact, Canaanite society was a patchwork of city-states, although many of the outlying areas were somewhat more sparsely populated.

So when the Israelites invaded the land, they took possession of developed cities, not just land. Using Hebrew names, Joshua listed dozens of these captured settlements (Josh. 15:21–63; 18:21–19:48; 21:1–40) which the people continued to conquer into the period of the judges (Judg. 1:8–26).

Thus the Promised Land was urban too, not just rural. God gave it to His people complete with walled cities, houses, cisterns, water systems, trees, and vineyards. All of these urban assets were gifts from God.

However, the gifts were given under certain conditions, which Moses spelled out (Deut. 6:12–19). The main condition was faithfulness to the Lord. If Israel continued to follow God when they came into possession of the cities, then it would "be righteousness" for them (Deut. 6:25).

Believers who live in cities today can take encouragement from Israel's experience. Just as God placed His people in an early urban society to live out His ways, so God has placed many, if not most, of His people today in urban settings to live out His ways. Following God in the city is not only possible, it's vital!

Safety in the City

A common view among many people today is that the countryside is a place of peace and safety, while cities are a breeding ground of danger and violence. However, urban crime notwithstanding, the Bible presents a view of the city as a place of safety and civilization. One of the clearest examples of this perspective is the cities of refuge in Israel (Deut. 4:41).

It is interesting that God provided cities to harbor "manslayers." Instead of running away from a community, the suspect was encouraged to run toward one. The obvious implication is that the citizens of the city would be able to protect the person and ensure a fair hearing, rather than leave him in the open to be preyed upon by the dead person's relatives.

If cities have become dangerous today, it is not because cities are inherently dangerous. More likely it has something to do with the loss of that community life which cities by their nature encourage. Thus the answer to urban crime is not to move to the country, but to reclaim the ability to live alongside one's neighbor in a mutually beneficial way (compare Lev. 19:18). God certainly desires His people to be involved in that effort.

URBAN MINISTRY

Jesus—A City Preacher

Popular opinion frequently regards the Bible in general and the ministry of Jesus in particular in rural terms. Perhaps it's the Christmas story, with its quaint references to a donkey, a manger, and shepherds. Perhaps it's the memorable parables, such as the sower and the seed, the wheat and the weeds, and the prodigal son. Perhaps it's because of Jesus' origins in a small town. Whatever the cause, the popular image of Jesus and His world seems fixed on a rural environment. But that is somewhat misleading.

Palestine in Jesus' day was undergoing rapid urban development. Its population of around two and a half to three million people lived in numerous preindustrial cities and towns that revolved around Jerusalem, the hub of the region. The Holy City had a population conservatively estimated by modern scholars at between fifty-five thousand and ninety thousand. (Josephus, a first-century Jewish historian, placed the number at three million; the Talmud gives an incredible twelve million.)

So as Jesus carried out His ministry, He focused on the urban centers of Palestine (Matt. 9:35; 11:1; Luke 4:43; 13:22) and visited

Jerusalem at least three times. This brought Him into contact with a greater number and wider variety of people than He would have encountered in a purely rural campaign— women, soldiers, religious leaders, the rich, merchants, tax collectors, Gentiles, prostitutes, beggars, and the poor. These He attracted in large crowds as He visited each city.

Jesus' urban strategy established a model for His disciples and the early church. When He sent the disciples on preaching tours, He directed them toward cities (Matt. 10:5, 11–14; Luke 10:1, 8–16). And later, the movement spread throughout the Roman Empire by us-

ing an urban strategy that planted communities of believers in no less than forty cities by the end of the first century.

In light of the vital role that cities played in the ministry of Jesus, we who follow Him today need to ask: What are we doing to relate the message of Christ to our increasingly urban, multicultural, and pluralistic world? Our Lord's example in urban Palestine has much to teach us.

Paul's Urban Strategy

Ephesus. Corinth. Antioch. Athens. Iconium. Lystra. Derbe. Philippi. For most people today, names like these indicate merely

URBAN LIVING

dots on a map. But they were major cities in the Roman world, centers of influence that attracted Christian messengers such as Paul (Acts 16:4). The message of Christ was a message for the city—for its marketplace, arts, academies, councils, courts, prisons, temples, and synagogues.

Paul was from the beautiful coastal seaport of Tarsus, "no mean city" as he described it (Acts 21:39; see Acts 11:25), with an estimated half-million residents. He was trained in Jerusalem, one of the largest cities in the Eastern Mediterranean. Thus he was no stranger to city life. In fact, as a spokesperson for the Christian movement, he preferred working in urban centers. This strategy offered several advantages:

1. *He could use a common language, Greek.* Older ethnic languages prevailed among rural peoples, but multicultural city dwellers spoke to each other in *koiṇ* ("common") Greek.

2. *He could anticipate greater receptivity.* Urban peoples were perhaps more likely to entertain new ideas and consider change.

3. *He could influence networks.* As crossroads of communication and commerce, cities tended to amplify the Christian message to their surrounding areas.

4. *He could affect multiple ethnic groups.* The gospel is inclusive and multiethnic, uniting people of every background. Cities brought into close proximity Jews and Gentiles, men and women, rich and poor. The message of Christ brought them together.

5. *He could reach the workplace.* As a tentmaker, Paul identified with the great numbers of artisans who populated Roman cities. In fact, urban areas were often divided into districts according to crafts, and workers formed guilds to enhance their trades. Paul used these coalitions to advantage in spreading the message.

6. *He could make use of the Roman legal system.* Paul believed that his message had relevance for the political, economic, and religious institutions of his day. As a Roman citizen, he expected—and even demanded—justice. He also used the courts to attract a larger audience for the gospel.

Paul intentionally went to the cities. The gospel he proclaimed had implications for an urban setting. To him, the message of Christ spoke not only to the private individual, but to public society as well. Given the increasingly urban nature of the modern world, he would likely urge Christians today to pay attention to cities. Those who want to have influence will benefit from a careful study of Paul's urban strategy.

Rome or Bust

When Paul declared, "I must also see Rome" (Acts 19:21), he wasn't talking about a tourist excursion; he was stating his bold intention to penetrate the capital of his world with the gospel. To him, Rome was a symbol of the center of power, the system that was driving the world. Jerusalem may have been important as a starting point, but the goal was Rome.

In the center of Rome was a tall, marble obelisk indicating the distance from that point to every town in the empire—a graphic reminder of just how important Rome viewed itself. But Paul seemed to have a reverse model of that. Wherever he was, an internal marker seemed to remind him how far he was from Rome and how intent he was on getting there. The cities that he visited—including Jerusalem—became mileposts on his way to Rome.

The audacity of his plan is rather shocking: A tiny group living on the periphery of the Roman Empire aimed to conquer the cities and even the capital of the mightiest empire in world history with its new and strange beliefs. Incredibly, the movement prevailed!

That stunning achievement compels believers today to ask: What is our Rome? What are the forces shaping our world today? What is our strategy for gospel penetration? If Paul were alive today, where would he be headed as the strategic center of influence? Perhaps to the megacities of our world, like Mexico City with its twenty-four million people, half under the age of fifteen. Perhaps to Tokyo, the second largest city in the world and a major influence on the world's economy.

The point is that modern Christians walk in a tradition of people who declared, "We must get to Rome!" In the same way, we must not stay in our Jerusalems, our homes, our cultures. We are here for influence. We are here to spread the gospel.

The City Is the Lord's!

The truth that all of the earth and all of its people ultimately belong to the Lord (Ps. 24:1) has profound implications for God's people today. One is that cities belong to God. City councils and agencies may manage them, but God is the Lord of the city (Ps. 24:7–10).

What this means for Christians in metropolitan areas is that the city has value. Some look at the city as little more than a stronghold of Satan and a headquarters of evil. For that reason, they write off the city as worthless and hopeless. Better to live in the suburbs or the country, "away" from the corrupt and corrupting urban lifestyle.

Without question, Satan is alive and well and at work in the city. But occupation is not the same as ownership. The city belongs to God, not Satan. That makes it valuable real estate, because it is a place where God's glory can be expressed (Ps. 24:7).

How? Through God's people who live there. If the city belongs to God, then it makes sense that God's people belong in the city. Not all of them, certainly. But there is no reason to abandon the city, because the Lord has not abandoned it.

For more on this topic, see **CITIES**, *"At Home in the City," page 62.*

URBAN RENEWAL

(*see* Community Development)

V

VALUES

Confused About Greatness

Significance is a tricky achievement. Too often it is built upon fame, money, marketing, power, position, or possessions.

The disciples were caught up in a value system based on these things, which caused them to compete with each other (Mark 9:34). In fact, the dispute over greatness resurfaced later (Mark 10:35–45). The quest for significance through power was an insidious problem.

Jesus noticed His followers' thinking and challenged it (Mark 9:35). He pointed out that true greatness is in serving others rather than outdoing them. Later He suggested the same thing to a rich ruler (Mark 10:21).

To drive His point home, Jesus gathered a child in His arms and said that to welcome a child is to welcome both Christ and His Father (Mark 9:36–37). No wonder the apostle Paul, in writing to believers in Galatia, identified many childlike characteristics as highly valued works of the Spirit (Gal. 5:22–25). He contrasted those traits with some ugly ones that often accompany competition (Gal. 5:16–21).

Do you need to rework your value system? Are you addicted to fame and fortune? A good test is to ask yourself, *Where do children and the poor stand among my priorities?*

For more on this topic, see **CHILDREN**, *"Pass On the Story," page 54.*

VENGEANCE

(*see* Revenge)

VIOLENCE

A New Way to Respond

In the Sermon on the Mount, Jesus appears to make some stark, seemingly impossible demands: God's people should never use force in self-defense (Matt. 5:39); they should never contest a lawsuit (5:40); they should comply with every type of demand (Matt. 5:41); and they should lend without reserve (Matt. 5:42). Could Jesus possibly be serious?

To be sure, some circumstances call for resistance and self-defense. The Law specifically sanctioned self-protection when there was no other apparent recourse (Ex. 22:2). Likewise, Jesus Himself protested when He was slapped (John 18:22–23).

But He warned against the needless use of force, particularly in revenge. In self-defense the alternative to resistance may be injury or death. But in vengeance one inflicts harm, even though immediate danger is past. A slap on the cheek is little more than an insult. There's no place for violence in response to that.

In the case of lawsuits (Matt. 5:40), the Law permitted demanding a tunic (or shirt) in pledge for a loan, but prohibited taking a cloak (or coat) overnight, because it was needed for warmth (Ex. 22:26–27). However, Jesus' listeners commonly pressed for the cloak—for ruinous damages. But Christ's point was that if lawsuits have to go to extremes, they ought to be in the extreme of charity.

What about going the second mile (Matt. 5:41)? The word *compels* is a technical term meaning "to requisition or press into service." Roman soldiers could press a private citizen into service to help carry a burden—but for no further than one mile. Jesus challenged His followers to go beyond the law. Imagine the reputation that Christians would have if we always did twice what the law required! What would tax auditors think if we not only followed the rules, but paid more than the law required?

Throughout Matthew 5:17–48, Jesus speaks in stark contrasts and strong hyperboles (overstatements for the sake of emphasis). The key to understanding this section is to keep in mind the major thrust of His teaching: good not evil, grace not vengeance, love not hatred. That is the morality of Christ.

For more on this topic, see CRUELTY, "Bloody Assyria," page 96.

VISION
Beyond Data—Vision

Our world has entered the "information age." Never before has humanity known so much. Yet as Moses and the Israelites discovered at Kadesh Barnea, possessing facts does not necessarily lead to wisdom. For that we need leaders with vision.

Apparently only two of the men that Israel sent to "spy out the land of Canaan" (Num. 13:2, 17) were visionary leaders. The rest became depressed by their data. Actually, the English term "spy" is a bit misleading. The twelve tribal representatives were not engaged in cloak-and-dagger espionage. They were more like explorers and land surveyors. Many of the details of their work are laid out in Numbers 34 and became the basis for apportioning the land forty years later.

But as chapters 13–14 show, even though these men had the technical skill to assess the lay of the land, most of them lacked the vision and courage needed to take hold of it. Despite God's repeated promises to help His people by driving out the Canaanites, these men lost faith in Him. Indeed, they lost faith in themselves: "We were like grasshoppers in our own sight" (Num. 13:33).

Thus, twelve experts read the same data, but ten reached a different conclusion than the other two. What was the difference? Vision. All twelve could see that this was indeed a "land flowing with milk and honey." Likewise, all twelve could see the powerful forces to be overcome if they were to take possession of the land. But ten could not see past those immediate obstacles. The other two did. They were looking to a God who was more powerful than all of the Canaanites put together (had He not defeated the Egyptians?), a God who had pledged Himself to deliver the land to His people.

Today's world cries out for leaders with vision. There is no lack of data. But the question remains whether we interpret the data according to our own human limitations, or whether we factor in the power and promises of God. If not, we doom ourselves, like Israel, to aimless "wandering."

A Sense of Mission

Almost by definition, leaders have some end to which they are headed. This sense of mission helps to guide their decisions and determine their strategy.

Nehemiah's mission grew out of his knowledge of the Law and his awareness that the destruction of Jerusalem had come about through God's judgment of his people's sins (Neh. 1:5–8). At the same time, he knew that God was willing to forgive their sins and restore them to the land (Neh. 1:9). Therefore Nehemiah determined that he would see to the rebuilding of Jerusalem, in accordance with the Lord's promises, and he began to devise a strategy toward that end (Neh. 1:10–11).

It is important to note that Nehemiah did not dream up a sense of mission out of his own agenda or self-interest. He responded to the news of Jerusalem's plight with tears, prayer, fasting, humility, and seeking the Lord's will (Neh. 1:4). As he prepared to go before the king, he probably did not know exactly what he should say or do, only that he needed to go to Jerusalem. Nor could he have known all that he would encounter once he arrived at the ruined city.

Nevertheless, convinced that God wanted the Holy City to be revived, Nehemiah stepped forward as a change agent, and his leadership proved strategic.

If you are in a leadership position, have you identified the overarching mission to which you are committed? Is it a worthwhile endeavor? Is it something that you believe God wants you to accomplish?

VOCATION
Called into the World

Should followers of Christ withdraw from the world to set up their own exclusive communities or retreat from society into "Chris-

tian ghettos"? Not if they are to fulfill Christ's prayer in John 17:18. Engagement, not isolation, is His desire.

Some early Christians sought refuge in the catacombs of Rome. But that practice was only temporary, and they were forced there only by the most extreme persecutions. Normally, they could be found actively participating in the society. Jesus sends us into the world to make an impact (see Matt. 5:13–16). The New Testament gives us plenty of examples to follow:

1. *Jesus.* The Lord Himself came into the world to offer a new relationship with God. He didn't have to. He could have remained in His heavenly position. But He was determined to follow God's call into the world. He came to earth to die for us, and to deliver to a rebellious humanity God's offer of forgiveness, love, and acceptance (Phil. 2:5–8).

VISION

2. *Paul.* The church's greatest messenger started out hating anyone who followed Jesus. Yet Christ Himself stopped him in his vengeful tracks and redirected his life to become a globetrotting messenger of faith and forgiveness. He crisscrossed the Roman Empire, bringing the gospel to dozens of cities and towns. He also challenged others to live, work, and witness among the lost (1 Cor. 4:16–20).

3. *Peter.* Peter struggled throughout his life to break out of the separatist mentality he had grown up with. He didn't like the prospect of suffering and rejection, and at times took steps to forestall it (see Mark 8:31–38; Luke 22:54–62; John 18:10–11). He liked even less the idea of sharing God's good news of salvation with Samaritans and Gentiles. But Christ kept calling Peter back to re-engage the world (Acts 10). He finally learned the necessity and the value of suffering (1 Pet. 4:1–2) and called others to do likewise (1 Pet. 2:11–12).

4. *Barnabas.* A respected landowner, Barnabas enjoyed a relatively "safe" calling as a leader of the infant church in Jerusalem. But he accepted an assignment to visit Antioch and investigate rumors of Gentile converts to the predominantly Jewish movement. Sure enough, he found that God was bringing all nations into the fellowship. So he sought out Paul, an unknown new believer, to help him establish the new converts in the faith (Acts 11:19–26). Later, they traveled to Jerusalem to defend and extend this new "worldly" thrust in the growing work of God (15:1–33).

"Called" to a New Purpose

Nowadays people often speak of a "calling" to signify a career that one has made a lifelong passion, a vocation to which one feels deeply committed. In a similar way, many people use the term "calling" in connection with vocational Christian work. For instance, members of the clergy often describe their "call" to the ministry, a conviction that God has led them into that particular career to accomplish certain work for Him.

Hebrews tells us that all of us as believers partake of "the heavenly calling" (Heb. 3:1). The Greek word translated "calling" comes from *kaleo,* meaning to call, invite, or summon. The word and its derivatives are used often in the New Testament. There is no single, definitive discussion of calling, but we can gain a fuller understanding by looking at some of the ways in which this subject is treated. For example, calling is used in connection with:

- An invitation to classes of people for salvation (Mark 2:17; 1 Cor. 1:9, 24; 2 Thess. 2:13–14).
- An invitation to individuals for salvation (Gal. 1:15–16; 2 Tim. 1:9).
- A summons to a Christlike lifestyle (Eph. 4:1; 1 Thess. 2:12).
- A designation of believers' position with God (1 Pet. 2:9; 1 John 3:1) or their identity with Christ, especially when it means suffering (1 Pet. 2:21; James 2:7).

Vocation or calling is the sense of identification with Christ and with other believers that Hebrews emphasizes when it calls us "holy brethren, partakers of the heavenly calling" (Heb. 3:1). Christ became human like us (Heb. 2:14, 17) in order that we might become like Him—alive, free from sin, and holy.

One overriding theme for all of these treatments of calling is that the call of God is a summons to people to come to Him through faith in Christ and to live as servants of His kingdom. Thus, salvation from sin and obedience to God are at the heart of what "calling" means in the New Testament.

Our calling has important implications for our jobs and careers. For one thing, it means a change of bosses: as God's children, we ultimately serve Christ. It also means a change of conduct and character: as Christ's followers, we need to work with a Christlike "workstyle" (see Titus 2:9–10). And it means a new motivation when it comes to our paycheck: we work not only to meet our own needs, but to have money to meet the needs of others.

No matter what we do for work—whether "full-time" vocational Christian work or "secular," everyday work—we are all called to serve Christ. In the end, what makes the issue of calling important is not us, but the One who calls us.

Who's Your Boss?

He had a menial, dead-end job. They assigned him tasks that no one else wanted—the "dumb work," the dirty work, the dangerous work. They called him out at all hours of the day and night to satisfy the whims of his supervisors. He had little hope for advancement. In fact, he'd be lucky just to keep his job; plenty of others stood in line, ready to replace him. Whether he even lived or died mattered little. He was a first-century Roman slave.

Yet he mattered to God, and his work mattered, too. In writing to this lowly worker (Col. 3:22–24), Paul redefined his occupational status: he was not just a Roman slave, he was an employee of Christ the Lord! That makes all the difference.

So it is for any Christian in the workplace. You may work for a giant multinational corporation or a mom-'n'-pop pizza parlor. You may have fifteen levels of bureaucracy over you, or be self-employed. It doesn't matter. Ultimately, Christ is your Boss. Consider what that means:

1. *Christ gives you work to do.* Work is a gift from God. He has created you in His image to be a worker, giving you skills and abilities to accomplish His purposes. He has also sovereignly placed you in your occupation to do His work there. Even if your job is as lowly as a Roman slave's, it still has value and dignity to Christ.

2. *Christ is your Boss, but He uses human supervisors.* According to Colossians 3, people in authority over you are actually human representatives of Christ. They may not act very Christlike. But in working for them, you are ultimately working for Christ. Do you follow their instructions? Do you shirk your job when they're not around? Are you more interested in impressing them to gain approval and advancement than in getting the job done? How would your work ethic change if you saw Christ as your supervisor?

3. *Christ asks you to put your heart into your work.* If you serve Christ in your job, you have more reason than anyone else to work with integrity and enthusiasm. The job itself may be unchallenging or unpleasant. But Christ asks you to do it with dignity, to the best of your ability, as though working for Christ Himself.

4. *Christ will reward you for good, faithful work.* This passage says that Christ will review your work someday. You can expect praise and reward for working in a Christlike manner.

*For more on this topic, see **SPIRITUAL GIFTS**, "Gifts and Vocations," page 377.*

W

WAR

A Just War, or Just a War?

Throughout history, people of faith have struggled to identify the conditions, if any, under which war is justifiable. All agree that war is a terrible evil, but many have felt that under some circumstances, it is unavoidable. In ancient Persia, thanks to the courage of Queen Esther and the permission of King Ahasuerus (Esth. 8:3–6, 11), the Jews fought a limited war of revenge on their enemies until they had destroyed almost all of them (Esth. 9:1–5).

Was this bloodshed justifiable? It would be if measured against a set of criteria developed by church leaders Augustine in the fifth century and Aquinas in the thirteenth century.

According to that tradition, a particular war is a "just war," and not "just a war," if it passes a number of tests, as follows:

- A just war pursues a "just cause" or "right intention," such as self-defense, in the face of an obvious, one-sided evil; this assumes that those who engage in the "just war" have mostly righteous purposes as their motives.
- A just war is declared and directed by a "competent government authority."
- A just war is joined as a last resort only after exhausting all peaceful means such as diplomatic channels, economic sanctions, and the like.
- A just war must conform to the "law of proportionality"—the "greater good" or

W

"lesser of two evils"; that is, the anticipated good results must outweigh the actual bad effects of damage done.

- A just war must be "redemptive," that is, fought in a way that leaves room for the two warring parties to reconcile when the war is over.
- A just war is always "discriminate" and fought in terms of "limited engagement" that precludes looting, massacres, or engagements that would harm noncombatants.
- A just war must be waged with at least a "probability" of winning.
- A just war must allow exemption for conscientious objectors.

It would be instructive to measure the wars fought over the centuries against these principles. And assessing potential conflicts by using these guidelines (or similar ones) coud help nations limit military involvements to situations that are truly worth fighting for.

Israel's Holy War

Wars are fought for many reasons, but the Israelites' war against the Canaanites was fought because the Lord told them to fight it (Deut. 20:16). This means that the campaign fit the definition of a "holy war," a war that God declares, fights, leads, and wins. Similar engagements were carried out against the Amorites (Ex. 17:16) and Midianites (Num. 31:1–3).

Ancient Israel did not have a standing army like the Egyptians, Assyrians, or Babylonians. Nor did it have chariots, horses, or sophisticated weaponry prior to the monarchy. Instead, the Israelites were to trust primarily in the Lord, who promised to fight on their behalf. In fact, even after Israel acquired military hardware and expertise, the nation was still told to rely on God to bring about victory.

The Lord Himself would be the defender of Israel. Even though the nation's men were often mustered to battle, it was to be the Lord fighting through them, as well as for them. In fact, defeat usually occurred as a result of disobedience against God.

For this reason, Israelite warriors were expected to consecrate themselves to God. Often they were to do so by abstaining from certain activities, such as drinking or sexual relations. And those who were distracted by

fear, a recent marriage, a new house, or a newly planted vineyard were told to remain at home (Deut. 20:5–9).

Because a holy war was primarily God's war, certain rules of engagement applied. For example, if a besieged city surrendered, the occupants were to be spared, though they would become servants of the Israelites (Deut. 20:10–11). Likewise, the natural environment of the battlefield was to be preserved as much as possible (Deut. 20:19–20).

The battles in which the Lord called for the utter destruction of the enemy were mainly fought against the Canaanites (Deut. 20:16). These pagan tribes had once been friends and neighbors of the patriarchs, but after centuries of idolatry, they stood under the judgment of the Lord. In calling for their annihilation, the Lord was purifying the land of their religion and culture in order to replace it with those of His own choosing.

This holy war fulfilled God's promises to Abraham (Gen. 15:18–21). But it was also a unique campaign in human history in that God never again called for His people to exterminate a society. Down through history, religious leaders may have claimed that the Lord was calling them and their followers to fight a holy war, but time and again those claims have proven false. Holy war is no longer an option for God's people. He uses other means to bring about change in the societies of the world—primarily the influence of changed individuals (Rom. 12:2; 1 Thess. 1:6–10).

A Picture of Warfare

The Book of Nahum vividly describes the scene of Nineveh's fall (Nah. 2:3–12). The prophet's graphic images of flashing swords and racing chariots (Nah. 2:3–4, 3:3), walls collapsing like sand castles (Nah. 2:6), and the devastating loss of human life (Nah. 2:10; 3:3, 10) accurately portray the horrors visited on the city by the Babylonians.

Unlike much of ancient literature, the Bible does not glamorize war. It paints a grimly realistic picture to show that war is an outcome of humanity's rebellion against God. The Lord takes no delight in watching human armies clash. However, sometimes in judgment He removes His restraining hand, exposing people and nations to their own unbridled destruction of each other. This was the case for Nineveh.

Largely because of its strategic location, the land of Canaan was the site of numerous conflicts in Bible times. Two major highways ran through the territory. Over the centuries, various armies traveled back and forth across these roads, challenging each other for control of the Middle East.

The Sounds of Urban Destruction

The sounds of modern warfare include the scream of jet aircraft, the chopping rhythm of helicopters, the concussion of bombs exploding, and the rapid-fire blast of assault rifles. By contrast, the noise of ancient warfare was primarily the sound of human beings crying out either in victory or defeat.

The din of battle can be heard in Isaiah's vivid description of the fall of Jerusalem:

- shouting from the rooftops (Is. 22:1);
- the thud of arrows shot by armies of skilled archers (Is. 22:2–3);
- the moaning and weeping of captives (Is. 22:3–4);
- the pounding of battering rams on city gates and walls (Is. 22:5);
- clamor for help that never comes (Is. 22:5);
- the thundering of chariots and the neighing of horses (Is. 22:6–7); and
- the collapse of houses in order to furnish building materials for fortifying the walls (Is. 22:10).

Hollywood films sometimes recreate battle scenes like these, but we can perhaps gain a more gripping impression of what Jerusalem's "day of trouble and treading down and perplexity" (Is. 22:5) must have been like by listening to the shouts and screams that come from modern-day battlegrounds in cities torn by civil strife. To hear the wail of the wounded and the moans of those in mourning is to catch an echo of the human pain unleashed whenever cities are destroyed.

The Disgrace of the Defeated

When ancient cities fell to attacking armies, the survivors generally suffered cruelly at the hands of their captors. Jeremiah mentions some of the indignities faced by the people of Judah after the fall of Jerusalem (Lam. 5:11–14). Elsewhere, the prophet tells us that King Zedekiah was made to watch his sons being put to death before he was blinded and led away in chains to Babylon.

However, cruel as the Babylonians were, they were probably more lenient than their predecessors, the Assyrians. Surviving records of Assyrian military victories tell of severe atrocities. Captives were often beheaded or had their arms, legs, or hands cut off. Some were staked to the ground while their tormentors disemboweled them. Others were impaled on sharply pointed poles erected outside the walls of the conquered cities.

The main point of these detestable cruelties was to humiliate the conquered and to deter other enemies from resisting Assyrian demands.

The Season of War

As any military strategist knows, the advantage is usually to the aggressor, the army that takes the offensive and uses the element of surprise. For that reason, ancient kings tended to make war in the spring of the year (2 Sam. 11:1), when road conditions were most favorable and troops could move quickly and without warning to an enemy.

In Palestine, the rainy season occurs during the cool winter months. Summers are very hot, and the fall is marked by unpredictable thunderstorms off the Mediterranean. Thus the spring was the best season for kings to engage in warfare.

WASTE DISPOSAL

(*see* Sanitation)

WEALTH

Getting Beyond Wealth

Jesus said it would be hard for the rich to enter the kingdom of heaven (Matt. 19:23). The remark has led some to believe that rich people can't enter the kingdom, and others to feel that Jesus was opposed to wealth and the wealthy. But Matthew's response to Jesus' call (9:9–13) contradicts both of those assumptions.

The incident recorded here contrasts sharply with Jesus' encounter with the rich young ruler (Matt. 19:16–30; Mark 10:17–31;

Luke 8:18–30). In many ways, the ruler seemed to make a more likely prospect than Matthew for membership in Jesus' burgeoning movement.

Yet despite the young ruler's apparent edge, it was Matthew who ended up following Jesus. The other "went away sorrowful" (Matt. 19:22). What accounts for the difference? For one thing, the wealthy young man clearly perceived himself as already righteous (Matt. 19:17–20). He felt that he was able to meet God's requirements on his own merits (Matt. 19:16). But no one had to convince Matthew that he needed the Great Physician (Matt. 9:11–12). As a tax collector, he was among the most despised members of Jewish society.

Yet there was a more fundamental difference between these two men—a difference that depended on Jesus' attitude more than on theirs. In calling Matthew but turning away the rich young ruler, Jesus demonstrated precisely this point: salvation depends on the mercy of God, not on the merits or sacrifice of people.

The crucial difference between the rich man who followed and the rich man who rejected was the merciful choice of God. Of course, none of us knows that choice beforehand. Therefore, we as believers need to be equally eager to present the gospel of Christ to everyone, rich or poor, wise or foolish, mighty or weak.

Greatest of All

The writer's claim that he had more possessions "than all who were in Jerusalem before me" (Eccl. 2:7) is consistent with reports of Solomon's wealth (1 Kin. 3:13; 10:23). Furthermore, in addition to riches, Solomon possessed extraordinary wisdom (Eccl. 3:12; 1 Kin. 4:29–34), which the writer of Ecclesiastes also had (Eccl. 2:9).

The irony is that Solomon, who enjoyed greater wisdom and wealth than any of the Israelite kings, came to great spiritual ruin because of his foolish choices regarding idolatry (1 Kin. 11:1–13). Ecclesiastes does not reflect that spiritual apostasy. However, is it possible that Solomon's disillusionment with pleasure and knowledge, which eventually caused him to "hate life" (Eccl. 2:1–17), might

have been a contributing factor in turning his heart to other gods? Scripture does not say. But the tragic fact remains that one of the greatest of Israel's kings had his kingdom come to "vanity" because he forsook the God who had given him all that he possessed.

Wealth's Temptation

For us who live in a materialistic culture, it's good to recognize that the desire for wealth and all that it symbolizes—prestige, power, luxury, authority—can be a powerful tool in Satan's hands. It was one of three strategies that the devil used to try to draw Christ away from His mission (Matt. 4:8–10).

Are you tempted by desires that are closely tied to wealth? If so, Christ's response in verse 10 challenges you to ask: Who or what are you going to worship and serve?

*For more on this topic, see **POSSESSIONS**, "A Man Who Almost Had It All," page 307.*

WEDDINGS
At Home in the City

Ever since the time of Cain (Gen. 4:17), one of the main purposes of human communities and of the rule of law has been to keep the family from disintegrating. This principle lies behind the Mosaic laws concerning questions of marital purity (Deut. 22:13–21).

According to the marriage customs of the day, a wedding celebration lasted eight days, after which the husband and wife retreated to their home to consummate the marriage. If the husband then alleged that his wife was not a virgin—whether as a legitimate complaint or as an excuse to annul the marriage—he could not just divorce her, abandon her, or take revenge on his in-laws. He had to take his case before the elders of the city, who placed the woman's parents—not the woman—on trial (Gen. 22:15). The elders would examine evidence as to the woman's sexual activity prior to marriage, and render a ruling (Gen. 22:17–21).

Thus God held the city, its leaders, and its legal system accountable to uphold the rights of women. This guarantee of due process for them set ancient Israel apart from other Middle Eastern cultures. Marriage was considered to be not just a private covenant between two consenting adults, but a legal commitment publicly honored by the city. This was appropriate, because cities had a vested interest in healthy marriages and families. City and family went together—and still do today.

For more on this topic, see HOSPITALITY, "Rude Rejection," page 204.

WEIGHT CONTROL

(*see* Dieting; Fasting)

WELFARE

(*see* Disadvantaged Persons)

WIDOWS
Effective Care for the Needy

Followers of Christ have the potential to be among the world's most effective agents for social service. They have the example of Christ to follow. They have the motivation of doing compassionate work in His name. They have the structure, community life, and pooled resources of their congregations. And they have the model of the early church, which provided standards for the systematic, ongoing care of widows (1 Tim. 5:3–22).

We can learn a great deal about delivering services to the needy by carefully observing the principles that Paul set forth for Timothy and the believers at Ephesus. For example:

1. The care described here was regular and ongoing for people who were "taken into the number" (1 Tim. 5:9), that is, put on a list of continuing recipients of the church's support. Presumably, the church was to give short-term support to people who needed help until they could get back on their feet, but not to able-bodied people who refused to work to support themselves (compare 2 Thess. 3:10).

2. The care was for "widows who are really widows" (1 Tim. 5:3). The Old Testament described a widow as a woman who had no one to support her and therefore depended on the protection of the community (Ex. 22:22–24; Deut. 14:28–29; 24:17–22; 26:12–13). If a widow had able-bodied children or grandchildren, she needed to depend on them for provision, not the church (1 Tim. 5:4).

3. A widow who was "taken into the number" incurred certain responsibilities in order to maintain her eligibility for the church's charity. For example, she needed to be frugal lest someone reproach her for living an extravagant lifestyle and the fellowship for supporting it (1 Tim. 5:6–7). Likewise, she needed to meet certain criteria related to her earlier life and character (1 Tim. 5:9–10). The point was not to keep a widow out of the program, but to ensure that she served her fellow believers in every way she could if she was going to receive support.

4. Younger widows were expected to remarry and, as was common for that day, bear children (who presumably would care for their parents in old age). Again, the church needed to avoid offering long-term support to someone who had other options. To do so might contribute to wantonness, idleness, and gossip (1 Tim. 5:11–14).

These instructions to Timothy mirror principles about systematic aid found elsewhere in Scripture. For example, Paul told the Corinthians that financial support should go only to the truly poor. Likewise, the aim of providing care is to give people enough food, clothing, and other aid for survival and health. It is not intended to give anyone a free ride, even less to underwrite an inflated standard of living (2 Cor. 8:13–15; 1 Tim. 6:6–10).

First Timothy 5 specifically addresses the care of widows, but its principles apply to a much broader range of human need. By using this and other biblical texts to develop social programs, believers can effectively render care in a way that honors the name of Christ and provides real help to needy people.

Concern for Widows

Widows tended to have a rough lot in the ancient world. The widow who cried out to Elisha typified the situation: her husband had died, leaving her with a big debt and the prospect of poverty. Moved by her plight, Elisha sought to help (2 Kin. 4:2). The compassion shown by this prophet of God demonstrates the Lord's concern for widows, especially those who have little means of support or protection.

Numerous other incidents and passages in Scripture offer ways for God's people to reach out to women left in dire straits:

- The Law of Moses told landowners to allow widows and other needy people to glean in their fields (Deut. 24:19–22).

W

- The Book of Ruth in the Old Testament focuses on the dilemma of two widows, Naomi and Ruth, who were destined for poverty until God provided a wealthy man, Boaz, to care for them both.
- David provided housing and support for his ten concubines who had been violated by Absalom, who lived as "widows until their death" (2 Sam. 20:3).
- Elijah the prophet provided for a needy widow at Zarephath through a miracle (1 Kin. 17:8–24).
- Jesus often ministered to the needs of widows and held them up as examples of faithfulness or as people deserving care and respect; He condemned the Pharisees for their mistreatment of widows (Mark 12:41–44; Luke 7:11–17; 18:1–8; 20:46–47).
- The early church showed compassion to widows and other needy members by selling land and using the proceeds for assistance; it also developed a system to assure equality in the care (Acts 4:34–37; 6:1–7).
- James defined "pure religion" partly in terms of how believers treat widows (James 1:27).

Feasting Off the Poor

Jesus chastised the Pharisees for growing fat at the expense of widows (Matt. 23:14). Unfortunately, not much has changed from that day to this. We still see people with lots of power but few scruples grow rich by dislodging widows and other less powerful folks from what little they own.

Sadly, there are loan sharks and other flimflam artists who con the poor. But there are also more respectable businesspeople whose activities can hurt the powerless. For example, occasionally some "urban renewal projects" have driven the poor from one slum to another in a frantic search for housing that costs more than before.

Then there are those who buy, sell, close down, and bankrupt companies with little regard for the impact on workers or communities, and whose only motive appears to be personal financial gain.

Jesus never condemned business or investment. But His stiff rebuke of the Pharisees challenges any of us involved in finance and deal-making to carefully weigh the ethics of our choices. Woe to us if we devour the resources of the disadvantaged.

*For more on this topic, see **MIRACLES**, "The Widow's Oil," page 269; **ORPHANS**, "Protect the Widows and Orphans!" page 286.*

WISDOM
Courting Wisdom

The father of Proverbs 4 counsels his son that above all else, he needs to "get wisdom" (Prov. 4:7), because she offers great blessings and honor "when you embrace her" (Prov. 4:8). This advice is typical in Proverbs, where wisdom is often personified as a woman (Prov. 1:20–21; 3:13–18; 4:8–9; 7:4; 8:1–11; 9:1–12). Young men especially are urged to court and embrace wisdom as a man would "embrace" a woman in a romantic relationship. They are to fall in love with her and make her the object of their affection, devotion, and loyalty.

Note also that the person in Proverbs who best displays wisdom in the "man's world" of the marketplace is the virtuous woman of Proverbs 31.

The Greatest Value

It is one thing to be educated. It is quite another thing to have wisdom. Many jobs require educational degrees and certification, and studies show that the better educated one is, the higher one's income is likely to be. However, wisdom is even more valuable than either advanced learning or the riches that it often brings (Prov. 8:10–11).

Why is wisdom worth more than anything else one could desire? Why does Proverbs tell us that whatever we do, we should get wisdom (Prov. 4:5–7)? It is because wisdom yields benefits that go far beyond material comfort and convenience. Notice how Proverbs describes wisdom:

- Wisdom comes from God Himself (Prov. 8:22), is from everlasting (Prov. 8:23), and has existed from the beginning (Prov. 8:23–30).
- Wisdom results in prudence (Prov. 8:5, 12), understanding (Prov. 8:5), excellent things (Prov. 8:6), truth (Prov. 8:7), hatred of wickedness (Prov. 8:7), righteousness

(Prov. 8:8), knowledge (Prov. 8:12), discretion (Prov. 8:12), and fear of the Lord (Prov. 8:13).

- Wisdom yields riches and honor (Prov. 8:11, 18), blesses the wise (Prov. 8:32, 34), and gives life to the wise (Prov. 8:35).

Beyond Human Understanding

It seems incredible that God would tell Abraham to "take . . . your son, your only son Isaac, whom you love," and offer him up as a sacrifice (Gen. 22:2). What sort of God would ask such a thing? What sort of God would test a man's faith with such a weighty request?

It was a severe test of Abraham's faith. Perhaps most of us would have failed the test. We might even have rejected God as cruel and bloodthirsty. But Abraham believed God. Though the sacrifice of Isaac seemed to go against God's promise of an heir, Abraham believed that God would still fulfill His Word, even if it required Him to raise Isaac from the dead (Rom. 4:17).

The request was also a harsh lesson that all of life comes from and belongs to God (Gen. 2:7; Job 27:3; 33:4). In essence, life is merely on loan to us, both as parents and children. God can ask for its return at any time. So in that respect, the request to slay Isaac was similar to the difficult period that Abram and Sarai endured as they waited for the birth of this very son (Gen. 18:1–15; 21:1–7). Their lives and the lives of any children they might have were in the hands of God.

Let there be no mistake: God abhors human sacrifice, as many Old Testament passages make clear (for example, Lev. 18:21; 20:2; Deut. 12:31; Ps. 106:35–38; Ezek. 20:30–31). So when Abraham was about to slay his son, God stopped him short of the actual sacrifice and provided an alternative in Isaac's place. It proved to Abraham that his faith was well-placed: God is the God of mercy.

He is also the God of wisdom. He sometimes makes what to us may seem like strange requests. But if like Abraham we will believe and obey, He will reward our faith with His goodness and righteousness.

In Wisdom He Has Made Us

One of the most fundamental and far-reaching truths of Scripture is that God is the

THE WIDOW'S MITE

WIDOWS

W

Creator of the universe (Prov. 3:19–20). Like his father David before him (Ps. 8), Solomon realized the significance of this truth. He affirmed it early in Proverbs in order to emphasize that true wisdom is not of human origin, but comes from the Lord who made all things.

An important implication of God being the Creator is that He is King over all the people of the world. In wisdom He has brought every person into existence. Therefore, everyone owes ultimate allegiance to the Lord, an allegiance that transcends family, tribal, ethnic, or national claims. It is not that these are unimportant. But wisdom says that each of us needs to fear the Lord first and foremost (Prov. 1:7). Anyone can follow God's ways, and everyone is accountable to the Creator. Is that the wisdom that you are pursuing?

The All-Wise King

A list of Solomon's political, administrative, military, and architectural achievements would be one of the most impressive of the ancient world. Under his leadership, Israel expanded its influence from the Euphrates to the Mediterranean, and from Asia Minor to the Gulf of Aqaba and Egypt.

Yet underlying all of Solomon's accomplishments was a God-given wisdom for which he was renowned in his own day and is remembered today:

- The judgment that he rendered in the case of the harlots and the child won the respect of the entire nation (1 Kin. 3:16–28).
- His wisdom was said to surpass that of all other known wise men of his day (1 Kin. 4:30–31).
- He gave three thousand proverbs (1 Kin. 4:32), many of which are contained in the Book of Proverbs.
- He composed one thousand five songs (1 Kin. 4:32), including Psalms 72 and 127.
- He demonstrated competencies in botany, horticulture, zoology, and ichthyology (1 Kin. 4:33; compare Prov. 30:24–31; Eccl. 2:4–6).
- Visitors from throughout the world traveled to Jerusalem to hear his opinion (1 Kin. 4:34), including the queen of Sheba (1 Kin. 10:1–9).

- He was the originator of most of the Book of Proverbs and all of Ecclesiastes and the Song of Solomon; several pieces of extrabiblical literature are attributed to him as well.
- Folktales from ancient Israel, Arabia, and Ethiopia celebrate Solomon's wisdom and even ascribe magical powers to him.

Practical Living

The purpose of Proverbs is straightforward: "to know wisdom" (Prov. 1:2). It is common to conceive of wisdom as either an advanced form of knowledge or learning, or else a rare sense of deep understanding and insight. This view of wisdom has a touch of the mystical about it, as if those who possess it had in some way tapped into profound, enigmatic truths from ages past.

However, there is no mystery about the wisdom talked about in Proverbs, nor is it necessarily limited to a privileged few. The wisdom that Proverbs mentions more than forty times and that Ecclesiastes mentions twenty-seven times is the Hebrew *chokmah*, which means something like "the skill of living." This wisdom is practical, not esoteric. It means that a person knows how to live in a responsible, productive, and prosperous way.

From that standpoint, the wisdom of Proverbs has a lot in common with what we might call common sense, or even "street smarts." It is an understanding of the way the world works. The issue is not so much what one knows intellectually, but what one does practically. It is truth applied.

That is why Proverbs deals with so many day-to-day issues of life, especially those involving moral choices and other decisions that affect the future. The wise person (Hebrew *chakam*) avoids evil and promotes good by observing what others have chosen and then pursuing a course of action based on the outcomes. Thus the Proverbs are not so much promises of God as they are observations and principles about how life works.

WITCHCRAFT

(*see* Occult)

WITNESSING

A Straightforward Approach

Many people in today's culture have grown cynical about religion. So as we believers think about presenting the gospel to others, we need to be careful to make our message credible and straightforward.

Paul mentions two dangers that he avoided so as not to compromise his credibility (1 Thess. 2:5): the use of "flattering words," which amounts to telling people what they want to hear, and "a cloak for covetousness," which involves hidden motives. To use either of these approaches is to deceive people. That's unacceptable for someone who presents himself as a representative of Christ.

The key to Paul's integrity was his realization that God Himself had entrusted him with the message (1 Thess. 2:4). The task of taking the gospel to the Gentiles was not something that Paul had thought up, but a calling from God (Gal. 1:11–17). Thus his aim was not to please people, but God.

Nor did he need to worry about his material well-being, even less to covet what others had. As a messenger of God, he could rely on God to provide for his needs and remain content in whatever circumstances came his way (Phil. 4:11–12). (This is not to suggest that Paul was irresponsible; he earned his living through his occupation as a tentmaker.)

As we consider ways in which to communicate Christ to people around us, what obstacles to our credibility might there be? Are there things about our methods or motives that conflict with the message with which we've been entrusted?

A Witness at Work

At Athens Paul addressed the Greeks in three very different settings—the synagogue, the Areopagus (the supreme tribunal), and the agora, or marketplace. This required three different approaches and points to Paul's great ability in the rhetorical arts.

It's particularly interesting that Paul spoke out in the marketplace. As there apparently were few if any believers in Athens, he had to work "from the outside in" to present the gospel to Athenian workers. By contrast, believers today work in all levels of industry and commerce.

Paul's example raises a challenging question: Are you willing—and prepared—to represent Christ and His message and values where you work? Your faith cannot be a purely personal affair. God has appointed you to your workplace to carry the message of Christ to your coworkers and customers, just as he appointed Paul to go to the agora of Athens.

Sharing Faith Within the Family

If you ever feel discouraged because family, friends, or coworkers refuse to accept the gospel, you may take some comfort from the fact that even Jesus' own brothers did not believe that He was the Christ (John 7:5). Even though they had seen His miracles and listened to His teaching, they still balked at the idea of placing faith in Jesus as the Son of God.

This is important to notice, because it shows that the person who hears the gospel bears responsibility for responding in faith, while the person who shares the gospel bears responsibility for communicating with faithfulness. If we as believers ever start holding ourselves responsible for whether unbelievers accept or reject the message of Christ, we are headed for trouble!

That's not to suggest that we can be careless in our witness or ignore our credibility. Notice that Jesus' brothers rejected Him *in spite of* His works and words. Is that true of us? Or do people dismiss our faith because our lives show little evidence that what we say we believe is true or that it makes any difference to us?

Eventually, at least some of Jesus' brothers did believe in Him. James, probably the oldest, became a leader in the church (Acts 15:13–21) and wrote the New Testament letter that bears his name. Likewise, the author of Jude may have been the half brother of Jesus. Ultimately, both urged Christians to practice and defend their *faith* (James 2:2–26; Jude 3).

From Garbage Dumps to High-Rises

The modern world shows an increasing gap between the extremely rich and the extremely poor. In some large cities today, people literally live beside or even on top of garbage dumps within plain sight of posh high-rises. Each morning, the bodies of those who have starved to death are removed from the streets before chauffeured limousines pass by, carrying the powerful to their appointments.

In a way, this is the kind of scene depicted in David's allusion to the "gates of death" and the "gates of the daughter of Zion" (Ps. 9:13–14). Just outside the city of Zion (Jerusalem) was a garbage dump known as Gehenna, the valley of Hinnom (see Josh. 18:16). The city's refuse was burned there day and night. (Centuries after David, Jesus would often mention the site as a fitting image of hell.)

By contrast, the "gates of the daughter of Zion" represented the power center of Jerusalem. The city gates were where major business transactions were made, where court judges announced their decisions, where city elders deliberated, where vows of marriage and other commitments were witnessed, and where caravans were unloaded.

So for David to be "lifted up" from the gates of death so that he could praise God in the gates of Zion suggests a dramatic deliverance, a complete reversal of his situation. Faced with utter ruin and disaster, he is rescued by God. In response, he resolves to go to the "city hall" of the day and tell everyone what God has done for him.

What has God done for you? Are you making it known to your acquaintances and publicizing it far and wide? Christian witness is not just a private transaction in a church or confessional; it calls for a public presence and proclamation in the "gates" of the modern world.

Witnessing Through Commerce

Springtime on the Mediterranean meant the return of cargo-laden ships from Alexandria, Egypt. They used westerly winds to deliver their goods to the empire's key ports.

Paul was transported from Malta to Rome on one such vessel, a voyage that covered one hundred eighty nautical miles in less than two days at sea (Acts 28:11). On the journey he was able to visit three important cities and continue his movement-building work: Syracuse; the dominant city of Sicily; Rhegium, a key harbor town on the Italian side of the Strait of Messina; and Puteoli, gateway to southern Italy, just thirty-three miles from Rome.

Throughout Christian history, the gospel has invariably traveled the routes of commerce. For example, many have been introduced to the Good News through the witness of:

- merchants doing business in foreign countries;
- employees of multinational corporations stationed overseas;
- consultants advising governments and businesses worldwide;
- medical personnel serving in developing nations;
- faculty and students studying and teaching around the world; and
- soldiers in foreign lands during war or occupation.

Are you taking advantage of strategic opportunities to influence others with the message of Christ through your networks?

Making Your Faith Available

Do you find some of your coworkers or neighbors totally uninterested in the Christian faith? Are some even openly hostile? Have you become a target for their venom?

Jesus called us to be His witnesses (Acts 1:6–8), but that is not a call to convert others. Conversion is the responsibility of the Holy Spirit (John 16:8–11). That means that we need not measure our success in witnessing by the number who respond. If that were the case, Jesus would have often been considered a failure: many who heard Him—and even some who followed Him—turned out to be uninterested (John 6:60–66).

The fact is that people are in various conditions when it comes to spiritual matters, as Jesus' story of the four kinds of soils illustrates (Mark 4:3–20). One thing we as "farmers" can't do is change the soil. But we can offer good seed and do the best we can to nurture whatever faith sprouts up (1 Cor. 3:7–9). One way to do that is by continually working out our faith in day-to-day life (Phil. 2:12–13; James 2:14–26), making it available for others to consider rather than hiding it (Mark 4:21–23). How others react is between them and God.

That's not to suggest that we should be detached or uncaring about others and their responses. Scripture challenges us to love others as we have been loved. One way is to make available to them our experience of faith—and make ourselves available to God to be used with anybody, anywhere, anytime.

We ought to avoid the trap of evaluating our faith by how others respond to us. The Spirit of God converts people—we don't. If we do, our converts are on shaky ground. The story is told of an evangelist traveling on an airplane who sat across the aisle from a noisy drunk. After watching the fellow carry on for a while, the minister's seatmate turned and sarcastically remarked, "I understand he's one of your converts!"

The evangelist replied, "Must be. If he were God's, he wouldn't act that way." [[dieresis]]

Some Basics of Witness

What exactly does it mean to "witness"? Many people associate the term with street evangelism. But street preachers can sometimes alienate people, although the boldness of their faith is acknowledged by all. What else, then, is needed for someone to be an effective representative for Christ?

John was one of Jesus' closest associates. In this first chapter of his first letter, John notes several basic elements of what it means to communicate Christ to others:

- Our message grows out of our knowledge and experience of Christ (1 John 1:1–4).
- We make clear to others what we have heard from Christ (1:5).
- We live out our faith on a continuous basis, thereby avoiding lives that contradict our message (1 John 1:6–7). "Walk" is a metaphor for living used often in the New Testament (for example, John 8:12; Rom. 4:12; Col. 3:7).
- When we fall short (as we all will, 1 John 1:10), we own up to it, avoiding deception about our walk or Christ's work (1 John 1:8–10).

Truthfulness, clarity, consistency, and honesty should be basic qualities of Christ's followers. They are things that last in the eyes of God, and they matter most to those evaluating the faith. We should offer nothing less.

The Road Less Traveled

For Jews in Jesus' day, the main road to Jerusalem went around Samaria. But He intentionally went *through* Samaria (John 4:4), where He taught His disciples a lesson in cross-cultural communication.

Finding a woman at Jacob's well in Sychar (John 4:5–7), Jesus struck up a conversation which quickly turned personal. Before long, the woman was on the verge of conversion. But Jesus understood that in her culture women lacked authority to make substantive decisions on their own. Those were made by men, often tribally, within clans. In fact, it was unusual for a man, particularly a rabbi, to hold serious conversation with a woman in public, as Jesus was doing. Perhaps that's one reason why the woman left as soon as the disciples showed up (John 4:27–28).

However, another reason was so that she could go and tell her "significant others," her network of family and friends, about Jesus (John 4:28–30). The woman left her waterpot at the well, maybe because she was in a hurry, though she may have left it there to avoid having to carry it around; after all, she clearly intended to return. At any rate, John 4:28 specifically points out that she approached "the men" in the community first—perhaps a clue that they were indeed the decision makers.

But it was also true that she had been married to, or had lived with or been intimate with, a number of the men in that clan (John 4:17–18). In that respect, she was like many public assistance mothers today living in common-law marriages. Those connections might have made her a unique "gatekeeper" or social organizer in the community. She could unlock the village for Jesus. Once she did, He stayed there for two days (John 4:43).

What does Jesus' example say about communicating the gospel message today? Northern European and American cultures tend to value individual choice. But elsewhere, many cultures are more clannish. Inter- and intra-family relationships have a powerful bearing on how the message will be received. Western believers need to respect that and use it to advantage as they cross over into cultures different from their own.

Jesus followed the less-traveled road directly into Samaria to bring not just an individual woman, but an entire community to faith. Have you chosen the road less traveled to walk with Jesus into cultures different from your own?

Why Nineveh Repented

Like Saul of Tarsus in the New Testament (Acts 9:1–22), the Assyrians of Nineveh were perhaps the least likely people of their day to repent of sin and turn to God. Yet when Jonah came preaching the Lord's imminent judgment (Jon. 3:4), they believed God and immediately proclaimed a fast to show their sincere sorrow for wickedness and idolatry (Jon. 3:5–9).

Ultimately, who can say why the Ninevites repented? Many factors may have accounted for their sudden change of attitude. Yet we know that God has a way of drawing people, and of arranging events so people are more likely to turn toward Him. Financial pressures, political turmoil, natural disasters, sickness—such things often cause people to take stock of their relationship with the Almighty. The case of Nineveh shows that this is true for nations as well as individuals.

Assyria in Jonah's day was perhaps ideally primed to hear and respond to a message of repentance. The empire was in decline (temporarily) due to uprisings among its vassal states and political turmoil at home. The exact date of Jonah's visit is unknown, but it is believed to have occurred around 759 B.C., on the heels of several important events:

- The death of Shalmaneser IV (about 773 B.C.). The king was young and left no successor. This created political instability.
- A famine in Nineveh (about 765 B.C.).
- A military defeat (about 763 B.C.), which coincided with a total eclipse of the sun—for the Assyrians, a sure sign of ill fortune.
- Floods following the eclipse.
- A famine (about 759 B.C.).
- An earthquake said to have occurred about the same time.

In light of these troubling phenomena, it is not surprising that the Assyrians listened to Jonah's message. Like the sailors in the storm who cried out to whatever gods might save them (Jon. 1:5–6), the Ninevites were probably willing to try anything to return some stability to their land. They heeded the Lord's warning, and He withheld judgment (Jon. 4:10).

Nineveh's repentance is instructive for Christians today. Like Jonah, we have been commissioned to take the gospel of repentance and salvation to the nations of the world (Mark 16:15–16). In doing so, it might be well to consider a strategy of targeted evangelism. Efforts would seem likely to be more effective in areas where recent political upheaval and natural disasters have created instability and more openness to a message of grace. If God has been preparing hearts beforehand, it is reasonable to expect greater success under such circumstances.

Jesus' Style of Witnessing

Does evangelism make you nervous? If so, it will help to study carefully how Jesus interacted with people. Whom did He meet? How did He connect with them? Where did the encounters take place? Who initiated contact? What happened in the conversation?

In many situations, Jesus initiated the conversations with people. Examples include a Samaritan woman (John 4:7–42) and a crippled beggar (John 5:1–15). In other cases, the other party started the discussion. Examples include a rich young ruler (Matt. 19:16–30), a demoniac (Mark 5:1–20), Jairus, a synagogue ruler (Mark 5:21–43), and a hemorrhaging woman (Mark 5:24–34). Other conversations were triggered by third parties. Examples include a tax collectors and other "sinners," invited to a party by Matthew (Matt. 9:9–13), Herod, introduced by Pilate (Luke 23:6–16), Nathaniel, invited by Philip (John 1:45–51), and an adulterous woman brought by the scribes (John 8:1–11)

The majority of Jesus' interactions occurred in the workplace: with James and John (Matt. 4:21–22), with a Samaritan woman (John 4:7–42), with a lame man (John 5:1–15). Other interactions occurred in homes: at Peter's house with his mother-in-law (Mark 1:29–31), with a Syro-Phoenician woman (Mark 7:24–30), and at Zacchaeus's house (Luke 19:1–10). Few interactions took place in religious settings. He did not need a special environment or control over the circumstances to discuss things of eternal significance.

Jesus asked questions in more than half of His conversations with people: an adulterous woman (John 8:1–11), the scribes (Luke 5:17–26), His mother and brothers (Matt. 12:46–50), and the Pharisees (Luke 6:6–11)

Jesus connected with people's thoughts and feelings. He understood that new ideas need to be connected with existing frames of reference if they are to last. He seldom pressed for "closure" or a decision. Instead, He understood that time is required for ideas to simmer before people will act on them.

What can we learn from Jesus' example?

- Jesus knew how to take initiative.
- Jesus responded to the initiatives of others.
- Jesus left room in His schedule for interruptions by friends and others enlisting His help.
- Jesus usually met people on their own turf.
- Jesus was interested in establishing common ground with others.

Witnessing is a science, an art, and a mystery. It involves connecting your faith with people's experience in a way that they can understand it, in their own time and manner. It means cooperating with whatever God's Spirit may be doing with them and leaving the results to Him.

For more on this topic, see **COMMUNITY SERVICE,** *"Faith Impacts the World," page 76;* **KINDNESS,** *"Blessings for the Unbelievers," page 236.*

WOMEN

A Rabbi for Women, Too

Luke mentions that Jesus had a following among the women of His day (Luke 23:49). From what we know about Jewish culture in the first century, their presence and loyalty probably offended many Jews.

Jewish tradition frowned upon women studying with rabbis. Some rabbis actually considered it sinful to teach women the Law. Women were permitted in the synagogues, but custom required them to sit apart from the men. Menstruation made them unclean

each month according to the Law (Lev. 15:19). Women were often viewed as the cause of men's sexual sins. To prevent any temptation, Jewish men were instructed not to speak to a woman in public—even to one's wife. And they were never to touch a woman in public.

But not only did Jesus speak to women in public (John 4:27), He dared to take them by the hand (Mark 5:41). He encouraged a woman who desired to follow Him, even when it conflicted with her household duties (Luke 10:42). And as He tried to help people understand the kingdom of God, He used illustrations that women as well as men could relate to.

Though excluded from the inner courts of the temple, Jewish women were welcome among Jesus' followers. He showed that rules of "clean" and "unclean" no longer determined who could approach God. He had come to open a new way, and everyone was welcome to participate. In doing so, He turned the world upside down.

What about your world? Do you see people—whether women or men—the way Jesus does? What one change would you need to make to treat someone more like the Savior did?

The Model Woman

Proverbs 31:10–31 is an acrostic poem, in which the first word of each line begins with a successive letter of the Hebrew alphabet. This poem is part of the instruction that King Lemuel's mother gave to teach her son about wisdom (Prov. 31:1). In describing the "virtuous wife," Lemuel's mother was showing what wisdom looks like when it is lived out in everyday life.

Why is the woman of Proverbs 31 more valuable than rare jewels (Prov. 31:10)? It is because of her wisdom, her ability to live life in a responsible, productive, and prosperous way (see Prov. 1:2). The Book of Proverbs often personifies wisdom as a woman (Prov. 8:1–11), and also describes wisdom as more valuable than any riches (Prov. 3:15; 8:11).

Thus it is no surprise that the woman of Proverbs 31 earns praise in the most public of places, the gates of the city (Prov. 31:31), which in her day represented a combination of city hall and the marketplace. She is a woman whose hard work brings material rewards (Prov. 31:13–16, 21–22). Proverbs promises that whoever seeks and finds wisdom will also find wealth, happiness, honor, and long life. This woman is an example of how those promises are fulfilled.

It is worth noting that this woman pursues what are sometimes thought of as traditional female jobs, such as making clothes (Prov. 31:13, 19), as well as nontraditional work, such as real estate investment, farming, and merchandising (Prov. 31:16, 18). Furthermore, her energies are directed not only toward providing for her family and household (Prov. 31:11, 14–15, 27), but also toward meeting the needs of people in the community (Prov. 31:20).

In short, the woman of Proverbs 31 is a model, for both women and men, of a way of living that brings fulfillment and contentment. She exhibits a lifestyle of work and love, based on godly wisdom.

Women and Work in the Ancient World

Paul's observation that a married woman must care about "the things of the world" (1 Cor. 7:34) hints at the busy lives that first-century women lived, especially in the large cities of the Roman Empire.

The New Testament shows that women carried out a wide range of tasks: for example, drawing water, grinding grain, manufacturing tents, hosting guests, governing and influencing civic affairs, making clothes, teaching, prophesying and filling other spiritual functions, burying the dead, and doing the work of slaves, to name but a few. Additional evidence from the period reveals that women also served as wool workers, midwives, hairdressers, nurses, vendors, entertainers, political leaders, and even construction workers, among many other occupations.

If a woman was among the upper classes, she enjoyed relative economic security and social privileges. According to the Roman ideal, her role in society was to marry a citizen, produce legitimate heirs for him, and manage the household according to his orders. However, by the first century few families attained that ideal.

Wealthy women used slaves to perform such household tasks as cooking, making clothes, washing laundry, and caring for children. Slaves also functioned as nurses, midwives, hairdressers, stenographers, and secretaries, and it was common for a high-ranking slave to be designated the household manager.

Female slaves were not only considered to be household property, but sexual property as well. The master of the house could legally force a slave to have sex with him, or with anyone he chose. Any children that she bore became his property. In this way a citizen could increase his number of slaves.

Women who were former slaves, or freeborn, lacked the economic security of either the citizen or the slave. Nevertheless, many women sought to buy their way out of slavery. Some of these working-class women earned their living as vendors, selling fish, grain, vegetables, clothing, or perfume. Others became wet nurses, and some chose to become entertainers or prostitutes, occupations that were considered beneath the dignity of respectable women.

Many Shades of Bible Women

The record of Leah and Rachel (Gen. 29:31–35) stands out among the writings and stories that survive from ancient times. As near as we can tell, many cultures in the ancient world viewed women as little more than property. Furthermore, the men who recorded the literature of those times tended to overlook the presence and significance of their female counterparts.

By contrast, the Bible not only includes women but tells about their leadership, contributions, and feelings, and not just their sins and failures. Overall, Scripture provides an honest account of women as well as men in a fallen world.

- Eve, the first woman, chose to eat what God had forbidden, resulting in expulsion from the Garden of Eden and separation from God (Gen. 2:18–4:26).
- Sarah bore a child late in life in fulfillment of God's covenant promise (Gen. 17:15–18:15; 20:1–21:13; 23:1–2).
- Hagar was a slave who was abused by her mistress; but God remembered and rescued her (Gen. 16:1–16; 21:9–21).
- Rebekah was a cunning woman who perceived a way to capture her husband Isaac's blessing for her favorite son (Gen. 24:1–67; 25:20–26; 27:5–46).
- Tamar was a widow who resorted to prostitution to obtain justice and support from her father-in-law (Gen. 38:1–20).
- Potiphar's wife was a vindictive temptress who used sexual harassment to slander an innocent man (Gen. 39:7–20).

*For more on this topic, see **MALE-FEMALE RELATIONSHIPS**, "Every Man King," page 252.*

WORDS

(*see* Talk)

WORK

A Responsibility to Work

God wants Christians to take responsibility to provide for their material needs and those of their families. In fact, 2 Thessalonians 3:10 states this as a command.

God has created a world of resources for this purpose. He gives us authority, along with strength and skills, to use those resources to earn our living. Work is His gift to us, a means of supplying what we need.

Obviously, there are times when grown children must care for their parents or grandparents (Mark 7:9–13; 1 Tim. 5:4). Likewise, the church community sometimes must assume responsibility for those in need. But responsibility always starts with the individual, as this passage makes plain.

Earlier, in 1 Thessalonians 4:12, Paul explains why: (1) Because of the testimony that Christians have among unbelievers. Believers who beg, borrow unnecessarily, or steal discredit Christ and the church. (2) Because God doesn't want His children to "lack" what they need. He doesn't call us to poverty, but to adequacy.

Every Breath You Take

People frequently use the term "Mother Nature" to describe the natural laws that bring order and predictability to the world. But Paul reminds us that Christ is ultimately the One who holds things together (Col. 1:17), not some impersonal force or random chance. We depend on Him for every breath we draw. Since the first day of creation, He has been sustaining the world and providing for His creatures (Neh. 9:6; Ps. 36:6; Heb. 1:3).

That lends tremendous dignity to human labor, especially since God has placed humanity over the creation as His managers. He values work that seeks to understand and oversee this world—for example, the work of the climatologist who studies the impact of humans on global ecology; the physicist who looks into the makeup of the atom and the application of that knowledge to human needs; and the publisher who helps distribute information and ideas to people. Jobs like these reflect God's work as Creator, and those who do them are actually partners with Christ in maintaining His creation.

God the Worker

The Bible opens with God (Gen. 1:1), and the first thing we read about God is that He created the heavens and the earth. In other words, God first appears in Scripture as a Worker.

Consider the many kinds of work that God did in forming the world: artist, designer, strategic planner, organizer, project developer, assessor, zoologist, biologist, chemist, linguist, programmer, materials specialist, engineer, and waste management technician, to name but a few.

What sort of job did He do? The record says that it was "good" (Gen. 1:4, 10, 12, 18, 21, 25) and "very good" (Gen. 1:31).

However, God's work did not end with the creation of Adam and Eve. His continues to work by providing for His creatures (Ps. 104:27; 136:25; 145:15–16; Matt. 6:11), sustaining the creation (Neh. 9:6; Ps. 36:6; Col. 1:17; Heb. 1:3), and bringing salvation to people (John 5:17; Eph. 1:7).

This picture of God as a Worker holds far-reaching implications for every worker today. For example, it shows us that:

- Work is inherently good.
- Working with and reshaping what God has already created is an important activity. It pleases God. It matters to Him.
- Whether we call our work "sacred" or "secular," all legitimate work reflects the activity of God.
- God is honored in His work, and we are to honor Him by doing the work He has given us to do in a way that pleases Him.

Is Work a Curse?

What was the curse that God put on creation (Gen. 3:17–19)? One of the most stubborn myths in Western culture is that God imposed work as a curse to punish Adam and Eve's sin. As a result, some people view work as something evil. Scripture does not support that idea:

1. *God Himself is a worker.* The fact that God works shows that work is not evil, since by definition God cannot do evil. On the contrary, work is an activity that God carries out.

2. *God created people in His image to be His coworkers.* He gives us ability and authority to manage His creation.

3. *God established work before the Fall.* Genesis 1–2 record how God created the world. The account tells how He placed the first humans in a garden "to tend and keep it" (Gen. 2:15). This work assignment was given *before* sin entered the world and God pronounced the curse (Gen. 3). Obviously, then, work cannot be a result of the Fall since people were working before the Fall.

4. *God commends work even after the Fall.* If work were evil in and of itself, God would never encourage people to engage in it. But He does. For example, He told Noah and his

family the same thing He told Adam and Eve—to have dominion over the earth (Gen. 9:1–7). In the New Testament, Christians are commanded to work (Col. 3:23; 1 Thess. 4:11).

5. *Work itself was not cursed in the Fall.* A careful reading of Genesis 3:17–19 shows that God cursed the *ground* as a result of Adam's sin—but not work: "Cursed is the *ground* for your sake; in toil you shall eat of it" (emphasis added).

Notice three ways that the curse affected work: (1) Work had been a joy, but now it would be "toil." People would feel burdened down by it, and even come to hate it. (2) "Thorns and thistles" would hamper people's efforts to exercise dominion. In other words, the earth would not be as cooperative as it had been. (3) People would have to "sweat" to accomplish their tasks. Work would require enormous effort and energy.

Most of us know all too well how burdensome work can be. Workplace stresses and pressures, occupational hazards, the daily grind, office politics, crushing boredom, endless routine, disappointments, setbacks, catastrophes, frustration, cutthroat competition, fraud, deception, injustice—there is no end of evils connected with work. But work itself is not evil. Far from calling it a curse, the Bible calls work and its fruit a gift from God (Eccl. 3:13; 5:18–19).

Coworkers with God

Do you know that your job is an extension of God's rule over the world? That's what Psalm 8 means when it says that God has given people "dominion," or authority, over His works (Ps. 8:6). The psalmist is looking back to the Creation account (Gen. 1:26–30), where God made people in His image to be His coworkers in overseeing the creation. Consider what that means:

1. *You bear the very image of God.* Like Him, you are a person, which means you have dignity and value. You matter. Who you are and what you do are significant. God has created you for a reason, which gives your life ultimate meaning and purpose.

2. *You are created to be a worker.* God is a worker, and since you are made in His image, your work expresses something of who He is and what He wants done in the world. Work (activity that advances your own well-being or that of someone else, or that manages the creation in a godly way) reflects the work that God does. That means your work has dignity and value. It matters to God.

3. *You are God's coworker.* Genesis 1:26–30 makes it clear that God wants people to manage the world. He gives us authority to "subdue" the earth—to cultivate and develop it, bring it under our control, use it to meet our needs, explore its wonders, and learn to cooperate with its natural laws. He also gives us "dominion" over every plant and animal for similar purposes.

Your job can help accomplish that mandate, as you use your God-given skills and opportunities. He views your work as having not only dignity, but purpose and direction as well. He wants you to accomplish meaningful tasks as you labor with a godly work ethic. Ultimately, He wants you to bring Him glory as a faithful manager of the resources and responsibilities He has placed under your control. By approaching work from this perspective, you can find fulfillment and motivation as a partner with God Himself.

Reconnecting Our Work with God's Work

Psalm 90 reminds us of a profound and lasting truth: that God is eternal and unchanging, while humanity is destined to die. Yet it is interesting that in drawing the psalm to a close, Moses asks God to show His own work to His people by establishing the work of their hands (Ps. 90:16–17). In this way Moses shows a connection between God's work and people's day-to-day work.

In essence, Moses was praying that God would invest the labors of His people with meaning, significance, and purpose. Too often, everyday work is seen as dreary drudgery, or, at the opposite extreme, it is a selfish pursuit of personal ambition. By reconnecting our work with God's work, we can avoid either pitfall. Our work can become a testimony to God's goodness and a means of conveying His grace to everyone touched by our efforts.

What might that mean for your day-to-day work, whatever it may be? What would the blessing of God mean for your tasks? How might others recognize the results of re-connecting your work with God's work?

The Spirituality of Everyday Work

What does Colossians 3:1–2 imply about everyday work? Is it possible to hold a "secular" job and still "seek those things which are above" rather than "things on the earth"? The issue is spirituality—the capacity to know and respond to God. How is it possible to bring spirituality into "secular" work? Here are some points to consider:

1. *If Christ is Lord over all of life, then He must be Lord over work, too.* Colossians 3 does not distinguish between the sacred and the secular, but between the life that Christ offers (the "things above") and its alternative—spiritual death apart from Him (the "things on the earth"). Spirituality has to do with conduct and character, not just vocation. It also has to do with the lordship of Christ. Christ is Lord over all of creation (Col. 1:15–18). Therefore, He is Lord over work. Whatever we do for work, we should do it "in the name of the Lord Jesus" (Col. 3:17)—with a concern for His approval and in a manner that honors Him.

2. *The Spirit empowers us to live and work with Christlikeness.* Spirituality has to do with character and conduct, regardless of where we work. Christ gives the Holy Spirit to help us live in a way that pleases Him (Gal. 5:16–25). This has great implications for how we do our jobs, our "workstyle" (see Titus 2:9–10). Furthermore, Scripture calls us "temples" of the Holy Spirit (1 Cor. 6:19). We can expect the Spirit to enable us to use our God-given skills and abilities to bring glory to God.

3. *God values our work even when the product has no eternal value.* A common measure of the significance of a job is its perceived value. Will the work "last"? Will it "really count" for eternity? The assumption is that God values work for eternity, but not work for the here and now.

By this measure, the work of ministers and missionaries has eternal value because it deals with the spiritual, eternal needs of people. By contrast, the work of the shoe sales-man, bank teller, or secretary has only limited value, because it meets only earthly needs. The implication of this line of reasoning is

that this kind of work doesn't really "count" to God.

But this way of thinking overlooks several important truths:

- God Himself has created a world which is time-bound and temporary (2 Pet. 3:10–11). Yet He values His work, declaring it to be good by its very nature (Gen. 1:31; Ps. 119:68; Acts 14:17).
- God promises rewards to people in everyday jobs, based on their attitude and conduct (Eph. 6:7–9; Col. 3:23–4:1).
- God cares about the everyday needs of people as well as their spiritual needs. He cares whether people have food, clothing, shelter, and so forth.
- God cares about people, who will enter eternity. To the extent that a job serves the needs of people, He values it because He values people.

What Are You Working For?

Why do you go to your job? If it is only to draw a paycheck, that is not enough—at least, not according to the Bible's teaching on work. Earning a living is important, but it is only part of God's intention for work. Ultimately, God calls His people to be signposts pointing toward His kingdom, not just functionaries in the world's system. Through our job-related responsibilities, we have an opportunity to be like the citizens of Zion: "priests of the LORD" and "servants of our God" (Is. 61:6), carrying out His assignments wherever He has placed us.

In Isaiah 61:4–9, priests and servants have some very interesting work to do:

- They rebuild ruined buildings.
- They restore that which has been desolated.
- They repair ruined cities.
- They recover what has been lost from previous generations.
- They produce food by working together with former strangers and people of other nationalities.
- They no longer bear shame, but rather receive honor and even double honor.
- They rejoice in the assignments given to them.
- They will be known and respected.

According to Isaiah, these workers were intended to be God's priests, doing good for the creation and benefiting from the rewards of their labors (Is. 61:6). Likewise, that perspective should turn our jobs into holy assignments from God. And why not? God wants us to be holy in all that we do. Any of us can serve Him through the day-to-day responsibilities and relationships that He has given us. We can give Him the gift of worship as we carry out our tasks.

WORKAHOLISM

(see Burnout; Rest and Recreation)

WORKMANSHIP

Faithful Workmanship

The carpenters, builders, and masons making repairs to the temple were so trustworthy that they needed no accounting for their work (2 Kin. 22:7). What a marvelous example! Scripture has honored these faithful workers by recording Josiah's assessment of them for all time.

Imagine if you were one of the workers hired to do temple repairs. Based on your past performance, would your work be so well done and your character so honest that no one needed to check up on whether you were doing the job with integrity?

The world needs trustworthy workers today more than ever. Why not commit yourself to the pursuit of quality and honesty in your workmanship?

WORKPLACE

A Model for the Workplace

If you work in today's marketplace, you may wonder at times how your faith applies in a tough business environment. If so, it helps to study the life of Joseph. He is an excellent model in Scripture for how to honor God in a "secular" workplace.

Consider Joseph's circumstances. He was cut off from his family. He was part of a culture that worshiped pagan gods, and apparently he alone worshiped the true God. Thus he had no support system for his beliefs or values and no one to turn to for godly counsel as he made far-reaching decisions.

How did Joseph maintain his faith in such an environment? Consider several ways:

1. *He maintained his integrity.* Joseph steadfastly resisted the sexual advances of Potiphar's wife (Gen. 39:7–10). He realized that moral compromise would have been an offense not only against his master, but even worse, against God. He remained committed to what he knew was right, despite the consequences.

2. *He kept doing his best even when the situation was the worst.* Unjustly thrown into prison, Joseph easily could have become bitter at God. Instead, he kept doing what God had designed Him to do—exercising authority, even in prison (Gen. 39:22–23).

3. *He carried out the task he was given.* Promoted to Pharaoh's right hand, Joseph was faithful in the responsibility. He wisely planned for the coming famine and managed the Egyptian economy in a way that saved many lives (Gen. 41:46–49, 53–57). He recognized that the work itself was what God wanted him to do.

4. *He used his power and influence compassionately.* Joseph could have used his position as an opportunity to "pay back" his enemies, such as his brothers, the slave traders, and Potiphar's wife. Instead, he used his power to bring reconciliation (Gen. 45:3–15; 50:20).

God used Joseph's faithfulness to preserve the children of Jacob (Israel) in order to fulfill His promise to Abraham (Gen. 45:5–8). In the same way, God intends to use believers today in positions great and small to accomplish His purposes. Therefore, it is crucial that we honor God through our work. Like Joseph, we need to be people of whom there can be no doubt—we are those "in whom is the Spirit of God" (Gen. 41:38).

The Spirit in the Workplace

Do you think of the Holy Spirit as present in your workplace? Do you think that He is even concerned about your work? As the people of Israel began to build the tabernacle, the Spirit was actively involved with the workers and their project (Ex. 35:31–36:1)—as He was in the Bible's first "construction project," the creation of the world (Gen. 1:2).

The Spirit of God is said to be the source of the many skills and abilities required for the design and construction of the taber-

W

nacle—metalwork, jewelry making, carpentry, engraving, weaving, and other related talents. Notice some of the characteristics of these Spirit-driven workers:

- They were men and women (Ex. 35:20–22, 25).
- Their hearts were "willing" or "stirred" (Ex. 35:5, 21–22, 26), meaning that they were motivated to accomplish the task.
- They were skilled or "gifted" by God to carry out their various assignments (Ex. 35:10, 25, 34–35; 36:1–2).
- They were generous with their skills, as well as their possessions, in order to get the job done (Ex. 35:5, 22, 29; 36:3–7), which suggests that they were hard and loyal workers.
- The finished product shows that excellence was a hallmark of their work.

We see that the Spirit gives talents, and also character. How can you demonstrate the fruit of the Holy Spirit in your workplace (Gal. 5:16–26)? Carefully consider your character, relationships, skills, and productivity in light of these qualities. The same Spirit who was available to the ancient Israelite workers is ready to help you carry out your work to the the glory of God!

Workplace Witness

Our jobs put us in touch with people like no other activity. For forty or more hours a week we toil, laugh, struggle, and interact with others to accomplish tasks. For that reason, many Christians view their workplace as a primary platform for spreading the gospel. Is that legitimate?

It is certainly legitimate to treat our workplace as an opportunity for unbelievers to see Christianity by looking at us. Indeed, Paul challenges us to display a godly workstyle for that reason (Titus 2:9–10). However, we must never emphasize verbal witness to the detriment of our work, as if God sends us into the work world only to use it as a platform for evangelism.

Employers rightly look down on workers who are intruders, deceivers, or sluggards. In Ephesians 6:5–9, Paul challenges us to work with "sincerity of heart" and to pay close attention to the work itself, which he

calls "doing the will of God." That's what impresses one's employer, as well as God.

For more on this topic, see **FEAR,** *"Fear in the Workplace," page 154.*

WORLD HUNGER

(*see* Hunger)

WORLD MISSIONS

A House of Prayer for All Nations

Solomon's prayer of dedication for the temple at Jerusalem showed that Israel's God was a God for all nations. The king anticipated that foreigners from all over the world would be drawn to the house of worship. So he asked God to honor their prayers in order that "all peoples of the earth may know Your name and fear You" (1 Kin. 8:41–43).

One early answer to Solomon's prayer was a visit by the queen of Sheba (1 Kin. 10:1–13), who had heard of the splendors of Solomon's kingdom but wanted to see them for herself. After reviewing his accomplishments, she praised God for what he had done for Israel (1 Kin. 10:9). Other visitors had similar reactions.

The temple was located at Jerusalem, but as Jesus pointed out (quoting Isaiah), it was meant to be "a house of prayer for *all* nations" (Is. 56:7; Mark 11:17, emphasis added). Likewise, Israel was to be a blessing to the nations and a light showing the way toward the one true God (Gen. 12:1–3; Is. 51:4).

Similarly, Jesus teaches His followers to be a light to the nations (Matt. 5:14–16). Rather than bringing people to a central place of worship, believers—who are themselves temples of the Holy Spirit (1 Cor. 6:19–20)—are to go to the ends of the earth, taking the good news of God's grace to all the peoples of the world).

"Many People"

Who were the "many people to be saved alive" encompassed by Joseph's statement (Gen. 50:20)? Certainly they included Jacob's family, said to be at least seventy persons (Gen. 46:27; Ex. 1:5). Joseph's position in Egypt enabled him to save this group from starvation (Gen. 45:5–8). Yet many more people than just Joseph's family benefited from his presence in Egypt. God used Joseph to rescue Pharaoh and the Egyptians from the famine (Gen. 41:53–55). In fact, as a result of Joseph's wise planning and management, people from all countries in that part of the world were able to find food in Egypt (Gen. 41:56–57).

But God's goodness through Joseph did not stop there. Because the Israelites were preserved in Egypt, they eventually became a great nation (Ex. 1:7), in fulfillment of God's promise to Abraham (Gen. 12:2; 15:5). In turn, it was through the Israelites that God brought Jesus into the world, and through Him made salvation available to every person and nation (John 3:17; Rom. 3:21–26, 29).

Given this perspective, we can see that the "many people" far exceeded even those that Joseph probably had in mind. In fact, Christians today are among the "many" who have benefited from the good purposes carried out by Joseph. This suggests that the Old Testament is not only about God's dealings with the Israelites, but about God's plan to reach the entire world through the Israelites. God's purpose has always been to "save alive" as many people as possible by bringing them into right relationship with Him.

Great Among the Nations

If you've ever wondered what God is up to, and what the purpose of history is, the Lord's word through Malachi spells it out: "My name shall be great among the Gentiles [or nations]" (Mal. 1:11). This is the God's great plan. He is literally making history into "His story."

There are several ways God is making His name great, and known by every person and nation. One way is that behind the scenes, He orchestrates the rise and fall of governments and rulers. They may think their power is their own, and it may appear to the rest of the world that they are in control. But God is sovereign, and He installs and disposes of authorities in a way that moves His plan forward.

Another way that God is making His name known is through Christians. Jesus sent His followers to make disciples of "all the nations" (Matt. 28:19). That means taking the gospel to the ends of the earth. It also means living the gospel right where we are, in our homes, workplaces, and communities.

By all means, God is going to make His name great among the nations. That has been His purpose throughout history. Someday, when history draws to a close, every person on earth will know the Lord's name; everyone will admit, either in joy or in shame, that He alone is Lord (Phil. 2:10–11). In the meantime, are you helping to make His name great among the nations *right now?*

Spiritual Superhighway

Developed nations are currently building an "information superhighway" to link societies together through interactive computer technology. Isaiah described what could be called a "spiritual superhighway" that would eventually link former enemies to each other and to the Lord (Is. 19:23–25).

In Isaiah's time, Judah was flanked by two empires. To the north and east lay Assyria, a fierce, ambitious nation that dominated the Near East. To the south and west was Egypt, the ancient nemesis of the Israelites, but by then an aging superpower that was collapsing in upon itself through civil war and political strife.

Isaiah had already predicted the eventual demise of Egypt (Is. 19:1–15) and Assyria (Is. 10:5–12). Yet the prophet offered a word of hope even in the midst of God's judgment. "In that day" the Lord would bring into existence a highway of commerce and peace extending from Egypt to Assyria, passing through a revived Israel. Egyptians and Assyrians would join with Israelites to worship God together. The highway would pass through cities that had repented of their idolatry and set up altars to the Lord (Is. 19:18–19).

When will this spiritual superhighway come about? Its completion still lies in the future, but one might say that portions of it are already being constructed. In fact, the groundwork was laid when God allowed Israel and Judah to be taken into captivity. Jews were scattered among the cities of the ancient world, not only in Assyria and Babylon, but in Egypt and other Mediterranean cities as well. For example, by Jesus' day, some two million Jews are believed to have lived at Alexandria.

W

This set the stage for the spread of the gospel following the day of Pentecost (Acts 2). Following Peter's sermon, thousands of religious pilgrims responded to the message about Christ and took their newfound faith with them when they returned to their lands.

As in Isaiah's day and the days of the early church, Christ's people today are called to take the gospel to the cities of the world. By doing so, we help to build a "spiritual superhighway" that will ultimately connect not only the Middle East, but the entire world to each other and to the Lord.

For All the Nations

Jesus sent His followers to make disciples of all the nations (Matt. 28:19). That mandate may seem obvious to us today. After all, we live at the end of two thousand years of Christian outreach based on this and similar passages. Christianity now is an overwhelmingly Gentile religion subscribed to by roughly one-third of the world's population. And with modern technology, it appears to be a relatively simple task to expand that outreach even further.

Yet in many ways we are just like Jesus' original disciples. They wanted a local hero, a Messiah just for Israel, one who would follow their customs and confirm their prejudices. So they were no doubt stunned by the scope and far-reaching implications of the global, cross-cultural vision that Jesus now presented. He was turning out to be more than the King of the Jews; He was the international Christ, the Savior of the entire world.

It's easy to pay lip service to the idea that Jesus cares for the whole world. But isn't it easier to follow a Christ that fits comfortably into our own culture? Culture is the key. Jesus told His Galilean followers to "make disciples," and they did—Jewish disciples. But they experienced culture shock when the Holy Spirit brought new groups into the fellowship, including Hellenist disciples (Acts 6:1–7), Samaritan disciples (Acts 8:4–25), and eventually even Gentile disciples (Acts 10:1–11:18; 15:1–21).

Today the bulk of new disciples are non-white and non-Western. Not surprisingly, they bring very different cultural perspectives into the church. So one of the greatest challenges believers will face in the coming years is the same one that the original disciples faced at the inauguration of the movement: not only to believe but to accept that Jesus really is for all the nations.

WORRY

Don't Worry!

Of the texts in Scripture that discuss money and work, Matthew 6:19–34 are among the most frequently cited. Unfortunately, they are often used to imply that Jesus was against money and considered everyday work a distraction to things that "really" matter.

However, a careful reader will notice that Jesus condemned worry, not work (Matt. 6:25, 27–28, 31, 34). He never told us to stop working. Rather, He called us to correctly focus our faith on God, the ultimate supplier of our needs (Matt. 6:32).

God provides for people in many ways. The most common is through everyday work. He expects us to work diligently with whatever resources He gives us (2 Thess. 3:6–12). Of course, sometimes that normal means of provision fails for a variety of reasons: ill health, divorce from or death of a provider, loss of a job, natural disaster, changing markets, and other circumstances beyond our control.

It is precisely the fear of those possibilities that tempts us to worry so much and forget about trusting God. Why rely on Him, we figure, if He can't keep us from troubles like that? Why not just rely on ourselves and trust to our own devices? All the while we forget that God never promised that we wouldn't face hard times, and that He has many ways to help us through them when we do: family members, church communities, neighbors, charities, inheritances, even public agencies and nonprofit groups.

Certainly we need to pay attention to our physical and material needs. But Jesus urged us to stop worrying about things so that they dominate our lives and values. We can't do that and serve God at the same time (Matt. 6:24). Instead, we need to redirect our focus onto God's kingdom and righteousness (Matt. 6:33). That means adopting the values of the King and bringing Him into our work and lives. Jesus said that's what "really" matters.

For more on this topic, see INTROSPEC-TION, "Avoiding Morbid Introspection," page 229.

WORSHIP

A New Way to Worship

What is the proper way to worship God? For those who had grown up in the religious climate of Ephesus before the gospel, Christian worship called for altogether different behavior than they were used to practicing. So Paul offered guidelines for worship to the men and women in the Ephesian church (1 Tim. 2:8–15).

Ephesus was world-renowned for its magnificent temple of Artemis. Pagan cults flourished there, along with occult practices. In fact, books with magic recipes came to be known as "Ephesian books."

Nevertheless, the gospel bore great fruit there and the community of believers grew rapidly. Yet some of the new converts brought their old way of life into the church and began teaching other doctrines (1 Tim. 1:3–7). When it came to worship, many were used to wild rites and festivals. Ephesian women were particularly unacquainted with public behavior, having been excluded for the most part from public gatherings, except pagan rituals.

So Paul described the correct way of worship. Men, who were apparently given to anger and doubts, needed to stop wrangling and start praying (1 Tim. 2:8). Likewise, women needed to focus on godliness and good works rather than clothing, jewelry, and hairstyles (1 Tim. 2:9–10). And because some were apparently disruptive, they needed to practice restraint (1 Tim. 2:11)—not necessarily complete silence, but "quiet" (as the word is translated in 2 Thess. 3:12), since they likely participated in the prayers and other expressive parts of the worship gatherings (compare 1 Cor. 11:5; Eph. 5:19).

Today the message of Christ continues to attract people from a variety of backgrounds. Some, like the Ephesians, need to learn for the first time about worshiping God. Others bring cultural norms and expectations that are worth using in the worship experience, so long as they preserve biblical guidelines such as those that Paul gave to the Ephesians.

God Responds to Worship

Scripture assures us that God notices and responds when we worship Him. That worship may be as formal and elaborate as the ceremony to dedicate the temple (2 Chr. 5:12–13), or it may be as simple and spontaneous as the worship of the early church, which often met in people's homes (Acts 2:42, 46–47). What matters is not the setting or the program so much as the content of the worship and the heart attitude of the worshipers (John 4:21–24).

It is interesting to compare the account of the temple's dedication in 2 Chronicles 5–7 with the account in 1 Kings 8. Second Chronicles provides less detail until it comes to the singers and trumpeters. Then it shows how the musicians' harmony in pitch and purpose brought the ceremony to its climax (2 Chr. 5:13), and God responded by blessing the occasion and the temple itself with His glory and presence (2 Chr. 5:14).

The New Testament makes no mention of early Christians engaging in anything like the carefully scripted and rehearsed ritual that the Hebrews practiced. Nevertheless, God responded to the Christians' worship with similar assurances of His presence and power (for example, Acts 4:31).

So we are encouraged to worship the Lord in whatever ways are appropriate to the circumstance. He invites us to "come before His presence with singing" (Ps. 100:2)—whether that means painstakingly detailed ceremonies led by professional singers and musicians, or simple prayers and songs of heartfelt praise. Either way, He longs for us to "enter His gates with thanksgiving, and into His courts with praise" (Ps. 100:4).

For more on this topic, see SERVICE, "From Worship to Service," page 364; SYMBOLS, "The Danger of Relics," page 390.

WORSHIP CENTERS

A Building, More or Less

Have you ever been tempted to think of a church building as either more or less important than it really is? Solomon's prayer of dedication helps us gain a proper perspective on how to view houses of worship.

On the one hand, Solomon's temple was just a building. As such, it could not possibly

W

contain the Lord (2 Chr. 6:18). On the other hand, it was a site which God had chosen to bless with His presence (2 Chr. 6:6). Thus the temple became a hallowed symbol that stood for God (2 Chr. 6:20).

By the time of Jesus, however, people had distorted Solomon's balanced perspective. Some treated the temple as more than a building. Whereas Solomon's temple was dedicated as a house of prayer for all nations (2 Chr. 6:32–33; compare Is. 56:7), the temple of Jesus' day restricted Gentiles to an outer court, called the Court of the Gentiles. Notices in Greek and Latin were posted to warn Gentiles that they risked death if they trespassed into the inner courts.

On the other hand, some treated the temple as less than a house of prayer. Jesus strongly criticized the money changers for turning the site into a "den of thieves" (Mark 11:17), and He rebuked the Pharisees for their lack of respect for what the temple symbolized (Matt. 23:15–22).

It helps to keep these errors in mind as we think about the significance and symbolism of church buildings today. Like the temple, no church structure can lay sole claim to being the house of God. At the same time, church buildings and what goes on in them are intended to point to God. So how we treat these sanctuaries in many ways reveals our attitude toward God.

A Place to Be Forgiven

For the Hebrews, there was only one place to worship God by offering sacrifices—at the tabernacle (Lev. 17:8–9). This is not to say that one could not worship God elsewhere. But to make atonement for sin, one had to come to the altar, where a priest offered up a sacrifice according to the highly detailed instructions in the Law.

Believers today are fortunate. Our high priest, Jesus, offered a sacrifice for our sins once and for all when He died on the Cross (Heb. 10:11–14). As a result, we can receive forgiveness for sins anytime, anyplace. We are not required to go to a specific location for this purpose, nor does the Bible prescribe a certain ritual. We need only draw near to God through Christ with a "true heart" and confess our sins (Heb. 10:19–22).

A Worship Center

Sometimes people speak of a sanctuary, or place of worship, as "God's house." That can be a bit misleading, for the Lord does not need a house to live in. He is Spirit and is everywhere present (Ps. 139:7–10; John 4:24).

Why, then, did God instruct His people to build a worship center, "that I may dwell among them" (Ex. 25:8)? Perhaps it was not because He needed a place to live, but because they needed a place to worship. The sanctuary, or tabernacle, was for their benefit more than His—as becomes apparent when we look at the minute details given for the construction (Ex. 25–31).

The former slaves of Egypt had probably seen incredible temples and monuments in the empire along the Nile. Indeed, the Israelites may have helped to construct some of them. Yet now they were refugees in the wilderness, with no centralized location at which to worship the God who had delivered them from bondage. So they must have been inspired—and awed—to hear God's plans for a beautiful worship center of their own, complete with finely crafted accessories.

Not only was the tabernacle a work of art, but its construction involved the entire community. In, fact, it showed that the ordained priests were not the only Spirit-filled leaders in Israel: so were the artists and craftsmen who led the project (Ex. 31:1–11). It was their wisdom, management ability, and technical expertise, not just Moses', that made it possible for the people to do the work (Ex. 39:42).

Likewise, the "financing" of the tabernacle was also a community effort. It's interesting that Moses proposed both a free-will donation, or "love offering" (Ex. 25:2–9), and a "flat tax" (Ex. 30:12–16) to pay for the project. As a result, rich and poor alike shared the cost—and therefore the ownership.

Groups of believers today can learn a number of lessons about worship from Israel's experience with the tabernacle. One of the most important is that if everyone participates in the financing and construction of a worship center, then everyone will have a greater sense of participation in the worship that takes place there. Everyone can know that, like Israel, they have built a sanctuary for God and He has come to dwell among them.

Sparing No Expense

Whenever modern-day churches draw up plans and budgets for buildings in which to worship, they face an age-old tension: what is appropriate for a worship center in terms of size, materials, beauty, and expense? For Solomon, there seems to have been only one answer to that question as he proposed to build God's temple: spare no expense! Consider the costliness of Solomon's temple:

- It was made of the most precious of building materials, many of them imported: cedar (1 Kin. 5:6), quarried stone (1 Kin. 5:15–18), gold (1 Kin. 6:20–22), olive wood (1 Kin. 6:23–28, 31–33), cypress (1 Kin. 6:34), and bronze (1 Kin. 7:13–47).
- The project employed thirty thousand laborers (1 Kin. 5:13), one hundred fifty thousand stonemasons and haulers (1 Kin. 5:15), and three thousand three hundred supervisors (1 Kin. 5:16).
- The temple was paneled with cedar, some of which was ornately carved (1 Kin. 6:9, 15–18).
- Its floors and walls were overlaid with gold (1 Kin. 6:20–22).
- It was furnished with items of finely crafted wood and gold (1 Kin. 6:23–35; 7:48–50).
- So much bronze was used that its weight (and therefore cost) was not determined (1 Kin. 7:45–47).
- The work continued nonstop for seven years (1 Kin. 6:37–38).

Was Solomon justified in incurring such an expense? The question is not easily answered.

On the one hand, the project contributed to a number of problems of Solomon's reign: heavy taxation, a growing underclass of foreigners, and the depletion of the forests of Lebanon. The temple was not the sole cause of these troubles (1 Kin. 9:15–19). But it was built with a policy of "only the best" that seemed to typify the Solomonic empire.

On the other hand, Solomon apparently recognized that architecture is not neutral; it makes a statement. The temple was a remarkable work of art, built to the glory of God (1 Kin. 8:12–13). God apparently approved of Solomon's achievement, for He blessed the sanctuary with His presence (1 Kin. 8:10–11).

Yet even as the construction went forward, the Lord reminded His builder that what mattered was not a house of cedar and gold, but the keeping of the Law (1 Kin. 6:11–13). Perhaps that is the most important architectural principle of all when it comes to houses of worship: it is not the size, beauty, or expense of the structure, but the sincere devotion and obedience of those who worship in the structure. After all, the Lord does not dwell only in sanctuaries built by people, but in the people themselves (1 Kin. 8:27; Acts 7:48; 17:24; 1 Cor. 6:19–20).

WORTH OF PERSONS

A Value on Life

God instructed Noah to bring into the ark two of every creature that had the "breath of life" (Gen. 7:15), along with his family. In this way God preserved His creatures from total destruction. This shows that God places a high value on life itself.

This is important to remember as we read the Old Testament. To some, Scripture seems needlessly bloody and violent. But is it really any more violent than most of the cultures that have existed throughout history, or even around the world today? Actually, bloodshed and wickedness are the norm; protracted periods of peace are the exception.

So if we live in one of those exceptional societies and enjoy relative peace and prosperity, we ought not to let that color our perceptions of the biblical record. Scripture shows us a realistic picture of humanity: on the whole, we are plagued by sin, evil, and death.

Yet the Bible also reveals that our Creator places value on life. He was "grieved in His heart" to see people giving themselves over to wickedness (Gen. 6:6). In fact, after the flood He established a code to enforce the protection of people's lives (Gen. 9:5–6). In the same spirit, Christ later appealed for His followers to engage in peacemaking (Matt. 5:9). The biblical record is clear: life is a gift from God, a treasure to be cherished and honored.

Unworthy, but Not Worthless

Bildad's portrait of man as a maggot and a worm (Job 25:6) was hardly flattering. But it's important to notice that he was making a

W

statement about people's moral standing before God (Job 25:4) rather than their relative worth as creatures.

Scripture supports Bildad's assertion that no one is pure who is "born of a woman." Sin pollutes every one of us, so that from our earliest days our lives are corrupted by evil (Gen. 8:21; Ps. 51:5; Rom. 5:12). Even our faltering attempts at righteousness are nothing but filthy rags (Is. 64:6). With the singular exception of Christ Himself, this fallen condition extends to every one of us (53:6; Rom. 3:10, 23), and makes us unworthy to stand before a holy God.

Yet though we are unworthy, we are not worthless. We have been created by God in His own image (Gen. 1:26–27; Ps. 8:5; 139:13–16), which establishes our inherent worth and gives us dignity. Moreover, God so loved us that despite our rebellion and hostility, He sent Jesus to rescue us from sin and retrieve our humanity from corruption. And when we turn to Jesus for the forgiveness of our sin, we become children of God and fellow-heirs of Christ's glory (Eph. 1:11–12).

Thus our worth as people is totally derived from God—a truth that helps to correct any distortions we may have about our "self-esteem." On the one hand, we need not live with the attitude, "I'm worthless. I'm a nothing." God does not see us that way. On the other hand, there's no room for exalting ourselves by denying our sin, setting ourselves up as little gods, and demanding our own way. A healthy self-image is important, but we can get into trouble by ignoring the natural human tendency toward pride.

Scripture urges us to strike a healthy balance between these two extremes. It tells us to regard ourselves as neither too low nor too high, but with honesty and realism (Rom. 12:3; 1 Cor. 12:15–19).

Y

YOUTH

Young People at Risk

Youth is supposed to be a time of energy and vitality. But what happens when extreme circumstances sap the life out of young people, robbing them of enthusiasm and rendering them too weak to go on?

God has pledged Himself to help young people at risk (Is. 40:30–31), as well as those who are lowly and despised, poor and needy, thirsty and hungry (Is. 41:17). This concern for people living on the margins of life is a theme that punctuates and permeates Isaiah's prophecy. And more often than not he urges people of power and means to do something about the needs of their at-risk neighbors.

In Isaiah 40–41, the prophet speaks directly to these needy people. In his day, they were the weary ones who were held captive in Babylon. They were on a long road home, having had their land taken away and their lives turned upside down. Isaiah assured them that they could expect God's help in relocation, relief, and redevelopment that would re-build their lives and economy and bless their land with renewed prosperity (Is. 41:18–19; compare Ps. 104:13–16; Is. 30:25; 44:3–4).

If you work with young people at risk for "fainting" from the demands of life, or if you yourself are close to giving up because of the circumstances weighing you down, you can take comfort from God's promises for strength. The key is "waiting on the Lord" (Is. 40:31), expecting Him to supply what you cannot.

"I'm Too Young!"

Young people can easily feel intimidated in the presence of older adults, especially if they must perform a solo activity or take a stand for a principle. When Jeremiah was called by God to serve as His prophet to Judah and the nations, he complained that he was too young (Jer. 1:6). Perhaps he was imagining how the stern faces of his elders would look when he announced that God was going to judge them for their sins.

Like Jeremiah, you may feel intimidated by older coworkers and superiors, members of your community, or relatives. Perhaps you are new on the job or have just graduated from school, or maybe you have just settled in a new community. As the young newcomer, you may be afraid to "make waves," especially if living according to biblical values goes against the prevailing culture. But consider these suggestions:

• Remember that you are God's representative—in your community, on the job, in your family. Ultimately you are where you are to seek His glory, not your own power or prestige.
• Listen carefully for God's instructions to you. They normally come through prayer,

reading and studying the Bible, and paying attention to the advice of seasoned believers who have walked the path before you.
• Place confidence in God's power and provision. The Lord will use your skills and abilities, but in His way, in His time, and for His glory.

For more on this topic, see **PARENT-YOUTH RELATIONSHIPS,** *"An Age-old Battle," page 290;* **SINGING,** *"A Song for Young People," page 370.*

YOUTH-PARENT RELATIONSHIPS
(*see* Parent-Youth Relationships)

YOUTH

—GUIDE TO SUBJECTS AND ARTICLES—